INDEX TO POETRY IN
POPULAR PERIODICALS,
1955-1959

INDEX TO POETRY IN POPULAR PERIODICALS, 1955–1959

Compiled by
JEFFERSON D. CASKEY

GREENWOOD PRESS
Westport, Connecticut • London, England

Library of Congress Cataloging in Publication Data

Caskey, Jefferson D.
  Index to poetry in popular periodicals, 1955-1959.

  Includes index.
  1. American poetry—20th century—Periodicals—
Indexes. 2. American periodicals—Indexes. I. Title.
Z1231.P7C37 1984 [PS301] 016.811'008 83-22584
ISBN 0-313-22227-4 (lib. bdg.)

Library of Congress Catalog Card Number: 83-22584
ISBN: 0-313-22227-4

First published in 1984

Greenwood Press
A division of Congressional Information Service, Inc.
88 Post Road West, Westport, Connecticut 06881

Printed in the United States of America

10 9 8 7 6 5 4 3 2 1

To my faithful wife
Louise Huffaker Caskey

CONTENTS

PREFACE

Index to Poetry in Popular Periodicals, 1955-1959, is an author, title, first-line, and subject analysis of over 7,000 poems that were published in periodicals over a five-year period. The periodicals indexed in H. W. Wilson's *Reader's Guide to Periodical Literature* were used as a basis for this research.

The search for these poems revealed a wide range of subjects—love, hate, joy, sadness, marriage, divorce, war, rumors of war, quests for peace, racial unrest, and myriads of others. In the poems that were published during this five-year period, virtually every facet of human concern is expressed.

Most of the periodicals searched were for casual, light, or practical reading such as *Field and Stream, Saturday Evening Post,* and *Ladies' Home Journal;* but others were erudite or professional, such as *Poetry, Yale Review, Atlantic Monthly,* and *American Libraries.*

Many of the poems that were located were by outstanding poets or by poets who became famous after some of their first efforts were published. There were poems by poets who wrote very little; and there were poems by persons who did not profess to be poets at all.

When the compiler and interested reference librarians discovered that most of the poems in these periodicals were either lost or would soon be lost to the world of poetry because of a lack of bibliographic control, the *Index to Poetry* had its beginning.

Index to Poetry was developed with a twofold purpose in mind. First, the only partial bibliographic control for poems published in general periodicals for many years was the *Reader's Guide to Periodical Literature.* This indexing service gave author-title coverage of the poems along with the other materials which were indexed. The indexing of poetry was discontinued by H. W. Wilson with the publication of Volume 21 of *Readers' Guide,* which had indexed poetry in periodicals from March 1955 to February 1957.

The second purpose of the *Index to Poetry* is to supplement other existing poetry indexes which may or may not have included the indexing of poetry published in periodicals. There is *Granger's Index to Poetry* (Columbia University Press) which does not index periodical poetry; *Chicorel Index to Poetry in Collections* (Chicorel Library Publishing Corporation); and *American Periodical Verse* (Scarecrow Press), which from 1971 has indexed poetry published primarily in scholarly journals and little magazines.

ACKNOWLEDGMENTS

Many individuals contributed to making *Index to Poetry in Popular Periodicals* a reality: Gretchen Caskey, Louise Huffaker Caskey, Dr. Vera Grinstead Guthrie, Dr. William R. Hourigan, Constance Caskey Huff, Paul Kobasa, Rodney Rogers, Adolfina Simpson, Debby Smith, Dr. Robert C. Smith, Dan R. Twaddle, and Dr. Earl Wassom. Pat Mize worked long hours using her knowledge as a professional librarian in assisting with the editing, organizing, and typing of the Title Index entries of this manuscript.

Much friendly and capable assistance came from librarians in these libraries: Enoch Pratt Free Library, Joint University Libraries, Vanderbilt University, Kentucky Wesleyan College Learning Center, Louisville Public Library, Nashville Public Library, University of Kentucky Libraries, University of Louisville Libraries, and Western Kentucky University Library.

There was also assistance and encouragement from the Faculty Research Committee of Western Kentucky University.

To all of them the compiler is deeply grateful.

Jefferson D. Caskey

ABBREVIATIONS OF PERIODICALS INDEXED

A	*America*	Hb	*Hobbies*
AA	*American Artist*	Hl	*Holiday*
AC	*American City*	Hr	*Horizon*
AF	*American Forests*	Hn	*Hornbook*
AH	*American Heritage*	HG	*House and Garden*
AI	*American Imago*	HB	*House Beautiful*
AL	*American Libraries*	LHJ	*Ladies Home Journal*
AB	*ALA Bulletin*	L	*Life*
AS	*American Scholar*	M	*McCall's*
AN	*Art News*	N	*Nation*
At	*Atlantic*	NaR	*National Review*
BHG	*Better Homes and Gardens*	NHB	*Negro History Bulletin*
CA	*Camping*	NR	*New Republic*
CC	*Christian Century*	NY	*New Yorker*
CT	*Christianity Today*	PM	*Parents Magazine*
CH	*Clearing House*	P	*Poetry*
C	*Commentary*	R	*Redbook*
Co	*Commonweal*	SEP	*Saturday Evening Post*
EJ	*English Journal*	SR	*Saturday Review*
FS	*Field and Stream*	TH	*Today's Health*
GH	*Good Housekeeping*	WLB	*Wilson Library Bulletin*
H	*Harper's*	YR	*Yale Review*
HBR	*Harvard Business Review*		

A NOTE ON HOW TO USE THE *INDEX*

The entries in the *Index* are divided into four sections: Title Index, First-Line Index, Author Index, and Subject Index.

Along with these four categories, it will be important to locate the Abbreviations of Periodicals Indexed on page xiii. This list and the Title Index are the keys to locating a poem from the information given in the other indexes.

The following example will illustrate how the *Index* is arranged.

TITLE INDEX ENTRIES

The Title Index gives the entry number, the full title of the poem, the poet's surname with first and middle initials, and an abbreviated form of the periodical followed by volume number, date of issue, and the page(s) on which the poem may be located. (See example below.)

FIRST-LINE INDEX ENTRIES

The First-Line Index entries give the first line of the poem followed by the corresponding Title Index entry number. For example:

A one-night world of fairy lights and music: 15.

AUTHOR INDEX ENTRIES

The elements of the Author Index entries are: the author's surname, first name, middle initial in all capital letters, followed by an alphabetical listing the poem followed by the corresponding Title Index entry number. For example:

NEAME, ALAN: An Academic Occasion, 15; Conversation Piece, 1191; Correcting, 1234.

SUBJECT INDEX ENTRIES

The Subject Index entries give the subject headings in all capital letters. Following the subject heading are the corresponding Title Index entry numbers and authors' names. For example:

GRADUATION: 15, Neame A.; 3248, Kissler, J.S.; 4211, Jaffray, N.R.

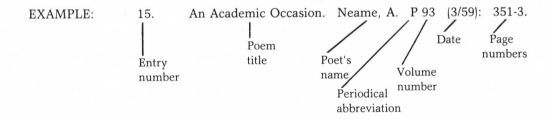

EXAMPLE: 15. An Academic Occasion. Neame, A. P 93 (3/59): 351-3.

Entry number / Poem title / Poet's name / Periodical abbreviation / Volume number / Date / Page numbers

INDEX TO POETRY IN POPULAR PERIODICALS, 1955–1959

TITLE INDEX

1. A+ Stockdale, A. B. BHG 33 (11/55): 201.
2. Abandoned. Abse, D. C 24 (10/57): 350-1.
3. Abandoned Home. Lawson, D. E. SEP 232 (7/18/59): 50.
4. Abandoned Orchard. Barker, E. SR 39 (4/14/56): 59.
5. Ablutions. Meredith, W. NY 33 (6/22/57): 81.
6. About Courbet. O'Hara, F. AN 56 (1/58): 44-51.
7. Abraham. Berrigan, D. Co 69 (1/16/59): 405.
8. Abraham. Schwartz, D. C 27 (3/59): 221-2.
9. Abroad and at Home. Swift, J. GH 141 (11/55): 14.
10. Absent-Minded Professor. Nemerov, H. N 184 (3/9/57): 222.
11. Absentee Landlordism. Ponsot, M. A 93 (9/17/55): 594.
12. Absolutely Roomy. Weiss, T. P 87 (12/55): 162-3.
13. Absentions. Ashberry, J. P 89 (3/57): 341.
14. Abundance. Ciardi, J. At 204 (7/59): 42-5.
15. An Academic Occasion. Neame, A. P. 93 (3/59): 351-3.
16. The Academic Overture. Lattimore, R. H 216 (5/58): 50.
17. Academic Procession. Watt, W. W. NY 33 (6/8/55): 10.
18. Academic Spring. Hillyer, R. SR 38 (6/18/55): 10.
19. The Academician. Jaffray, N. R. SEP 227 (2/19/55): 114.
20. Acceptance. Merrill, H. SEP 231 (2/14/59): 82.
21. The Accounting. Townsend, O. E. CC 76 (11/25/59): 1367.
22. Achievement Report--First Grade. Jenkins, B. H. LHJ 73 (10/56): 153.
23. Acquired Taste. Lineaweaver, M. LHJ 75 (11/59): 119.
24. Acrobat. Armour, R. SEP 231 (9/27/58): 73.
25. Across the Brown River. Kinnell, G. P 85 (1/55): 210.
26. Across the Valley. Baro, G. N 188 (1/10/59): 36.
27. An Act of Her Own. Chadbourne, M. SR 39 (4/21/56): 18.
28. Adagia. Stevens, W. SR 40 (7/20/57): 14.
29. Adagio for Jazz. Perry, R. P 91 (10/57): 21-2.
30. Adagio: On a Summer's Beach. Dejong, D. C. P 86 (4/55): 25-6.
31. Adam. Booth, P. P 85 (3/55): 340-1.
32. Adam. Feldman, I. C 25 (6/58): 527.
33. Adam. Afterward. Ponsot, M.A. 98 (3/22/58): 725.
34. The Adamses. Sagittarius. NR 138 (4/14/58): 7.
35. Added Problem. Richstone, M. SEP 229 (6/8/57): 54.
36. Address to the Fates. Thompson, D. B. SEP 230 (11/2/57): 86.
37. An Address to the Holder of Some High Government Office. Whittemore, R. YR 45 (12/55): 246-8.
38. Address to the Senior Class. Jennison, C. S. At 199 (6/57): 95.
39. Adieu to That Trip for Two. Jennison, C. S. LHJ 73 (6/56): 169.
40. Adjustment. Warsaw, I. SEP 232 (10/17/59): 69.
41. An Administrator's Prayer for the New Year. Katz, R. L. HBR 35 (1/2/57): 136.
42. Admonition. Milbrath, M. M. SEP 230 (8/3/57): 62.
43. Adolescence. Olivier, R. LHJ 72 (2/55): 135.
44. Adoption. Miller, M. B. SEP 227 (2/19/55): 46.
45. The Advantage of Me. Emmons, D. SEP 232 (7/4/59): 61.
46. Advent. Carter, A. H. CC 76 (12/16/59): 1464.
47. Advent. Nunc Est Hora....McCarthy, L. A. 100 (12/13/58): 342.
48. Advent Song. Warwick, D. A 98 (12/21/57): 375.
49. Adventure. Clark, N. M. SEP 230 (3/29/58): 84.
50. Advertisement. Kessler, S. SR 39 (5/26/56): 26.
51. Advice. Buchanan, P. GH 148 (5/59): 116.
52. Advice for a Wedding. Kanfer, A. H 213 (11/56): 69.
53. Advice from a Comic Book. Honig, E. SR 39 (7/21/56): 24.

57. Advice to a Prophet. Wilbur, R. NY 35 (4/4/
    59): 40.
58. Advice to a Strong Man with Weak Knees.
    Lieberman, E. SEP 228 (7/2/55): 65.
59. Advice to Another Man's Son. Summers, H.
    SR 41 (9/6/58): 25.
60. Advice to be Ignored. Parrish, M.M. SEP 229
    (11/17/56): 145.
61. Advice to Commuters. Dickinson, P. At 203
    (4/59): 145.
62. Advice to Husbands. Herz, B. SEP 232 (10/17/
    59): 124.
63. Advice to Lovers as Dancers. Tyler, P. P 86
    (8/55): 258-9.
64. Advice to Travelers. Gibson, W. SR 39 (5/5/
    56): 26.
65. Advice to Writers for the Daily Press.
    Harris, J.C. GH 140 (2/55): 28.
66. Aesthetic for Benetto Gulgo. Middleton, C.
    P 87 (1/56): 232.
67. Affairs No Longer Foreign. Harvey, M.G. SEP
    227 (2/26/55): 115.
68. Affinities. Stoutenberg, A. SR 39 (7/28/56):
    28.
69. Africa. Diop, D. At 203 (4/59): 80.
70. African Prophecy. Smith, H.A. CC 76 (1/7/59):
    8.
71. African Violet. Kilkeary, G. SEP 228 (3/24/
    56): 129.
72. After a Night Vigil with a Sick Child.
    Smith, J.J. SEP 231 (5/23/59): 107.
73. After a Visit. Roberts, D. YR 46 (Aut/56):
    74.
74. After All. Fandel, J. A 96 (3/9/57): 648.
75. After Christmas. Lattimore, R. NR 139 (12/
    29/58): 19.
76. After Christmas. McDonnell, T.P. A 92 (1/1/
    55): 362.
77. After Columbus. Sullivan, X.X. A 100 (3/7/
    59): 655.
78. After Consulting My Yellow Pages. Wagoner,
    D. NY 35 (10/17/59): 44.
79. After Decision. Edelman, K. SEP 231 (9/27/
    58): 122.
80. After-Dinner Speaker. Neely, L. SEP 230
    (2/8/58): 66.
81. After Dylan Thomas. Johnson, C. Co 69 (12/
    5/58): 257.
82. After Evening Milking. Everson, R.G. At 195
    (2/55): 60.
83. After Four Years. Sarton, M. At 197 (3/56):
    53.
84. After Ice Storm. Ebright, F. SEP 229 (1/5/
    57): 68.
85. After Long Waiting. Rubin, M. SEP 231 (4/
    18/59): 103.
86. After-Luncheon Speaker. Otis, A.F. SEP 231
    (12/13/58): 98.
87. After Rain. Page, P.K. P 89 (11/56): 100.
88. After Reading Keats' Letters. Corman, C.
    P 88 (6/56): 152.
89. After Some Years. Merwin, W.S. H 214 (6/57):
    45.
90. After Speaking of One Who Died a Long Time
    Ago. Colum, P. P 94 (6/59): 179.
91. After Spring. Crouse, M.L. SEP 228 (3/24/
    56): 66.
92. After the Agony in the Garden. Hine, D. Co
    63 (3/23/56): 642.
93. After the Bomb. Corke, H. N 188 (1/10/59):
    38.

94. After the Burst. Coxe, L.O. P 91 (1/58):
    225-6.
95. After the Death of Her Mother. Rukeyser, M.
    P 86 (4/55): 4.
96. After the Flood. Merwin, W.S. NR 135 (7/23/
    56): 19.
97. After the Quarrel. Facos, J. SEP 228 (5/19/
    56): 172.
98. After the Rain. Corke, H. NY 35 (5/23/59):
    39.
99. After the Second Flood. Lehman, W. At 199
    (3/57): 116.
100. After Work. Eckman, F. P 93 (12/58): 164.
101. Afternoon. Kondo, A. P 88 (5/56): 84.
102. The Afternoon as an Aria. Stefanile, F.
     P 87 (10/55): 17.
103. Afternoon in the Animal Kingdom. Flaumenhaft,
     A.S. CH 34 (9/59): 35.
104. Afternoon in the Library. Parker, B.E. GH
     142 (10/56): 13.
105. Afternoon in the Thirties. Kennedy, M. LHJ
     74 (6/57): 120.
106. Afternoon Moon. Potter, M. SEP 230 (8/24/
     57): 62.
107. An Afternoon with a Poet. O'Gorman, N. P 93
     (12/58): 169-70.
108. Afterthoughts on the Lovers. Mueller, L.
     P 94 (8/59): 295.
109. Afterward.... Abel, L. C 23 (6/57): 579.
110. Against Seasons. Mezey, R. NY 35 (2/28/59):
     107.
111. Against That Time, if Ever That Time Come.
     Moss, H. C 22 (11/56): 447.
112. Against the Wind. Gilboa, A. P 92 (7/58):
     248.
113. Age of Discovery. Johnson, L. P 87 (2/56):
     271-2.
114. Age of Miracles. Coblentz, S.A. CC 75 (9/
     10/58): 1024.
115. Aged Eight and Three. Nathan, N. LHJ 75
     (4/58): 188.
116. The Ageing Athlete. Weiss, N. P 88 (8/56):
     317.
117. Agenda. Richstone, M. SEP 229 (5/18/57): 46.
118. Aging Process. Grenville, R.H. SEP 229 (2/
     2/57): 82.
119. Agnus Dei. Hilberry, C. CC 76 (6/3/59): 666.
120. Agonia. Russo, P.G. CC 74 (3/27/57): 389.
121. Agreement with Sir Charles Sedley. Howard,
     R. P 87 (1/56): 221-2.
122. Ah How My Cat Benjamin. Leet, P.M. H 214
     (3/57): 36.
123. Ah Moon. Kinnell, G. P 87 (3/56): 349-50.
124. Ahab on His Wedding Night. Burns, J. P 85
     (3/55): 342-3.
125. Aim. Freeman, J.D. GH 143 (7/56): 28.
126. The Aim's the Same. Cutler, G.B. SEP 231
     (12/27/58): 43.
127. Air-Borne Missy. Hammer, P. SEP 232 (10/17/
     59): 106.
128. Air for a Plastic Hautboy. Knowlton, R.A.
     NY 32 (1/12/57): 28.
129. The Alarm. Wright, J. P 92 (8/58): 282.
130. Alas! Scott, W.T. SR 39 (7/7/56): 13.
131. Alas! Farewell! Graham, E. LHJ 76 (1/59): 81.
132. Albert Einstein on the Violin. Haber, L.
     C 24 (7/57): 19.
133. Alewives Pool. Kinnell, G. P 85 (1/55):
     212-3.
134. Alexandrina. Donnelly, D. P 86 (8/55): 249-
     51.

135. Alfred Lord Tennyson. Whittemore, R. P 86
    (9/55): 313-4.
136. Alias and Milisande; or, Gammon Me Once,
    Gammon Me Twice, You Can Count Gammoning
    Me Thrice. Nash, O. NY 33 (4/27/57): 32.
137. Alike to Thee. Ely, E.S. CT 2 (7/21/58): 11.
138. All at Sea, See, C, Si, Ci, (C) [c].
    Sturges, G.M. WLB 29 (1/55): 363
139. All Fool's Eve. Avison, M. P 91 (12/57):
    173.
140. The All Forgiving. Coblentz, S.A. CC 75
    (12/10/58): 1428.
141. All Hail! Kruse, R. WLB 29 (4/55): 613.
142. All Hallows Eve. McCarthy, L. A 98 (11/2/
    57): 133.
143. All Is Dust. Hagelstange, R. P 88 (7/56):
    255-6.
144. All Joking Aside. Jaffray, N.R. SEP 229
    (6/29/57): 34.
145. All Mornings Brief. Roseliep, R. Co 68 (7/
    25/58): 417.
146. All My Knowing. Beach, J.W. P 87 (2/56):
    288-90.
147. All Souls. Sarton, M. H 215 (11/57): 49.
148. All That Glitters is Not Me. Hammer, P.
    SEP 229 (11/17/56): 88.
149. All the Blue April. Hess, M.W. SEP 227 (4/
    23/55): 127.
150. All the Leaves That Fall. Kahn, H. SEP 230
    (10/5/57): 58.
151. All the Rivers of Eden. Cotter, J.F. A 96
    (1/5/57): 395.
152. All the World's a Library. Godley, M. WLB
    29 (4/55): 609.
153. The Allergic. Stoutenburg, A. NY 33 (3/30/
    57): 129.
154. Alliance. Graham, E. LHJ 72 (12/55): 178.
155. All's Noel That Ends Noel, or Incompati-
    bility Is the Spice of Christmas. Nash, O.
    NY 33 (12/14/57): 42.
156. Alma Mater, Forget Me. Cole, W. At 196 (10/
    55): 102.
157. Almanac. Swenson, M. NY 33 (4/6/57): 154.
158. The Almanac of Time. Thomas, D. P 87 (11/
    55): 90.
159. Almost Bliss. Usk, T. SEP 232 (12/12/59):
    84.
160. Alone. Bohm, E. SEP 228 (4/14/56): 103.
161. Alone Awake. Merrill, H. SEP 231 (5/23/59):
    52.
162. Alone in the House. Quentin, A.R. At 204
    (7/59): 86.
163. Along About March. Eisenlohr, L. SEP 230
    (3/1/58): 79.
164. Along the Shore. Pierce, E.L. CC 76 (8/19/
    59): 947.
165. Aloud. Sward, R. SR 39 (10/27/56): 12.
166. Alpine View. Cane, M. SR 39 (4/7/56): 33.
167. Alternatives. Jamieson, J. CT 1 (9/30/57):
    14.
168. Always Room for One More. Graham, E. LHJ 75
    (6/58): 153.
169. Amagansett Beach. Engle, P. P 86 (8/55):
    273.
170. The Ambassadors. Burford, W. P 95 (11/59):
    78.
171. Ambiguity. Rank, M.O. SEP 232 (11/28/59):
    81.
172. Ameliorating Possibility. Patrice, A. SEP
    230 (5/10/58): 142.
173. America. Simpson, L. SR 39 (5/5/56): 24.
174. America to Hungary, 1956. Coxe, L.O. NR 135
    (12/17/56): 28.
175. An American in the Thieves' Market. Simpson,
    L. AS 28 (Summ/59): 322.
176. American Prayer. Pierce, E.L. CC 72 (6/29/
    55): 752.
177. American Primitive. Keller, M. SEP 231 (7/
    5/58): 67.
178. An American Summer. Hay, J. P 86 (4/55): 21.
179. American Valhalla. Flaumenhaft, A.S. CH 34
    (10/59): 73.
180. Amiss. Lamb, M.W. LHJ 73 (5/56): 155.
181. Among the Paeligni. Humphries, R. P 90
    (9/57): 371.
182. Among the Traffic Dead. Rennert, M. SR 41
    (5/3/58): 30.
183. Amos. Hall, D. P 88 (7/56): 229.
184. The Amphitheatre--Arles. Lister, R.P. NY 34
    (7/26/58): 62.
185. Amusement Park. Collins, B.F. SEP 230 (3/
    15/58): 50.
186. Ana Making Cheese Straws. Blackwell, H.G.
    SEP 232 (10/31/59): 97.
187. Anacreontic. Rattray, D. N 186 (1/18/58):
    55.
188. The Anaesthetic. Galler, D. N 189 (9/26/59):
    178.
189. The Analyst's Lament. Stern, M.P. At 199
    (3/57): 90.
190. The Ancient Dark. McIlnay, R.D. N 184 (4/
    27/57): 375.
191. The Ancient Dunes. Stork, C.W. SR 38 (3/26/
    55): 18.
192. The Ancient Heroes and the Pilot. Hughes,
    T. P 90 (8/57): 280-1.
193. The Ancient Quest. Coblentz, S.A. CC 73
    (1/4/56): 13.
194. And Everywhere Ghost. Hanson, P. P 93 (10/
    58): 22-3.
195. And Goe the Fooles Among. Laing, D. N 188
    (4/25/59): 383.
196. And I Say the Hell with It. Hammer, P. H 216
    (2/58): 54.
197. And in the Fifty-First Year of That Century,
    While My Brother Cried in the Trench,
    While My Enemy Glared from the Cave.
    Plutzik, H. YR 44 (6/55): 566-7.
198. And It Happens That Spirit. Shimoni, D.
    P 92 (7/58): 208.
199. And Mary Sang. Cotter, J.F. A 102 (12/12/
    59): 352.
200. And One Small Leaf. Kahn, H. LHJ 72 (9/55):
    90.
201. And Say We Are Not Lost. Shook, B. LHJ 74
    (2/57): 98.
202. And Smile, Smile, Smile. Bentley, E. N 185
    (11/16/57): 366.
203. And So It Was. Van Doren, M. N 188 (4/25/
    59): 370.
204. And Step. Ignatow, D. P 93 (11/58): 83.
205. And the Time Were May. Coatsworth, E. LHJ
    73 (5/56): 194.
206. And the Virgin. Bode, C. P 91 (2/58): 300.
207. And This Is Hallelujah. Lilly, O. CC 76
    (10/7/59): 1142.
208. And Thomas Knows. Lilly, O. CC 75 (7/23/58):
    851.
209. And You Know. Ashbery, J. P 87 (12/55):
    149-51.

210. Andaluz, I-IV. Belitt, B. P 89 (11/56): 74-80.
211. Anecdote in the Parque Espana. Urdang, C. P 91 (11/57): 96.
212. Anecdote of 2 A.M. Wain, J. P 92 (6/58): 163.
213. The Anesthetic. Galler, D. N 189 (9/26/59): 178.
214. The Angel of the Maze. Dickey, J. P 86 (6/55): 147-53.
215. The Angels. Humphries, R. N 183 (12/15/56): 524.
216. Angels at Breakfast. Lister, R.P. NY 35 (10/24/59): 120.
217. Anger of the Bull. Hull, O.M. P 88 (9/56): 357.
218. Angle. McCrane, J. SR 38 (12/17/55): 22.
219. Angler Emeritus. Ellis, C. SEP 231 (8/30/58): 65.
220. Anima. Eberhart, R. NR 134 (4/30/56): 17.
221. The Animal. Abbe, G. At 201 (3/58): 47.
222. The Animal Inside the Animal. Jacobsen, J. P 91 (1/58): 229-31.
223. Animal Reaction. Schiff, L.K. BHG 37 (9/59): 87.
224. The Animals. Jacobsen, J. Co 68 (8/15/58): 498.
225. The Animals' Carol. Maris Stella, Sr. A 96 (12/29/56): 373.
226. Animated Leaves. Collins, M.G. SEP 230 (9/28/57): 143.
227. Annabel Lee. Poe, E.A. GH 141 (9/55): 14.
228. The Annihilation of Nothing. Gunn, T. P 93 (10/58): 4.
229. Anniversary. Abse, D. P 86 (9/55): 317-8.
230. Anniversary. Isler, B. SEP 230 (2/15/58): 65.
231. Anniversary. Lattimore, R. NY 32 (6/16/56): 35.
232. Anniversary. Ponsot, M. P 90 (6/57): 136.
233. Anniversary Birds. Beum, R. P 91 (2/58): 299.
234. Anniversary Challenge. Shaw, E.W. AF 61 (4/55): 41.
235. Anniversary Eve. Graham, E. LHJ 73 (2/56): 132.
236. Anniversary Song. Raskin, A. GH 142 (4/56): 164.
237. Anno Domini. Clark, L.S. CC 74 (11/6/57): 1312.
238. Annual Complaint. Pratt, W.W. SEP 229 (6/29/57): 34.
239. Annual Garden. Leibrand, E. SEP 230 (5/3/58): 49.
240. Annunciation. Van Allen, G.R. CC 73 (7/11/56): 847.
241. L'Annunciazione: from Bellini. O'Gorman, N. P 90 (8/57): 299.
242. Anomalous Oyster. Heringman, B. N 185 (9/14/57): 140.
243. Another Summer. Merchant, J. SEP 229 (10/13/56): 137.
244. Another Teacher. Whittemore, R. P 86 (9/55): 315.
245. Another Third. Garrigue, J. P 93 (12/58): 135.
246. Anoukis and Later Jeanne. Char, R. P 89 (3/57): 336.
247. Anselmic. Janes, K. CC 72 (8/10/55): 923.
248. Answer at Easter. Grover, K.A. SEP 231 (3/28/59): 116.
249. Answered. Edelman, K. SEP 229 (5/18/57): 102.
250. Answers Please. Ringstad, M.E. WLB 33 (5/59): 632.
251. An Antarctic Hymn. Ciardi, J. SR 42 (1/17/59): 71.
252. Antecedents. Tomlinson, C. P 91 (10/57): 28-35.
253. The Anthropologist. Jones, H.M. At 203 (1/59): 89.
254. Antipiscatorial. Adams, F.P. GH 142 (2/56): 43.
255. Anti-Poem. Laing, D. N 188 (6/13/59): 539.
256. Anti-Romantic. Ponsot, M. P 91 (3/58): 353.
257. Anxiety. Carruth, H. N 186 (4/26/58): 364.
258. Any Summer Afternoon. M. Maura, Sr. YR 48 (3/59): 401.
259. Anybody for Money? Nash, O. NY 32 (2/25/56): 30.
260. Anyone for Nothing? Eisenlohr, L. SEP 230 (3/15/58): 103.
261. Apartness. White, G. LHJ 75 (11/58): 131.
262. Apocalypse. Foster, R. YR 45 (12/55): 249-51.
263. Apocalypse. Ozick, C. C 28 (9/59): 242.
264. Apocalyptic. Delattre, P.H. Co 70 (5/29/59): 226.
265. Apologia Pro Vita Nostra. Sloan, J. C 21 (6/56): 554.
266. Apologia Pro Vita Sua. Ryskind, M. NaR 4 (10/26/57): 379.
267. Apologies to W.S. Gilbert and Most Directors of Libraries. Anonymous, D.Q. LJ 83 (9/15/58): 2363.
268. Apology for No Poems. Gibson, W. H 217 (8/58): 49.
269. Apology to Poets. Dunn, M.B. GH 142 (5/56): 184.
270. The Apotheosis of Alexander. Feldman, I. A 195 (2/55): 58-9.
271. Apple-Blossom Vandal. Savage, F.H. SEP 231 (5/9/59): 58.
272. The Apple Eaters. Russo, L.I. LHJ 73 (9/56): 153.
273. Apple Time. Jacobson, E. LHJ 76 (10/59): 128.
274. Appointment. Kahn, H. LHJ 72 (8/55): 91.
275. The Approach to Thebes. Kunitz, S. P 90 (4/57): 4-5.
276. L'Apres-Midi d'Un Homme. Sandeen, E. P 89 (12/56): 143-4.
277. Apricot in a City Courtyard. Brasier, V. LHJ 72 (3/55): 200.
278. April. Merrill, H. SEP 227 (4/2/55): 75.
279. April. Quinn, J.R. SEP 230 (4/12/58): 70.
280. April Bus to Richmond. Nixon, J. NY 35 (4/4/59): 129.
281. April 15 Complaint. Chadwick, H. SEP 230 (4/12/58): 88.
282. April Fool. Oppenheimer, J.L. N 188 (4/4/59): 300.
283. April in England. Sabe, K. P 85 (3/55): 369.
284. April in the Country. De Jong, D.C. NR 138 (4/28/58): 14.
285. April in Vermont. Freneau, I.D. SEP 227 (4/16/55): 111.
286. April Night. Friedrich, G. CC 74 (4/10/57): 448.
287. April Snow. Saunders, K. SEP 229 (4/13/57): 103.
288. April Song. Hazen, B.S. LHJ 76 (4/59): 141.

289. April Testament. McNeill, L. SEP 231 (4/4/ 49): 98.

290. Apron Strings. Gohn, G.E. BHG 34 (5/56): 350.

291. An Arabian Valentine. Muldoon, E. LHJ 76 (2/59): 123.

292. An Arab's Appeal to His Steed. Sagittarius. NR 139 (8/4/58): 17.

293. Arbor Vitae. Coxe, L.O. NR 135 (9/10/56): 17.

294. Argument for Attics. Farnham, J. SEP 229 (4/27/57): 62.

295. Aristobulus. Cavafy, C. C 19 (2/55): 119.

296. Aristotle to Phyllis. Hollander, J. P 94 (4/59): 19-24.

297. The Arizona Desert, Filmed. Golffing, F. P 91 (1/58): 232.

298. The Ark. Macpherson, J. P 89 (2/57): 267-70.

299. Arkansas. Bowie, B.M. NR 138 (4/21/58): 19.

300. Arkansas Children. Johnson, G.D. NHB 21 (4/58): 152.

301. The Armadillo - Brazil. Bishop, E. NY 33 (6/22/57): 24.

302. Armored Car. Kroll, E. H 214 (4/57): 37.

303. Arms and the Man. Lattimore, R. NR 140 (6/ 1/59): 17.

304. Around the Mountain. Graves, R. NY 34 (7/ 5/58): 26.

305. Arriving 6:25. Kempher, R.M. SEP 231 (12/ 20/58): 77.

306. The Arrogance of Ignorance. Askue, R.P. CH 29 (1/55): 311.

307. Art Appreciation. Schiff, L. BHG 36 (11/58): 159.

308. Art for Art. Kessler, E. SR 42 (2/7/59): 14.

309. An Art of Poetry. O'Gorman, N. P 92 (4/58): 8-9.

310. Art of Teaching. Solovay, J.C. CH 33 (9/58): 6.

311. Art of the Sonnet: VI. Orlovitz, G. P 91 (11/57): 94.

312. Art of the Sonnet: IX. Orlovitz, G. P 90 (4/57): 21.

313. Art of the Sonnet: XXIX. Orlovitz, G. P 88 (9/56): 375.

314. Art of the Sonnet: LV. Orlovitz, G. P 91 (11/57): 94-5.

315. Art of the Sonnet: LVI. Orlovitz, G. P 91 (11/57): 95.

316. Art Song. Nemerov, H. P 88 (9/56): 388.

317. Artesian Spring. Quinn, J.R. SEP 228 (1/2/ 56): 113.

318. The Artist. Crews, J. P 88 (4/56): 17.

319. The Artist. Stepanchev, S. N 189 (8/1/59): 56.

320. The Artist. Williams, W.C. SR 41 (10/11/58): 38.

321. The Artist and the Nude. Stepanchev, S. P 90 (5/57): 88.

322. Artistic Appreciation. Douglass, S. LHJ 74 (5/57): 118.

323. Artist's Testimony. MacKinstry, E. Hn 33 (4/57): 116.

324. As a Wild Bird. Galbraith, G.S. LHJ 76 (11/ 59): 16.

325. As Brooks Rush Headlong. Galbraith, G.S. SEP 231 (11/1/58): 102.

326. As Flowers Are. Kunitz, S. SR 39 (5/5/56): 24.

327. As If. Kreymborg, A. SR 40 (11/9/57): 17.

328. As in a Mirror, Dimly. Janes, K. CC 74 (1/ 16/57): 72.

329. As Peter Loved. Dudley, J.H. CC 74 (1/16/ 57): 72.

330. As Petrarch Coming. Roseliep, R. Co 67 (3/ 14/58): 615.

331. As Pippa Lilted. Stafford, W. P 91 (1/58): 250.

332. As Real As Life. Stone, R. P 87 (10/55): 31.

333. As Sometimes in a Tale. Coblentz, S.A. CC 73 (4/11/56): 452.

334. As Through a Misted Glass. Steinman, D.B. CC 72 (11/23/55): 1361.

335. ...As Tidy Does. Westgate, H. WLB 34 (12/ 59): 303.

336. As to Beauty. Speer, C.A. SEP 231 (8/30/58): 57.

337. As We Forgive--. Giordan, A.R. SEP 229 (9/ 22/56): 115.

338. As You Make It. Bartlett, E. C 26 (9/58): 219.

339. Ascendance. Galler, D. P 92 (4/58): 39.

340. Ascension. Martaugh, I.A. A 100 (3/21/59): 713.

341. The Ascensions. Pillin, W. P 91 (11/57): 104-5.

342. Ash Can. Dufault, P.K. H 212 (5/56): 35.

343. Ash Wednesday. Awad, J. A 92 (3/19/55): 649.

344. Asiatic Flew. Eff, J. NaR 4 (10/5/57): 299.

345. Ask Any Aunt. Richstone, M. TH 33 (5/55): 53.

346. Aspects of Spring in Greater Boston. Starbuck, G. NY 34 (4/12/58): 48.

347. Aspects of Venus. Bentley, B.S. P 94 (4/ 59): 27-9.

348. Aspiration. Lee, C. SEP 231 (12/6/58): 69.

349. Assembling the Family. Hillyer, R. At 202 (10/58): 50.

350. Assembly Line. Stoutenburg, A. SR 41 (12/ 6/58): 56.

351. Assist. Usk, T. SEP 228 (9/24/55): 119.

352. Astrology. Cassity, T. P 94 (4/59): 34.

353. The Asylum. Carruth, H. P 91 (1/58): 219-24.

354. At a Patched Window. Katz, M. C 21 (2/56): 175.

355. At a Summer Hotel. Gardner, I. NY 33 (8/10/ 57): 26.

356. At Acatitlan. Cutler, B. CC 72 (11/2/55): 1267.

357. At Bay. Walton, E.L. P 91 (11/57): 88.

358. At Delft. Tomlinson, C. NY 35 (12/5/59): 48.

359. At Earle Birney's School. Stafford, W. P 94 (7/59): 229-31.

360. At Eventide. Mansfield, M.A. NHB 22 (2/59): 107.

361. At Hearne. Bernard, O. P 86 (5/55): 75.

362. At Kent Everybody Reads. AB 52 (2/58): 103.

363. At Lyons. Takenaka, I. P 88 (5/56): 77.

364. At Majority. Rich, A.C. NY 32 (3/17/56): 40.

365. At Mamallapuram. Merrill, J. P 91 (2/58): 283.

366. At Milton's Imagined Grave. Rosen, S. P 86 (6/55): 154.

367. At No Loss for Words. Galbraith, G.S. SEP 229 (4/13/57): 46.

368. At Son-Up. Schlitzer, S. SEP 229 (3/16/57): 46.

369. At Summer's End. Liddell, B.C. GH 142 (10/ 56): 13.

370. At the Banquet. Schlitzer, S. SEP 229 (3/2/ 57): 40.

371. At the Book's Ending. Coblentz, S.A. CC 75 (9/17/58): 1052.
372. At the Border. Kessler, S. SR 41 (4/12/58): 67.
373. At the Crossroad. Blackburn, P. N 187 (12/6/58): 429.
374. At the Custer Monument. Stafford, W. SR 39 (11/13/56): 21.
375. At the Death of Roy Campbell. Wright, D. P 92 (4/58): 25-6.
376. At the Executed Murderer's Grave. Wright, J. P 92 (8/58): 277-80.
377. At the Jewish New Year. Rich, A.C. NY 32 (9/1/56): 28.
378. At the Kaiser's Villa. Wright, D. P 95 (11/59): 86-7.
379. At the Old Place. Stafford, W. P 91 (1/58): 250.
380. At the Shore. Oakes, N.E. SR 41 (11/22/58): 38.
381. At the Tombs of the House of Savoy. Smith, W.J. P 91 (10/57): 8.
382. An Atmosphere. Fleming, H. P 95 (12/59): 161-2.
383. Atomic Institute. Huntiers, K. SR 38 (6/4/55): 29.
384. Atomic Submarine. Bracker, M. SR 39 (2/4/56): 39.
385. Attending. Rago, H. P 91 (10/57): 4-6.
386. Attention: Book-of-the-Month Club. McGinley, P. NY 34 (5/10/58): 38.
387. Attention with Intention. Van Hise, A. AS 28 (Aut/59): 457.
388. Attitudes. Eberhart, R. P 88 (8/56): 318.
389. Au 'Voir. Galbraith, G.S. SEP 229 (11/17/56): 61.
390. Aubade. Friedrich, G. CC 72 (6/29/55): 752.
391. Aubade. Jerome, J. N 181 (9/10/55): 230.
392. Aubade. Laing, D. N 187 (10/25/58): 299.
393. Aubade. Lamb, M.W. LHJ 72 (5/55): 108.
394. Aubade. Prasad, J. P 93 (1/59): 257.
395. Aubade. Wheelock, J.H. NY 32 (6/30/56): 23.
396. Aubade at the Zama Replacement Depot. Wright, J. P 89 (3/57): 353-4.
397. Aubade: The Desert. Bock, F. P 93 (10/58): 32-33.
398. Auction at the Hillside Farm. Mack, R. SEP 229 (1/26/57): 92.
399. Augeias and I. Graves, R. H 216 (6/58): 35.
400. August. Crook, K. SEP 232 (8/1/59): 77.
401. August 1. Lindeman, J. P 91 (1/58): 242-3.
402. August 2. Lindeman, J. P 91 (1/58): 243.
403. August 5. Lindeman, J. P 91 (1/58): 244.
404. August Moon. Friedrich, G. SR 38 (8/20/55): 16.
405. August Rain. Heafield, K. CC 75 (7/30/58): 873.
406. August Song. Shook, B. LHJ 74 (8/57): 105.
407. August Sun. Duncan, R. P 91 (3/58): 384.
408. Augustine. Stafford, W. P 91 (1/58): 251.
409. Auld Lang Syne. Krausz, S. SEP 229 (1/5/57): 75.
410. Aunt Mabel. Geiger, D. P 88 (4/56): 24.
411. Auschwitz. Enrico, H. N 185 (11/16/57): 350.
412. Authority. Douglass, S. LHJ 75 (9/58): 153.
413. Autobiography. Hartley, R.E. SEP 228 (5/12/56): 55.
414. Autobiography in the Year 1952. Amihai, Y. C 27 (5/59): 386.
415. Auto-psychography. Pessoa, F. P 87 (10/55): 26.

416. Autumn. Craig, R.B. NHB 19 (1/56): 87.
417. Autumn. Dickinson, E. GH 141 (11/55): 14.
418. Autumn. Robertson, P.A. Hn 35 (10/59): 406.
419. Autumn. Tomlinson, C. P 94 (4/59): 8-10.
420. Autumn and After. Velton, W. P 88 (9/56): 380.
421. Autumn Beach. Bohm, E. LHJ 72 (10/55): 112.
422. Autumn Chapter in a Novel. Gunn, T. P 86 (6/55): 136-7.
423. Autumn Duet. Petite, I. LHJ 76 (6/59): 164.
424. An Autumn in a Word. Ferlinghetti, L. N 189 (8/15/59): 80.
425. Autumn in Another State. Hollander, J. NR 137 (11/11/57): 17.
426. Autumn Leaves. Ginsberg, L. EJ 45 (9/56): 356.
427. Autumn Love. Hearst, J. LHJ 76 (11/59): 114.
428. Autumn Moment. Zlotnik, H. EJ 47 (10/58): 397.
429. Autumn Nymphal. Coxe, L.O. NR 137 (10/7/57): 18.
430. Autumn on Cape Cod. Starbuck, G. SR 42 (2/21/59): 48.
431. Autumn on the Skyline Drive. Drewry, C. SEP 232 (10/31/59): 51.
432. Autumn Song. Taylor, A. LHJ 75 (10/58): 195.
433. An Autumn Walk. Bynner, W. At 202 (9/58): 36.
434. An Autumn Wood. Todd, R. H 215 (10/57): 51.
435. Autumnals. Friedrich, G. SR 38 (11/19/55): 44.
436. The Avant Garde. Lowenfels, W. N 187 (10/25/58): 296.
437. Averages: A Pantomime. Honig, E. SR 40 (5/11/57): 19.
438. The Awakened. Jacobson, E. SEP 228 (3/3/56): 76.
439. Awful Thought. Peck, J. SEP 232 (7/11/59): 39.
440. Awkward Attitude. Sagittarius. NR 138 (2/3/58): 7.
441. The B-Hive. Berigan, B. SR 39 (3/17/56): 41.
442. The B Minor Mass. Grayer, R. SR 42 (4/18/59): 22.
443. A Babe Is Born. SR 38 (12/3/55): 36.
444. The Baby. Raskin, S. SEP 227 (3/12/55): 80.
445. Baby Sitter. Landeweer, E. SEP 232 (8/15/59): 83.
446. Baby Sitting Grandma. Parrish, M.M. LHJ 76 (2/59): 83.
447. Baby Spoon. Smith, L.C. SEP 230 (3/8/58): 98.
448. Bach at a Funeral Service. Delattre, P.H. CC 74 (7/31/57): 917.
449. Bach in Sacred Heart Chapel. Mary Virginia, Sr. A 94 (10/29/55): 130.
450. Bachelor. Meredith, W. P 88 (6/56): 165.
451. Back. Witt, H. P 90 (4/57): 11-2.
452. Back Again from Yucca Flats. Kelley, R.S. NR 139 (8/18/58): 28.
453. The Back of Mine Hand to Mine Host. Nash, O. NY 35 (9/19/59): 40.
454. The Back of My Mind to You! Talman, T. BHG 34 (10/56): 235.
455. The Back Road. Graves, S.B. SEP 228 (6/2/56): 104.
456. Back to Nature. Armour, R. NY 34 (3/15/58): 121.
457. Back to the Engine. Green, F.P. NY 33 (10/19/57): 153.

458. Back-yard Barbecue. Thorson, S. SEP 228 (8/6/55): 71.
459. Backlog. Armstrong, P. SEP 232 (8/8/59): 49.
460. Backward Glance. Constantine, J. LHJ 76 (7/59): 38.
461. Backward Psalm. Petrie, P. NR 135 (12/31/56): 17.
462. Bad Dream. Gill, B. NY 35 (3/7/59): 131.
463. Bad Script. Neely, L. SEP 229 (11/24/56): 84.
464. A Ball Is for Throwing. Rich, A. P 90 (8/57): 303.
465. Ballad. McFarland, E. LHJ 72 (3/55): 179.
466. Ballad. McGahey, J. P 93 (11/58): 78-9.
467. Ballad for Montogomery. Waterman, W. NHB 19 (4/56): 158.
468. A Ballad for Holy Week. Sullivan, D. At 197 (2/56): 51.
469. The Ballad of Longwood Glen. Nabokov, V. NY 33 (7/6/57): 27.
470. Ballad of the Ikendick. Ciardi, J. N 187 (9/13/58): 136.
471. Ballad of the Mermaid of Zennor. Watkins, V. P 95 (10/59): 11-14.
472. Ballad of the Red Giants. Hansen, J. At 204 (7/59): 88.
473. Ballad of the World's Kindness. Brecht, B. NR 135 (9/24/56): 21.
474. A Ballad--The Lake of the Dismal Swamp. Moore, T. SR 38 (8/6/55): 39.
475. Ballade at Eight Bells. McCord, D. NY 32 (4/14/55): 38.
476. Ballade for the Birds. McCord, D. SR 41 (6/14/58): 46.
477. Ballade of a Tropical Cruise. Thornton, W. NY 31 (1/14/56): 99.
478. Ballade of a Voice Crying. Tobin, J.E. A 93 (5/28/55): 242.
479. Ballade of the Early Seas. Myers, E.L. P 91 (12/57): 184.
480. Ballade of the Peace Conferences. Noyes, A. NaR 1 (1/18/56): 17.
481. Ballade to a Book Borrower. Solovay, J.C. WLB 31 (1/57): 387.
482. Ballade to Be Read in the Medici Gardens. Stock, R. P 92 (4/58): 13-5.
483. Ballade to Venus. Goodman, P. AN 57 (5/58): 29.
484. Ballet Slippers. Matthews, A.C. SEP 229 (2/23/57): 203.
485. Baltimore. Nash, O. Hl 21 (3/57): 88-93.
486. Baltimore Summer. Raynor, O. P 87 (1/56): 230-1.
487. Bamboo. Hall, D. P 86 (8/55): 268-9.
488. Banjo Boomer. Stevens, W. At 195 (3/55): 66.
489. Banquet Bore. Schlitzer, S. SEP 228 (4/28/56): 147.
490. Barbecue. Sward, R.S. P 94 (5/59): 85.
491. Barberous. Talman, T. SEP 227 (4/16/55): 100.
492. Barbershops. Burr, H. SEP 231 (4/4/59): 158.
493. Bare Trap. Emmons, D. SEP 228 (8/6/55): 48.
494. Bare Tree. Lindbergh, A.M. At 195 (3/55): 56.
495. Barefoot Road. Peterson, R.D. SEP 229 (7/28/56): 64.
496. Barely Visible. Saunders, K. SEP 232 (9/19/59): 119.
497. The Bargain. Galbraith, G.S. LHJ 76 (3/59): 188.
498. Bargain Hunter. Neely, L. SEP 227 (4/23/55): 133.
499. Barges on the Hudson. Deutsch, B. P 87 (12/55): 147.
500. A Barn, a School, or a Church. Walsh, C. LHJ 75 (8/58): 122.
501. Baroque Epigram. Tyler, P. P 88 (6/56): 150-1.
502. The Barracuda. Eff, J. NaR 6 (7/5/58): 61.
503. Barred Islands. Booth, P. YR 44 (6/55): 568.
504. Bars and the Bear. Engle, J.D., Jr. SEP 229 (3/9/57): 74.
505. The Base that Mac. Built. Sagittarius. NR 138 (3/31/58): 8.
506. The Basket-Maker. Colum, P. At 200 (12/57): 66-7.
507. The Bass. Plutzik, H. YR 44 (6/55): 565.
508. The Bat. Eff, J. NaR 6 (7/5/58): 61.
509. The Bat. Zilles, L. NY 32 (10/20/56): 177.
510. The Bath. McFarland, E. LHJ 76 (2/59): 33.
511. The Bather. Wolf, L. Co 64 (6/1/56): 225.
512. The Battenkill in Winter. Nemerov, H. P 88 (9/56): 385.
513. The Battle of Bonn. Sagittarius. NR 137 (9/23/57): 10.
514. Battle of the Box Tops. Jennison, C.S. SEP 230 (6/7/58): 140.
515. Battle-Piece. Belitt, B. P 95 (11/59): 69-74.
516. Bawdry Embraced. Hughes, T. P 88 (8/56): 295-7.
517. Bay Windows. Quinn, J.R. SEP 231 (10/4/58): 58.
518. Be Constant, My Love. Lineaweaver, M. LHJ 76 (12/59): 86.
519. Be My Valentine. Sagittarius. NR 138 (2/17/58): 7.
520. Be Still. Pierce, E.L. CC 74 (7/10/57): 842.
521. Beach Baubles. De Vito, E.B. SEP 229 (6/22/57): 61.
522. Beach Plums. McFarland, E. LHJ 72 (8/55): 138.
523. Beach Site. Landeweer, E. SEP 229 (5/25/57): 80.
524. Beach Talk. Maccaig, N. P 86 (5/55): 81.
525. The Bean Eaters. Brooks, G. P 94 (9/59): 373-5.
526. Bear. Merwin, W.S. P 85 (1/55): 214-6.
527. The Bear Who Came to Dinner. Stoutenburg, A. SR 41 (4/12/58): 69.
528. Beasts. Pillin, W. P 86 (9/56): 334.
529. Beat. Delattre, P.H. CC 76 (7/15/59): 828.
530. Beatitude for Steven. Ellis, C. SEP 228 (2/18/56): 56.
531. A Beautiful Day at Jerusalem's Mills. Solomon, M. P 94 (6/59): 168-9.
532. Beauty. Rothenberg, R. Hn 35 (8/59): 280.
533. Beauty and the Beast. Clower, J. P 93 (10/58): 7-8.
534. Beauty and the Beast. Tomlinson, C. P 88 (9/56): 348-50.
535. Beauty-Blind. Nash, M. SEP 229 (10/20/56): 146.
536. The Beauty of Job's Daughters. MacPherson, J. P 93 (12/58): 146.
537. Because I Live. Ames, E. H 213 (2/56): 67.
538. Because Noni Trespassed in the Night. O'Gorman, N. P 92 (4/58): 3-4.
539. Because You Would Not Bend. Morgan, L.S. LHJ 74 (3/57): 220.

540. The Beda Flower. Han, U.T. At 201 (2/58): 112.
541. Bedrock. Carruth, H. P 93 (3/59): 357-8.
542. Bedtime. Eisenlohr, L. SEP 231 (4/4/59): 78.
543. Bedtime Rhyme. Galbraith, G.S. SEP 228 (6/9/56): 141.
544. Bedtime Story. Solovay, J.C. CH 32 (11/57): 154.
545. The Bee. Fandel, J. Co 70 (9/18/59): 514.
546. Bee Stings Cure Arthritis. Rosenberg, J.L. At 203 (6/59): 59.
547. The Beech Wood. Sarton, M. LHJ 72 (10/55): 100.
548. The Bees. Donaldson, S. LHJ 75 (9/59): 113.
549. A Beethoven Dance. Conrad, S. NR 133 (10/31/55): 25.
550. The Beetle. Galler, D. P 92 (4/58): 34-5.
551. Before Good Night. Brasier, V. LHJ 76 (4/59): 156.
552. Before the Cathedral. Iris, S. P 91 (11/57): 101.
553. Before the First Opening. Papatzonis, T. At 195 (6/55): 105.
554. Before We Mother-Naked Fall. Thomas, D. P 87 (11/55): 89-90.
555. Before Your Third. Muir, E.A. At 197 (5/56): 55.
556. The Beggar's Manuscript. McFarland, E. LHJ 73 (7/56): 131.
557. The Beginning of Wisdom. Pierce, E.L. CC 75 (1/8/58): 40.
558. Behavior That Gives Who Away? Or Whom. Watt, W.W. NY 35 (8/1/59): 22.
559. Behind Science. Rawlins, W. CC 74 (4/3/57): 419.
560. Behind the Umpires Backs the Stars Relax. Nash, O. L 39 (9/5/55): 85.
561. Behold the Yogi. Lee, M.L. GH 148 (3/59): 211.
562. Behold Your King. Mary Cathlin, Sr. A 92 (3/19/55): 649.
563. Being. Grace, W.J. A 96 (3/9/57): 646.
564. Being Married. Moraes, D. P 93 (1/59): 250.
565. Bejeweled Callers. Long, E.E. SEP 229 (6/15/57): 55.
566. Belated Thanks. Merchant, J. SEP 231 (11/29/58): 98.
567. Belief. Miles, J. NR 134 (4/30/56): 22.
568. Bell Buoy. Merwin, W.S. N 184 (4/27/57): 368.
569. Bell Song. Freeman, J.T. LHJ 73 (4/56): 111.
570. Belladonna. Holmes, D. SR 41 (11/1/58): 22.
571. Below the Lighthouse. Dickey, J. P 94 (7/59): 232-5.
572. Bendix. Updike, J. NY 33 (2/15/58): 30.
573. Beneath This White. Seager, R.W. SEP 232 (12/19/59): 47.
574. Benediction. Viereck, P. P 85 (2/55): 255.
575. Benefit Performance. Warsaw, I. SEP 231 (8/2/58): 57.
576. Benevolent Boss. Heath, C. SEP 230 (6/28/58): 125.
577. A Benison on C.S. Jennison. Clapp, D. At 198 (8/56): 25.
578. Berceuse. Ebright, F. At 201 (4/58): 99.
579. Berceuse. Pillin, W. P 86 (9/55): 335.
580. Berceuse. Ponsot, M. P 90 (6/57): 132.
581. Berg. Miles, J. P 94 (6/59): 146.
582. Best Loved of Africa. Danner, M. P 89 (10/56): 23.

583. The Best Minds of What Bloody Generation. Weales, G. NR 138 (4/7/58): 18.
584. Best Time of Day. Chadwick, H. SEP 228 (4/21/56): 81.
585. Bethlehem Was Small. Jacobs, F.B. LHJ 75 (12/59): 160.
586. Betrayal. Moffitt, J. SR 39 (11/24/56): 33.
587. Betrayed. Bangham, M.D. CC 72 (8/31/55): 991.
588. Between Christmas and Good Friday. Eckhart, A.R. CC 74 (1/30/57): 128.
589. Between Classes. Willis, S.D. EJ 48 (3/59): 122.
590. Between Friends. Usk, T. SEP 229 (11/24/56): 100.
591. Between Ironwood and the Sea. Scott, W.T. P 89 (1/57): 226-7.
592. Between the Airbase and the Radar Tower. Coxe, L.O. NR 140 (4/6/59): 20.
593. Between the City and the Sea. DeLongchamps, J. P 90 (8/57): 284.
594. Between Them and Portugal. Kumin, M.W. SR 41 (8/9/58): 27.
595. Between Town and City. Nathan, L. P 89 (10/56): 19-22.
596. Between Two Worlds. Apin, R. At 197 (6/56): 163.
597. Between Worlds. Cone, L.O. N 187 (9/27/58): 176.
598. Beware--Friendly Dog. Armknecht, R.F. SEP 228 (4/14/56): 128.
599. Beware, Saunterer, of This Desperado, a Mr. Bones, a Bad Actor. Plutzik, H. YR 44 (6/55): 565-6.
600. Beyond Her Depth. Broughton, J. P 92 (4/58): 11.
601. Beyond the Hunting Woods. Justice, D. NY 32 (7/7/56): 73.
602. The Big Buck and the Little Buck. Herschberger, R. P 86 (6/55): 141.
603. Big Claus and Little Claus. Burke, K. N 182 (4/14/56): 331.
604. Big Dam. Moses, W.R. P 91 (12/57): 166.
605. Big Dipper. Landeweer, E. SEP 230 (7/27/57): 73.
606. Big Wheel. Otis, A.F. SEP 231 (7/26/58): 73.
607. The Biggest Thing. Galbraith, G.S. LHJ 74 (7/57): 129.
608. Binding the Dragon. Sarton, M. N 183 (11/10/56): 410.
609. Biographical. Fadiman, C. SR 40 (6/1/57): 24.
610. Biology, I Love You. Carlisle, I. GH 142 (3/56): 28.
611. Bird Feeding Young. Ginsberg, L. CH 33 (3/59): 428.
612. Bird of Paradox. Otis, A.F. SEP 231 (1/17/59): 66.
613. Bird of Prey. Grenville, R.H. SEP 229 (10/13/56): 122.
614. Bird Song. Dicker, H. N 182 (6/2/56): 473.
615. The Birds Begin to Gather. Coatsworth, E. LHJ 74 (9/57): 154.
616. Birds on a Telegraph Wire. Coblentz, S.A. CC 72 (9/7/55): 1022.
617. Birds Waking. Merwin, W.S. NY 32 (4/14/56): 44.
618. Birth. Gilboa, A. P 92 (7/58): 248-9.
619. The Birth. Meireles, C. At 197 (2/56): 128.
620. Birth. Schwartz, S.S. P 89 (11/56): 82.

621. Birth. Takahashi, S. P 88 (5/56): 89.
622. The Birth of Athena. Clower, J. P 93 (10/58): 9.
623. The Birth of Venus. Carruth, H. P 93 (3/59): 358-9.
624. The Birth of Venus. Rukeyser, M. N 183 (11/10/56): 399.
625. The Birth of Venus. Urdang, C. P 89 (11/56): 105.
626. Birthday. Merwin, W.S. N 186 (4/26/58): 367.
627. The Birthday-Cake Glockenspiel. Henley, E. LHJ 72 (11/55): 177.
628. A Birthday Candle. Justice, D. NY 33 (3/16/57): 152.
629. Birthday Card. Broughton, J. P 92 (4/58): 12.
630. Birthday Gift. Gibbs, E. SEP 231 (10/18/58): 97.
631. Birthday Observance. Nathan, L. NY 35 (5/9/59): 46.
632. Birthday Roses. Eisenlohr, L. SEP 230 (5/24/58): 51.
633. The Bite. Kumin, W. H 219 (7/59): 84.
634. Biting Remarks. Lazarus, P. TH 33 (8/55): 22.
635. A Bitter Life. Updike, J. NY 31 (1/7/56): 26.
636. Bitter the Cup. Kreiser, M. LHJ 73 (11/56): 183.
637. Bitter Thoughts on Receiving a Slice of Cordelia's Wedding Cake. Graves, R. NY 33 (7/27/57): 34.
638. Bittersweet. Albright, R.L. LHJ 72 (10/55): 132.
639. Black and White. Longfellow, E.B. SEP 228 (8/13/55): 84.
640. Black Cross. Fussell, E. P 86 (5/55): 91.
641. Blest Crib! Blest Cross! Patrick, J.G. CC 75 (12/17/58): 1455.
642. Black Eyes. Chi, L. NY 34 (3/8/58): 112.
643. Black Jackets. Gunn, T. P 93 (10/58): 2-3.
644. Black Jess. Dufault, P.K. NY 35 (5/30/59): 27.
645. Black Water and Bright Air. Carrier, C. NY 31 (1/21/56): 90.
646. Blackboard Jungle. Stokely, J. N 182 (5/12/56): 404.
647. Blackboard Room. Wolcott, K. SEP 229 (11/3/56): 87.
648. Blast Off. Singer, H. P 94 (8/59): 286-7.
649. Bless. Holmes, J. LHJ 72 (11/55): 109.
650. Blessed Is the Man. Moore, M. LHJ 73 (8/56): 101.
651. Blind Child. Cotter, J.F. A 94 (12/17/55): 334.
652. Blind, I Speak to the Cigarette. DeLongchamps, J. P 90 (8/57): 285.
653. The Blind Lead the Blind. Brown, S. NY 33 (5/25/57): 44.
654. The Blind Man. Marx, R. P 86 (8/55): 281.
655. A Blind Man's Bluff. Belvin, W. P 85 (2/55): 255-6.
656. Blizzard in March. Mansfield, M. SEP 229 (3/9/57): 90.
657. Blked. Updike, J. NY 34 (6/21/58): 90.
658. Blood. Morris, H. P 88 (7/56): 214-5.
659. The Blood. O'Gorman, N. P 93 (12/58): 171.
660. The Blow Lands. Gordon, D. N 180 (8/20/55): 159.
661. Blowing Weather. Merchant, J. SEP 227 (2/19/55): 125.

662. Blue and White. Morais, V. At 197 (2/56): 108.
663. A Blue Day. Koehler, G.S. P 95 (12/59): 156.
664. The Blue-Eyed Daisy. McFarland, E. LHJ 72 (4/55): 182.
665. Blue-Eyed Grass. Turner, E.E. LHJ 75 (7/58): 113.
666. The Blue Fire of April. Trott, R.C. LHJ 75 (4/58): 91.
667. Blue Fox. Ote, T. P 88 (5/56): 96.
668. The Blue Grains. Eberhart, R. P 95 (10/59): 2.
669. Blue Grosbeaks. Jacobson, E. SEP 230 (6/28/58): 46.
670. Blue Heron. Miner, V.S. SEP 229 (2/9/57): 107.
671. Blue Jay. Goodman, M.W. SEP 229 (6/1/57): 103.
672. Blue Monday. Grenville, R.H. SEP 229 (5/25/57): 61.
673. The Blue Saint of Brecon. Duryee, M.B. SR 38 (6/4/55): 35.
674. The Blue Tablecloth. Marz, R. P 95 (10/59): 9.
675. The Blue Tree. Scott, W.T. P 87 (2/56): 270.
676. Blueberry Girl. Abbe, G. SR 39 (5/5/56): 26.
677. Boat Whistle Blues. Conklin, B.S. LHJ 72 (9/55): 201.
678. Boating at Yaddo. Herschberger, R. P 86 (6/55): 143.
679. Boats on the Marne. Montale, E. P 92 (5/58): 100-1.
680. Boatyard in Spring. Brown, S. NY 33 (4/13/57): 44.
681. The Body Builder. Nash, O. L 39 (9/5/55): 90.
682. Body of Waking. Rukeyser, M. P 86 (4/55): 1-2.
683. Boiling Eggs. Moss, H. NR 134 (5/21/56): 20.
684. Bone. Morris, H. P 88 (7/56): 212-3.
685. Bone China. Lister, R.P. NY 33 (1/25/58): 30.
686. Bone Dance. Duncan, R. P 95 (10/59): 33-5.
687. Bone Thoughts on a Dry Day: Chicago. Starbuck, G. NY 33 (10/19/57): 50.
688. Bonfire. Hess, M.W. SEP 230 (11/23/57): 53.
689. A Book. Ellis, S. WLB 30 (4/56): 644.
690. Book Borrower. Solovay, J.C. WLB 31 (4/57): 645.
691. Book Burial. Shapiro, K. NR 139 (12/1/58): 18.
692. Book Buyer's Plea. Yudkin, Mrs. S. SR 39 (6/2/56): 14.
693. Book Gluttony. Field, A. WLB 31 (1/57): 387.
694. The Book of Kells. Colum, P. At 196 (7/55): 53.
695. Book Reviewers Lament. Kime, H.C. WLB 29 (1/55): 367.
696. Book Reviews. Kruse, R.E. WLB 29 (4/55): 613.
697. Book Shelf. Ringstad, M.E. WLB 32 (4/58): 594.
698. Books. Ringstad, M.E. WLB 32 (2/58): 419.
699. Books. Shores, W.M. WLB 30 (11/55): 262.
700. Books on Exhibit. Ringstad, M.E. WLB 33 (12/58): 305.
701. Boom. Nemerov, H. N 186 (1/25/58): 81.
702. Boor But Honest. Stewart, M. SEP 229 (11/10/56): 55.
703. Bootless Speculations. McGinley, P. NY 33 (10/5/57): 49.

704. Borrowing Bookworms. Reinert, D.E. WLB 31 (10/56): 184.
705. Boston. Moore, M. LHJ 76 (1/59): 88.
706. Botanical Garden. Witt, H. P 90 (4/57): 13.
707. A Botanical Trope. Meredith, W. P 88 (6/56): 167.
708. Boulevards in Autumn. Rizzardi, A. P 94 (8/59): 319.
709. A Bouquet from a Fellow-Roseman. Graves, R. NY 32 (6/30/56): 30.
710. Bout. Whitt, M.W. SEP 232 (12/12/59): 102.
711. Boy and Parade. Moore, R. SR 40 (7/6/57): 29.
712. Boy and Pool. Bruce, C. SEP 229 (8/11/56): 77.
713. The Boy and the Watch. Zimmerman, E.H. SEP 231 (10/4/58): 106.
714. Boy at Piano. Isler, B. SEP 228 (8/27/55): 70.
715. Boy Buried on Sunday. Marz, R. P 86 (8/55): 280.
716. Boy in a Monastery. McCarthy, L. A 96 (3/9/57): 647.
717. Boy in a Museum. Bohm, E. GH 142 (3/56): 28.
718. Boy in Church. Hutchinson, R. At 199 (2/57): 54.
719. Boy in Clover. Faubion, D. SEP 228 (7/23/55): 91.
720. Boy Meets Bath. Armour, R. TH 34 (1/56): 28.
721. Boy on Bike. Lee, M.L. GH 142 (5/56): 184.
722. Boy, Reading. Counselman, M.E. SEP 228 (5/19/56): 150.
723. Boy Riding Forward Backward. Francis, R. SR 39 (3/10/56): 13.
724. Boy with a Basket Ball. Freeman, A.D. SR 41 (7/5/58): 10.
725. Boy with a Kerosene Lamp. Moody, M.H. LHJ 75 (8/59): 129.
726. Boy with Snake. Crown, R. P 90 (6/57): 159.
727. Bracketeer. Eisenlohr, L. SEP 231 (8/11/59): 55.
728. Braemar. Kinnell, G. P 87 (3/56): 352.
729. Braggadocio. Collins, M.G. SEP 231 (9/27/58): 86.
730. The Brahms. Morris, H. P 88 (7/56): 218.
731. Braille. Mullins, T.Y. CT 3 (2/2/59): 8.
732. The Branches of Water or Desire. Dugan, A. P 88 (4/56): 7-10.
733. The Brave Names. Singer, H. P 94 (8/59): 284.
734. Brave Valentine. Milbrath, M.M. SEP 227 (2/12/55): 82.
735. The Bravery of Love. Stafford, W. P 88 (9/56): 364.
736. The Breach. Middleton, C. SEP 231 (6/13/59): 72.
737. Bread. Levertov, D. N 188 (6/13/59): 543.
738. Breakfast in Bed in the Hospital. Ciardi, J. H 219 (8/59): 26.
739. A Breast Humming. Crawford, J., Jr. P 94 (5/59): 103.
740. Breath. Morris, H. P 88 (7/56): 216-7.
741. Bride in Eden. Adrian, V.H. SEP 229 (9/15/56): 109.
742. The Bride Is a Motive of Melody. Eaton, C.E. P 89 (3/57): 343-4.
743. Bridegroom. Blanchard, E. SEP 227 (6/4/55): 64.
744. The Bride's Complaint. Mueller, L. P 94 (8/59): 294.

745. Bride's Winter. Singleton, M.E. SEP 229 (3/2/57): 96.
746. The Bridge. Abbe, G. P 88 (9/56): 372.
747. The Bridge. Lister, R.P. At 199 (2/57): 88.
748. Bridge Park. Petrie, P. NY 33 (8/24/57): 74.
749. Bridges. Dicker, H. N 184 (3/30/57): 282.
750. Brief Definition of a Sunday Nap. Chadwick, H. SEP 228 (9/10/55): 121.
751. Brief Description of Hoarded String. Armour, R. SEP 228 (6/30/56): 79.
752. A Brief Guide to Rhyming; or, How Be the Little Busy Doth? Nash, O. NY 32 (2/9/57): 33.
753. Brief Lives in Not So Brief--I. Nash, O. NY 35 (10/31/59): 49.
754. Brief Lives in Not So Brief--II. Nash, O. NY 35 (11/7/59): 50.
755. Brief Lives in Not So Brief--III. Nash, O. NY 35 (11/14/59): 50.
756. Brief Love. Savage, F.H. LHJ 75 (11/58): 91.
757. Brief Note to a Creditor. Grenville, R.H. SEP 230 (10/11/57): 118.
758. Brief Summary of the Events Leading Up to the Explosion. Rittell, H. SEP 228 (7/23/55): 99.
759. Bright Gravity. Nicholl, L.T. AS 26 (Spr/57): 195.
760. Brighten the Corner. Galbraith, G.S. SEP 228 (6/16/56): 93.
761. A Brighter Hellas. Berkeley, D.S. CT 3 (4/13/59): 14.
762. Bringing Up Parents. Richstone, M. SEP 230 (5/17/58): 132.
763. Broader the Lawn in Those Summers. Nicholl, L.T. AS 28 (Summ/59): 341.
764. Broadway Harlequin. Feldman, I. NR 141 (10/5/59): 20.
765. The Broken Music Box. Lee, C. SEP 232 (8/1/59): 65.
766. Brotherhood. Razaf, A. NHB 20 (12/56): 76.
767. Brotherly Eden. Trent, L. CC 72 (7/27/55): 868.
768. Brotherly Love. Hughes, L. N 183 (8/18/56): 142.
769. Brought to Love. Duncan, R. P 91 (3/58): 377.
770. Brown. Brand, M. NY 35 (4/11/59): 44.
771. Brown, All of the Autumn. Stefanile, F. P 87 (10/55): 18.
772. Brown Moment. Engle, J.D., Jr. SEP 232 (9/5/59): 80.
773. Brown Mountain. Sorrentino, G. N 188 (5/23/59): 482.
774. Brown Study. Lister, R.P. At 200 (10/57): 171.
775. A Brueghel Nativity. Williams, W.C. N 186 (5/31/58): 499.
776. The Brute! Pennington, P. SEP 229 (4/20/57): 46.
777. Bucolic. Merwin, W.S. N 186 (2/8/58): 125.
778. Budapest. McCallister, C. Co 71 (10/16/59): 77.
779. Budapest: November 1, 1956. Hubert, A.M. C 24 (11/56): 402.
780. Bufo, Vulgaris. Ciardi, J. H 213 (10/56): 38.
781. Bug Talk. Houghton, F.A. At 201 (2/58): 62.
782. Build Well That House. Flint, L. GH 148 (5/59): 251.
783. The Builder of Houses. Cooper, J. P 93 (10/58): 19-21.

784. Builders. Corbin, J. Hb 63 (10/59): 131.
785. Building Estate. Johnson, G. CC 76 (1/18/ 59): 195.
786. Building Problem. Schiff, L.K. SEP 230 (1/ 18/58): 87.
787. The Bulganin Boat Song. Cortes, D. At 198 (11/56): 115.
788. The Bull of Bendylaw. Plath, S. Hn 35 (4/ 59): 148.
789. Bullfighter Story. Carson, A. P 86 (5/55): 92-3.
790. Bullfrog. Hughes, T. NY 35 (8/8/59): 26.
791. Bunch of Wild Flowers. Zilles, L. NY 32 (7/7/56): 67.
792. The Burial. Doherty, K.F. A 95 (6/2/56): 244.
793. Burned Forest. Barker, S.O. SEP 230 (2/22/ 58): 50.
794. Burning Mountain. Merwin, W.S. NY 33 (1/25/ 58): 36.
795. Burning the Cat. Merwin, W.S. H 211 (10/55): 71.
796. Bus Journey. Ebright, F. SEP 229 (7/14/56): 82.
797. Bus to Marienlund. Sandeen, E. P 95 (11/ 59): 100.
798. The Buses Headed for Scranton. Nash, O. NY 32 (3/10/56): 40.
799. The Bush. Coxe, L.O. P 91 (1/58): 228.
800. Business Offices. Coblentz, S.A. CC 72 (3/ 9/55): 296.
801. Busy Child. Frost, F. GH 149 (10/59): 235.
802. The Busy Man. Mullins, T.Y. CT 2 (1/6/58): 7.
803. But Doctor--. Bonaluto, L.M. SEP 228 (5/12/ 56): 127.
804. But Honey, It Wasn't Like That! Jaffray, N.R. SEP 230 (5/31/58): 90.
805. But Soft.... Sagittarius. NR 138 (1/20/58): 5.
806. But Utamaro: Secretly. Tyler, P. AN 57 (3/ 58): 44.
807. But What Was Beauty? Coatsworth, E. LHJ 74 (2/57): 131.
808. Butterflies. Chapin, K.G. P 92 (5/58): 77.
809. Butterfly. Blackwell, H.G. GH 142 (6/56): 119.
810. Butterfly. Burns, R.G. NY 35 (5/30/59): 98.
811. Butterfly. Smith, W.J. At 200 (9/57): 93.
812. Butterfly Collection. Hicky, D.W. SEP 231 (6/27/59): 61.
813. By Any Name. Mary Immaculata, Sr. A 98 (10/ 12/57): 40.
814. By Auto & Camera in Navajo Country. Honig, E. SR 39 (7/14/56): 19.
815. By Coincidence. Galbraith, G.S. SEP 230 (9/ 28/57): 82.
816. By Marriage I Make Evil. Hull, O.M. P 92 (9/58): 354.
817. By Saint Callixtus' Tomb. Posner, D.L. P 90 (8/57): 274.
818. By the Ancient Castle at Komoro. Shimazaki, T. P 88 (5/56): 73.
819. By the Fire. Merrill, H. SEP 228 (9/17/55): 54.
820. By the Marsh. Tanaka, F. P 88 (5/56): 65.
821. Byroad. Harrington, H. SEP 230 (8/14/57): 179.
822. The Cabin Builders. Johnson, W.R. P 86 (9/ 55): 331.

823. A Cabin Summer. Buchwald, E.B. AS 27 (Summ/ 58): 318-20.
824. Cacti. Gardener, W. NY 32 (4/28/56): 110.
825. The Cactus. Bandeira, M. At 197 (2/56): 139.
826. The Cage. Dudek, L. SR 41 (10/25/58): 34.
827. Cain. Cordan, W. P 88 (7/56): 254.
828. Cairo. Lerner, M. NR 139 (8/18/58): 24.
829. Calenture. Reid, A. NY 34 (7/19/58): 28.
830. The Calico Cat. Cresson, A. GH 142 (11/56): 13.
831. California, an Ode. Gibbs, B. P 91 (12/57): 152-6.
832. Caligula's Dream. Updike, J. Co 68 (6/27/ 58): 327.
833. Call of the Jungfrau. Eff, J. NaR 5 (2/15/ 58): 156.
834. Calligraphy. Seferis, G. At 195 (6/55): 159.
835. Calling Heaven, Line 2, Ring 4. Gibbons, A. LHJ 74 (10/57): 134.
836. Calling the Child. Shapiro, K. NY 34 (5/ 31/58): 34.
837. Calling the Turn. Power, J.W. BHG 33 (2/ 55): 21.
838. Cambridge. O'Hara, F. P 90 (5/57): 90.
839. Camel. Derwood, G. P 85 (2/55): 268.
840. Camel. Merwin, W.S. P 85 (1/55): 217-9.
841. Camel. Smith, W.J. At 200 (9/57): 93.
842. The Camel Bells of Jericho. Pillowe, W.C.S. Hb 63 (2/59): 45.
843. Camel-Bird. Datta, S. P 93 (1/59): 218-9.
844. Camelot. Watkins, V. P 89 (3/57): 338-40.
845. Camera Piece. Wangsgaard, E.W. SEP 228 (8/27/55): 54.
846. Campaign Note. Merwin, W.S. N 183 (12/1/ 56): 482.
847. Campaign Song. Lemon, R. NY 32 (8/18/56): 90.
848. A Campus in Summer. Whittemore, R. NR 140 (6/15/59): 16.
849. Canada: Case History. Birney, E. SR 42 (10/ 24/59): 54.
850. Canada Warbler. Kinnell, G. P 87 (3/56): 349.
851. Cancion de Las Siete Doncellas. Blackburn, P. N 185 (11/16/57): 355.
852. Candle in the Wind. Walker, C.T. CC 72 (12/ 7/55): 1425.
853. Candle Star. Brown, L.R. GH 149 (11/59): 223.
854. Candlelighter. Elmer, F.D., Jr. CC 72 (10/ 26/55): 1235.
855. Candles of the Heart. Pack, R. C 21 (6/56): 508.
856. Candy for a Little Mexican Boy. LHJ 75 (9/ 59): 115.
857. A Canon for Two Voices. Carruth, H. P 89 (3/57): 366.
858. The Cantankerous One. Roethke, T. NY 33 (11/30/57): 50.
859. Canticle. Roseliep, R. A 99 (4/26/58): 144.
860. Canticle in October. MacLow, J. C 24 (7/ 57): 74.
861. Canticle of the Columns. Valery, P. P 94 (4/59): 1-4.
862. Canto XVIII. MacNeice, L. NR 132 (5/16/55): 26-7.
863. Canzonetta. Gardner, I. At 195 (4/55): 90.
864. Capacity. Updike, J. NY 32 (1/5/57): 29.
865. Cape Dread. Merwin, W.S. N 183 (11/10/56): 391.

866. Capercaille, Ave Atque Vaille. Nash, O. NY 35 (4/25/59): 48.
867. Captain Bud. Lister, R.P. NY 35 (5/9/59): 42.
868. The Captain of Sand Dredge. Rainer, D. SR 39 (5/5/56): 23.
869. Captain Slocum in West Tisbury for W.M.T. Todd, R. SR 42 (9/19/59): 41.
870. The Car Barn Under Coogan's Bluff. Goodman, P. P 88 (8/56): 306.
871. Card Trick. Alkus, M. SEP 229 (12/8/56): 70.
872. Cards, Cards, Cards. Lockhart, M.L. WLB 29 (1/55): 367.
873. Care. Miles, J. NY 35 (11/7/59): 176.
874. Caretaker. Freeman, A.D. SEP 232 (7/4/59): 47.
875. Caribbean. Hall, D. P 92 (6/58): 170.
876. Carillon. Thompson, J.B. CC 76 (9/2/59): 994.
877. Carlsbad Caverns. Barker, S.O. SEP 230 (10/19/57): 92.
878. A Carol. Thorley, W. LHJ 73 (12/56): 116.
879. A Carol for Palm Sunday. Waugaman, C. CT 3 (3/2/59): 11.
880. Carol for the Christmas Angels. Maris Stella, Sr. A 102 (12/19-26/59): 374.
881. A Carol Out of Season. Deutsch, B. NY 31 (1/7/56): 71.
882. Carol: To a Child. Hilberry, C. CC 76 (12/16/59): 1464.
883. The Carousel. Galler, D. P 92 (4/58): 35-6.
884. Carpenter-Wise. Lilly, O. CC 74 (8/28/57): 1007.
885. Case History. Burke, K. N 183 (7/7/56): 21.
886. A Case of Premeditated Compatability. Hammer, P. GH 140 (5/55): 99.
887. The Case of the Helping Hand. Moreland, G. B. and Smith, Mrs. T.L. LJ 80 (4/15/55): 844-5.
888. Cash Reserve. Galbraith, G.S. BHG 36 (2/58): 9.
889. Cassandra. L'Heureux, J. Co 69 (2/27/59): 566.
890. Castra. Colt, B. YR 48 (9/58): 78-81.
891. The Casualty. Hughes, T. P 94 (8/59): 279-80.
892. Cat. Smith, W.J. SR 38 (12/10/55): 19.
893. Cat and Mouse. Hughes, T. P 94 (8/59): 297.
894. Cat and the Autumn Stars. Frost, F. A 95 (9/22/56): 591.
895. Cat Cay. Perry, R. P 91 (10/57): 20.
896. Cat-Faith. Reid, A. P 93 (2/59): 293-4.
897. Cat Nap. Freeman, A.D. SEP 232 (12/5/59): 86.
898. Cat on the Walk. Long, E.E. SEP 229 (3/23/57): 120.
899. The Cat Sat on the Mat. Mottram, E. P 93 (2/59): 306-7.
900. The Catalog Is 'Only Secondarily a Reference Tool'. Reed, S.R. LJ 81 (1/1/56): 23-4.
901. The Catalpa. Bell, C.G. LHJ 74 (5/57): 178.
902. Catamount. Huff, R. At 201 (4/58): 74.
903. Catch What You Can. Garrigue, J. SR 39 (10/13/56): 25.
904. Cathay. Loehlin, J. H 210 (2/55): 50.
905. The Cathedral. Miller, H.A. CT 1 (9/16/57): 8.
906. Catkind. Graves, R. H 219 (10/59): 77.
907. Cats. Hitchcock, A. SR 40 (1/12/57): 10.

908. Catty Commuter. Small, H. SEP 229 (10/13/56): 151.
909. Cause and Effect. Swenson, M. N 182 (3/10/56): 200.
910. Caw-Cus. McNeill, L. SEP 229 (9/22/56): 58.
911. A Celebration. Hoffman, D.G. LHJ 76 (1/59): 94.
912. A Celebration. Rago, H. A 93 (5/21/55): 212.
913. A Cellar Song. Reaney, J. P 94 (9/59): 380.
914. Center of Gravity. Armour, R. SEP 231 (4/25/59): 78.
915. Central Park Spring. Solum, S. SR 38 (5/14/55): 18.
916. Certain Things. Smith, R.P. GH 142 (4/56): 164.
917. Certified. Merchant, J. SEP 230 (10/19/57): 61.
918. Chaconne. Perry, R.L. P 92 (6/58): 155-6.
919. Chagall's Ebony Horse. Swan, J. AS 26 (Aut/57): 459.
920. Chair, Dog, and Clock. Corke, H. NY 35 (6/27/59): 26.
921. Challenge. Trent, L. CC 75 (4/9/58): 438.
922. Challenge. Wheeler, P.M. CC 76 (8/5/59): 900.
923. A Challenge to Teachers. Robbins, B.B. CH 30 (10/55): 89.
924. The Chance. Holmes, J. N 184 (2/16/57): 143.
925. The Change. Weiss, T. N 187 (11/22/58): 387.
926. A Change in the Weather. Burrows, E.G. P 93 (11/58): 90.
927. A Change in the Weather. Gibbs, R. LHJ 75 (7/59): 72.
928. Change of Hearts. Emmons, D. SEP 230 (2/15/58): 77.
929. Chant at Aquidneck: Pars Verna. Fandel, J. P 92 (9/58): 359.
930. Chanty. Beum, R. P 91 (2/58): 298.
931. Chapel. Delattre, P.H. CC 76 (3/4/59): 260.
932. Charade. Lougee, D. P 86 (7/55): 235-6.
933. Charge and Countercharge. Collins, I.J. SEP 227 (3/5/55): 98.
934. Charles Darwin. Whittemore, R. P 86 (9/55): 312-3.
935. Charles Peguy. Touster, S. P 89 (1/57): 238-9.
936. Charm. Donnelly, D. P 88 (8/56): 298.
937. Charm for the Tooth-Ache. Murry, P. P 92 (4/58): 18.
938. A Charm of Goldfinches, A Writhe of Worms. Lineaweaver, M. H 218 (2/59): 60.
939. A Charm to Be Whispered. Carke, H. N 184 (6/8/57): 503.
940. Charmed Circle. Gleason, M. SEP 230 (1/18/58): 65.
941. Charms. Aucort, J. LHJ 73 (9/56): 102.
942. Chart 1203. Booth, P. P 88 (7/56): 239.
943. Charter Member. Tenney, J.H. SEP 231 (6/27/59): 82.
944. Chartres: July 1955. Chandler, D. Co 69 (1/9/59): 384.
945. Chateau de Muzot. Tomlinson, C. P 92 (5/58): 104-5.
946. Checkers. Marx, A. SEP 230 (5/10/58): 52.
947. Checkmate. Fitzsimmons, T. NR 137 (9/23/57): 17.
948. Cheerful Company. Cresson, A. SEP 229 (4/27/57): 124.
949. Chemiseration. Armstrong, P. SEP 231 (10/25/58): 53.

950. Cherry-Pie Paradox. Merchant, J. SEP 231 (2/21/59): 96.

951. The Cherry Tree in a Storm. Schevill, J. NR 132 (6/20/55): 20.

952. The Chess Dance. Garrigue, J. P 90 (9/57): 337-40.

953. Chez Cythera. Tyler, P. P 86 (8/55): 259-61.

954. Chiaroscuro. Thompson, J.B. CC 76 (10/14/59): 1181.

955. Chicago. Mary Faith, Sr. A 97 (9/28/57): 677.

956. Chicago Dynamic. Sandburg, C. L 43 (11/4/57): 107-10.

957. Chickens the Weasel Killed. Stafford, W. P 91 (1/58): 249.

958. The Child. Boyson, E. C 26 (11/58): 382.

959. Child. Sandeen, E. NY 33 (6/8/57): 101.

960. Child Adopted. Faubion, D. SEP 229 (3/9/57): 83.

961. Child and the Tide. Chapin, K.G. NR 139 (10/13/58): 19.

962. Child at Dusk. Taylor, A.D. LHJ 74 (12/57): 146.

963. A Child at Play. Cotter, J.F. A 93 (9/17/55): 593-4.

964. A Child at Winter Sunset. Van Doren, M. At 204 (11/59): 75.

965. A Child Ill. Betjeman, J. H 213 (7/56): 69.

966. Child in a Sandbox. Johnson, W.M. SEP 228 (8/13/55): 87.

967. Child of Light. Cotter, J.F. A 94 (12/24/55): 357.

968. The Child of Many Winters. Haag, J. SR 42 (1/17/59): 61.

969. Child on a Beach. Chaffee, E.A. SEP 231 (8/9/58): 69.

970. Child on a Pullman. Krieger, R. At 199 (2/57): 53.

971. Child on a Streetcar. Harrington, H. SEP 231 (8/16/58): 89.

972. Child, Play Not in the Sand. Ratliff, H., Jr. CC 73 (11/21/56): 1352.

973. Child Running. Frost, F. A 95 (4/28/56): 111.

974. Child Singing. Grenville, R.H. SEP 230 (12/21/57): 72.

975. The Child Whose Name is Love. La Bombard, J. At 197 (1/56): 46.

976. Childhood. Drummond de Andrade, C. At 197 (2/56): 160.

977. Childhood. O'Gorman, N. P 88 (6/56): 162-3.

978. The Children. Marz, R. P 95 (10/59): 8.

979. Children and Leaves. Solomon, M. P 91 (11/57): 98.

980. Children Defy the Winter King. Nathan, L. P 91 (3/58): 375.

981. Children of God. Kraft, V.A. CC 72 (8/24/55): 967.

982. Children of Light. Huff, R. At 198 (10/56): 60.

983. Children Selecting Books in a Library. Jarrell, R. NR 132 (2/23/55): 23.

984. Children Sliding. Abbe, G. GH 140 (3/55): 99.

985. Children, the Sandbar, That Summer. Rukeyser, M. P 86 (4/55): 3.

986. The Children's Innocent and Infinite Window. Schwartz, D. NR 132 (1/3/55): 19.

987. Children's Recital. Richstone, M. SEP 229 (12/8/56): 60.

988. Children's Menu. Isler, B. BHG 33 (5/55): 207.

989. Child's Game. Jerome, J. SR 41 (2/15/58): 25.

990. A Child's Valentine. Stockdale, A.B. GH 142 (2/56): 44.

991. Child's Voice. Averitt, E. LHJ 75 (4/58): 30.

992. China Is an Island. Sagittarius. NR 139 (9/1/58): 7.

993. Chinese Baby Asleep. Donnelly, D. LHJ 76 (3/59): 43.

994. The Chinese Doll. Lal, P. P 93 (1/59): 247.

995. The Chinese Horse. Perry, R. P 95 (12/59): 171.

996. The Chinese Kite. Solomon, M. P 89 (3/57): 357.

997. Chinese Poetry. Hitchcock, A. P 92 (9/58): 358.

998. Choice. Langland, J. P 89 (3/57): 358-9.

999. The Choice of Weapons. Kunitz, S. NR 135 (7/2/56): 18.

1000. The Choir and Music of Solitude and Silence. Schwartz, D. NR 141 (9/28/59): 27.

1001. Les Choise--Neige. Lewin, R.A. NY 34 (2/22/58): 134.

1002. Chokecherries. Montague, J.L. NY 32 (9/15/56): 152.

1003. The Cholthoi Panel. Beum, R. P 90 (5/57): 81.

1004. Choosing the Site. Church, R. At 202 (10/58): 70-1.

1005. Chores with Robert Frost. Bulkeley, M. SR 39 (3/24/56): 27.

1006. Chosen and Appointed Path. Smith, J.C. CT 2 (10/28/57): 19.

1007. Chosen Roads. Keith, J.J. SR 38 (1/8/55): 28.

1008. Christ Church Meadows, Oxford. Hall, D. NY 33 (10/5/57): 44.

1009. A Christening. Belvin, W. P 89 (1/57): 218.

1010. Christening. Warwick, D. A 100 (1/17/59): 467.

1011. Christian Patriots, Inc. Stokely, J. N 182 (5/12/56): 404.

1012. Christmas. Magaret, H. A 98 (12/21/57): 375.

1013. Christmas. Olson, C. N 188 (1/3/59): 18.

1014. Christmas Card List. Clark, L.C. SEP 231 (12/13/58): 80.

1015. A Christmas Child. Engle, P. BHG 37 (12/59): 10.

1016. Christmas Day in the Morning. Shotwell, J.T. SR 38 (12/24/55): 6.

1017. Christmas Day is Come. Wadding L. SR 38 (12/3/55): 16.

1018. Christmas Eve at Chartres. Hare, W. At 196 (12/55): 46-7.

1019. Christmas Greeting. Patrick, J.G. CC 72 (12/7/55): 1429.

1020. Christmas Harvest. McDonnell, T.P. A 94 (12/24/55): 358.

1021. A Christmas Legend. McGinley, P. M 87 (12/59): 28.

1022. Christmas List. Longfellow, I.B. SEP 232 (12/12/59): 47.

1023. Christmas Lullaby. Koppes, Sr. M.C. A 96 (12/22/56): 351.

1024. Christmas Poem. Cummings, E.E. At 198 (12/56): 55.

1025. Christmas Presents from a Little Girl. Dunn, M.B. GH 142 (12/57): 8.

1026. Christmas Problem. Blackwell, P.J. SEP 229 (12/1/56): 83.

1027. Christmas Questions. Doyle, M. M 87 (12/59): 168.

1028. Christmas Symbol. Lennen, E. CC 72 (12/21/55): 1493.

1029. The Christmas Trees. Owen, J. Hn 33 (12/57): 531.

1030. Christoforo Colombo. Wallace, R.A. SR 39 (12/15/56): 21.

1031. Chronic Necessities. Chadwick, H. SEP 230 (8/24/57): 98.

1032. Chronicle. Zlotnik, H. EJ 45 (10/56): 408.

1033. Chronology. Cassity, T. P 86 (8/55): 275.

1034. Chrysalis. Webb, M.H. AS 28 (Spr/59): 183-84.

1035. The Church in Search Thereof. Molton, W.L. CC 73 (3/14/56): 332.

1036. The Church of San Antonio de La Florida. Petrie, P. NY 34 (2/7/59): 30.

1037. Church Supper. Kroll, E. H 214 (4/57): 37.

1038. Cicada. Stoutenburg, A. NY 33 (8/3/57): 24.

1039. The Cigar Store Indian's Gift to the Puritans. Carroll, P. P 94 (5/59): 93.

1040. Cinquain. Schulz, H.A. CC 76 (9/30/59): 1114.

1041. Cinquain: Easter Morning. Mullins, T.Y. CT 3 (3/16/59): 6.

1042. Circus. Blackwell, P.J. SEP 227 (6/4/56): 114.

1043. Circus Clown. Grenville, R.H. SEP 229 (4/20/57): 109.

1044. Circus in Three Rings. Plath, S. At 196 (8/55): 68.

1045. The Citadel. Galbraith, G.S. SEP 229 (10/27/56): 105.

1046. Cities of Refuge. Bangham, M.D. CC 74 (6/5/57): 705.

1047. A Citizen Looks at the Female Figures on an Ancient Jar. Burke, K. N 183 (10/27/56): 352.

1048. Citrus Country. Isler, B. SEP 227 (1/15/55): 61.

1049. Citrus Harvest. Isler, B. SEP 229 (2/23/57): 88.

1050. City Afternoon. Howes, B. NR 140 (1/12/59): 20.

1051. City Late. Gemmell, J. P 86 (5/55): 80.

1052. City Life. Heller, C.E. Hb 63 (9/59): 125.

1053. City Science. Bishop, M. NY 32 (3/31/56): 66.

1054. City View. Matthews, A.C. SEP 231 (6/20/59): 65.

1055. City Woman. Leibrand, E. SEP 229 (8/24/56): 48.

1056. Civil Defender. Starbuck, G. NR 136 (4/8/57): 17.

1057. Civil War House: England. Simpson, R.A. P 95 (11/59): 96.

1058. Civilities of Lamplight. Tomlinson, C. P 90 (4/57): 10.

1059. Clairvoyance. Stoutenburg, A. SR 40 (4/27/57): 22.

1060. Clam Diggers. Eberhart, R. LHJ 75 (7/58): 126.

1061. Clara Bodfish. Squires, R. P 90 (5/57): 93-4.

1062. Clarence Darrow. Masters, E.L. NR 136 (9/27/57): 16.

1063. Class of '58. Grenville, R.H. SEP 230 (12/28/57): 39.

1064. The Class Will Come to Order. Kunitz, S. N 184 (6/29/57): 571.

1065. Classroom Heaven. Solovay, J.C. CH 30 (10/55): 97.

1066. Clatter. Grenville, R.H. SEP 229 (12/56): 48.

1067. Claustrophobia. Rawlins, W. CC 75 (7/30/58): 873.

1068. Clay. Dell, G.F. At 202 (7/58): 71.

1069. Clay God. Burford, W. P 95 (11/59): 78.

1070. Clearance. Lee, M.L. GH 142 (8/56): 121.

1071. Clerihews. Fadiman, C. NY 32 (5/5/56): 37.

1072. Clerihewsful. Fadiman, C. SR 40 (6/1/57): 24.

1073. Cliche'. Davidson, G. SR 38 (12/3/55): 29.

1074. Cliff Idyll. Freneau, I.D. SEP 228 (4/28/56): 102.

1075. Cliptomaniac. Parrish, M.M. SEP 228 (1/21/56): 50.

1076. The Clock. Hanes, H.R. SEP 228 (3/24/56): 119.

1077. The Clock. Quinn, J.R. GH 142 (3/56): 28.

1078. Clock and Three Candles. Walton, E.L. P 94 (5/59): 89.

1079. The Clock Hart. Sobiloff, H. P 92 (6/58): 164.

1080. A Clock Without Hands. Nemerov, H. P 88 (9/56): 382.

1081. Close-Up. Ammons, A.R. P 93 (3/59): 372-3.

1082. Closed Shop. Merrill, H. SEP 228 (6/16/56): 131.

1083. Closing Prayer. Patrick, J.G. CC 72 (7/6/55): 784.

1084. Closing the Cabin. Merrill, H. SEP 232 (9/26/59): 47.

1085. Closing the Resort. Denney, R. NR 132 (3/14/55): 20.

1086. Clothes Tree. Rosenfield, L. At 198 (12/56): 111.

1087. The Cloud. Sagittarius. NR 137 (9/30/57): 8.

1088. Cloud Above the Land. Harvey, R.E. SEP 228 (6/30/56): 75.

1089. Cloud of an Ancient Rage. Hassmer, W. P 90 (4/57): 27.

1090. Cloud-Seeding. Nemerov, H. P 88 (9/56): 382.

1091. The Clouds of Spring. Lynch, B. Hn 33 (6/57): 234.

1092. The Clown: He Dances in the Clearing by Night. Guthrie, R. N 185 (11/2/57): 307.

1093. The Clown's Heart. Morris, H. P 93 (12/58): 158-9.

1094. The Clown's Report on Satyrs. Guthrie, R. N 187 (11/22/58): 388.

1095. The Coast at Grand Isle. Cassity, T. P 94 (4/59): 35-6.

1096. Coast Flight. Hare, W. At 199 (1/57): 80.

1097. Coast Route: California. Spingarn, L.P. SR 39 (3/3/56): 10.

1098. A Coat for My Mother. Wood, A. YR 45 (9/55): 104-5.

1099. The Cock of Confidence. Witt, H. NR 136 (5/27/57): 27.

1100. Cocktail Party. Gibson, D. SEP 231 (6/6/59): 55.

1101. Cocktails. Salinger, H. SR 39 (9/1/56): 32.

1102. Code of Honor. Stokely, J. N 182 (5/12/56): 404.

1103. Cognizance of All We Know. Van Hise, A. AS 28 (Aut/59): 466.

1104. Cokkils. Smith, S.G. P 88 (4/56): 36.

1105. Colchis Bay. Grenville, R.H. SEP 230 (5/10/58): 95.

1106. A Cold Day on the Marx-Engels Platz, East Berlin. MacInnes, M. N 188 (1/3/59): 14.

1107. The Cold Divinities. Wright, J. YR 47 (12/57): 236-7.

1108. Cold Facts. Raskin, A. BHG 35 (3/57): 120.

1109. The Cold Glass Door. Tanaka, F. P 88 (5/56): 66.

1110. Cold Iron. Kipling, R. HBR 34 (5-6/56): 93.

1111. Cold Journey. Rorty, J. SR 41 (6/4/58): 26.

1112. Cold Proposition. Kerman, F.G. SEP 229 (1/26/57): 95.

1113. Cold Reception. Merrill, H. SEP 231 (6/6/59): 102.

1114. Cold-War Bulletin from the Cultural Front. Starbuck, G. H 218 (2/59): 89.

1115. Cold-Weather Love. Everson, R.G. SR 41 (10/18/58): 56.

1116. Colette. Engle, P. P 88 (8/56): 321-3.

1117. A Collection of Epitaphs. P., R.I. AH 9 (4/58): 112.

1118. College Town. Weismiller, E. H 214 (3/57): 80.

1119. College Walk, Postwar. Fall, D. N 186 (6/7/58): 520.

1120. Colman the Hermit. McGinley, P. Co 66 (9/20/57): 617.

1121. Colonel Johnson's Ride. Huff, R. At 202 (7/58): 58.

1122. Color. Cane, M. AS 26 (Aut/57): 442.

1123. Color Chart. Schulberg, L. SEP 232 (10/17/59): 145.

1124. Color in the Cold. Longchamps, J.de LHJ 75 (12/59): 89.

1125. The Colosseum. Watkins, V. N 84 (2/9/57): 127.

1126. Columbia the Abbot. McGinley, P. Co 67 (10/25/57): 93.

1127. Combat Cultural. Moore, M. NY 35 (6/6/59): 40.

1128. Come, Come, Kerouac! My Generation Is Beater Than Yours. Nash, O. NY 35 (4/4/59): 45.

1129. Come Green Again. Scott, W.T. N 184 (6/22/57): 551.

1130. Come Home. McCarthy, L. A 94 (12/24/55): 358.

1131. Come Soon, Come Now. Pierce, E.L. CC 75 (7/30/58): 875.

1132. Come Summer. Coles, C.L. LHJ 75 (7/58): 83.

1133. Comet Crossing Ahead. Rosenfield, L. SEP 231 (8/2/58): 46.

1134. Coming Attraction. Rosenfield, L. SEP 229 (5/25/57): 91.

1135. Coming Down. Morse, S.F. P 90 (7/57): 206-7.

1136. Coming of Air Age. Summers, H.,Jr. SR 40 (9/14/57): 54.

1137. Coming of the Bridal Wind. Levine, R. P 87 (3/56): 353.

1138. Comma Il Faut. Solovay, J.C. EJ 42 (4/58): 194.

1139. Comme on Voit Sur la Branche. Ronsard, P.de P 85 (1/55): 200.

1140. Comment in Re Girls Who Look Good Enough to Eat. Pennington, S. SEP 229 (6/8/57): 80.

1141. Comment on Cows. Armour, R. SEP 228 (6/23/56): 91.

1142. Committees. Gaertner, J. At 200 (10/57): 189.

1143. Committees in Heaven? Cully, K.B. CT 3 (5/11/59): 12.

1144. The Communion. Levertov, D. P 94 (7/59): 245.

1145. Communion. Ward, W.A. CC 72 (2/23/55): 237.

1146. Communion Meditation. Pierce, E.L. CC 72 (5/11/55): 563.

1147. Commuter's Sentence. Raskin, A. SEP 228 (4/28/56): 138.

1148. Companion. Richstone, M. SEP 231 (8/23/58): 48.

1149. Companions. Balch, B.J. SEP 230 (7/20/57): 51.

1150. Companions. Stoutenburg, A. SR 39 (12/8/56): 12.

1151. Companions in the Garden. Char, R. P 94 (4/59): 37-40.

1152. A Company of Mine Is Nature. Seg, K.D. Hn 32 (2/56): 25.

1153. Comparison of Flowers. Gill, J.J. P 86 (6/55): 157-9.

1154. Compassion. Delattre, P.H. CC 76 (2/23/59): 225.

1155. Compassion. Eckhardt, A.R. CC 72 (11/16/55): 1328.

1156. Compensation. Malody, B.M. EJ 44 (12/55): 536.

1157. Complaint at the Library. Hodges, E.J. WLB 32 (12/57): 296.

1158. Complaint Department. Merrill, H. SEP 229 (11/17/56): 125.

1159. The Complaint of a Young Priest. O'Gorman, N. P 93 (12/58): 172-3.

1160. The Complete Cycle of Government Social Planning. Stroup, W.H. NR 6 (1/31/59): 493.

1161. Complex Autumnal. Kizer, C. P 87 (1/56): 208-9.

1162. Compliment. Richstone, M. SEP 231 (4/4/59): 114.

1163. Complin. Hamilton, H. N 187 (11/29/58): 413.

1164. Component. Janes, K. CC 76 (8/26/59): 966.

1165. Components. Ream, D.C. CT 1 (3/18/57): 5.

1166. Comrades of Silence. Supervielle, J. At 201 (6/58): 44.

1167. Conception. Ponsot, M. A 93 (5/21/55): 213.

1168. Concerning the Guest Towel. Brasier, V. SEP 230 (11/16/57): 143.

1169. Concerning Weather. Summers, H., Jr. AS 27 (Spr/58): 182.

1170. Concert. Ginsberg, L. EJ 44 (12/55): 524.

1171. Condensation. Sweet, A.P. WLB 31 (1/57): 395.

1172. Confession. Stone, R. P 89 (1/57): 211.

1173. Confession Concerning My Troubles With the Straight-and-Narrow Path. Wheeler, R. SEP 232 (11/7/59): 66.

1174. Confessions of Zilpah. Haber, L. C 22 (7/56): 27.

1175. Confetti for a Red Haired Bride. Bagg, R. P 92 (9/58): 365-6.

1176. Confidential to Wives. Chadwick, H. BHG 33 (5/55): 251.

1177. Conformer. Kahn, H. AS 24 (Aut/55): 458.

1178. Confusion. Cregeen, S. N 184 (6/15/57): 528.

1179. Congo. Smith, H.A. CC 74 (1/9/57): 40.

1180. Congratulations. Wolf, L. C 28 (10/59): 323.

1181. Congratulations, Commiserations and So Forth. Lemon, R.C. NY 33 (5/4/57): 143.

1182. A Congressman's Prayer. Adams, J.Q. AH 9 (12/57): 128.

1183. Conjure. Miles, J. P 92 (6/58): 141.

1184. Connection in October. Levant, H. P 89 (12/56): 167.

1185. The Conqueror. Smith, J.J. SEP 231 (4/4/59): 153.

1186. Conscience. Lilly, O. CC 74 (4/24/57): 513.

1187. Conscience. Raiziss, S. Co 63 (12/9/55): 257.

1188. Conscience. Richstone, M. SEP 230 (11/9/57): 122.

1189. Conscience. Usk, T. SEP 230 (4/26/58): 128.

1190. Conscience Struck. Armour, R. BHG 35 (2/57): 112.

1191. Conservation Piece, 1957. Neame, A. P 91 (2/58): 315-6.

1192. Conservatives. Armour, R. SEP 229 (1/26/57): 87.

1193. A Consolation. Drewry, C. SR 38 (10/15/55): 15.

1194. Consolation. Ford, E. LHJ 73 (10/56): 180.

1195. Consolation. Grenville, R.H. SEP 232 (11/28/59): 53.

1196. Consolation to the Returning Fighters Against the Floods. Chu, T. At 204 (12/59): 79.

1197. Consolations. Plutzik, H. N 187 (12/20/58): 484.

1198. Conspicuous Variation. Galbraith, G.S. LHJ 75 (10/59): 140.

1199. Conspiracy. Eisenlohr, L. SEP 231 (12/20/58): 58.

1200. Conspirators. Havard, P. SEP 229 (1/19/57): 75.

1201. The Constant Merchandising Manager to His Love. Martin, P. SEP 227 (2/5/55): 81.

1202. The Constant Reviewer. Mumford, O. WLB 29 (5/55): 726.

1203. Constellation of the Tree. Donnelly, D. A 101 (5/30/59): 394.

1204. Constellations. Rizzardi, A. P 94 (8/59): 321.

1205. Constitutional. Starbuck, G. NR 139 (9/29/58): 20.

1206. The Constructed Space. Graham, W.S. P 93 (10/58): 30.

1207. Contemplative Blossom. Galbraith, G.S. SEP 232 (8/15/59): 78.

1208. Contentment. Mary Davida, Sr. A 94 (12/24/55): 358.

1209. Continuity. Brisco, P. LHJ 75 (9/58): 25.

1210. Continuity. Ponsot, M. A 99 (7/12/58): 413.

1211. Contrary Things. Mack, R. SEP 228 (10/8/55): 91.

1212. A Contrite Heart. Mullins, T.Y. CC 75 (10/8/58): 1143.

1213. Convalescent. Armour, R. SEP 228 (10/8/55): 82.

1214. Convalescent. Burger, O.K. GH 142 (5/56): 184.

1215. The Convent Bell. Drake, L.B. Co 69 (12/12/58): 290.

1216. Convention Wives. Brown, D. SEP 231 (6/6/59): 84.

1217. Conversation. Galbraith, G.S. SEP 230 (7/20/57): 73.

1218. Conversation English. Matthews, T.S. H 211 (10/55): 77.

1219. Conversation in Black and White. Sarton, M. N 187 (11/1/58): 305.

1220. Conversation with a Child. Cotter, J.F. A 98 (11/16/57): 209.

1221. Conversational Taboo. De Vito, E.B. LHJ 74 (4/57): 111.

1222. Conviction. De Leeuw, C. N 180 (1/29/55): 102.

1223. Convoy. Booth, P. P 92 (5/58): 83-4.

1224. Cook's Detour. Lamport, F. H 213 (9/56): 67.

1225. Cool Comment. Warsaw, I. SEP 230 (3/22/58): 60.

1226. Cooling System. Hammer, P. GH 141 (9/55): 103.

1227. Coquette. Isler, B. SEP 228 (4/7/56): 82.

1228. Coral. Char, R. P 89 (3/57): 337.

1229. The Coral Reef. Pierce, E.L. CC 74 (7/3/57): 815.

1230. Cornucopia. McNeill, L. SEP 229 (10/20/56): 141.

1231. The Coronation. Watkins, V. P 88 (6/56): 140.

1232. Corps de Ballet. Merwin, W.S. P 87 (3/56): 325-7.

1233. Corpus Mundi. Clower, J. P 93 (10/58): 5-6.

1234. Correcting. Neame, A. P 93 (3/59): 353-4.

1235. Correction. Engle, J.D.,Jr. LHJ 73 (8/56): 129.

1236. Correspondence. Kreymborg, A. SR 38 (6/25/55): 14.

1237. Correspondence. McFarland, E. LHJ 73 (5/56): 135.

1238. The Corridor. Gunn, T. P 86 (6/55): 137-9.

1239. Cortaron Tres Arboles. Blackburn, P. N 185 (11/16/57): 363.

1240. The Cosmos. Cane, M. SR 38 (12/10/55): 27.

1241. Cotton Fields by Moonlight. Hicky, D.W. SEP 232 (9/26/59): 66.

1242. Cottontail in Snow. Duryee, M.B. SR 38 (12/3/55): 48.

1243. Could I Believe. Milne, E. P 88 (6/56): 127.

1244. Counsel to Budding Aesthetes. Duffy, D. NR 6 (8/16/58): 138.

1245. Count the Kittens. PM 33 (7/58): 106.

1246. Count Twenty. Jaffray, N.R. GH 148 (3/59): 44.

1247. Counterpoint. Janes, K. CC 72 (10/26/55): 1232.

1248. Counterpoint. Kahn, H. AS 24 (Aut/55): 458.

1249. The Countershadow. Booth, P. NY 34 (1/24/59): 78.

1250. The Country. Kondo, A. P 88 (5/56): 83.

1251. Country Auction. Dell, G.F. At 198 (10/56): 64.

1252. Country Boredom. Van Doren, M. N 185 (8/3/57): 55.

1253. Country Girl in April. Brand, M. LHJ 73 (4/56): 18.

1254. Country Hills. Franklin, J.M. SEP 231 (11/29/58): 106.

1255. The Country Store. Thomson, C.A. GH 140 (3/55): 99.

1256. Country Town at Night. Strachen, E. McK. SEP 231 (12/6/58): 103.

1257. County Twenty. Jaffray, N.R. GH 148 (3/59): 44.

1258. County Well Curb. Clark, L.S. CC 72 (10/26/55): 1235.

1259. Couple. Stone, W. NY 35 (8/1/59): 26.

1260. Courteous Counter-Attack. Raskin, A. SEP 230 (3/29/58): 96.
1261. A Courtly Poem. Swan, J. NY 35 (10/10/59): 157.
1262. Courtship Unencumbered. Jaffray, N.R. GH 149 (11/59): 8.
1263. Cow at Her Own Drinking Fountain. Lape, F. H 212 (2/56): 42.
1264. Cow Country. Barker, S.O. SEP 230 (12/4/57): 72.
1265. Cowboy Cookin'. Barker, S.O. SEP 229 (9/1/56): 72.
1266. Cowboys. Engle, P. GH 141 (11/55): 46.
1267. Coyote Night. Jacobson, E. SEP 232 (11/7/59): 56.
1268. Crab Apples. Zilles, L. NY 32 (9/22/56): 144.
1269. Crab Grass. Kroll, E. H 214 (4/57): 37.
1270. Crabbing. Levine, N. At 204 (8/59): 48-9.
1271. Cradock Newton. Tomlinson, C. P 92 (5/58): 104.
1272. The Crane. Watkins, V. P 92 (6/58): 144-5.
1273. Created. Harrington, H. SEP 232 (12/12/59): 109.
1274. The Creation. Cutler, B. CC 73 (2/8/56): 169.
1275. The Creation. Pack, R. C 26 (8/58): 140-1.
1276. Creature of Custom. Gleason, H.W. SEP 228 (2/18/56): 104.
1277. Credo! Ellis, C. M 86 (8/59): 134.
1278. Creek Song. Brand, M. N 187 (8/30/58): 94.
1279. The Crematory. Ashman, R. P 89 (10/56): 26.
1280. Crickets. Cane, M. SR 38 (1/22/55): 28.
1281. The Crisis. Wagoner, D. P 88 (6/56): 138.
1282. Crison on the Hill. Sandeen, E. Co 61 (4/1/55): 676.
1283. Criteria. Jaffray, N.R. SEP 232 (9/19/59): 58.
1284. Critical Situation. Barker, S.O. SEP 232 (9/12/59): 113.
1285. Critique for Our Times. Carter, A.H. CC 76 (10/14/59): 1181.
1286. Cro-co-dile. Jacobsen, E. GH 141 (7/55): 40.
1287. The Cross. Bing, J. CC 76 (12/2/59): 1400.
1288. The Cross. Golffing, F. P 88 (6/56): 158.
1289. Cross Against the Sky. Russo, P.G. CC 73 (10/24/56): 1225.
1290. The Cross in the Cup. Patrick, J.G. CC 74 (4/17/57): 489.
1291. Crossing the Ice. Merrill, H. SEP 230 (1/18/58): 73.
1292. The Crossroads. Galler, D. N 186 (3/15/58): 242.
1293. Crow. Dufault, P.K. NY 32 (3/24/56): 36.
1294. Crow. Grenville, R.H. SEP 230 (5/24/58): 98.
1295. Crow's Nest. Armknecht, R.F. SEP 228 (5/19/56): 101.
1296. The Crucifix in the Filing Cabinet. Shapiro, K. P 90 (8/57): 267-8.
1297. Crude Reply to a Classic Question. Grenville, R.H. SEP 229 (1/5/57): 38.
1298. The Cruse. Nicholl, L.T. NY 34 (4/19/58): 124.
1299. Crush Hour. Schiff, L.K. SEP 230 (11/23/57): 96.
1300. Crusoe. Boylan, R. SR 40 (9/21/57): 40.
1301. Cry of the Heart. Love, A. SEP 232 (12/5/59): 51.

1302. Crying in the Wilderness. Bunner, F.N. CC 73 (8/22/56): 969.
1303. Crying Shame. Grenville, R.H. SEP 228 (2/25/56): 61.
1304. Cuban Woman Confronts the Sea. Rainer, D. N 183 (11/10/56): 397.
1305. Cuckold Contented. Koshland, M. At 203 (4/59): 47.
1306. The Cuckoo Clock. Gorman, F. Hn 35 (10/59): 406.
1307. Cuckoo Clock. Weiss, N. P 92 (8/58): 303.
1308. Cultivate Your Garden. Enzensberger, H.M. P 88 (7/56): 250-1.
1309. Cupid Reappraised. Magee, I. SEP 231 (4/11/59): 84.
1310. Cupid's Chant. Schwartz, D. NR 141 (7/27/59): 29.
1311. The Cure. Swan, J. NY 35 (5/23/59): 95.
1312. Curiosity. Reid, A. NY 35 (11/14/59): 54.
1313. Curious. Armour, R. SEP 231 (3/21/59): 108.
1314. The Curious Case of the Tongue Which Would not Wag. Lemon, R. SR 41 (7/19/58): 5.
1315. A Curious Song. Graham, E. LHJ 72 (5/55): 180.
1316. A Curse. Feldman, I. NR 140 (4/13/59): 17.
1317. Curtains. Sagittarius. NR 137 (12/30/57): 5.
1318. A Cut of Copernicus. Glaze, A. P 87 (2/56): 281-2.
1319. Cycle. Kahn, H. LHJ 72 (11/55): 172.
1320. The Cycles. Delattre, P.H. CC 76 (7/16/59): 828.
1321. The Cyclist. Morris, H. P 91 (12/57): 187-8.
1322. The Cynic. Galbraith, G.S. SEP 229 (8/4/56): 58.
1323. The Cynical Librarian. Gnash, O. WLB 30 (1/56): 401.
1324. Cyprus Calling. Sagittarius. NR 137 (9/16/57): 8.
1325. Cytherea's Isle. Mann, I.R. EJ 44 (9/55): 329.
1326. Daddy's Turn. Francis, L.V. LHJ 74 (12/57): 108.
1327. Daguerreotype. Parry, M. At 202 (8/58): 62-3.
1328. Daily We Touch Omniscience. Wolf, M. CC 73 (10/31/56): 1260.
1329. Damascus Road. Schmidt, W.J. CC 73 (12/19/56): 1477.
1330. Damayanti. Rajan, B. P 93 (1/59): 246.
1331. The Dance. Rawlins, W. CC 74 (5/29/57): 683.
1332. The Dance. Zweig, P.L. C 22 (11/56): 400.
1333. Dance, Dance. Cotter, J.F. A 99 (7/26/58): 453.
1334. The Dance of Spring. Cole, C. Hn 33 (6/57): 253.
1335. Dance of the Macabre Mice. Stevens, W. NR 133 (8/15/55): 21.
1336. The Dancer's Reply. Nemerov, H. P 91 (11/57): 77.
1337. Dangerous Inflation. Galbraith, G.S. SEP 229 (11/24/56): 91.
1338. Danse Macabre. Greer, S. P 85 (2/55): 258-9.
1339. Danseur Apache. Seager, R.W. SEP 231 (3/7/59): 68.
1340. Daphnis. Witt, H. P 91 (12/57): 178-9.
1341. The Dark and the Fair. Kunitz, S. P 90 (4/57): 1-2.

1342. Dark Mirror. Doherty, K.F. A 98 (3/15/58): 694.

1343. The Dark the Darkness. Corke, H. N 188 (4/25/59): 390.

1344. The Dark Wood. Feinstein, H. AI 14 (Wint/57): 344.

1345. The Dark Wood. Wheelock, J.H. AS24 (Spr/55): 180.

1346. A Darkening Threshold. Hassmer, W. P 93 (12/58): 151-2.

1347. Darkness Needing Light. Cully, K.B. CC 75 (10/15/58): 1181.

1348. Darling, It Frightens Me! Pasternak, B. NR 139 (11/24/58): 19.

1349. Date Town. Isler, B. SEP 229 (5/18/57): 82.

1350. Dateline: December 25. Galbraith, G.S. GH 149 (12/59): 8.

1351. Daughter of a Son. Berning, H.D. SEP 228 (8/20/55): 95.

1352. Daughter to Mother. de la Mare, W. LHJ 72 (2/55): 92.

1353. Daughters Who Lose Their Mothers. Mansfield, M. LHJ 75 (9/59): 153.

1354. David. Wright, J. YR 46 (12/56): 222-3.

1355. David's Boyhood. Rich, A. P 90 (8/57): 302.

1356. Dawn. Cardarelli, V. At 202 (12/58): 118.

1357. Dawn in Kensington Gardens. Lister, R.P. NY 35 (11/21/59): 173.

1358. Dawn Patrol. Douglass, S. LHJ 75 (11/59): 194.

1359. Day After Labor Day. Mergard, J.C. SEP 231 (8/30/58): 44.

1360. The Day Begins. Chaffee, E.A. SEP 229 (8/24/56): 70.

1361. A Day for Hunting. Simon, J. SR 40 (11/9/57): 18.

1362. A Day in Early Winter. Ray, L. At 200 (8/57): 45.

1363. Day in Gold. Goodman, M.W. SEP 229 (9/56): 143.

1364. The Day of Days. Smith, O.J. CT 3 (1/19/59): 8.

1365. The Day of the Dead. Finkel, D. P 91 (1/58): 236-7.

1366. A Day on a Cruise. Nash, O. Hl 23 (3/58): 64.

1367. A Day on the Big Branch. Nemerov, H. P 91 (11/57): 71-4.

1368. Day Unto Day. Friedrich, G. CC 72 (7/20/55): 839.

1369. Daybreak. Embirokos, A. At 195 (6/55): 146.

1370. The Days of Love. Burford, W. P 90 (6/57): 164-7.

1371. Days of the Sun. Grover, K.A. SEP 229 (8/18/56): 81.

1372. Deaconing Is an Honorable Profession. Moore, M. P 86 (8/55): 272.

1373. The Dead at Rest Standishtown and Settler's Harbor. NR 135 (9/17/56): 19.

1374. Dead Bird. Redgrove, P. P 90 (6/57): 153.

1375. Dead Reckoning. Hatch, F.W. At 196 (9/55): 92.

1376. Deaf-Mutes at a Ball Game. Jacobsen, J. SR 42 (7/18/59): 60.

1377. De Angelis. Mary Therese, Sr. A 96 (3/9/57): 647.

1378. Dear Departing Guests. Galbraith, G.S. LHJ 72 (1/55): 78.

1379. Death and Resurrection. Jones, M.E. CC 74 (4/17/57): 489.

1380. Death and Resurrection. Kenseth, A. AS 28 (Summ/59): 359.

1381. Death and the Maiden. Fitzgerald, G. P 88 (4/56): 25.

1382. Death and the Maiden. Nemerov, H. P 94 (9/59): 396-7.

1383. Death Fugue. Celan, P. C 19 (3/55): 242-3.

1384. Death in the Back Yard. Holmes, J. SR 41 (7/26/58): 27.

1385. Death Is a Cup. Tate, V.D. SR 38 (2/5/55): 16.

1386. Death of a Frog. Hagiwara, S. P 88 (5/56): 103.

1387. Death of a Good Neighbor. De Vito, E.B. SEP 227 (2/26/55): 129.

1388. Death of a Librarian. Sloan, J. C 24 (9/57): 253.

1389. Death of a Maker. Sandeen, E. P 85 (2/55): 260-1.

1390. Death of a Nun. Stein, G. A 94 (12/10/55): 313.

1391. The Death of a Poet. Joshi, U. P 93 (1/59): 230.

1392. The Death of a Public Servant. Kizer, C. NR 136 (4/22/57): 17.

1393. Death of a Vermont Farm Woman. Howes, B. P 94 (9/59): 359.

1394. Death of Another Swan--Miami. Lang, V.R. P 89 (3/57): 369-70.

1395. The Death of Atahuallpa. Larraud, V. P 85 (2/55): 252-3.

1396. The Death of Myth-Making. Plath, S. P 94 (9/59): 370.

1397. The Death of Southwell. Logan, J. P 85 (2/55): 278-82.

1398. The Death of Vitellozzo Vitelli. Feldman, I. SR 40 (1/19/57): 26.

1399. Death Paints a Picture. Ashbery, J. and Koch, K. AN 57 (9/58): 24.

1400. Death Unmourned. Dana, D. SR 38 (7/23/55): 18.

1401. Death Wish. Nicholl, L.T. AS 26 (Spr/57): 196.

1402. Debate: Question, Quarry, Dream. Warren, R.P. YR 47 (6/58): 498-9.

1403. December. Richardson, D.L. AS 25 (Wint/55-6): 28.

1404. December Tenth. Kreymborg, A. P 87 (12/55): 154.

1405. Dec. 25, 1886. Claudel, P. P 87 (12/55): 143-6.

1406. Deception. Myhre, S.P. CC 72 (9/7/55): 1022.

1407. Deception Island. Merwin, W.S. NY 32 (11/17/56): 54.

1408. Deceptive Sounds. Laneweer, E. SEP 230 (6/14/58): 86.

1409. Decision. Frazee-Bower, H. SEP 231 (6/6/59): 47.

1410. The Decision. Roethke, T. YR 48 (9/58): 78.

1411. Declamation After the Three Bears. Garrigue, J. P 86 (8/55): 284-6.

1412. Declaration of Dependence. Raskin, A. SEP 228 (5/19/56): 156.

1413. A Dedication. Engle, P. P 95 (10/59): 27.

1414. Dedication. Watkins, V. N 187 (7/5/58): 15.

1415. Dedication to Elvis Presley. Pathan, P. NY 33 (2/15/58): 78.

1416. Deep Deep. Goldin, J. CC 74 (6/5/57): 706.

1417. A Deep Discussion. Moore, R. SR 41 (4/12/58): 68.

1418. Deep Hour. Dockry, M.McA. SEP 229 (9/8/56): 76.

1419. Deep-Rooted. Merrill, H. SEP 228 (10/1/55): 123.

1420. Deep South Kensington. Treymayne, P. At 198 (8/56): 66.

1421. Deeper Than Knowledge. Cully, K.B. CC 75 (4/2/58): 407.

1422. The Deer Come Down. Barker, S.O. SEP 230 (11/2/57): 46.

1423. The Deer Come Down. Mundell, W.D. SR 38 (12/3/55): 35.

1424. Deer Hunt. Jerome, J. P 86 (5/55): 84.

1425. Deer in the Garden. Jacobson, E. SEP 227 (6/4/55): 50.

1426. Defenestration. Lister, R.P. NY 32 (9/8/56): 40.

1427. The Defense Rests. Jones, C. GH 142 (8/56): 121.

1428. The Defense Rests. Merrill, H. SEP 232 (11/14/59): 67.

1429. Defenseless. Clark, L.S. CC 73 (8/8/56): 920.

1430. Definition Arrived at While Looking in a Mirror. Chadwick, H. SEP 228 (2/4/56): 63.

1431. Definition of Creative Art. Pasternak, B. NR 140 (1/5/59): 19.

1432. Degrees of Charity. Spacks, B.B. At 204 (12/59): 145.

1433. Deities and Beasts. Updike, J. NR 140 (3/30/59): 17.

1434. The Delay. Krieger, R. P 89 (11/56): 103.

1435. Delayed Fuse. Everson, R.G. At 200 (12/57): 177.

1436. Delayed Reaction. Nelson, T. LHJ 75 (11/59): 137.

1437. Delilah. Clark, L.S. CC 73 (7/25/56): 871.

1438. Delinquent Son. Pierce, E.L. CC 74 (2/13/57): 196.

1439. Delivered from a Heaviness of Love. Longchamps, J.de. P 89 (12/56): 156.

1440. Delivery Room. Howes, B. P 89 (12/56): 139.

1441. Demands of the Muse. Watkins, V. P 92 (6/58): 146-7.

1442. Demeter. Gibbs, B. NR 135 (8/6/56): 17.

1443. Demons and a Poet. Kaneko, M. P 88 (5/56): 72.

1444. Denise. Hale, R.B. NY 34 (3/8/58): 111.

1445. The Departure. Levertov, D. P 93 (10/58): 10-11.

1446. Departure. Petrie, P. P 95 (12/59): 155.

1447. Departure. Plath, S. N 188 (3/7/59): 212.

1448. Departure, Off the Congo. Ackerson, J. CC 72 (1/19/55): 73.

1449. Departure: September. Van Doren, M. H 215 (9/57): 51.

1450. Depression. Carruth, H. P 93 (3/59): 359-60.

1451. Descending Landscape. Bynner, W. SR 38 (9/3/55): 31.

1452. The Descent. Kinnell, G. P 92 (5/58): 85-8.

1453. A Description of the Sea for Lina Lenzi Who Has Never Seen It. O'Gorman, N. P 93 (12/58): 167-9.

1454. Desegregation. Calkins, T.V. CC 72 (9/7/55): 1019.

1455. The Desert. Chamberlin, E. SEP 230 (3/8/58): 61.

1456. Desert Doubles. Collins, M.G. SEP 230 (6/21/58): 54.

1457. Desert Quail. Smythe, D. SEP 227 (3/19/55): 124.

1458. Desert Soliloquy. Martinek, J. N 185 (8/3/57): 57.

1459. Designing Women. Galbraith, G.S. SEP 227 (6/11/55): 55.

1460. Designs on a Point of View. Everwine, P. P 91 (10/57): 23.

1461. Desire not the Night. Cotter, J.F. Co 63 (12/2/55): 229.

1462. Desiring Other Selves. Stepenchev, S. P 88 (6/56): 155.

1463. Destruction of Asshur. Dana, D. SR 39 (4/14/56): 34.

1464. The Destructive Will. Shapiro, H. C 21 (3/56): 268.

1465. Details from the Nativity Scene. Lattimore, R. NR 139 (12/27/58): 14-5.

1466. Determination. Moorhead, J.K. CC 73 (8/29/56): 994.

1467. The Devil of My Dreams. Barnstone, W. N 185 (12/7/57): 444.

1468. The Devil Shamed. Hay, S.H. SR 40 (10/26/57): 6.

1469. Deya (Mallorca). Earle, V. SR 40 (8/24/57): 19.

1470. Diagon. Berry, W. P 93 (2/59): 313-9.

1471. Dialectic of Love. Bell, C.G. N 181 (9/3/55): 201.

1472. Dialog in the Dark Tower. Garrigue, J. P 93 (12/58): 136-8.

1473. A Dialog of Stars. Cotter, J.F. A 99 (7/5/58): 391.

1474. Dialogue. Goldberg, L. P 92 (7/58): 238.

1475. Dialogue. Miles, J. P 94 (6/59): 145-6.

1476. Dialogue from La Ville. Claudel, P. P 87 (12/55): 130-2.

1477. A Dialogue in the Stoneworks. Ciardi, J. At 203 (5/59): 62.

1478. The Diamond Cutters. Rich, A.C. At 195 (4/55): 55.

1479. The Diamond Dude. Nash, O. L 39 (9/5/55): 91.

1480. The Diamond Hunter. Pierce, E.L. CC 72 (11/16/55): 1334.

1481. Diana. Fiscalini, J. Co 67 (10/11/57): 42.

1482. Diary of Dreams. Mary Gilbert, Sr. GH 141 (9/55): 103.

1483. Dick Straightup. Hughes, T. At 204 (12/59): 136-7.

1484. Dictator's Democracy. Sagittarius. NR 139 (12/1/58): 7.

1485. Didactic Poem. Stepanchev, S. N 183 (10/6/56): 289.

1486. The Difference. Hecht, R. SR 39 (5/5/56): 24.

1487. The Difference Between a Little Boy and His Dad. Chadwick, H. SEP 228 (9/24/55): 109.

1488. Different Substance. Chadwick, H. SEP 227 (5/7/55): 57.

1489. Digging a Neighbor's Grave. Hay, J. P 86 (4/55): 22.

1490. Dilemma. Carter, R.H. WLB 33 (9/58): 48.

1491. Diminishing Returns. Turner, D.G. At 202 (10/58): 100.

1492. Diner. Kroll, E. H 214 (4/57): 37.

1493. Dining Out. Henry, J. LHJ 75 (4/58): 167.

1494. Directions Out of a Dream. Wright, J. P 89 (3/57): 355-6.

1495. Directions to the Armorer. Olson, E. NY 35 (11/14/59): 191.
1496. A Dirge. O'Gorman, N. P 92 (4/58): 2-3.
1497. Dirge. Ostroff, A. P 92 (8/58): 300.
1498. Dirge. Roethke, T. AS 28 (Summ/59): 293-5.
1499. Dirge for a Performing Lion. Dunsany, L. SEP 228 (2/18/56): 117.
1500. Disasters of War: Goya at the Museum. Deutsch, B. NY 33 (4/27/57): 122.
1501. Disciple. Congdon, A.K. CC 76 (5/20/59): 613.
1502. Discontinuous Poems. Caeiro, A. P 87 (10/55): 27-8.
1503. A Discovery. Freneau, I.D. SEP 230 (4/5/58): 75.
1504. Disguises. Jennings, E. N 184 (4/20/57): 352.
1505. A Dish of Skylarks. Hagiwara, S. P 88 (5/56): 104.
1506. Dishpan Dirge. Schiff, L.K. TH 33 (1/55): 25.
1507. Displaced Person. Galbraith, G.S. LHJ 75 (7/59): 107.
1508. Dissemblers. Mary Honora, Sr. Co 69 (12/26/58): 343.
1509. Distaff. Gleason, H.W. SEP (5/23/59): 59.
1510. The Distance Spills Itself. Bat-Miriam, Y. P 92 (7/58): 229.
1511. A Distant View of the School. Maruyama, K. P 88 (5/56): 90.
1512. Disturbing the Peace. Merrill, H. SEP 229 (1/12/57): 51.
1513. Diver. Hilberry, C. At 199 (2/57): 54.
1514. Dives and Lazarus. Pierce, E.L. CC 74 (7/24/57): 887.
1515. Dividing Lines. Blackwell, P.J. SEP 227 (2/12/55): 87.
1516. The Divine Dancers. Tagliabue, J. P 86 (5/55): 82-3.
1517. Divine Decline. Rosenteur, P.I. TH 33 (6/55): 47.
1518. The Divine Insect. Wheelock, J.H. NY 35 (9/5/59): 30.
1519. Divorce. Walsh, C. NR 140 (4/20/59): 16.
1520. Do Good Works, Up to Twenty Per Cent Adjusted Gross Income. Bishop, M. NY 34 (4/12/58): 144.
1521. Do-It-Myself-Analysis. Warfel, H. SEP 232 (10/3/59): 96.
1522. Do Not Stop Playing. Pierce, E.L. CC 72 (1/26/55): 109.
1523. Do Re Mi of Young Watching and Waiting. De Jong, D.C. P 91 (10/57): 13.
1524. Do What Thy Manhood Bids Thee Do. Burton, R. GH 141 (7/55): 40.
1525. Do You Know Him? Honig, E. SR 42 (9/19/59): 42.
1526. Do You Remember? D., H. At 201 (4/58): 42.
1527. Do You Remember? De Jong, D.C. N 189 (12/19/59): 476.
1528. Doctor. Markle, M. TH 34 (4/56): 63.
1529. Doctor in the House. Markle, M. TH 35 (12/57): 36.
1530. Doctor Johnson. Posner, D.L. P 90 (8/57): 278.
1531. Dog. Smith, W.J. SR 38 (12/10/55): 18.
1532. Dog With Flea. Landeweer, E. SEP 229 (7/7/56): 67.
1533. Dogwood. Lindbergh, A.M. LHJ 73 (10/56): 110.

1534. The Doings of Love. De Jong, D.C. LHJ 76 (11/59): 141.
1535. Domes. Berrigan, D.J. A 98 (10/19/57): 72.
1536. Domestic Dawn. Spark, M. SR 40 (4/13/57): 30.
1537. Domestic Dilemma. Grenville, R.H. SEP 229 (3/16/57): 144.
1538. Domestic Poem. Barker, G. P 86 (4/55): 8-9.
1539. Don Juan Tenorio and the Man of Stone. Campbell, R. NR 2 (5/30/56): 11.
1540. Don't Go. Engle, P. GH 142 (4/56): 18.
1541. Don't Let Suburbia Disturbia. Jennison, C.S. At 195 (5/55): 90.
1542. Don't Look Now, But There's Something Behind the Curtain. Nash, O. NY 33 (2/1/58): 36.
1543. Don't Tread on Us. Laing, D. N 188 (1/31/59): 107.
1544. The Door (I). Creeley, R. P 94 (4/59): 12.
1545. The Door (II). Creeley, R. P 94 (4/59): 15-8.
1546. Door Knobs. Schiff, L.K. TH 35 (7/57): 54.
1547. Door Marked Maternity. Ward, M.E. GH 140 (5/55): 99.
1548. The Door That Won't Close. Singleton, M.E. SEP 230 (4/19/58): 52.
1549. Doorway Delay. Grabisch, P.L. BHG 35 (1/57): 119.
1550. Dottissimi Signori: Giacomo Leopardi. Gregory, H. N 187 (12/29/58): 479.
1551. Double Deficiency. Galbraith, G.S. SEP 229 (10/13/56): 146.
1552. Double Entry. Richman, F.B. LHJ 75 (5/58): 144.
1553. Double Talk. Armour, R. SEP 232 (8/15/59): 91.
1554. Double Trouble. Alkus, M. SEP 232 (11/14/59): 104.
1555. The Dove of the Seas. Barker, G. P 88 (8/56): 287.
1556. Dover: Believing in Kings. Dickey, J. P 92 (8/58): 283-90.
1557. The Doves of My Eyes. Mohanty, G.P. P 93 (1/59): 241-2.
1558. Down at the Docks. Koch, K. P 90 (7/57): 201.
1559. Downpour. Middleton, C. SEP 231 (8/16/58): 56.
1560. Doxology in Surburbia. Overmyer, B.H. CC 76 (12/23/59): 1502.
1561. Dozer's Dilemma. Spring, A.T. SEP 231 (6/13/59): 47.
1562. Dr. Choumayyil's Cat. Abdough, T. At 198 (10/56): 189.
1563. Dragonfly Dream. Andrews, M. SR 38 (9/3/55): 33.
1564. Drawing of a Little Girl by a Little Boy. Donnelly, D. NY 34 (3/15/58): 38.
1565. The Dread and the Fear of the Mind and Others. Schwartz, D. NR 140 (2/2/59): 18.
1566. A Dream. Ciardi, J. At 202 (11/58): 74-5.
1567. Dream. Miles, J. P 94 (6/59): 145.
1568. A Dream of Birds. Hemphill, G. YR 46 (6/57): 568-9.
1569. A Dream of Governors. Simpson, L. NY 33 (9/21/57): 40.
1570. A Dream of Life. Shapiro, H. C 24 (8/57): 163.
1571. Dream of Liverpool, England. McGovern, M. At 198 (11/56): 60-1.

1572. Dream of the Pastoral Poet. Stow, R. At 200 (8/57): 46-7.
1573. Dream with Clam-Diggers. Plath, S. P 89 (1/57): 232-3.
1574. The Dreamers. Freeman, J.T. LHJ 72 (2/55): 130.
1575. Dreams. Moss, H. NY 35 (11/7/59): 56.
1576. Dreams. Nash, O. NY 35 (11/7/59): 56.
1577. Dreams Dreamed. Boyle, K. SR 42 (4/4/59): 24.
1578. Dream's End. Conklin, B.S. LHJ 72 (5/55): 112.
1579. Dreams Pass Before My Sight As Blossoms Fall. Ranko (1726-1798). L 40 (4/30/56): 96-7.
1580. The Dressing of a Young Girl. Holmes, T. P 90 (7/57): 214-5.
1581. The Dressmaker's Workroom. Smith, W.J. P 91 (10/57): 7-8.
1582. The Drifting Man. Lucy, S. At 203 (2/59): 67.
1583. Driftwood Arrangement. Isler, B. SEP 232 (10/17/59): 97.
1584. Drinking at Dusk. Golffing, F. P 87 (10/55): 53.
1585. Drone. Drake, L.B. At 195 (6/55): 38.
1586. The Drowned. Brown, H. P 90 (6/57): 139-40.
1587. The Drowned Woman. Hughes, T. P 89 (2/57): 296-7.
1588. Drugstore Bookstand. McGonigal, M. GH 142 (12/56): 8.
1589. The Drummer Boy. Nash, O. L 39 (9/5/55): 86.
1590. Dry Gold. Golffing, F. P 87 (10/55): 34.
1591. Dry Water Hole. Miles, L.E. SEP 229 (1/19/57): 48.
1592. Duck Blind. Landeweer, E. SEP 230 (12/7/57): 143.
1593. The Dumb Show. Moss, H. NY 35 (3/21/59): 48.
1594. Dunbarton. Lowell, R. NR 140 (1/19/59): 16.
1595. Dunce's Song. Van Doren, M. H 216 (3/58): 32.
1596. During an Absence. Gunn, T. P 86 (6/55): 125-6.
1597. Dusk of May. Bell, C.G. LHJ 72 (5/55): 86.
1598. The Dutchman's-Pipe Vine. Hoskins, K. N 183 (11/10/56): 418.
1599. The Dye Is Cast. Galbraith, G.S. BHG 37 (1/59): 26.
1600. The Dying Man. Roethke, T. At 197 (5/56): 48-9.
1601. Dylan Thomas, 1914-1953. Thomas, R. AS 24 (Spr/55): 180-1.
1602. E = mc^2. Aller, C. CT 2 (6/23/58): 10.
1603. E:mc^2. Speiser, M. N 180 (8/6/55): 113.
1604. E=mc^2. White, P.J. CC 75 (12/10/58): 1428.
1605. Each Winter. Merchant, J. SEP 229 (12/1/56): 111.
1606. Eachaton. Delattre, P.H. CC 76 (7/15/59): 828.
1607. Earliness at the Cape. Deutsch, B. NY 32 (6/30/56): 75.
1608. An Early Call. Whittemore, R. SR 41 (11/22/58): 39.
1609. Early Clearing of Fog. Smythe, D. SEP 231 (5/1.59): 103.
1610. The Early Flower. Roethke, T. NY 35 (4/25/59): 44.
1611. Early in the Morning. Simpson, L. AS 24 (Summ/55): 325-6.

1612. Early Maples. Richter, H. SEP 229 (4/20/57): 94.
1613. Early Morning. Beach, J.W. P 89 (1/57): 229.
1614. Early Morning. Karandikar, V. P 93 (1/59): 239-40.
1615. Early One Morning. Hicks, J.V. SEP 231 (10/25/58): 80.
1616. Early Supper. Howes, B. NY 32 (11/10/56): 56.
1617. Earrings for the Virgin. Cassity, T. P 86 (8/55): 275-6.
1618. Earth. McGhee, M. SR 38 (12/24/55): 17.
1619. Earth Hates an Emptiness. Slavitt, D.R. YR 46 (1/57): 568.
1620. The Earth Is Not an Old Woman. Satyarthi, D. P 93 (1/59): 228-9.
1621. Earth, Sea, and Sky: 1919. Freeman, J. AS 24 (Summ/55): 321.
1622. Earth-Sparrow. Kinnell, G. N 187 (11/15/58): 366.
1623. Earth Walker. Frost, F. A 96 (3/9/57): 647.
1624. Earth Was Their Banker. Stuart, J. AF 63 (6/57): 42.
1625. Earthbound. Goodman, M.W. SEP 231 (5/16/59): 59.
1626. Earthling. McNeill, L. SEP 229 (5/25/57): 85.
1627. Earthling, Aged Ten. Rittell, H. SEP 227 (1/15/55): 59.
1628. Earthly Love. Bennett, J. P 90 (5/57): 73-7.
1629. Earthquakes, Kona, Hawaii. Shiffert, E. NY 35 (4/25/59): 38.
1630. Earth's Passion. Lee, C. SEP 232 (9/12/59): 49.
1631. East River. Balliett, W. NY 32 (3/10/56): 86.
1632. Easter. Laing, D. SR 38 (4/9/55): 20.
1633. Easter. Swartz, R.T. At 203 (3/59): 112.
1634. Easter Among Four Children. O'Gorman, N. P 92 (4/58): 1-2.
1635. Easter Carol. Patrick, J.G. CC 72 (4/6/55): 423.
1636. An Easter Riddle Song. Beloof, R. P 87 (3/56): 334.
1637. Easter Sea. Lilly, O. CC 74 (6/19/57): 753.
1638. Easter Vigil. Mary of Our Lady of Charity. A 93 (4/2/55): 18.
1639. Easter Wings. Herbert, G. A 97 (4/20/57): 59.
1640. Easy Directions. Taylor, M. SEP 231 (9/6/58): 70.
1641. Easy Does It...Or Does It? Galbraith, G.S. LHJ 75 (5/58): 82.
1642. Eat Every Crumb, Chum. Rosenfield, L. SEP 232 (10/8/59): 148.
1643. Eating Fish. Johnston, G. At 203 (2/59): 107.
1644. Ecce Homo. Lewars, J.S. A 98 (3/22/58): 725.
1645. Ecce Homo. Patrick, J. CC 73 (2/29/56): 271.
1646. Echo. Hardy, E.S. AS 28 (Aut/59): 458.
1647. Echo. Whitt, M.W. SEP 229 (11/24/56): 69.
1648. Eclogue for Rachel. Johnson, C. AS 24 (Spr/55): 181-2.
1649. Edelweiss. Nathan, L. N 186 (5/3/58): 398.
1650. Eden. Wiggam, L. LHJ 72 (1/55): 103.
1651. Eden, Afterward. Earle, V. SEP 227 (6/18/55): 73.

1652. Edgar, Solus. Morse, S.F. P 87 (3/56): 338.
1653. The Edge of Sleep. Francis, M. SEP 231 (3/21/59): 64.
1654. Edith Cavell. Hull, O.M. P 88 (9/56): 360.
1655. Editions of a Poet. Fandel, J. NaR 4 (11/30/57): 501.
1656. Effective Footwork. Blackwell, P.J. SEP 229 (7/28/56): 91.
1657. Eglantine: A Souvenir. Dejong, D.C. P 86 (4/55): 24-5.
1658. Ego. Booth, P. NY 31 (2/11/56): 104.
1659. Ego. Solum, S. SEP 229 (2/23/57): 46.
1660. The Egotist. Galbraith, G.S. SEP 229 (6/8/57): 101.
1661. Egotist. Stefanile, F. H 217 (9/58): 75.
1662. El Dorado. Burford, W. P 88 (8/56): 304.
1663. The Elect and the Damned. Koval, A. P 88 (7/56): 252.
1664. The Election. Gustafson, R. N 186 (3/22/58): 263.
1665. Election-Year Commentary. Lee, C. SEP 229 (8/4/56): 46.
1666. Electroencephalograph--Hyperventilation. Thornton, M.B. SR 42 (7/11/59): 17.
1667. Elegy. Berrigan, D. P 94 (7/59): 232-3.
1668. Elegy. Berry, W. P 91 (3/58): 357.
1669. Elegy. Boultenhouse, C. P 91 (1/58): 241.
1670. Elegy. Ciardi, J. P 86 (5/55): 69-70.
1671. Elegy. Coxe, L.O. P 88 (8/59): 300.
1672. Elegy. Ostroff, A. P 89 (12/56): 151.
1673. Elegy. Rosenthal, R.A. At 203 (2/59): 65.
1674. Elegy. Thomas, D. At 197 (5/56): 42-5.
1675. Elegy for a Distant Relative. Wagoner, D. P 90 (9/57): 373-4.
1676. Elegy for a Nature Poet. Nemerov, H. NY 35 (12/12/59): 50.
1677. Elegy for an Unrelated Cousin. Petrie, P. P 93 (10/58): 27-8.
1678. Elegy for Dylan Thomas. Sitwell, E. P 87 (11/55): 63-7.
1679. Elegy for Sally. Hart, H. SR 42 (9/12/59): 47.
1680. Elegy for Simon Corl, Botanist. Wagoner, D. SR 42 (9/19/59): 41.
1681. Elegy in a Dream. Morse, S.F. P 87 (3/56): 337.
1682. An Elegy Long After. Carrier, C. NY 33 (3/2/57): 30.
1683. Elegy on a Personal Pronoun. Feinstein, H. AI 14 (Wint/57): 344.
1684. Elegy Upon a Certificate of Birth. Maddow, B. P 85 (1/55): 194-5.
1685. The Elephant. Eff, J. NaR 6 (7/5/58): 60.
1686. Eleutheria. Wright, J. At 198 (8/56): 68.
1687. Eleventh Commandment. Holmes, J. H 213 (10/56): 53-4.
1688. The Elizabethan Maid. Bevington, H. NY 32 (10/20/56): 140.
1689. Ella Mason and Her Eleven Cats. Plath, S. P 90 (7/57): 233-6.
1690. Elles-Mereland. Birney, E. At 203 (6/59): 64.
1691. Elocution at Thirty. Fleming, H. P 92 (8/58): 293-4.
1692. Emancipated. Davidson, J.F. CC 73 (6/6/56): 692.
1693. Embryo Tycoon. Buchanan, P. SEP 230 (3/1/58): 95.
1694. Emerson. Kroll, E. H 211 (9/55): 80.
1695. Emigree. Burrows, E.G. P 87 (12/55): 158-60.
1696. Emily Dickinson and Patanjali Examine a New Soul. Huff, R. SR 40 (5/4/57): 28.
1697. Emotions Recollected in Late-Cenozoic Tranquility. Sack, J. NY 33 (8/24/57): 38.
1698. Empty House. Crawford, J., Jr. P 94 (5/59): 101.
1699. The Empty House. Mundell, W.D. LHJ 73 (3/56): 189.
1700. Empty House. Newbold, F. LHJ 76 (4/59): 121.
1701. The Enchanted Cottage. Eisenlohr, L. SEP 230 (11/23/57): 142.
1702. Enclosed. McFarland, E. LHJ 75 (8/58): 101.
1703. The Enclosure. Dickey, J. P 94 (7/59): 218-20.
1704. Encore. Harrison, H. C 19 (2/55): 150.
1705. Encounter. Clancy, J.P. A 97 (7/20/57): 425.
1706. Encounter. Ogilvie, J. AS 28 (Spr/59): 194.
1707. Encounter at Salerno. Koehler, G.S. P 95 (12/59): 157-8.
1708. The End of a Perfect Lesson. Mary Dolores, Sr. EJ 44 (2/55): 96.
1709. End of the Road. Coxe, L.O. P 88 (8/56): 302-3.
1710. End of the Weekend. Eisenlohr, L. SEP 230 (7/20/57): 59.
1711. The End of the World. Rowland, S., Jr. CC 74 (11/13/57): 1346.
1712. End of Vacation. Davidson, J.F. CC 76 (8/26/59): 963.
1713. Endless Exit. Rosenfield, L. SEP 230 (2/15/58): 52.
1714. The Enemy. Morse, S.F. P 87 (3/56): 336.
1715. Energy Likes Company. Blackwell, P.J. SEP 231 (1/10/59): 52.
1716. The Engines Never Quite Die Away. Gibbs, B. N 184 (3/9/57): 216.
1717. English Assignment: Poem. Singleton, M.E. SEP 231 (4/18/59): 73.
1718. An English Cathedral. Gibbs, B.R. SEP 229 (9/8/56): 129.
1719. The English Teacher. Mooney, A.L. EJ 44 (5/55): 294.
1720. An English Teacher. Whittemore, R. P 86 (9/55): 314-5.
1721. Enigma. Cooper, J.C. CC 74 (5/22/57): 654.
1722. Enki. Subbarao, N. P 93 (1/59): 223.
1723. The Enlisted Man. Graves, R. NY 34 (5/24/58): 115.
1724. Environment, and More. Lennen, E. CC 72 (8/10/55): 919.
1725. Epigraphical Note. Lattimore, R. N 182 (4/28/56): 369.
1726. Epiphany of Prayer. Powers, J. A 94 (1/21/56): 453.
1727. Episcopal Confession. Redman, B.R. SR 41 (9/6/58): 27.
1728. Epitaph. Gray, T. AA 19 (11/55): 45.
1729. Epitaph. Mellichamp, L. SR 42 (9/19/59): 6.
1730. Epitaph. Morgan, F. P 94 (4/59): 32.
1731. Epitaph. Morgan, F. P 94 (4/59): 33.
1732. Epitaph. Smith, N. SEP 229 (12/15/56): 70.
1733. Epitaph. Wagoner, D. P 88 (6/56): 139.
1734. Epitaph. Walton, E.L. P 94 (5/59): 90.
1735. Epitaph for a Librarian. Solovay, J.C. WLB 32 (2/58): 427.
1736. Epitaph for Fire and Water. Plath, S. P 89 (1/57): 236-7.
1737. Epitaph to an Old Book. Reinert, D.E. WLB 33 (10/58): 162.

1738. Epithalamium. Weinstein, A. P 87 (12/55): 157.

1739. Eppur Si Muove? Hillyer, R. AS 28 (Wint/58-9): 165.

1740. Equine Lines. Jacobson, E. SEP 229 (6/15/57): 46.

1741. Equinox. Balliett, W. NY 32 (3/24/56): 125.

1742. Erinna and the Waters. Watkins, V. P 88 (6/56): 141-2.

1743. Erinna to Sappho. Wright, J. P 92 (8/58): 281.

1744. Eros and Agape. Cully, K.B. CC 75 (10/8/58): 1139.

1745. The Errand. Jenney, L.E. SEP 229 (11/10/56): 103.

1746. Escapist. Heath, A.R. CC 74 (11/13/57): 1348.

1747. Eschaton. Delattre, P.H. CC 76 (7/15/59): 828.

1748. The Esquimaux Have No Word for Divorce. Merriam, E. N 185 (8/17/57): 78.

1749. An Essay Upon Excess. Sylvester, W. Co 71 (10/9/59): 46-7.

1750. Essentials. Grenville, R.H. SEP 229 (2/16/57): 95.

1751. Established Lovers. Graves, R. At 204 (10/59): 44.

1752. Estre Indigent. Ronsard, P. de. P 85 (1/55): 201.

1753. Et Renovabis Faciem Terrae. Schneider, E. F. A 101 (8/29/59): 651.

1754. The Eternal Return. Hillyer, R. NY 33 (3/9/57): 30.

1755. Eternal South. Keith, J.J. SR 38 (11/26/55): 30.

1756. Etruria. Viereck, P. NR 135 (8/13/56): 17.

1757. Eucalyptus Dance. Lieberman, L. N 188 (5/2/59): 410.

1758. Europa. Guthrie, R. N 185 (11/30/57): 408.

1759. Eve Beyond Eden. Kay, E.DeY. N 182 (6/16/56): 517.

1760. The Eve of Bergunder. Burgunder, R. AS 24 (Summ/55): 323-4.

1761. Even--. Lindbergh, A.M. LHJ 73 (9/56): 74.

1762. Even. Schiff, L.K. GH 149 (11/59): 8.

1763. Even in Eden. Douglass, S. LHJ 75 (8/59): 84.

1764. Even in Your Doggerel. Warsaw, I. At 197 (1/56): 91.

1765. Even So the Adolescent. Ames, B. SEP 228 (7/23/55): 56.

1766. Even Stones. Lilly, O. CC 73 (2/1/56): 136.

1767. Even the Ivy Isn't Free Any More. Kremer, B.G. SEP 232 (10/24/59): 61.

1768. Evening. Wright, J. NY 33 (7/27/57): 61.

1769. Evening Landscape, One Day in Winter. Tanaka, F. P 88 (5/56): 64.

1770. Evening of Whirlwind. Gilboa, A. P 92 (7/58): 252.

1771. Evening Picture. Shapiro, J. SR 40 (3/16/57): 6-7.

1772. Evening Song. Kraus, S. LHJ 75 (10/58): 90.

1773. Evening Song for Mothers. Jennison, C.S. LHJ 73 (2/56): 165.

1774. Event. Fisher, L.E. SEP 227 (1/8/55): 67.

1775. Ever to Scourges. Mary Jeremy, Sr. P 89 (11/56): 81.

1776. Evergreen. Langland, J. NY 31 (2/18/56): 34.

1777. Evergreen, Northwest. Bryan, R. SEP 231 (9/27/58): 56.

1778. The Everlasting Light. Doyle, M. GH 148 (6/59): 166.

1779. The Everlasting Surge. Barker, S.O. SEP 230 (6/14/58): 110.

1780. Every Summer's Children. Collier, M.D. SEP 231 (6/20/59): 50.

1781. Everywhere. Nationek, H. CC 75 (9/10/58): 1024.

1782. Eve's Eden. Hoskins, K. NY 34 (8/16/58): 28.

1783. Ex-Baby. Fisher, L.E. SEP 230 (3/22/58): 47.

1784. Ex-Basketball Player. Updike, J. NY 33 (7/6/57): 62.

1785. Ex-GI at the Show of Berlin Paintings. Griffin, H. AN 56 (1/58): 44.

1786. Ex Libris. Feine, V.B. At 202 (9/58): 86.

1787. The Excavator. Creekmore, H. NR 140 (5/20/59): 16.

1788. Excelsior. Crews, J. P 91 (1/58): 240.

1789. Excelsior. Sagittarius. NR 138 (3/17/58): 4.

1790. Excerpt from Debout. U Tam'si, T. At 203 (4/59): 84.

1791. Excerpt from Narcissus--Parallel of Art. Thornton, M.B. SR 40 (7/6/57): 9.

1792. Excerpt from 'Seamarks.' Perse, St.J. At 201 (6/58): 59.

1793. Exchange. Waddington, M. H 216 (5/58): 58.

1794. The Execrators. Galler, D. N 188 (4/25/59): 386.

1795. Executive. Schlitzer, S. SEP 230 (7/27/57): 65.

1796. The Exegesis. Olson, E. P 91 (3/58): 350.

1797. The Exegete. Scrutton, K.T. A 96 (3/9/57): 647.

1798. Exercise in Aesthetics. Scott, W.T. NR 132 (4/25/55): 20.

1799. Exercise in Pessimism. Yellem, S. At 196 (11/55): 109.

1800. Exercise in Rime. Carter, R. WLB 33 (10/58): 164.

1801. The Exhibition. Beum, R. P 90 (5/57): 81-2.

1802. The Exile. Rubin, L. Co 69 (1/16/59): 411.

1803. The Exile. Wolf, L. Co 66 (8/23/57): 539.

1804. Eximious Old Friendships Are. Ely, G. P 92 (9/58): 368.

1805. Existentialist. Tracy, P.E. CC 76 (4/8/59): 418.

1806. Exodus. Rich, A. At 203 (6/59): 45.

1807. Exorcism. Friend, R. NY 33 (5/25/57): 113.

1808. Expanding North. Grenville, R.H. SEP 229 (10/27/56): 115.

1809. The Expectation. Holmes, J. H 219 (9/59): 79.

1810. Expecting the Barbarians. Kavafis, C. At 195 (6/55): 126.

1811. Expense Amount. Schiff, L.K. SEP 231 (2/7/59): 94.

1812. Expensive Victory. Blackwell, P.J. SEP 228 (5/5/56): 102.

1813. The Explorer. Brooks, G. H 219 (9/59): 35.

1814. Extra Mileage. Pratt, W.W. SEP 231 (8/9/58): 56.

1815. The Eye. Bentley, N. P 86 (9/55): 328.

1816. Eye-Filling Motes Blown Abroad by a Rather Large Wind During a Public Speech. Tadlock, M. SR 39 (2/18/56): 25.

1817. An Eye for an Eye. Standish, J.S. At 201 (5/58): 93.

1818. The Eyelid Has Its Storms. O'Hara, F. P 87 (10/55): 11.

1819. The Eyes of the Drowned. Merwin, W.S. NY 32 (3/3/56): 37.

1820. Ezra Pound in Paris and Elsewhere. Guthrie, R. N 185 (11/16/57): 345.

1821. Fable for Blackboard. Starbuck, G. H 216 (6/58): 52.

1822. Fable for Flipped Lid. Starbuck, G. H 215 (12/57): 65.

1823. The Face. Kogure, K. P 88 (5/56): 69.

1824. Face of the Earth. Burford, W. P 92 (6/58): 172-3.

1825. The Face of the Fisherman. Hollerer, W. At 199 (3/57): 149.

1826. Faces. Eckhardt, A.R. CC 72 (6/29/55): 752.

1827. Faces and Landscapes. Merwin, W.S. N 182 (4/14/56): 308.

1828. Facets. Baird, M. LHJ 73 (11/56): 32.

1829. Facsimile. Golden, L. SEP 227 (2/12/55): 101.

1830. The Fact Is. Usk, T. SEP 232 (11/7/59): 92.

1831. The Fact Is the Sweetest Dream That Labor Knows. Tagliabue, J. P 95 (10/59): 18.

1832. The Factory. Mayo, E.L. P 92 (6/58): 167-8.

1833. The Failure of the Mask. Dicker, H. N 183 (9/8/56): 205.

1834. The Fair Sex. Galbraith, G.S. LHJ 75 (9/58): 79.

1835. Fairlight Brittain, R. H 218 (4/59): 56.

1836. Fairy May. Kunz, M. Hn 34 (4/58): 127.

1837. Faith of My Father. McGovern, M. At 201 (5/58): 58-9.

1838. The Faithful Lover. Armknecht, R.F. SEP 229 (6/8/57): 97.

1839. The Fall. Pack, R. C 26 (8/58): 141.

1840. Fall. Petrie, P. NR 139 (10/20/58): 18.

1841. Fall Guy. Galbraith, G.S. LHJ 76 (8/59): 110.

1842. Fall in Corrales. Wilbur, R. N 182 (1/21/56): 53.

1843. Fall Morning. Montague, J.L. H 219 (12/59): 56.

1844. Fall of Leaf. Coxe, L.O. P 90 (7/57): 227.

1845. Fall of Snow. Loeser, K. NY 31 (1/14/56): 28.

1846. Fallout. Slemp, J.C. CC 75 (1/29/58): 131.

1847. Fall's Alarm. Emmons, D. SEP 230 (9/21/57): 63.

1848. False Alarm. Sagittarius. NR 137 (10/18/57): 7.

1849. Falsehood. Rubenstein, R. Hn 35 (4/59): 157.

1850. The Family. Hagiwara, K. P 88 (5/56): 87.

1851. Family Doctor. Kenny, N. TH 33 (2/55): 11.

1852. Family Evening. Huws, D. NY 34 (4/5/58): 115.

1853. A Family Group. Birnbaum, H. P 87 (10/55): 8-10.

1854. Family Lineup. Richstone, M. SEP 227 (4/9/55): 126.

1855. Family Scenes. Neely, L. SEP 229 (11/10/56): 83.

1856. Famine. Everson, L. P 88 (9/56): 370.

1857. Fan-Piece. Corker, H. NY 33 (12/28/57): 30.

1858. A Farewell. Andrews, M. GH 142 (9/56): 46.

1859. Farewell to My Soldier-Friend. Tze-Chiang, C. P 90 (4/57): 28.

1860. The Farm. Fleming, H. P 95 (12/59): 159.

1861. Farm at Evening. Harrington, H. SEP 231 (12/13/58): 64.

1862. The Farm, Early Morning. Todd, R. AS 28 (Wint/58-59): 59-60.

1863. The Farm on the Great Plain. Stafford, W. P 91 (1/58): 248-9.

1864. Farm Sale. Rauth, M.T. SEP 229 (9/15/56): 125.

1865. Farm Widow. Collins, M.G. SEP 231 (1/31/59): 76.

1866. Farm Wife Dead. Griffith, E.V. SEP 229 (4/6/57): 148.

1867. The Farmer. Wright, J. P 92 (8/58): 281.

1868. Farmer by the Sea. Duncan, L. SEP 228 (8/20/55): 65.

1869. The Farmer's Wife. Sexton, A. H 218 (5/59): 60.

1870. Fashion Note for March 21. Rittell, H. SEP 227 (3/19/55): 114.

1871. Fashion Picture. Richstone, M. SEP 228 (2/4/56): 93.

1872. Faster! Faster! Caswell, O. NaR 4 (12/7/57): 518.

1873. Fastidity or Phobia. Ireland, T. TH 33 (10/55): 63.

1874. Fat Chance. Hammer, P. SEP 231 (5/23/59): 103.

1875. The Fat Lady. Carruth, H. P 87 (3/56): 355-9.

1876. A Fat Man Dies. Abbe, G. SR 40 (8/24/57): 35.

1877. Fate. Rothenberg, J. C 26 (6/58): 41.

1878. Father. Kaplan, M. NY 33 (6/15/57): 102.

1879. Father Lord, R.I.P. Dever, J. A 93 (5/21/55): 213.

1880. Father of Twins. Neely, L. SEP 227 (1/1/55): 52.

1881. Father to Son. Gottlieb, S. C 19 (1/55): 73.

1882. Fatherly Advice. Jaffray, N.R. SEP 229 (5/11/57): 50.

1883. Fathers. Raiziss, S. P 88 (9/56): 361.

1884. Fathers and Sons. Petrie, P. P 88 (4/56): 20.

1885. The Father's Body. Dickey, J. P 89 (12/56): 145-9.

1886. Fauna of the Sky. Supervielle, J. At 201 (6/58): 107.

1887. The Fear. King, F. NY 34 (7/12/58): 81.

1888. Fear Is a Formal Matter. Kanfer, A. P 94 (4/59): 31.

1889. Fear of Falling. Gibson, W. NY 32 (12/29/56): 58.

1890. The Feast of Stephen. Johnson, C. Co 62 (5/13/55): 146.

1891. Feast of the Ram's Horn. Shapiro, H. C 21 (1/56): 32.

1892. The Feather and the Song. Goddard, H.C. LHJ 73 (4/56): 144.

1893. Feathered Etiquette. Raskin, S. SEP 230 (3/15/58): 67.

1894. February Landscape. Hicky, D.W. SEP 228 (2/4/56): 75.

1895. February Second. Sutin, H.G. SEP 231 (1/31/59): 88.

1896. Fee Fi Ho Hum, No Wonder Baby Sucks His Thumb. Nash, O. NY 32 (3/24/56): 30.

1897. Feeding the Chickens. Deutsch, B. SR 39 (3/17/56): 22.

1898. Feeling Low. Armour, R. BHG 36 (7/58): 91.

1899. The Feet of the Mayor of Clay. White, E.B. NY 32 (9/29/56): 32.

1900. Feline Felicity. Armour, R. SEP 227 (5/14/55): 135.

1901. Feline Sea. Nickerson, L.A. SEP 229 (6/8/57): 50.

1902. Fellow-Creatures, Tray and Outre. NY 33 (10/12/57): 42.
1903. Fellow Feeling. Richards, I.A. At 204 (10/59): 47.
1904. Female Fashion Expert. De Vito, E.B. SEP 229 (4/6/57): 76.
1905. The Female of the Beaches. Galbraith, G.S. SEP 230 (8/3/57): 42.
1906. Femine Figure. Barker, S.O. SEP 230 (9/14/57): 78.
1907. Feminine Figuring. Parrish, M.M. SEP 230 (2/8/58): 72.
1908. Feminine Privilege. Rosenfield, L. SEP 228 (4/14/56): 137.
1909. Fences. Houston, D.L. NHB 20 (12/56): 71.
1910. Festival. Kitagawa, F. P 88 (5/56): 85.
1911. The Fever. Graves, R. At 199 (5/57): 35.
1912. A Few Objections Concerning Elections. Jennison, C.S. At 197 (6/56): 88.
1913. Few Things Unnerve Me Like People Who Serve Me. Jennison, C.S. At 201 (2/58): 90.
1914. A Few Ways of Pulling Apart a Poem. Whittemore, R. NR 137 (12/8/57): 15.
1915. Field Marshall, Retired. Coxe, L.O. NY 35 (9/5/59): 34.
1916. Fields of Flowers. Galler, D. P 94 (4/59): 23-4.
1917. The Fields of November. Van Doren, M. At 204 (11/59): 75.
1918. Fifth Child. Bridgman, B. LHJ 73 (8/56): 81.
1919. Fifth Wheel. Armour, R. SEP 230 (6/7/58): 128.
1920. A Figure for J.V. Meer. Garrigue, J. P 86 (8/55): 282-3.
1921. Figure in the Distance. Nathan, L. P 90 (5/57): 78.
1922. The Figurehead. Stallman, R.W. NR 138 (1/20/58): 16.
1923. Figures in a Garden. Kroll, E. NY 35 (4/4/59): 160.
1924. Figures of Farewell. Baro, G. P 92 (9/58): 357.
1925. Filing Cabinet. Schlitzer, S. SEP 229 (2/2/57): 40.
1926. Final Arbiter. Zylstra, M. CT 4 (10/26/59): 15.
1927. The Final View of Henry Two. Eff, J. NaR 4 (9/21/57): 250.
1928. Finale. Schiff, L. TH 34 (4/56): 52.
1929. Financial Autobiography. Talman, T. SEP 229 (10/27/56): 98.
1930. Financially Speaking. Schlitzer, S. SEP 229 (4/27/57): 54.
1931. Finder, Please Return to Henry Thoreau. Beston, E.C. SR 38 (12/17/55): 17.
1932. Finders Keepers. Richardson, D.L. LHJ 75 (1/58): 58.
1933. Fine Fix. Wheeler, R. SEP 229 (12/15/56): 49.
1934. A Fine Small Blanket. Rubin, M. SEP 231 (11/15/58): 51.
1935. Fingers. Traad, M. At 198 (10/56): 175.
1936. Fingers in the Nesting Box. Graves, R. NY 34 (3/29/58): 104.
1937. Fire. Jamieson, L.J. SEP 229 (1/19/57): 13.
1938. The Fire at Alexandria. Weiss, T. P 94 (6/59): 150-1.
1939. Fire Island Walking Song. K., E.F. NY 33 (8/31/57): 53.

1940. Fire with Fire. Galbraith, G.S. LHJ 73 (5/56): 101.
1941. Fireflies. Cotter, J.F. A 99 (9/27/58): 670.
1942. Firefly: A Japanese Romance. Murray, P. P 85 (1/55): 208-9.
1943. Fires. Hale, O. LHJ 74 (10/57): 212.
1944. First Apartment. Taylor, A. LHJ 76 (6/59): 156.
1945. First Birds--Like the Eyes of a Girl Hidden. Shusetsu (18th Century). L 40 (4/30/56): 94-5.
1946. First Birthday. Landeweer, E. SEP 230 (8/31/57): 69.
1947. First-Born. Gall, A. SEP 227 (5/28/55): 128.
1948. First-Born. Smith, B.F. LHJ 74 (8/57): 116.
1949. First Call. Hicks, J.V. SEP 230 (3/8/58): 73.
1950. First Came the Lion-Rider. Patchen, K. P 86 (5/55): 72-3.
1951. The First Carol. Larsson, R.E.F. Co 71 (12/25/59): 369.
1952. First Cold Snap. Montgomery, M. LHJ 75 (11/58): 115.
1953. First Come First Serviced. Rosenfield, L. SEP 232 (9/26/59): 69.
1954. First Communion. Cotter, J.F. A 93 (8/13/55): 474.
1955. First Communion. Delattre, P.H. CC 76 (5/13/59): 575.
1956. First Day at the Beach. Raskin, S. SEP 227 (6/25/55): 62.
1957. The First Easter: Two Views. Jellema, R. CT 3 (3/16/59): 15.
1958. First Fashion. Thorson, S.W. SEP 229 (1/26/57): 68.
1959. First Flight. Singleton, M.E. SEP 230 (11/23/57): 70.
1960. The First Friends' Meeting. Groom, I. CC 74 (6/26/57): 788.
1961. First Gathering. Farjeon, E. Hn 35 (4/59): 109.
1962. First Grader in Library. Craven, M. WLB 32 (4/58): 567.
1963. First Haircut. Isler, B. SEP 227 (1/22/55): 45.
1964. First Leaf. Heath, C. SEP 231 (3/14/59): 49.
1965. First Love. Shimazaki, T. P 88 (5/56): 73.
1966. First Mass. Quinn, C. A 99 (5/17/58): 226.
1967. The First Morning of Cancer. Dickey, J. P 90 (5/57): 97-102.
1968. First Physicist. Platt, J.R. 218 (1/59): 77.
1969. First Quarrel. Grenville, R.H. SEP 228 (7/16/55): 66.
1970. The First Rain of Spring. Kumin, M.W. NY 35 (3/28/59): 30.
1971. First Reader. Hilberry, C. SR 42 (10/10/59): 55.
1972. First Reader. Rubin, L. SR 40 (9/14/57): 50.
1973. First Snow. Riggs, D.C. SEP 231 (11/22/58): 58.
1974. First Snow. Walton, E.L. Co 67 (12/6/57): 253.
1975. First Snowfall. Sloat, C. GH 148 (1/59): 143.
1976. First Song. Ungaretti, G. At 202 (12/58): 161.

1977. The First Spring. Stockdale, A.B. SEP 229 (5/11/57): 82.

1978. First Swallow. Landeweer, E. SEP 229 (4/27/57): 158.

1979. First Things Come First. Auden, W.H. NY 33 (3/9/57): 38.

1980. The First Time. Shapiro, K. P 90 (8/57): 266-7.

1981. First Touch of Spring in the Plaza Mayor, Madrid. Templin, E.H. Co 70 (6/5/59): 255.

1982. First Wrist Watch. Grenville, R.H. SEP 228 (6/23/56): 109.

1983. Fish. Townsend, E. NY 34 (2/21/59): 113.

1984. The Fish That Got to Stay. Kelley, R.S. SEP 229 (9/8/56): 114.

1985. The Fish-Vendor. Meredith, W. P 87 (10/55): 13.

1986. The Fisher. Glazier, L. NY 32 (6/2/56): 129.

1987. Fisherman's Love Song. Savage, F.H. SEP 231 (2/2]/59): 82.

1988. The Fishermen. Merwin, W.S. NY 31 (1/28/56): 32.

1989. Fishermen on a Foggy Day. Pinkney, D.C. AS 26 (Wint/1956-57): 37-8.

1990. Fishing Line. Chadwick, H. SEP 229 (9/15/56): 68.

1991. Fission. Delattre, P.H. CC 75 (1/1/58): 12.

1992. Fitting Comment. Heath, C. SEP 231 (7/19/58): 52.

1993. Five P.M. McGinley, P.D. SEP 231 (5/9/59): 80.

1994. Five Poems. Dahlberg, E. P 95 (12/59): 144-8.

1995. Five-Year-Old. Grenville, R.H. SEP 227 (5/7/55): 101.

1996. Fixer of Midnight, and Other Portraits. Denney, R. P 86 (8/55): 254-5.

1997. A Fixture. Swenson, M. NY 35 (11/14/59): 132.

1998. Flagpole. Carruth, H. NY 33 (1/18/58): 74.

1999. Flattery. Galbraith, G.S. SEP 227 (3/12/55): 52.

2000. Flemish Artists, Fifteenth Century. Drake, L.B. At 195 (2/55): 57.

2001. Flesh Can Say Loudly. Nader, A. CC 73 (4/18/56): 485.

2002. Flickerphobia. Pugh, S.S. TH 33 (3/55): 28.

2003. Flight and Return. Stepanchev, S. N 185 (7/6/57): 15.

2004. Flight by Instruments. Jerome, J. SR 41 (9/20/58): 25.

2005. Flight Landing at Night. Hughes, D.G. SEP 227 (2/19/55): 117.

2006. Flight of Finches. Howard, S. SEP 232 (9/19/59): 88.

2007. Flight of the One-Eyed Bat. Smith, W.J. NR 135 (9/24/56): 18.

2008. Flight of the Wild Geese. Pierce, E.L. CC 72 (11/30/57): 1396.

2009. Flight Report. Graves, R. SR 41 (8/9/58): 30.

2010. Flight to Cytherea. Simpson, L. AS 27 (Spr/58): 213-4.

2011. A Flirting Hat. Stepanchev, S. P 88 (6/56): 157.

2012. A Flock of Guinea Hens Seen from a Car. Welty, E. NY 33 (4/20/57): 35.

2013. Flood. Carter, M.A. CC 72 (5/11/55): 561.

2014. Flood Valley. Rukeyser, M. N 184 (3/30/57): 279.

2015. Florence. Nims, J.F. P 89 (11/56): 83-6.

2016. Florence. Norse, H. P 89 (11/56): 92-7.

2017. Florence: At the Villa Jernyngham. Sitwell, O. H 216 (2/58): 68-71.

2018. Florida. Moss, H. NY 34 (1/31/59): 26.

2019. A Floridian Museum of Art. Whittemore, R. NR 138 (5/26/58): 19.

2020. A Flower At Five. Marsh, C. TH 36 (4/58): 63.

2021. Flower Is My Proper Name--Watch the Dancing Sleeves of My Twirling Kimono. So-in (1605-1681). L 40 (4/30/56): 92-3.

2022. The Flower Pot. Shimoni, D. P 92 (7/58): 206.

2023. The Flowering. Fandel, J. Co 62 (9/23/55): 612.

2024. Flowering Antler. Krieger, R. P 93 (12/58): 153-4.

2025. Flowering Sudden. L'Heureux, J. Co 71 (12/25/59): 373.

2026. Flowers. Berrigan, D.J. A 98 (10/26/57): 111.

2027. Flowers and Spice. Collins, M.G. LHJ 76 (7/59): 126.

2028. Fly in the Car. Otis, A.F. SEP 229 (11/10/56): 129.

2029. The Foal of Medusa. Keller, M. NY 33 (9/28/57): 44.

2030. Focus. Gibson, W. N 183 (8/11/56): 121.

2031. Fog. Merwin, W.S. N 183 (7/14/56): 42.

2032. Foghorn. Merwin, W.S. NY 34 (5/24/58): 99.

2033. Folding Money. Armour, R. SEP 227 (2/5/55): 45.

2034. Food for Fire, Food for Thought. Duncan, R. P 95 (10/59): 29-30.

2035. The Food of Love. Eisenlohr, L. SEP 231 (5/16/59): 50.

2036. Food, Shelter, and Clothing Slumber Song. Dawson, E.L. LHJ 73 (8/56): 71.

2037. Footnote. Kemp, L. SR 39 (12/22/56): 36.

2038. Footnote. Norman, C. N 185 (7/6/57): 20.

2039. A Footnote on Saintliness. Brotherson, R. P 93 (11/58): 69.

2040. Footnote to a Revolution. Morse, S.F. P 90 (7/57): 205.

2041. For a Child's Book of Courtesy. Mary Ada, Sr. A 96 (10/20/56): 73.

2042. For a Congressman's Tombstone. Solovay, J.C. CH 34 (10/59): 112.

2043. For a Daughter, Learning to Sew. McGonigal, M. M 86 (8/59): 98.

2044. For a Deaf Girl. Silkin, J. P 91 (11/57): 82-3.

2045. For a Friend Who Died Alone. Blum, M. NR 135 (9/3/56): 19.

2046. For a Girl Killed at Sea. Thomas, C., Jr. P 87 (10/55): 14.

2047. For a Golden Jubilarian. Barrett, A. A 94 (11/12/55): 179.

2048. For a New Friend. Redman, P.D. SEP 232 (12/12/59): 73.

2049. For a Second Marriage. Merrill, J. P 87 (2/56): 298.

2050. For a Still-Born Child. Ponsot, M. P 90 (6/57): 132.

2051. For a Twenty-Fifth Birthday. Whitbread, T. H 216 (3/58): 84.

2052. For a Wordfarer. Humphries, R. P 86 (6/56): 145.

2053. For an Agnostic. Lilly, O. CC 74 (2/13/57): 192.
2054. For an April Day. Mary Faith, Sr. A 101 (4/18/59): 221.
2055. For Bernard De Voto. Ciardi, J. SR 39 (4/14/56): 14.
2056. For Blake's Angels. Galler, D. P 94 (4/59): 22.
2057. For Businessmen Only. Margaret, H. A 100 (2/7/59): 543.
2058. For Captain Walter Phillips, U.S.M.C. Morris, J.N. P 87 (1/56): 205.
2059. For Certain Idaho Babies. Henley, E. LHJ 72 (10/55): 58.
2060. For Christmas and the New Year. Carter, A.H. CC 76 (12/23/59): 1499.
2061. For Clarice. Brooks, G. H 219 (12/59): 69.
2062. For Earth Alone. Clark, L.S. CC 72 (3/30/55): 397.
2063. For Easter Island or Another Island. Dickey, W.H. P 85 (3/55): 335.
2064. For Elizabeth Bleecker Averell, D. 20 June 1957. Ponsot, M. P 91 (3/58): 352.
2065. For Ezra Pound. Ciardi, J. AS 26 (Aut/57): 428.
2066. For Ezra Pound. O'Gorman, N. P 93 (12/58): 171.
2067. For Falling Asleep. Merchant, J. SEP 228 (5/12/56): 117.
2068. For Father. Gall, A. GH 142 (5/56): 184.
2069. For Flooded Yard. Van Slyke, B. SR 42 (1/10/59): 69.
2070. For Gift of Sky. Clark, L.S. CC 73 (10/24/56): 1225.
2071. For Helen Keller. Perreau-Saussine, R. P 90 (7/57): 219.
2072. For Helen Keller. Pierce, E.L. CC 73 (7/11/56): 825.
2073. For Her Who Carried My Child. Wright, J. P 88 (4/56): 1-2.
2074. For He's a Jolly Good Fellow. GH 141 (7/55): 40.
2075. For His Father. Poster, W.S. C 25 (5/58): 397.
2076. For I Have Known Your Love. Graham, E. LHJ 74 (8/57): 121.
2077. For Isaac Rosenfeld. Ray, D. N 184 (1/26/57): 82.
2078. For James Dean. O'Hara, F. P 87 (3/56): 335-41.
2079. For Janice and Kenneth to Voyage. O'Hara, F. P 87 (3/56): 345.
2080. For Joan of Arc. Cotter, J.F. A 95 (4/28/56): 111.
2081. For Jonathan. Urdang, C. P 91 (11/57): 97.
2082. For MHS. Stuart, J. SR 38 (11/19/55): 33.
2083. For Mrs. Cadwallader. Wolf, L. P 92 (6/58): 151-2.
2084. For Music. Cully, K.B. CC 73 (4/25/56): 507.
2085. For My Brother: 'Other Systems Must Exist'. Ponsot, M. P 91 (3/58): 356.
2086. For My Mother. Acret, J. SEP 227 (5/7/55): 149.
2087. For My Son: Twenty. Dell, G.F. At 203 (6/59): 52.
2088. For My Son's Birthday. Coxe, L.O. NR 140 (6/22/59): 18.
2089. For None But the Lonely. Liddell, B.C. GH 140 (4/55): 16.

2090. For One Impatient to Know All. Richardson, D.L. CC 74 (6/5/57): 703.
2091. For One Who Has Lost a Son. Richardson, D.L. CC 74 (7/3/57): 819.
2092. For Peter Who Cried Because He Could Not Catch the Moth. Donnelly, D. P 88 (8/56): 299.
2093. For Pleasant Dreams. Merchant, J. SEP 231 (8/9/58): 83.
2094. For Pop. Gold, A.R. C 27 (4/59): 291.
2095. For Rachel. Fearing, B. N 186 (1/25/58): 85.
2096. For Richer. Fitzpatrick, A. A 101 (5/9/59): 300.
2097. For Ring-Givers. Reid, A. NY 32 (2/9/57): 108.
2098. For Robert Graves. Galler, D. P 90 (5/57): 86-7.
2099. For Sister Mary Apolline. Dana, R.P. P 91 (10/57): 17-9.
2100. For Steven at Three. Lee, M.L. SEP 231 (5/30/59): 79.
2101. For Students Away at Christmas. Roseliep, R. A 98 (12/21/57): 375.
2102. For T.S.E. Only. Plutzik, H. AS 24 (Spr/55): 183-5.
2103. For That Unjourneyed Man and Visioned Sea. Morris, H. P 87 (2/56): 274-5.
2104. For the Circuit of the Orpheum and the Isis. Garrigue, J. NR 140 (5/11/59): 18.
2105. For the Defense. Baird, M. LHJ 74 (5/57): 222.
2106. For the Demolition of a Theater. Olson, E. P 91 (3/58): 351.
2107. For the Queen of Franklin High. Bock, F. P 93 (10/58): 31.
2108. For the State of Minnesota. Hansen, C. H 213 (7/56): 58.
2109. For Wendy. Freeman, J.T. LHJ 74 (11/57): 102.
2110. For What Is Foreign. Bernard, O. P 86 (5/55): 74.
2111. For Whom the Siren Screams. Carlisle, T.J. CC 73 (12/5/56): 1416.
2112. For Whom the Times Chimes. Eff, J. NaR 4 (8/24/57): 157.
2113. For You. Mok, S. LHJ 74 (4/57): 207.
2114. Forbidden Equation. May, J.B. N 187 (8/2/58): 54.
2115. Forbidden Flight. Abbe, G. SR 38 (10/29/55): 23.
2116. Force-Fed. Galbraith, G.S. SEP 231 (12/27/58): 73.
2117. Foreboding. Dorheim, R.N. BHG 33 (12/55): 186.
2118. Forecast. Nemerov, H. NY 31 (2/11/56): 38.
2119. Forecast Colder. Grenier, M.B. LHJ 76 (9/59): 20.
2120. Foreign Affairs. Kunitz, S. NY 34 (3/15/58): 47.
2121. The Forest. Nissenson, C.A. Hn 34 (4/58): 126.
2122. The Forest and the Town. McCulloch, W.F. AF 62 (7/56): 40-1.
2123. The Forge of the Solstice. Watkins, V. P 91 (10/57): 24-5.
2124. Forget It. GH 141 (9/55): 14.
2125. Forgive Me Nothing. Booth, P. LHJ 74 (9/57): 165.
2126. Forgotten Light. Everson, R.G. At 201 (2/58): 89.

2127. Form 1040. Kellogg, K. BHG 33 (4/55): 117.
2128. Form 1040 Blues. Halacy, D.S., Jr. SEP 229 (4/6/57): 142.
2129. The Forms of Blindness. Squires, R. P 90 (5/57): 95.
2130. Formula for Sleep. Farnham, J. SEP 227 (6/18/55): 129.
2131. The Forsaken. Conklin, B.S. LHJ 72 (11/55): 44.
2132. Forsythia. Landeweer, E. SEP 230 (3/22/58): 90.
2133. Fort Tryon Park. Gustafson, R. SR 42 (10/24/59): 54.
2134. Fortitude. Cunliffe, C. LHJ 72 (9/55): 188.
2135. Fortune. Cocteau, J. At 201 (6/58): 81.
2136. Fortune and I. Wheeler, R. SEP 232 (8/1/59): 68.
2137. Fortune's Mist. Eberhart, R. N 186 (6/7/58): 518.
2138. Forty Days. Pierce, E.L. CC 76 (1/18/59): 195.
2139. 48 B.C. Gerlach, L.J. AS 25 (Spr/56): 161-2.
2140. 42nd Street Library. Hale, O. LHJ 76 (11/59): 163.
2141. The Fountain. Gibbs, B. P 93 (3/59): 363.
2142. Fountains. Thornton, L.M. SEP 232 (7/18/59): 70.
2143. Four. Gibbs, E. SEP 228 (7/9/55): 66.
2144. The Four Faces of My Cousin. Jacobsen, J. Co 69 (1/23/59): 433.
2145. Four Ghosts. Zaturenska, M. P 95 (11/59): 103.
2146. Four Midrashim for Passover. Fiedler, L.A. C 27 (1/59): 116.
2147. Four O'Clock. Gilbert, P.C. GH 140 (5/55): 99.
2148. Four Poems. Court, A.B. P 92 (5/58): 92-5.
2149. Four Poems of Martial. Pitts, D. P 91 (12/57): 157-9.
2150. Four Unromantic Portraits. Urdang, C. P 94 (5/59): 94-7.
2151. Four Views in Praise of Reality. Chang, D. AS 25 (Wint/55-56): 67-8.
2152. Four-Year-Old Fingers. Hammer, P. SEP 231 (3/28/59): 82.
2153. The Fourth Day. Molton, W.L. CC 74 (4/3/57): 422.
2154. The Fourth of July. Nemerov, H. N 182 (7/30/56): 553.
2155. The Fourth of July. Solomon, M. P 94 (6/59): 166-7.
2156. The Fourth R. Sagittarius. NR 138 (1/13/58): 16.
2157. Fox. Blackwell, H.G. SEP 228 (1/7/56): 53.
2158. The Fox. Huws, D. N 189 (11/14/59): 352.
2159. Fox Barking Late. Smythe, D. SEP 229 (6/1/57): 62.
2160. Foyer Trap. Feine, V.B. At 197 (3/56): 94.
2161. The Fragile Time. Merrill, H. SEP 231 (10/4/58): 82.
2162. Fragments. Benn, G. At 199 (3/57): 187.
2163. Frankly Speaking. Sagittarius. NR 138 (3/3/58): 15.
2164. Free Will. Gogarty, O.St.J. LHJ 73 (9/56): 36.
2165. Freedom's Morning Star. Norton, A.C. NHB 20 (2/57): 111-2.
2166. Freight Trains. Avery, L. SEP 230 (9/14/57): 87.
2167. The French in Cyprus, 1956. Lukacs, J.A. C 23 (1/57): 71.

2168. Friday Night Cantata. Victor, F. C 26 (10/58): 307.
2169. Friday So Soon. Scott, W.T. SR 39 (7/28/56): 24.
2170. A Friend Indeed. Armour, R. SEP 229 (5/25/57): 50.
2171. A Friend Revisited. Hall, D. NR 133 (10/31/55): 19.
2172. Friends. Smith, H.A. CC 74 (6/26/57): 784.
2173. Friends. Weiss, N. P 95 (12/59): 167.
2174. Friends of My Bones. Greig, M. N 185 (11/9/57): 331.
2175. The Fritillary. Updike, J. NY 35 (8/15/59): 28.
2176. Fritz Gulda Takes the 'A' Train. Smith, C.E. SR 39 (8/25/56): 48.
2177. Frog Autumn. Plath, S. N 188 (1/24/59): 74.
2178. Frog Dream. Reid, A. At 204 (8/59): 69.
2179. From a Sermon on the Five Afflictions (Derush Naeh). Shapiro, H. C 21 (2/56): 32.
2180. From 'A Summer Sequence'. Tyler, P. P 93 (12/58): 155.
2181. From a Wandering Jew. Feldman, I. C 27 (5/59): 376-7.
2182. From American Panels. Kroll, E. N 186 (5/10/58): 418.
2183. From an Editor. Howe, M.A.DeW. SR 38 (3/5/55): 19.
2184. From an Exotic Country. Singer, H. P 94 (8/59): 282.
2185. From As Far As Once. Hanson, P. P 90 (7/57): 226.
2186. From Bad Dreams. Justice, D. P 95 (12/59): 149-51.
2187. From Bed to Worse. Hammer, P. SEP 229 (7/7/56): 71.
2188. From 'Delta Return'. Bell, C.G. P 87 (2/56): 283-6.
2189. From 'Die Schuldlosen'. Broch, H. C 24 (12/57): 538-41.
2190. From 'Feeding-Pieces'. Redgrove, P. P 94 (9/59): 372.
2191. From 'Letter to J.M.'. Perry, R. P 93 (2/59): 296.
2192. From Morning-Glory to Petersburg. Rich, A. NY 33 (7/13/57): 34.
2193. From Music to Mire. Burrows, E.G. P 93 (11/58): 88-9.
2194. From 'Nude Fire'. Alterman, N. P 92 (7/58): 235.
2195. From 'On the Flowering'. Goldberg, L. P 92 (7/58): 242-4.
2196. From 'Paterson V'. Williams, W.C. P 92 (9/58): 341-5.
2197. From 'Poems to Preserve the Years at Home'. Lang, V.R. P 89 (3/57): 370-1.
2198. From Sun-God to Mushroom Cloud. Coblentz, S.A. CC 75 (9/24/58): 1071.
2199. From the 'Adagia'. Stevens, W. P 90 (4/57): 40-4.
2200. From the Ardent Forest. Mandelbaum, A. P 86 (5/55): 86.
2201. From the 'Art Poetique'. Claudel, P. P 87 (12/55): 133-4.
2202. ...from the Book of Hours. Rilke, R.M. NR 134 (4/30/56): 24.
2203. From 'The Fantast in the City'. Weiss, N. P 92 (8/58): 302.
2204. From the Garden. Coles, C.L. LHJ 72 (6/55): 75.

2205. From the Gradual Grass. Stafford, W. N 189 (7/18/59): 34.

2206. From the Greek. Weinstein, A. AN 56 (1/58): 44.

2207. From the North. Horner, J. H 213 (8/56): 33.

2208. From the Office Window. Swenson, M. SR 42 (9/19/59): 41.

2209. From 'The Pomegranite'. Levine, R. P 87 (3/56): 354.

2210. From 'The Ten Plagues of Egypt'. Alterman, N. P 92 (7/58): 236-7.

2211. From the Window Down. Coxe, L.O. NY 32 (7/14/56): 20.

2212. From 'Toil'. Shlonsky, A. P 92 (7/58): 224-6.

2213. The Frontier. Corke, H. NY 32 (2/2/57): 30.

2214. Frontispiece. Swenson, M. P 88 (6/56): 153-4.

2215. Frost. Rubenstein, R. Hn 34 (4/58): 127.

2216. Frozen Assets. Galbraith, G.S. LHJ 75 (6/58): 87.

2217. The Frozen Lake. Bentley, B. At 204 (12/59): 135.

2218. The Frozen Lake. Strickhausen, H. P 90 (9/57): 358-9.

2219. Fruit. Iwai, S. P 88 (5/56): 71.

2220. The Fruited Month. Shneur, Z. P 92 (7/58): 211.

2221. Fruition. Coblentz, S.A. CC 175 (1/1/58): 12.

2222. Fulfillment. Jacobs, F.B. LHJ 75 (2/58): 118.

2223. Full Circle. Ronalson, J.M. SR 38 (4/2/55): 12.

2224. Full Circle. Talman, T. GH 142 (4/56): 18.

2225. A Full Heart. Bock, F. YR 49 (9/59): 93.

2226. Fun at the Dentist's. Miner, V.S. EJ 47 (9/58): 348.

2227. Fundamental Flaw. Bradey, B. GH 149 (11/59): 8.

2228. Fund-amentalism. Crumpet, P. NR 3 (6/22/57): 597.

2229. Future Homestead. Briley, A. GH 142 (2/56): 43.

2230. Future Partners. Graves, S.B. SEP 231 (9/20/58): 124.

2231. Futures. Eberhart, R. N 182 (4/21/56): 343.

2232. G.I. Reprise. Poster, W.S. C 23 (2/57): 160.

2233. G.I.'s in Classroom. Ginsberg, L. CH 31 (3/57): 428.

2234. Galilee. MacDonald, W. CC 74 (9/25/57): 1135.

2235. The Gallery. Howes, B. NY 34 (4/5/58): 32.

2236. Gambling for His Seamless Robe. Nichols, E.H. CT 2 (11/11/57): 10.

2237. The Game. Dickey, J. P 94 (7/59): 211-2.

2238. Gannets' Bath. Sparshott, F. N 186 (3/8/58): 216.

2239. Garden. Bynner, W. SR 38 (9/24/55): 9.

2240. The Garden. Josephs, L. P 95 (11/59): 90.

2241. The Garden. Posner, D.L. P 90 (8/57): 276.

2242. The Garden. Thorley, W. LHJ 74 (6/57): 191.

2243. The Garden. Zaturenska, M. Co 66 (8/23/57): 519.

2244. The Garden Enclosed. Berry, V. P 86 (7/55): 230.

2245. The Garden God. Eberhart, R. N 186 (2/22/58): 160.

2246. The Garden of Delights. Coleman, E. P 94 (6/59): 178.

2247. Garden of My Childhood. Chang, K.C. AS 26 (Summ/57): 303-4.

2248. A Garden Shut. Macpherson, J. P 90 (9/57): 341-2.

2249. The Garden Snail. Wallace, R.A. NY 32 (9/8/56): 98.

2250. Gardener. Quentin, A.R. SEP 231 (5/23/59): 47.

2251. The Gardener. Wheelock, J.H. NY 33 (7/27/57): 29.

2252. The Gardener Outside a College Window. Gibbs, B. NY 32 (11/24/56): 138.

2253. Gargoyles. Lister, R.P. At 202 (11/58): 182.

2254. Garland for You: Poem. Warren, R.P. YR 47 (6/58): 494-5.

2255. Garment of Grace. Edelman, K. SEP 229 (12/22/56): 74.

2256. Gather Up the Fragments.... Pierce, E.L. CC 75 (5/14/58): 588.

2257. The Gathered Crumbs. Kahn, H. LHJ 76 (6/59): 166.

2258. Gay Leaf. Streit, C. LHJ 75 (10/58): 141.

2259. The Gazebos. Honig, E. N 84 (2/16/57): 146.

2260. The Geese. Eff, J. NR 6 (7/5/58): 60.

2261. The Geese. Todd, R. AS 28 (Wint/58-59): 59.

2262. Gemini. Strickhausen, H. P 95 (10/59): 20-1.

2263. The Generations. Jacobs, F.B. SEP 232 (9/19/59): 61.

2264. The Generous Heart. Merchant, J. SEP 227 (2/12/55): 95.

2265. Genesis. Seaburg, C. CC 76 (10/11/59): 1307.

2266. Genesis Revisited. Warwick, D. A 100 (10/11/58): 47.

2267. The Gentle Yes. Squires, P. NY 31 (2/4/56): 66.

2268. Gentlemen Never Go Bareheaded. Appel, W. BHG 33 (6/55): 167.

2269. George Gordon of Gight. Ciardi, J. SR 41 (1/4/58): 15.

2270. Georges Rouault: Processions. Gill, M. Co 68 (8/29/58): 54.

2271. A Gesture by a Lady with an Assumed Name. Wright, J. P 88 (4/56): 4-5.

2272. Gethsemane. Bernhardt, V. CC 72 (3/23/55): 360.

2273. Getting the Drift. Galbraith, G.S. GH 149 (9/59): 14.

2274. Ghazal. Morabadi, J. Poetry 93 (1/59): 235-7.

2275. The Ghost. Scott, W.T. P 85 (2/55): 275.

2276. The Ghost With Curly Hair. York, E.B. SEP 229 (10/27/56): 128.

2277. Ghosts. Reid, A. NY 34 (4/5/58): 36.

2278. Ghosts of the Missionaries. Starbuck, G. SR 42 (5/16/59): 69.

2279. The Giant Yea. Weiss, T. P 89 (10/58): 14-7.

2280. Giants. Lance, C. Hn 35 (10/59): 407.

2281. Gielgud Reading Lear. Dufault, P.K. SR 42 (5/9/59): 22.

2282. The Gift. Balliett, W. NY 33 (1/4/58): 51.

2283. The Gift. Doyle, M. SEP 231 (4/25/59): 66.

2284. Gift. Mary Ignatia, Sr. A 96 (12/22/56): 351.

2285. Gift of Gab. Morris, M. SEP 232 (10/10/59): 55.

2286. Gift of God. White, P.J. CC 74 (2/6/57): 167.

2287. A Gift of Great Value. Creeley, R. P 94 (4/59): 12.

2288. The Gift of Oneself. Larraud, V. P 85 (2/55): 250-1.

2289. A Gift of Song. Engle, P. GH 148 (3/59): 44.

2290. Gifted. McFarland, E. LHJ 76 (5/59): 33.

2291. Gifts. Smith, B.F. M 86 (8/59): 118.

2292. The Gifts of the Oracle. Milne, E. P 88 (6/56): 128-30.

2293. Gigue. Koch, K. P 89 (11/56): 91.

2294. Giovanni and the Indians. Page, P.K. P 89 (11/56): 101-2.

2295. The Giraffe. Kanfer, A. P 91 (2/58): 294-5.

2296. The Giraffe. Perry, R.L. P 87 (1/56): 210.

2297. Girandole. Donnelly, D. NY 34 (5/17/58): 42.

2298. The Girl at Play. Cotter, J.F. A 96 (10/6/56): 12.

2299. Girl in Love. DeVito, E.B. SEP 231 (6/27/59): 106.

2300. Girl With a Diamond. DeVito, E.B. SEP 230 (11/9/57): 94.

2301. Girl With a New Doll. Landeweer, E. SEP 231 (7/12/58): 121.

2302. Girl's Eye View of Relatives. McGinley, P. NY 34 (1/17/59): 27.

2303. The Girls I Remember. White, S. SEP 232 (8/8/59): 54.

2304. Girls in a Pony Cart. Graham, E. LHJ 74 (2/57): 173.

2305. Give Kindness Grandly. Galbraith, G.S. SEP 229 (4/20/57): 122.

2306. Give Me a Book for Traveling. Gates, C. WLB 33 (4/59): 578.

2307. Give Me My Name. Lineaweaver, M. LHJ 73 (10/56): 202.

2308. Give Me That Book, Worm. Warsaw, J. GH 142 (1/56): 42.

2309. Give Us Another Slice. Jones, E.O. NaR 6 (4/11/59): 647.

2310. A Glance at the Album. Burr, G. P 86 (8/55): 277.

2311. Glass Grain. Tomlinson, C. P 90 (4/57): 9.

2312. Glasses. Updike, J. NY 33 (4/20/57): 139.

2313. The Glassy Look. Brasier, V. SEP 230 (9/28/57): 76.

2314. Gleanings. Shimoni, D. P 92 (7/58): 207.

2315. Glimpse of Three Children on a Picnic. Dufault, P.K. NY 32 (6/23/56): 28.

2316. Global Strands. Stewart, C.W. WLB 32 (2/58): 429.

2317. Gloria in Excelsis. Cunningham, D.J. CC 76 (12/16/59): 1464.

2318. Gloss on a Text from the Mansions. Johnson, C. Co 69 (3/6/59): 598.

2319. Go Tell Her That You Love Her. Freeman, J.D. M 86 (8/59): 108.

2320. Goal. Richstone, M. BHG 35 (5/57): 231.

2321. The Goat. Saba, U. At 202 (12/58): 181.

2322. A Gobbler's Lament for Gobblers. Congdon, T. SEP 231 (11/22/58): 78.

2323. God and Man. Patrick, J.G. CC 72 (10/12/55): 1169.

2324. God of Grace and God of Glory. Fosdick, H.E. CC 75 (5/21/58): 611.

2325. The God Who Spoke to Darkness. Barbee, F.M. CT 1 (5/27/57): 10.

2326. Godchildren. Meredith, W. NY 32 (2/16/57): 134.

2327. Goddess of the Doorbell. Crawford, J.,Jr. P 94 (5/59): 103.

2328. God's Dimension. Taylor, J.R. CT 1 (6/24/57): 10.

2329. God's Music. Scovel, M. CC 72 (7/6/55): 784.

2330. Godspeed. Weiss, T. N 184 (1/19/57): 63.

2331. Gogglehead. Marshall, L.G. SR 39 (6/9/56): 20.

2332. Going Away. McFarland, E. LHJ 74 (11/57): 137.

2333. Going Away. Nemerov, H. AS 28 (Summ/59): 308-9.

2334. Going to Bed. Creeley, R. P 94 (4/59): 14.

2335. Gold Morning, Sweet Prince. Schwartz, D. NR 140 (5/25/59): 15.

2336. Golden Anniversary. Walton, E.L. P 91 (11/57): 84.

2337. Golden Palace. Lister, R.P. At 195 (1/55): 52.

2338. Golf Widows' Lament. Waldman, S. SR 41 (2/1/58): 9.

2339. The Gone. Stuart, J. LHJ 75 (11/58): 28.

2340. Gone to Pot. Chadwick, H. SEP 227 (6/18/55): 55.

2341. Good-By Before Dawn. Nakano, S. P 88 (5/56): 80-1.

2342. Good-Bye, My Fancy. Whitman, W. L 39 (6/20/55): 120.

2343. Good Friday. Pierce, E.L. CC 73 (3/21/56): 365.

2344. Good Friday: 1954. Booth, P. NR 132 (4/55): 23.

2345. Good Friday, 1955. Patrick, J.G. CC 72 (3/30/55): 391.

2346. Good Friday--Burying a Jay. Hansen, J. SR 40 (2/16/57): 22.

2347. Good-Gracious Living. Young, J. BHG 34 (1/56): 140.

2348. A Good Man's Dying. Singer, H. P 94 (8/59): 281.

2349. Good Morning, Love! Blackburn, P. N 187 (7/5/58): 18.

2350. Good Night to a Little Girl. Dufault, P.K. At 204 (7/59): 68.

2351. The Good Old Days. Lazarus, P. SEP 229 (11/24/56): 114.

2352. Goodman Up for Election. Kanfer, A. YR 49 (12/59): 244-5.

2353. The Goodnight. Simpson, L. NY 34 (1/24/59): 38.

2354. Goose Pond. Kunitz, S. P 97 (2/56): 257-8.

2355. The Gorilla. Eff, J. NaR 6 (7/5/58): 61.

2356. Gossips. Smith, W.J. NR 134 (5/7/56): 21.

2357. Got Wise. Starbuck, G.S. SEP 229 (7/14/56): 58.

2358. Grab Bag. Collins, B.F. SEP 229 (3/23/57): 50.

2359. Grace After Meals. Henley, E. LHJ 73 (4/56): 174.

2360. The Grace O God and the Meth Drinker. Smith, S.G. P 88 (4/56): 40-2.

2361. The Graces of Autumn. Galler, D. P 87 (1/56): 202.

2362. Gracious Lady. Armknecht, R. SEP 232 (8/8/59): 38.

2363. Grackle Days. Moses, W.R. P 91 (12/57): 167.

2364. The Graduation Exercise Recollected. Moynahan, J. P 94 (7/59): 237.

2365. The Graiae. Squires, R. P 95 (10/59): 24.

2366. Grammar on a Clear Day. Zlotnik, H. EJ 45 (5/56): 256.

2367. Grand Abacus. Ashbery, J. P 87 (12/55): 152-3.

2368. Grand Canyon. Hartley, R.E. SEP 229 (11/17/56): 141.

2369. The Grand Canyon. Noyes, A. A 99 (7/26/58): 455.

2370. Grand Concert by the Lake. Vazakas, B. N 188 (2/21/59): 174.

2371. Grand Opera Land. Levy, N. SR 41 (9/20/58): 6.

2372. Grandfather's Belief. Merchant, J.H. LHJ 74 (11/57): 148.

2373. Grandfather's Farm. Hearst, J. SEP 232 (8/29/59): 43.

2374. Grandmother. Donnelly, M. LHJ 76 (8/59): 133.

2375. Grandmother. Hall, J.B. P 88 (6/56): 160-1.

2376. Grandmother. MacNeil, M.A. A 101 (4/18/59): 223.

2377. Grandmother. Mitchel, H. LHJ 74 (4/57): 177.

2378. Grandmother's Granddaughter. Jacobs, E.L. LHJ 74 (5/57): 219.

2379. Granton. Smith, S.G. P 88 (4/56): 33-5.

2380. The Grape Leaf. Nicholl, L.T. SR 38 (9/10/55): 48.

2381. Grapes. Ridgely, D. GH 140 (4/55): 16.

2382. Grapes from Thorns. Mary Immaculata, Sr. A 94 (11/12/55): 185.

2383. Grass. Holmes, J. SR 39 (2/18/56): 27.

2384. The Grass, Alas. Emmons, D. At 202 (8/58): 91.

2385. The Grass, the Flowers, and the Word of God. Carlisle, T.J. CC 72 (3/9/55): 299.

2386. The Grasses Are Cut Down. Farber, N. NY 35 (9/26/59): 40.

2387. A Grasshopper. Wilbur, R. NY 35 (8/26/59): 34.

2388. Grassy Sound. Ammons, A.R. P 93 (3/59): 373-4.

2389. Graubunden Cape Ann. Singer, H. P 87 (2/56): 292.

2390. Graven Images. Hunter, K. N 184 (4/27/57): 380.

2391. The Graveyard at Genoa. Masters, M. P 88 (7/56): 223-4.

2392. Gravity. McNeill, L. SEP 230 (1/25/58): 92.

2393. The Gravity of Spilt Milk. Broughton, J. P 92 (4/58): 10.

2394. The Great Bear. Hollander, J. NY 33 (2/1/58): 30.

2395. The Great Birds. Patchen, K. P 86 (5/55): 71.

2396. The Great Black Hound Upstairs. Goodman, P. P 92 (9/58): 377.

2397. The Great Blue Heron. Kizer, C. P 92 (4/58): 28-9.

2398. The Great Event Is Science.... Frost, R. SR 42 (3/21/59): 18.

2399. A Great Fall. Marshall, C.B. NR 140 (6/1/59): 19.

2400. Great Farm. Booth, P. P 85 (3/55): 340.

2401. Great Grandfather, Clamdiggers, and Homer. O'Gorman, N. P 95 (11/59): 82-4.

2402. The Great Healer. Gibson, W. NY 32 (12/15/56): 73.

2403. The Great Lakes. Hull, O.M. P 88 (9/56): 358-9.

2404. The Great of Heart. Lieberman, E. GH 141 (9/55): 103.

2405. The Great River and Small. Hope, W. SR 42 (7/25/59): 18.

2406. Great Spruce Head Island. Porter, F. P 85 (2/55): 328-9.

2407. The Great Vox: A Dumb Show. Galler, D. P 87 (1/56): 200-1.

2408. The Great Wave: Hokusai. Finkel, D. P 93 (2/59): 312.

2409. The Greater Music. Weiss, T. N 184 (5/4/57): 398.

2410. Greek Coins. Donnelly, D. P 86 (8/55): 252-3.

2411. The Greek Drama in Translation. Weales, G. At 195 (4/55): 72.

2412. A Greek Trireme. Decavalles, A. P 88 (8/56): 310.

2413. The Green and the Black. Bailey, A. NY 32 (11/24/56): 56.

2414. Green and White. Lattimore, R. P 95 (11/59): 75.

2415. Green As the Rice at Humpty Don. Lister, R.P. NY 34 (4/19/58): 116.

2416. Green Eulogy. Blackwell, H.G. SEP 231 (8/16/58): 64.

2417. Green-Eyed View. Warsaw, I. SEP 229 (6/29/57): 44.

2418. Green Girls. Richter, H. NY 33 (6/29/57): 32.

2419. Green I Walk. Carrier, W. P 93 (3/59): 375.

2420. Green Light. Fabstein, W.E. GH 149 (12/59): 8.

2421. The Green Lodger. Nathan, L. NR 137 (7/1/57): 19.

2422. A Green Place. Smith, W.J. P 90 (4/57): 35.

2423. A Green Pride. Humphries, R. LHJ 73 (1/56): 66.

2424. The Green Refrain. Huss, A. P 92 (7/58): 257.

2425. Green River. Stuart, J. AF 63 (12/57): 32.

2426. Green Song. Booth, P. P 88 (7/56): 238.

2427. Green Song. Sarton, M. NY 32 (8/11/56): 59.

2428. Greenhouse Grandpa. Landeweer, E. SEP 232 (11/21/59): 89.

2429. Greetings (Belated). Usk, T. SEP 228 (4/21/56): 72.

2430. Greetings, Friends! Sullivan, F. NY 32 (12/22/56): 20.

2431. Greetings Given. Sullivan, G. SEP 229 (6/22/57): 13.

2432. The Gregarious Age. Hillyer, R. NY 33 (2/8/58): 101.

2433. Gresham's Law. Booth, P. SR 39 (5/5/56): 27.

2434. Grid Gripe. Emmons, H. SEP 232 (10/10/59): 48.

2435. Gridiron Heroics. Talman, T. SEP 228 (10/1/55): 76.

2436. Grief. Dana, D. SR 38 (5/21/55): 47.

2437. Grief. Weiss, N. P 88 (8/56): 316.

2438. Grieving House. Kahn, H. SEP 227 (5/21/55): 113.

2439. Grim Pruner. Trent, L. CC 72 (1/5/55): 15.

2440. Grocery List. Kumin, M.W. BHG 34 (6/56): 136.

2441. Ground Mole. Cosbey, R.C. SEP 232 (8/8/58): 79.

2442. A Group of Verse. Reznikoff, C. C 20 (7/55): 28-9.

2443. Growing. Dodge, H.G. CC 73 (1/11/56): 49.

2444. Growing Daughters. Kumin, M.W. SEP 229 (9/8/56): 60.

2445. Growing, Flying, Happening. Reid, A. NY 34 (5/24/58): 34.

2446. Grown-Up Note. De Vito, E.B. SEP 228 (7/2/55): 71.

2447. Growth. Ponsot, M. A 93 (5/21/55): 212.

2448. Grudge. Usk, T. TH 35 (9/57): 47.

2449. The Guardian Angels. Schmidt, A.F. At 197 (2/56): 124.

2450. Guess I'll Get Used To It. Richman, F.B. SEP 231 (1/59): 76.

2451. The Guest. Balch, B.J. SEP 230 (5/31/58): 52.

2452. Guest. Stewart, M.S. SEP 231 (7/19/58): 70.

2453. The Guests. Zukofsky, L. P 87 (3/56): 346-8.

2454. The Gullible Budget. Magee, I. SEP 229 (11/3/56): 107.

2455. Gulls. Weiss, N. P 95 (12/59): 166.

2456. The Gunfighters. Urdang, C. H 217 (9/58): 35.

2457. Gus: The Theatre Cat. Eliot, T.S. L 45 (11/24/58): 110.

2458. The Gypsy Moth. Berg, S. NY 35 (11/28/59): 54.

2459. Hadrian's Lullaby. Winslow, A.G. H 213 (10/56): 44.

2460. Hadrian's Villa. Rich, A.C. At 196 (10/55): 48.

2461. The Hag. Hughes, T. N 183 (8/18/56): 144.

2462. Hagar. Pinkerfeld-Amir, A. P 92 (7/58): 232-4.

2463. Haitian Endymion. Cassity, T. P 94 (4/59): 35.

2464. The Half Alive. Abrahams, R.D. SEP 228 (1/28/56): 111.

2465. Half Past Two. Richstone, M. TH 34 (3/56): 55.

2466. Halfway. Kumin, M.W. H 218 (1/59): 37.

2467. Hall of Fame. Ryskind, M. NaR 3 (5/4/57): 427.

2468. Halloween Do-It-Yourself. Congdon, T. SEP 231 (10/25/58): 125.

2469. Hand and Glove. Parrish, M.M. SEP 228 (3/3/56): 73.

2470. The Hand of God. Heafield, K. CC 75 (11/5/58): 1273.

2471. The Handcar. Abbe, G. SR 41 (10/11/58): 47.

2472. Handle with Care. Francis, L.V. LHJ 74 (6/57): 181.

2473. Hands. Cotter, J.F. A 99 (7/5/58): 390.

2474. Hands to Match the Mind. Hunter, E.W. CC 72 (1/12/55): 43.

2475. Handy Rule of Thumb. Merchant, J. GH 149 (11/59): 215.

2476. The Hangman. Moss, S. P 85 (1/55): 204.

2477. A Happening. Levertov, D. P 93 (10/58): 10-11.

2478. A Happy Christmas Hop of Mr. Leaper. Nash, O. Hl 26 (12/59): 78.

2479. Happy Ending. De Vito, E.B. LHJ 74 (3/57): 148.

2480. The Happy Housewife. Rudd, L.C. SEP 231 (4/4/59): 52.

2481. Hard Lines on a Soft Touch. Starbuck, G. LHJ 75 (7/58): 69.

2482. The Hard Structure of the World. Eberhart, R. N 188 (4/25/59): 368.

2483. Hardly Worth It. Stewart, M. SEP 229 (11/24/56): 60.

2484. Hark, Hark, the Lark. Bishop, M. NY 34 (3/22/58): 96.

2485. Hark, Hark, the Lark. Stone, H. LHJ 73 (5/56): 96.

2486. Hark, Hark, the Lark. Welch, M.deL. At 196 (12/55): 62.

2487. A Harmony, with Stars. Reid, A. At 202 (9/58): 72.

2488. Harriet's Train Again. Fennell, R.E. NHB 22 (1/59): 95.

2489. Hart Crane. Lowenfels, W. N 183 (9/15/56): 225.

2490. Harvard Revisited. Hanford, J.H. AS 28 (Aut/59): 432.

2491. Harvest. Oerke, A. NY 32 (10/13/56): 48.

2492. Harvest. Walton, E.L. NY 35 (11/28/59): 49.

2493. Hasty Judgment. Grenville, R.H. SEP 231 (1/6/59): 51.

2494. Hat Bar. Weston, M. NY 32 (12/15/56): 138.

2495. Have Baby Will Travel. McFarland, E. LHJ 74 (10/57): 128.

2496. Have I Forgotten Anything? Blackwell, P.J. SEP 228 (9/17/55): 93.

2497. Have You Ever Known Children Watching an Old-Time Movie? Kline, L.W. EJ 45 (5/56): 268.

2498. Having a Miserable Time (Glad You're Not Here!) Emmons, D. SEP 229 (6/29/57): 34.

2499. Havre de Grace. Chandler, D. At 202 (8/58): 64.

2500. The Hawk and the Lizard. Frumkin, G. SR 40 (8/31/57): 21.

2501. The Hawk in the Storm. Hughes, T. At 199 (2/57): 53.

2502. Hawk on the Roadside. Oerke, A. NY 34 (2/14/59): 97.

2503. The Hawk's Victim. Todd, R. NY 32 (2/2/57): 86.

2504. Haying Before Storm. Rukeyser, M. N 183 (11/24/56): 461.

2505. The Hayloft. Schoeberlein, M. GH 142 (9/56): 42.

2506. He Came with Music. Frazee-Bower, H. CT 3 (6/8/59): 11.

2507. He Cracked a Word. Curnow, A. P 86 (9/56): 343.

2508. He Descended into Hell. Pierce, E.L. CC 74 (4/17/57): 487.

2509. He Speaks a Critic Speaks. Sandburg, H. H 219 (9/59): 56.

2510. He Was Despised and Rejected. Pierce, E.L. CC 74 (5/8/57): 588.

2511. He Wears His Years.... Richardson, D.L. CC 73 (2/29/56): 269.

2512. The Head Librarian. Foss, S.W. LJ 84 (9/1/59): 2447.

2513. Head of the House. Askue, R.P. SEP 232 (8/22/59): 77.

2514. Head of the House. McGinley, P.D. SEP 232 (9/12/59): 97.

2515. Head Wind. Kozmenuik, N. SEP 232 (11/21/59): 54.

2516. Headwork. Alkus, M. SEP 227 (1/8/55): 58.

2517. Healthy, Wealthy and Grumpy. Talman, T. SEP 229 (10/13/56): 115.

2518. A Heap of Difference. Galbraith, G.S. SEP 229 (2/9/57): 40.

2519. Heard and Not Seen. Schlitzer, S. SEP 229 (4/27/57): 133.

2520. Hearing Aid. Usk, T. SEP 229 (2/23/57): 120.

2521. Heart Cry. Jacobson, E. TH 35 (12/57): 351.

2522. The Heart Flies Home. Stuart, J. LHJ 75 (5/58): 160.

2523. The Heart on the Sand. Bock, F. P 88 (7/56): 219.

2524. Hearth Fire. Hart, M.A. SEP 229 (11/17/56): 95.

2525. Heartlight. Galbraith, G.S. SEP 228 (9/24/55): 74.

2526. Heat of Snow. Hollander, J. At 201 (2/58): 62.

2527. Heat of the Sun. Claudel, P. P 87 (12/55): 132-3.

2528. Heat Rave. Schiff, L.K. SEP 230 (8/10/57): 67.

2529. Heat Raves on the Airways. Eisenlohr, L. SEP 231 (7/19/58): 73.

2530. Heat Storm. Grenville, R.H. SEP 230 (8/3/57): 68.

2531. Heat Wave. Lazarus, P. SEP 229 (8/11/56): 81.

2532. Heaven. Weiss, N. C 22 (7/56): 74.

2533. Heavy, Heavy, But Not Too Heavy. Galbraith, G.S. SEP 228 (3/10/56): 117.

2534. Height of Affection. Armour, R. BHG 34 (9/56): 101.

2535. Heirlooms. Miner, V.S. SEP 229 (5/25/57): 185.

2536. Heirlooms. Walker, F.C. GH 148 (2/59): 159.

2537. Hell-Diver. Hilberry, C. NY 35 (4/11/59): 79.

2538. The Hellenic World. Drake, L.B. At 200 (10/57): 44-5.

2539. Helpful Hint on Keeping Friends. Chadwick, H. SEP 228 (3/3/56): 108.

2540. Henri Matisse. Langland, J. N 180 (4/30/55): 369.

2541. Her Love As a North. Gustafson, R. N 187 (8/2/58): 58.

2542. Her Side. Jaffray, N.R. SEP 229 (4/6/57): 46.

2543. Heraldry. Hoffman, D.C. NR 133 (10/10/55): 20.

2544. The Herd. Creeley, R. P 94 (4/59): 11.

2545. The Herdsman. Caeiro, A. P 87 (10/55): 29.

2546. Here. Witt, H. N 189 (10/10/59): 216.

2547. Here Are Roses. Triem, E. P 89 (2/57): 273.

2548. Here I Am! Rosenfield, L. SEP 229 (2/2/57): 72.

2549. Here I Belong. Stanley, I. SEP 228 (9/17/55): 90.

2550. Here in a Teardrop. Coblentz, S.A. CC 75 (3/12/58): 308.

2551. Here in Katmandu. Justice, D. P 88 (9/56): 366-7.

2552. Here Is a Candle to Light You to Bed.... Gardner, I. NR 132 (5/9/55): 21.

2553. Here Live Your Life Out. Graves, R. NY 35 (3/28/59): 34.

2554. Here Lovely. McGrath, J.J. A 97 (9/14/57): 624.

2555. Heritage of Words. Nickerson, V. TH 33 (9/55): 43.

2556. The Hermit. Galbraith, G.S. SEP 229 (1/12/57): 60.

2557. The Hermitage. O'Connor, F. Co 66 (6/14/57): 273.

2558. Hero. Coblentz, S.A. CC 74 (5/29/57): 679.

2559. Hero of the Yellow Pages. Galbraith, G.S. LHJ 75 (10/58): 122.

2560. Hero Speech. Rukeyser, M. P 91 (2/58): 292-3.

2561. Heroes and Worms. Barker, G. P 88 (8/56): 288.

2562. Heroes in Their Prime. Graves, R. NY 35 (5/23/59): 42.

2563. Hero's Winter. Coxe, L.O. NY 32 (11/3/56): 44.

2564. Herring-Gull. Wheelock, J.H. AS 25 (Summ/56): 306.

2565. He's Learning to Dress. Anthony, E. GH 148 (3/59): 168.

2566. Hey, Hey! Make Way for the Latest Model. Cole, B. SR 39 (11/24/56): 8.

2567. Hey, Who Put This Hoofprint on the Counterpane? Pedrick, J. H 213 (10/56): 75.

2568. Hibernation. Hopkins, F. SEP 227 (3/12/55): 120.

2569. Le Hibou Et La Poussiquette. Stergmuller, F. NY 35 (6/20/59): 38.

2570. Hidden, Lost or Right Where It Belongs? Emmons, D. and Douglass, S. SEP 231 (3/14/59): 83.

2571. Hidden Page. Barker, S.O. SEP 231 (12/13/58): 108.

2572. Hieroglyphics. Smith, L.C. SEP 227 (2/5/55): 61.

2573. High Altitude. Kilkeary, G. SEP 228 (7/2/55): 59.

2574. High Fidelity. Gunn, T. P 86 (6/55): 139.

2575. High Finance in the Suburbs. Russell, F. NaR 5 (1/25/58): 83.

2576. The High Malady. Pasternak, B. SR 41 (12/13/58): 12-3.

2577. High Morning. Rubin, M. SEP 230 (9/7/57): 77.

2578. High Note. Ellert, M.M. SEP 231 (5/2/59): 73.

2579. High Place, Southwest. Armknecht, R.F. SEP 231 (6/6/59): 107.

2580. The High Price of Daffodils. Stolorow, H.R. At 203 (3/59): 81.

2581. High School Choir. Jacobs, E.L. GH 141 (10/55): 111.

2582. The Highway. Merwin, W.S. P 89 (3/59): 348.

2583. Highway Construction. Chapin, C.E. At 199 (5/57): 92.

2584. The Hike. Weiss, N. P 85 (1/55): 207.

2585. The Hill. Creeley, R. P 94 (4/59): 11.

2586. Hills of My Youth. Richter, H. SEP 230 (11/23/57): 123.

2587. The Hindu Painter Prepares to Paint. Carruth, H. SR 40 (5/18/57): 32.

2588. Hint to a Young Man Getting Nowhere. Lieberman, E. SEP 232 (8/15/59): 57.

2589. Hint to Anybody's Husband. Galbraith, G.S. SEP 229 (2/23/57): 109.

2590. His Going. Stewart, A. LHJ 74 (5/57): 228.

2591. His--or Ours? Haines, J.A. CC 72 (1/19/55): 79.

2592. Historian. Hughes, T. N 187 (11/15/58): 364.

2593. The Historian. Jones, H.M. At 203 (1/59): 89.

2594. Historical Footnote. Daiches, D. NY 32 (10/13/56): 137.

2595. A History. Stepanchev, S. N 84 (2/27/57): 169.

2596. History Revisited. Gleason, M. SEP 229 (3/16/57): 63.

2597. Hobbema and the Casks. Spingarn, L.P. SR 41 (8/30/58): 26.

2598. Hobby. SEP 231 (1/6/59): 13.

2599. Hokusai. Hughes, D.J. At 201 (2/58): 60.

2600. Holding the Mirror Up to Nature. Nemerov, H. P 91 (11/57): 75.

2601. Holiday House. Carlisle, T.J. Hn 35 (12/59): 496.

2602. Holler Guy. Nash, O. L 39 (9/5/55): 85.

2603. Holly and Hickory. Warren, R.P. SR 41 (11/22/58): 37.

2604. Holy Beggars. Pillin, W. P 91 (11/57): 105-6.

2605. Holy Innocents 1956. McGuire, J.V. A 96 (12/22/56): 351.

2606. Homage. Carter, R. WLB 33 (2/59): 416.

2607. Homage to Don Marquis. Watt, W.W. NY 34 (6/7/58): 30.

2608. Homage to the King's Choir. Nathan, L. P 91 (3/58): 375-6.

2609. Home. Kessler, E. AS 27 (Spr/58): 227.

2610. Home. Vance, E.G. LHJ 72 (6/55): 154.

2611. Home for Christmas. Jeans, M.T. GH 142 (12/56): 8.

2612. Home Groan. Emmons, D. SEP 229 (2/23/57): 40.

2613. Home Groan. Vesely, R.S. TH 34 (8/56): 44.

2614. Home Movie. Stone, R. P 87 (10/55): 32.

2615. Home Thoughts. Armour, R. SEP 231 (11/22/58): 89.

2616. Home Town. Miner, V.S. LHJ 72 (11/55): 148.

2617. Home with the Evening Tide. Hicky, D.W. SEP 231 (9/27/58): 109.

2618. The Homecoming. Hooper, P. AS 26 (Spr/57): 207.

2619. Homecoming. Krieger, R. N 185 (9/14/57): 135.

2620. Homecoming. Swan, J. NY 35 (8/8/59): 30.

2621. Homesteader. Grenville, R.H. SEP 228 (5/5/56): 126.

2622. Homework. Anthony, E. GH 142 (3/56): 140.

2623. Honest, Anyhow. Barker, S.O. SEP 228 (3/10/56): 67.

2624. Honey. Blackwell, H.G. SR 38 (7/16/55): 64.

2625. The Honeybees. Langland, J. LHJ 73 (8/56): 14.

2626. The Hoofer. Abrams, C. L 39 (9/5/55): 87.

2627. The Hooked Rug. Zilles, L. At 201 (4/58): 48.

2628. Hoot Owls. Eberhart, R. N 185 (12/7/57): 437.

2629. Hope. Goldsmith, O. GH 140 (1/55): 28.

2630. Hope. Longfellow, I.B. SEP 231 (2/14/59): 75.

2631. Hope is the Thing with Feathers. Dickinson, E. GH 141 (8/55): 25.

2632. Horace to Tibullus. Highet, G. H 212 (4/56): 48.

2633. Horizon Organ. Carter, M.A. CC 75 (10/22/58): 1208.

2634. Horizon Thong. Abbe, G. At 196 (11/55): 46.

2635. L'Horloge. Conway, M.D. A 95 (5/5/56): 138.

2636. Horn Blower. De Vito, E.B. SEP 230 (6/14/58): 116.

2637. Horoscope. Kumin, M.W. GH 142 (1/56): 42.

2638. Hors D'Oeuvres. Talman, T. GH 142 (7/56): 28.

2639. The Horse. Koch, K. P 89 (11/56): 87-8.

2640. A Horse and a Landscape. Kitagawa, F. P 88 (5/56): 86.

2641. Horse and Donkey. Pierce, E.L. CC 73 (4/4/56): 416.

2642. The Horses. Guillen, J. AS 28 (Summ/59): 296.

2643. The Hostage. Coxe, L.O. P 90 (7/57): 228.

2644. Hostess Who's the Toastess of the Town. De Vito, E.B. SEP 230 (5/31/58): 68.

2645. The Hot-Rods Ride at Dusk. Zitner, S.P. N 185 (11/16/57): 352.

2646. Hotel de Dieu. Morris, H. P 94 (9/59): 391-5.

2647. The Hour and the Arrow. Wilson, D.C. LHJ 72 (4/55): 104.

2648. The Hour Before the Coming of the Night. Fleming, H. P 92 (8/58): 295.

2649. The House. Debee, R. P 93 (1/59): 211.

2650. The House. Sward, R.S. P 89 (2/57): 290.

2651. The House of Bread. Patrick, J.G. CC 74 (12/25/57): 1535.

2652. A House of Friends. Wright, D. P 92 (4/58): 27.

2653. The House of the Seven Gables. Warren, J.E. Jr. EJ 48 (9/59): 303.

2654. House of the Warm Woods. Dawson, E.L. LHJ 75 (10/58): 175.

2655. House Plans. Kilkeary, G. SEP 228 (6/2/56): 75.

2656. Housebroke. Starbuck, G.S. LHJ 75 (3/58): 20.

2657. The Housewife. Amma, B. P 93 (1/59): 258.

2658. Housewife. Lieberman, L. SR 42 (5/9/59): 50.

2659. Housewife to Husband. Lincoln, A. SEP 232 (11/28/59): 106.

2660. A Housewife's Time. Fasel, I. GH 148 (6/59): 230.

2661. How Are You, George? Romine, R. TH 33 (11/55): 51.

2662. How Come? Talman, T. SEP 227 (4/9/55): 60.

2663. How Cooly Refreshing. Natsume, S. At 195 (1/55): 164.

2664. How Dare They Make My Mountain a Molehill? Collins, I.J. SEP 228 (9/10/55): 68.

2665. How Fair. McFarland, E. LHJ 72 (6/55): 81.

2666. How Fortunate. Laughlin, J. P 89 (12/56): 150.

2667. How Guess? Ward, M.W. SEP 231 (5/30/59): 73.

2668. How Many Leaves? Merchant, J. SEP 231 (6/13/59): 85.

2669. How My True Love Proposed to Me. Thorpe, B. LHJ 74 (9/57): 95.

2670. How Shall I Measure You? Mary Timothy, Sr. Co 70 (9/11/59): 495.

2671. How Shall I Sing Again. Iris, S. P 91 (11/57): 102.

2672. How Silently. Lilly, O. CC 73 (5/9/56): 583.

2673. How Slow Spring Is! Payne, A.B. SEP 231 (5/2/59): 46.

2674. How Slow the Day. SEP 231 (8/3/59): 8.

2675. How So Lovely Walks the Wind. Woods, J. P 91 (12/57): 177.

2676. How Still the Hawk. Tomlinson, C. N 189 (12/12/59): 456.

2677. How the Beasts Keep Christmas. McGinley, P. At 202 (12/58): 41.

2678. How To Be Charming Though Farming. Jennison, C.S. At 196 (10/55): 106.

2679. How to Harass a Hitchcock. Nash, O. HG 110 (12/56): 43.

2680. How to Harry a Husband. Nash, O. NY 32 (6/2/56): 32.

2681. How to Lose Friends and Influence Nobody. Hammer, P. SEP 229 (6/8/57): 46.

2682. How to Reduce. Chadwick, H. SEP 232 (11/21/ 59): 121.

2683. How to Start a War. McGinley, P. AS 28 (Aut/59): 445-6.

2684. How to Tell a Kitchen from a Cuisine: Take a Quick Look at Ours. Nash, O. HG 111 (4/ 57): 184.

2685. How Walks My Love? Conklin, B.S. LHJ 73 (4/ 56): 130.

2686. However Casually You May Go. Mary Paulinus, Sr. A 94 (10/29/55): 130.

2687. Hugh Latimer. Ellis, E.K. CC 73 (7/4/56): 800-2.

2688. Hulks. Shenton, E. SEP 227 (3/12/55): 137.

2689. The Human Condition. Gunn, T. P 86 (6/55): 127-8.

2690. Human Condition. Mary Aquin, Sr. A 100 (1/ 3/59): 404.

2691. Human Interest Story. Greer, S. P 85 (2/ 55): 256-7.

2692. The Human Weave. Barker, S.O. SEP 230 (4/ 26/58): 82.

2693. A Hummingbird. Coffin, R.P.T. SEP 227 (6/ 11/55): 66.

2694. Hummingbird. Rosenberg, J.L. NY 34 (8/2/ 58): 30.

2695. Hunger. Bunner, F.N. CC 72 (5/25/55): 619.

2696. The Hunt. Weiss, N. P 88 (8/56): 316.

2697. The Hunter. Adler, L. P 88 (9/56): 377.

2698. Hunter, Immobile. Jacobsen, J. Co 70 (9/ 25/59): 541.

2699. Hunters of the Dusk. Jacobson, E. SR 38 (10/22/55): 21.

2700. Hunting Song. Brand, M. N 186 (4/26/58): 376.

2701. Hunting Tale. Johnson, W.R. P 86 (9/55): 330.

2702. The Hurt of Autumn. Donaldson, S. LHJ 76 (10/59): 106.

2703. Husbandry. Fandel, J. Co 67 (11/29/57): 226.

2704. Husbands Are Like That. Armour, R. BHG 33 (10/55): 110.

2705. The Hush of Autumn. McBrown, G.P. NHB 19 (1/56): 87.

2706. Hydrocephalus. Hetznecker, W. A 100 (2/28/ 59): 633.

2707. Hydrogen Age. Coblentz, S.A. CC 72 (3/2/ 55): 267.

2708. Hymn for the Church Dilettante. Hunter, R.E. CC 76 (10/7/59): 1142.

2709. A Hymn to the Creator. Cutler, B. CC 72 (1/12/55): 45.

2710. I. McGrane, J. N 188 (5/23/59): 484.

2711. I Also Love Thee Proserpine: A Romantic Elegy. Carruth, H. P 89 (3/57): 362-5.

2712. I Always Say There's No Place Like New York in the Summer, or That Cottage Small by a Waterfall Was Snapped up Last February. Nash, O. HG 109 (6/56): 63.

2713. I Am an Up-To-Date Librarian. Young, V.G. WLB 33 (3/59): 507.

2714. I Am in Babylon Dying. Grossman, A. P 90 (6/57): 146.

2715. I As Charles IX. Nixon, J.,Jr. SR 41 (11/ 22/58): 38.

2716. I Being Man. Huntley, J. LHJ 76 (4/59): 145.

2717. I Being Woman. Hunter, N. LHJ 75 (3/58): 163.

2718. I Believe in Your Country. Hull, O.M. P 92 (9/58): 352-3.

2719. I Burn and Recognize Imminence. Giuliani, A. P 94 (8/59): 313.

2720. I Can't Win. Avery, L. SEP 231 (5/16/59): 91.

2721. I Change Time and Think of Margaret. Fiedler, L.A. P 90 (8/57): 295.

2722. I Chop Down Trees. Hall, D. SR 40 (6/29/ 57): 15.

2723. I Didn't Catch the Face. Buchanan, P. SEP (7/7/56): 47.

2724. I Do Not See Myself. Horiguchi, D. At 195 (1/55): 107.

2725. I Don't Decry Hi-Fi, But--. Otis, A.F. SEP 232 (12/19/59): 67.

2726. I Dreamed I Saw Lord Daniels. Cuney, W. NHB 21 (4/58): 158.

2727. I Dreamed in a City Dark As Paris. Simpson, L. SR 39 (6/23/56): 10.

2728. I Dreamt the Negro, Beautiful as Night. Walsh, P.B. P 85 (1/55): 193.

2729. I Felt. Ignatow, D. P 93 (11/58): 84.

2730. I Force Myself to Watch the Scenery. Fiedler, L.A. P 90 (8/57): 294.

2731. I Gathered. Oerke, A. NY 33 (7/13/57): 67.

2732. I Hate to Say Good-By. Rosenfield, L. SEP 232 (10/24/59): 116.

2733. I Hate Winter. Woolley, I.H. SEP 229 (1/ 12/57): 67.

2734. I Have Singled Out a Tree. Peel, D. GH 141 (10/55): 111.

2735. I Hear America Singing. Whitman, W. L 38 (6/20/55): 115.

2736. I Hear America Swinging. Smith, C.E. SR 39 (6/16/56): 40.

2737. I Hold the Book. Frazee-Bower, H. CT 2 (3/ 17/58): 13.

2738. I Know a Girl. Anthony, E. GH 142 (8/56): 178.

2739. I Know the Night No Longer. Elytis, O. At 195 (6/55): 141.

2740. I Light My Candle from Their Torches. Bennett, E.W. WLB 30 (5/56): 685.

2741. I Like Pink. Grossman, M. Hn 32 (6/56): 219.

2742. I Live Quietly. Wheeler, R. SEP 229 (3/16/ 57): 46.

2743. I Must Have Dozed Off. Power, J.W. BHG 34 (4/56): 360.

2744. I Mustn't Forget. Anthony, E. GH 142 (10/ 56): 241.

2745. I Never Knew a Night So Black. Bangs, J.K. GH 141 (9/55): 14.

2746. I Never Lost Faith in Angels. De Jong, D.C. P 94 (9/59): 384.

2747. I Rest in His Love. Frazee-Bower, H. CT 1 (9/2/57): 12.

2748. I Saw a White Bird Once. Yosano, A. At 195 (1/55): 147.

2749. I Saw the Invisible. Coblentz, S.A. CC 72 (8/31/55): 991.

2750. I Saw the Muses. Sinisgalli, L. At 202 (12/ 58): 170.

2751. I Saw Us. Der Hovanessian, D. H 210 (3/55): 41.

2752. I Saw You Stand Lonely.... Rawlins, W. CC 75 (8/20/58): 947.

2753. I Scarcely See But Feel You Now at First. Toland, P. LHJ 75 (1/58): 99.

2754. I Shall Come to You. Shook, B. LHJ 75 (4/58): 126.
2755. I Sometimes Think. Lister, R.P. NY 35 (5/2/59): 127.
2756. I Spy, or, The Depravity of Privacy. Nash, O. HG 111 (1/57): 12.
2757. I Stand and Wait. Wheeler, R. SEP 230 (10/26/57): 52.
2758. I Stand Upon a Dike. Ignatow, D. SR 39 (7/28/56): 12.
2759. I Stole the Mad Woman's Love, the Mad Woman Said. Roskolenko, H. P 89 (10/56): 30.
2760. I Thought I'd Tell You. Todrin, B. LHJ 75 (11/59): 146.
2761. I Too Arose. Palmer, H. CT 3 (3/16/59): 12.
2762. I Too Have Lived in Arcadia. Lang, V.R. P 86 (4/55): 27-40.
2763. I, Too, Shall Sing. Ardayne, J.C. GH 142 (9/56): 46.
2764. I Wake But It Is Always the Wrong Time. Fiedler, L.A. P 90 (8/57): 294.
2765. I Wander Lonely in the Crowd. Atherton, J. AS 27 (Wint/57-58): 48.
2766. I Will Not Let You Go. Tagore, R. P 93 (1/59): 203-8.
2767. I Will Suffer from What My Father suffered from. Hagiwara, K. P 88 (5/56): 88.
2768. I Wish It Were April. Coatsworth, E. GH 142 (4/56): 164.
2769. I Won't!--Or Will I? Anthony, E. GH 142 (12/56): 203.
2770. I Would Go Home Again. Pasternak, B. NR 139 (11/10/58): 20.
2771. Icarus. Mayo, E.L. P 92 (6/58): 167.
2772. Ice At Last. Johnston, G. NY 32 (12/22/56): 63.
2773. Ice Cream. Wolf, L. Co 67 (11/1/57): 121.
2774. Ice-Cream Cones. Armour, R. SEP 228 (1/28/56): 66.
2775. The Iceberg. Merwin, W.S. NY 32 (5/5/56): 30.
2776. The Icehouse. Abbe, G. At 204 (10/59): 72.
2777. Ich Am of Irlaunde. Brinnin, J.M. NY 32 (8/25/56): 30.
2778. Icos. Tomlinson, C. P 88 (9/58): 350.
2779. I'd Cancel His Poetic License. Nash, V. SR 38 (5/14/55): 12.
2780. I'd Just Like to Know. Jaffray, N.R. SEP 227 (5/7/55): 74.
2781. I'd Like To Be a Firefly. Frost, T. Hn 35 (8/59): 280.
2782. I'd Rather Be. GH 140 (4/55): 40.
2783. Ides of March. O'Kearney, J. N 182 (3/24/56): 235.
2784. The Idiot. Ashbery, J. P 91 (10/57): 165.
2785. Idiot's Delight. Eff, J. NaR 4 (12/14/57): 545.
2786. Idyll. Longchamps, J.de P 85 (1/55): 203.
2787. Idyll. Updike, J. NY 35 (10/10/59): 50.
2788. If...? Graham, J. GH 141 (7/55): 40.
2789. If Harold Ross Had His Way. Black, S.M. NR 141 (12/21/59): 20-2.
2790. If I Could Breathe. McFarland, E. LHJ 74 (12/57): 12.
2791. If I Should Die Before I Wake. Mezey, R. NY 33 (9/14/57): 47.
2792. If the Bright Bird. Bernard, O. P 86 (5/55): 75.
2793. If They Show Me a Stone and I Say Stone. Gilboa, A. P 92 (7/58): 252.

2794. If We Were Water Voice. La Bombard, J. P 92 (5/58): 90-1.
2795. If You Are a Stranger Here. Graham, E. LHJ 76 (3/59): 107.
2796. If You Believe the Commercials. Chadwick, H. BHG 37 (4/59): 189.
2797. If You But Dreamed It. Van Doren, M. H 215 (7/57): 27.
2798. If You Came. Dunbar, V.E. LHJ 72 (1/55): 130.
2799. If You Can. Moss, H. NY 35 (8/15/59): 24.
2800. If You Have an Appointment for April, Break It. Pedrick, J. H 212 (4/56): 77.
2801. If You Will. Richardson, D.L. LHJ 76 (8/59): 118.
2802. Ignis Dominae. Laing, D. N 185 (11/16/57): 362.
2803. Ignis Fabuous. Jones, E.E. NaR 1 (4/11/56): 23.
2804. Il Capitano, the Fencing Master. Sitwell, O. NY 33 (2/23/57): 35.
2805. Il Va Neiger. Jammes, F. P 89 (12/56): 157.
2806. I'll Always Love You. Martin, P. LHJ 74 (4/57): 97.
2807. I'll Eat My Split-Level Turkey in the Breezeway. Nash, O. HG 108 (12/55): 96-9.
2808. Illumination. Turnbull, A.S. GH 141 (10/55): 111.
2809. Illusion. Tremayne, P. At 200 (9/57): 72.
2810. I'm Dreaming of a White Daisy. Wright, P. GH 140 (4/55): 16.
2811. I'm Glad You Asked That Question, Because It Shows You in Your True Colors. Nash, O. NY 35 (2/21/59): 36.
2812. I'm Growing Old. Saxe, J.G. GH 140 (5/55): 40.
2813. I'm Here. Roethke, T. NY 32 (12/15/56): 39.
2814. I'm Home. Engle, P. LHJ 72 (9/55): 160.
2815. I'm Just an In-Between. Baxter, J. CH 33 (12/58): 245.
2816. The Imbecile. Finkel, D. P 91 (1/58): 237-8.
2817. Imitation of Nature. Jerome, J. At 200 (11/57): 257.
2818. Immanence. Clark, L.S. CC 74 (10/16/57): 1229.
2819. Immigrant. Drake, C.C. P 89 (11/56): 99.
2820. Impasse. Young, N. CC 73 (1/11/56): 46.
2821. An Imperial Tanka. His Majesty the Emperor of Japan. At 195 (1/55): 121.
2822. The Important Personages. Smith, A.J.M. N 185 (12/7/57): 440.
2823. Impressions of My Father. Masters, M. P 93 (11/58): 91-4.
2824. Improper Name. Herz, B. SEP 232 (10/3/59): 162.
2825. The Improvement of Prayer. Sandeen, E. P 85 (2/55): 260-1.
2826. In a Day of Menaced Freedom. Coblentz, S.A. CC 72 (5/4/55): 527.
2827. In a Dream I Spoke. Pillin, W. P 91 (11/57): 103-4.
2828. In a Drugstore. Robin, R. SR 40 (4/13/57): 30.
2829. In a Dutch Town. Dejong, D.C. N 184 (1/26/57): 83.
2830. In a Gallery of Oriental Art. Pierce, E.L. CC 76 (6/3/59): 666.
2831. In a Great Library. Greene, C.S. WLB 32 (6/58): 725.
2832. In a Greek New Testament. Wood, N.R. CT 1 (3/18/57): 11.

2833. In a Hospital Nursery. Adrian, V.H. SEP 229 (7/14/56): 97.

2834. In a Liberal Arts Building. Stone, R. N 186 (2/22/58): 173.

2835. In a Manner of Speaking. Ellyson, L. At 199 (4/57): 92.

2836. In a Parlor Containing a Table. Kinnell, G. N 189 (8/29/59): 98.

2837. In a Railway Compartment. Fuller, J. P 93 (10/58): 17.

2838. In a Textile Factory. Che, S. At 204 (12/59): 94.

2839. In a Wet Season. McInery, R. A 99 (4/26/58): 144.

2840. In After Time. Eberhart, R. N 187 (12/27/58): 500.

2841. In Alien Land. Moreljono, J. At 197 (6/56): 105.

2842. In an Old Blacksmith Shop. Jacobs, E.L. SEP 231 (9/13/58): 83.

2843. In Answer to Your Question, Son.... Congdon, T. SEP 231 (4/4/59): 69.

2844. The In-Betweener. Laurence, R. SR 39 (6/2/56): 4.

2845. In Burnt Autumn. Garrigue, J. NR 134 (4/30/56): 21.

2846. In Childhood's Chair. Friar, K. P 90 (7/57): 217-8.

2847. In China I Learned About Gardens. Moore, M. SR 38 (11/5/55): 16.

2848. In Concert. Arnold, L. SEP 232 (10/31/59): 69.

2849. In Conclusion. Murphy, W.J. NY 34 (1/3/59): 71.

2850. In Dear Detail, By Ideal Light. Stafford, W. P 94 (7/59): 227-8.

2851. In Defense of a Green Christmas. Dean, E. GH 142 (12/56): 8.

2852. In Defense of Colds. Petrie, P. P 90 (8/57): 296-7.

2853. In Defense of Living in the North. Emans, E.V. SEP 230 (12/28/57): 56.

2854. In Defense of Metaphysics. Tomlinson, C. P 92 (5/58): 105.

2855. In Defense of Superficiality. Olson, E. NY 33 (10/26/57): 46.

2856. In Dry Fields Daniel Walks. Lynch, J.A. Co 68 (9/5/58): 561.

2857. In Easy Dark. Barker, E. AS 28 (Wint/58-59): 72.

2858. In Egypt. Enrico, H. C 28 (12/59): 527.

2859. In Flames of Fire. Beck, V.E. CT 3 (9/14/59): 8.

2860. In Heaven All Were Dancing. Lilly, O. CC 76 (5/20/59): 613.

2861. In Her Song She Is Alone. Swan, J. NY 33 (8/10/57): 30.

2862. In Her Splendor Islanded. Paz, O. P 92 (6/58): 171.

2863. In India. Shapiro, K. NY 32 (9/22/56): 42.

2864. In Laws and Lust. Salinger, H. SR 42 (4/18/59): 14.

2865. In Lieu of a Press Agent. Blackwell, H.G. GH 140 (4/55): 16.

2866. In Love with You. Koch, K. P 86 (4/55): 18-20.

2867. In Loving Evidence. Moody, M.H. SEP 231 (12/13/58): 52.

2868. In Memoriam: 1954. Freeman, J. AS 24 (Summ/55): 321-3.

2869. In Memoriam Wallace Stevens. Smith, W.J. P 90 (4/57): 37.

2870. In Memoriam--Wyndham Lewis. Russell, P. P 91 (1/58): 255.

2871. In Memory of an Over-Ambitious Poem. Moore, R. SR 41 (3/15/58): 24.

2872. In Memory of Anton Webern, Dead. Mueller, L. P 92 (4/58): 20-1.

2873. In Memory of Augusta Hall. Hall, D. LHJ 72 (8/55): 69.

2874. In Memory of Dylan Thomas. Barker, E. At 195 (2/55): 60.

2875. In Memory of Pfc. R.N. Rock, F. P 86 (7/55): 234.

2876. In Memory of Sister Virgilia of the Sacred Heart. O'Gorman, N. P 92 (4/58): 5.

2877. In Memory of Two Friends. Masefield, J. SR 38 (5/7/55): 32.

2878. In Miniature. Singleton, M.E. SEP 232 (11/14/59): 78.

2879. In Moonlight, Somewhere, They Are Singing. Warren, R.P. SR 41 (11/22/58): 37.

2880. In My Beginnings. Giller, A. C 20 (8/55): 108.

2881. In October. McNeill, L. SEP 230 (10/26/57): 96.

2882. In Our Town. MacNeil, M.A. A 100 (1/3/59): 399.

2883. In Passage Tropical. Walton, E.L. P 94 (5/59): 91.

2884. In Perspective. Coblentz, S.A. CC 75 (1/8/58): 44.

2885. In Poems. Casey, K. P 95 (10/59): 23.

2886. In Praise of $C_{10}H_9O_5)_x$. Updike, J. NY 35 (5/16/59): 44.

2887. In Praise of Newspaper Verse. Moore, R. SR 41 (9/20/58): 36.

2888. In Redwoods. Witt, H. NR 141 (9/21/59): 21.

2889. In Reply to Your Query, Sincerely. Graham, E. LHJ 75 (1/58): 88.

2890. In Santa Maria del Popolo. Gunn, T. P 93 (10/58): 1-2.

2891. In Search of Man. Ghiselin, B. P 90 (6/57): 156-7.

2892. In Spring. MacCollom, J. SR 38 (6/11/55): 13.

2893. In That Weird Continent. Coblentz, S.A. CC 75 (7/23/58): 851.

2894. In the Beginning. Hoffman, D.G. P 89 (1/57): 221-2.

2895. In the Birdhouse. Hemley, C. NR 132 (6/13/55): 22.

2896. In the Blossoms of a Village the City is Lost. Motonari (1497-1571). L 40 (4/30/56): 88-9.

2897. In the Days When Purple Was New. Pomeroy, R. P 91 (11/57): 90.

2898. In the Desperate Hours. Freeman, J.T. LHJ 72 (7/55): 113.

2899. In the Fall. MacDiarmid, H. N 187 (11/1/58): 308.

2900. In the Garden. Merrill, H. SEP 228 (5/26/56): 88.

2901. In the Garden. Weinstein, A. SR 39 (5/5/56): 25.

2902. In the Gray Light. Greenberg, E. C 25 (4/58): 312-3.

2903. In the Heart of a Shell. Lineaweaver, M. LHJ 72 (8/55): 80.

2904. In the Hot Wind. Lamdan, Y. P 92 (7/58): 217-9.

2905. In the Hydrogen Age. Coblentz, S.A. CC 74 (1/23/57): 107.

2906. In the Light of Autumn. Merwin, W.S. N 183 (9/29/56): 272.

2907. In the Line Storm. Morse, S.F. P 90 (7/57): 207-8.

2908. In the Lions' Den. Hay, S.H. SR 41 (4/26/58): 10.

2909. In the Madness of Age. Stone, R. P 89 (1/57): 214.

2910. In the Manger, Christmas Day. Grebanier, B.D. A 96 (12/22/56): 351.

2911. In the Maze. Galler, D. P 94 (4/59): 25.

2912. In the Midst of Life I Petition Thee. Cooper, J.C. CT 2 (7/7/58): 6.

2913. In the Morning. Frimet, H. AS 27 (Wint/57-58): 62.

2914. In the Morning You Always Come Back. di Giovanni, N.T. N 187 (9/13/58): 135.

2915. In the Orchard. Friend, R. SR 40 (9/28/57): 15.

2916. In the Pink. Antolini, M.F. SEP 229 (7/21/56): 88.

2917. In the Public Gardens. Betjeman, J. NY 33 (1/4/58): 20.

2918. In the Same Club Chair. MacKaye, P. NY 32 (9/29/56): 116.

2919. In the Snake Park. Plomer, W. NY 35 (9/12/59): 50.

2920. In the Thriving Season. Mueller, L. P 94 (8/59): 293.

2921. In the Time of Fall. Gustafson, R. N 189 (10/24/59): 256.

2922. In the World-Crowded Corner of a Stall. O'Connell, R. A 94 (12/24/55): 357.

2923. In Those Days. Wolf, L. C 28 (10/59): 322.

2924. In Time Like Air. Sarton, M. NY 32 (5/12/56): 42.

2925. In Time of Gold. D., H. P 91 (12/57): 149-50.

2926. In Various Alleys Zig Zagging with Dilapidated and Sometimes Squeeking Bicycles Does Not the Buddha Spirit Surprise Us? Tagliabue, J. P 95 (10/59): 17.

2927. Inactive File. Seifer, D. GH 149 (8/59): 53.

2928. Inasmuch. Clark, L.S. CT 3 (6/8/59): 17.

2929. The Inattentive. Erba, L. P 94 (8/59): 309, 11.

2930. Inaudibles. Kraft, V.A. CC 72 (1/12/55): 41.

2931. Incantatory Poem. Garrigue, J. P 90 (9/57): 335-7.

2932. Incident at Calvary. McDonnell, T.P. A 92 (3/19/55): 650.

2933. Incident at High Chair. Chadwick, H. SEP 228 (1/21/56): 106.

2934. Incinerator. Van Doren, M. H 215 (7/57): 27.

2935. Inclined To Be Lenient. Usk, T. TH 35 (7/57): 48.

2936. Incompatibilities. Hughes, T. N 185 (7/20/57): 34.

2937. Incomplete Dishwasher. Armour, R. BHG 33 (4/55): 147.

2938. Inconsistency. Power, J.W. LHJ 73 (2/56): 149.

2939. Inconstancies. Sullivan, D. A 95 (6/2/56): 244.

2940. Incorrigibles. Perkins, D. YR 47 (12/57): 237-8.

2941. Increment. Miles, J. P 92 (6/58): 190.

2942. Indian Slummer. Rosenfield, L. At 200 (7/57): 94.

2943. Indian Summer. Richardson, D.L. AS 25 (Aut/56): 410.

2944. Indian Summer. Ward, M.W. SEP 230 (10/19/57): 52.

2945. Indian Summer Day. Balch, B.J. SEP 231 (10/18/58): 60.

2946. The Indians. Bangham. M.D. CC 73 (1/11/56): 46.

2947. Indians. Fandel, J. NY 35 (7/25/59): 79.

2948. Individual. Merchant, J. SEP 229 (4/6/57): 85.

2949. Inevitable. Soule, J.C. BHG 35 (5/57): 170.

2950. Inexpensive Remedy. Galbraith, G.S. SEP 230 (4/5/58): 92.

2951. The Infant Jesus of Prague. Claudel, P. P 87 (12/55): 136-7.

2952. Infernal Equinox. Hammer, P. SEP 227 (3/19/55): 128.

2953. Influenza. Van Horn, R.G. N 185 (11/23/57): 395.

2954. Inland Angler. Ellis, C. SEP 230 (5/10/58): 129.

2955. Inner Fire. Baldwin, L.M. CC 72 (10/55): 1136.

2956. The Innkeeper's Story. Cooper, J. H 217 (12/58): 71.

2957. The Innocence and Windows of Children and Childhood. Schwartz, D. NR 132 (1/10/55): 19.

2958. The Innocents. Vazakas, B. P 86 (6/55): 146.

2959. Inquire of the Wind. Natsume, S. At 195 (1/55): 164.

2960. An Inquiry Into the Ultimate Loneliness. Frumlein, G. SR 42 (6/20/59): 19.

2961. The Insatiate. McFarland, E. LHJ 76 (9/59): 30.

2962. Inscription on Grave of a Horse Thief. GH 140 (5/55): 40.

2963. Inscription on the Flyleaf of a Bible. Abse, D. C 20 (9/55): 200.

2964. Inscriptions on Chinese Paintings. Bynner, W. P 89 (1/57): 240-3.

2965. The Insects. Kelley, R.S. NY 32 (6/30/59): 63.

2966. Inseparable. Ford, E. LHJ 76 (1/59): 77.

2967. Inside Athens. Gottlier, H.J. N 189 (10/17/59): 238.

2968. Inside Story. Murphy, W.J. NY 33 (10/12/57): 155.

2969. Inside the Angel. Macpherson, J. P 90 (9/57): 345.

2970. Inside the Shadow. Goldin, J. CC 74 (9/4/57): 1035.

2971. Inside the Snow. Robson, E.N. SR 24 (2/7/59): 51.

2972. Insomnia. Lund, M.G. CC 76 (7/1/59): 965.

2973. Insomnia. Quasimodo, S. At 202 (12/58): 144.

2974. Inspiration. Miller, H.A. CT 1 (9/16/57): 8.

2975. Inspiration. Ryskind, M. NaR 3 (6/18/57): 573.

2976. Inspired Race. Sawyer, D.J. CC 76 (8/26/59): 963.

2977. Instance of the Leaf. Perkins, D. YR 47 (12/57): 238.

2978. The Instant in the Eye. Vance, T. P 87 (1/56): 196-8.

2979. Instead of a Journey. Humburge, M. NY 35 (10/31/59): 155.

2980. Instructions for Acting: Drunk Scene. Jerome, J. SR 42 (6/27/59): 28.

2981. Instructions for Chaperons at a Teen-age Party. Armour, R. SEP 230 (10/19/57): 123.

2982. Instrument Approach. Fairbairn, D. SEP 230 (5/17/58): 86.

2983. Intellectual Observation. Wheeler, R. SEP 229 (5/18/57): 92.

2984. Intelligence Test. Merchant, J. SEP 229 (4/6/57): 152.

2985. Intercessor. Molton, W.L. CC 76 (11/25/59): 1370.

2986. Interest-Bearing. Talman, T. GH 142 (1/56): 42.

2987. Interior. Smith, W.J. P 90 (4/57): 37.

2988. Interior Day. Nicholl, L.T. AS 26 (Spr/57): 195.

2989. The Interior of Roses. Rilke, R.M. NR 134 (3/12/56): 25.

2990. Interlude. White, C.N. L 45 (8/4/58): 5.

2991. Interval Before Autumn. Henritzy, S.M. SEP 230 (9/14/57): 157.

2992. The Interview. Galler, D. N 189 (12/5/59): 423.

2993. Into November. McGonigal, M. SEP 232 (11/7/59): 75.

2994. Into the Stone. Dickey, J. P 94 (7/59): 225-6.

2995. Into the Wind. Scott, W. SR 40 (2/9/57): 41.

2996. Introvert's Lament. Galbraith, G.S. At 202 (7/58): 90.

2997. Intruder. Jacobson, E. SR 38 (7/9/55): 17.

2998. The Intruder. Kizer, C. P 89 (12/56): 161-2.

2999. The Invasion. Burger, O.K. NY 35 (6/27/59): 68.

3000. Invasion. Stoutenberg, A. SR 40 (4/13/57): 30.

3001. The Inventors. Char, R. P 89 (3/57): 333-4.

3002. The Invisible Line. McNeill, L. SEP 231 (2/21/59): 99.

3003. Invitation. Hanes, L. SEP 228 (3/31/56): 75.

3004. Invitation. Mok, S.M. LHJ 74 (7/57): 135.

3005. Invitation to Dalliance. Brasier, V. TH 35 (5/57): 20.

3006. Invocation. Sarton, M. SR 38 (3/12/55): 18.

3007. Involuntary. Merrill, H. SEP 230 (11/30/57): 53.

3008. Iowa and the West. Miles, J. P 94 (6/59): 141-4.

3009. Ipswich Ballad. Frost, F. At 202 (10/58): 105.

3010. Iris, at the Piano. Swenson, M. NY 34 (4/19/58): 44.

3011. Iron Bedstead. Moody, M.H. GH 142 (4/56): 18.

3012. Iron Curtain. Stokely, J. N 182 (5/12/56): 404.

3013. The Iron Gate. Davidson, L.K. CT 2 (10/14/57): 7.

3014. Iron Mirror. Laing, A. SR 42 (6/27/59): 17.

3015. The Irresistible Intention. Kraft, V.A. CC 72 (1/55): 75.

3016. Irreverent Thought. R., W.A. NaR 7 (5/23/59): 83.

3017. Irritant Incarnate. Galbraith, G.S. At 199 (4/57): 93.

3018. The Irritated Office. Stock, R. P 92 (4/58): 15.

3019. Is uar geimred; atracht gaeth. Merwin, W.S. N 187 (12/27/58): 501.

3020. Isaac. Gilboa, A. P 92 (7/58): 249.

3021. Isaiah's Coal. Nims, J.F. Co 71 (10/16/59): 66.

3022. Ishmaelites. Coblentz, S.A. CC 76 (7/1/59): 965.

3023. Island. Zlotnik, H. EJ 44 (4/55): 227.

3024. The Island in the Evening. Porter, F. P 85 (3/55): 326-7.

3025. The Island-Maker. Marz, R. SR 40 (5/4/57): 19.

3026. Island Song. Freeman, J.T. LHJ 73 (8/56): 114.

3027. The Islanders. Booth, P. H 218 (4/59): 41.

3028. Islanders. Braun, R.E. SR 39 (9/22/56): 38.

3029. Islands. Pillin, W. P 91 (11/57): 103-4.

3030. The Isles of Greece. Capetanakis, D. At 195 (6/55): 125.

3031. Isolation. Coblentz, S.A. CC 74 (5/22/57): 654.

3032. Israel. Lamdan, Y. P 92 (7/58): 220.

3033. It Figures. Eisenlohr, L. SEP 231 (3/21/59): 73.

3034. It Happened One Friday. Street, R. WLB 33 (4/59): 585.

3035. It Hardly Pays. Wheeler, R. SEP 230 (4/19/58): 136.

3036. It Is a Wind Where All Was Still. Corke, H. NY 33 (5/4/57): 36.

3037. It Is June, This Jesting Heat. Mezey, R. P 90 (5/57): 83-4.

3038. It Is Not Necessary. Angoff, C. CC 75 (9/3/58): 995.

3039. It Is Time for Plain Speaking. Hoffman, D.G. N 181 (11/5/55): 402.

3040. It Isn't a Job: It's a Position. Emmons, D. SEP 230 (11/16/57): 107.

3041. It Looks Like a Beautiful Day. Middleton, C. LHJ 76 (4/59): 176.

3042. It Was the Last of the Parades. Simpson, L. NY 35 (5/30/59): 30.

3043. It Won't Be Yours Again. Robertson, G.V. CT 4 (12/7/59): 10.

3044. It Works Both Ways. Collins, I.J. SEP 228 (8/27/55): 91.

3045. It Works Both Ways. Jaffray, N.R. SEP 231 (1/24/59): 54.

3046. It Would Have Been Quicker to Walk. Nash, O. NY 32 (9/8/56): 36.

3047. Italian. Miles, J. P 92 (6/58): 141.

3048. Italian Lesson. Merrill, J. P 91 (2/58): 285.

3049. Italian Market. Nicolas, C. SR 39 (11/10/56): 19.

3050. Ithaka. Scott, T. P 89 (2/57): 302-4.

3051. It's a Constant Battle! Chadwick, R. SEP 231 (8/1/59): 44.

3052. It's a Pleasure! Schlitzer, S. SEP 229 (9/1/56): 67.

3053. It's All in the Raising. Armknecht, R.F. SEP 228 (8/20/55): 79.

3054. It's 'Cause You Get Excited. Anthony, E. GH 142 (9/56): 166.

3055. It's Easy to Please a Child. Jennison, C.S. LHJ 73 (12/56): 180.

3056. It's Impolite to Change the Subject. Armknecht, R.F. BHG 34 (12/56): 133.

3057. It's in the Bag. Alkus, M. SEP 231 (9/20/58): 119.

3058. It's Later Than I Think. Wright, A. LHJ 75 (2/58): 96.

3059. It's My Turn to Snooze in the Hammock. Pratt, W.W. SEP 229 (7/21/56): 55.

3060. It's Too Darn Quiet! Eisenlohr, L. SEP 231 (7/5/58): 81.

3061. It's Your Ego, but It's My Id. Pedrick, J. H 211 (10/55): 66.

3062. Iuvenes Dum Sumus. Hall, D. At 195 (1/55): 90.

3063. I've Had a Superfluity of Yankee Ingenuity. Jennison, C.S. At 203 (3/59): 98.

3064. The Ivory Wanderer. Swann, T.B. LHJ 75 (12/58): 119.

3065. J. Holmes, T. P 94 (6/59): 174-5.

3066. Jack. Updike, J. NY 33 (10/19/57): 134.

3067. Jack and the Other Jack. Hall, D. N 186 (4/12/58): 330.

3068. Jacob. Kanfer, A. P 85 (12/55): 205.

3069. The Jaguar. Hughes, T. P 90 (8/57): 281-2.

3070. Jake's Wharf. Booth, P. NY 34 (3/1/58): 38.

3071. Jamaica. Hall, D. P 86 (8/55): 267-8.

3072. Jane. Galbraith, G.S. SEP 230 (10/5/57): 96.

3073. The Janitor's Face. De Jong, D.C. P 91 (10/57): 11-2.

3074. January. Johnson, G. A 100 (1/17/59): 458.

3075. January. Wallace, R.A. NY 31 (1/7/56): 53.

3076. January Afternoon. Wooten, P. SEP 227 (1/8/55): 81.

3077. January Fog. Palen, J.M. SEP 229 (1/19/57): 81.

3078. January Night. Frost, F. SR 39 (1/14/56): 23.

3079. January Thaw. Raner, D. SR 38 (1/15/55): 18.

3080. Japan That Sank Under the Sea. Sato, S. P 88 (5/56): 107.

3081. Jays in the Wood. Solomon, M. P 88 (8/56): 313.

3082. Je Faisois ces Sonnets. Ronsard, P.de P 85 (1/55): 202.

3083. Jealous. Fuller, J. P 93 (10/58): 17-18.

3084. Jeeped Molasses. Merchant, J. SEP 229 (10/27/56): 109.

3085. Jennie Missed Me. Bentley, G. SR 39 (6/2/56): 4.

3086. Jeremiad. Delattre, P.H. Co 71 (11/13/59): 201.

3087. A Jeremiad. Flatto, E. C 22 (9/56): 248.

3088. Jericho. Galler, D. P 92 (4/58): 41.

3089. Jerusalem Is a Hill City. Shlonsky, A. P 92 (7/58): 227.

3090. Jerusalem, Vermont. Gleason, M. SEP 231 (8/2/58): 64.

3091. Jesu, Joy of Man's Desiring. Fitzgerald, R. NY 32 (12/22/56): 26.

3092. Jesu's Toy. Thorley, W. LHJ 73 (4/56): 115.

3093. Jesus Wrote with His Finger on the Ground. Pierce, E.L. CC 75 (7/16/58): 826.

3094. Jet-Age Dilemma. Coblentz, S.A. CC 75 (12/3/58): 1393.

3095. Jet-Vapor Trail. Dufault, P.K. NY 32 (2/25/56): 36.

3096. A Jew Walks in Westminster Abbey. Hodes, A. C 21 (2/56): 126-7.

3097. The Jewels and the Gracchi. Hollander, J. P 87 (1/56): 217.

3098. Jezebel. Clark, L.S. CC 72 (7/6/55): 789.

3099. Joan and Darby. Graves, R. NY 35 (12/12/59): 54.

3100. Job. Cooper, J.C. CC 75 (11/5/58): 1266.

3101. Job's Anger. Ignatow, D. P 93 (11/58): 84.

3102. Jochebed Mourns for Moses. Tr. by Roth, C. C 28 (10/59): 347-8.

3103. John Brown's Bodies. Burford, W. SR 40 (11/16/57): 49.

3104. John Hancock. Hale, O. SR 38 (10/22/55): 10.

3105. John Otto. Merwin, W.S. NY 34 (3/29/58): 30.

3106. The Jokesmith. Smith, F. L 39 (9/5/55): 89.

3107. Jonah and the Whale. Swan, J. AS 28 (Summ/59): 364-6.

3108. Jongleur de Dieu. Delattre, P.H. CC 74 (10/2/57): 1168.

3109. Joseph. Galler, D. P 92 (4/58): 40-1.

3110. Joshua Tree. Ammons, A.R. P 93 (3/59): 371-2.

3111. Journey. Bynner, W. SR 38 (8/20/55): 26.

3112. The Journey. Rawlins, W. CC 76 (1/14/59): 42.

3113. Journey in the Tessellated Corn. Myers, E.L. P 91 (12/57): 181-3.

3114. The Journey to Golgotha. Rao, K.R. P 93 (1/59): 252-3.

3115. Journey to the Holy Land. Pierce, E.L. CC 76 (12/23/59): 1501.

3116. Journey Toward Evening. McGinley, P. NY 34 (2/7/59): 115.

3117. Joy and the Presence of Snakes. Moore, R. P 85 (3/55): 347-8.

3118. Joyce's Grave. Coleman, E. P 92 (8/58): 291.

3119. Jubilee. Cotter, J.F. A 99 (7/5/58): 301.

3120. July Day. Deutsch, B. P 86 (7/55): 231.

3121. July Escapist. Witt, H. LHJ 76 (7/59): 128.

3122. July Fourth Memory. Merrill, H. SEP 229 (7/7/56): 73.

3123. July 4, 1984: Ode Written in Newspeak. Ryskind, M. NaR 7 (7/4/59): 177.

3124. July Mountain. Stevens, W. At 195 (4/55): 42.

3125. June. Freeman, J.D. GH 142 (6/56): 119.

3126. June Hot Spell. Bradbury, B. SEP 230 (6/7/58): 61.

3127. The Jungfrau in Season Bricht wi Eternal Whiteness Is Natheless Raped by the Bruts O a Cloud O Witness. Smith, S.G. P 88 (4/56): 37-9.

3128. Junior Grows Wise. Usk, T. SEP 232 (8/29/59): 72.

3129. Junior Partner. Heath, C. SEP 230 (3/29/58): 56.

3130. Just a Hobby. Chadwick, H. BHG 34 (3/56): 243.

3131. Just Before Class. Kline, L.W. EJ 46 (2/57): 111.

3132. Just Before Dawn. Averitt, E. SEP 232 (8/22/59): 71.

3133. Just Between You and I. Solovay, J.C. CH 32 (9/57): 3.

3134. Just His Dish. Galbraith, G.S. SEP 228 (4/28/56): 122.

3135. Just in Case. Minck, G.S. SEP 228 (1/7/56): 74.

3136. Just in From the Cold. Souster, R. P 94 (8/59): 301.

3137. Justus ut Palma. Gordon, W.M. A 93 (9/10/55): 565.

3138. Juveniles. Stone, R. P 89 (1/57): 213.

3139. Kaleidoscopic. Hirshman, R. N 186 (2/22/58): 168.

3140. Kanheri Caves. Moraes, D. P 93 (1/59): 251.

3141. The Kate. McFarland, E. LHJ 72 (1/55): 122.

3142. Katherine. Stewart, M.S. LHJ 75 (7/58): 24.

3143. Kathleen Ferrier (1912-1953). Fawcett, B. SR 38 (5/28/55): 36-

3144. Katie. O'Doherty, B. P 87 (1/56): 227-8.

3145. Keel-boatman's Horn. Knoepfle, J. P 93 (12/58): 148.

3146. Keeping up with the Youngsters. Schlitzer, S. SEP 230 (2/8/58): 86.

3147. Kenneths. Updike, J. NY 34 (7/5/58): 59.

3148. Kenossis 1955. Eckhardt, A.R. CC 72 (3/2/55): 267.

3149. Keraunograph. Carruth, H. N 186 (5/3/58): 400.

3150. The Key. Carruth, H. NR 138 (1/6/58): 18.

3151. Key Note. Wheeler, R. SEP 229 (9/8/56): 105.

3152. Key Pattern. Nicholl, L.T. SR 38 (5/28/55): 19.

3153. Key to Accomplishment. Chadwick, H. SEP 231 (7/5/58): 52.

3154. Key to His Confidence. Usk, T. SEP 228 (6/23/56): 75.

3155. Key West. Kadow, A. P 89 (1/57): 225.

3156. Khan of the Sunflowers. Nixon, J.,Jr. NR 141 (8/24/59): 29.

3157. The Khazar Poet. Haber, L. C 21 (4/56): 358.

3158. Killdeer Crying. Landeweer, E. SEP 228 (9/17/55): 50.

3159. Kind Design. Collins, M.G. LHJ 75 (11/58): 156.

3160. A Kind of Music. Van Duyn, M. P 93 (12/58): 139.

3161. A Kind of View. Morse, S.F. P 90 (7/57): 209.

3162. Kind Offices. Johnston, G. H 210 (2/55): 73.

3163. Kind Sir: These Woods. Sexton, A. H 219 (11/59): 40.

3164. Kind Word. Richstone, M. SEP 229 (3/23/57): 40.

3165. A Kind Word for Winter. Collins, B.F. SEP 231 (2/7/59): 68.

3166. Kindergarten. Goodman, M.W. SEP 229 (10/6/56): 77.

3167. King Midas. Moss, H. P 90 (5/57): 67-72.

3168. The King of Asine. Seferis, G. At 195 (6/55): 158-9.

3169. The King of Evil. Coblentz, S.A. CC 73 (8/22/56): 967.

3170. King Salmon. Huff, R. At 197 (6/56): 53.

3171. Kingdom of Daylight. Cotter, J.F. A 94 (3/31/56): 717-9.

3172. The Kingdom of Poetry. Schwartz, D. P 92 (5/58): 63-6.

3173. King's Mountain. Rukeyser, M. P 86 (4/55): 5-6.

3174. The Kiss. Hall, D. P 93 (10/58): 29.

3175. Kitchen Sink. Armour, R. GH 142 (8/56): 121.

3176. Kite Flying. Pomeroy, R. P 93 (2/59): 303.

3177. A Kite Is a Victim. Cohen, L. SR 42 (10/24/59): 54.

3178. Kitty Hawk. Frost, R. At 200 (11/57): 52-6.

3179. Kline and Stein. Fox, I. AN 56 (1/58): 43.

3180. A Knee-Length Trapeze. Lamport, F. H 218 (2/59): 49.

3181. Knight, with Umbrella. Olson, E. NY 33 (2/1/58): 72.

3182. Knightly Behavior. Magee, I. SEP 231 (10/25/58): 58.

3183. Knock for Luck. Armknecht, R.F. SEP 228 (3/31/56): 97.

3184. Know-How. Laing, A. N 186 (3/15/58): 241.

3185. Know Something. Wood, J.P. LHJ 74 (3/57): 163.

3186. Know Thyself. Razaf, A. NHB 18 (4/55): 169.

3187. The Knowledge of Light. Rago, H. P 91 (10/57): 1-3.

3188. Known Room. Merchant, J. SEP 230 (3/1/58): 68.

3189. Kokoro. Hughes, D.J. P 94 (9/59): 379.

3190. Kunlun. Tse-Tung, M. At 204 (12/59): 54-5.

3191. The LP Catalog: An Appreciation. Leviant, C. NY 32 (6/23/56): 60.

3192. Labor-Saving System. Parrish, M.M. SEP 229 (10/27/56): 65.

3193. Laboratory Poem. Merrill, J. P 91 (2/58): 284.

3194. The Ladder. Baro, G. NY 34 (6/7/58): 93.

3195. Lady Dancing in the Street. Weinstein, A. SR 39 (7/14/56): 38.

3196. Lady Day. Mastin, F.R. SR 38 (4/23/55): 10.

3197. Lady in Waiting. Franklin, J.M. SEP 228 (2/11/56): 60.

3198. Lady Is a Lady. Holmes, J. SR 41 (11/22/58): 38.

3199. Lady with Trowel and Basket. Schofield, D.H. SEP 227 (5/21/55): 54.

3200. Laine. Bagg, R. P 90 (6/57): 148-50.

3201. Lake Allen: Summer 1954. Ostroff, A. P 85 (3/55): 323-4.

3202. Lake Beaver. La Follette, M.W. P 88 (4/56): 27.

3203. Lake Change. Merrill, H. SEP 229 (12/8/56): 111.

3204. The Lake Eternal. Pierce, E.L. CC 74 (8/21/57): 987.

3205. A Lake Scene. Swenson, M. P 91 (2/58): 301-2.

3206. Lakes Learn from the Season. Pomeroy, R. P 91 (11/57): 89.

3207. The Lame Heart. Giuliani, A. P 94 (8/59): 315, 7.

3208. Lament. MacLeod, N. P 91 (12/57): 168-9.

3209. Lament for a Lost Morning. Richstone, M. SEP 230 (9/28/57): 110.

3210. Lament for a Shining Past. Wheeler, R. SEP 231 (5/16/59): 102.

3211. Lament for an Old Pressman. Frumbin, G. P 95 (12/59): 164.

3212. Lament for Heroes. Brennan, F. SR 42 (4/18/59): 10.

3213. Lament for Our Failure to Improve Ancient Skills. Gass, W.H. N 187 (8/2/58): 56.

3214. The Lament of Llywarch Hen. Humphries, R. P 97 (2/56): 263-4.

3215. Lament of the Wife of a Psychoanalyst. Saroyan, S. At 196 (12/55): 106.

3216. The Lamp, and Heliodora. Triem, E. P 89 (2/57): 272.

3217. Land and Sea. Erba, L. P 94 (8/59): 311.
3218. The Land of Cockayne. Barker, E. At 196 (10/55): 71.
3219. A Land of Settled Government. Tennyson, A. HBR 36 (3-4/58): 136.
3220. Landed: A Valentine. Howard, R. P 87 (1/56): 220.
3221. Landfall. Burrows, E.G. P 91 (2/58): 297.
3222. The Landfall. Dickey, J. P 94 (7/59): 213-5.
3223. Landfall. Dugan, A. P 88 (4/56): 11-2.
3224. Landing on the Moon. Swenson, M. N 187 (9/6/58): 118.
3225. Landscape. Zilles, L. At 196 (8/55): 66.
3226. Landscape Finally with Figure. Jacobsen, J. Co 68 (9/19/58): 615.
3227. Landscape for a Wife. Legler, P. P 93 (2/59): 289-90.
3228. Landscape Near Salt Lake. Nichols, D. NR 135 (11/12/56): 22.
3229. The Landscape of Love. McGinley, P. LHJ 76 (2/59): 150.
3230. Landscape: Ragged Key. Perry, R.L. P 92 (6/58): 156-9.
3231. Landscape with Bo Tree. Burrows, E.G. P 93 (11/58): 87-8.
3232. Landscape with Story. Lattimore, R. P 88 (4/56): 15.
3233. Landscapes There Are. Berrigan, D.J. A 98 (10/26/57): 111.
3234. The Lane. Ely, G. P 92 (9/58): 367.
3235. L'Ane Savant. Jammes, F. P 89 (12/56): 159.
3236. Languages I Never Mastered: Hotelese. Rosenfield, L. GH 149 (11/59): 8.
3237. The Lantern. Rubin, M. CT 2 (5/26/58): 9.
3238. Laocoon and the Bomb. Weiss, N. P 92 (8/58): 302.
3239. The Lark. Bynner, W. SR 38 (9/10/55): 20.
3240. Last Classic Scene. Dickey, W. SR 39 (10/6/56): 44.
3241. Last Day. Shah, R. P 93 (1/59): 231.
3242. The Last Entries in the Journal. Olson, E. P 91 (3/58): 343-7.
3243. The Last Hero. Coxe, L.O. P 95 (11/59): 139-43.
3244. The Last Marriage. Everson, L. P 88 (9/56): 370-1.
3245. Last One In. Solomon, M. P 91 (11/57): 99-100.
3246. Last Resource. Hoskins, K. N 187 (9/27/58): 178.
3247. Last Things, I, II. Sandeen, E. P 95 (11/59): 97-8.
3248. The Last Time. Kissler, J.S. EJ 48 (12/59): 510.
3249. Last Wisdom. Nationek, H. CC 75 (4/2/58): 399.
3250. Last Words for a Sunken Ship. Parone, E. NY 32 (11/24/56): 50.
3251. The Last Words of the President of the Gourmet Society. Lemon, R. SR 41 (8/16/58): 5.
3252. Latch Fast, Cargo Down. Rago, H. LHJ 74 (10/57): 120.
3253. A Late Elegy for a Baseball Player. Stefanile, F. P 87 (10/55): 15.
3254. Late Frost. Grenville, R.H. SEP 231 (4/11/59): 44.
3255. Late Grace. St. Simon, Sr. A 96 (3/9/57): 648.
3256. Late Lake. Merrill, H. SEP 230 (8/10/57): 80.
3257. Late Last Night. Gregor, A. N 189 (8/29/59): 100.
3258. Late Marriage. Hammer, P. SEP 228 (3/10/56): 125.
3259. Late Song. Chapin, K.G. P 92 (5/58): 78.
3260. Late Spring. Ross, N.W. NY 32 (4/21/56): 93.
3261. Late Summer. Eberhart, R. P 95 (10/59): 5-6.
3262. The Lately Mockingbird. Witt, H. P 85 (2/55): 268.
3263. Latin Lecturer. Moore, R. P 89 (1/57): 205-7.
3264. Latter Day Psalm. Mary Paulinus, Sr. A 92 (1/29/55): 453.
3265. A l'Aube. Benon, E. N 187 (12/27/58): 504.
3266. Laugh and Learn. Solovay, J.C. EJ 47 (1/58): 24.
3267. Laugharne Churchyard in 1954. Todd, R. P 88 (8/56): 293-4.
3268. Launched. Petrie, P. NR 136 (3/11/57): 19.
3269. Launching Platform. Merrill, H. SEP 229 (3/30/57): 48.
3270. Laundry. Stone, R. NY 34 (6/28/58): 30.
3271. Lavender. Goodman, P. P 94 (8/59): 290.
3272. Law and the New Order. Thompson, D.B. SR 39 (6/2/56): 4.
3273. Law of Motion. Burford, W. P 95 (11/59): 80.
3274. The Laws. Hecht, R. SR 41 (2/8/58): 24.
3275. The Laying Away of Ornament. Henley, E. At 200 (12/57): 179.
3276. Lazy...Me? Chadwick, H. BHG 35 (3/57): 207.
3277. Lazy Poet to His Girl. GH 140 (3/55): 16.
3278. Leading the Parade. Heath, C. SEP 231 (5/2/59): 79.
3279. Leaf. Darcy, L. CC 73 (3/21/56): 360.
3280. Leap. Loring, H.R. CC 73 (8/1/56): 900.
3281. Leap-Year Lyric. Grenville, R.H. SEP 229 (9/29/56): 123.
3282. Least Likely to Succeed. Canady, J.W. SEP 231 (5/30/59): 67.
3283. Leaves at Night. Moore, R. SR 40 (10/5/57): 16.
3284. Leaving Haifa. Hodes, A. C 21 (2/56): 127.
3285. Leaving Ringshall: A Quodlibet. Ridler, A. P 85 (2/55): 283-7.
3286. Lecture to the Geophysical Society. Posner, D. SR 42 (10/17/59): 84.
3287. Left at the Lift. Rose, E.K. SEP 231 (12/27/58): 69.
3288. Legacy. Barker, M.L. CT 2 (10/28/57): 13.
3289. Legacy. Kahn, H. GH 142 (5/56): 184.
3290. The Legacy. Marz, R. P 90 (6/57): 163.
3291. Legacy in Brass. Farnham, J. LHJ 72 (5/55): 166.
3292. Legal Reform. Gunn, T. P 86 (6/55): 134-5.
3293. Legal Separation. Seifer, D. GH 149 (8/59): 53.
3294. Legend. Fandel, J. Co 68 (7/11/58): 371.
3295. The Legend of Success, the Salesman's Story. Simpson, L. NY 35 (2/28/59): 26.
3296. Leilah. Lattimore, R. P 88 (4/56): 14-5.
3297. Lemonade Stand. Daerr, M. BHG 33 (7/55): 121.
3298. The Lens Grinder. Fleming, H. P 89 (10/56): 25.
3299. Lent. Coxe, L.O. N 184 (4/6/57): 304.
3300. Lenten Chant. Sullivan, W. A 98 (3/8/58): 670.

3301. Leonard Da Vinci's. Moore, M. NY 35 (7/8/59): 22.

3302. The Lesson. Rubin, L. SR 40 (5/25/57): 20.

3303. A Lesson for Beautiful Women. Reid, A. NY 34 (4/19/58): 40.

3304. Lesson in Anatomy. Posner, D.L. P 90 (8/57): 274-5.

3305. Lesson in Bone-Song. Morgan, J. A 97 (8/10/57): 485.

3306. Lesson in Philosophy. Quinn, J.R. SEP 231 (11/29/58): 73.

3307. A Lesson in Vengeance. Plath, S. P 94 (9/59): 371.

3308. Let Love Consume. Richardson, D.L. AS 26 (Summ/57): 324.

3309. Let Me Whirl Suns. Lilly, O. CC 75 (12/10/58): 1428.

3310. Let No Tree Wither. Lineaweaver, M. LHJ 72 (5/55): 102.

3311. Let the Judgment Be. Rachel. P 92 (7/58): 214.

3312. Let Them Ask Their Husbands. Laing, D. N 186 (1/4/58): 15.

3313. Letdown. Bolton, B. SEP 227 (3/26/55): 51.

3314. Let's Face It. Schiff, L.K. SEP 230 (10/19/57): 116.

3315. Let's Face It. Talman, T. SEP 229 (9/8/56): 122.

3316. Let's Face It. Zacks, H.A. LHJ 73 (4/56): 160.

3317. Let's Get This Straight. Armour, R. GH 141 (10/55): 111.

3318. Let's Kiss. Zilles, L. LHJ 76 (5/59): 102.

3319. Let's Stop at the Next Gas Station. Jaffray, N.R. SEP 228 (9/10/55): 88.

3320. Letter. Kahn, H. LHJ 74 (12/57): 92.

3321. The Letter. Seager, R.W. M 86 (8/59): 94.

3322. Letter. Smith, W.J. P 90 (4/57): 38.

3323. A Letter for Allhallows. Dufault, P.K. NY 32 (10/27/56): 30.

3324. Letter from a Deep-South Village. Hicky, D.W. GH 142 (6/56): 119.

3325. Letter from a Distant Land. Booth, P. P 87 (10/55): 19-25.

3326. Letter from America. Kessler, S. SR 40 (5/18/57): 19.

3327. Letter from Berkeley. Ostroff, A. P 85 (3/55): 322.

3328. Letter from Home. Lineaweaver, M. LHJ 73 (2/56): 14.

3329. A Letter from the Center. Burke, K. P 93 (10/58): 14-5.

3330. Letter from Verona. Collins, B.F. SEP 230 (2/1/58): 64.

3331. Letter Man. Lindeman, J. P 95 (11/59): 88-9.

3332. The Letter: Morning. Rago, H. P 85 (10/55): 9.

3333. A Letter Not Written. Montale, E. P 92 (5/58): 103.

3334. Letter to a Country Cousin. Chaffee, E.A. GH 141 (10/55): 111.

3335. Letter to a Former Neighbor. Evans, V.M. GH 140 (3/55): 99.

3336. Letter to an American. Squires, R. NR 137 (11/18/57): 18.

3337. Letter to My Husband from a Distant City. Reingold, N.K. GH 142 (3/56): 28.

3338. A Letter to V.R. Lang. Napier, J.T. P 90 (6/57): 155.

3339. Letter Written Standing in a Train. Weiss, N. P 95 (12/59): 168.

3340. The Leveler. Gleason, H.W. GH 148 (2/59): 152.

3341. The Lever. Singleton, M.E. CC 76 (1/28/59): 107.

3342. Liberals on the Loose. Barker, S.O. SEP 229 (6/29/57): 73.

3343. Librarian. Avrett, R. WLB 33 (2/59): 442.

3344. A Librarian in Today's School. Banning, E.I. WLB 32 (4/58): 573.

3345. Librarian's Charade. Ashby, D. WLB 30 (10/55): 173.

3346. Librarian's Nightmare. Trosper, G. WLB 32 (9/57): 49.

3347. The Library. Davis, O.L.,Jr. WLB 31 (1/57): 394.

3348. The Library. Hug, R.A. WLB 31 (11/56): 266.

3349. The Library. Knight, J.A. WLB 30 (1/56): 405.

3350. The Library. Short, D. and McIlwaine, P. WLB 32 (10/57): 169-70.

3351. Library Lady. Ringstad, M.E. WLB 31 (4/57): 629.

3352. Library Lament. Sharp, H.S. LJ 84 (1/15/59): 144.

3353. Library Lament. Sharp, H.S. LJ 84 (3/1/59): 691.

3354. Library Lament. Sharp, H.S. LJ 84 (3/15/59): 824.

3355. Library Lament. Sharp, H.S. LJ 84 (5/15/59): 1589.

3356. Library Lament. Sharp, H.S. LJ 84 (6/1/59): 1746.

3357. Library Lament. Sharp, H.S. LJ 83 (6/15/58): 1871.

3358. Library Lament. Sharp, H.S. LJ 84 (7/59): 2124.

3359. Library Lament. Sharp, H.S. LJ 83 (10/15/58): 2796.

3360. Library Memories. Klitzke, L.W. WLB 30 (9/55): 72.

3361. Library Period. Ringstad, M.E. WLB 32 (10/57): 139.

3362. Libris Meis. Liotta, J. WLB 33 (9/58): 41.

3363. Life. Scott, S. CT 3 (1/19/59): 18.

3364. Life and Literature. Tovatt, A. EJ 46 (2/57): 122.

3365. Life at a Premium. Jennison, C.S. At 202 (11/58): 180.

3366. Life Begins at Forty? Chadwick, H. SEP 230 (12/7/57): 95.

3367. Life from a Goldfish Bowl. Johnston, G. At 197 (5/56): 92.

3368. Life Insurance. Lieberman, L. SR 42 (5/2/59): 22.

3369. Life of a King. Moore, R. P 89 (1/57): 208-9.

3370. The Life of the Party. Douglass, S. LHJ 74 (11/57): 125.

3371. Life of the Virgin. Marz, R. P 88 (6/56): 131.

3372. Life's a Wild-Plum Tree. Wangsgaard, E.W. SEP 228 (5/5/56): 112.

3373. Life's Race. Boggs, W.A. CH 32 (9/57): 27.

3374. Lift High Our Souls. Sharp, L.B. Ca 31 (10/59): 34.

3375. Light. Blackburn, P. N 187 (11/1/58): 326.

3376. Light. Smith, H.A. CC 76 (12/30/59): 1523.

3377. Light and Dark. Moss, H. NY 35 (6/27/59): 32.

3378. Light and Shadow. Stuart, J. SR 38 (8/20/55): 18.

3379. Light Bulb: Lares. Zitner, S.P. P 90 (7/57): 220.

3380. Light from Above. Eberhart, R. P 95 (10/59): 1-2.

3381. A Light to Bring Us Safe. Carlisle, T.J. LHJ 76 (6/59): 101.

3382. Lights Off - Light's On. Landeweer, E. SEP 230 (2/1/58): 81.

3383. Lignum Vitae. Howes, B. P 90 (6/57): 131.

3384. Like Adamant. Macpherson, J. P 90 (9/57): 344.

3385. Like Country Gardens and the Shepherd's Hey. Vazakas, B. SR 42 (9/19/59): 43.

3386. Like Proud Women. Kelley, R.S. SEP 228 (6/16/56): 110.

3387. Like This Before You Just As I Am. Bat-Miriam, Y. P 92 (7/58): 228.

3388. Like Two Old Theologians. Kanfer, A. P 88 (7/56): 232.

3389. The Lilac Bush. Lineaweaver, M. AS 24 (Spr/55): 182-3.

3390. Lilac Parasols. Swann, T.B. LHJ 76 (5/59): 179.

3391. Lilacs. Kinnell, G. P 85 (1/55): 211.

3392. Lilacs Are a Brief Affair. Miner, V.S. EJ 48 (4/59): 190.

3393. Lily. Weiss, N. P 85 (1/55): 206.

3394. Limbo Culture. Auden, W.H. At 200 (11/57): 132.

3395. Limited Vista. Gleason, H.W. LHJ 75 (11/58): 145.

3396. Lincoln Christening. Ross, G. SEP 231 (2/14/59): 56.

3397. Lincoln's Tailor. Perrings, M. SEP 229 (2/9/57): 102.

3398. A Line Dragging Down. Carter, M.A. CC 75 (10/8/58): 1143.

3399. Line of Most Resistance. Spring, A.T. SEP 228 (7/9/55): 85.

3400. Line of Trucks. Eisenlohr, L. SEP 230 (4/12/58): 49.

3401. Line Post West. Griffith, E.V. SEP 230 (7/6/57): 47.

3402. The Linen Bands. Roseliep, R. Co 67 (1/17/58): 407.

3403. Lines. White, E.B. NY 33 (8/31/57): 32.

3404. Lines at the Death of a Child. Logan, J. Co 63 (3/16/56): 615.

3405. Lines for a Book. Gunn, T. P 86 (6/55): 130.

3406. Lines for a Dangerous Day. Wagoner, D. P 88 (6/56): 137-8.

3407. Lines for a Little Man. Milbrath, M.M. GH 149 (12/59): 184.

3408. Lines for a One Hundredth Birthday. Shaw, G.B. SR 39 (7/21/56): 7.

3409. Lines for a Young Wanderer in Mexico. Logan, J. P 94 (6/59): 164.

3410. Lines for an Anniversary. Chang, D. AS 25 (Wint/55-56): 66.

3411. Lines for an Educated Spaniel. Bracken, P. SEP 232 (7/25/59): 50.

3412. Lines for Holy Week. Davidson, J.F. CC 76 (3/25/59): 355.

3413. Lines for My Grandmother's Death. Greenwood, R. YR 46 (12/56): 225.

3414. Lines for the Ancient Scribes. Shapiro, H. SR 39 (10/27/56): 20.

3415. Lines Found Under a Blotter. MacAfee, H. YR 45 (6/56): 497.

3416. Lines in Which I Try to Modify a View Held by Many Women. SEP 230 (3/8/58): 88.

3417. Lines on a Bus to a Young Matron Across the Aisle. Evans, V.M. GH 148 (2/59): 183.

3418. Lines on a Half-Painted House. Kumin, M.W. SEP 227 (1/22/55): 98.

3419. Lines on a Very Special Librarian. WLB 31 (3/57): 555.

3420. Lines Suggested by a Pecunious Librarian. Brown, J.C. WLB 30 (11/55): 302.

3421. Lines to a Boy Regarding His Dog. Anthony, E. GH 148 (6/59): 110.

3422. Lines to a Christmas Angel. Stein, E.G. GH 142 (12/56): 8.

3423. Lines to a Goldfish. Blackwell, P.J. SEP 229 (11/17/56): 115.

3424. Lines to Elizabeth. Guntert, J. LHJ 74 (2/57): 88.

3425. Lines to Four Small Children. Henry, J. LHJ 75 (1/58): 116.

3426. Lines to His Son on Reaching Adolescence. Logan, J.B. Co 71 (11/13/59): 208.

3427. Lines to Myself at 6:30 A.M. Schlitzer, S. SEP 228 (1/28/56): 101.

3428. Lines to Nora. Johnson, L. LHJ 76 (12/59): 87.

3429. Lines Which Will Probably Go Unappreciated. Armknecht, R.F. SEP 230 (3/22/58): 106.

3430. Lines With a High Moral Tone. Galbraith, G.S. LHJ 72 (5/55): 129.

3431. Lines Written After Reading Keats Whose Name Is Writ in Water. Nicholl, L.T. SR 38 (10/29/55): 30.

3432. Links in a Chain. Morse, S.F. NY 34 (6/28/58): 26.

3433. The Lion. Fiedler, L.A. P 85 (1/55): 197.

3434. Lion. Gibbs, B. P 93 (3/59): 365.

3435. Lion. Smith, W.J. At 200 (9/57): 93.

3436. A Lion Named Passion. Hollander, J. NR 141 (12/28/59): 21.

3437. Liquidation Sale. Bell, C.G. C 20 (7/55): 8.

3438. Liscot's Horses. Campbell, R. NaR 1 (2/29/56): 8.

3439. The Listener. Mastin, F.R. SR 38 (4/2/55): 19.

3440. A Listener's Guide to the Birds. White, E.B. NY 35 (7/4/59): 8-9.

3441. A Listening Prayer. Marley, F.J. CC 75 (7/23/58): 849.

3442. Litany for a Man-Child. Giordan, A.R. LHJ 74 (6/57): 118.

3443. Litany of the Apathetic. Bradford, B. CC 75 (10/29/58): 1238.

3444. Litany of the Matrons. Lehon, A. A 92 (3/22/55): 622.

3445. Litany on an Edifice Complex. Bradford, B. CC 75 (11/5/58): 1266.

3446. Literary. Fadiman, C. SR 40 (6/1/57): 24.

3447. A Little Book of Hours. Murray, P. At 201 (1/58): 39.

3448. The Little Book's Story. Dugan, M.M. WLB 29 (11/54): 243.

3449. Little Boys. Ginsberg, L. CH 30 (9/55): 35.

3450. Little Boys' Kisses. Le Vinson, F.G. BHG 33 (4/55): 245.

3451. The Little Candy Store. Galler, D. C 20 (7/55): 63.

3452. The Little Dark One. Henley, E. LHJ 74 (10/57): 33.

3453. Little Elegy. Galbraith, G.S. SEP 228 (6/30/56): 60.

3454. The Little Girl. Hawes, E.B. LHJ 73 (2/56): 91.

3455. Little Girl at the Piano. Franklin, J.M. SEP 230 (8/24/57): 81.

3456. A Little Girl on Her Way to School. Wright, J. P 88 (4/56): 3-4.

3457. Little Girl Skipping. Armour, R. SEP 227 (1/1/55): 36.

3458. Little Harpe's Head. Knoepfle, J. P 93 (12/58): 149.

3459. Little Hearth Song. Kelley, R.S. SEP 230 (12/14/57): 49.

3460. Little Homily. Galbraith, G.S. BHG 34 (2/56): 101.

3461. A Little, If Not Much. Turner, E.D. N 185 (10/19/57): 271.

3462. A Little Knowledge Is a Dwindling Thing. Nelson, T. GH 148 (6/59): 160.

3463. A Little Liking. McFarland, E. LHJ 75 (9/58): 91.

3464. A Little Morning Music. Schwartz, D. NY 35 (4/18/59): 44.

3465. A Little Night Music. McGinley, P. At 200 (11/57): 162.

3466. A Little Ode. Green, F.P. NY 33 (5/4/57): 30.

3467. Little Oranges. Sorrentino, G. N 187 (12/6/58): 435.

3468. Little Pitchers Spill Plenty. Galbraith, G.S. SEP 232 (9/19/59): 105.

3469. Little Song. Fuller, E.R. CC 73 (10/3/56): 1127.

3470. A Little to the Left, Please. Strachan, E. M. SEP 231 (6/13/59): 91.

3471. Little Traditionalist. Hammer, P. SEP 229 (12/29/56): 70.

3472. Little Trip. Van Doren, M. H 215 (6/57): 27.

3473. The Little Winter Garden. Weiss, T. P 89 (10/56): 17-8.

3474. Littoral Zone. Hagiwara, S. P 88 (5/56): 103.

3475. Lives in Spite. Singer, H. P 94 (8/59): 292.

3476. Lives of Great Men All Remind Us. Starbuck, G.S. SEP 230 (8/17/57): 45.

3477. Living in Time. Reid, A. P 93 (2/59): 291-2.

3478. Living Power. Calkins, T.V. CC 72 (9/7/55): 1019.

3479. Living Room at Nine P.M. Karns, H. SEP 229 (6/22/57): 72.

3480. The Lizard. Eff, J. NaR 6 (7/5/58): 60.

3481. Lo! A Child Is Born. MacDiarmid, H. N 185 (8/17/57): 72.

3482. Loafer. Armour, R. BHG 35 (10/57): 138.

3483. Local Places. Moss, H. NY 32 (4/21/56): 36.

3484. Local Showers. Warsaw, I. SEP 229 (10/13/56): 111.

3485. Location. Miles, J. P 94 (6/59): 147.

3486. The Lock of Weeping. Gilboa, A. P 92 (7/58): 252.

3487. Locks. Koch, K. P 90 (7/57): 199-200.

3488. The Locust. Walter, E. LHJ 73 (7/56): 84.

3489. The Lodestar. Patrick, J.G. CC 73 (12/19/56): 472.

3490. Lodestone. Virden, H. CC 75 (9/17/58): 1052.

3491. Loft. Strobel, M. SR 42 (8/22/59): 23.

3492. Loneliness. Berrigan, D. Co 71 (12/11/59): 317.

3493. Loneliness. Carter, M. LHJ 76 (4/59): 24.

3494. The Lonely Fugitive. Kanfer, A. P 91 (2/58): 294.

3495. Long August. Faubion, D. SEP 228 (8/13/55): 61.

3496. The Long Clock. Sampley, A.M. SR 38 (12/3/55): 32.

3497. Long, Darwin, and Others. Dufault, P.K. NY 35 (5/9/59): 98.

3498. Long Lines. Goodman, P. P 90 (7/57): 210.

3499. The Long March. Tse-Tung, M. At 204 (12/59): 54.

3500. Long View. Kreymborg, A. SR 38 (2/19/55): 15.

3501. The Long Walk. Galler, D. NY 33 (7/20/57): 24.

3502. Longer Faces. Chadwick, H. BHG 33 (6/55): 225.

3503. Look Alikes. Barnes, K. LHJ 73 (6/56): 126.

3504. Look Alikes. Coatsworth, E. LHJ 73 (6/56): 126.

3505. Look Alikes: By the Shore. Coatsworth, E. LHJ 73 (8/56): 31.

3506. Look at Prosperity. Barker, S.O. SEP 229 (5/4/57): 122.

3507. Look, Ma--No Leaves! Ward, L.B. GH 148 (2/59): 171.

3508. Look to It, Then, My Soul! Howe, M.A.D. SR 38 (10/22/55): 20.

3509. Look Within My Heart. Neely, A. NHB 20 (12/56): 76.

3510. Looking at the X-Rays Taken. Vennendaal, C. Co 69 (11/14/58): 201.

3511. Looking Down. Nathan, L. P 93 (3/59): 378-9.

3512. Looking for Firewood. Everson, R.G. At 198 (7/56): 91.

3513. Looking Out to Sea. Morse, S.F. At 200 (7/57): 80.

3514. Lord Clive. Whittemore, R. P 86 (9/55): 311-2.

3515. Lord of Darkness. Elmer, F.D.,Jr. CC 76 (3/4/59): 262.

3516. Lore. Nemerov, H. N 182 (4/14/56): 318.

3517. Lore. Stafford, W. SR 39 (8/4/56): 34.

3518. The Loser. Merchant, J. SEP 227 (4/23/55): 50.

3519. The Loser. Rich, A. N 187 (9/20/58): 158.

3520. Losing Phase. Galbraith, G.S. BHG 34 (4/56): 250.

3521. Loss. Feldman, I. P 87 (2/56): 287.

3522. Loss. Petrie, P. NR 141 (7/13/59): 19.

3523. Loss of Hearing. Finkel, D. P 93 (2/59): 311.

3524. Lost and Found. Thomas, R. NY 35 (6/6/59): 46.

3525. Lost and Sound. Talman, T. BHG 34 (9/56): 215.

3526. The Lost Children. Sloan, J. C 23 (3/57): 230.

3527. Lost Country. Jenkins, O. SR 38 (6/18/55): 21.

3528. Lost Heritage. Gaines, C. C 19 (4/55): 367.

3529. Lost Heritage: II. Gaines, C. C 22 (8/56): 125.

3530. The Lost Ingredient. Sexton, A. YR 48 (6/59): 559.

3531. Lost Objects. Stanford, A. P 87 (1/56): 206.

3532. Lost Stolen Strayed. Laing, D. At 198 (7/56): 91.

3533. The Lost Stone. Galbraith, G.S. SEP 231 (8/23/58): 58.

3534. Lost Voices. Merwin, W.S. N 188 (2/14/59): 143.

3535. Lot's Wife. Clark, L.S. CC 72 (11/2/55): 1264.

3536. Lot's Wife. Thompson, J.B. CC 75 (9/3/58): 992.

3537. Lotteria, Lotteria. Cassity, T. P 91 (2/58): 306.

3538. The Lottery. Blackburn, P. N 186 (4/26/58): 356.

3539. Louisiana Foxhunt. Hardy, J.E. P 93 (10/58): 24-5.

3540. Lourdes: A Poem. Clancy, J.P. Co 68 (5/9/58): 151.

3541. Loushan Pass. Tse-Tung, M. At 204 (12/59): 54.

3542. Love Among the Ruins. Eberhart, R. N 183 (10/13/56): 310.

3543. Love and a Season. Scott, W.T. P 85 (2/55): 277.

3544. Love Birds. Smith, W.J. P 91 (10/57): 9-10.

3545. Love 'Em--And Leave 'Em. Jaffray, N.R. GH 141 (10/55): 111.

3546. A Love for God. Langland, J. SR 41 (4/12/58): 66.

3547. Love Gift. Grenville, R.H. SEP 228 (1/28/56): 63.

3548. Love in a Grotto; or, The Scorpion's Court-ship. Schevill, J. N 184 (6/29/57): 574.

3549. Love in a New Light. Wheeler, R. SEP 229 (2/23/57): 74.

3550. Love Is the Maker of Mankind.... Tremayne, P. At 198 (8/56): 67.

3551. Love Letter for the 24th of November. McGinley, P. GH 141 (11/55): 57.

3552. Love Poem II. Pomeroy, R. P 91 (11/57): 93.

3553. Love Sick. Putnam, J.C. LHJ 75 (9/58): 125.

3554. Love Song. Friedrich, G. CC 72 (8/17/55): 948.

3555. Love Song. Kizer, C. P 93 (3/59): 383.

3556. Love Song for Middle Age. Savage, F.H. SEP 232 (8/29/59): 39.

3557. Love, the First Decade. Jerome, J. SR 41 (4/12/58): 66.

3558. Love Will Distract Me No More. Galbraith, G.S. SEP 230 (5/10/58): 72.

3559. Lover of Puppets. Wilbur, R. NY 33 (4/13/57): 40.

3560. The Lovers. Crews, J. P 85 (3/55): 337.

3561. Lovers. Golden, L. SEP 230 (8/10/57): 49.

3562. Lovers. McFarland, E. LHJ 76 (6/59): 152.

3563. The Lovers. Smith, W.J. NR 141 (11/30/59): 20.

3564. The Lover's Ghost. Simpson, L. NY 33 (9/7/57): 107.

3565. Love's Harvest. Stafford, J. LHJ 74 (5/57): 163.

3566. Love's Island. Kaiser, W. NY 32 (3/17/56): 154.

3567. Love's Legacy. Redman, P.D. SEP 230 (4/12/58): 97.

3568. Love's Map. Justice, D. P 95 (12/59): 152.

3569. Love's Messages. Lee, A.M. SEP 230 (8/17/57): 90.

3570. Love's Progress. Roethke, T. NR 132 (4/11/55): 27.

3571. Love's Worth. Louchheim, K. H 215 (8/57): 53.

3572. Love's Youth. Smith, M.C. R 105 (1/55): 102.

3573. Low and Behold! Rosenfield, L. At 202 (7/58): 89.

3574. Low Chairs: Beware! Brosier, V. TH 33 (11/55): 46.

3575. Low-Cost Holocaust. Galbraith, G.S. SEP 231 (10/11/58): 49.

3576. Low Tide. White, C.N. L 45 (8/4/58): 5.

3577. The Lowest Place. Rossetti, C.G. CT 2 (1/20/58): 11.

3578. Loyalty. Jacobs, E.L. SEP 230 (2/1/58): 57.

3579. Loyalty Does Pay. Rosenfield, L. SEP 231 (11/15/58): 110.

3580. Lucifer in Anytown. McDonnell, T.P. A 93 (5/28/55): 241-2.

3581. Lucinda. Conklin, B.S. LHJ 73 (3/56): 202.

3582. Lucky Lady. Otis, A.F. SEP 230 (9/14/57): 87.

3583. Lullaby. Gibson, W. H 218 (2/59): 73.

3584. A Lullaby. Howes, B. P 89 (12/56): 137.

3585. Lullaby. Merriam, E. N 187 (10/4/58): 198.

3586. Lullaby. Rich, A.C. LHJ 73 (8/56): 140.

3587. Lullaby for a Baby Bookworm. Engen, E. WLB 33 (10/58): 145.

3588. Lullaby for a Monday Night. McKee, G. SEP 230 (7/13/57): 67.

3589. Lullaby for a Rainy Day. McFarland, E. LHJ 72 (10/55): 120.

3590. Lullaby Through the Side of the Mouth. Wagoner, D. YR 46 (12/56): 227.

3591. Lullaby to Myself. Renon, E. AS 25 (Spr/56): 176.

3592. The Lumber Baron. Cassity, T. P 94 (4/59): 36.

3593. Lunar Tune. Burr, G. P 86 (8/55): 278.

3594. Lupercalia. Hughes, T. P 94 (8/59): 298-300.

3595. Lycanthropy Revisited. Hall, D. P 86 (8/55): 265-6.

3596. Lydia. Plunkett, P.M. A 96 (12/15/56): 330.

3597. The Lyf So Short.... NR 134 (1/16/56): 27.

3598. Lying Awake. Snodgrass, W.D. NY 35 (6/13/59): 36.

3599. Lyric. Orlovitz, G. N 184 (2/23/57): 173.

3600. Lyric. Viereck, P. H 211 (7/55): 38.

3601. A Lyric for Lovers. Lamb, M.W. LHJ 72 (10/55): 185.

3602. Lyricist. Halacy, D.S.,Jr. SEP 227 (6/4/55): 109.

3603. Macbeth on Being Told the Queen is Dead. Shakespeare, W. GH 140 (5/55): 40.

3604. Mad Day in March. Levine, P. NY 34 (3/29/58): 38.

3605. Madeline's Christmas. Bemelmans, L. GH 141 (12/55): 74-5.

3606. The Madonna of the Ill-Favored. Farnash, H. A 98 (12/21/57): 374.

3607. Madrigal: For Judith. Langland, J. At 198 (7/56): 44.

3608. Magi and Manger. Besch, R. SEP 232 (12/19/59): 90.

3609. The Magical Harvest. Kelley, R.S. SEP 230 (10/5/57): 66.

3610. The Magician. Nash, O. L 39 (9/5/55): 88.

3611. Magnetic Attractions. Galbraith, G.S. GH 149 (11/59): 8.

3612. The Magpie. Swan, J. NY 35 (11/21/59): 48.
3613. Mahler. Gross, H. C 19 (5/55): 450.
3614. Maid Service. Mergard, J.C. SEP 230 (4/19/58): 102.
3615. The Maiden Shrouded as a Deer. Vance, T. N 189 (11/14/59): 344.
3616. Major. GH 140 (1/55): 28.
3617. Major Cameron and Miss Cairns. Sitwell, O. NY 33 (2/23/57): 34.
3618. Make Me No Lazy Love. Farber, N. P 91 (1/58): 245.
3619. Make Mine People. Kline, L.W. EJ 45 (11/56): 485.
3620. Make Room for Me. Pratt, W.W. SEP 230 (2/15/58): 100.
3621. Mama Turns the Tables. Constant, B.B. SEP 232 (11/21/59): 100.
3622. Mamma's Dream House. Henry, J. LHJ 76 (1/59): 70.
3623. The Mammoth. Wallace, R.A. NY 33 (2/23/57): 71.
3624. The Man. McGowan, L. Hn 32 (8/56): 277.
3625. Man. Woodrum, L. CC 75 (5/28/58): 641.
3626. Man at a Window. Hecht, R. P 92 (6/58): 160.
3627. The Man from the Top of the Mind. Wagoner, D. P 90 (9/57): 374-5.
3628. The Man in the Aisle Seat. Galbraith, G.S. At 201 (1/58): 85.
3629. Man of Authority. Raskin, A. SEP 227 (4/2/55): 54.
3630. Man of My Time. Enrico, H. N 182 (6/2/56): 474.
3631. Man on the Bridge. Grenville, R.H. SEP 231 (7/19/58): 44.
3632. Man Overboard. Koehler, G.S. P 95 (12/59): 157.
3633. Man-Versus Housekeeping. Merrill, H. SEP 232 (10/31/59): 72.
3634. The Man Who Hid His Own Front Door. McKinstry, E. Hn 33 (4/57): 112.
3635. The Man Whose Pharynx Was Bad. Stevens, W. NR 133 (8/15/55): 21.
3636. Mañana. Freeman, B.K. SEP 229 (12/1/56): 129.
3637. Manger Scene. Cooke, R. SR 42 (1/31/59): 16.
3638. The Manicure. Moore, R. P 89 (1/57): 207-8.
3639. Manning an Observation Post in a Remote Area in Maine. Graves, S.B. SEP 228 (3/17/56): 88.
3640. A Man's Length Shadow. Jacobs, E.L. SEP 230 (11/9/57): 142.
3641. Mansion at Sundown. Masters, M. P 90 (9/57): 365-6.
3642. Manuelzinho. Bishop, E. NY 32 (5/26/56): 32.
3643. Map. Engle, P. GH 141 (9/55): 103.
3644. A Map of Europe: Some Paintings by Vermeer. Bailey, A. NY 33 (6/8/57): 32.
3645. The Map of Water. Woods, J. P 89 (1/57): 215.
3646. Maraeld. Smith, S.G. P 88 (4/56): 31-2.
3647. The Marauders. Hillyer, R. NY 33 (6/29/57): 63.
3648. March at Night. Jacobson, E. SEP 227 (5/7/55): 124.
3649. March, My Lion. Thomson, M. NY 35 (3/21/59): 111.
3650. March Scene (With Applause). Ford, E. LHJ 73 (3/56): 101.
3651. March Snowfall. Richter, H.C. SEP 228 (3/3/56): 60.
3652. March Twilight. Bogan, L. NY 33 (3/23/57): 32.
3653. March Wind. Graham, R. SEP 229 (3/16/57): 89.
3654. Margaret Was Stranger. Secrist, M. GH 142 (6/56): 119.
3655. The Margin. Booth, P. SR 39 (12/29/56): 16.
3656. Marginal Note on a Milk Bill. Galbraith, G.S. LHJ 75 (4/58): 112.
3657. Marginals. Lattimore, R. P 88 (4/56): 14.
3658. Marianne. Sagittarius. NR 138 (6/16/58): 5.
3659. Marin. Booth, P. NY 35 (9/2/59): 182.
3660. Marine. Kroll, E. H 214 (4/57): 37.
3661. Marine Mood. Raiziss, S. P 88 (9/56): 362.
3662. A Mark of Resistance. Rich, A. P 90 (8/57): 304.
3663. Marked Men. Chadwick, H. SEP 228 (5/26/56): 66.
3664. The Markers. Reinert, D. WLB 30 (2/56): 461.
3665. Marooned. Millyer, R. H 219 (11/59): 75.
3666. A Marriage. Moss, H. P 89 (10/56): 12-3.
3667. Marriage. Yamanguchi, B. P 88 (5/56): 67.
3668. The Marriage of Mankind. F., H.P. NY 33 (10/26/57): 193.
3669. Marriage's First Paradox. Congdon, T. SEP 232 (10/10/59): 89.
3670. Marsh at Night. Jacobson, E. SEP 227 (5/7/55): 124.
3671. Marsh Night. Hicky, D.W. SEP 229 (12/29/56): 35.
3672. Marta, for Example. Schluneger, F.E. CC 76 (3/4/59): 260.
3673. Martha Jane. Lamb, M.W. LHJ 74 (3/57): 118.
3674. Marthe. Rexroth, K. N 186 (4/26/58): 359.
3675. Martin Luther. McGinley, P. At 200 (7/57): 98.
3676. Martinis at the Schneiders'. Noll, B. At 201 (2/58): 59.
3677. The Martyrdom of Bishop Ferrar. Hughes, T. P 90 (8/57): 282-3.
3678. Mary to the Dead Christ. Hazo, S.J. Co 67 (2/21/58): 538.
3679. Mary Tudor's Song. Coatsworth, E. LHJ 72 (5/55): 158.
3680. Mary's Lamb. Galbraith, G.S. LHJ 74 (2/57): 109.
3681. The Mask. Barker, E. SR 38 (9/10/55): 54.
3682. The Mask of Winter. Watkins, V. P 91 (10/57): 25-7.
3683. Masked Man. Pierce, E.L. CC 74 (7/31/57): 911.
3684. Masquerade. Jaffray, N.R. SEP 230 (5/17/58): 99.
3685. Masquerade Night. Ebright, F. SEP 230 (10/26/57): 67.
3686. Massu S' En Va T' En Guerre! Sagittarius. NR 138 (5/26/58): 7.
3687. Master. Dejong, D.C. P 86 (4/55): 23.
3688. The Master. Merwin, W.S. P 87 (3/56): 323-5.
3689. Master Musician. Lilly, O. CC 74 (10/16/57): 1231.
3690. Matadora. Crews, J. P 85 (3/55): 337-8.
3691. The Mate. Stokely, J. At 198 (8/56): 65.
3692. Mate, to the Skipper. Bradbury, B. SEP 231 (1/3/59): 79.
3693. Materia Medica. Gleason, M. SEP 229 (4/13/57): 106.

3694. Material Change. Holloway, R. SEP 229 (2/9/57): 40.

3695. A Materialist Pictures Man. Coblentz, S.A. CC 74 (10/2/57): 1168.

3696. Maternity Ward. Richstone, M. SEP 227 (6/25/55): 47.

3697. Mathematics of Encounter. Gardner, I. NR 132 (5/9/55): 21.

3698. Matinee. Mayhall, J. NR 133 (12/26/55): 17.

3699. Matlock Bath. Betjeman, J. NY 35 (3/4/59): 40.

3700. A Matter of Discipline. Grenville, R.H. SEP 229 (4/27/57): 109.

3701. A Matter of Distribution. Eisenlohr, L. SEP 230 (4/26/58): 109.

3702. Matter of Fact. Hall, D. P 86 (8/55): 263-5.

3703. Matter of (Golf) Course. Emmons, D. SEP 229 (8/18/56): 89.

3704. The Mausoleum. Tomlinson, C. P 88 (9/56): 354-6.

3705. May I Be One. Mok, S. LHJ 73 (5/56): 38.

3706. The Mayflower Sails Again. Jaffray, N.R. SEP 229 (2/16/57): 42.

3707. The Meadow. Horner, J. NY 33 (6/29/57): 67.

3708. Meadow Incident. Cane, M. AS 27 (Summ/58): 298.

3709. A Meadow Moreover. Powers, J. A 92 (1/8/55): 382.

3710. Meadow Remembered. Burr, G. P 86 (8/55): 279.

3711. Meadows and Mesas. Kelley, R.S. SEP 229 (7/28/56): 55.

3712. Meal Timing. Armour, R. BHG 33 (10/55): 105.

3713. The Measure. Stanford, A. P 87 (1/56): 207.

3714. The Measure. Williams, W.C. N 186 (5/31/58): 499.

3715. A Measure of Reason. Bartlett, E. SR 38 (2/12/55): 12.

3716. Measurements. Clark, L.S. CT 2 (4/28/58): 5.

3717. The Mediators, the Peace-Makers. Amihai, Y. P 92 (7/58): 255.

3718. Medical College: Levant. Neame, A. P 91 (2/58): 313-5.

3719. Medical School Red-Letter Day. De Vito, E.B. SEP 232 (10/3/59): 109.

3720. Meditation. Herschberger, R. N 186 (1/25/58): 84.

3721. Meditation. Hough, E.J. CT 2 (3/31/58): 25.

3722. Meditation.... Neely, L. SEP 227 (6/25/55): 97.

3723. Meditation at Midnight. Wurdemann, A. SEP 231 (5/2/59): 100.

3724. Meditations on the Humanities. Jones, H.M. SR 39 (5/5/56): 24.

3725. The Mediterranean. Montale, E. At 202 (12/58): 186.

3726. The Medium. Morris, H. P 91 (12/57): 189-90.

3727. Meet the Mrs. Richstone, M. SEP 230 (1/25/58): 48.

3728. Meeting. Alisjahbana, S.T. At 197 (6/56): 121.

3729. The Meeting. Bogan, L. NY 33 (2/9/57): 36.

3730. Meeting. Christopher, J. Co 70 (4/24/59): 100.

3731. Meeting. Freeman, A.D. NR 136 (3/25/57): 17.

3732. A Meeting. Lewis, C.D. NY 33 (10/19/57): 42.

3733. Meeting. Neame, A. P 93 (3/59): 355-6.

3734. The Meeting-Place of the Colors. Gibbs, B. P 93 (3/59): 364-5.

3735. Meeting You at the Piers. Koch, K. P 89 (11/56): 90.

3736. Meeting You on the Street Today. Nardi, M. LHJ 73 (10/56): 162.

3737. Meetings. Merchant, J. GH 141 (9/55): 103.

3738. Mein Grossfader's Mamma Goosen. Morrah, D. SEP 229 (3/16/57): 46.

3739. Melanie Rose. Powell, D.K. SEP 229 (5/4/57): 72.

3740. Melchior Vulpius. Moore, M. At 201 (1/58): 59.

3741. Memento. Hagelstange, R. At 199 (3/57): 120.

3742. Memento Mori. Howard, S. N 185 (9/28/57): 198.

3743. Mementos. Barker, S.O. R 104 (12/54): 90.

3744. Memo to the Hungarian Patriots. Auslander, J. SEP 229 (3/30/57): 28.

3745. Memorial Day. Chaffee, E.A. LHJ 73 (5/56): 116.

3746. Memorial Inscriptions. Rosenthal, M.L. N 187 (11/15/58): 367.

3747. Memorial Window: 1946-56. Kirstein, L. N 182 (6/2/56): 467.

3748. Memories. Justice, L. NHB 22 (3/59): 139.

3749. Memories of Childhood. Matran, K. At 198 (10/56): 136.

3750. Memory. Grenville, R.H. GH 148 (3/59): 229.

3751. Memory. Lee, C. SEP 228 (2/25/56): 125.

3752. Memory. Malody, B.M. EJ 45 (1/56): 25.

3753. The Memory. Masters, M. P 86 (9/55): 321.

3754. Memory. Roethke, T. At 197 (4/56): 41.

3755. Memory of Paris. Ciardi, J. N 183 (9/15/56): 226.

3756. Men of Letters. Stevens, G. SR 40 (2/23/57): 8-10.

3757. The Men That Don't Fit In. Service, R. GH 141 (8/55): 25.

3758. The Menagerie Goes for a Walk. Rosenthal, R.A. At 204 (9/59): 72.

3759. The Mendicants. Brasler, V. SEP 232 (12/5/59): 77.

3760. Mental Note Made at the Annual Banquet. Pennington, P. SEP 229 (3/30/57): 40.

3761. Mention of God's Name. Strachan, E.M. CT 2 (8/18/58): 6.

3762. Menu Maneuvers. Jacobson, E. TH 35 (8/57): 32.

3763. Mercy. Merwin, W.S. P 89 (3/59): 346-7.

3764. Mercy Is Its Own Reward. Ryskind, M. NaR 5 (4/12/58): 341.

3765. Mercy's Dark Shadow. Weaver, B. CC 72 (11/9/55): 1301.

3766. Merioneth, Wales. Humphries, R. NY 32 (5/5/56): 145.

3767. Merlin in the Cave: He Speculates Without a Book. Gunn, T. P 86 (6/55): 131-4.

3768. Merrill's Brook. Scott, W.T. P 97 (2/56): 269.

3769. Merrimack County. Hall, D. NY 35 (8/22/55): 96.

3770. Merry Christmas. Spear, G.B. WLB 30 (12/55): 324.

3771. Merry Christmas and Bon Voyage. Nash, O. H1 22 (12/57): 84-5.

3772. A Merry Heart. Nichols, D. NR 136 (6/3/57): 19.

3773. The Mesa Land. Kelley, R.S. NY 32 (10/27/56): 157.

3774. The Mess of Pottage. Ryskind, M. NaR 3 (5/18/57): 476.

3775. The Message of the Bells. Gray, E.L. CC 75 (9/17/58): 1052.

3776. Messenger. Flexner, H. At 197 (3/56): 72.

3777. Messmuk. Sears, G. FS 60 (7/55): 128.

3778. Mestrovic. Sweeney, F. A 94 (10/29/55): 130.

3779. Metamorphosis. Duncan, R. P 91 (3/58): 379-81.

3780. Metamorphosis. Plath, S. P 89 (1/57): 234.

3781. Metamorphosis. Sarton, M. LHJ 73 (5/56): 175.

3782. Metaphysical. Fitzgerald, R. P 89 (2/57): 271.

3783. Meteor Shower. Smythe, D. SEP 229 (1/5/57): 52.

3784. Mexican Holiday. Landeweer, E. SEP 231 (1/10/59): 65.

3785. A Mexican in Passing. Nathan, L. P 90 (5/57): 79.

3786. Mexican Poems. Tagliabue, J. P 89 (3/59): 349-52.

3787. Mexican Profile. Bartlett, E. H 210 (6/55): 38.

3788. Mexico Picnic, October 31. Summers, H.,Jr. SR 40 (1/12/57): 54.

3789. Michelangelo's Moses. Lilly, O. CC 73 (10/3/56): 1132.

3790. Mid-Autumn Evening. Lilly, O. SR 39 (4/21/56): 24.

3791. Mid-Morning for Sheba. Tiempo, E.L. P 89 (1/57): 224.

3792. Mid-November. Ross, G. SEP 231 (11/15/58): 72.

3793. Mid Winter. Walton, E.L. Co 71 (12/18/59): 342.

3794. The Middle-Aged. Rich, A.C. H 211 (8/55): 42.

3795. The Middle Passage. Gordon, D. P 86 (9/55): 322-3.

3796. Midmorning Snack. Isler, B. BHG 33 (11/55): 240.

3797. Midnight. Clark, N.M. SEP 230 (5/10/58): 89.

3798. Midnight. Fichman, Y. P 92 (7/58): 205.

3799. Midnight Train. Riordan, A. SEP 231 (7/5/58): 87.

3800. Midnight Zero. Merrill, H. SEP 228 (1/14/56): 83.

3801. Midsummer. Bronk, W. P 86 (5/55): 85.

3802. Mid-summer. Lindbergh, A.M. At 200 (12/57): 44.

3803. Midsummer Invitation. Merchant, J. SEP 230 (7/27/57): 58.

3804. Midsummer Night. Bevington, H. NY 35 (7/8/59): 61.

3805. Midsummer Night. Guenther, C. N 188 (2/7/59): 124.

3806. Midsummer-Night Christmas. Merrill, H. SEP 231 (7/12/58): 128.

3807. Midsummer Thames. Roche, P. SR 38 (7/23/55): 25.

3808. Midwinter Flight. Howes, B. LHJ 75 (12/58): 24.

3809. The Migration. Wagoner, D. P 90 (9/57): 372-3.

3810. Milestone. Power, J.W. SEP 229 (5/18/57): 46.

3811. Military Funeral. Thomas, M.B. SR 38 (4/16/55): 23.

3812. The Mill of Death. Rexroth, K. N 186 (4/12/58): 327.

3813. Milordo Inglese. Sitwell, O. At 202 (7/58): 46-9.

3814. The Mind Is an Ancient and Famous Capital. Schwartz, D. NR 139 (12/15/58): 17.

3815. The Minister of Finance. Stepanchev, S. N 186 (4/5/58): 300.

3816. Minor Realism for a Major Poet. Welch, M. deL. N 186 (2/15/58): 144.

3817. Minotaur. Redman, B.R. SR 38 (10/1/55): 9.

3818. Minstrel. Huff, R. SR 39 (9/29/56): 24.

3819. The Minstrel in Search of a Legend. Carter, R.A. P 86 (5/55): 87-90.

3820. Miracle. Calkins, T.V. CC 73 (2/29/56): 267.

3821. Miracle. Goodman, M.W. SEP 230 (1/25/58): 86.

3822. The Miracle. Pasternak, B. CC 76 (9/23/59): 1081.

3823. Miracle in the Back Yard. Brooks, E. SEP 232 (7/25/59): 50.

3824. Mirage. Barker, E. SR 38 (10/1/55): 20.

3825. Mirror. Merrill, J. P 91 (2/58): 281-2.

3826. The Mirror. Posner, D.L. P 90 (8/57): 275.

3827. Mirror. Stokely, J. N 182 (5/12/56): 404.

3828. A Mirror, A Window, A Pool. Josephs, L. P 95 (11/59): 91.

3829. The Mirroring Transparencies. Brown, D.C. NY 35 (7/11/59): 24.

3830. Misfiled. Sweet, A.P. WLB 31 (1/57): 398.

3831. The Misogynists. Roseliep, R. EJ 47 (11/58): 486.

3832. Miss Balch's Letter to China. Balch, E. N 180 (5/14/55): 418.

3833. Miss Elderli Dora Des Moines,--One March. Sward, R.S. P 91 (12/57): 185.

3834. Missa Solemnis. Vazakas, B. SR 41 (7/19/58): 30.

3835. Missing. Coblentz, S.A. CC 74 (2/20/57): 223.

3836. Missing Invention. Rosenfield, L. SEP 227 (1/1/55): 56.

3837. Mississippi. Ward, M.W. SEP 229 (9/22/56): 81.

3838. The Misstep. White, E.B. NY 34 (7/12/58): 28.

3839. The Mist from Tree to Tree. Gregor, A. C 28 (9/59): 213.

3840. Mistral. Howes, B. NY 32 (2/16/57): 36.

3841. Mistress Franklin's Son. Briggs, O.H. SEP 228 (1/21/56): 73.

3842. Mists. Coblentz, S.A. CC 76 (7/15/59): 827.

3843. Misty Meeting. Merrill, H. SEP 230 (7/20/57): 78.

3844. Misunderstanding. Burrowes, E. CC 75 (3/5/58): 277.

3845. Mnemesis. Tadlock, M. N 183 (7/28/56): 85.

3846. Mnemosyne and Me. Johns, V. SEP 227 (4/21/5): 13.

3847. Moan from the Doghouse. Ellert, M.McK. SEP 231 (3/28/59): 109.

3848. Moaning Dove. Basch, H.F. SR 38 (11/5/55): 14.

3849. Mobile of Birds. Updike, J. NY 35 (12/19/59): 32.

3850. A Mobile of Carved Wooden Fish. Nemerov, H. P 88 (9/56): 386.

3851. The Mockery. Galler, D. YR 45 (6/56): 561-2.

3852. Mockingbird's Reveille. Isler, B. SEP 229 (3/16/57): 139.

3853. A Mode of Hangings. Gregor, A. P 89 (10/56): 29.

3854. Model for a New World. Alkus, M. SEP 230 (3/29/58): 46.

3855. The Moderate. Updike, J. NY 34 (1/10/59): 103.

3856. Modern Conveniences. Chadwick, H. SEP 229 (11/3/56): 119.

3857. Modern Diagnosis. Galbraith, G.S. SEP 230 (9/21/57): 108.

3858. Modern Mother Goose. Jennison, C.S. LHJ 73 (7/56): 124.

3859. Modern Science. Boggs, W.A. CC 75 (9/24/58): 1079.

3860. A Modest Mound of Bones. Updike, J. Co 66 (4/26/57): 92.

3861. The Moment. Kirrup, G.S. P 93 (1/59): 259-61.

3862. The Moment Clearly. Kumin, M.W. LHJ 76 (5/59): 26.

3863. Moment in Time. Cully, K.B. CC 73 (2/1/56): 139.

3864. Moment of Incarnation. Cotter, J.F. A 94 (10/15/55): 72.

3865. Moment of Truth. De Vito, E.B. NY 31 (1/21/56): 32.

3866. Moment Toward Spring. Hearst, J. LHJ 76 (3/59): 28.

3867. Moments in America: First Letter from New Albion. Rockwell, M. SR 41 (10/11/58): 42.

3868. Monday's Vision. Fandel, J. Co 63 (10/7/55): 10.

3869. Mondican. Carruth, H. AN 57 (9/58): 25.

3870. The Mondrian. Solomon, M. P 86 (4/55): 10-11.

3871. Monet's Venice. Norse, H. AN 56 (1/58): 43.

3872. Money. Kearns, B.S. GH 140 (2/55): 28.

3873. Monks at Recreation: 13th Century. Co 69 (1/9/59): 391.

3874. Monologue for the Good Friday Christ. Logan, J. Co 62 (4/8/55): 10.

3875. The Monster Who Loved the Hero. Pack, R. SR 42 (10/10/59): 48.

3876. Monsterama Movies and Me. Congdon, T. SEP 231 (9/20/58): 80.

3877. The Month of February. Gillis, W.E. CH 29 (2/55): 337.

3878. Moods. Matthews, T.S. NY 33 (2/15/58): 114.

3879. Moody Music. Blackwell, P.J. SEP 229 (6/8/57): 46.

3880. The Moon. Sato, S. P 88 (5/56): 92.

3881. The Moon. Zilles, L. NY 32 (1/5/57): 53.

3882. Moon Dawn. Hartley, R.E. SEP 230 (4/12/58): 61.

3883. The Moon in Your Hands. D., H. NY 33 (7/20/57): 29.

3884. Moon Road. Adams, M.R. SEP 228 (4/14/56): 165.

3885. Moon Song for a Night in May. Lipton, L. At 203 (5/59): 49.

3886. The Moonlight. Bock, F. P 93 (10/58): 31-2.

3887. Moonlight Dance. Jacobson, E. SEP 228 (8/6/55): 100.

3888. Moontide Low. Philbrick, C. N 189 (9/12/59): 135.

3889. Moral Spontaneity: A Love Poem. Ely, G. P 92 (9/58): 369.

3890. The Morality of Poetry. Wright, J. P 90 (9/57): 360-2.

3891. More Essential Than Lanolin. Rosenfield, L. SEP 232 (11/14/59): 116.

3892. More Foreign Cities. Tomlinson, C. P 90 (4/57): 8.

3893. More Like the Sea. Berrigan, D. P 92 (8/58): 301.

3894. More Research, Please. Ellis, C. SEP 229 (5/11/57): 72.

3895. The Morning. Cotter, J.F. A 99 (4/26/58): 144.

3896. Morning. Pausch, E. P 93 (11/58): 68.

3897. Morning. Tigner, H.S. CC 74 (7/17/57): 863.

3898. Morning After Storm. Merrill, H. SEP 230 (5/17/58): 65.

3899. Morning Becomes Electric. Hammer, P. SEP 231 (3/7/59): 90.

3900. Morning Care of Husbands. Merchant, J. SEP 230 (11/30/57): 107.

3901. Morning Draws Near. Wheelock, J.H. At 198 (7/56): 61.

3902. Morning Hymn to a Dark Girl. Wright, J. P 86 (9/55): 347-8.

3903. A Morning in Spain. Reid, A. At 202 (11/58): 112.

3904. Morning in Spring. Ginsberg, L. At 195 (4/55): 57.

3905. A Morning Letter. Duncan, R. P 90 (9/57): 350-1.

3906. Morning Mass--Tsuruma, Japan. Bryan, B. A 93 (9/17/55): 594.

3907. The Morning Moon. Morris, H. NR 135 (11/26/56): 20.

3908. Morning--O. Austin, D. At 204 (8/59): 47.

3909. Morning on the St. John's. Cooper, J. NY 33 (6/15/57): 36.

3910. The Morning Porches. Hall, D. P 88 (7/56): 228.

3911. Morning Song. Moffitt, J. At 203 (3/59): 54.

3912. Morning Song. Vance, T. N 188 (4/18/59): 350.

3913. Morning Stroll. Moffitt, J. SR 39 (12/15/56): 21.

3914. Mortal. Frost, F. SR 38 (6/18/55): 20.

3915. Moses. Gilboa, A. P 92 (7/58): 250.

3916. Moses. Kanfer, A. P 91 (2/58): 296.

3917. The Most. Greene, J.C. SEP 228 (5/19/56): 129.

3918. The Moth. Barker, S.O. SEP 228 (2/25/56): 116.

3919. Mother. Heller, C.E. Hb 63 (5/58): 73.

3920. Mother at Poker. Weiss, N. C 28 (8/59): 148.

3921. Mother Gorden's Round. Rukeyser, M. P 86 (4/55): 6-7.

3922. Mother Hubbard's Cupboard. Wolking, E.W. At 204 (12/59): 142.

3923. Mother into Child. Petrie, P. P 93 (10/58): 27-8.

3924. Mother of the Bride. Greenville, R.H. GH 141 (11/55): 46.

3925. Mother Told Me So. Marx, A. LHJ 76 (1/59): 74.

3926. Mother Tongue. Armour, R. NY 32 (5/26/56): 74.

3927. The Mother Tongue. Nash, O. NY 33 (11/9/57): 46.

3928. Mother Views a Holiday. Richstone, M. SEP 230 (12/7/57): 133.

3929. A Mother's Brand of Logic. Richstone, M. SEP 228 (6/9/56): 85.

3930. Mother's Needlework. Jennison, C.S. LHJ 73 (5/56): 146.

3931. Mothers of the Ages Past. Miner, V.S. SR 41 (8/2/58): 2.

3932. The Motor and the Man. Coblentz, S.A. CC 73 (8/29/56): 991.

3933. Mots Justes. Russell, P. P 92 (9/58): 351.

3934. Motto for an Uncompleted Monument. Pitchford, K. N 184 (6/22/57): 554.

3935. Mountain Afternoon. Long, E.E. SEP 229 (8/20/55): 54.

3936. Mountain Burial. Penny, L. SEP 231 (10/25/58): 68.

3937. Mountain Fire, Thornbush. Shapiro, H. C 28 (7/59): 28.

3938. Mountain Homestead. Jacobson, E. SEP 227 (3/5/55): 64.

3939. The Mountain Is Stripped. Ignatow, D. P 93 (11/58): 82.

3940. Mountain Passage. Knowlton, R.A. SR 41 (1/25/58): 30.

3941. Mountain River--And Even the Stones Sing Poems to the Blossoms. Onitsura (1661-1738). L 40 (4/30/56): 90-1.

3942. Mountain Saddle. Landeweer, E. SEP 228 (8/13/55): 69.

3943. A Mountain Standing Strong. Kanfer, A. P 91 (2/58): 295.

3944. A Mountain Stream. Russell, P. P 92 (9/58): 349-50.

3945. Mountain Summer. Schwartz, D. P 94 (5/59): 104.

3946. Mountain View. Lougee, D. P 95 (11/59): 163.

3947. Mountains and Lowlands. Powell, D.K. SEP 230 (11/16/57): 84.

3948. The Mounted Bell. Cassity, T. P 91 (2/58): 308.

3949. Mournful Numbers. Usk, T. SEP 231 (7/12/58): 52.

3950. The Move to California. Stafford, W. P 90 (4/57): 14-7.

3951. Movement in the Peach Orchard. Nathan, L. N 183 (9/22/56): 248.

3952. A Movement of Peoples. O'Gorman, N. P 92 (4/58): 6.

3953. Movies More Fattening Than Ever. Rosenfield, L. SEP 229 (1/26/57): 40.

3954. Moving Inland. Rich, A. NY 33 (9/21/57): 46.

3955. Moving Lights. Rosenberg, J.L. At 203 (5/59): 80.

3956. The Moving Man. Lucy, S. At 203 (2/59): 66.

3957. Mozart in Heaven. Bandeira, M. At 197 (2/56): 139.

3958. Mr. and Mrs. Whittemore, R. NR 138 (5/12/58): 17.

3959. Mr. and Mrs. Billings. Hall, D. NR 139 (9/8/58): 17.

3960. Mr. High-Mind. Updike, J. NY 32 (4/28/56): 44.

3961. Mr. Mammon. Ignatow, D. C 22 (10/56): 360.

3962. Mr. Mammon. Ignatow, D. N 186 (6/28/58): 591.

3963. Mr. Middlegreens, Etc. Sward, R. P 91 (12/57): 186.

3964. Mr. Moto, I Presume. Gordon, R. WLB 32 (3/58): 500.

3965. Mr. Smith (With Nods to Mr. Lear and Mr. Eliot). Smith, W.J. NY 33 (3/2/57): 36.

3966. Mr. Tantripp's Day. Jacobsen, J. P 86 (4/55): 14-5.

3967. Mrs. Tortoise and Mr. Hare. Schiff, L.K. GH 149 (12/59): 8.

3968. Ms. Found Under a Servette in a Lonely Home. Nash, O. NY 32 (9/22/56): 49.

3969. The Mud-Pie Set. Galbraith, G.S. SEP 229 (5/18/57): 46.

3970. The Multitude of His Mercies. Lindsay, M. CT 3 (2/16/59): 5.

3971. Murder a la Mode. Russell, S.R. SR 40 (3/14/57): 8.

3972. Murder Mystery. Wagoner, D. P 89 (2/59): 276-7.

3973. The Murder of William Remington. Nemerov, H. N 185 (12/28/57): 488.

3974. Murder Within the Law. Allen, E.J. AC 72 (9/57): 155.

3975. The Murderer. Wright, J. H 215 (7/57): 64.

3976. The Murmuring Fountains, Rome. Ackerson, J. At 196 (7/55): 71.

3977. The Muse in Rose Street. Smith, S.G. P 88 (4/56): 28-30.

3978. A Muse of Water. Kizer, C. P 93 (3/59): 380-2.

3979. Museum. Tanikawa, S. P 88 (5/56): 70.

3980. Museum Musing. Bonaluto, L.M. SEP 228 (1/28/56): 97.

3981. Museum Piece. Carruth, H. NR 138 (5/5/58): 18.

3982. Music Box. Stevenson, C.T. LHJ 72 (8/55): 14.

3983. The Musician. Lister, R.P. At 198 (9/56): 65.

3984. The Musk Ox and the Musk. Lister, R.P. NY 32 (9/29/56): 120.

3985. Musky Ducks on the Pond. Sabe, K. R 105 (2/55): 8.

3986. Mussel Hunter at Rock Harbor. Plath, S. NY 34 (8/9/58): 22.

3987. Mustn't! Jacobson, E. SEP 230 (6/21/58): 101.

3988. Mutiny with Bounty; Considered Reflections on TV, Without Color. Young, S. SR 38 (9/17/55): 12.

3989. My Car. Ellert, M.McK. SEP 227 (3/26/55): 70.

3990. My Correspondence, Alas. Galbraith, G.S. SEP 230 (8/31/57): 53.

3991. My Daughter Very Ill. Goodman, P. P 90 (7/57): 211.

3992. My Dream Was Real. Freeman, J.T. LHJ 74 (5/57): 183.

3993. My Ego. Warsaw, I. SEP 231 (2/7/59): 48.

3994. My Father. Macaulay, J.C. CT 1 (2/8/57): 25.

3995. My Father and My Son. Gibson, D. SEP 231 (3/14/59): 98.

3996. My Father Died in Alexandria. Haber, L. C 25 (4/58): 349.

3997. My Father Is Working Still and I Am Working. Pierce, E.L. CC 75 (10/15/58): 1175.

3998. My Father's Benediction. Crown, R. CT 3 (1/5/59): 11.

3999. My Father's Death. Sarton, M. H 214 (4/57): 82.

4000. My Glass Brother. Dana, R.P. P 85 (1/55): 196-7.

4001. My Grandfather's Rules for Holy Living. Wolf, L. C 24 (7/57): 41.

4002. My Grandmother's Ghost. Wright, J. NY 32 (6/9/56): 92.

4003. My Grandmother's Province. Weinstein, A. At 196 (8/55): 65.

4004. My Heart Has Loved but Once. Zimmerman, E. H. LHJ 74 (6/57): 141.

4005. My Lord and My Heart. Pierotti, D.L. CC 72 (8/10/55): 923.

4006. My Love. Creeley, R. P 94 (4/59): 13.

4007. My Love Is a Many-Splintered Thing. Hammer, P. SEP 230 (8/31/57): 73.

4008. My Love Lies Down Tonight. Doyle, C. N 188 (4/25/59): 375.

4009. My Malenkovy Baby. Eff, J. NaR 4 (7/27/57): 106.

4010. My Message. Panigrahi, K.C. P 93 (1/59): 243.

4011. My Mother. Wolf, L. C 28 (10/59): 322.

4012. My Mother's Father. Halpern, M. C 21 (5/56): 468.

4013. My Muse. Larraud, V. P 85 (2/55): 249-50.

4014. My Only Jo. McFarland, E. LHJ 72 (9/55): 115.

4015. My Satellite. Jaffray, N.R. SEP 231 (9/13/58): 94.

4016. My Seahorse. Legg, L. Hn 35 (6/59): 202.

4017. My Six Toothbrushes. McGinley, P. AS 28 (Summ/59): 320-1.

4018. My Son. Kaplan, M. SEP 231 (5/16/59): 68.

4019. My Thrifty Wife. Chadwick, H. SEP 227 (1/15/55): 70.

4020. My Uncle's Books. Victor, F. C 24 (7/57): 14.

4021. Mycene. Saly, J. At 196 (8/55): 67.

4022. Myself and Thou from Theatres or the Night. Morris, H. P 94 (9/59): 389-91.

4023. Mysterious Gift. Galbraith, G.S. SEP 228 (2/11/56): 90.

4024. Myth. O'Gorman, N. Co 69 (11/7/58): 150.

4025. The Mythmakers. Coxe, L.O. P 88 (8/56): 301.

4026. N.Y. Tanka. Deutsch, B. N 188 (6/27/59): 584.

4027. Nails for Petals. D., H. P 91 (12/57): 150.

4028. The Naked and the Nude. Graves, R. NY 32 (2/16/57): 105.

4029. The Nameless Color. Little, K.D. SR 38 (7/9/55): 29.

4030. The Nameless Ocean. Jenkins, D. P 86 (5/55): 77.

4031. The Names. Creeley, R. P 94 (4/59): 13.

4032. Names of Michalishek. Katz, M. C 27 (2/59): 132-3.

4033. Nancy Revisited. Rennert, M. SR 39 (10/13/56): 21.

4034. Nantucket. Chadbourne, M. SR 39 (2/25/56): 20.

4035. Naples. Ciardi, J. N 181 (10/1/55): 287.

4036. Naples. Langland, J. SR 39 (5/5/56): 24.

4037. Narcissus. Packard, A.A. EJ 47 (4/58): 222.

4038. Narcissus and the Star. Barker, G. P 88 (8/56): 290.

4039. Narrative Dirge for Wind Instruments. Wrenn, P.W. NY 32 (10/29/56): 146.

4040. A Narrow Squeak. Smith, A.J.M. N 184 (6/1/57): 483.

4041. Native Village. Tanaka, F. P 88 (5/56): 63.

4042. Natural History. Levine, R. SR 39 (2/25/56): 25.

4043. Nature Walks. Nash, O. NY 32 (12/1/59): 56.

4044. Nature's Carolers. McBrown, G.P. NHB 18 (1/55): 92.

4045. Navaho Woman at Day's End. Long, E.E. LHJ 74 (4/57): 151.

4046. Nazareth. Patrick, J.G. CC 72 (10/5/55): 1136.

4047. Near, in Mountains. Stewart, A. LHJ 72 (7/55): 130.

4048. Neat Feat. Chadwick, H. SEP 231 (1/17/59): 38.

4049. Neat Trick. Galbraith, G.S. SEP 228 (6/2/56): 72.

4050. Necessary Evil. Henry, J. LHJ 75 (2/58): 83.

4051. Neck and Neck. Galbraith, G.S. SEP 229 (6/15/57): 127.

4052. The Need for Candles. Victor, F. C 25 (1/58): 7.

4053. Negative. Jerome, J. SR 41 (10/18/58): 20.

4054. The Negro Speaks. Razaf, A. NHB 22 (1/59): 82.

4055. Neighbor's Garden. Grenville, R.H. SEP 229 (8/4/56): 70.

4056. Nessmuk. Sears, G. FS 60 (7/55): 128.

4057. Nests. Lamb, M.W. LHJ 72 (11/55): 16.

4058. Nests Are Made to Fly From. McGrath, C.J., Jr. A 101 (9/28/59): 765.

4059. The Neutralist. Armour, R. SEP 228 (5/26/56): 97.

4060. Never as Men. Giordan, A.R. SR 38 (3/5/55): 35.

4061. Never Counsel a Lovely Lady. Kanfer, A. P 88 (7/56): 233.

4062. Never Let Your Pride. Galbraith, G.S. GH 142 (3/56): 28.

4063. Never Scoff. Ewing, A. LHJ 75 (8/58): 97.

4064. Never Show Defiance Toward a Kitchen Appliance. Jennison, C.S. At 204 (8/59): 90.

4065. Never Take His Love for Granted. Alleman, E.C. GH 142 (7/56): 52.

4066. Never the Truth. Chadbourne, M. SR 39 (3/24/56): 17.

4067. Nevermore. Sagittarius. NR 137 (9/9/57): on cover.

4068. New Bethlehem, Pa. Houghton, F.A. At 201 (2/58): 60.

4069. New Bread. Schoeberlein, M.S. LHJ 72 (12/55): 170.

4070. New Car in the Family. Schlitzer, S. SEP 229 (8/4/56): 82.

4071. New Chitons for Old Gods. McCord, D. H 213 (9/56): 72.

4072. New Coin. Coffin, R.P.T. GH 141 (10/55): 111.

4073. New Construction. Koehler, G.S. P 90 (4/57): 23-4.

4074. The New Emigration. Boyle, K. N 183 (9/22/56): 246.

4075. A New Explanation of the Quietude and Talkativeness of Trees. Plutzik, H. SR 41 (10/4/58): 32.

4076. The New Grass. Mary Davida, Sr. A 100 (12/13/58): 339.

4077. New Hampshire Eclogue. Golffing, F. C 27 (6/59): 512.

4078. The New Heavens. Coblentz, S.A. CC 74 (5/
      22/57): 648.
4079. New Home. Keith, J.J. A 95 (6/30/56): 324.
4080. New Homes. Lattimore, R. H 214 (6/57): 74.
4081. New House. Blackwell, H.G. SEP 228 (5/19/
      56): 84.
4082. The New Houses. Collins, B.F. SEP 228 (3/
      31/56): 125.
4083. New Look. Carleton, S.K. LHJ 75 (8/58):
      115.
4084. New Look in Divas. De Vito, E.B. SEP 230
      (9/7/57): 52.
4085. New Moon. Quinn, J.R. SEP 229 (4/27/57):
      165.
4086. New Moon. Savage, F.H. SEP (4/18/59): 95.
4087. The New Muse. Moira, Sr. SR 42 (12/19/59):
      5.
4088. The New Ordained. Doherty, K.F. A 100 (3/
      7/59): 658.
4089. The New Overcoat. Weiss, N. P 88 (8/56):
      317.
4090. The New Road of Koide. Hagiwara, S. At 195
      (1/55): 140.
4091. A New System of Water Purification. Fast,
      N. NY 33 (4/13/57): 139.
4092. New Teacher, First Day of School. Congdon,
      T. SEP 232 (9/5/59): 70.
4093. New Technique. Armour, R. SR 42 (8/15/59):
      35.
4094. The New Year. Clark, L.S. CC 74 (1/2/57):
      7.
4095. New Year's Resolution Made the Week Before
      Christmas. Alkus, M. SEP 229 (12/22/56):
      69.
4096. Newlyweds. Armknecht, R.F. SEP 230 (9/28/
      57): 125.
4097. News from Our Town. Nardi, M. AS 24 (Aut/
      55): 326-7.
4098. News from the Cabin. Swenson, M. NY 34 (7/
      26/58): 29.
4099. News from the Home Front. Raskin, A. LHJ
      76 (9/59): 116.
4100. News from the Islands. Brinnin, J.M. NY 34
      (2/22/58): 38.
4101. News Item: Chimpanzee Escapes from Zoo in
      Antwerp. Sandeen, E. P 95 (11/59): 99.
4102. News Item: Science Now Reveals 'Busy Bee'
      Really Lazy. Mortimer, J. At 203 (6/59):
      90.
4103. News of the World. Ridler, A. A 90 (8/57):
      286-90.
4104. The News Photo. Ignatow, D. N 185 (9/28/
      57): 201.
4105. Nice People. Sagittarius. NR 139 (9/29/58):
      6.
4106. A Niche for the Architect. Nixon, J.,Jr.
      NY 33 (2/8/58): 110.
4107. Night. Irvine, J. LHJ 76 (9/59): 107.
4108. Night at the Ocean: A Walk. Jenkins, D. P
      86 (5/55): 76.
4109. Night Creek. Schierloh, S. SEP 232 (4/29/
      59): 61.
4110. Night Letter. Galler, D. YR 45 (6/56): 560-
      61.
4111. Night Music for Old Men. Davis, S. AS 28
      (Aut/59): 474.
4112. Night of Fog. McKee, Gladys. SEP 230 (7/6/
      57): 64.
4113. The Night of the Tornado. Jacobs, E.L. SEP
      227 (6/8/55): 118.

4114. Night Patterns. Isler, B. SEP 230 (3/22/
      58): 83.
4115. Night Plight of an Urbanite. Magee, I. SEP
      231 (1/17/59): 61.
4116. Night Scene. Neame, A. P 91 (2/58): 318-9.
4117. Night Shift. Armknecht, R.F. SEP 228 (9/
      24/55): 124.
4118. Night Shift. Frost, F. A 95 (7/7/56): 347.
4119. Night Sounds. Clower, J. P 93 (10/58): 5-6.
4120. Night Speech. Hutchinson, R. At 199 (2/57):
      52.
4121. Night Talk. Garrigue, J. NY 33 (7/13/57):
      30.
4122. Night Thoughts Over a Sick Child. Levine,
      P. P 93 (11/58): 95-6.
4123. The Night Watch. Merrill, H. SEP 227 (6/
      25/55): 129.
4124. The Night Wind. Galbraith, G.S. LHJ 72 (6/
      55): 114.
4125. The Night You Slept. Di Giovanni, N.T. NR
      141 (9/21/59): 18.
4126. Nightcoach from Salzburg. Witt, H. At 197
      (2/56): 50.
4127. The Nightingale Has Not Come. Yosano, A.
      At 195 (1/55): 147.
4128. Nightmare in the Color Red. Solovay, J.C.
      EJ 46 (5/57): 261-2.
4129. Nightpiece. Wright, J. P 90 (9/57): 363-4.
4130. Nigrei Sum, Sed Formosa. Sullivan, D. A 96
      (3/9/57): 646.
4131. Nikko Kekko, Beautiful Nikko. Morris, J.N.
      P 87 (1/56): 203.
4132. Nimrod. Johnson, L. P 89 (1/57): 228.
4133. Nine Little Niggers. Sagittarius. NR 137
      (10/7/57): 6.
4134. Nine Months Making. Mueller, L. P 92 (4/
      58): 21.
4135. Nineteen Seventeen. Burrows, E.G. P 93 (11/
      58): 89-90.
4136. 1934. Hall, D. SR 41 (8/16/58): 20.
4137. No. Goodman, P. P 92 (9/58): 375.
4138. No Better Than a Withered Daffodil. Moore,
      M. AN 58 (3/59): 44.
4139. No Conformity, to Enormity! Nash, O. NY 34
      (2/22/58): 34.
4140. No Date in the Desert. Sagittarius. NR 137
      (11/4/57): 6.
4141. No Daughter of Mine. Philbrick, C. SR 41
      (7/5/58): 24.
4142. No Ifs, Ands, or Buts. Galbraith, G.S. GH
      149 (10/59): 8.
4143. No Interference. Schlitzer, S. SEP 228 (3/
      3/56): 113.
4144. No Laughing Matter. Grenville, R.H. SEP 230
      (6/7/58): 109.
4145. No Letter Today. Feine, V.B. At 199 (1/57):
      91.
4146. No Little Problems. Brasier, V. TH 33 (7/
      55): 54.
4147. No Man but One. Cotter, J.F. A 99 (4/19/
      58): 113.
4148. No Matter What Disguise You Work. Carleton,
      S.K. LHJ 73 (1/56): 74.
4149. No Need. Workman, M.T. CC 73 (1/18/56): 76.
4150. No Previous Experience Necessary. Blackwell,
      P.J. SEP 228 (6/16/56): 65.
4151. No Progress, Please. Roche, L. WLB 32 (6/
      58): 719.
4152. No Purple Bovine Have I Spied (Nor Any
      Other Shade, Beside). Raskin, A. GH 142
      (1/56): 42.

4153. No Secrets. Sagittarius. NR 137 (11/25/57): 8.

4154. No Storms Trouble This Part of the Key. Bock, F. P 93 (10/58): 34.

4155. No Sugar. Otis, A.F. SEP 232 (9/19/59): 72.

4156. No Thanks, Dear. Merrill, H. SEP 232 (9/6/59): 53.

4157. No Time for Remorse. Sarabhai, B. P 93 (1/59): 248-9.

4158. No Way Out. Pugh, S.S. TH 33 (4/55): 50.

4159. Noah. Delattre, P.H. CC 74 (9/25/57): 1131.

4160. Noah's Ark. Langland, J. LHJ 73 (6/56): 94.

4161. Nobody Here But Us. Abrahams, W. P 88 (8/56): 308-9.

4162. Nocturnal Aerial Act. Schenker, D. N 187 (11/22/58): 390.

4163. Nocturne. Friedrich, G. CC 74 (11/13/57): 1348.

4164. Nocturne of the Dead Adolescent. di Giovanni, N.T. N 185 (11/16/57): 358.

4165. Nocturne: Traveling Salesman in a Hotel Bedroom. Warren, R.P. AS 28 (Summ/59): 306-7.

4166. Nocturne with Ghosts. Pillin, W. P 86 (9/55): 336-7.

4167. Noel. Tongue, M. CC 72 (12/7/55): 1458.

4168. Noname Road. Rizzardi, A. P 94 (8/59): 323.

4169. None the Wiser. Bannon, M.M. LHJ 72 (2/55): 102.

4170. Nonprofit. Maguire, C.E. A 96 (12/15/56): 329.

4171. Nonsense Rhyme. Landau, B.M. Hn 35 (4/59): 156.

4172. Noon Fire. Greer, S. P 92 (9/58): 360-1.

4173. Norma. Grossman, A. P 90 (6/57): 145.

4174. North China and the Children. Lattimore, R. NR 139 (11/24/58): 16.

4175. The North of Wales. Morris, H. P 85 (1/55): 220.

4176. Northern River Port. Warsaw, I. SEP 228 (4/14/56): 175.

4177. A Northern View. Merrill, H. SEP 227 (2/26/55): 47.

4178. The Nose of Gogol. Schevill, J. N 186 (6/28/58): 587.

4179. Nosegay. Long, E.E. SEP 229 (5/11/57): 134.

4180. Nostalgia. Farrar, J. SR 38 (12/17/55): 30.

4181. Nostalgia. Muyoshi, T. P 88 (5/56): 79.

4182. Nostalgia. Rottmann, B.C. SEP 231 (5/16/59): 82.

4183. Not All Is So Simple. Shalom, S. P 92 (7/58): 231.

4184. Not As a Stranger. Clark, L.S. CC 73 (9/12/56): 1049.

4185. Not for Babes. Smith, L.C. SEP 227 (4/23/55): 123.

4186. Not Gold, But Only Man Can Make. Emerson, R.W. Hb 63 (8/59): 86.

4187. Not Love. Schulberg, L. SEP 231 (9/13/58): 113.

4188. Not No. Richards, I.A. YR 46 (12/56): 226.

4189. Not Quite a Poem on Togetherness in the Witherness. Gerkle, W.F. H 214 (5/57): 77.

4190. Not Ready to Go Yet. Schlitzer, S. SEP 227 (6/8/55): 63.

4191. Not So Big. Avery, L. SEP 232 (10/31/59): 83.

4192. Not So Measly. Stewart, M. SEP 229 (8/18/56): 92.

4193. Not So Sure. Secrist, M. LHJ 74 (8/57): 108.

4194. Not to Be Stilled. Freedman, C.P. CC 74 (5/22/57): 651.

4195. Not Too Distant Shore. Bathgate, J. CC 72 (4/6/55): 417.

4196. Not Yet the New Adam. Triem, E. P 89 (2/57): 274.

4197. Notation. Garrigue, J. P 93 (12/58): 136.

4198. Notation in Haste. Lieberman, E. At 200 (10/57): 191.

4199. A Note. Parker, D.H. CC 76 (10/21/59): 1213.

4200. A Note from the Coast. Reid, A. NY 32 (12/15/56): 192.

4201. Note in November. Rauth, M.T. N 189 (11/7/59): 334.

4202. A Note on Hart Crane. Loche, E. SR 39 (8/18/56): 28.

4203. Note on Stenographers. Armour, R. SEP 229 (6/1/57): 91.

4204. Note on the Land N. Lattimore, R. P 88 (4/56): 16.

4205. Note to a Librarian. Stefanski, S. WLB 30 (10/55): 176.

4206. Note to My Husband. Liddell, B.C. SEP 229 (12/8/56): 94.

4207. Note to Wang Wei. Berryman, J. NY 34 (8/2/58): 59.

4208. Note to Weekend Guests. Emmons, D. SEP 229 (6/1/57): 36.

4209. Note With a Jar of Jam. Emans, E.V. SEP 231 (1/17/59): 52.

4210. Notes for a Poem. Carrier, C. AS 24 (Wint/54-55): 46.

4211. Notes for a Valedictory Address. Jaffray, N.R. SEP 227 (6/4/55): 47.

4212. Notes from Underground. Garrigue, J. NY 33 (5/11/57): 42.

4213. Notes on the Cap-Pistol Set. Blanchard, E. SEP 230 (8/17/57): 85.

4214. Nothing. Graves, R. SR 41 (4/12/58): 69.

4215. Nothing. Vail, B. SR 41 (10/11/58): 27.

4216. Nothing Before Something. Sturges, G.M. WLB 29 (1/55): 363.

4217. Nothing But the Truth. Lazarus, H. TH 35 (3/57): 30.

4218. Nothing Is Immune. Angoff, C. CC 76 (1/28/59): 107.

4219. A Notice to My Emotions. Sobiloff, H. P 92 (6/58): 165.

4220. Notre Dame de Chartres. Meredith, W. SR 40 (7/20/57): 15.

4221. Notre Dame Perfected by Reflection. Witt, H. P 88 (9/56): 373.

4222. The Nourishment of Memory. Abbe, G. SR 42 (11/21/59): 59.

4223. A Novelist. Hall, D. H 211 (12/55): 57.

4224. The Novelist at Home in New Jersey. Pomeroy, R. P 91 (11/57): 92.

4225. November. Mary Faith, Sr. A 100 (11/15/58): 204.

4226. November Anniversary. Bulkeley, M. SR 38 (11/22/55): 12.

4227. November Day. Averitt, E. SEP 231 (11/8/58): 81.

4228. November, Early. Souster, R. P 94 (8/59): 301.

4229. November in Windham. Porter, K.A. H 211 (11/55): 44.

4230. November: Indian Summer. Carruth, H. NY 33 (11/30/57): 150.

4231. November Night. Love, A. SEP 232 (11/21/59): 82.

4232. Now: A Definition. Galbraith, G.S. SEP 227 (4/2/55): 108.

4233. Now a Satellites. Ginsberg, L. CH 30 (3/56): 394.

4234. Now and Then. France, W.B. SEP 227 (6/4/55): 40.

4235. Now Autumn. Galbraith, G.S. LHJ 73 (10/56): 129.

4236. A Now Famous Escape. Krieger, R. P 89 (11/56): 104.

4237. Now It Is Light.... O'Hara, F. P 87 (10/55): 12.

4238. Now Must the Mind Write. Walton, E.L. P 91 (11/57): 87.

4239. Now Satellites. Ginsberg, L. CH 33 (11/58): 164.

4240. Now Side by Side. Hall, D. SR 40 (3/9/57): 15.

4241. Now Song. Gaines, C. C 22 (8/56): 125.

4242. Now When the Waters Press in Force. Amihai, Y. C 28 (11/59): 430.

4243. Now You Have Said Good-by. Ewing, A. GH 148 (2/59): 165.

4244. Nudge. Hurd, P.S. SR 38 (2/26/55): 30.

4245. Nuit Blanche. Hoskins, K. N 186 (4/26/58): 365.

4246. Number One. Chadwick, H. SEP 231 (7/12/58): 104.

4247. Nuptial Knot. Wheeler, R. SEP 231 (5/2/59): 85.

4248. Nurse at the White Cove. White, J. YR 44 (6/55): 566-7.

4249. Nursery, 1956. Enright, E. SR 39 (12/8/56): 21.

4250. Nursery Rhyme. McCarthy, M.W. LHJ 74 (6/57): 101.

4251. Nursery Rhyme. McFarland, E. LHJ 73 (12/56): 141.

4252. Nursery Story: Modern Version. Montague, J. N 186 (2/1/58): 108.

4253. 'O' Antiphons. Mary Honora, Sr. A 102 (12/12/59): 355.

4254. O Captain! My Captain! Sagittarius. NR 139 (11/24/58): 5.

4255. O Darkly in the Summer's Eye. La Bombard, J. At 200 (7/57): 58.

4256. O Death Where Is Thy Sting. Davidson, J.F. CC 75 (2/19/58): 220.

4257. O for the Boy. Latham, J. At 200 (7/58): 58.

4258. O for the Child. Friedrich, G. CC 72 (12/21/55): 1493.

4259. O! It Used To Be Such a Pleasure. Wolf, L. C 29 (10/59): 323.

4260. O Jerusalem, Jerusalem. Pierce, E.L. CC 75 (4/9/58): 438.

4261. O Little Town. Frankenberg, L. At 204 (12/59): 113.

4262. O Now the Drenched Land Wakes. Patchen, K. P 86 (5/55): 73.

4263. O Pearl and Breasted World. Barker, G. P 88 (8/56): 289.

4264. O She Is As Lovely--Often. Patchen, K. P 86 (5/55): 72.

4265. OAA Check. Tyler, R.L. N 185 (10/12/57): 252.

4266. Oafishness Sells Good, Like an Advertisement Should. Nash, O. NY 32 (11/3/56): 48.

4267. Oak. Humphries, R. P 97 (2/56): 264-5.

4268. Obiter Dicta. Ryskind, M. NaR 5 (6/14/58): 562.

4269. Obiter Dicta on the Inside Story. NaR 5 (5/17/58): 463.

4270. Objection. Merrill, H. SEP 227 (1/1/55): 44.

4271. Objective-Tester. Lazarus, A.L. EJ 44 (3/55): 147.

4272. Oblation. Bangham, M.R. CC 72 (2/16/55): 206.

4273. Obscure Incident. Morton, D. AS 24 (Aut/55): 457.

4274. The Observatory. Hollander, J. P 90 (7/57): 221-3.

4275. Obsolete. Ignatow, D. N 188 (3/14/59): 233.

4276. Occasional Intelligence by Radar. MacLeod, N. P 91 (12/57): 168.

4277. Occupied! Armour, R. SEP 230 (4/12/58): 106.

4278. The Ocean. Winston, W.J. Hn 34 (4/58): 126.

4279. Ocean Voyage. Bohm, E. SEP 228 (9/10/55): 63.

4280. Ochre Yellow. Hedden, M. AS 27 (Wint/57-58): 133.

4281. O'Clock. Fitzell, L. N 180 (6/11/55): 497.

4282. October. Dean, A. LHJ 75 (10/59): 111.

4283. October. Long, E.E. LHJ 72 (10/55): 146.

4284. October. Longfellow, I.B. SEP 228 (10/1/55): 87.

4285. October. Pomeroy, R. NY 35 (10/10/59): 42.

4286. October Escapade. Grenville, R.H. SEP 232 (10/3/59): 85.

4287. October Fly. Edey, M. SR 38 (10/15/55): 28.

4288. October Morning. Grenville, R.H. SEP 230 (10/12/57): 59.

4289. October Robbers. Jacobs, E.L. SEP 229 (10/6/56): 114.

4290. October Wisdom. McKee, G. GH 142 (10/56): 13.

4291. October's Man of Gold. Eaton, C.E. N 185 (10/12/57): 247.

4292. Odalisque. Watson, R.W. AS 28 (Summ/59): 360-3.

4293. Ode. Casey, K. P 95 (10/59): 22.

4294. Ode for a Windy Afternoon. Pack, R. AS 27 (Spr/58): 195-6.

4295. Ode 3. Brown, H. P 93 (12/58): 165-6.

4296. Ode to a Half Persian Cat. Ground, Y. SEP 230 (4/5/58): 65.

4297. Ode to a Retiring Editor. Ulman, R. WLB 32 (5/58): 669.

4298. Ode to Mill Hoyland. Chatterton, T. NR 135 (12/17/56): 29.

4299. Ode to Swansea. Watkins, V. At 203 (4/59): 118.

4300. Ode to the Finnish Dead at Hietaniemi Heroes' Cemetery. Walsh, C. LHJ 76 (9/59): 131.

4301. Ode to the Memory of Paul Wightman, Painter. Golffing, F. N 185 (9/7/57): 114.

4302. Ode to the New Tenant on the Top Floor. Wilbur, N.G. SEP 231 (12/6/58): 52.

4303. Ode to Walt Whitman. Garcia Lorda, F. P 85 (1/55): 187.

4304. Odes. Pessoa, F. P 87 (10/55): 26.

4305. Odessa Gal. Stokely, J. N 182 (5/12/56): 404.

4306. Odysseus. Merwin, W.S. H 215 (10/57): 29.

4307. Of a Winter Evening. Frost, R. SR 41 (3/15/58): 66.

4308. Of All the Many Things Which Give Love Rise. Lee, M. LHJ 76 (6/59): 95.

4309. Of Asphodel. Williams. W.C. P 86 (5/55): 99-107.

4310. Of Cats. Hughes, T. H 216 (6/58): 30.

4311. Of Course Not! Andrews, G.C. SEP 230 (12/7/57): 59.

4312. Of Digests. Wall, M.B. WLB 29 (9/54): 78.

4313. Of Girls and Beaux. Wheeler, R. SEP 230 (1/11/58): 85.

4314. Of Heroes. Stone, R. P 87 (10/58): 30.

4315. Of Highways and Byways. Bracken, P. SEP 227 (4/23/55): 62.

4316. Of History, Fiction, Language. Ciardi, J. N 183 (9/1/56): 184.

4317. Of Hunger for the Coming. St. John of the Cross. A 98 (2/22/58): 600.

4318. Of Joy. Renon, E. AS 25 (Summ/56): 281.

4319. Of Matters Marital and Martial. Bracken, P. SEP 227 (3/12/55): 108.

4320. Of Matters Small and Great. Bracken, P. SEP 227 (4/30/55): 54.

4321. Of Mops and Men. Galbraith, G.S. SEP 229 (4/27/57): 54.

4322. Of Mrs. Bird Bishop and the Beyond. Lape, F. H 210 (1/55): 46.

4323. Of Objects Considered As Fortresses in a Baleful Space. Plutzik, H. YR 44 (6/55): 564.

4324. Of Peaks and Parables. Kelley, R.S. SEP 229 (6/22/57): 104.

4325. Of Reefs and Marital Waters. Bracken, P. SEP 227 (4/9/55): 96.

4326. Of Scents and Sensibility. Bracken, P. SEP 227 (3/5/55): 92.

4327. Of Space and Time. Cardozo, N. At 200 (10/57): 66.

4328. Of Such Is the Kingdom. Rittell, H. SEP 228 (7/16/55): 78.

4329. Of the Annunciation. Nims, J.F. Co 67 (12/27/57): 339.

4330. Of the Bride and the Bargain. Bracken, P. SEP 229 (4/27/57): 135.

4331. Of the Budget and the Shining Chariot. Bracken, P. SEP 227 (4/2/55): 64.

4332. Of the Festivity. Dickey, W. P 92 (8/58): 296-8.

4333. Of the Hammer and Its Habitat. Bracken, P. SEP 227 (5/7/55): 127.

4334. Of the Husband and the Telephone Belle. Bracken, P. SEP 229 (6/8/59): 122.

4335. Of the Husband, the Wife, and the Inner Ear. Bracken, P. SEP 229 (5/18/57): 105.

4336. Of the Incarnation. St. John of the Cross. A 98 (2/22/58): 600.

4337. Of the Lady and the Household Law. Bracken, P. SEP 229 (4/6/57): 66.

4338. Of the Male and the Status Quo. Bracken, P. SEP 227 (4/16/55): 81.

4339. Of the Man and the Plan. Bracken, P. SEP 227 (5/14/55): 70.

4340. Of the Monday Mood and the Man. Bracken, P. SEP 229 (4/13/57): 97.

4341. Of the Most Holy Trinity. Nims, J.F. Co 67 (12/27/57): 339.

4342. Of the Nativity. Nims, J.F. Co 67 (12/27/57): 339.

4343. Of the Tortoise and the Hare. Bracken, P. SEP 227 (3/19/55): 87.

4344. Of the Vine Which Clingeth. Bracken, P. SEP 229 (4/20/57): 54.

4345. Of the Warrior Upon His Shield. Bracken, P. SEP 227 (2/26/59): 110.

4346. Of the Wife and Haute Cuisine. Bracken, P. SEP 229 (6/1/57): 72.

4347. Of the Wife and the Big Picture. Bracken, P. SEP 229 (6/15/57): 86.

4348. Of the Wife, the Hyacinth, the Loaf of Bread. Bracken, P SEP 229 (5/4/57): 115.

4349. Of Time and the River. Wolfe, T. Ne 45 (1/24/55): 34.

4350. Of Water Come to Water. Bell, C.G. C 21 (4/56): 343.

4351. Off Key. Wheeler, R. SEP 229 (11/19/56): 90.

4352. Off Marblehead. Hollander, J. NY 35 (8/29/59): 34.

4353. Off New London. Koehler, G.S. YR 46 (6/57): 569-70.

4354. Off Point Lotus. Kunitz, S. P 97 (2/56): 258.

4355. Office Party. McGinley, P. LHJ 75 (12/58): 71.

4356. Offspring Cleaning. Wade, E.A. TH 33 (8/55): 47.

4357. Often at Night. McGinley, P. M 86 (8/59): 68-9.

4358. L'Ogre a L' Estime. Murry, P. P 92 (4/58): 16-7.

4359. Oh, Baby! Antolini, M.F. SEP 227 (6/18/55): 85.

4360. Oh, Had I Known It Once For All. Pasternak, B. NR 139 (11/10/58): 20.

4361. Oh, I Rode Right Through Childhood. Graham, E. LHJ 74 (6/57): 14.

4362. Oh, My Aching Baccalaureate. Eisenlohr, L. SEP 229 (6/1/57): 36.

4363. Oh, Shade and Lemonade. Pogue, D.E. SEP 228 (6/30/56): 108.

4364. Oh! That the Desert Were My Dwelling Place. Bryon, G.G.N.B. GH 140 (1/55): 28.

4365. Oh, Tidings of Comfort and Joy. Sollis, L. At 202 (12/58): 106.

4366. Oh, Uncouth Lover! Jones, I.H. LHJ 73 (11/56): 212.

4367. Oil Tanker. Landeweer, E. SEP 230 (5/3/58): 90.

4368. Okaru and Kampei. Kitahara, H. P 88 (5/56): 100-1.

4369. Old Autograph Album. Lieberman, E. GH 142 (2/56): 44.

4370. The Old Blind Man in Spring. Schevill, J. P 86 (9/55): 320.

4371. Old Books. Snell, T. WLB 31 (5/57): 705.

4372. An Old Bootblack in the Cafeteria. Stefanile, F. P 87 (10/55): 16.

4373. The Old Chair. Kelly, M. Hb 63 (3/59): 101.

4374. Old Chapel: A Poem in Favor of the World. Clark, D.R. P 88 (6/56): 144.

4375. An Old Chinese Zen Traveller Often Depicted in Sumi-E Carrying a Large Dim White Bag Like a Light Cloud. Tagliabue, J. P 95 (10/59): 19.

4376. Old Clothes. Wood, J.P. LHJ 73 (12/56): 170.

4377. The Old Dowser. Freeman, A.D. SEP 231 (8/23/58): 70.

4378. The Old Duke. Engels, J. P 95 (12/59): 165.

4379. Old Earth. Merrill, H. SEP 231 (10/18/58): 120.

4380. Old Faces of '56. Updike, J. NY 32 (10/27/56): 36.

4381. The Old Familiar Faces. Lister, R.P. NY 32 (11/17/56): 216.

4382. Old Father Mountain. Weismiller, E. At 196 (7/55): 32.

4383. The Old Fishstation. Gale, V. P 87 (1/56): 214.

4384. Old Folks at Home. Wright, J.A. SEP 229 (4/13/57): 126.

4385. Old Folks at the Home. Bishop, M. NY 33 (1/11/58): 106.

4386. Old Gentlemen Rising. Hemphill, G. YR 49 (9/59): 246.

4387. Old Granary Burying Ground. Freeman, A.D. SR 39 (5/5/56): 25.

4388. The Old Horse-Breaker. Campbell, R. NaR 1 (11/26/55): 23.

4389. Old House. Redgrove, P. P 90 (6/57): 153-4.

4390. Old Houseboats. Nickerson, V. SEP 228 (2/25/56): 122.

4391. Old Jubal. Merrill, H. At 200 (8/57): 63.

4392. An Old Liberal Looks to the New Year, 1953. Burke, K. N 181 (10/8/55): 308.

4393. Old Love. Trail, J. GH 149 (12/59): 122.

4394. Old Man. Harper, J. SR 41 (2/22/58): 32.

4395. The Old Man. Macpherson, J. P 90 (9/57): 342.

4396. Old Man at Desk. Keith, J.J. A 101 (6/20/59): 453.

4397. Old Man, Phantom Dog. Eckman, F. P 93 (12/58): 162-3.

4398. An Old Man's August. Morris, J.N. NY 34 (8/9/58): 69.

4399. Old Man's Song. MacGillivray, A. A 95 (6/2/56): 244.

4400. Old Men in Church. Long, E.E. SEP 227 (3/19/55): 121.

4401. Old Men Observing Small Boy Crying. De Jong, D.C. P 92 (9/58): 371-3.

4402. Old Nun Recalls God. Stein, G. A 94 (12/17/55): 335.

4403. Old Orange Trees. Faubion, D. SEP 229 (12/8/56): 102.

4404. The Old Order. Biel, N. N 189 (9/19/59): 158.

4405. An Old Palestinian Donkey. Engle, P. BHG 36 (4/58): 8.

4406. Old Rome. Singer, H. P 87 (2/56): 291.

4407. The Old Soldiers' Home. Nemerov, H. At 196 (9/55): 62.

4408. Old Song. McFarland, E. LHJ 75 (4/58): 169.

4409. An Old Song. Walton, E.L. P 91 (11/57): 85-6.

4410. Old Summer. Longfellow, I.B. SEP 229 (9/15/56): 68.

4411. Old Tears in Galilee. Galbraith, G.S. LHJ 73 (4/56): 52.

4412. Old War-Dreams. Whitman, W. L 38 (6/20/55): 116.

4413. Old Wharves. Ebright, F. SEP 229 (10/6/56): 95.

4414. Old Woman on a Fine Day. Ward, M.W. SEP 230 (5/17/58): 53.

4415. The Old Woman's Song. Barnes, K. LHJ 72 (8/55): 105.

4416. An Old Woman's Words to Her Young Cat. Hall, C. P 90 (9/57): 356.

4417. Old World Dialogue. Graves, R. H 218 (3/59): 58.

4418. The Olive Tree. Shapiro, K. P 90 (8/57): 268.

4419. Oliver Would Twist. Flaumenhaft, A.S. EJ 45 (11/56): 506.

4420. The Olympic Girl. Betjeman, J. H 212 (1/56): 55.

4421. Oman the Diver. Haring, P. P 86 (9/55): 341.

4422. On a Book. Liotta, J. WLB 34 (12/59): 281.

4423. On a Cage of Mice. Holmes, J. H 218 (5/59): 57.

4424. On a Certain Spinster. Galbraith, G.S. SEP 229 (9/15/56): 117.

4425. On a Child Who Lived One Minute. Kennedy, X.J. NY 34 (3/8/58): 42.

4426. On a Dial. Batchelder, A. LHJ 72 (8/55): 122.

4427. On a Gray Afternoon. Newbold, F. LHJ 75 (11/58): 23.

4428. On a Horse and a Goat. Lister, R.P. At 197 (2/56): 88.

4429. On a Horse Carved in Wood. Hall, D. N 184 (6/29/57): 573.

4430. On a Literary Censor. Solovay, J.C. CH 31 (5/57): 522.

4431. On a Mountain. O'Hara, F. P 90 (5/57): 91-2.

4432. On a Philosophical System. Wright, C.T. H 213 (11/56): 76.

4433. On a Portrait of Wallace Stevens. D'Andrade, D. N 185 (7/20/57): 40.

4434. On a Prize Crucifix by a Student Sculptor. Logan, J. Co 69 (11/14/58): 170.

4435. On a Recollected Road. Gilboa, A. P 92 (7/58): 251.

4436. On an Irreparable Piano. Aucourt, J. LHJ 72 (1/55): 119.

4437. On an Old Album. Coblentz, S.A. CC 72 (5/25/55): 616.

4438. On Ash Wednesday. Lennen, E. CC 74 (3/6/57): 287.

4439. On Beauty. Benek, M. N 185 (9/14/57): 138.

4440. On Becoming of Age. Holmes, T. P 92 (4/58): 31-2.

4441. On Boarding the Dog. Dean, E. SEP 228 (7/30/55): 82.

4442. On Buying by Mail (Antiques, That Is). La Rue, D. Hb 63 (3/59): 101.

4443. On Carley Ridge. Wolf, L. C 25 (1/58): 61.

4444. On Certain Wits. Nemerov, H. N 187 (9/6/58): 119.

4445. On Closer Inspection. Usk, T. SEP 229 (3/30/57): 67.

4446. On Completing His Hundredth Year. Summers, H.,Jr. SR 42 (8/8/59): 33.

4447. On David's Portrait of a Grandniece. O'Gorman, N. Co 66 (7/12/57): 374.

4448. On Drinking English Beer. Lister, R.P. NY 34 (3/22/58): 38.

4449. On Educational Toys and Fun with a Purpose. Molloy, R.B. SEP 231 (6/27/59): 50.

4450. On Equality. Fein, R. N 184 (4/20/57): 347.

4451. On Falling Asleep by Firelight. Meredith, W. NY 33 (12/21/57): 33.

4452. On Falling Asleep in a Mountain Cabin. Howes, B. P 94 (9/59): 360.

4453. On First Looking at the Chap's Homer. Hammer, P. LHJ 75 (8/59): 100.

4454. On First Looking in on Blodgett's Keats' 'Chapman's Homer'. YR 49 (12/59): 245.

4455. On Friendship. Pepler, L.J. CT 2 (9/15/58): 10.

4456. On Getting to Work at 8:10 A.M. Gabler, C. M. SEP 227 (1/8/55): 68.

4457. On Hallowe'en. Pessin, C. Hn 32 (10/56): 367.

4458. On Having Meant Well. Galbraith, G.S. At 195 (1/55): 96.

4459. On Having the Bachache. Lister, R.P. At 204 (9/59): 76.

4460. On Hearing Certain Words. Merchant, J. SEP 229 (6/15/57): 96.

4461. On Hearing Frederick Play the Apassionata. Pillin, W. P 86 (9/55): 338.

4462. On Hearing the Monologue of a Deaf Poet. Abse, D. P 89 (2/57): 279-80.

4463. On Her Third New Year. Hamilton, H.E. SR 39 (5/5/56): 26.

4464. On His Marks. Armour, R. BHG 34 (6/56): 97.

4465. On His Robust and Slatternly Muse. Lister, R.P. At 200 (7/57): 92.

4466. On Inheriting an Empty House on Coney Island. Atherton, J. YR 47 (9/57): 74-5.

4467. On Installing an American Kitchen in Lower Austria. Auden, W.H. NY 35 (3/7/59): 34.

4468. On Knowing Nothing. Smith, A.J.M. N 182 (3/24/56): 240.

4469. On Listening to Music with Two Minds. Lister, R.P. NY 33 (5/25/57): 92.

4470. On Looking East to the Sea Without a Sunset Behind Me. Ciardi, J. P 86 (5/55): 66-8.

4471. On Making Friends. Armknecht, R.F. SEP 228 (9/3/55): 66.

4472. On Man Considered as an Instrument for Hurting. Abel, L. AN 58 (3/59): 44.

4473. On Minding One's Own Business. Wright, J. H 217 (7/58): 21.

4474. On Moving Into a New House. Isler, B. BHG 37 (3/59): 79.

4475. On My Thirty-Fifth Birthday. Nicholson, N. H 210 (4/55): 67.

4476. On Not Knowing What Lies About Us. Clark, J.A. NaR 3 (1/19/57): 64.

4477. On Not Knowing Yiddish. Victor, F. C 28 (8/59): 167.

4478. On Opening a Wedding Invitation. Eisenlohr, L. SEP 230 (10/19/57): 84.

4479. On Passing a Small Place on Fifth Avenue Where a Building Once Was. Lemon, R. SR 42 (7/18/59): 30.

4480. On Penitencia Creek. Stafford, W. P 91 (1/58): 252.

4481. On Playing Games with the Children. Bryan, R. SEP 231 (12/20/58): 65.

4482. On Prescience. Golffing, F. P 88 (6/56): 159.

4483. On Rachmaninoff's Birthday. O'Hara, F. P 87 (3/56): 343.

4484. On Reading a Collection of Essays on Baudelaire. Starbuck, G. N 188 (2/28/59): 191.

4485. On Reading Shakespeare Near a Window. Cuomo, G. SR 39 (5/5/56): 25.

4486. On Refusing Secrets. Galbraith, G.S. SEP 229 (3/16/57): 79.

4487. On Re-Reading Hawthorne. McCarthy, L. A 100 (3/21/59): 711.

4488. On Returning. McGinley, P.D. GH 142 (3/56): 28.

4489. On Second Thought. Krausz, S. SEP 228 (3/31/56): 52.

4490. On Seeing Larry Rivers' 'Washington Crossing the Delaware' at the Museum of Modern Art. O'Hara, F. P 87 (3/56): 342.

4491. On Seeing My Great-Aunt in a Funeral Parlor. Chang, D.C. AS 28 (Wint/58-59): 37-8.

4492. On Seeing the Sun Rise Seven Times. Lister, R.P. NY 33 (6/15/57): 30.

4493. On Taking a Shower. Nixon, J.,Jr. SR 39 (2/25/56): 28.

4494. On the Adoption: An Anniversary. Sandeen, E. P 85 (2/55): 262-3.

4495. On the Birth of Jeffrey to William and Barbara Harding. Ciardi, J. LHJ 72 (8/55): 132.

4496. On the Bridge. Sato, S. P 88 (5/56): 105-6.

4497. On the Curve-Edge. Evans, A.H. NY 35 (11/21/59): 52.

4498. On the Death of a Student Hopelessly Failing My Course. Cuomo, G. SR 42 (1/3/59): 20.

4499. On the Death of a Test Pilot: A Footnote. Legler, P. P 88 (9/56): 381.

4500. On the Death of an Ordinary Person. Hudson, D. N 184 (3/16/57): 240.

4501. On the Decline of Oracles. Plath, S. P 94 (9/59): 368-9.

4502. On the Difficulty of Conjuring up a Dryad. Plath, S. P 90 (7/57): 235-6.

4503. On the Difficulty of Justice. Vance, T. P 89 (2/57): 285-6.

4504. On the Difficulty of Obtaining Potions. Moss, H. NR 136 (2/4/57): 19.

4505. On the Edge. Levertov, D. N 188 (1/24/59): 75.

4506. On the Eighth Day. Kenny, H. NaR 3 (5/11/57): 446.

4507. On the Grass. Armour, R. BHG 34 (5/56): 337.

4508. On the High Cost of Primroses. Galbraith, G.S. SEP 230 (12/14/57): 77.

4509. On the Lake. Goodman, P. P 94 (8/59): 291.

4510. On the Late Hungarian Massacre. Davis, F.M. CT 1 (6/24/57): 13.

4511. On the Ninth Psalm. Wirt, S.E. CC 72 (1/26/55): 111.

4512. On the Occasion of the First Edition of Mr. T.S. Eliot's 'The Cultivation of Christmas Trees.' NR 135 (10/15/56): 28.

4513. On the Other Hand. Chadwick, H. SEP 230 (9/21/57): 94.

4514. On the Passing of a Sternwheel Tow. Knoepfle, J. P 93 (12/58): 147-8.

4515. On the Poet William Carlos Williams. Langton, D. N 182 (4/14/56): 322.

4516. On the Road to Bethlehem. Meissner, W.W. A 96 (1/5/57): 393.

4517. On the Run. Armour, R. BHG 35 (6/57): 159.

4518. On the Scrawled Wall. Montale, E. P 92 (5/58): 97.

4519. On the Site of the Old Lafayette. Moss, H. SR 39 (5/5/56): 26.

4520. On the Spot. Richstone, M. BHG 36 (10/58): 130.

4521. On the State of the Art. Nathan, R. SR 38 (9/10/55): 32.

4522. On the Tip of the Tongue. Douglass, S. LHJ 75 (3/58): 140.

4523. On the Unreality of Toothache. Lister, R.P. NY 33 (1/4/58): 59.

4524. On the Welsh Marches. Stone, W. NY 35 (9/26/59): 161.

4525. On the Youth of England Corrupted by Coffee. Lister, R.P. NY 32 (1/5/57): 60.

4526. On This Day. Goldberg, L. P 92 (7/58): 240.

4527. On This Wall, in This Town, in Their Own State. Engle, P. L 40 (5/28/56): 95-105.

4528. On Tobey's Road. Mundell, W.D. At 198 (8/56): 89.

4529. On Torrance Beach. Fort, C.L. SEP 232 (8/22/59): 60.

4530. On Trying to Stay a Bachelor. Chadwick, H. SEP 230 (4/5/58): 122.

4531. On Various Errors. Witt, H. P 91 (12/57): 179.

4532. On Viewing an Empty Classroom Early in the Morning. Bastone, J. EJ 44 (10/55): 423.

4533. On Waking in Rome. Lynch, J.A. Co 68 (4/25/58): 104.

4534. On Womanhood. Gokak, V.K. P 93 (1/59): 262-64.

4535. Once Beautiful as a Wave. Barker, E. SR 38 (3/12/55): 16.

4536. Once Over, Weekly. Gleason, H.W. SEP 231 (3/7/59): 76.

4537. Once the Wind. Van Doren, M. At 202 (7/58): 33.

4538. Once Upon a Summer. Grenville, R.H. GH 142 (7/56): 28.

4539. One A.M.: Bleury and Mayor. Souster, R. P 94 (8/59): 302.

4540. The One and the Many. Coblentz, S.A. CC 76 (12/2/59): 1400.

4541. One and the Other. Char, R. At 201 (6/58): 105.

4542. The One Dull Thing You Did Was to Die, Fletcher. Ciardi, J. SR 41 (11/22/58): 38.

4543. One Flame. Carter, M.A. CC 72 (9/7/55): 1016.

4544. 104 Boulevard Saint-Germain. Pitchford, K. NY 34 (5/17/58): 46.

4545. 151st Psalm. Shapiro, K. P 90 (8/57): 269.

4546. One Kind of Colloquy. Hillyer, R. At 199 (1/57): 43.

4547. One Light, One Love. Cully, K.B. CC 74 (5/29/57): 681.

4548. One Little Difference. Chadwick, H. SEP 227 (3/5/55): 87.

4549. One More Chore. Penny, L. SEP 231 (5/23/59): 121.

4550. One More Day. Johnson, J.M. GH 142 (10/56): 12.

4551. One on a Hearth. Jacobson, E. GH 142 (11/56): 13.

4552. One Place. Janson, E. LHJ 73 (4/56): 59.

4553. The One-Room Apartment. Bramley, W. LHJ 72 (3/55): 211.

4554. One Small Quirk. Jacobs, E.L. SEP 230 (10/5/57): 75.

4555. One Step. Heafield, K. CC 76 (11/25/59): 1367.

4556. One Sundry Thing. Weiss, T. P 94 (6/59): 151-2.

4557. One Thing Is Sure the Heavens Declare. Cooper, J.C. CC 74 (9/18/57): 1103.

4558. One Thing Thou Lackest. Fretz, J.H. CC 76 (2/23/59): 225.

4559. One Third of a Dream. Garrigue, J. P 93 (12/58): 135.

4560. One Volume Soiled. Ridland, J.M. NY 32 (9/15/56): 88.

4561. One Way Out. Gordon, R. WLB 31 (11/56): 270.

4562. One Way Out. Schiff, L.K. SEP 230 (11/2/57): 98.

4563. One Word for Four Seasons. Wheldon, J. AS 24 (Spr/55): 185.

4564. The One-Year-Old. Updike, J. LHJ 74 (3/57): 172.

4565. Only Begotten Son. Bradley, S. CC 76 (12/16/59): 1464.

4566. The Only Granite. Root, M.E. NaR 2 (8/1/56): 12.

4567. Only in the Dream. Eberhart, R. P 88 (8/56): 319.

4568. Open Letter to Santa. Ryskind, M. NaR 4 (12/21/57): 563.

4569. Open Saturdays. Atherton, J. SR 39 (4/18/56): 31.

4570. Ophelia Sings Under Observation. Young, A. SR 38 (11/26/55): 14.

4571. Opinions. Galbraith, G.S. SEP 230 (5/24/58): 73.

4572. Opposite Opinions. Chadwick, H. BHG 33 (3/55): 183.

4573. Or Turn to Stone. Freeman, J.T. LHJ 73 (11/56): 98.

4574. The Orange Picker. Ignatow, D. SR 39 (6/30/56): 8.

4575. Oranges Three, Lemons Two. Krolow, K. P 88 (7/56): 253.

4576. The Orator. Waddington, M. N 184 (4/20/57): 350.

4577. Orbit. Lamport, F. H 211 (9/55): 33.

4578. Orchard. Hubler, R.G. At 197 (4/56): 63.

4579. Orchard. Stone, R. P 89 (1/57): 212.

4580. Order. Hay, J. P 86 (4/55): 22.

4581. Orizons. Birnbaum, H. P 94 (6/59): 156-63.

4582. Ornithology in a World of Flux. Warren, R. P. SR 41 (11/22/58): 37.

4583. Orphan Bride. Spencer, B.S. SEP 232 (10/3/59): 111.

4584. Orpheus. Scott, T. P 86 (5/55): 94-5.

4585. Orpheus. Slavitt, D.R. YR 46 (6/57): 566-7.

4586. Orpheus Before Hades. Dickey, J. NY 35 (12/5/59): 52.

4587. Orpheus with His Lute. Untermeyer, L. At 196 (9/55): 51-2.

4588. Orthodoxy. Paddack, M. A 93 (4/9/55): 46.

4589. The Other. Dickey, J. YR 48 (3/59): 398-400.

4590. The Other Lives. Pack, R. H 217 (8/58): 80.

4591. The Other Tree. Merwin, W.S. P 86 (7/55): 228-9.

4592. Ouch! Stockdale, A.B. SEP 228 (10/8/55): 62.

4593. Our Brother's Keeper. Bender, B.B. CC 74 (5/1/57): 558.

4594. Our City Is Guarded by Automatic Rockets. Stafford, W. P 91 (1/58): 354.

4595. Our Clouds. Ritter, D. Hn 33 (6/57): 234.

4596. Our Common Humanity. Russo, P.G. CC 74 (1/23/57): 107.

4597. Our Den. Armour, R. BHG 34 (6/56): 245.

4598. Our Lady of Advent. Claude of Jesus, Sr. A 98 (11/30/57): 277.

4599. Our Lady of the Migrant. Conway, M.D. A 93 (5/28/55): 241.

4600. Our Lady of the Word. Mary Immaculata, Sr. A 101 (8/22/59): 635.

4601. Our Lady, Patron of Arts. Taylor, S.W. A 97 (6/15/57): 324.

4602. Our Maidservant. Sato, S. P 88 (5/56): 93.

4603. Our Mutual Friend. Creason, A. SEP 228 (5/12/56): 78.

4604. Our Stairs. Anthony, E. GH 149 (10/59): 154.

4605. Our Youth. Ashberg, J. P 91 (10/57): 163-5.

4606. Out of a War of Wits. Thomas, D. P 87 (11/55): 84-5.

4607. Out of Many Songs. Coblentz, S.A. CC 74 (2/20/57): 229.

4608. Out of My Reach. Collins, I.J. SEP 227 (5/21/55): 62.

4609. Out of Sight. Averitt, E. LHJ 75 (5/58): 14.

4610. Out of Sight. Galbraith, G.S. SEP 228 (4/7/56): 73.

4611. Out of the Black. Duncan, R. N 188 (4/25/59): 365.

4612. Out of the Cradle Endlessly Rocking. Whitman, W. L 38 (6/20/55): 115.

4613. Out of the Pit. Cassity, T. P 91 (2/58): 307.

4614. Out of the Window into Moonlight. Pomeroy, R. P 91 (11/57): 91.

4615. The Outcast. Liotta, J. WLB 30 (11/55): 272.

4616. Outdoors One Makes Most Strange, My Lady. Galler, D. P 87 (1/56): 199-200.

4617. The Outer Banks. Drewry, C. SR 38 (8/13/55): 17.

4618. Outer Doubt. Richter, H.C. SEP 231 (7/12/58): 75.

4619. Outer Drive. Honig, E. SR 40 (7/20/57): 17.

4620. Outline of a Lecture for Seniors Too Actively Engaged in Athletics. Roseliep, R. EJ 48 (10/59): 416.

4621. Outlook, Uncertain. Reid, A. At 204 (10/59): 58.

4622. The Outsider. Graves, R. H 214 (5/57): 72.

4623. Over Grave Flowers. Morris, J.N. P 87 (1/56): 204.

4624. Overhaul. Armour, R. SEP 227 (5/28/55): 75.

4625. Overhearing. Stafford, W. N 189 (10/24/59): 255.

4626. The Overlooked Anniversary. Neely, L. SEP 231 (7/26/58): 76.

4627. Overshoe Exchange. Smith, B.L. LHJ (2/59): 79.

4628. Oversight. Coblentz, S.A. CC 72 (1/5/55): 13.

4629. Oversupplied. Zimmerman, E.H. SEP 230 (6/28/58): 103.

4630. Overwrought. Schiff, L.K. SEP 229 (2/2/57): 40.

4631. Owed to a Bookbinder. Sutherland, W. WLB 31 (4/57): 653.

4632. Owed to the Country Road. Seager, R.W. SEP 232 (9/15/59): 55.

4633. Oxford 16 October 1555. Dickey, W.H. P 85 (3/55): 336.

4634. Oxfordshire Song. Chapin, K.G. LHJ 76 (11/59): 44.

4635. Oyez! Riddle, M. N 188 (4/11/59): 324.

4636. Oyster Farm. Landeweer, E. SEP 231 (9/13/58): 122.

4637. P.S. to a Letter of Recommendation. Eisenlohr, L. SEP 230 (8/17/57): 59.

4638. Pacific 101: The Ranch by the Sea. Levine, R. SR 41 (8/23/58): 14.

4639. Package Deal. Galbraith, G.S. LHJ 74 (3/57): 218.

4640. Package Deal. Nelson, T. GH 149 (12/59): 181.

4641. Pageant. Pierce, E.L. CC 74 (12/18/57): 1507.

4642. Paging Mr. Paterson. Scott, W.T. N 188 (4/25/59): 372.

4643. Pain. Grossman, A. P 90 (6/57): 147.

4644. Pain. Van Hise, A. AS 25 (Summ/56): 329.

4645. The Painted Lady. Danner, M. P 89 (10/56): 23.

4646. The Painter. Ashbery, J. P 87 (12/55): 154-5.

4647. The Painter. Jennings, E. P 90 (6/57): 151.

4648. Painting a Mountain Stream. Nemerov, H. P 91 (11/57): 79-80.

4649. Painting of a Courtesan on a Roof at Venice. Singer, H. P 87 (2/56): 293.

4650. A Pair of Hands. Sarton, M. At 198 (9/56): 63.

4651. The Palms. Whittemore, R. P 92 (9/58): 347.

4652. Panorama. Trent, L. CC 72 (10/5/55): 1136.

4653. The Panther. Eff, J. NaR 6 (7/5/58): 61.

4654. Par. Workman, M.T. CC 73 (1/11/56): 40.

4655. Parable. Berrigan, D. P 94 (7/59): 233.

4656. A Parable. Smith, W.J. P 87 (10/55): 7.

4657. Parable for April. Adrian, V.H. SEP 230 (4/26/58): 57.

4658. Parable of Animus and Anima. Claudel, P. P 87 (12/55): 141-8.

4659. Parables. Mary Madeleva, Sr. A 100 (12/13/58): 344.

4660. The Parade. Hammer, P. GH 142 (3/56): 28.

4661. Parade. Neely, L. SEP 229 (2/2/57): 91.

4662. Paradise. Anwar, C. At 197 (6/56): 123.

4663. Paradise. Austin, D. YR 46 (12/56): 224-5.

4664. Paradise. Menashe, S. Co 68 (8/8/58): 465.

4665. Paradise for Sale. Nash, O. NY 35 (7/25/59): 34.

4666. Paradise Regained. Thornton, M.B. SR 42 (2/14/59): 37.

4667. Paradise Retained. Galbraith, G.S. SEP 229 (7/14/56): 53.

4668. Les Parapluies: Renoir. Morris, H. P 85 (1/55): 223-4.

4669. Parents' Progress. Neely, L. SEP 229 (5/11/57): 109.

4670. Paris Sky. Drouet, M. L 40 (2/13/56): 53.

4671. Park Orator. Lilly, O. SR 39 (5/5/56): 24.

4672. Parlor Travels. Wuebker, K. LHJ 74 (2/57): 166.

4673. Paroled. Lilly, O. CC 74 (9/25/57): 1133.

4674. Parson Turell's Legacy. GH 140 (2/55): 28.

4675. Part-Time Aristocrat. Johnson, A.S. SEP 230 (10/5/57): 51.

4676. Part-Time Calendar. Adams, M.R. SEP 231 (3/7/59): 96.

4677. The Parting. Hay, S.H. SR 38 (4/30/55): 14.

4678. Parting. Walujati. At 197 (6/56): 144.

4679. Party Spirit. Schlitzer, S. SEP 230 (11/16/57): 76.

4680. Pascal in the Schoolroom: A Rephrasing. Camp, J. EJ 46 (4/57): 216.

4681. Passed by Customs. Miner, V.S. SEP 228 (9/3/55): 82.

4682. The Passenger. Howe, M. At 195 (6/55): 64.

4683. Passing East of Hartford. Kroll, E. P 90 (4/57): 22.

4684. The Passing of the Days. Astier, M. CC 75 (12/3/58): 1393.

4685. The Passing of Time. Shenton, E. SEP 232 (9/12/59): 71.

4686. Passing Reflection. Vesely, R.S. TH 33 (8/55): 59.

4687. The Passing Remark. Mundell, W.D. At 197 (4/56): 96.

4688. The Passing Storm. Pasternak, B. NR 139 (11/3/58): 17.

4689. Passion. Richardson, D.L. CC 72 (6/15/55): 703.

4690. A Passionate Commissar to His Love. Viereck, P. SR 38 (7/23/55): 31.

4691. The Passionate (Union) Shepherd to His Love. Counselman, M.E. SEP 227 (3/26/55): 44.

4692. Passover. Wolf, L. C 23 (5/57): 418.

4693. Passover in Jerusalem. Hameiri, A. P 92 (7/58): 213.

4694. The Past. Goodman, P. P 92 (9/58): 375.

4695. Past All Understanding. Boynton, S.C. CT 2 (7/21/58): 24.

4696. Past Midwinter. Nathan, N. SEP 230 (2/22/58): 82.

4697. Past Misunderstanding. Lennen, E. SEP 230 (3/22/58): 68.

4698. The Pastel Girls. Morrison, J. LHJ 75 (8/58): 64.

4699. The Pastor and the Lady. McGinley, P. AS 28 (Aut/59): 444-6.

4700. Pastoral. Barnes, K. NY 35 (9/19/59): 46.

4701. Pastoral. Meredith, W. P 88 (6/56): 166.

4702. Pastoral. Ross, L.T. At 199 (6/57): 100.

4703. A Pastor's Sermon to Himself. Schreiber, A. CT 1 (6/10/57): 15.

4704. Patchwork Weather. Grenville, R.H. SEP 232 (9/12/59): 89.

4705. Pater Noster in Winter. Sandeen, E. P 89 (12/56): 142.

4706. The Path to the Barn. Van Slyke, B. SEP 229 (12/22/56): 40.

4707. The Patina of Memories. Cresson, A. GH 140 (3/55): 99.

4708. The Patriarch. Singer, S. C 26 (12/58): 507.

4709. Patrol. Pomeroy, R. P 93 (2/59): 301-2.

4710. The Patterned Fields. Lister, R.P. NY 33 (9/14/57): 145.

4711. Paul Before Agrippa. Hazo, S. Co 70 (8/28/59): 444.

4712. Paulinus of Nola. Cotter, J.F. A 95 (7/14/56): 365.

4713. The Paulownia Tree. Marz, R. P 90 (6/57): 162.

4714. The Paupers. di Giovanni, N.T. N 187 (12/13/58): 458.

4715. Pavan for a Young Duchess at Christmastide. Carruth, H. NR 135 (12/24/56): 20.

4716. Pavan on a Beach. De Jong, D.C. P 89 (2/57): 300-1.

4717. Pavana in Avila. Mary Jeremy, Sr. A 93 (9/24/55): 621.

4718. Pavane. Bernard, O. P 86 (5/55): 74.

4719. Pavane. Perry, R. P 87 (1/57): 212.

4720. The Pax. Loyal, G. A 93 (7/23/55): 413.

4721. Pay-Off. Otis, A.F. SEP 230 (2/22/58): 102.

4722. Peace. Trent, L. CC 76 (12/2/59): 1404.

4723. Peace. White, H.S. N 184 (5/18/57): 444.

4724. Peace and Prayer. Gray, E. CT 1 (6/10/57): 10.

4725. Peace and the Pacific. Koehler, G.S. P 90 (4/57): 24.

4726. The Peaceable Kingdom. Morse, S.F. P 92 (5/58): 74.

4727. Peacock. Landeweer, E. SEP 230 (9/28/57): 98.

4728. Peacock. Witt, H. SR 41 (2/15/58): 42.

4729. Pearl of Great Price. Grace, W. A 93 (9/24/55): 621.

4730. The Peasant. Wolf, L. NY 33 (4/20/57): 92.

4731. Peasant's Dance. SEP 231 (6/10/58): 11.

4732. Pecadillo. Mullins, T.Y. CC 76 (9/16/59): 1054.

4733. Pecuniary, Aren't We? Clark, J.A. NaR 4 (12/21/57): 569.

4734. Pedagogic Logic. Henry, J. EJ 44 (12/55): 550.

4735. The Peddler. Ginsberg, L. CH 34 (12/59): 213.

4736. Peepers. Cane, M. AS 28 (Spr/57): 164.

4737. Peer Gynt. Kinnell, G. P 87 (3/56): 350-1.

4738. Penalty. Hymes, D. N 186 (2/22/58): 170.

4739. Penelope. Bagg, R. At 200 (8/57): 48.

4740. Penitential Sonnet. McCarthy, L. A 93 (4/2/55): 17-8.

4741. Penny Arcade. Atherton, J. NY 33 (9/28/57): 134.

4742. Penny Wise and Found Foolish. Watt, W.W. NY 35 (9/12/59): 56.

4743. Peonies. Quinn, J.R. LHJ 72 (5/55): 14.

4744. People. Donnelly, D. P 90 (8/57): 270-3.

4745. People Are So Inconsistent. Otis, A.F. SEP 229 (6/8/57): 84.

4746. People in Vogue. Kessler, J. C 25 (1/58): 67.

4747. Perception. Van Hise, A. AS 25 (Wint/55-56): 128.

4748. Perennial Landscape. Donnelly, D. P 86 (8/55): 251-2.

4749. Perennial Problem. Wheeler, R. SEP 231 (10/18/58): 64.

4750. Perfect Passenger. Armour, R. BHG 35 (6/57): 38.

4751. The Performance. Dickey, J. P 94 (7/59): 220-1.

4752. Perfumes. Speer, C.A. SEP 231 (7/26/58): 81.

4753. Peri Poietikes. Zukofsky, L. N 187 (11/7/58): 336.

4754. Perils of Modern Living. F., H.P. NY 32 (11/10/56): 52.

4755. Period. Richstone, M. SEP 229 (3/2/57): 48.

4756. A Periphrasis. Morse, S.F. NY 35 (4/18/59): 107.

4757. Permanently. Koch, K. P 89 (11/56): 89.

4758. A Perpetual Memory. Patstone, A.J. CT 2 (4/14/58): 15.

4759. The Perpetual Painter. Armour, R. SEP 229 (3/23/57): 93.

4760. Persephone. Hopkins, G.M. A 97 (8/3/57): 465.

4761. The Persimmon Tree. Solomon, M. P 94 (6/59): 167.

4762. Persona Non Grata. Sagittarius. NR 138 (6/30/58): 9.

4763. Personae. Touster, S. C 26 (8/58): 106.

4764. Personal Glossary. De Vito, E.B. SEP 230 (11/30/57): 72.

4765. Personals. Swift, M.J. LJ 84 (5/15/59): 1573.

4766. Personnel Problems. Brooks, H.B. WLB 30 (11/55): 274.

4767. Perspective. Mergard, J.C. SEP 231 (2/14/59): 45.

4768. Pertaiho. Tse-Tung, M. At 204 (12/59): 55.

4769. A Pertinent Observation. Todd, R. AS 27 (Aut/58): 422.

4770. Pertinent to My Heart. Rainer, D. AS 24 (Aut/55): 434.

4771. Pessimist's Plaint. Barker, S.O. SEP 229 (10/6/56): 62.

4772. The Pestle. Tiempo, E.L. P 89 (1/57): 223.

4773. Pet Aversion. Lund, D.H. LHJ 76 (5/59): 154.

4774. Pet Theory. Wheeler, R. SEP 229 (10/6/56): 57.

4775. Peter the Rock. O'Connell, R. A 98 (3/29/58): 751.

4776. Petition to This Room, to Allow One to Work. Gibbs, B. P 90 (6/57): 142-3.

4777. Petticoat Convention. Hammer, P. SEP 229 (10/27/56): 80.

4778. Petticoat Fever. Richstone, M. SEP 229 (12/29/56): 53.

4779. The Ph.D. Learns About Love. Steiner, S. SR 39 (12/1/56): 20.

4780. Pharisaic. Janes, K. CC 74 (7/10/57): 844.

4781. The Phase That Fazes. Raskin, S. SEP 227 (6/11/55): 115.

4782. Philander Musing. Jerome, J. H 218 (3/59): 71.

4783. Philatelist's Prayer at Twilight. Ebright, F. NY 32 (4/7/56): 123.

4784. Philistines in Hired Rooms. Bradley, S. CC 76 (12/9/59): 1437.

4785. Philological. Updike, J. NY 33 (4/6/57): 109.

4786. The Philosopher. Jones, H.M. At 203 (1/59): 89.

4787. Philosophic Thought Based on Income, Lack of. Graham, E. LHJ 75 (2/58): 131.

4788. Philosophy. Bangs, J.K. GH 140 (4/55): 40.

4789. Phobia Suburbia. Polikoff, B.G. BHG 35 (11/57): 177.

4790. Phoenix. Posner, D. H 217 (8/58): 23.

4791. The Phoenix. Whitman, R. At 198 (8/56): 67.

4792. The Phoenix and the Garden. Aiken, C. NR 139 (12/8/58): 20.

4793. The Phoenix Too Frequent. Owen, G. EJ 47 (9/58): 333.

4794. Photographs of the Poets. Shapiro, K. NY 32 (6/2/56): 36.

4795. Pianists. Gibbs, B. NY 34 (3/1/58): 32.

4796. Piano Lesson. Burns, M.G.G. LHJ 72 (6/55): 100.

4797. Piazza Di Spagna, 26. Witt, H. SR 40 (8/17/57): 17.

4798. Picasso at Vallauris. Lohf, K.A. P 94 (4/59): 26.

4799. Pick and Choose. Lister, R.P. At 202 (10/58): 98.

4800. Pick Me Green. Hallock, K. TH 33 (2/55): 52.

4801. Picnic. Mary Maura, Sr. A 102 (11/14/59): 191.

4802. The Picnic of Othello. Bock, F. P 93 (10/58): 33.

4803. A Picture. Nemerov, H. N 187 (9/20/58): 157.

4804. Picture in Rain. Howard, F.M. NY 32 (12/8/56): 54.

4805. The Picture Is Turned Toward the Wall. Graham, C. GH 140 (4/55): 40.

4806. A Piece of Happiness. Rich, A. NY 33 (11/9/57): 50.

4807. The Pied Piper. Ashbery, J. P 87 (12/55): 153.

4808. Pierian Thirst. Sweet, A.P. WLB 31 (10/56): 186.

4809. Pierrot to Columbine. Orr, C. LHJ 73 (9/56): 224.

4810. Pieta. Rennert, M. SR 40 (10/12/57): 58.

4811. Pieta. Zaturenska, M. Co 70 (9/18/59): 514.

4812. Pig. Saunders, K. SEP 231 (6/3/59): 81.

4813. Pigeon Key. Perry, R.L. P 87 (1/56): 211.

4814. Pigs in Clover. Manker, D. GH 142 (9/56): 46.

4815. The Pillow and the Book. Lattimore, R. P 95 (11/59): 76.

4816. Pinch of Sage. Johnson, C.H. SEP 229 (5/25/57): 50.

4817. Pinnacle. Clark, D.R. P 92 (6/58): 154.

4818. Pioneers. Mansfield, M. SR 39 (4/7/56): 30.

4819. Pioneers! O Pioneers! Whitman, W. L 38 (6/20/55): 119.

4820. The Pious Squire Regrets His Year's Sins of Lust. Levant, H. P 89 (12/56): 166.

4821. Pipe and Strings. Lister, R.P. At 203 (1/59): 88.

4822. Piper. Dufault, P.K. NY 32 (10/6/56): 157.

4823. Pique-Dame. Lang, V.R. P 89 (3/57): 368-9.

4824. Pity God. Scovel, M. CC 73 (11/7/56): 1325.

4825. Pizzicato. Abbe, G. SR 41 (9/27/58): 59.

4826. Plainsong. Nicholl, L.T. AS 27 (Aut/58): 436.

4827. Plaint for the Death of Guillen Peraza. Merwin, W.S. N 186 (5/10/58): 420.

4828. Plaint of a Darker Brother. Willis. P. NHB 22 (2/59): 108.

4829. Plaint of the Poet in an Ignorant Age. Kizer, C. P 93 (3/59): 384-5.

4830. A Plan of Self Subjection. Gunn, T. P 86 (6/55): 128-9.

4831. A Plant of High Altitudes. Shiffert, E. SR 42 (10/12/59): 62.

4832. Planting a Mailbox. Updike, J. NY 33 (5/11/57): 103.

4833. Platform Before the Castle. Winslow, A.G. H 216 (4/58): 38.

4834. The Platonist Sees Snakes at an Ideal Moment. Witt, H. P 88 (9/56): 374.

4835. The Plausible. Cane, M. SR 38 (10/29/55): 24.

4836. Playthings. Coblentz, S.A. CC 72 (2/2/55): 174.

4837. Plaza de Toros, Iowa. Stoutenburg, A. N 186 (3/15/58): 238.

4838. A Plea for Alias. Schevill, J. NR 132 (6/13/55): 19.

4839. Plea to Boys and Girls. Graves, R. At 199 (2/57): 59.

4840. Please, Dear. (Soon, Dear!) Milbrath, M.M. GH 148 (5/59): 217.

4841. Please, Don't Ask Me for a Loan. Wheeler, R. SEP 231 (3/28/59): 77.

4842. Please Don't Mention Another Tension. Jennison, C.S. At 198 (8/56): 91.

4843. Please, Father! The Neighbors Will Hear You! Janke, D. SEP 228 (3/31/56): 106.

4844. Please Mr. Filson. Watkins, A.E. WLB 31 (4/57): 652.

4845. Pleasures of the Imagination. Levant, H. P 89 (12/56): 166-7.

4846. The Pledge. McNeill, L. GH 148 (1/59): 154.

4847. Pledge. Pritam, A. P 93 (1/59): 226-7.

4848. Plucking the Stars. Chin-tsai, P. At 204 (12/59): 94.

4849. The Pocket. Wesley, C.C. GH 142 (6/56): 119.

4850. Poe-tatory. Fadiman, C. SR 40 (6/1/57): 24.

4851. Poem. Amihai, Y. P 92 (7/58): 256.

4852. Poem. Elliott, G. NR 133 (8/22/55): 19.

4853. Poem. Gilman, M. N 187 (7/1/58): 19.

4854. Poem. Graybeal, M. P 93 (11/58): 74.

4855. Poem. Kondo, A. P 88 (5/56): 82.

4856. Poem. Lang, V.R. P 89 (3/57): 367.

4857. Poem. Lang, V.R. P 89 (3/57): 372.

4858. The Poem. Melo Neto, J.C. At 197 (2/56): 146.

4859. A Poem. Menashe, S. Co 65 (12/28/56): 335.

4860. A Poem. Miller, D. C 19 (6/55): 594.

4861. Poem. Morgan, F. P 94 (4/59): 33.

4862. Poem. O'Doherty, B. P 87 (1/56): 228-9.

4863. Poem. O'Hara, F. P 90 (5/57): 92.

4864. Poem. Roethke, T. NR 133 (9/12/55): 19.

4865. Poem. Schwartz, D. C 25 (5/58): 400.

4866. Poem. Schwartz, D. NR 141 (10/19/59): 24.

4867. Poem. Schwartz, J. Co 70 (9/18/59): 487.

4868. Poem. Stuart, J. SR 39 (2/18/56): 49.

4869. Poem. Thornton, M.B. SR 40 (1/26/57): 16.

4870. Poem. Weiss, S. P 86 (7/55): 232.

4871. Poem. Williams, W.C. N 187 (11/1/58): 310.

4872. Poem. Wilson, C.A. P 94 (7/59): 238.

4873. Poem. Woods, J. P 94 (7/59): 234.

4874. Poem. Wylie, P.C. GH 142 (5/56): 184.

4875. A Poem About a Prince. O'Gorman, N. P 86 (9/55): 344-5.

4876. Poem and Message. Abse, D. P 86 (9/55): 319.

4877. Poem at Equinox. Corke, H. NY 34 (3/22/58): 30.

4878. Poem at Thirty. Woods, J. P 91 (12/57): 176-7.

4879. Poem by Water. Woods, J. P 89 (1/57): 216-7.

4880. Poem for a Child Who Slept Too Long. Disher, N. LHJ 73 (9/56): 213.

4881. Poem for a Commencement. Moore, R. P 93 (11/58): 65-7.

4882. Poem for a Festival of Art at the Boston Public Gardens. MacLeish, A. SR 39 (7/28/56): 11.

4883. Poem for an Afternoon. Balch, B.J. SR 40 (4/6/57): 11.

4884. Poem for Con. Merber, K.K. P 95 (11/59): 92-3.

4885. A Poem for Elizabeth. Clancy, J.P. Co 70 (8/14/59): 417.

4886. Poem for Men Only. Hammer, P. GH 143 (8/56): 121.

4887. Poem for Pigtails. McKee, G. GH 142 (1/56): 42.

4888. A Poem for S--. Stefanile, F. P 91 (1/58): 233-4.

4889. Poem for You. Pack, R. NY 33 (5/11/57): 49.

4890. Poem Found in a Grass Catcher. Galbraith, G.S. BHG 35 (10/57): 159.

4891. A Poem of Gratitude. Boyle, K. P 93 (3/59): 376.

4892. Poems for My Cousin. Jacobsen, J. P 94 (5/59): 82-4.

4893. Poems from a Hospital. O'Doherty, B. P 87 (1/56): 224-7.

4894. The Poem's Words. Marz, R. P 90 (6/57): 163.

4895. Poemscapes. Patchen, K. P 89 (10/56): 31-42.

4896. Poet. Smith, W.J. NR 134 (5/7/56): 21.

4897. The Poet. Touster, S. P 89 (1/57): 239.

4898. The Poet (After 'L'Ultima Rinunzia' of Guido Gozzano, 1883-1916). Stefanile, F. SR 41 (5/24/58): 35.

4899. The Poet at Seven. Justice, D. H 219 (7/59): 48.

4900. Poet Cornered. De Kay, O.,Jr. H 215 (8/57): 43.

4901. Poet on Horseback. Hanford, J.H. AS 28 (Aut/59): 432.

4902. The Poet Who Lived with His Words. Morse, S.F. SR 39 (8/11/56): 11.

4903. Poetry. Farjeon, E. Hn 35 (4/59): 104.

4904. Poetry and Pedantry. Honig, E. P 90 (6/57): 160.

4905. Poetry Defined. Holmes, J. SR 41 (3/1/58): 20.

4906. Poetry Going Out. Kitasono, K. At 195 (1/55): 151.

4907. Poetry 1948. Engonopoulos, N. At 195 (6/55): 148.

4908. Poetry on Wheels. BHG 35 (1/57): 39.

4909. Poetry Reading. Kaplan, M. SR 39 (5/5/56): 25.

4910. The Poet's Brain. Burford, W. P 95 (11/59): 79.

4911. Poet's Wish. Larraud, V. P 85 (2/55): 254.

4912. Pole Vault. Murano, S. P 88 (5/56): 78.

4913. Policeman Song. Anthony, E. GH 142 (2/56): 111.

4914. Policy Statement. Bernard, S. N 187 (10/11/58): 200.

4915. Political Agreement. Lazarus, P. SEP 229 (10/5/56): 117.

4916. The Political Prophet. Glaze, A. SR 39 (7/14/56): 26.

4917. Political Reflection. Nemerov, H. P 88 (9/56): 387.

4918. Political-Science Note. Galbraith, G.S. SEP 228 (5/12/56): 121.

4919. Pompeii. Grossman, A. P 94 (7/59): 239.

4920. Pompes Funebres. Smith, W.J. NR 138 (6/23/58): 19.

4921. The Pond. Steiner, S. SR 41 (12/13/58): 17.

4922. Ponte Veneziano. Tomlinson, C. P 88 (9/56): 353.

4923. The Poodle. Solomon, M. P 88 (8/56): 315.

4924. Poor Me! Pratt, W.W. SEP 230 (4/26/58): 65.

4925. Poor Parents' Almanac. Brasier, V. TH 34 (2/56): 49.

4926. The Poplar's Shadow. Swenson, M. NY 34 (5/10/58): 138.

4927. Poppies. Shneur, Z. P 92 (7/58): 212.

4928. The Popular Magazines. Whittemore, R. NR 138 (1/13/58): 18.

4929. Popular Pastime. Barker, S.O. SEP 230 (8/24/57): 92.

4930. A Popular Score. Schwartz, D. NR 139 (12/1/58): 16.

4931. Port of Call. Howes, B. NR 138 (6/30/58): 20.

4932. Portage. La Follette, M.W. P 88 (4/56): 26.

4933. Portovenere. Rizzardi, A. P 94 (8/59): 321.

4934. Portrait. Dugan, A. P 88 (4/56): 10.

4935. The Portrait. Johnson, G. A 97 (9/21/57): 651.

4936. Portrait. Walton, E.L. P 91 (11/57): 86.

4937. Portrait for Mother. Watts, H. LHJ 74 (1/56): 81.

4938. Portrait in Winter. Chapin, K.G. NR 136 (1/14/57): 19.

4939. Portrait of a High Court Judge. Rawlins, W. CC 74 (9/4/57): 1033.

4940. Portrait of a Jew. Cavafy, C. C 19 (6/55): 561.

4941. Portrait of a Philadelphian. J., H. H 210 (4/55): 62.

4942. Portrait of a Poet. Humphries, R. N 182 (4/14/56): 326.

4943. Portrait of Alethea, a Quakeress. Young, A. SR 38 (1/29/55): 16.

4944. Portrait of an Enthusiast. Armour, R. SEP 229 (3/9/57): 63.

4945. The Portrait of Gertrude Stein. Neville, H. C 25 (3/58): 260.

4946. Portrait of Lucifer. Pierce, E.L. CC 72 (3/2/55): 264.

4947. Portrait of the Boy as Artist. Howes, B. NR 135 (11/5/56): 22.

4948. Posies from a Second Childhood. Nash, O. NY 32 (4/7/56): 32.

4949. Positive Thinking. Douglass, S. LHJ 75 (1/58): 68.

4950. The Possibility. Turnoy, B. P 93 (11/58): 73.

4951. Possum Agonistes. Eliot, T.S. NaR 3 (1/5/57): 19.

4952. Post-Blizzard Report. Neely, L. SEP 227 (1/29/55): 92.

4953. Post-Vacation Pibroch. Jacobs, F.B. NY 32 (9/8/56): 123.

4954. Postcard Harlequin. Nichols, D. NR 141 (11/23/59): 19.

4955. Postlude to Mendelssohn. Strong, J.H. SEP 231 (11/22/58): 118.

4956. The Postman. Carlile, J. GH 142 (2/56): 44.

4957. Postmortem of a Solon: State Level. De Jong, D.C. NR 141 (11/9/59): 23.

4958. Postscript to a No Visitors Sign. Galbraith, G.S. SEP 231 (4/18/59): 50.

4959. Postscript to Rain. Emans, E.V. SEP 229 (5/4/57): 74.

4960. A Pot of Geraniums. Brasier, V. SEP 230 (4/19/58): 90.

4961. Potent Fluid. Brasier, V. SEP 230 (7/13/56): 89.

4962. A Potted Watch Never Boils. Nash, O. NY 34 (8/9/58): 28.

4963. Pottery. Woodrum, L. CT 3 (8/3/59): 5.

4964. Potting the Plants. Thomas, D. LHJ 75 (8/59): 74.

4965. Pounding the Clothes. Tze-Chiang, C. P 90 (4/57): 28.

4966. Prairie Mother. Stanley, I. SEP 228 (2/25/56): 110.

4967. Prairie Spring. Grenville, R.H. SEP 231 (5/23/59): 65.

4968. Praise for a Tom Cat. Parkinson, T. N 184 (6/22/57): 553.

4969. A Praise for the Sun. Wolf, L. P 92 (6/58): 152.

4970. A Praise to Good Poets in a Bad Age. Ciardi, J. SR 39 (8/11/56): 13.

4971. Praise We Great Men. Sitwell, E. At 204 (11/59): 97.

4972. A Prayer. Brenneman, J. BHG 34 (3/56): 154.

4973. Prayer. Coleridge, H. GH 140 (2/55): 28.

4974. Prayer. Hamizah, A. At 197 (6/56): 158.

4975. Prayer at a Place of Learning. Heafield, K. CC 75 (6/11/58): 690.

4976. Prayer for a Better World. Benet, S.V. PM 30 (7/55): 31.

4977. Prayer for a Child in a Hospital. Griffith, H.M. GH 140 (4/55): 16.

4978. Prayer for a Little Girl. Osborne, A. LHJ 72 (12/55): 26.

4979. Prayer for a New Daughter. Fasel, I. GH 148 (5/59): 120.

4980. Prayer for Cowards. Werner, H.C. GH 148 (1/59): 151.

4981. Prayer for Peace. Patrick, J.G. CC 72 (11/16/55): 1335.

4982. A Prayer for the South. Nash, A. CC 73 (4/4/56): 416.

4983. A Prayer for the United Nations. Ferry, A.J. CC 73 (10/17/56): 1193.

4984. Prayer, for the Useless Days. Pierce, E.L. CC 73 (11/21/56): 1356.

4985. Prayer for an Aged Man. Davidson, L. CC 74 (1/2/57): 7.

4986. A Prayer of Gratitude. Hager, W.H. CC 75 (8/6/58): 900.

4987. Precarious Serene. Walton, E.L. N 185 (9/7/57): 115.

4988. Preferred Treatment. Smith, L.C. SEP 229 (9/15/56): 77.

4989. Pregnancy. Kock, K. P 87 (2/56): 259-62.

4990. Pregnant Woman. Butler, D. P 94 (6/59): 176.

4991. Prelude. Avison, M. P 93 (3/59): 366-8.

4992. Prelude. Pillin, W. N 185 (9/21/57): 182.

4993. A Prelude For the Feast of St. Agnes. Merton, T. Co 63 (12/23/55): 304.

4994. Premonition at Twilight. Levine, P. C 26 (12/58): 533.

4995. A Prenatal Prayer. Finks, J.W. TH 33 (4/55): 38.

4996. The Preparation. Logan, J. SR 39 (5/5/56): 24.

4997. Preparing for a Love Nest on the Plains. De Jong, D.C. P 91 (10/57): 14.

4998. The Presence of Their Honor. Singer, H. P 87 (2/56): 294.

4999. Present Tension. Blackwell, P.J. SEP 229 (6/29/57): 34.

5000. A Presentation of Two Birds to My Son. Wright, J. P 85 (1/55): 198-9.

5001. A Pretty Girl. Dugan, A. SR 39 (8/18/56): 12.

5002. Pretty Words. Wylie, E. EJ 46 (3/57): 160.

5003. The Price of Leisure. Richstone, M. SEP 227 (2/19/55): 102.

5004. The Pride of Life. Jennings, E. N 186 (4/26/58): 362.

5005. The Pride of the Morning. Jones, T.H. P 85 (2/55): 264.

5006. Priest to Certain Penitents. Roseliep, R. A 94 (12/31/55): 379.

5007. Primary Notion. Morgan, F. P 94 (4/59): 32.

5008. A Primer of the Daily Round. Nemerov, H. NY 33 (10/12/57): 46.

5009. Primitive Art. Hicks, J.C. BHG 33 (2/55): 169.

5010. The Principal Part of a Python. Ciardi, J. LHJ 72 (12/55): 31.

5011. Principles of Flight. Clower, J. P 93 (10/58): 6-7.

5012. The Prior Buyer. Talman, T. SEP 229 (12/15/56): 97.

5013. Prismatic Psyche. Tyler, P. P 88 (6/56): 149.

5014. The Prisoner of War Returns Through the Underground. Vance, T. P 87 (1/56): 192-6.

5015. Prisoners. Kabir, H. P 93 (1/59): 220.

5016. Private and Profane. Ponsot, M. P 90 (6/57): 134-5.

5017. The Private Meeting Place. Wright, J. NY 34 (1/3/59): 28.

5018. Private Pantomime. Stone, R. P 89 (1/57): 213.

5019. A Private World. Roditi, E. P 94 (6/59): 177.

5020. Prize Hen. Grenville, R.H. SEP 230 (4/26/58): 117.

5021. A Problem in History. Wallace, R.A. NY 33 (6/11/57): 28.

5022. Problem in June. Redman, P.D. SEP 231 (6/6/59): 71.

5023. A Problem in Morals. Moss, H. N 184 (6/1/57): 486.

5024. Processional. Catheron, L. At 197 (6/56): 64.

5025. Prodigal Son. Coxe, L.O. P 86 (6/55): 155.

5026. A Professor Goes Fishing. Ellis, C. SEP 228 (5/5/56): 84.

5027. Professor X: Composite Portrait. Ryskind, A.H. NaR 2 (9/8/56): 9.

5028. The Professor's Farewell. Mary Jeremy, Sr. SR 38 (6/4/55): 38.

5029. Profit and Loss. Smith, N. SEP 228 (5/12/56): 131.

5030. Prognosis. Starbuck, G. NR 138 (2/10/58): 19.

5031. Progress. Bentley, E. N 185 (11/16/57): 366.

5032. Progress. Eisenlohr, L. SEP 231 (10/11/58): 71.

5033. Progress in Poverty. Seifer, D. GH 149 (8/59): 53.

5034. Progressive Education. Royster, S. EJ 46 (1/57): 31.

5035. Progressive School: Fourth Grade. Ryskind, M. NaR 39 (5/4/57): 427.

5036. A Projection. Whittemore, R. YR 45 (12/55): 249-51.

5037. Proletarian Pastorales. Riddle, M. N 185 (12/28/57): 502.

5038. Prologue at Midnight. Merwin, W.S. N 186 (2/22/58): 164.

5039. Promises. Warren, R.P. YR 46 (3/57): 321-40.

5040. Prompt Pardon. Galbraith, G.S. SEP 230 (11/2/57): 76.

5041. Proof of My Tact. Jaffray, N.R. SEP 230 (5/3/58): 55.

5042. The Property of Saint Jerome. Swartz, R.T. SR 40 (10/5/57): 24.

5043. Property Rights. Schlitzer, S. SEP 229 (6/15/57): 70.

5044. A Prophecy for Pedestrians. Schneider, E.F. A 101 (8/22/59): 632.

5045. The Prophet. Ratliff, H.,Jr. CC 74 (1/9/57): 42.

5046. The Prophet Announces. Shapiro, H. C 23 (1/57): 10.

5047. The Prophets. Richardson, D.L. CC 72 (5/18/55): 594.

5048. Proserpine. Freeman, J.T. LHJ 72 (4/55): 91.

5049. The Prospect. Mullins, T.Y. CC 75 (7/30/58): 875.

5050. Protest. Burket, G.B. TH 34 (9/56): 46.

5051. Protest. Burket, G.B. TH 35 (10/57): 47.

5052. Proteus. Hillyer, R. NY 32 (2/9/57): 99.

5053. Prothalamium. Morris, H. P 90 (4/57): 19-20.

5054. Proud Steps. Feighny, G.F. GH 142 (4/56): 164.

5055. Provision. Winchester, C.W. CC 73 (11/28/56): 1387.

5056. Pruning Vines. Todd, R. AS 28 (Wint/58-59): 60.

5057. A Psalm. Merton, T. Co 69 (10/24/58): 89.

5058. A Psalm for the Magi. Muldoon, R.J. A 98 (12/21/57): 375.

5059. The Psalm of Comfort. Wood, M.A. CC 74 (5/15/57): 616.

5060. Psalm of Love. Facos, J. SEP 230 (1/4/58): 67.

5061. The Psychoanalyst. Jones, H.M. At 203 (1/59): 89.

5062. Psychoemantics. Feinstein, H. AI 14 (Wint/57): 344.

5063. Public Nuisance. Jacobson, E. SEP 232 (12/19/59): 89.

5064. Publius Vergilius Maro, the Madison Avenue Hick. Updike, J. NY 32 (3/31/56): 32.

5065. Puerto Rico Song. Williams, W.C. NY 33 (9/14/57): 94.

5066. Pup at a Parade. Bellows, S.B. SEP 227 (5/21/55): 123.

5067. The Pure Passion. Laing, D. N 187 (9/27/58): 175.

5068. Purely Nominal. Elmer, I. At 196 (11/55): 104.

5069. The Puritan Conflict. Henley, E. P 86 (6/55): 162-7.

5070. Le Puritain et La Putain. Bogardus, E. P 91 (12/57): 160-2.

5071. Purity. Whittemore, R. N 187 (12/6/58): 432.

5072. Pursuit. Plath, S. At 199 (1/57): 65.

5073. Pursuit of Happiness. Dewhurst, S.H. SEP 227 (3/12/55): 48.

5074. Put It This Way. Jones, F.P. SEP 228 (1/14/56): 63.

5075. Put It This Way. Jones, F.P. SEP 228 (1/21/56): 110.

5076. Put Me Into the Breach. Karni, Y. P 92 (7/57): 210.

5077. Put on Guard. Char, R. P 89 (3/57): 335.

5078. Put-Out. Philbrick, C. SR 42 (5/30/59): 17.

5079. The Puzzler. Nash, O. L 39 (9/5/55): 88.

5080. Pygmalion. Friend, R. SR 40 (10/19/57): 53.

5081. The Pyromaniac. Porter, F. P 85 (3/55): 325.

5082. Quae Lucis Miseris Tam Dira Cupido? Dickey, W.H. P 85 (3/55): 333-5.

5083. Quand Meme. Carrier, C. AS 28 (Summ/59): 356.

5084. Quand Verrai- Je Les Iles.... Jammes, F. P 89 (12/56): 156.

5085. The Quarrel of the Mountain with the Wood. Ginsberg, L. CH 32 (5/58): 537.

5086. The Quarter. Cassity, T. P 89 (3/57): 361.

5087. The Queen of Sheba Says Farewell. Mueller, L. NY 34 (5/24/58): 38.

5088. Queen's Summer Song. Bennett, P.A. At 202 (8/58): 63.

5089. Query. Turnoy, B. P 93 (10/58): 72.

5090. Query: To Cornelia. Rittell, H. GH 140 (4/55): 16.

5091. The Quest. Cumin, M.W. GH 141 (9/55): 103.

5092. Question. Culbert, A.C. LHJ 75 (5/58): 112.

5093. Question Heir. Gaskill, M. BHG 34 (3/56): 280.

5094. Question of Light. Sullivan, A.M. A 94 (12/10/55): 306.

5095. Question of Survival. Tobin, J.E. A 93 (9/17/55): 594.

5096. The Questioner. Lipton, L. At 201 (3/58): 53.

5097. Questions for Us and Coronado. Scott, W.T. P 97 (2/56): 268.

5098. Questions of Travel. Bishop, E. NY 31 (1/21/56): 40.

5099. The Quick and the Dead. Johnson, L. P 87 (2/56): 272-3.

5100. Quick Change. Domoff, J. BHG 33 (4/55): 344.

5101. Quilt. Updike, J. NY 33 (11/16/57): 54.

5102. Quit Kidding, Dear! Chadwick, H. SEP 230 (10/11/57): 125.

5103. The Quiz. Goodreau, W.J. Co 68 (7/4/58): 347.

5104. Quomodo Sola Sedet Civitas. Carroll, P. P 88 (7/56): 230-1.

5105. Quota. Richstone, M. SEP 229 (5/4/57): 42.

5106. Rachel. Clark, L.S. CC 72 (11/9/55): 1301.

5107. A Rack of Paperbacks. Updike, J. NY 33 (3/23/57): 124.

5108. Radiated Man. Jacobsen, J. Co 68 (8/1/58): 442.

5109. The Radical. Caton, P.W. CC 73 (10/31/56): 1263.

5110. Radio. O'Hara, F. P 87 (3/56): 344.

5111. The Radio Under the Bed. Whittemore, R. NY 34 (7/19/58): 45.

5112. The Raft. Lloyd, D. AS 25 (Wint/55-56): 36-7.

5113. Raftery. Colum, P. P 94 (6/59): 180-1.

5114. Ragout Robert. Lee, M. GH 149 (7/59): 108.

5115. Rain. Armour, R. BHG 33 (4/55): 138.

5116. The Rain. Blevins, H. Hn 32 (8/56): 277.

5117. Rain. Ciardi, J. LHJ 76 (2/59): 19.

5118. The Rain. Creeley, R. N 189 (11/14/59): 363.

5119. Rain. Levine, R. SR 39 (5/5/56): 23.

5120. Rain. Moss, H. NY 32 (8/25/56): 36.

5121. Rain. Nabokov, V. NY 32 (4/21/56): 43.

5122. Rain. Nishiwaki, J. P 88 (5/56): 75.

5123. Rain Before Noon. Burger, O.K. NY 33 (4/13/57): 104.

5124. Rain Crow. Berry, W. P 89 (2/57): 291-2.

5125. Rain in Jackson Heights. Humphries, R. P 90 (9/57): 370.

5126. The Rain in Spain. Reid, A. NY 34 (6/28/58): 68.

5127. A Rain-Like Costume. Horiguchi, D. At 195 (1/55): 107.

5128. A Rain Song. Scollard, C. GH 140 (1/55): 28.

5129. Rain Talk. Landeweer, E. SEP 227 (3/19/55): 97.

5130. The Rainbow. Landers, D. Hn 32 (8/56): 276.

5131. Rainbow, Rainbow.... Fleming, H. P 95 (12/59): 162.

5132. Rainfall on 'The Puritans'. Masters, M. P 88 (7/56): 222.

5133. Rainy Season. Blackwell, H.G. SEP 227 (6/25/55): 55.

5134. Range Calf. Landeweer, E. SEP 228 (5/19/56): 82.

5135. Raphael Archangel. Maris Stella, Sr. A 99 (4/26/58): 144.

5136. Rapunzel! Rapunzel! Ellis, C. GH 141 (9/56): 103.

5137. Rapunzel, Rapunzel, Let's Down Our Hair. Nash, O. NY 33 (3/16/57): 32.

5138. Raspberry Canes. Riggs, D.C. LHJ 76 (3/59): 153.

5139. A Rat of Rabit. Witt, H. NR 140 (6/15/59): 20.

5140. Rat Race. Blagden, R. NY 33 (11/23/57): 156.

5141. Ratio. Kessler, S. SR 40 (11/2/57): 17.

5142. The Raying Fog. Witt, H. NR 137 (12/6/57): 19.

5143. Re--. Duncan, R. P 91 (3/58): 382.

5144. The Reactionary. Sellers, R.Z. LJ 83 (3/1/58): 713.

5145. Reactionary History. Nemerov, H. N 183 (11/10/56): 414.

5146. Reading Dante With Ionians. O'Gorman, N. Co 71 (10/16/59): 70.

5147. Reading Rousset's L'Univers Concentrationnaire'. Feldman, I. C 25 (4/58): 305.

5148. Ready Remark. Wheeler, R. SEP 229 (5/25/57): 50.

5149. Real, False, Cultured. Raiziss, S. SR 42 (9/5/59): 17.

5150. Real Name. Bonnefoy, Y. At 201 (6/58): 54.

5151. Reality. Smith, H.A. CC 74 (5/22/57): 648.

5152. Reappraisal. Coblentz, S.A. CC 73 (1/25/56): 107.

5153. Reasonable Answer to a Reasonable Question. Richstone, D. and M. SEP 232 (12/5/59): 62.

5154. The Rebel. Adib, A. At 198 (10/56): 141.

5155. The Rebel. Galbraith, G.S. SEP 230 (1/18/58): 53.

5156. A Rebel. Stepanchev, S. N 184 (5/11/57): 428.

5157. Rebirth. Thornton, M.B. SR 42 (3/14/59): 20.

5158. Recess Ended. Hopkins, F. SEP 227 (3/26/55): 63.

5159. Recipe for Mystery Writing. Thompson, D.B. SEP 229 (6/15/57): 113.

5160. Reciprocal. Mergard, J. SEP 229 (3/16/57): 137.

5161. Reciprocal. Richstone, M. SEP 230 (6/28/58): 91.

5162. Recital. Baker, D.W. P 91 (3/58): 370.

5163. Recital. Merrill, H. SEP 229 (10/6/56): 124.

5164. The Recluse. Haag, J. NY 33 (12/14/57): 140.

5165. The Recognition. Wagoner, D. P 92 (5/58): 70.

5166. Recollection of a Very Young Oracle. Galbraith, G.S. SEP 229 (4/6/57): 134.

5167. Recollections of Gulliver: The Inquiring Reporter in Lilliput. Atherton, J. AS 28 (Wint/58-59): 21-4.

5168. Recollections of Octobers. Langland, J. SR 40 (8/10/57): 37.

5169. Recovery. Thomas, A. At 199 (2/57): 52.

5170. Recovery Discovery. Emmons, D. SEP 230 (1/18/58): 89.

5171. Red and Brown. Colvin, F. LHJ 72 (11/55): 120.

5172. Red and White. Root, M.E. NaR 2 (8/1/56): 12.

5173. Red and White Television. Kelly, R.S. SR 42 (6/6/59): 36.

5174. Redbird in the South. Freneau, I.D. SEP 230 (11/9/57): 130.

5175. Redbird: Late Winter. Hess, M.W. SEP 229 (2/9/57): 93.

5176. Redeemable in Full. Congdon, T. SEP 230 (1/4/58): 76.

5177. Reed Jarnagin. Stokely, J. N 182 (5/12/56): 404.

5178. Reeds. Tomlinson, C. P 88 (9/56): 351.

5179. Reel. Updike, J. NY 34 (5/3/58): 133.

5180. The Reference Librarian. Foss, S.W. LJ 84 (12/15/59): 3827.

5181. Reflection. Stafford, W. LHJ 74 (3/57): 186.

5182. Reflection. Workman, M.T. CC 72 (9/21/55): 1088.

5183. Reflection on the Date of a Book: October 26. Logan, J. P 88 (9/56): 368-9.

5184. Reflection on the Innate Fairness of Words. Edwards, B. NaR 6 (3/14/59): 590.

5185. Reflections. Tomlinson, C. P 88 (9/56): 350-1.

5186. Reflections in a Slum. MacDiarmid, H. N 184 (3/2/57): 193.

5187. Reflections of a Busy Mother. Pasley, L.F. TH 34 (6/56): 34.

5188. Reflections on Christmas. Sansone, E. M 87 (12/59): 131.

5189. Reflections on Guernsey. Mary Madeleine Sophie, Sr. A 93 (5/7/55): 156.

5190. Refusal. Burrowes, E. CC 72 (9/14/55): 1054.

5191. Refusal for Heaven. McGahey, J. P 93 (11/58): 79-81.

5192. A Refusal to Mourn, Etc. Frankenberg, L. H 216 (1/58): 47.

5193. Regard the Roach. Fleischer, L. At 201 (3/58): 107.

5194. Regarding the Ash-Tray Attitude of a Certain Hostess. Otis, A. SEP 232 (10/24/59): 98.

5195. Regardless. Love, A. SEP 232 (8/28/59): 77.

5196. Regards the Changes. Hedden, M. AS 26 (Sum/57): 314.

5197. Regents of the Night. D., H. P 94 (5/59): 71-3.

5198. Rehabilitation Center. Kumin, M.W. SR 42 (9/19/59): 42.

5199. The Reign in Spain. Sagittarius. NR 139 (7/7/58): 10.

5200. Relative. Huhn, J. BHG 33 (9/55): 259.

5201. Relatively Speaking. Galbraith, G.S. SEP 229 (10/6/56): 128.

5202. Relaxation. Lister, R.P. At 201 (1/58): 87.

5203. Release. Graham, E. LHJ 74 (5/57): 131.

5204. The Release. Keith, J.J. A 101 (8/22/59): 635.

5205. Relic. Hughes, T. H 217 (11/58): 36.

5206. Religious Articles. Hall, D. SR 40 (12/28/57): 6.

5207. Reluctant Host. Jaffray, N.R. SEP 228 (7/30/55): 92.

5208. Remarkable Mutation. Galbraith, G.S. SEP 229 (12/1/56): 131.

5209. Remarks from the Man on the Stein End at the Second Carry. Van Keuren, W.G. NY 33 (9/21/57): 118.

5210. Remarks on the Occasion of Love. Hall, D. SR 40 (7/20/57): 16.

5211. Remember? Anthony, E. GH 142 (7/56): 142.

5212. Remembering John Marin. Nichols, D. NR 134 (6/25/56): 19.

5213. Remembrance for Rosemary. Mounts, C.E. LHJ 72 (1/55): 114.

5214. Remembrance of Beginnings of Things. Goldberg, L. P 92 (7/58): 239.

5215. Reminder. Kessler, S. SR 40 (1/26/57): 17.

5216. Reminder from the Recipient. Lazarus, P. SEP 229 (11/3/56): 109.

5217. Reminder in September. Spring, A.T. SEP 231 (9/20/58): 56.

5218. Remorse. Jaffray, N.R. SEP 229 (11/24/56): 147.

5219. Remorse in Our Time. Weaver, B. CC 72 (3/30/55): 391.

5220. Rendezvous. Facos, J. SEP 228 (7/30/55): 94.

5221. Rendezvous. Jacobson, E. SEP 229 (8/18/56): 44.

5222. Renegades. Coblentz, S.A. CC 72 (10/12/55): 1169.

5223. The Renewal. Roethke, T. NY 34 (4/26/58): 103.

5224. Renoir Girl. Mills, B. N 189 (8/29/59): 94.

5225. The Rented Garden. Nall, B. N 187 (10/11/58): 216.

5226. Repeat--and Present. Schnitzer, S. SEP 228 (2/11/56): 64.

5227. Repentance. Colby, W.H. CT 2 (8/18/58): 12.

5228. Reply to Demonic Assult. Cully, K.B. CC 76 (1/28/59): 105.

5229. Report Retort. Merchant, J. SEP 229 (11/24/56): 135.

5230. Repose. Delattre, P.H. CC 76 (6/17/59): 721.

5231. Representing Far Places. Stafford, W. N 187 (12/20/58): 483.

5232. Request for a Little Miracle. Bowser, I.W. SEP 227 (5/28/55): 81.

5233. Request for Quiet. Engle, J.D.,Jr. SEP 229 (12/8/56): 124.

5234. Requiem. Hurshman, R. N 183 (9/8/56): 204.

5235. Requiem. Merrill, H. SEP 230 (10/19/57): 100.

5236. Requiem for a Nun. L'Heureux, J. Co 70 (6/19/59): 304.

5237. Requiem for an Abstract Artist. Kessler, J. P 89 (2/57): 293-4.

5238. A Requiem for Hungary. Ciardi, J. N 184 (4/27/57): 363.

5239. Requiem to the Remains of Library Books. Ringstad, M. WLB 31 (1/57): 380.

5240. Rescue Party. Cassin, M. NR 136 (2/18/57): 17.

5241. The Reservoir. Adler, L. N 184 (2/9/57): 123.

5242. Residue. Galbraith, G.S. LHJ 74 (6/57): 201.

5243. Resolution. Pomeroy, R. P 93 (2/59): 304-5.

5244. Respite. Marshall, L.G. AS 25 (Summ/56): 330.

5245. Responsibilities. Hoskins, K. YR 47 (3/58): 416-9.

5246. Responsibility. Burket, G.B. CC 72 (4/6/55): 423.

5247. Rest Period. Galbraith, G.S. SEP 230 (2/15/58): 110.

5248. Resume. Rosenthal, M.S. N 187 (7/19/58): 35.

5249. Resurrection. McCoy, C.S. CC 74 (11/20/57): 1380.

5250. The Resurrection of Animals. O'Gorman, N. P 88 (6/56): 163-4.

5251. Retired. Merchant, J. SEP 232 (12/12/59): 58.

5252. Retired Colonel. Vesely, R.S. SEP 227 (4/30/55): 122.

5253. Retired Missionary. Collier, M.D. SEP 231 (3/14/59): 64.

5254. Retort. Hall, F. SEP 229 (2/9/57): 112.

5255. Retort While Shoveling Snow. Goodman, M.W. SEP 230 (1/4/58): 44.

5256. Retreat Poems. Caedman, Sr. A 95 (9/15/56): 563.

5257. Retribution. Coblentz, S.A. CC 75 (6/25/58): 746.

5258. Return from Bethlehem. Burrowes, E. CC 73 (1/11/56): 43.

5259. The Return from Nontauk. Howard, R. NY 36 (10/13/56): 132.

5260. A Return from the Wars. Bock, F. YR 45 (6/56): 562.

5261. Return Mail. Eisenlohr, L. SEP 231 (10/18/58): 110.

5262. The Return of Odysseus. Kazantzakis, N. At 195 (6/55): 110-12.

5263. Return of the Lover. Bowen, D. P 88 (4/56): 23.

5264. Return of the Native. Rorty, J. H 216 (4/58): 57.

5265. Return to Earth. Green, F.P. NY 32 (6/9/56): 131.

5266. Return to Love. Carruth, H. N 188 (5/9/59): 432.

5267. Return to Strangeness. Laing, D. SR 38 (7/2/55): 20.

5268. The Returner. Hart, R.L. P 87 (3/56): 332-33.

5269. Returning to Roots of First Feeling. Duncan, R. P 95 (10/59): 35.

5270. Reunion. Thomas, M.M. SEP 228 (5/26/56): 123.

5271. Reunion Recollected. Swan, J. NY 33 (12/28/57): 57.

5272. Rev. Alfred J. Barrett, S.J. Fitzgerald, J.E. A 94 (11/26/55): 227.

5273. Reveille. Facos, J. SEP 228 (6/23/56): 103.

5274. The Revelation. D., H. N 185 (8/31/57): 94.

5275. Revelation. Isler, B. SEP 231 (10/25/58): 133.

5276. Revelation. Zawadsky, P. SEP 228 (10/1/55): 104.

5277. Revelation According to the Beloved. Stock, R. P 92 (4/58): 13.

5278. Revenge. Congdon, T. SEP 230 (2/22/58): 57.

5279. Reverse Allure. Blackwell, H.G. SEP 230 (5/24/58): 102.

5280. Reverse Harvest. Kelley, R.S. SEP 228 (8/27/55): 84.

5281. The Reviewer to Himself. Rosenthal, M.L. N 189 (11/14/59): 358.

5282. Revisited Waters. Watkins, V. P 92 (6/58): 147-8.

5283. A Revolution of Grandmothers. Lister, R.P. SR 39 (11/24/56): 23.

5284. Rewards in the First Grade. Hartich, A. LHJ 75 (10/58): 180.

5285. A Rhinoceros and a Lion. Maruyama, K. P 88 (5/56): 91.

5286. Rhyme for April. Gordon, R. SR 39 (4/14/56): 58.

5287. A Rhyme Without a Moral. Akins, Z. LHJ 75 (7/58): 96.

5288. Rhymers Mein Grossfader Made: Ein Oldischer Frau. Morrah, D. SEP 229 (6/8/57): 46.

5289. Rice Pounding Songs. Zaw, U.K. At 201 (2/58): 125.

5290. Rich Boy's Birthday Through a Window. Avison, M. P 91 (12/57): 175.

5291. Richard in England. Moore, R. P 93 (11/58): 63-5.

5292. Richard Rolle's Lament for the Passion. Mary Jeremy, Sr. A 97 (9/14/57): 619.

5293. Riches. Eberhart, R. P 95 (10/59): 6-7.

5294. The Riddle. Friend, R. SR 39 (12/8/56): 48.

5295. Riddle Song for Tad. McFarland, E. LHJ 73 (9/56): 182.

5296. A Ride to the Sea. Duncan, R. P 90 (9/57): 354-5.

5297. Right on My Toes. Krausz, S. SEP 230 (7/20/57): 94.

5298. Rimbaud: On His Muse. Moran, M. At 196 (8/55): 68.

5299. Rimer, Penna. Merwin, W.S. H 215 (11/57): 72.

5300. The Ring in Grandfather's Nose. Nash, O. GH 142 (8/56): 39.

5301. A Ring of Changes. Levertov, D. P 94 (7/59): 240-4.

5302. Ring out the Old, Ring in the New, But Don't Get Caught in Between. Nash, O. NY 32 (12/29/56): 28.

5303. Rioting for a Fall. Neely, L. SEP 228 (10/8/55): 76.

5304. Riposte. Neame, A. P 91 (2/58): 317.

5305. Rise and Shine. Lattimore, R. NY 33 (4/6/57): 29.

5306. The Risen Eyelid. Bagg, R. P 92 (9/58): 364-5.

5307. The Rites. Kumin, M.W. NY 33 (5/18/57): 67.

5308. Rites in October. Petrie, P. P 95 (12/59): 153.

5309. Ritournelle, Paris 1948. Ponsot, M. P 90 (6/57): 133-4.

5310. The River. Crews, J. P 91 (1/58): 239.

5311. The River Belle. Facos, J. SEP 227 (1/8/55): 76.

5312. River Daughter. Engle, P. NY 32 (5/19/56): 111.

5313. The River from the Bridge. Lee, C. SEP 232 (11/14/59): 54.

5314. A River to Cross. Perrings, M. SEP 231 (11/15/58): 99.

5315. The River Voyagers. Zaturenska, M. P 95 (11/59): 102.

5316. The River Was the Emblem of All Beauty: All. Schwartz, D. P 94 (5/59): 108.

5317. Rivers Are Not Patient in Duress. Boyle, R. SEP 227 (1/8/55): 75.

5318. The Road. Taylor, K.P.A. P 89 (10/56): 27-8.

5319. The Road Back. Sexton, A. NY 35 (8/29/59): 30.

5320. The Road from Emmaus. Cotter, J.F. A 99 (7/5/58): 391.

5321. Road Through Forest. Speer, C.A. SEP 228 (8/6/55): 96.

5322. Road to Spaakistan. Sagittarius. NR 138 (5/12/58): 8.

5323. Roadside Phone Booth. Moody, M.H. LHJ 75 (10/59): 132.

5324. Roarers in a Ring. Hughes, T. N 183 (12/22/56): 543.

5325. The Robin Tree. Merrill, H. SEP 231 (4/18/59): 66.

5326. Robin's Secret. Freeman, J.T. LHJ 72 (1/55): 17.

5327. Rock. Langland, J. SR 40 (2/29/57): 21.

5328. The Rock. Magaret, H. A 100 (12/6/58): 316.

5329. The Rock. Padgaonkar, M. P 93 (1/59): 238.

5330. Rock-and-Roll Session. McGinley, P. At 202 (11/58): 81.

5331. The Rock Pool. Barker, E. At 199 (4/57): 70.

5332. Rock Wren. Walton, E.L. P 91 (11/57): 87-8.

5333. Rocky Mountain Town. Dreyer, C.W. SEP 231 (5/59): 49.

5334. Roman Candle. Ames, B. SEP 228 (7/2/55): 90.

5335. The Roman Forum. Jennings, E. NY 34 (5/3/ 58): 36.

5336. Roman Ghetto. Norse, H. C 25 (2/58): 140-1.

5337. The Roman Soldier. Lattimore, R. NR 141 (9/ 28/59): 22.

5338. Romantic Lament. McCarthy, L. A 95 (6/30/ 56): 326.

5339. La Ronde. Sagittarius. NR 138 (4/28/58): 8.

5340. The Roofers. Hemschemeyer, J. At 202 (8/ 58): 61-2.

5341. Rooftrees. Colvin, F. SEP 229 (6/15/57): 109.

5342. Rooks. Feringhetti, L. N 84 (2/23/57): 160.

5343. The Room. Berg, S. P 91 (2/58): 309-10.

5344. The Room. Levertov, D. P 93 (10/58): 13.

5345. Room for Rent. Brandon, W. SEP 232 (10/17/ 59): 177.

5346. A Room in the Villa. Smith, W.J. NY 34 (1/ 7/56): 20.

5347. The Rooster and the Sun. Merrill, H. SEP 228 (4/56): 112.

5348. Root. Thornton, M.B. SR 38 (10/8/55): 16.

5349. Rooted. Lilly, O. CC 72 (6/1/55): 647.

5350. The Rose and the Body of the Rose. O'Gorman, N. P 86 (9/55): 345-6.

5351. The Rose and the Rod. Barker, G. P 88 (8/ 56): 288.

5352. The Rose and the Sun. Zitner, S. AS 24 Aut/55): 459.

5353. The Rose Is Both. Galbraith, G.S. LHJ 73 (7/56): 100.

5354. Roses for My Grandmother. Josephs, L. C 26 (12/58): 498.

5355. Rotten Log. Landeweer, E. SEP 230 (6/28/ 58): 120.

5356. Rotting Trees. Levine, P. C 27 (4/59): 316.

5357. A Rough Wall. Goodman, P. P 92 (9/58): 376.

5358. Rough Winds Do Shake the Darling Buds of May. Hiller, R. NY 33 (5/11/57): 146.

5359. Roundling. Pardue, I.M. BHG 37 (1/59): 96.

5360. Route. Dufault, P.K. NY 33 (11/16/57): 138.

5361. Route. Singleton, M.E. CC 74 (6/26/57): 786.

5362. The Routine. Blackburn, P. N 188 (4/25/59): 394.

5363. Routine. Richstone, M. SEP 229 (7/7/56): 77.

5364. Routine Assignment. Kessler, J. P 91 (3/ 58): 364.

5365. Rover Recumbent. Jacobson, E. At 196 (8/ 55): 91.

5366. The Roving Eye. Newbold, F. LHJ 76 (6/59): 32.

5367. Row. Pomeroy, R. NY 32 (9/22/56): 156.

5368. Ruach. Delattre, P.H. CC 75 (7/16/58): 829.

5369. Rubbish Heap by the Euphrates. Ackerson, J. CC 72 (1/26/55): 111.

5370. The Ruby Yacht of Paramount. Malcolm, D. and Winn, J. NR 137 (9/16/57): 19.

5371. Rude Awakening. Galbraith, G.S. BHG 34 (10/ 56): 105.

5372. Rued Awakening. Brown, J. SEP 232 (9/12/ 59): 105.

5373. Rueful Reflection. Chaffee, E.A. LHJ 73 (1/56): 59.

5374. Rules. Logue, C. H 218 (6/59): 71.

5375. The Run: A Parable for Tired Teachers. Montgomery, M. EJ 48 (1/59): 87.

5376. Runes. Nemerov, H. P 93 (2/59): 281-8.

5377. Running a Temperature. Woods, J. SR 41 (3/ 15/58): 63.

5378. Rural Night. Beyer, W. BHG 36 (7/58): 81.

5379. Rural Reflections. Rich, A. H 216 (3/58): 57.

5380. Ruth. Weiss, N. C 25 (1/58): 15.

5381. Rx. Schiff, L.K. TH 34 (7/56): 49.

5382. Rx for Joyce Cary. Van Horn, R.G. N 184 (5/11/57): 420.

5383. *S. Hammer, P. GH 142 (6/56): 119.

5384. S.P.Q.R.--A Letter from Rome. Ciardi, J. P 91 (2/58): 287-90.

5385. S.S. Tungus--Midnight. Richardson, D.L. CC 76 (12/16/59): 1469.

5386. The Sacred Wood. Laing, D. SR 40 (2/9/57): 48.

5387. The Sad Dragon. Steel, N. Hn 35 (4/59): 157.

5388. Sad-Libber. White, S. SEP 231 (4/4/59): 125.

5389. Safe. Jacobson, E. TH 35 (9/57): 58.

5390. Sage. Coblentz, S.A. CC 73 (4/18/56): 482.

5391. The Sage. Levertov, D. N 187 (11/1/58): 325.

5392. Sailboat at Sunset. Hicky, D.W. SEP 231 (5/30/59): 46.

5393. Sailboat, Your Secret. Francis, R. P 86 (7/55): 233.

5394. Sailing Away. Pasternak, Boris. NR 140 (5/ 4/59): 19.

5395. The Saint. Feldman, I. C 22 (12/56): 557.

5396. Saint. Richardson, D.L. CC 73 (3/28/56): 395.

5397. Saint Andrew. Magaret, H. A 100 (10/11/58): 43.

5398. St. Basil to the Elder Harmatius. Wolf, L. Co 66 (8/16/57): 494.

5399. St. Christopher. Bogan, L. AN 57 (9/58): 24.

5400. Saint Francis Borgia, or a Refutation for Heredity. McGinley, P. A 94 (1/28/56): 478.

5401. Saint Francis in the Square. Salomon, I.L. A 97 (9/14/57): 625.

5402. Saint John Baptist. Berrigan, D. P 94 (7/ 59): 231.

5403. Saint Joseph. Claudel, P. P 87 (12/55): 140.

5404. Saint Martin's Infirmary. Lynch, J.A. Co 70 (5/8/59): 148.

5405. St. Paul in Arabia. Janes, K. Co 70 (5/15/ 59): 183.

5406. St. Paul of the Epistles. Richardson, D.L. CC 73 (8/22/56): 969.

5407. St. Philip and the Martyrs of Japan. Logan, J. Co 68 (9/12/58): 586.

5408. Saint Sebastian. Merwin, W.S. H 211 (9/55): 85.

5409. St. Valentine's Day. Ericson, A. LHJ 73 (2/56): 173.

5410. Saints. Baro, G. P 92 (9/58): 355.

5411. Salamander. Merrill, H. SEP 231 (7/26/58): 44.

5412. The Salesman. Frumkin, G. SR 42 (9/19/59): 41.

5413. Salesmanship. Cooper, B.B. SEP 227 (5/14/ 55): 128.

5414. Salmon Run. Grenville, R.H. SEP 231 (9/20/ 58): 106.

5415. Salome. Merrill, J. P 87 (2/56): 295-7.

5416. The Same Old Cracked Tune. Mary Gilbert, Sr. A 102 (11/7/59): 156.

5417. Same Old Jazz. McGrath, T. P 86 (6/55): 156.

5418. Samela. Greene, R. Hb 63 (5/58): 129.

5419. Sanctuary. Bauer, G.L. TH 33 (5/55): 57.

5420. The Sandcastle. Drouet, M. LHJ 75 (8/58): 75.

5421. Sandpipers. Nemerov, H. NY 32 (8/4/56): 22.

5422. Sans Souci. Mueller, L. SR 40 (7/20/57): 16.

5423. Santa Without Strings. Sagittarius. NR 137 (12/23/57): 6.

5424. Sanvies Island. Stafford, W. SR 39 (11/17/56): 72.

5425. Sapphires. Goodman, M.W. SR 38 (2/5/55): 17.

5426. Sappho's Child. Wright, J. P 86 (9/55): 352.

5427. Sarabande. Nemerov, H. P 91 (11/57): 78.

5428. Sarah. Schwartz, D. C 27 (3/59): 222.

5429. Sartorial. Fadiman, C. SR 40 (6/1/57): 24.

5430. Satan on Economics. Belvin, W. P 89 (1/57): 219-20.

5431. Saturday Eight O'Clock. Roethke, T. LHJ 76 (11/59): 130.

5432. Saturday's Child. Hammer, P. H 218 (6/59): 77.

5433. The Satyrs. Williams, W.C. N 186 (5/31/58): 498-9.

5434. The Savage Flutes. Chapin, K.G. N 184 (6/8/57): 504.

5435. Saybrook Point. Burrows, E.G. At 197 (2/56): 49.

5436. Sayings from the Northern Ice. Stafford, W. P 88 (9/56): 363.

5437. Sayonara. White, G. LHJ 76 (1/59): 26.

5438. Scance Macabre. Kober, A. SEP 229 (6/22/57): 40.

5439. The Scar. Hillyer, R. NY 32 (12/29/56): 22.

5440. Scarecrow. Armour, R. SEP 231 (7/12/58): 66.

5441. Scarecrow in a Winter Field. Grenville, R. H. SEP 227 (1/15/55): 89.

5442. Scarecrow Trees. Jacobson, E. SEP 231 (6/13/59): 54.

5443. Scarred Earth. Clark, L.S. CC 74 (11/13/57): 1344.

5444. Scenario. Galler, D. N 187 (8/16/58): 79.

5445. Scenic. Updike, J. NY 33 (3/9/57): 94.

5446. Scenic Routes. Johnson, F. GH 148 (11/58): 13.

5447. The Scholars. Kenny, H.A. SR 41 (3/15/58): 60.

5448. School. Ginsberg, L. CH 30 (1/56): 285.

5449. School Bus. Freneau, I.D. SEP 227 (1/8/55): 50.

5450. The School of Life. Kreymborg, A. NR 135 (11/19/56): 20.

5451. School Performance. Isler, B. BHG 33 (5/55): 139.

5452. The School Play. Alleman, E.C. GH 142 (2/56): 43.

5453. School's in, School's Out. Mitchel, H. SEP 231 (1/3/59): 59.

5454. Scientific Fact. Wheeler, R. SEP 229 (1/26/57): 47.

5455. The Scientific Viewpoint. Schenck, H.,Jr. H 218 (5/59): 69.

5456. Scorned. Richstone, M. SEP 230 (4/5/58): 104.

5457. A Scot Dreams of Heaven. Johnson, H.W. SEP 227 (6/11/55): 154.

5458. Scrap Mettle. Raskin, A. GH 142 (11/56): 13.

5459. Screech Owl. Benet, L. SR 38 (10/22/55): 40.

5460. Screech Owl. Russo, L.I. SEP 227 (3/26/55): 124.

5461. Scrod Is Sliced Cod. Taylor, M. SEP 230 (10/12/57): 52.

5462. Scrolls. Winslow, A.G. H 213 (12/56): 62.

5463. Scrooge Rides Again. Nash, O. Hl 24 (12/58): front cover and 75.

5464. The Sea. Burgess, J. Hl 25 (12/59): 128.

5465. The Sea and the Secret. Byron, E. SEP 229 (4/6/57): 122.

5466. Sea Born. Landeweer, E. SEP 228 (6/23/56): 63.

5467. Sea Changes. Lattimore, R. P 88 (4/56): 13.

5468. Sea Gulls. Stefanile, F. P 91 (1/58): 235.

5469. The Sea Gulls.... Tagliabue, J. P 97 (2/56): 266.

5470. Sea Gulls on an English Cliff. Gibbs, B.R. SEP 227 (1/29/55): 101.

5471. Sea in October. Stewart, M.S. SEP 231 (10/18/58): 80.

5472. The Sea Lavender. Burford, W. P 95 (11/59): 77.

5473. Sea Mark. Frost, F. H 210 (3/55): 66.

5474. Sea Monster. Merwin, W.S. N 184 (4/13/57): 326.

5475. Sea of Baal, Sea of Mammon. Perse, St.-J. P 86 (7/55): 189-227.

5476. Sea Place. Bohm, E. SEP 229 (8/11/56): 55.

5477. Sea Trauma. Eaton, C.E. N 184 (1/5/57): 25.

5478. Sea Wife. Merwin, W.S. H 214 (2/57): 80.

5479. Seamarks. Perse, St.J. YR 44 (3/55): 389-40.

5480. The Searchers. Berkowitz, R. At 196 (8/55): 66.

5481. Seasalter. Sparshott, F. P 92 (6/58): 161-2.

5482. Seascape. Deutsch, B. NY 34 (5/31/58): 93.

5483. Seascape. Frezza, L. P 94 (8/59): 329.

5484. Seaside Golf. Betjeman, J. H 213 (7/56): 69.

5485. Seasonal Disturbance. Alkus, M. SEP 231 (9/13/58): 68.

5486. Season's Greetings. Cogley, J. Co 69 (12/26/58): 339.

5487. Season's Greetings, Etc. Swift, M.J. WLB 33 (12/58): 303.

5488. A Seated Figure. Hull, O.M. P 92 (9/58): 353.

5489. Second Chorus. Merrill, H. SEP 230 (5/3/58): 100.

5490. Second Coming. Moffitt, J. At 197 (4/56): 55.

5491. Second Dog. Smith, B.F. GH 142 (10/56): 13.

5492. The Second-Fated. Graves, R. NR 136 (1/7/57): 17.

5493. Second Winter. Plath, S. LHJ 75 (12/58): 143.

5494. Second Wonder. Nicholl, L.T. AS 24 (Aut/55): 456-7.

5495. The Secondary Players. Baro, G. P 92 (9/58): 356.

5496. The Secret. Bendre, D.R. P 93 (1/59): 265.

5497. Secret. Senge, M. P 88 (5/58): 76.

5498. The Secret Religionist. Grossman, A. P 90 (6/57): 144.

5499. The Sectarian. Burket, G.B. CC 72 (11/30/55): 1396.

5500. The Secular View. Bentley, E. N 185 (11/16/57): 366.

5501. Sediment. Lilly, O. CC 75 (6/4/58): 667.

5502. See Too the Morning Come. Strand, M. YR 48 (6/59): 560-1.

5503. Seeing-Eye Dog. Carlisle, T.J. SEP 231 (6/20/59): 88.

5504. Seek Haven. Zeldis, C. C 25 (1/58): 29.

5505. 'Seek Ye'. Clark, L.S. CC 72 (10/19/55): 1206.

5506. Seems Like We Must Be Somewhere Else. Levertov, D. P 93 (10/58): 12.

5507. Seen Some Years Later. Kreiser, M. LHJ 73 (10/56): 175.

5508. The Seer. Lilly, O. CC 74 (2/20/57): 232.

5509. The Seiners. Booth, P. P 88 (7/56): 241-2.

5510. A Seizure of Couplets. Galbraith, G.S. At 198 (11/56): 65.

5511. The Self and the Weather. Whittemore, R. N 188 (4/25/59): 380.

5512. The Self-Appointed. Golden, L. SEP 230 (9/14/57): 134.

5513. Self As an Eye. Squires, R. P 90 (5/57): 96.

5514. Self-Criticism (or Ultima Ratio). Sagittarius. NR 140 (1/26/59): 16.

5515. Self-Portraiture. Coblentz, S.A. CC 73 (11/14/56): 1327.

5516. A Semblance. Ignatow, D. P 93 (11/58): 83.

5517. Send Flowers. Galbraith, G.S. LHJ 73 (6/56): 53.

5518. Send Six Box Tops. White, S. SEP 231 (12/6/58): 90.

5519. Sendai Sequence. Kirkup, J. NY 35 (10/3/59): 46.

5520. A Sense of Hugging Oneself. Birnbaum, H. P 91 (3/58): 361.

5521. The Sensible Voyage. Saunders, J. NY 33 (3/16/57): 97.

5522. The Sensualist. Updike, J. NY 332 (2/16/57): 30.

5523. Sentiments. Richstone, M. SEP 228 (4/14/56): 188.

5524. Sentry. Delattre, P.H. Co 69 (3/27/59): 666.

5525. Separation. Carnicelli, T. LHJ 74 (6/57): 155.

5526. September Afternoon. Carpenter, M.H. GH 142 (9/56): 46.

5527. September Grasses. Thompson, D.B. SEP 230 (9/14/57): 104.

5528. The Septic Pencil. Peters, H.J. CH 32 (3/58): 410.

5529. Sequence. Kahn, H. LHJ 73 (5/56): 50.

5530. Serenade. Bentley, G. SR 39 (6/2/56): 4.

5531. Serenade in Black. Berry, W. P 91 (3/58): 360.

5532. Serenity Is Not Enough. Bartlett, F. WLB 32 (9/57): 43.

5533. A Serious Case. Van Duyn, M. P 93 (12/58): 140-4.

5534. A Sermon. Ciardi, J. LHJ 75 (2/58): 154.

5535. Sermon for Today. Elmer, F.D.,Jr. CC 73 (5/9/56): 583.

5536. Sermon of Our Century. Elmer, F.D.,Jr. CC 75 (11/26/58): 1365.

5537. Serpent's Teeth. Galbraith, G.S. LHJ 72 (7/55): 122.

5538. Service Rendered. Swift, M.J. LJ 84 (3/15/59): 1573.

5539. Services. Stefanile, F. P 94 (9/59): 382.

5540. Sestina. Bishop, E. NY 32 (9/15/56): 46.

5541. Sestina at the Sea. Sylvester, W. P 92 (9/58): 362-3.

5542. A Sestina for Georges de La Tour. Todd, R. AN 58 (3/59): 45.

5543. A Set of Seasons. Hall, D. AS 26 (Aut/57): 416.

5544. Setting-Up Exercises. Talman, T. SEP 228 (7/16/55): 86.

5545. Seven Poems for Marthe, My Wife. Rexroth, K. P 89 (10/56): 1-8.

5546. Seven Streams of Nevis. Kinnell, G. P 90 (9/57): 346-9.

5547. Seven-Tenths Cloud. Dicker, H. N 84 (2/16/57): 145.

5548. Seven Times One Are Seven. Hillyer, R. At 204 (9/59): 48.

5549. Seventeen. Galbraith, G.S. LHJ 73 (12/56): 159.

5550. The Seventeen-Year Locusts. Clark, D.C. AS 28 (Spr/59): 151.

5551. The Shad. Nash, O. HG 111 (5/57): 41.

5552. Shadow Dancer. Jacobson, E. SR 38 (3/19/55): 16.

5553. Shadowbrook Revisited. McCarthy, L. A 95 (7/14/56): 365.

5554. Shadows. Coblentz, S.A. CC 72 (12/28/55): 1523.

5555. Shadows. Stuart, J. AF 64 (9/58): 24.

5556. Shadows in the Air. Krolow, K. At 199 (3/57): 171.

5557. Shag. Booth, P. P 88 (7/56): 240-1.

5558. Shakuhachi and Samisen. Lister, R.P. NY 34 (1/24/59): 99.

5559. Shall I Compare Thee to a Summer's Day? Moss, H. C 22 (11/56): 447.

5560. The Shampoo. Bishop, E. NR 133 (7/11/55): 19.

5561. The Shape of Death. Swenson, M. N 181 (8/27/55): 181.

5562. The Shape of Things. Warsaw, I. SEP 231 (3/21/59): 87.

5563. Shape of Things to Come. Congdon, T. SEP 232 (9/26/59): 101.

5564. Share My World. Johnson, G.D. NHB 21 (4/58): 152.

5565. Shared Joy. Burket, G.B. CC 73 (8/29/56): 991.

5566. She. Wilbur, R. At 202 (11/58): 42.

5567. She Has a Way of Putting Things. Anthony, E. GH 142 (6/56): 132.

5568. She Is Asleep. Carmi, T. P 92 (7/58): 258.

5569. Sheepshape. Dodson, S. SEP 228 (6/16/56): 56.

5570. The Shell. Merchant, J. SEP 228 (6/30/56): 91.

5571. The Shellpicker. Perry, R. P 93 (2/59): 295-6.

5572. Shells. Nemerov, H. N 182 (5/19/56): 436.

5573. Shelter. Derwood, G. P 85 (2/55): 270.

5574. Sheltered by Your Light. Kahn, H. GH 148 (4/59): 142.

5575. Shepherd. Stafford, W. P 91 (1/58): 249.

5576. Shepherd Song. Hicks, J.V. SEP 231 (12/20/58): 49.

5577. Shepherds at Advent. Crites, S. CC 76 (11/25/59): 1370.

5578. The Shield. Weiss, T. P 91 (12/57): 170-1.

5579. Shiloh's Seed. Thomas, D. P 87 (11/55): 87-9.

5580. The Shimmer of Evil. Roethke, T. NR 133 (8/29/55): 19.

5581. Shine on, Little Wife. Armour, R. GH 149 (9/59): 14.

5582. Shipboard Dance. Miner, V.S. LHJ 74 (11/57): 127.

5583. The Shipwreck. Masefield, J. At 202 (11/58): 54-7.

5584. Shipwreck. Merwin, W.S. P 87 (3/56): 330-1.

5585. A Shirt-Silk from Havana. Morris, H. P 90 (4/57): 18-9.

5586. Shoal. Delattre, P.H. CC 76 (7/15/59): 828.

5587. Shoppers at a Clearance Sale. Fuller, E.R. SEP 229 (2/23/57): 98.

5588. Shopping Fatigue. Collins, I.J. SEP 229 (4/27/57): 137.

5589. Shore Line. Weaver, B. CC 73 (1/25/56): 104.

5590. Short Cut. Gleason, H.W. SEP 229 (1/5/57): 34.

5591. Short History. Weismiller, E. At 203 (3/59): 64.

5592. Short History of a Peace-Lover. McGinley, P. At 201 (3/58): 105.

5593. Short Short Story. Balch, B.J. LHJ 75 (9/58): 36.

5594. Shovel Dinosaur. Waring, R.L. SEP 229 (4/27/57): 85.

5595. Show Us the Father and It Sufficeth Us. Richardson, D.L. CC 72 (1/12/55): 49.

5596. The Shroud of Turin. Cotter, J.F. A 99 (7/5/58): 390.

5597. Sibling Hostility. Herschberger, R. N 185 (11/23/57): 392.

5598. The Sibyl. Golffing, F. P 93 (11/58): 85.

5599. The Sibyl. La Bombard, J. P 92 (5/58): 89-90.

5600. Sic Semper Mr. Sherman's Temper. Nash, O. NY 32 (12/15/56): 34.

5601. Sic Transit Gloria Mundi! Sweet, A.P. WLB 31 (4/57): 643.

5602. Sicily. Iqbal, M. P 93 (1/59): 233-4.

5603. Sick. Engle, P. P 86 (8/55): 274.

5604. Sickbed. Asher, E. P 94 (9/59): 378.

5605. Side Glances Along the Way. Smith, J. GH 148 (6/57): 13.

5606. Sidewalk Superintendents. Appel, W. SEP 227 (5/21/55): 154.

5607. Sierras. Jacobsen, E. SEP 228 (1/7/56): 84.

5608. Sigh of a Gardener's Wife. Merchant, J. SEP 229 (5/4/57): 95.

5609. Sight Unseen. Seager, R.W. SEP 232 (8/15/59): 43.

5610. The Sign. Eckman, F. P 90 (6/57): 158.

5611. Signal. Blackburn, P. N 186 (6/14/58): 548.

5612. The Signs. Dickey, J. P 94 (7/59): 215-8.

5613. Signs. Hite, W.G. At 199 (5/57): 91.

5614. Signs for Travelers. Johnson, W.R. P 86 (9/55): 329.

5615. Signs of Civilization. Seuss, Dr. SR 40 (1/26/57): 6.

5616. Signs of the Times. Bryan, R. WLB 33 (11/58): 225.

5617. Silence. Pomeroy, R. P 89 (2/57): 287.

5618. Silence Spoke with Your Voice. Goodman, R.T. At 203 (1/59): 61.

5619. Silent Partner. Romine, R. TH 36 (3/58): 41.

5620. The Silent Women. Kennedy, M. LHJ 75 (4/58): 102.

5621. Silently He Hung. Unruh, S. CC 73 (4/4/56): 422.

5622. Silhouette. Graham, E. LHJ 72 (6/55): 106.

5623. Silk of the Winds. Robson, E.M. SR 42 (2/7/59): 50.

5624. Similarity. Gates, C. WLB 33 (4/59): 578.

5625. A Simple Explanation of Certain Epistles. McGinley, P. AS 28 (Aut/59): 446.

5626. The Simple Life. Updike, J. NY 33 (1/18/58): 108.

5627. Simplicity. De Ford, S. CC 72 (10/5/55): 1141.

5628. Simultaneous Departure. Newmeyer, M.F. SEP 228 (7/30/55): 100.

5629. Sinai. Carruth, H. SR 40 (7/20/57): 14.

5630. Since We Shall Die, One Night, with the Radio On. Kessler, S. SR 41 (11/22/58): 39.

5631. Sincerity. Merton, T. P 89 (12/56): 140-1.

5632. Sing Kukla. Hammer, P. H 212 (6/56): 74.

5633. Sing, O Goddess, the Wrath. Winslow, A.G. H 210 (5/55): 69.

5634. Sing Song. Creeley, R. P 90 (8/57): 293.

5635. Singin' the Blues. Galbraith, G.S. SEP 229 (11/10/56): 59.

5636. Singing. Appleton, S. Co 68 (4/18/58): 77.

5637. Singing Voices. Coolidge. S. NHB 18 (1/55): 92.

5638. Singing Voices. Emerson, R.W. NHB 18 (5/55): 194.

5639. The Single Man. Adcock, J. L 39 (9/5/55): 88.

5640. A Single Man at the Fire. Holmes, T. P 90 (7/57): 215-6.

5641. Sink of Iniquity. Jaffray, N.R. SEP 231 (10/4/58): 74.

5642. The Sinner. Mullins, T.Y. CC 76 (2/11/59): 168.

5643. Siren. Wolf, L. C 27 (1/59): 56.

5644. The Siren of the Kitchen. Galler, D. C 26 (9/58): 200.

5645. Sirocco. Howes, B. SR 41 (7/12/58): 35.

5646. Sirvente. Blackburn, P. N 84 (2/23/57): 163-4.

5647. Sister. Kessler, S. SR 39 (8/25/56): 18.

5648. Sister of Charity. Jennings, E. P 90 (6/57): 152.

5649. Sisterly. Adler, L. P 88 (9/56): 376.

5650. Site. Grimm, E. N 181 (10/29/55): 366.

5651. The Site of Last Night's Fire. Davison, P.H. At 203 (6/59): 50.

5652. Situation of the Artist. Rosenberg, H. AN 57 (3/58): 44.

5653. Six A.M. Beum, R. P 90 (5/57): 82.

5654. 6 P.M. Stockdale, A.B. LHJ 74 (9/57): 147.

5655. Six Picassos. Laing, D. N 186 (4/12/58): 326.

5656. Sixth September. Starbuck, G. NR 137 (9/9/57): 18.

5657. Size 6. Richstone, M. SEP 227 (4/30/55): 98.

5658. Skaters. Stepanchev, S. N 188 (2/21/59): 170.

5659. Skating by Moonlight. Graves, M.H. SEP 231 (1/17/59): 69.

5660. Ski Run for Beginners. Barker, S.O. SEP 231 (12/6/58): 106.

5661. Skid Row. Mary Gilbert, Sr. A 94 (3/17/56): 664.

5662. Skin and Bone. Moss, H. N 183 (10/20/56): 332.

5663. Skin Divers. Armknecht, R.F. SEP 229 (11/3/56): 142.

5664. Skipping Rope. Lieberman, E. SEP 231 (8/23/58): 80.

5665. Sky Cottage. Merrill, H. SEP 232 (7/25/59): 83.

5666. The Sky Hung Idiot Blue. Nathan, L. P 87 (1/56): 223.

5667. A Sky of Late Summer. Rago, H. P 87 (12/55): 164-8.

5668. Sky-kemish River Running. Hugo, R.F. P 93 (2/59): 308-9.

5669. The Slapped Adolescent. Char, R. P 89 (3/57): 337.

5670. Sleep. Andayne, J.C. GH 149 (11/59): 275.

5671. Sleep at Dawn. Solum, S. SEP 227 (5/28/55): 126.

5672. The Sleepers and the Sun. Merrill, H. SEP 230 (4/5/58): 82.

5673. Sleeping. Fuller, J. P 93 (10/58): 16-7.

5674. Sleeping Beauty. Simpson, L. AS 24 (Summ/55): 324-5.

5675. The Sleeping Gipsy. Morse, S.F. At 196 (8/55): 67.

5676. Sleepwalkers. Crawford, J.,Jr. P 91 (12/57): 180.

5677. Sleepy Standing in the Sunny Windy Koku-bunji Station. Tagliabue, J. P 95 (10/59): 16.

5678. Sliding Scale. Lincoln, A. SEP 228 (5/26/56): 84.

5679. Slightly Frustrating. Chadwick, H. BHG 34 (6/56): 146.

5680. Slightly Souciant Song. Galbraith, G.S. LHJ 76 (6/59): 133.

5681. Slim Chance. Schliter, S. SEP 229 (5/18/57): 46.

5682. The Sling of Vision. Furlong, W. P 93 (11/58): 76-7.

5683. Slip Cover. Armour, R. BHG 33 (4/55): 125.

5684. The Sloth. Eff, J. NaR 6 (7/5/58): 60.

5685. Slow Motion. Armour, R. GH 149 (12/59): 8.

5686. Slow Starter. Galbraith, G.S. At 200 (11/57): 254.

5687. The Slug. Roethke, T. NR 133 (8/1/55): 18.

5688. A Sly Fox Waiting. Ford, E. GH 143 (7/56): 28.

5689. The Small. Roethke, T. NY 32 (9/8/56): 32.

5690. Small Colored Boy in the Subway. Deutsch, B. NY 33 (3/30/57): 36.

5691. Small Drum Majorette. Landeweer, E. SEP 230 (5/24/58): 58.

5692. Small Elegy. Moss, H. NY 32 (6/16/56): 32.

5693. Small Favor. Usk, T. SEP 229 (3/16/57): 99.

5694. Small Log House. Mack, R. GH 140 (5/55): 99.

5695. A Small Mountain Town. Tanaka, F. P 88 (5/56): 64.

5696. Small Protection. Nathan, N. SEP 231 (1/3/59): 64.

5697. Small Sad Song. Reid, A. NY 34 (1/10/59): 92.

5698. Small Tale of Summer. Thomas, M.B. SEP 228 (9/3/55): 50.

5699. Small Talker. Gleason, M. SEP 232 (11/28/59): 74.

5700. Small-Town Folks. Rubin, M. SEP 229 (3/30/57): 106.

5701. Small Towns. Havard, P. GH 141 (11/55): 46.

5702. Small Woman on Swallow Street. Merwin, W.S. P 89 (3/59): 345.

5703. Small World. Grenville, R.H. SEP 231 (11/8/58): 62.

5704. The Smallness and Strangeness. De Jong, D. C. P 94 (9/59): 388.

5705. Smells. Merchant, J. SEP 227 (3/5/55): 48.

5706. The Smiles of the Statues. Seferis, G. At 195 (6/55): 159.

5707. The Smoker's Hour. Hb 63 (8/58): 35.

5708. The Smoke's on You. Rosenfield, L. SEP 230 (6/28/58): 96.

5709. The Smooth Maroon Horse-Chestnut. Farber, N. SR 41 (9/20/58): 44.

5710. Snails. Earle, V. SEP 228 (6/9/56): 110.

5711. Snake. Witt, H. N 185 (8/3/57): 58.

5712. The Snake River in August. Denney, R. NR 132 (5/16/55): 24.

5713. Snapshot in a Teacher's Album. Evans, V.M. LHJ 73 (9/56): 140.

5714. Sneak Preview. Grenville, R.H. SEP 230 (7/6/57): 78.

5715. Sneak Thief. Craig, E.C. SEP 230 (12/14/57): 56.

5716. Sniper. Delattre, P.H. Co 69 (10/10/58): 45.

5717. The Snow. McKeehan, V. Hn 32 (8/56): 276.

5718. Snow. Petrie, P. P 90 (8/57): 297-8.

5719. Snow. Pierce, E.L. CC 72 (12/21/55): 1493.

5720. Snow. St.Martin, H. P 95 (11/59): 95.

5721. Snow Crystal. Heafield, K. CC 75 (3/26/58): 372.

5722. Snow Falls. Pasternak, B. GH 149 (12/59): 64.

5723. Snow Fire. Merrill, H. SEP 231 (1/24/59): 66.

5724. Snow-Flakes. Longfellow, H.W. GH 140 (2/55): 28.

5725. Snow Flowers. Freeman, J.D. GH 142 (1/56): 42.

5726. Snow Flurry at Midnight. Hazen, B.S. LHJ 76 (1/59): 108.

5727. The Snow Is Blue. Woods, C. SR 39 (5/5/56): 25.

5728. The Snow Lies Patched. Stuart, J. AF 63 (2/57): 24.

5729. The Snow-Man on the Moor. Plath, S. P 90 (7/57): 229-30.

5730. Snow Scene. Galler, D. P 90 (5/57): 85.

5731. Snow Scene. Mayo, E.L. N 184 (4/27/57): 364.

5732. Snow Storm. Stepanchev, S. N 189 (11/14/59): 362.

5733. Snowed Under. Fairchild, R. BHG 34 (11/56): 153.

5734. The Snowfall. Justice, D. N 189 (11/14/59): 350.

5735. Snowflakes. Donnelly, D. NY 34 (2/14/59): 34.

5736. Snowman. Berrigan, D. P 94 (7/59): 232.

5737. Snowy Heron. Ciardi, J. LHJ 73 (3/56): 144.

5738. So Beautiful Is the Tree of Night. Hanson, P. P 90 (7/57): 225.

5739. So Disappear. North, J.N. LHJ 73 (5/56): 201.

5740. So He Was Sung. Weiss, T. P 91 (12/57): 171-2.

5741. So Many Children. Galbraith, G.S. LHJ 74 (10/57): 205.

5742. So Much I've Known of Life. Stanton, A. CC 73 (6/13/56): 722.

5743. So Near Is God. Patrick, J.G. CC 72 (2/2/55): 139.

5744. Social Analysis. Manhelm, M. SEP 230 (8/3/57): 53.

5745. The Social Scientist. Jones, H.M. At 203 (1/59): 89.

5746. The Social Structure of Early Massachusetts. Ostrander, G.M. AH 9 (2/58): 112.

5747. Soeurs de Charite: March 1956. Brady, C.A. A 95 (7/14/56): 365.

5748. Soft Hope. Hirshman, R. N 184 (4/6/57): 302.

5749. Soft Song for Autumn. Hazen, B.S. LHJ 75 (10/58): 149.

5750. Soft Sounds. Emans, E.V. SEP 227 (6/11/55): 106.

5751. Soft Whips. Carter, M.A. CC 74 (4/10/57): 448.

5752. The Softer the Batter. Van Hise, A. AS 25 (Summ/56): 347.

5753. Softie. Collins, I.J. SEP 228 (2/25/56): 90.

5754. Soiree. Weiss, I.I. NY 32 (11/3/56): 195.

5755. Soldier. Whitt, M.W. SEP 230 (11/9/57): 84.

5756. Soldier on Leave. Ridland, J.M. At 204 (8/59): 50.

5757. A Soldier Rejects His Time Addressing His Contemporaries. Eberhart, R. N 187 (11/1/58): 315.

5758. Soldiers. Oga, T. P 88 (5/56): 98.

5759. Soldier's Mother. Zimmerman, E.H. LHJ 72 (2/55): 142.

5760. Sole the Fabled Dim Recess. Crews, J. P 88 (4/56): 18.

5761. Soleil. Morris, H. P 93 (12/58): 160-1.

5762. Solid Comfort. Updike, J. NY 31 (2/18/56): 93.

5763. Soliloquy in Cemetary of Per Lachaise. Garrigue, J. P 88 (7/56): 243-9.

5764. The Solipsist. McClintic, W. At 195 (4/55): 89.

5765. Solved the Hard Way. Chadwick, R. SEP 230 (3/8/58): 93.

5766. Somber Wonder. Trent, L. CC 72 (11/2/55): 1270.

5767. Some Burmese Riddle Verses. Wun, U. At 201 (2/58): 121.

5768. Some Figures for Who I Am. Ciardi, J. P 89 (12/56): 171-5.

5769. Some Poems. Tagliabue, J. P 91 (3/58): 371.

5770. Some Simple Measures in the American Idiom and the Variable Foot. Williams, W.C. P 93 (3/59): 386-91.

5771. Some Unsung Poems of Our Age. Joost, N. A 93 (8/20/55): 492.

5772. Somebody Has To. Talman, T. BHG 33 (5/55): 241.

5773. Somebody Has to Teach Them Their ZYX's. Cuomo, G. SR 40 (11/9/57): 33.

5774. Somebody's Been Parking in My Parking Space. Bishop, M. NY 31 (2/18/56): 30.

5775. Someone Talking to Himself. Wilbur, R. NY 34 (6/14/58): 34.

5776. Someone Walked Over My Grave. Menashe, S. YR 46 (Aut/56): 75.

5777. Something Different. Richstone, M. SEP 231 (2/28/59): 83.

5778. Something in the Day. Jacobs, E.L. SEP 228 (3/10/56): 61.

5779. Something Should Be Done About the Muses. Bishop, M. NY 33 (4/6/57): 35.

5780. Something You'd Say. Bruce, C. LHJ 73 (5/56): 220.

5781. Sometimes and After. D., H. P 91 (12/57): 151.

5782. Sometimes I Feel Like a Left-Handed Neutron. Bishop, M. NY 34 (2/14/59): 30.

5783. Somewhat Shaken. Chadwick, R. and H. SEP 230 (5/10/58): 113.

5784. Somnambulisma. Stevens, W. NR 133 (8/15/55): 21.

5785. Son of the Prairie. Barker, E.L.S. SR 38 (10/8/55): 28.

5786. Son Studying. Stewart, M.S. SEP 231 (3/21): 52.

5787. Song. Buchwald, E.B. H 216 (1/58): 61.

5788. Song. Burroway, J. At 200 (8/57): 45.

5789. Song. Coatsworth, E. LHJ 73 (3/56): 58.

5790. Song. Goodman, P. P 90 (7/57): 210.

5791. Song. Kay, E. N 184 (1/5/57): 24.

5792. Song. Kreymborg, A. SR 38 (3/26/55): 14.

5793. Song. McFarland, E. LHJ 74 (3/57): 51.

5794. Song. Sarton, M. N 182 (4/14/56): 330.

5795. Song. Scrutton, K. A 97 (5/25/57): 262.

5796. Song. Scrutton, K. A 100 (3/19/59): 687.

5797. Song. Snodgrass, W.D. NY 33 (6/22/57): 32.

5798. Song. Young, A. SR 38 (8/6/55): 22.

5799. Song After Seven Glasses of Picasso. Laing, D. N 185 (12/21/57): 479.

5800. Song Against Sorrow. Murray, P. P 89 (2/57): 289.

5801. Song and Me. Guri, H. P 92 (7/58): 247.

5802. Song at the End of Winter. Wagoner, D. P 89 (2/57): 277-8.

5803. Song Before Bedlam. Milbrath, M.M. SEP 230 (9/28/57): 154.

5804. Song Eden. Lilly, O. CC 75 (8/20/58): 947.

5805. Song for a Bad Night. Moffitt, J. At 200 (12/57): 73.

5806. Song for a Fifth Child. Hamilton, R.H. LHJ 75 (10/58): 186.

5807. Song for a Guitar. Fitzell, L. LHJ 73 (8/56): 92.

5808. Song for a Second Child. McKee, G. LHJ 75 (3/58): 200.

5809. Song for a September. Tuttle, S.W. SEP 230 (9/21/57): 77.

5810. Song for a Vigil. Whitman, R. At 200 (10/57): 50.

5811. Song for an American. Schneider, P.V. CC 75 (2/19/58): 216.

5812. Song for an Unknown Battle. Posner, D. NY 35 (9/19/59): 135.

5813. Song for Halloween. Gleason, H.W. GH 143 (11/56): 13.

5814. A Song for Mardi Gras. Humphries, R. NY 33 (3/2/57): 87.

5815. Song for Mid-August. McDonnel, T.P. A 95 (8/25/56): 486.

5816. Song for Music. Posner, D.L. P 90 (8/57): 277-8.

5817. Song for My Dead Grandmother. Weiss, N. C 28 (8/59): 148.

5818. Song for September. Wise, M.L. SR 38 (9/10/55): 12.

5819. Song for Strangers in Wales. Brinnin, J.M. NY 33 (1/18/58): 28.

5820. Song for Thanksgiving. Thompson, C.A. GH 141 (11/55): 46.

5821. A Song for the Passionate. O'Gorman, N. P 92 (4/58): 7.

5822. A Song for the Widow of Naim. Cotter, J.F. A 97 (6/8/57): 304.

5823. Song in a Cloud of Hands. Merwin, W.S. AS 28 (Summ/59): 342-3.

5824. Song in American Type. Updike, J. NY 33 (3/30/57): 30.

5825. Song of a Denatured Man. Riddle, M. N 183 (9/22/56): 252.

5826. Song of a Girl. Cantwell, E. LHJ 74 (5/57): 141.

5827. Song of a Little Experience. De Jong, D.C. P 92 (9/58): 373.

5828. Song of a Person of Puritan Extraction. Quentin, A.R. SEP 232 (7/4/59): 69.

5829. The Song of a Stone. Appleton, S. Co 69 (12/26/58): 343.

5830. Song of a Thorn Tree. Barnes, K. LHJ 72 (12/55): 88.

5831. A Song of Love-Longing. Murry, P. P 92 (4/58): 19.

5832. Song of Myself. Whitman, W. L 38 (6/20/55): 120.

5833. Song of Our Season. Bell, C.G. LHJ 72 (9/55): 141.

5834. Song of the Ants. Blackburn, P. N 186 (3/8/58): 210.

5835. Song of the Divine. Van Allen, G.R. CC 72 (9/7/55): 1016.

5836. Song of the Frightened Motorist. Armour, R. SEP 230 (3/8/58): 51.

5837. Song of the Hesitations. Blackburn, P. N 189 (9/12/59): 139.

5838. Song of the Open Road. Whitman, W. L 38 (6/20/55): 119.

5839. Song of the Passionate Psychologist to His Beloved. Eaton, W.H. AS 24 (Aut/55): 418.

5840. Song of the Stars. Dunbar, V.E. LHJ 72 (7/55): 88.

5841. Song of the Suburbs. Mack, R. LHJ 72 (7/55): 14.

5842. Song of the Thin Man. Murray, P. YR 46 (Aut/56): 75.

5843. The Song of Then. Lilly, O. CC 76 (1/7/57): 11.

5844. A Song Stricken from the Records. Moss, H. SR 42 (10/3/59): 28.

5845. Song to a Sacroiliac. Rosenteur, P.I. TH 33 (1/55): 40.

5846. A Song to Be Set to Music. Moss, H. P 89 (10/56): 11-2.

5847. Song to Cloud. Behn, H. Hn 33 (10/57): 389.

5848. Song Without a Name. Hagiwara, S. P 88 (3/56): 102.

5849. Song Without Words. Gregor, A. P 95 (5/58): 79-80.

5850. Song Yet Song. Gilboa, A. P 92 (7/58): 253.

5851. Songs for the Fourth Commandment. Mary Faith, Sr. A 102 (11/21/59): 235.

5852. Sonic Boom. Updike, J. NY 35 (8/8/59): 89.

5853. Sonnet. Amihai, Y. C 22 (12/56): 575.

5854. Sonnet. Amihai, Y. P 92 (7/58): 254.

5855. Sonnet. Burger, O.K. GH 142 (6/56): 119.

5856. Sonnet. Cantwell, E. LHJ 72 (5/55): 136.

5857. Sonnet. Constantinoff, R. At 202 (8/58): 64.

5858. Sonnet. Dale, E. N 185 (1/13/58): 48.

5859. Sonnet. de Kay, O.,Jr. LHJ 75 (8/58): 84.

5860. Sonnet. Kay, E. N 184 (1/12/57): 45.

5861. Sonnet. Lamb, M.W. LHJ 72 (3/55): 133.

5862. Sonnet. Schwartz, D. C 25 (5/58): 400.

5863. Sonnet XI. Perry, R. P 95 (12/59): 172.

5864. Sonnet XIII. Perry, R. P 95 (12/59): 174.

5865. Sonnet XXI. Beum, R. P 93 (2/59): 310.

5866. Sonnet by the Lakeside. Bagg, R. P 89 (11/56): 98.

5867. Sonnet for a Good Shepherd. Schluneger, F.E. GH 140 (3/55): 99.

5868. A Sonnet for Robert Frost But Not About Him. Ciardi, J. SR 42 (3/21/59): 20.

5869. Sonnet for the Good Warrior. Kinsey, R.L. LHJ 74 (12/57): 121.

5870. Sonnet in Search of an Author. Williams, W.C. N 182 (4/14/56): 313.

5871. Sonnet of the Shepherds. Crites, S. CC 76 (12/16/59): 1464.

5872. Sonnet on Nightmares. Manifold, J.S. N 182 (4/14/56): 317.

5873. Sonnet Right Off the Bat. Vega, L.de. SR 40 (7/20/57): 16.

5874. Sonnet to a Newborn Son. Rex, C.G. GH 140 (3/55): 99.

5875. Sonnet to My Father. Justice, D. H 219 (12/59): 77.

5876. Sonnets for Lent. Johnson, C. Co 61 (3/55): 580.

5877. Sonnets for the Space Age. Zylstra, M. CT 4 (12/7/59): 23.

5878. Sore Point. Emmons, D. SEP 230 (7/27/57): 96.

5879. Soren Kierkegaard. Rowse, A.L. H 217 (8/58): 75.

5880. The Sorrow of Kodio. Koshland, M. At 203 (4/59): 47.

5881. SOS. Balch, B.J. SEP 230 (5/17/58): 120.

5882. Soul Searching. Cooper, J.C. CC 75 (1/1/58): 16.

5883. Soul Searching. Cooper, J.C. CT 2 (10/14/57): 10.

5884. Souls Like Chisels. Rosenthal, M.L. N 189 (9/26/59): 180.

5885. Sound and Echo. Loeser, K. NY 32 (11/10/56): 122.

5886. Sound Approach. Emmons, D. SEP 231 (11/8/58): 141.

5887. Sound Defects. Galbraith, G.S. SEP 230 (4/26/58): 94.

5888. The Sound of Green. Engle, P. LHJ 75 (3/58): 188.

5889. The Sound of Love. Burrows, E.G. P 89 (12/56): 169-70.

5890. The Sound of Red. Engle, P. P 95 (10/59): 28.

5891. Soundings. Cuomo, G. N 183 (12/8/56): 503.

5892. Source. Rutledge, A. SEP 227 (2/26/55): 87.

5893. South Harpswell. Burford, W. P 95 (11/59): 79.

5894. Southern Gothic. Justice, D. P 92 (8/58): 292.

5895. Souvenir. Carleton, S.K. LHJ 73 (4/56): 197.

5896. Sow. Plath, S. P 90 (7/57): 231-3.

5897. Space Age Schooling. Armour, R. BHG 37 (10/59): 126.

5898. The Space Balloon. Burford, W. SR 40 (11/16/57): 23.

5899. The Space-Child's Mother Goose. Winsor, F. At 198 (12/56): 41-5.

5900. The Space-Child's Mother Goose. Winsor, F. At 200 (7/57): 46-9.

5901. Space Design. Levine, R. P 91 (2/58): 303-5.

5902. Space Travel. Lamb, E.S. SEP 231 (11/1/58): 82.

5903. Spain--III. Anzai, F. P 88 (5/56): 97.

5904. Span of Life. Russell, B.D. CC 72 (3/2/55): 264.

5905. A Spanish Landscape. Moss, S. P 86 (9/55): 324-7.

5906. A Spark of Laurel. Kunitz, S. P 90 (4/57): 3-4.

5907. The Sparrowmaker. Newton, V. Co 68 (5/16/58): 183.

5908. Sparrows. Carruth, H. NY 32 (12/8/56): 218.

5909. The Sparrows on Christmas Morning. Bock, F. CC 76 (12/16/59): 1464.

5910. Spartan. Usk, T. SEP 231 (4/4/59): 160.

5911. Speakable Bacle. Lamport, F. H 210 (1/55): 75.

5912. Speaking as a Parent. Grenville, R.H. SEP 230 (11/9/57): 147.

5913. Speaking Jesuswise. Rowland, S.,Jr. CC 75 (4/2/58): 402.

5914. Speaking of Islands. Justice, D. H 219 (8/59): 71.

5915. Speaking of Speakers. Spring, A.T. SEP 230 (3/15/58): 24.

5916. Speaking of Television. McGinley, P. NY 33 (5/25/57): 35.

5917. A Speckled Stone Mirror. Nemerov, H. P 88 (9/56): 384.

5918. Spectacular. Fadiman, C. SR 40 (6/1/57): 24.

5919. Speech for an Ideal Irish Election. Montague, J. P 94 (9/59): 376-7.

5920. Speech in an Orchard. Corke, H. NY 35 (5/16/59): 106.

5921. Speed, We Say. Rickeyser, M. SR 41 (4/12/58): 69.

5922. Spellbound. Harrington, H. SEP 232 (10/3/59): 133.

5923. The Spider. Eberhart, R. P 95 (10/59): 3.

5924. A Spider. Witt, H. NR 136 (3/4/57): 18.

5925. Spiders. Schwartz, D. NR 141 (7/6/59): 18.

5926. Spinal Discord. Lamport, F. H 218 (4/59): 47.

5927. The Spinner. Valery, P. P 94 (4/59): 4-5.

5928. Spirit of Rabbi Nachman. Shapiro, H. C 28 (10/59): 346.

5929. Spirit Sons, Spirit Lovers. Fisher, V. P 88 (7/56): 234-5.

5930. The Spirit's Name. Powers, J. A 93 (5/7/55): 156.

5931. Spiritual Journey. Grace, W.J. A 97 (9/14/57): 624.

5932. Spiritually Lost. Rolland, J. CC 73 (2/29/56): 269.

5933. The Spit. Gale, V. P 87 (1/56): 213.

5934. Spite. Koshland, M. At 203 (4/59): 47.

5935. Spite Fence. Long, E.E. SEP 230 (8/24/57): 101.

5936. The Splintered Streets. Brennan, J.P. AS 25 (Aut/56): 452.

5937. Split Root. Langland, J. LHJ 75 (4/58): 173.

5938. Spoiled by All My Tyrants. Stefanile, F.M. P 85 (3/55): 339.

5939. Spontaneous Bottle. Witt, H. P 93 (12/58): 156.

5940. Spoon-Feeding Rhyme. Galbraith, G.S. LHJ 75 (1/58): 96.

5941. Sportive Accolade. Eberhart, R. N 183 (9/8/56): 206.

5942. Sports Cars. Wheeler, R. SEP 227 (5/14/55): 91.

5943. Spray of Stars. Carter, M.A. CC 76 (2/23/59): 227.

5944. Spring. Bennett, P.L. SEP 227 (5/14/55): 94.

5945. Spring. Boyle, K. LHJ 74 (3/57): 211.

5946. The Spring. De Ford, S. CC 72 (9/7/55): 1016.

5947. The Spring. Guri, H. P 92 (7/58): 246.

5948. Spring. Lowenfels, W. N 186 (5/10/58): 426.

5949. The Spring. O'Gorman, N. P 95 (11/59): 85.

5950. Spring and Fall. Rainer, D. SR 38 (4/30/55): 15.

5951. Spring Cellar. McKee, G. SEP 229 (10/13/56): 87.

5952. Spring-Cleaning Notes. Franklin, J.M. SEP 227 (4/16/55): 119.

5953. Spring Comes to the Lending Library. Sitwell, O. NY 33 (2/23/57): 35.

5954. Spring Confession. Collins, I.J. SEP 227 (5/28/55): 114.

5955. Spring Day. Sarton, M. At 199 (4/57): 73.

5956. Spring Eclogue. Greet, A.H. NY 32 (3/17/56): 48.

5957. Spring Fever. Usk, T. SEP 231 (5/2/59): 57.

5958. Spring Freeze. Merchant, J. SEP 228 (4/14/56): 115.

5959. Spring Frogs. Landeweer, E. SEP 228 (4/21/56): 95.

5960. Spring Gray. Moffitt, J. NY 34 (5/10/58): 125.

5961. Spring Hearth. Singleton, M.E. SEP 231 (3/28/59): 52.

5962. Spring Interest. Stafford, W. NY 34 (5/17/58): 119.

5963. Spring Is a Looping-Free Time. Robbins, M. SR 40 (5/18/57): 14.

5964. Spring Magic. Ellis, C. SEP 228 (3/24/56): 87.

5965. Spring Morning. Norman, C. SR 38 (9/24/55): 17.

5966. Spring Morning. Simon, D. LHJ 76 (4/59): 12.

5967. Spring Mountain Climb. Eberhart, R. AS 28 (Summ/59): 354-5.

5968. Spring Near the Airbase. Coxe, L.O. N 183 (8/4/56): 101.

5969. Spring Nocturne. Galbraith, G.S. SEP 227 (5/21/55): 139.

5970. Spring Observation. Ellis, C. SEP 229 (5/25/57): 124.

5971. Spring on the Desert. Kelley, R.S. SEP 228 (4/7/56): 98.

5972. Spring Raking. Carruth, H. NR 136 (5/6/57): 17.

5973. Spring Song. Ginsberg, L. LHJ 76 (4/59): 58.

5974. Spring Sounds. Auxier, S. SEP 228 (4/28/56): 142.

5975. Spring Tide. Cousens, M. LHJ 72 (4/55): 122.

5976. Sprinkler System. White, E.F. SEP 229 (8/18/56): 85.

5977. The Sprinter's Sleep. Dickey, J. YR 47 (9/57): 72.

5978. Spurred to Action. Jaffray, N.R. GH 142 (7/56): 28.

5979. Sputnik. Pierce, E.L. CC 74 (12/18/57): 1504.

5980. Sputnik. Whittemore, R. NR 138 (3/17/58): 18.

5981. Squatter's Children. Bishop, E. NY 33 (3/23/57): 36.

5982. Squeaking Through. Armour, R. BHG 34 (10/56): 164.

5983. Squirrel. Swenson, M. SR 39 (5/5/56): 23.

5984. Stack Cracks. Spear, G.B. WLB 29 (5/55): 719.

5985. Stack Cracks. Spear, G.B. WLB 30 (9/55): 80.

5986. Stack Cracks. Spear, G.B. WLB 30 (10/55): 189.

5987. Stack Cracks. Spear, G.B. WLB 30 (11/55): 274.

5988. Stack Cracks. Spear, G.B. WLB 30 (12/55): 336.

5989. Stack Cracks. Spear, G.B. WLB 30 (1/56): 404.

5990. Stack Cracks. Spear, G.B. WLB 30 (2/56): 467.

5991. Stack Cracks. Spear, G.B. WLB 30 (3/56): 559.

5992. Stack Cracks. Spear, G.B. WLB 30 (4/56): 643.

5993. Stack Cracks. Spear, G.B. WLB 30 (5/56): 707.

5994. Stack Cracks. Spear, G.B. WLB 30 (6/56): 780.

5995. Stack Cracks. Spear, G.B. WLB 31 (12/56): 336.

5996. Stack Cracks. Spear, G.B. WLB 31 (1/57): 401.

5997. Stack Cracks. Spear, G.B. WLB 31 (2/57): 467.

5998. Stack Cracks. Spear, G.B. WLB 31 (5/57): 739.

5999. Stack Cracks. Spear, G.B. WLB 31 (6/57): 806.

6000. Stack Cracks. Spear, G.B. WLB 32 (9/57): 61.

6001. Stack Cracks. Spear, G.B. WLB 32 (11/57): 241.

6002. Stack Cracks. Spear, G.B. WLB 32 (12/57): 307.

6003. Stack Cracks. Spear, G.B. WLB 32 (1/58): 372.

6004. Stack Cracks. Spear, G.B. WLB 32 (2/58): 436.

6005. Stack Cracks. Spear, G.B. WLB 32 (3/58): 516.

6006. Stack Cracks. Spear, G.B. WLB 32 (4/58): 592.

6007. Stack Cracks. Spear, G.B. WLB 32 (5/58): 657.

6008. Stack Cracks. Spear, G.B. WLB 32 (6/58): 729.

6009. Stack Cracks. Spear, G.B. WLB 33 (9/58): 65.

6010. Stack Cracks. Spear, G.B. WLB 33 (10/58): 162.

6011. Stack Cracks. Spear, G.B. WLB 33 (11/58): 241.

6012. Stack Cracks. Spear, G.B. WLB 33 (12/58): 307.

6013. Stack Cracks. Spear, G.B. WLB 33 (1/59): 371.

6014. Stack Cracks. Spear, G.B. WLB 33 (2/59): 435.

6015. Stack Cracks. Spear, G.B. WLB 33 (3/59): 516.

6016. Stack Cracks. Spear, G.B. WLB 33 (4/59): 587.

6017. Stack Cracks. Spear, G.B. WLB 33 (5/59): 691.

6018. Stack Cracks. Spear, G.B. WLB 33 (6/59): 747.

6019. Stack Cracks. Spear, G.B. WLB 34 (9/59): 60.

6020. Stack Cracks. Spear, G.B. WLB 34 (10/59): 160.

6021. Stack Cracks. Spear, G.B. WLB 34 (11/59): 226.

6022. Stack Cracks. Spear, G.B. WLB 34 (12/59): 304.

6023. Stack Fever. Goodwell, R. and Anderson, F. LJ 84 (5/15/59): 1573.

6024. Stage Settings. Flynn, C.E. CT 2 (4/14/58): 10.

6025. Stance. Clower, J. P 93 (10/58): 9.

6026. A Stand of Pine. Belitt, B. P 91 (10/57): 16.

6027. Star Flight. Clark, L.S. CC 74 (11/13/57): 1350.

6028. The Star in the Hills. Stafford, W. H 215 (11/57): 59.

6029. Star Shower. Lineaweaver, M. SR 38 (12/10/55): 28.

6030. Star Time. Merchant, J. SEP 230 (11/9/57): 136.

6031. The Starlings. Hall, D. P 86 (8/55): 262.

6032. Stars Almost Escape Us. Berrigan, D. SR 40 (7/20/57): 15.

6033. Stars and a Frog. Merrill, H. SEP 230 (3/29/58): 93.

6034. The Stars and I. Lister, R.P. At 196 (7/55): 88.

6035. Starstruck. Jacobson, E. BHG 34 (6/56): 246.

6036. Start of School. Miner, V.S. EJ 45 (9/56): 356.

6037. Starting Point. Wheeler, R. SEP 229 (12/1/56): 58.

6038. The State. Gordon, D. AS 26 (Wint/56-57): 65-6.

6039. Statistical Blank. Galbraith, G.S. LHJ 76 (5/59): 140.

6040. Stature. Clark, L.S. CC 74 (11/20/57): 1377.

6041. Status Quo. Merrill, H. SEP 229 (11/3/56): 53.

6042. The Statutes in the Public Gardens. Nemerov, H. N 183 (8/25/56): 163.

6043. Stay of Sentence. Gleason, H.W. SEP 227 (4/2/55): 99.

6044. Steadfast. Heath, C. SEP 231 (11/1/58): 71.

6045. Steadfast Fever. Shaw, L.D. CT 1 (10/29/56): 15.

6046. Steady Girl. Jacobson, E. SEP 229 (5/4/57): 42.

6047. Step by Step. Kramer, A. NY 33 (1/25/58): 92.

6048. Step Lively, Please. Braley, B. SEP 230 (9/21/57): 124.

6049. Steppingstone. Isler, B. SEP 230 (11/2/57): 110.

6050. Steps for a Dancer. Nemerov, H. P 91 (11/57): 76.

6051. Sticks and Stones May Break My Bones, But Names Will Break My Heart. Nash, O. NY 35 (6/13/59): 30.

6052. Stiles. Pudney, J. NY 33 (4/27/57): 38.

6053. Still Life: Tankard, Sun, and Avocado Plant. Carroll, P. P 92 (5/58): 81-2.

6054. The Still Spirit. Eberhart, R. LHJ 75 (11/59): 152.

6055. Stillness. Gibbs, B.R. SEP 230 (1/11/58): 42.

6056. The Stoker. Shalom, S. P 92 (7/58): 230.

6057. The Stone-Breaker. Nirala. P 93 (1/59): 255-6.

6058. A Stone for Ravensbrueck. Heissenfuttel, E.G. SR 41 (11/29/58): 23.

6059. A Stony Field. Merrill, H. SEP 229 (5/18/57): 58.

6060. Stony Lonesome. Richman, F.B. SEP 227 (2/5/55): 50.

6061. Stopped Suddenly That He Is Beautiful. Ciardi, J. LHJ 76 (10/59): 34.

6062. Stopping to Write a Friend on a Thick Night. Wylie, P. SR 41 (5/10/58): 20.

6063. Store Thyself. Ratliff, H. CC 74 (3/20/57): 353.

6064. The Stork. Eff, J. NaR 6 (7/5/58): 61.

6065. Storm. Fandel, J. NR 138 (3/24/58): 18.

6066. Storm and After. Rothberg, L. N 187 (12/6/58): 430.

6067. Storm at Dingle. Sullivan, A.M. SR 38 (11/12/55): 18.

6068. A Storm from the East. Whittemore, R. NY 34 (4/26/58): 32.

6069. Storm in the Midlands. Huntress, K. SR 38 (7/30/55): 14.

6070. Storm Memory. Hughes, D. NY 32 (10/6/56): 42.

6071. A Storm of White. Duncan, R. P 93 (3/59): 369-70.

6072. The Storm Swallow. Bly, R. N 189 (12/26/59): 490.

6073. Storm Warning. Ireland, T. LHJ 74 (9/57): 182.

6074. Storm Warning. Lineaweaver, M. At 198 (9/56): 91.

6075. Storm Windows. Nemerov, H. N 183 (12/22/56): 543.

6076. Storm Worry. Long, E.E. SEP 227 (4/30/55): 68.

6077. Stormy Reception. Stoutenburg, A. N 185 (9/28/57): 199.

6078. Story for a Girl, Dien Tamaela. Anwar, C. At 197 (6/56): 113.

6079. Story-in-the-Making. Flint, L. M 86 (8/59): 134.

6080. The Strange Case of the Blight That Failed. Nash, O. NY 32 (10/13/56): 42.

6081. The Strange Case of the Lucrative Compromise. Nash, O. NY 32 (8/11/56): 24.

6082. The Strange Casement of the Poetic Apothecary. Nash, O. NY 33 (11/23/57): 52.

6083. Strange Christ. Davidson, L.K. CT 3 (11/24/58): 6.

6084. The Strange Horses. Everson, R.G. SR 42 (3/14/59): 16.

6085. Strange Species. Collins, I.J. SEP 228 (8/13/55): 64.

6086. Strangely Familiar. Richstone, M. SEP 229 (6/29/57): 79.

6087. The Stranger. Bernhardt, V. CC 72 (3/9/55): 296.

6088. Strangers. Jennings, E. N 187 (9/13/58): 138.

6089. The Strangest Chatter. Anthony, E. GH 142 (4/56): 112.

6090. Stratagems and Spoils. Schneider, E.F. A 101 (5/23/59): 371.

6091. Strategy at Six. Armknecht, R.F. SEP 230 (9/7/57): 47.

6092. A Straw Swan Under the Christmas Tree. Levertov, D. P 94 (7/59): 246.

6093. Stray. Collins, B.F. SEP 228 (2/4/56): 100.

6094. Stray Dog, Near Ecully. Avison, M. P 91 (12/57): 174.

6095. Streams. Auden, W.H. At 195 (5/55): 43-4.

6096. Streamside Spoor. Landeweer, E. SEP 229 (6/8/57): 130.

6097. The Street. Carruth, H. P 93 (3/59): 361-2.

6098. Street Song. Ekulkar, M. P 93 (1/59): 244.

6099. Strength. Freeman, J.D. GH 142 (8/56): 121.

6100. Strength Beyond the Day of Storm. Baldwin, L.M. CC 72 (9/14/55): 1049.

6101. The Stricken Heart. Benet, L. LHJ 76 (11/59): 51.

6102. The String. Dickey, J. P 94 (7/59): 222-3.

6103. The Stroke of Noon. Vance, T. P 89 (2/57): 283-4.

6104. Strokes. Stafford, W. SR 39 (9/29/56): 19.

6105. Strontium 90. Pierce, E.L. CC 75 (3/19/58): 338.

6106. Strumpet Song. Plath, S. P 89 (1/57): 233.

6107. Stubborn. Merrill, H. SEP 232 (8/22/59): 66.

6108. A Student, Departing for Christmas Vacation to Himself. Whitbread, T. H 217 (12/58): 30.

6109. Student Marginal on a Professor's Death. Roseliep, R. A 95 (4/28/56): 111.

6110. Suburban. Hooper, P. AS 26 (Summ/57): 334.

6111. Suburban Madrigal. Updike, J. NY 35 (4/25/59): 100.

6112. Suburban Song. Lee, M.L. LHJ 74 (7/57): 71.

6113. Suburban Spring. Zimskind, N. SR 40 (7/20/57): 14.

6114. Suburban Sunday. Posner, D.L. P 90 (8/57): 276.

6115. Suburbia. Hammer, P. SR 39 (4/28/56): 15.

6116. Subway Frustration. Zacks, H.A. SEP 228 (1/7/56): 83.

6117. Success. Hearst, J. P 92 (8/58): 299.

6118. The Success. Pack, R. AS 24 (Summ/55): 280.

6119. Such. Robin, R. SR 41 (4/12/58): 67.

6120. Such Force as Blinds the Giant. Eaton, C.E. P 92 (6/58): 153.

6121. Such Is Life. Richstone, M. SEP 231 (1/10/59): 47.

6122. Such Precious Things. Vance, E.G. SEP 231 (9/6/58): 74.

6123. Sudden Knowing. Armknecht, R.F. SEP 231 (9/20/58): 70.

6124. Suddenly April. Shook, B. LHJ 74 (4/57): 171.

6125. Suddenly in Summer. Shook, B. LHJ 75 (6/58): 108.

6126. Suerte. Blackburn, P. N 184 (2/2/57): 108.

6127. Suggestion from the Subject. Hammer, P. SEP 228 (8/13/55): 80.

6128. Suite for Wind Instruments. Perry, R. P 95 (12/59): 172-4.

6129. Suited. Merchant, J. SEP 228 (10/8/55): 127.

6130. Summary of the Man Situation at Any Summer Resort. SEP 229 (6/29/57): 34.

6131. Summary of the Situation. Galbraith, G.S. SEP 229 (9/8/56): 109.

6132. Summer. Kroll, E. SR 41 (8/9/58): 36.

6133. Summer. Levine, P. P 90 (4/57): 30-1.

6134. The Summer. O'Gorman, N. P 95 (11/59): 84.

6135. Summer Cape Song. Chapin, K.G. LHJ 72 (6/55): 145.

6136. Summer Chapel. Cunliffe, C. LHJ 73 (7/56): 61.

6137. Summer Entombed. Barnes, K. SR 38 (10/1/55): 12.

6138. The Summer Girls. Lineaweaver, M. LHJ 73 (1/56): 82.

6139. Summer Knowledge. Schwartz, D. P 94 (5/59): 109-10.

6140. The Summer Lake. Merrill, H. SEP 228 (7/16/55): 48.

6141. Summer Library Visits. Reinert, D.E. WLB 32 (4/58): 569.

6142. Summer Overhead. Isler, B. BHG 33 (6/55): 235.

6143. Summer Place. Scott, W.T. N 188 (1/31/59): 101.

6144. Summer Pond Romance. Mayhall, J. NR 134 (1/30/56): 18.

6145. Summer Remembered. Gardner, I. At 200 (9/57): 45.

6146. A Summer Rowing. Locke, E. YR 48 (12/58): 244.

6147. Summer Sequel. Alkus, M. SEP 228 (9/17/55): 105.

6148. Summer Slumber. Neely, L. BHG 33 (6/55): 153.

6149. Summer Song. Merwin, W.S. N 186 (4/19/58): 352.

6150. Summer Suspense. Neely, L. SEP 228 (7/16/55): 99.

6151. Summer Tourists. Barker, E. H 213 (8/56): 67.

6152. Summer Winds. Arnold, V. SEP 228 (7/30/55): 88.

6153. Summer's End. Hecht, R. P 86 (9/55): 332-3.

6154. Summer's Refrain. Keith, J.J. SR 38 (7/2/55): 5.

6155. A Summer's Tale. Galbraith, G.S. SEP 229 (6/15/57): 46.

6156. Summertime Insomniac. Long, E.E. SEP 232 (8/8/59): 57.

6157. Summit Time, and the Giving is Easy. Ryskind, A.H. NaR 5 (5/10/58): 443.

6158. The Sun. Nishiwaki, J. P 88 (5/56): 75.

6159. The Sunbathers. O'Gorman, N. P 89 (2/57): 281.

6160. Sunbathers. Sexton, A. NY 35 (6/13/59): 93.

6161. Sunbright on a City Way. White, H.S. N 189 (9/26/59): 179.

6162. Sunday. Necker, R. SR 41 (9/6/58): 32.

6163. Sunday Afternoon. Eisenlohr, L. SEP 231 (11/15/58): 126.

6164. Sunday in October. Eberhart, R. P 85 (2/55): 273.

6165. Sunday in the Country. Swenson, M. NR 134 (5/28/56): 18.

6166. Sunday in the Laboratory. Squires, R. P 95 (10/59): 24-5.

6167. Sunday Segment. Rorke, M. BHG 33 (5/55): 137.

6168. Sunderland. Nemerov, H. P 87 (10/55): 35-8.

6169. Sundial. Graham, E. LHJ 73 (9/56): 109.

6170. Sundown. Merrill, H. LHJ 72 (3/55): 113.

6171. A Sung Sonnet. Coughlin, P. At 204 (8/59): 50.

6172. Sunlight and Shadow. Mueller, L. P 92 (4/58): 23.

6173. Sunrise. Cunliffe, C. LHJ 74 (4/57): 143.

6174. Sunrise, the Bishop's Palace, Wells. Ackerson, J. CC 72 (10/5/55): 1136.

6175. Sunset on the 5:10. Kaplan, E.T. SEP 230 (2/1/58): 38.

6176. Superman. Galbraith, G.S. SEP 230 (11/9/57): 68.

6177. Supermarket Rider. Landeweer, E. SEP 230 (8/10/57): 72.

6178. Supernatural. Guha, N. P 93 (1/59): 214-5.

6179. Superseded Love Letters. Petrie, P. P 88 (4/56): 19.

6180. Suppertime. Grenville, R.H. SEP 229 (5/11/57): 64.

6181. The Supreme Crown. Gogarty, O.St.J. P 85 (2/55): 267.

6182. Sure-Fire Self-Starter. Chadwick, H. BHG 33 (4/55): 158.

6183. Sure of What the Birds Know. Fleming, H. P 89 (10/56): 24-5.

6184. Surface Reflection. Emmons, D. SEP 229 (11/24/56): 148.

6185. Surface Tension. Blackwell, P.J. SEP 232 (9/12/59): 76.

6186. Surgery Ward, December 8. Sandeen, E. P 95 (11/59): 100-1.

6187. Surgical Thoughts. Armstrong, P. SEP 232 (8/22/59): 51.

6188. Surmise. Moffitt, J. SR 40 (2/9/57): 15.

6189. Surplus. Darcy, L. SEP 229 (8/24/56): 61.

6190. Surprise. Moorhead, J.K. CC 73 (6/6/56): 692.

6191. Surprise Defeated. Anthony Marie, Sr. A 97 (8/10/57): 485.

6192. A Survey of the Italian Cinema. Brooks, G. SR 39 (6/2/56): 4.

6193. Survival. Kaplan, H. N 188 (4/11/59): 319.

6194. Survival. North, E. CC 76 (2/13/59): 197.

6195. Survivors. Congdon, T. SEP 230 (11/16/57): 58.

6196. The Survivors. Merwin, W.S. NR 138 (6/16/58): 20.

6197. The Survivors. Rich, A. NY 33 (12/21/57): 98.

6198. Susan's First Walk. Smith, B.F. LHJ 74 (3/57): 225.

6199. The Suspense. Middleton, C. P 97 (1/56): 233.

6200. Suspension. Deutsch, B. P 90 (6/57): 141.

6201. Suwanee River. Glaze, A. SR 40 (1/19/57): 44.

6202. The Swallowed Man. Quentin, A.R. At 204 (10/59): 84.

6203. Swan Song. Sterling, G. GH 141 (10/55): 14.

6204. Swansong of the Hyena. Barker, G. P 88 (8/56): 289.

6205. Sweater. Duke, T. SEP 232 (11/21/59): 130.

6206. A Sweeping Victory. Ward, L.B. GH 149 (7/59): 98.

6207. Sweet Grass. McFarland, E. LHJ 74 (9/57): 124.

6208. Sweet William's Breath. Van Doren, M. LHJ 76 (5/59): 119.

6209. Sweetheart in Jeans. Fairbion, D. SEP 229 (3/25/57): 76.

6210. Sweetly on the Ear Falls the Sound of the Sea. Bokudo (1660?-1715?). L 40 (4/30/56): 86-7.

6211. Swift. Schwartz, D. P 94 (5/59): 105-7.

6212. Swimmer Emerging. Perreau-Saussine, R. P 93 (10/58): 26.

6213. A Swimmer in the Air. Moss, H. P 89 (10/56): 9-11.

6214. The Sword. Dicker, H. N 183 (7/21/56): 65.

6215. Sybarite's Philosophy. Ryskind, M. NaR 3 (6/18/57): 572.

6216. The Sycamore. Grenville, R.H. SEP 228 (9/17/55): 132.

6217. Symbolism, or, Moby Dick Has Eaten of the Grapes of Wrath, and the Children's Teeth Are Set on Edge. EJ 48 (9/59): 325.

6218. A Sympathy, a Welcome. Berryman, J. NY 34 (8/9/58): 22.

6219. Sympathy, Please! Blackwell, P.J. SEP 230 (10/26/57): 55.

6220. The Syncretist. Koski, G. CC 73 (2/8/56): 172.

6221. Synthetic Age. De Vito, E.B. SEP 229 (3/2/57): 77.

6222. Sysyphus. Miles, J. NY 34 (5/31/58): 30.

6223. T.R. Hall, D. P 92 (6/58): 169.

6224. TV Tree. Freeman, A.D. SEP 230 (9/21/57): 50.

6225. A Table for One. White, E.B. NY 33 (2/23/57): 38.

6226. Table Talk. Nash, O. HG 111 (6/57): 18.

6227. Table Talk. Nash, O. HG 112 (11/57): 38.

6228. Table Talk. Nash, O. HG 112 (12/57): 8.

6229. Table Talk. Nash, O. HG 113 (4/58): 155.

6230. Table Tree. Potter, M.C. SEP 230 (12/21/57): 52.

6231. The Taciturn Type. Hammer, P. LHJ 75 (6/58): 78.

6232. The Tailor. Wolf, L. C 24 (10/57): 309.

6233. Tailor-Made. Blackwell, P.J. SEP 230 (6/14/58: 120.

6234. T'Ain't No Taint. Solovay, J.C. CH 32 (2/58): 366.

6235. Taiwan, Western Outpost. MacInnis, H.P. CC 75 (6/25/58): 748.

6236. Take It Easy. Talman, T. GH 140 (3/55): 99.

6237. Take the Rap. Braley, B. SEP 232 (10/17/59): 166.

6238. Take Thy Only Son. Powers, J. A 95 (9/15/56): 560.

6239. A Tale of a Poem and a Squash. Whittemore, R. P 92 (9/58): 346-7.

6240. A Tale of Isogonic Far Ago. Pell, J. At 196 (8/55): 89.

6241. Tale of Two Shortages. Warsaw, I. SEP 231 (2/21/59): 64.

6242. Taliesin and the Mockers. Watkins, V. P 87 (11/55): 75-9.

6243. Talking Books for the Blind. Barker, E.L.S. LJ 83 (10/15/58): 2798.

6244. Tall Are the Mountains of Christmas. Elmer, F.D.,Jr. CC 74 (12/18/57): 1507.

6245. Tall Little Girl. Brasier, V. LHJ 73 (10/56): 192.

6246. Tam Speaks. Robin, R. SR 39 (6/16/56): 27.

6247. The Tanager. Carrier, C. SR 38 (4/9/55): 25.

6248. Tanglewood Island. Jacobson, E. SEP 230 (6/7/58): 103.

6249. Tank Town. Atherton, J. NY 33 (7/27/57): 57.

6250. Tantalizing Morsel. Blackwell, P.J. SEP 227 (5/28/55): 53.

6251. Tantrum. Richstone, M. TH 35 (2/57): 44.

6252. Tao in the Yankee Stadium Bleachers. Updike, J. NY 32 (8/18/56): 28.

6253. Tap Nap. De Kay, O.,Jr. At 202 (7/58): 92.

6254. Tapestries at the Cloisters. Williams, W.C. AN 57 (5/58): 28.

6255. Tapestry Figures. Abrahams, W. P 88 (8/56): 307.

6256. Tardy Spring. Kahn, H. SEP 229 (3/23/57): 117.

6257. Tardy Tales. Reinert, D.E. WLB 31 (5/57): 729.

6258. Target. Usk, T. SEP 227 (2/12/55): 50.

6259. Targets. Marz, R. P 95 (10/59): 9.

6260. The Task. Morris, H. P 91 (12/57): 190-1.

6261. Tatami Floor. Yamanoguchi, B. P 88 (5/56): 68.

6262. Tavoy Evening. Pe, U.W. At 201 (2/58): 156.

6263. Taylor-Made. Redivivus, M.J. NaR 7 (12/5/59): 518.

6264. Teach Us to Pray. Terry, J. CT 3 (9/28/59): 8.

6265. The Teacher. Bevington, H. NY 35 (6/20/59): 87.

6266. Teacher. Carlisle, T.J. LHJ 76 (3/59): 96.

6267. Teacher Comes of Age. Flaumenhaft, A.S. EJ 44 (5/55): 294.

6268. Teachers All. Owen, G. EJ 46 (11/57): 507.

6269. Teacher's Pet. Owen, G. EJ 46 (4/57): 207.

6270. The Teaching Load. Wagoner, D. SR 42 (11/7/59): 43.

6271. Teaching Swift to Young Ladies. Dickey, W. P 94 (6/59): 165.

6272. Tears May Be Idle, But Women Aren't. Armour, R. SEP 229 (9/22/56): 123.

6273. Teasing the Nuns. Shapiro, K. P 90 (8/57): 265-6.

6274. Technologies. Starbuck, G. NY 35 (10/3/59): 42.

6275. Teen-Age Defense. Galbraith, G.S. SEP 228 (4/21/56): 101.

6276. Teens. Puneky, C. TH 35 (8/57): 26.

6277. The Tel at Givat Oz. Gisnet, A. C 19 (2/55): 170.

6278. Telephone. Freeman, J.T. LHJ 72 (3/55): 192.

6279. The Telephone Pad. Funk, M.R. LHJ 73 (11/56): 203.

6280. Telescope. Edelman, K. SEP 229 (6/29/57): 39.

6281. Television Transfer. Schiff, L.K. TH 34 (2/56): 59.

6282. Tell Me. Shook, B. LHJ 74 (12/57): 124.

6283. Tell Me a Story. Grenville, R.H. SEP 231 (10/11/58): 108.

6284. Tell That Neighbor Girl. Traad, M. At 198 (10/56): 175.

6285. The Telltale Moment. Weiss, T. P 94 (6/59): 153-4.

6286. Telmachos. Scott, T. P 86 (5/55): 96-8.

6287. Temper of Time. Plath, S. N 181 (8/6/55): 119.

6288. Temper Truth. Wheeler, R. SEP 230 (11/23/57): 84.

6289. The Temple of the Animals. Duncan, R. P 90 (9/57): 351-2.

6290. Temples in the Dark. Montgomery, J. N 185 (12/28/57): 504.

6291. Tempora Mutantur. Greenslet, F. At 200 (9/57): 91.

6292. Temporary Permanent. Seifer, D. GH 149 (8/59): 53.

6293. The Ten. Smith, W.J. NR 134 (4/30/56): 19.

6294. Tendons. Lilly, O. CC 72 (11/23/55): 1365.

6295. The Tennis. White, E.B. NY 32 (10/6/56): 46.

6296. Tense Situation. Wheeler, R. SEP 228 (6/9/56): 68.

6297. Tenth Anniversary. Freneau, I.D. LHJ 73 (1/56): 95.

6298. The Tenth One. Rosenthal, M.L. N 186 (2/22/58): 166.

6299. The Tenth Station of the Cross. Roseliep, R. A 92 (3/19/55): 649.

6300. Teresa. Sitwell, O. NY 33 (2/23/57): 34.

6301. Teresa de Cepeda. Hazo, S.J. Co 69 (10/17/58): 70.

6302. Terra Nova. Carrier, C. AS 24 (Wint/54-55): 45.

6303. La Terrace Dans La Pluie. Akins, Z. LHJ 76 (8/59): 12.

6304. Terrain. Morris, H. P 85 (1/55): 221-4.

6305. A Testament. Eberhart, R. P 95 (10/59): 4.

6306. Testament. Roseliep, R. Co 70 (8/28/59): 441.

6307. A Testament from 'Lieutenant Schmidt'. Pasternak, B. NR 140 (4/6/59): 14.

6308. Testament of Wonder. Hess, M.W. CC 75 (1/8/58): 44.

6309. Text for Grandma Moses. Olson, T. SR 39 (8/11/56): 26.

6310. Thank You. Koch, K. P 94 (5/59): 74-6.

6311. Thanks. Engle, J.D.,Jr. SEP 229 (11/24/56): 143.

6312. Thanksgiving. Koch, K. P 90 (7/57): 202-4.

6313. Thanksgiving Cup. Merrill, H. SEP 229 (11/24/56): 75.

6314. Thanksgiving in May. Howe, M.A.D. SR 39 (3/31/56): 10.

6315. Thanksgiving on Long Island. Nicolas, C. SR 40 (11/9/57): 25.

6316. A Thanksgiving Prayer. Hicky, D.W. GH 142 (11/56): 13.

6317. That Breakfast. Moran, M. At 198 (8/56): 54.

6318. That Miser, Fear. Stefanile, F. P 94 (9/59): 383.

6319. That Sense As in the Tragedies. Vliet, R.G. SR 40 (7/20/57): 15.

6320. That the Sestina Is What It Is Despite What It Is Not. Stock, R. P 90 (4/57): 25-6.

6321. That Which Is Found in Straw. Stebbing, F. CC 72 (11/30/55): 1392.

6322. That's Funny, I Used to Take a 38. White, S. SEP 232 (10/24/59): 125.

6323. That's Funny, She's a Big Girl Now. Lynn, P. GH 148 (4/59): 196.

6324. That's Funny, Wasn't It? Nash, O. At 199 (6/57): 54.

6325. That's Going Too Far. Chadwick, R. SEP 230 (12/28/57): 64.

6326. That's My Daughter. Treadwell, S. SEP 232 (7/18/59): 61.

6327. That's the Way It Goes. Wheeler, R. SEP 229 (7/28/56): 78.

6328. Thaw. Schofield, D.W. SEP 227 (3/26/55): 106.

6329. Theatrical Review. Douglass, S. SEP 231 (2/28/59): 65.

6330. Their Past Laughter Will Strike Them. Gilboa, A. P 92 (7/58): 253.

6331. Theme with Variations. Ryskind, M. NaR 5 (6/7/58): 532.

6332. Then and Now. Gogarty, O.St.J. GH 140 (5/55): 99.

6333. Then, Now, Hereafter. Morse, S.F. P 92 (5/58): 75-6.

6334. The Theology of Jonathan Edwards. McGinley, P. H 215 (10/57): 73.

6335. A Theory of Waves. Hollander, J. NY 32 (3/31/56): 38.

6336. Therapy. Morton, D. AS 25 (Aut/56): 458.

6337. There Are Other Lands. Shook, B. LHJ 75 (2/58): 28.

6338. There Are Places. Cunliffe, C. LHJ 73 (4/56): 137.

6339. There Goes My Child. Renon, E. AS 25 (Summ/56): 281-2.

6340. There Is a Railroad Track. De Jong, D.C. P 91 (10/57): 13.

6341. There Is a Time. Harrington, H. SEP 229 (2/16/57): 120.

6342. There Is But One. Hoffman, D.G. LHJ 76 (6/59): 21.

6343. There Is No Dew Tonight. Renon, E. N 188 (5/16/59): 460.

6344. There Once Was a Maiden of Siam. GH 141 (7/55): 40.

6345. There Was Once an Owl. Ciardi, J. LHJ 76 (3/59): 182.

6346. There Was Will. Jackson, W.S. SEP 229 (11/22/56): 81.

6347. There's Too Much Sea on the Big Sur. Duncan, R. P 90 (9/57): 352-3.

6348. Therese. L'Heureux, J. Co 69 (11/14/58): 175.

6349. These Faces. Hall, D. SR 41 (6/14/58): 42.

6350. These Friends of Yours. Everson, L. P 85 (3/55): 331-5.

6351. These Lovers Have Wandered.... Tagliabue, J. P 97 (2/56): 267.

6352. These Men. Booth, P. P 94 (5/59): 92.

6353. These Sons of Loveless Women. Thornton, M.B. SR 42 (2/29/59): 26.

6354. These Sunday Things. Schoeberlein, M. GH 142 (1/56): 42.

6355. They Are for the Living. Strachan, E.M. SEP 230 (12/7/57): 106.

6356. They Gave Him Vinegar to Drink. Sherwin, J.J. At 196 (8/55): 67.

6357. They Sing. Roethke, T. NY 32 (8/18/56): 22.

6358. They Uncovered the Roof. Pierce, E.L. CC 76 (3/25/59): 359.

6359. They're All in the Same Boat. Wheeler, R. SEP 229 (2/9/57): 61.

6360. The Thief. Kunitz, S. P 87 (2/56): 254-7.

6361. A Thief in the Night. Pierce, E.L. CC 76 (1/21/59): 78.

6362. Things Like This I Do Not Understand. Moore, M. LHJ 75 (5/58): 143.

6363. Things We Did That Meant Something. Stafford, W. P 91 (1/58): 252.

6364. The Things We Never Had Remain. Richardson, D.L. LHJ 74 (10/57): 125.

6365. Think of This. Eich, G. At 199 (3/57): 145.

6366. Thinner Sun. Weaver, B. CC 72 (8/31/55): 991.

6367. The Third Continent. Brulkar, M. P 93 (1/59): 245.

6368. Third Generation. Armknecht, R.F. SEP 229 (7/21/56): 63.

6369. Third-Grade Thanksgiving Project: Pilgrim Cut-outs. Ross, G. SEP 230 (11/30/57): 103.

6370. Third Madrigal. Derwood, G. P 85 (2/55): 271-2.

6371. The Third Poet. Little, K.D. SR 39 (4/7/56): 18.

6372. The Third Stair. Walton, E.L. N 188 (1/31/59): 104.

6373. The Third Tower. Mayo, E.L. P 92 (6/58): 166.

6374. Thirty-Fifth Spring. Mary Gilbert, Sr. SEP 230 (3/15/58): 97.

6375. Thirty Years in the Wrong Profession. Jaffray, N.R. SEP 229 (2/2/57): 40.

6376. This Christmas Pete's Fourteen. Freeman, J.D. M 87 (12/59): 180.

6377. This Edge of Autumn. Wangsgaard, E.W. SEP 231 (11/8/58): 118.

6378. This Garden. Friedrich, G. CC 74 (8/7/57): 941.

6379. This I Ask of Poetry. Eastman, F. CC 74 (5/8/57): 588.

6380. This Is Only the End. Carter, A.H. CC 76 (5/6/59): 549.

6381. This Is Remembered. Thomas, D. P 87 (11/55): 85-6.

6382. This Is the Beauty. Pustilnik, J. LHJ 76 (6/59): 75.

6383. This Is the Place. Stuart, J. SR 39 (4/21/56): 17.

6384. This Is the Sun You Know and Loved of Old. Tremayne, P. At 198 (8/56): 67.

6385. This Is the Way. Harrington, H. SEP 230 (11/16/57): 132.

6386. This Is to Walk. Frazee-Bower, H. SEP 229 (12/15/56): 104.

6387. This Isn't Spring. Kelley, R.S. SEP 228 (4/7/56): 98.

6388. This Light. Grace, W.J. A 94 (12/24/55): 357.

6389. This Morning. Galbraith, G.S. SEP 232 (9/5/59): 46.

6390. This Other Sleep. Jennings, L.N. SR 38 (1/1/55): 14.

6391. This Part of Ocean. Supervielle, J. At 201 (6/58): 63.

6392. This Side of Sanity. Henry, J. LHJ 73 (11/56): 113.

6393. This Side of Sanity. Henry, J. LHJ 74 (10/57): 106-7.

6394. This Swallow's Empire. Garrigue, J. P 93 (12/58): 133-4.

6395. This Thing Called Spring. Ellis, C. SEP 229 (4/27/57): 94.

6396. Thorn and Weed. Zimmerman, E.H. SEP 227 (1/29/55): 69.

6397. Thorn Leaves in March. Merwin, W.S. P 87 (3/56): 328-9.

6398. Those Abysses of Silence.... Tagliabue, J. P 97 (2/56): 266.

6399. Those New Year's Resolutions. Jaffray, N.R. SEP 227 (1/1/55): 35.

6400. Those Whom Death Leaves. Walton, E.L. P 91 (11/57): 84.

6401. Thou Shalt Have Trouble Trying Me. Herschberger, R. P 86 (6/55): 140.

6402. A Thought. Cooper, J.C. CC 74 (9/25/57): 1125.

6403. Thought. Liotta, J. WLB 32 (5/58): 649.

6404. The Thought-Fox. Hughes, T. NY 33 (8/31/57): 28.

6405. Thought in a Dentist's Waiting Room. Twiggs, D.E. SEP 232 (10/3/59): 152.

6406. Thought of an Icebox Raider. Neely, L. SEP 229 (10/13/56): 72.

6407. Thoughtful Junior. Eisenlohr, L. SEP 230 (5/10/58): 99.

6408. Thoughts After Stating I Hadn't Time to Serve on a Certain Committee. Parrish, M.M. SEP 229 (10/20/56): 91.

6409. Thoughts and the Billiard Balls. Noyes, A. NaR 3 (4/27/57): 399.

6410. Thoughts in a Doubting Time. Jacobs, C.H. SEP 231 (4/25/59): 93.

6411. The Thoughts of a Scholarly Sheperd. O'Gorman, N. Co 68 (8/22/58): 521.

6412. Thoughts of an Envious Housewife. Chadwick, R. SEP 229 (10/13/56): 65.

6413. Thoughts on a Motorcycle Policeman. White, S. SEP 232 (11/28/59): 83.

6414. Thoughts on Looking into a Thicket. Ciardi, J. P 86 (4/55): 27-40.

6415. Thoughts on Opening Someone Else's Medicine Cabinet. Jaffray, N.R. SEP 230 (3/58): 76.

6416. Thoughts on Rereading 'Don Juan'. Bishop, M. NY 33 (6/15/57): 108.

6417. Thoughts on Summer Reading. Hurianek, V. WLB 33 (4/59): 570.

6418. Thoughts on the Christmas Vacation. Lee, M. M 87 (12/59): 165.

6419. Thoughts While Cutting Grass. Goodman, M.W. SEP 230 (7/13/57): 47.

6420. Thoughts While Cutting Grass. Hammer, P. SEP 230 (1/4/58): 44.

6421. Thoughts While Waiting. Armour, R. SEP 228 (2/18/56): 77.

6422. A Thousand Paper Cranes. Yoneda, E. CC 75 (8/6/58): 903.

6423. A Thousandth Poem to Dylan Thomas. Ciardi, J. SR 39 (12/15/56): 21.

6424. Three from Gaius Valerius Catullus. Zukofsky, C. and L. P 94 (6/59): 148-9.

6425. Three Greek Virgins. Lattimore, R. P 92 (6/58): 149-50.

6426. The Three Little Pigs. Jenney, L.E. LHJ 75 (8/58): 119.

6427. Three Love Poems. Rayaprol, S. P 93 (1/59): 224-5.

6428. Three Masses of Christmas. Warwick, D. A 102 (12/19-26/59): 374.

6429. Three Nursery Rhymes. Warren, R.P. YR 47 (6/58): 495-8.

6430. Three Orpheus Songs. Fitzgerald, G. P 89 (12/56): 152-5.

6431. Three Phases of a Small Boy Helping With the Chores. White, S. SEP 232 (11/7/59): 106.

6432. Three Poems. Anderson, W. Hn 33 (8/57): 291.

6433. Three Poems. Menashe, S. H 219 (12/59): 89.

6434. Three Poems of St. John of the Cross. Nims, J.F. P 92 (8/58): 304-8.

6435. Three Poems to Jackson. Whittemore, R. P 94 (8/59): 305.

6436. Three Proverbs. Jefferson, R. At 198 (10/56): 189.

6437. Three Songs at Midsummer. Levine, R. P 86 (6/55): 160-1.

6438. Three Sonnets on Works of Art. Tyler, P. P 91 (1/58): 246-7.

6439. Three Sonnets to Time. Whittemore, R. P 94 (8/59): 303-4.

6440. Three Stages. Miles, J. P 92 (6/58): 139-40.

6441. Three Stages of Spring. Reid, A. NY 33 (3/30/57): 79.

6442. Three-Syllable Sonnet. Smith, W.J. NR 136 (3/18/57): 18.

6443. 3:35. Rigotti, C.J. CH 33 (2/59): 356.

6444. Three Valentines to the Wide World. Van Duyn, M. P 88 (7/56): 207-11.

6445. Three-Year-Old. Armknecht, R.F. SEP 232 (11/28/59): 70.

6446. Three-Year-Old. Peel, D. GH 142 (7/56): 28.

6447. Threes. Atherton, J. NY 33 (3/2/57): 103.

6448. Thrifty Lover. Morton, D. AS 26 (Summ/57): 359.

6449. Thriller. WLB 31 (3/57): 564.

6450. Thriller. Carlisle, T.J. WLB 32 (12/57): 288.

6451. Through a Glass, Brightly. Cochrane, P.G. CC 72 (3/9/55): 301.

6452. Through Tears in Antioch. Ackerson, J. CC 76 (12/9/59): 1437.

6453. Throwing the Apple. Eberhart, R. AN 58 (3/59): 45.

6454. The Thrush Returns to Find a Subdivision. Kroll, E. SR 42 (6/20/59): 33.

6455. Thrush Song at Dawn. Eberhart, R. P 88 (8/56): 320.

6456. Thrushes. Pasternak, B. NR 139 (11/10/58): 20.

6457. Thunder on the Left. Bishop, M. NY 33 (9/7/57): 30.

6458. Thursday Afternoon. Neame, A. P 91 (2/58): 311-12.

6459. Thus Speaketh Christ Our Lord. GH 140 (4/55): 40.

6460. Thyme Gallops Withal. Lamport, F. H 212 (1/56): 67.

6461. The Tide at Long Point. Swenson, M. NY 32 (7/7/56): 22.

6462. The Tide is Rising. Pierce, E.L. CC 73 (8/1/56): 900.

6463. The Tides of Emotion. Phillips, E. GH 142 (8/56): 121.

6464. Tied Intangibles. White, J. YR 44 (6/55): 567.

6465. The Tiger. Eff, J. NaR 6 (11/8/58): 297.

6466. Time. Pierce, E.L. CC 72 (9/21/55): 1088.

6467. Time. Rothenberg, R. Hn 35 (8/59): 280.

6468. Time and Atlantis. Zaturenska, M. N 183 (11/10/56): 402.

6469. Time and Space. Hitziz, W.M. SR 38 (12/3/55): 24.

6470. The Time Came. Swenson, M. N 185 (10/12/57): 250.

6471. Time for a Little Serious Talk Along Lines. McFarland, E. LHJ 75 (7/59): 108.

6472. Time Is Our Choice of How to Love and Why. Auden, W.H. A 97 (9/14/57): 624.

6473. Time Makes All People Necrophiliacs. Moore, M. LHJ 74 (11/57): 40.

6474. Time of Judgement. Decavalles, A. P 88 (8/56): 310.

6475. Time of Miracles. Harrington, H. CT 3 (4/27/59): 11.

6476. Time of Visitation. Pierce, E.L. CC 72 (4/13/55): 449.

6477. Time Off for Bad Behavior. Galbraith, G.S. LHJ 73 (11/56): 166.

6478. Time, the White Fox. Barker, E.L.S. SR 38 (11/5/55): 10.

6479. Time to Go In. Merrill, H. SEP 231 (11/1/58): 62.

6480. Time Was When Death. Van Doren, M. N 185 (9/7/57): 116.

6481. Timely Warning. Barker, S.O. SEP 229 (10/20/56): 67.

6482. Time's Out. Knoefle, J. P 93 (12/58): 150.

6483. The Timid Future. Wheelock, J.H. At 202 (11/58): 156.

6484. Timing. Usk, T. TH 35 (12/57): 48.

6485. The Tip-Off. Jaffray, N.R. SEP 228 (3/17/56): 110.

6486. Tip to Treasure. Longfellow, I.B. SEP 229 (10/13/56): 95.

6487. The Tipplers. Richter, H. SEP 231 (9/6/58): 64.

6488. Tiresias' Lament. Kay, E.deY. N 183 (11/10/56): 371.

6489. Tirzah. Cohen, Y. P 92 (7/58): 203-4.

6490. 'Tis Folly and 'Tis Wise. Solovay, J.C. CH 33 (10/58): 102.

6491. Tittle-Tattle. Chadwick, H. SEP 230 (5/17/58): 124.

6492. To a Blue-Jeaned Heart. Eldridge, J.C. LHJ 75 (9/58): 109.

6493. To a Caricaturist Who Got Me Wrong. Graves, R. NR 135 (12/17/56): 27.

6494. To a Certain Person. Batchelder, A. LHJ 72 (9/55): 112.

6495. To a Child Seen Skipping. Graham, E. LHJ 73 (4/56): 96.

6496. To a Fellow Shipmate. Davidson, J.F. CC 74 (10/16/57): 1229.

6497. To a First-Grade Desk. Stockdale, A.B. SEP 231 (9/6/58): 48.

6498. To a Fly in a Glass-Dome Car. Thompson, D. SEP 228 (6/16/56): 82.

6499. To a Friend. Pasternak, B. NR 140 (1/26/59): 19.

6500. To a Gentle Lover. Conklin, B.S. LHJ 72 (4/55): 156.

6501. To a Groundhog. Ardayne, J.C. NY 31 (1/28/56): 57.

6502. To a Hostess Saying Goodnight. Wright, J. SR 39 (5/5/55): 25.

6503. To a Husband on Father's Day. Frazee-Bower, H. SEP 230 (6/14/58): 72.

6504. To A.L. B., M.A. SR 38 (12/24/55): 19.

6505. To a Lost Child. Kahn, H. LHJ 75 (3/58): 120.

6506. To a Man Gazing at a Girl Gazing at an Ocean. Kelley, R.S. SEP 230 (3/22/58): 100.

6507. To a Marie Laurencin Girl. Coatsworth, E. LHJ 72 (6/55): 125.

6508. To a Misguided Maiden. Bryant, A. GH 148 (2/59): 138.

6509. To a Mouse. Galbraith, G.S. SEP 227 (1/1/55): 71.

6510. To a Nightingale. Groszmann, L. and Snodgrass, W.D. At 204 (11/59): 142.

6511. To a Passing Young Man. Isler, B. SEP 229 (1/26/57): 59.

6512. To a Real-Estate Agent. Darey, L. GH 142 (10/56): 13.

6513. To a Recent Believer. Golffing, F. P 88 (6/56): 159.

6514. To a Reluctant Student. Solovay, J.C. CH 33 (1/59): 270.

6515. To a Salesgirl Weary of Artificial Holiday Trees. Wright, J. NY 35 (12/19/59): 40.

6516. To a Scientist. Stuart, A.M. CC 73 (5/16/56): 609.

6517. To a Scientist Friend. Crown, R. CT 1 (12/24/56): 19.

6518. To a Second Child. Gibbs, E. SEP 230 (4/5/58): 52.

6519. To a Small Spider. Hackett, E.W. SEP 228 (7/2/55): 82.

6520. To a Son in Boot Camp. Kinnick, B.J. SEP 229 (1/12/57): 77.

6521. To a Too, Too Gracious Hostess. Galbraith, G.S. SEP 230 (6/21/58): 84.

6522. To a Used Auto Parts Dealer. Mayes, R.I. N 187 (10/25/58): 295.

6523. To a Woman Seen Eating the Evening Paper. Hall, C. P 90 (9/57): 357.

6524. To a Young Girl. Hazen, B.S. LHJ 75 (7/59): 136.

6525. To a Young Girl on a Premature Spring Day. Wright, J. NY 35 (3/14/59): 48.

6526. To a Youth Afraid. Solovay, J.C. CH 33 (5/59): 544.

6527. To an Agnostic. Marley, F.J. CC 75 (11/5/58): 1269.

6528. To an Atomic Scientist. Darcy, M.M. SR 42 (1/17/59): 12.

6529. To an Insect Entombed in a Tome. Solum, S. SR 38 (9/10/55): 16.

6530. To and On Other Intellectual Poets on Reading That the U.S.A.F. Had Sent a Team of Scientists to Africa to Learn Why Giraffes Do Not Black Out. Guthrie, R. N 185 (10/26/57): 292.

6531. To Apollo Musagetes. Hoskins, K. P 91 (11/57): 107-8.

6532. To Apologize. Sabe, K. LHJ 75 (11/59): 82.

6533. To Be a Child. Engle, P. LHJ 76 (10/59): 115.

6534. To Be Black, To Be Lost. Kahn, H. H 213 (11/56): 56.

6535. To Begin As the Rivers. Wells, M. P 93 (11/58): 70-1.

6536. To Bill Williams. Eberhart, R. N 186 (5/31/58): 501.

6537. To Break a Mirror. Hall, D. SR 39 (6/23/56): 40.

6538. To C, with Two Lines from Eluard. Zitner, S.P. N 184 (5/18/57): 443.

6539. To Carter G. Woodson--Historian. Johnson, G.D. NHB 18 (5/55): 194.

6540. To Certain Poets. Lowenfels, W. N 84 (2/2/57): 103.

6541. To Complicate Matters. Greenville, R.H. GH 148 (4/59): 186.

6542. To David, About His Education. Nemerov, H. N 187 (10/4/58): 195.

6543. To Edward Arlington Robinson. Obear, E.H. EJ 44 (10/55): 389.

6544. To Emily Dickinson. Moffitt, J. At 199 (3/57): 72.

6545. To Forget Me. Weiss, T. P 94 (6/59): 154-5.

6546. To Forget Self and All. Curnow, A. P 86 (9/55): 342-43.

6547. To Frederick Mistral (Neven). Campbell, R. NaR 1 (1/11/56): 21.

6548. To Galen Fisher. Harkness, G. CC 72 (1/19/55): 73.

6549. To Grownups Bearing Gifts. Lineaweaver, M. LHJ 72 (3/55): 124.

6550. To Helen, Being Weaned. Wells, A.M. NY 34 (4/26/58): 128.

6551. To Helen, with a Playbill. Eberhart, R. N 182 (4/7/56): 283.

6552. To J.B. Kessler, J. LHJ 74 (4/57): 117.

6553. To Judith. Ciardi, J. At 195 (1/55): 65.

6554. To Kate, Skating Better Than Her Date. Daiches, D. NY 32 (2/2/57): 34.

6555. To Live at All. Hoskins, K. N 187 (9/6/58): 116.

6556. To Love and to Cherish. Blackwelder, D.C. SEP 231 (9/6/58): 77.

6557. To Lucasta, About That War. Ciardi, J. P 91 (2/58): 290-91.

6558. To Mary of Bethany. Wilkinson, M. CC 75 (3/26/58): 372.

6559. To Michael Riviere, for His Second Son, Thomas. Silkin, J. P 91 (11/57): 81-2.

6560. To Mr. Liu Ya-tzu. Tse-Tung, M. At 204 (12/59): 55.

6561. To Mrs. Lindbergh. Fielding, W.K. SR 40 (2/9/57): 23-4.

6562. To My Child. Jilaveri, M. P 93 (1/59): 232.

6563. To My Father. O'Gorman, N. P 89 (2/57): 282.

6564. To My Friend Who Reads Braille. Lawson, D. CC 74 (6/12/57): 730.

6565. To My Friend Whose Parachute Did Not Open. Wagoner, D. P 92 (5/58): 69.

6566. To My Hostess at a Party. Castle, H. SEP 228 (6/23/56): 44.

6567. To My Husband, Hanging a Calendar. Emans, E.V. GH 148 (1/59): 132.

6568. To My Husband, Shaving. Rank, M.O. SEP 232 (7/11/59): 52.

6569. To My Neighbor. Raskin, A. SEP 228 (6/2/56): 49.

6570. To My Older Brother. Wright, J. P 92 (8/58): 280.

6571. To My Parents. Barkins, E. LHJ 74 (9/57): 109.

6572. To My Son, Who Is Grown and Gone. Petite, I. LHJ 76 (2/59): 134.

6573. To My Young Daughter. Fowler, E.M. TH 33 (12/55): 40.

6574. To Nearly Everybody. MacDiarmid, H. N 185 (10/19/57): 270.

6575. To One I Love. Boles, F. SEP 231 (1/24/59): 38.

6576. To One Who Walks Only on Boards and Wheels. Waugaman, C. CT 2 (1/20/58): 25.

6577. To Paint a Water-Lily. Hughes, T. P 94 (8/59): 297-98.

6578. To Praise a Man. Engle, P. L 46 (6/15/59): 15-6.

6579. To Prue, Below Sleep. Turner, A.T. At 201 (2/58): 61.

6580. To St. John the Evangelist. Appleton, S. Co 65 (3/8/57): 592.

6581. To Seek a Child. McCarthy, L. A 102 (12/19-26/59): 374.

6582. To Stella, Who Would Be 77. Singer, H. P 94 (8/59): 287-88.

6583. To Tabitha. Eaton, B. SR 39 (5/5/56): 25.

6584. To Teach or Not to Teach. Scholsser, J.J. CH 34 (11/59): 164.

6585. To the Author of a Travel Ad. Grenville, R.H. SEP 229 (6/22/57): 48.

6586. To the Bird. Sanzenbach, P. SR 42 (4/25/59): 15.

6587. To the Bureau of the Census. White, L.E. SR 42 (10/10/59): 46.

6588. To the Easter Dead. Stuart, G.C. CC 73 (3/28/56): 391.

6589. To the Evening Star. Blake, W. GH 140 (3/55): 16.

6590. To the First-Born. Parrish, M.M. SEP 229 (11/10/56): 121.

6591. To the First Grade Teacher. Henley, E. LHJ 74 (6/57): 44.

6592. To the Girls. Warsaw, I. SEP 229 (9/15/56): 78.

6593. To the Guillotine. Sagittarius. NR 137 (10/14/57): 9.

6594. To the Librarians of Montgomery, Alabama. Bentley, E. NR 140 (6/8/59): 8.

6595. To the Lifeless of the Party. Rosenfield, L. SEP 229 (3/30/57): 40.

6596. To the Lover. Hayden, R.L. LHJ 75 (11/58): 178.

6597. To the Painter Paul Klee. Plutzik, H. N 186 (3/1/58): 196.

6598. To the Plane Tree. Valery, P. P 94 (4/59): 5-7.

6599. To the Shades of Old Time Revolutionaires. Rosenthal, M.L. N 187 (9/20/58): 160.

6600. To the Snake. Levertov, D. P 93 (10/58): 19.

6601. To the Todas. Singer, H. P 94 (8/59): 284-85.

6602. To the Unnamed Lake. Kraft, V.A. CC 72 (1/12/55): 49.

6603. To Time. Miles, J. P 92 (6/58): 142-43.

6604. To Timothy. Zimmerman, E.H. SEP 227 (4/16/55): 143.

6605. To Vow. Duncan, R. P 91 (3/58): 378.

6606. To W.H. Auden on His Fiftieth Birthday. Howes, B. P 90 (6/57): 129-30.

6607. To Wit. Otis, A.F. SEP 227 (1/8/55): 42.

6608. The Toast. Siden, W. SR 42 (6/6/59): 34.

6609. Toast to 2000. Lister, R.P. At 200 (11/57): 118.

6610. Tobacco. Merwin, W.S. H 212 (2/56): 34.

6611. Toddler Free. Harrington, H. SEP 232 (8/8/59): 69.

6612. Toilers. Rutledge Archibald. LHJ 75 (2/58): 72.

6613. Told by a Gypsy. Grenville, R.H. GH 140 (5/55): 99.

6614. The Tomb. Pierce, E.L. CC 75 (8/13/58): 921.

6615. The Tomb of Stephane Mallarme. Golffing, F. P 93 (11/58): 86.

6616. Tome-Thoughts From the Times. Updike, J. NR 141 (8/10/59): 21.

6617. Tomorrow. Wood, J.P. LHJ 73 (11/56): 135.

6618. Too Old to Read. Van Doren, M. N 187 (7/19/58): 39.

6619. Too Polite for My Own Good. Brown, L. SEP 231 (3/14/59): 92.

6620. Top Secret. Armour, R. BHG 33 (5/55): 213.

6621. Topic Zone. Raskin, A. SEP 232 (9/5/59): 74.

6622. Topsy-Turvy. Richstone, M. SEP 231 (8/16/58): 93.

6623. Torch Song. Hammer, P. H 218 (1/59): 28.

6624. Tortoise. Hagiwara, S. P 88 (5/56): 102.

6625. The Total Calm. Booth, P. NY 33 (12/28/57): 26.

6626. A Tour of English Cathedrals in Summer (or Rainy Season). McGinley, P. NY 33 (8/3/57): 30-31.

6627. The Tourist on the Towers of Vision, 1957. Schevell, J. SR 41 (1/11/58): 68.

6628. Tourists. Moss, H. NY 33 (7/6/57): 32.

6629. The Tourist's Complaint to God: Yellowstone Park. Maino, J.G. N 185 (11/23/57): 396.

6630. Tourists from the City. Starbuck, G.S. At 202 (9/58): 85.

6631. The Tourists in Spain. Feldman, I. N 183 (8/11/56): 123.

6632. Touro Synagogue. Whitman, R. C 23 (4/57): 335.

6633. Towards Gethsemane. Molton, W.L. CC 73 (2/22/56): 239.

6634. The Tower. Muir, E. N 183 (11/10/56): 406.

6635. The Toxicologist. Van Valen, L. SR 41 (4/12/58): 69.

6636. Toy Windmill. Sandeen, E. P 85 (2/55): 261-62.

6637. The Toys. Levine, P. P 86 (5/55): 78-79.

6638. The Toys. Patmore, C. GH 140 (5/55): 40.

6639. Trader, Second Generation. Armour, R. BHG 33 (11/55): 193.

6640. Tragedia Minima. Decavalles, A. P 88 (8/56): 311-12.

6641. The Train Butcher. Ferril, H. H 211 (11/55): 71.

6642. Tramontana. Howes, B. P 89 (12/56): 136-37.

6643. Tranced. Moffitt, J. At 201 (3/58): 37.

6644. Tranquilizer for Mother. Shyer, L.F. SEP 231 (9/13/58): 97.

6645. Tranquilizers. Fleming, S. NY 32 (9/1/56): 85.

6646. Transatlantic Transports. Nash, O. Hl 26 (8/59): 46-47.

6647. Transcontinent. Hall, D. SR 42 (4/11/59): 26.

6648. Transformation Scene. Carrier, C. AS 24 (Wint/54-55): 47-48.

6649. Transience. Irvine, J. LHJ 76 (4/59): 99.

6650. Transmutation. Stanton, H.E. AS 26 (Aut/57): 448.

6651. Les Transparents. Char, R. P 87 (3/56): 316-22.

6652. The Trap. Franklin, G. SR 42 (11/21/59): 55.

6653. The Trap. Galler, D. N 187 (11/1/58): 312.

6654. Travail et Joie. Rich, A. P 90 (8/57): 304-5.

6655. Travel Log. De Jong, D.C. P 89 (2/57): 298.

6656. Travel Piece. Shapiro, H. N 181 (11/5/55): 394.

6657. Travel Trials. Smith, L.C. SEP 228 (10/1/55): 94.

6658. The Traveler. Chakravarty, A. P 93 (1/59): 221-22.

6659. Traveler's Song at Twilight. Douglass, S. BHG 37 (3/59): 125.

6660. Traveler's Tale. Pierce, E.L. CC 72 (10/5/55): 1136.

6661. Travelling Companions. Armour, R. NY 32 (5/5/56): 147.

6662. Travelogue. Sagittarius. NR 138 (1/27/58): 8.

6663. Treacherous Liberals. Sagittarius. NR 137 (11/11/57): 7.

6664. Treason with Reason. Galbraith, G.S. LHJ 74 (4/57): 123.

6665. Tree at Guadalupe Church, Santa Fe. Maris Stella, Sr. Co 69 (3/20/59): 641.

6666. The Tree House. Ford, E. GH 142 (1/56): 42.

6667. Tree of Knowledge. Clark, L.S. CC 72 (4/6/55): 419.

6668. The Tributary Seasons. Watkins, V. P 87 (11/55): 80-83.

6669. Tribute to My Mother. Counselman, M.E. SEP 230 (5/10/58): 121.

6670. A Tribute to W.H. Auden and His Vocabulary. Francis, R. NY 32 (8/4/56): 28.

6671. The Trigger Man. Kanfer, A. YR 48 (9/58): 81.

6672. Trinity. Heafield, K. CC 75 (4/2/58): 402.

6673. Trinity. Kemp, R.Z. CC 76 (1/7/59): 11.

6674. Trio in a Mirror. Donnelly, D. P 94 (9/59): 362-67.

6675. A Trip Through Yucatan. Weiss, T. YR 47 (9/57): 73-74.

6676. Triple Threat. Fairchild, R.B. BHG 37 (9/59): 94.

6677. Triptych. Aiken, C. At 204 (11/59): 80-83.

6678. Triptych. Hazo, S.J. Co 70 (4/3/59): 11.

6679. The Tristram Picnic. Corke, H. NY 32 (5/19/56): 36.

6680. The Triumph of Death. Borden, D. SR 39 (4/14/56): 64.

6681. The Triumph of Pride. Howes, B. P 89 (12/56): 360-61.

6682. The Triumph of Time. Howes, B. P 89 (12/56): 138.

6683. The Triumph of Truth. Howes, B. P 94 (9/59): 361.

6684. Trivialities of God. Carter, M.A. CC 74 (2/6/57): 159.

6685. Tropic of Advent. Jacobsen, J. Co 69 (12/19/58): 312.

6686. The Trouble with Shakespeare, You Remember Him. Nash, O. GH 141 (11/55): 46.

6687. The Trouble with Sunday Is Monday. Armour, R. SEP 229 (2/23/57): 40.

6688. Trout Flies. Todd, R. P 88 (8/56): 292.

6689. Troy in Green. Coffin, R.P.T. LHJ 72 (3/55): 176.

6690. Truck Stop by Night. Landeweer, E. SEP 230 (6/7/58): 81.

6691. Trucks. Grossman, A. P 89 (12/56): 168.

6692. True North. Eberhart, R. N 184 (3/16/57): 238.

6693. Trust in the Future! Coblentz, S.A. CC 75 (11/12/58): 1301.

6694. Tryst. Carleton, S.K. LHJ 75 (9/59): 155.

6695. A Tryst in Brobdingnag. Rich, A. NY 33 (1/4/58): 26.

6696. Tsokadze of Altitudo. Updike, J. NY 32 (2/25/56): 115.

6697. Tucking Him In. Long, E.E. SEP 230 (12/7/57): 66.

6698. Tulsa Speaks to Baltimore. Canaday, J.W. SEP 231 (8/2/58): 70.

6699. Turn of the Screw. Usk, T. SEP 229 (5/18/57): 73.

6700. Turn on the Light. De Ford, S. CC 75 (7/16/58): 826.

6701. Turning Point. Wheeler, R. SEP 227 (4/30/55): 133.

6702. Turpentine. Lister, R.P. NY 32 (10/20/56): 30.

6703. The Turtle. Williams, W.C. At 198 (9/56): 89.

6704. Tutee. Levy, N. At 199 (6/57): 94.

6705. Twain for Spring. Scrutton, K.T. A 95 (6/30/56): 324.

6706. 'Twas the Night Before Christmas. Moore, C. L 45 (12/22/58): 196.

6707. Twelfth Night, the Castle. Henley, E. LHJ 72 (1/55): 88.

6708. Twentieth Century Pastoral: Cow at Her Own Drinking Fountain. Lape, F. H 213 (2/56): 42.

6709. Twentieth Century Pastoral: Croquet. Lape, F. H 214 (1/57): 57.

6710. Twentieth Century Pastoral: The Simple Life. Lape, F. H 212 (3/56): 46.

6711. Twentieth Century Pastoral: Summer. Lape, F. H 213 (7/56): 33.

6712. Twenty-Six Brief Lectures on the History of Printing. Kaser, D. WLB 30 (1/56): 398.

6713. The 23rd Psalm. Ziegler, E.K. CC 73 (3/7/56): 300.

6714. Twenty Years After. Das, J. P 93 (1/59): 216-17.

6715. Twilight. Kahn, H. SEP 229 (11/10/56): 71.

6716. Twilight Moment. Trent, L. CC 76 (8/5/59): 900.

6717. Twinkling. Mayo, E.L. P 90 (9/57): 367.

6718. Two. Scott, W.T. NY 32 (1/12/57): 70.

6719. Two A.M. Manheim, M. SEP 230 (1/11/58): 93.

6720. Two Birds. Grenville, R.H. SEP 228 (4/7/56): 107.

6721. Two Citadels. Lindbergh, A.M. LHJ 73 (8/56): 120.

6722. The Two Cousins. Frezza, L. P 94 (8/59): 325, 327.

6723. The Two Faces of the Wind. Klopp, J. Hn 35 (4/59): 156.

6724. 2 for Theodore Roethke. McClure, M. P 87 (1/56): 218-19.

6725. Two Homilies. O'Gorman, N. Co 65 (3/15/57): 609.

6726. Two Leaves. Stuart, J. LHJ 72 (9/55): 209.

6727. Two-Legged Year. Merrill, H. SEP 230 (8/31/57): 44.

6728. Two Lives and Others. Scott, W.T. P 85 (2/55): 276.

6729. Two Moons. Cregeen, S. N 185 (10/26/57): 290.

6730. Two O'Clock Talk. Crane, C.L. LHJ 75 (1/58): 76.

6731. Two Octaves. Palamas, K. At 195 (6/55): 152.

6732. Two Plus Two Equals Furor. Raskin, S. BHG 34 (3/56): 130.

6733. Two Poems. Soles, M. P 94 (5/59): 78-81.

6734. Two Poems on Larger Topics. O'Gorman, N. P 95 (11/59): 81-82.

6735. Two Poems on the Way. Goodman, P. P 90 (7/57): 212-13.

6736. Two Ruthless Pieces. Whittemore, R. NR 138 (2/17/58): 17.

6737. Two Sides of a Street. Keegan, M. BHG 33 (5/55): 291.

6738. The Two Sisters. Muir, E. N 183 (11/10/56): 409.

6739. Two Sisters of Persephone. Plath, S. P 89 (1/57): 235-36.

6740. The Two Societies. Wheelock, J.H. NY 31 (2/4/55): 25.

6741. Two Songs for Lute. Woods, J. P 94 (7/59): 235.

6742. Two Steps of a Lame Man. Finkel, D. P 89 (3/57): 360.

6743. Two Unrelated Facts. Brown, H. P 90 (6/57): 138.

6744. Two Voices. McFarland, E. LHJ 75 (5/58): 95.

6745. Two Voices in a Cave. Morse, S.F. P 92 (5/58): 73.

6746. Two Voices in a Meadow. Wilbur, R. NY 33 (8/17/57): 26.

6747. Two-Way Revelation. Kernan, F.G. SEP 228 (5/26/56): 60.

6748. Two Ways. Mullins, T.Y. CT 3 (12/8/59): 12.

6749. Two Weeks in August. Heatherley, R.H. At 200 (8/57): 91.

6750. Two-Year-Old Talker. Landeweer, E. SEP 231 (6/13/59): 58.

6751. Tyburn. L'Heureux, J. Co 68 (7/18/58): 402.

6752. The Tycoon. Nash, O. L 39 (9/5/55): 87.

6753. The Typewriter Bird. Smith, W.J. NR 137 (7/29/57): 20.

6754. Uber Nacht. Scholes, K. NY 31 (1/28/56): 26.

6755. The Ugly Duckling. Kanfer, A. H 217 (11/58): 57.

6756. The Ugly Duckling. Rudolph, L. SEP 231 (3/14/59): 86.

6757. Ultimatum. Ryskind, M. NaR 5 (5/24/58): 484.

6758. The Umbrella. Hall, D. SR 40 (6/22/57): 21.

6759. Unaccustomed As I Am. Blackwell, P.J. SEP 229 (2/8/57): 83.

6760. Uncamouflaged. Merchant, J. SEP 228 (9/10/55): 160.

6761. Uncle Cal. Merwin, W.S. N 84 (3/2/57): 190.

6762. Uncle Hess. Merwin, W.S. NY 33 (10/26/57): 42.

6763. Uncles. Burrows, E.G. P 89 (12/56): 169.

6764. Uncles Are Good to Have. Amon, G. SEP 230 (9/21/57): 19.

6765. Unconcerned Employee. Dacy, M. SEP 230 (9/28/57): 19.

6766. Uncounted. Freedman, C.P. CC 74 (6/26/57): 786.

6767. Uncover Charge. Rosenfield, L. SEP 228 (9/3/55): 53.

6768. Uncreated Love. Cooper, J.C. CT 2 (3/17/58): 5.

6769. Under Ground. Duncan, R. P 95 (10/59): 31-33.

6770. Under the Boughs. Baro, G. N 187 (9/20/58): 155.

6771. Under the Cherry Blossom Trees There Are No Real Strangers. Issa (1763-1828). L 40 (4/30/56): 84-85.

6772. Under the Long Wind. Carruth, H. P 85 (3/55): 311-18.

6773. Under the Old One. Merwin, W.S. NY 33 (1/11/58): 31.

6774. Undergraduate Notes. Skinner, K. NR 134 (1/9/56): 18.

6775. Undine. Pfeiffer, E. N 186 (2/8/58): 124.

6776. Unearth the Man. Steiner, S. P 88 (6/56): 145.

6777. Unearthy Toy. Deutsch, B. P 92 (5/58): 71-72.

6778. Uneasy Lies.... Thatcher, M.K. NaR 5 (3/8/58): 227.

6779. Unembarrassed. Merchant, J. SEP 229 (9/1/56): 77.

6780. Unfair Competition. Steele, R.V. SEP 231 (2/7/59): 103.

6781. Unforgotten. Stuart, J. LHJ 75 (6/58): 125.

6782. Unfriendly Witness. Starbuck, G. NR 137 (10/28/57): 17.

6783. Unfurnished Room. Scott, W.T. NR 135 (10/1/56): 18.

6784. An Ungodly Appetite. Kelley, R.S. SEP 229 (9/29/56): 65.

6785. The Ungrateful Garden. Kizer, C. P 89 (12/56): 160.

6786. The Unhappy Farmer. Eisenlohr, L. SEP 231 (11/22/58): 110.

6787. Unhappy Landings. Armknecht, R.F. SEP 227 (6/11/55): 140.

6788. Unhappy Surprise. Pogue, D.E. SEP 229 (6/22/57): 93.

6789. Univac to Univac. Solomon, L.B. H 216 (3/58): 37.

6790. Unjust Desserts. Merchant, J. LHJ 75 (12/59): 94.

6791. Unlikely Clay. Patrick, J.G. CC 75 (4/23/58): 491.

6792. Unmelodious Song. Stepanchev, S. P 90 (5/57): 89.

6793. Unmolested Beauty. Turner, A.N. P 90 (4/57): 29.

6794. The Unprotected. Hearst, J. A 101 (9/26/59): 768.

6795. Unquiet Fourth. Whitt, M.W. SEP 230 (7/6/57): 81.

6796. Unreasonable Facsimile. Hammer, P. SEP 228 (9/2/55): 70.

6797. Unrecorded. Sikelianos, A. At 195 (6/55): 165.

6798. Unrest Home. Seifer, D. GH 149 (8/59): 53.

6799. Unsaid. Cox, M.S. CH 30 (11/55): 170.

6800. Unseen Beauty. Shaffer, T. NHB 21 (4/58): 163.

6801. The Unsettled Motorcyclist's Vision of His Death. Gunn, T. P 90 (4/57): 32-33.

6802. Unspoken Words. Elliott, M. GH 142 (4/56): 164.

6803. Unsubstantial Ghost. Chaffee, E.A. LHJ 74 (5/57): 158.

6804. Until You Came. Conklin, B.S. LHJ 72 (6/55): 86.

6805. Untimely Crows. Griffith, E.V. SEP 229 (5/4/57): 61.

6806. Unwilling Traveler. Merrill, H. SEP 232 (10/10/59): 68.

6807. The Unwise Goose. Merrill, H. SEP 229 (1/26/57): 72.

6808. Up Goethe's Path. Shneour, Z. C 27 (5/59): 434-35.

6809. Upon Reflection. Ellis, C. SEP 229 (10/27/56): 84.

6810. Upper Bay. Dicker, H. N 183 (10/6/56): 292.

6811. An Upper Left Central, Insisor. Todd, R. P 88 (8/56): 291.

6812. Upstairs Window. Harvard, P. SEP 230 (10/11/57): 84.

6813. Urban Archaeology. Jaffray, N.R. SEP 230 (7/27/57): 50.

6814. Urban Moral. Stephens, A. N 185 (10/26/57): 289.

6815. Urgent Spring. Stuart, J. SR 38 (3/19/55): 39.

6816. Uriah Heep Rides Again. Caswell, O. NaR 5 (1/4/58): 10.

6817. Uses of Intuition. Heath, C. SEP 231 (11/15/58): 120.

6818. The Usual Cloud. Lang, D. NY 34 (6/21/58): 34.

6819. Vacancy. Lamb, M.W. LHJ 72 (1/55): 96.

6820. Vacated Camps. Freneau, J.D. SEP 228 (9/10/55): 114.

6821. The Vacation. Kemp, L. P 89 (1/59): 230.

6822. Vacation. Walsh, F.O. BHG 33 (7/55): 121.

6823. Vacation Treasure. Johnson, V.B. EJ 46 (10/57): 455.

6824. Vacationing Housewife. Thompson, D.B. SEP 229 (10/6/56): 70.

6825. Valedictory of a Retiring Teacher. Patterson, E.M. CH 32 (2/58): 3367.

6826. A Valentine. WLB 30 (2/56): 467.

6827. Valentine. Petrie, P. SR 42 (12/12/59): 45.

6828. Valentine All Year. Jones, P. LHJ 76 (12/59): 18.

6829. A Valentine for Marianne Moore. Olson, E. P 91 (3/58): 348.

6830. Valentine for One Loved. Cully, K.B. CC 75 (2/12/58): 194.

6831. Valentine from a Young Gentleman of Verona. Humphries, R. LHJ 73 (2/56): 117.

6832. A Valentine in Crayons. Merrill, J. P 91 (2/58): 283.

6833. Valleys of the Night. Mack, R. SEP 229 (6/29/57): 88.

6834. Value. Galbraith, G.S. LHJ 74 (8/57): 92.
6835. Values. Merchant, J. SEP 228 (7/2/55): 48.
6836. Vanishing American. Grenville, R.H. SEP 230 (9/7/57): 90.
6837. Vanity. Victor, F. C 25 (4/58): 334.
6838. Variation. Akins, Z. LHJ 72 (10/55): 166.
6839. Variation on a Theme. Coe, A.C. At 197 (6/56): 92.
6840. Variations on a Neo-Classic Theme. Justice, D. P 88 (9/56): 365.
6841. Variations on a Theme. Jacobsen, J. Co 68 (9/5/58): 566.
6842. Variations on a Theme by John Donne. McCandless, J.H. CC 75 (9/3/58): 995.
6843. Variations on a Theme of Cavalcanti. Smith, A.J.M. N 186 (3/15/58): 236.
6844. Variations on a Voice. Middleton, C. SEP 231 (4/4/59): 105.
6845. Vast Light. Eberhart, R. N 183 (8/4/56): 104.
6846. Venture. Richardson, D.L. CC 72 (5/25/55): 616.
6847. Vernal Equinox. Moore, R. P 89 (1/57): 210.
6848. Verra la Morte. di Giovanni, N.T. N 186 (3/1/58): 191.
6849. Versatility. Bose, B. P 93 (1/59): 209-10.
6850. Verse for Christmas. Burrows, E. CC 76 (12/16/59): 1466.
6851. Versicle. Yborra, T.J., Jr. H 219 (8/59): 41.
6852. Vessels. McKay, C.C. At 201 (2/58): 62.
6853. Vi Connolly's Spring Song. Stewart, D. P 93 (11/58): 98-101.
6854. Via Southern Iowa. Merritt, V. SEP 229 (10/20/56): 78.
6855. Vice Verses. Lamport, F. SR 38 (6/4/55): 21.
6856. Vicious Cycle. Lee, M.L. LHJ 76 (2/59): 163.
6857. The Victim. Hillyer, R. NY 32 (6/16/56): 105.
6858. Victimae Paschali Laudes. O'Connell, R. Co 68 (4/11/58): 34.
6859. Victor Emanuel Monument (Rome). Norse, H. SR 40 (4/13/57): 51.
6860. Vientiane Journal. Perry, R. P 93 (2/59): 297-300.
6861. Le Vierge, le Vivace et le Bel Aujourd'hui. Smith, A.J.M. N 186 (1/11/58): 35.
6862. View. Miles, J. P 92 (6/58): 142.
6863. The View at Thome. Singer, H. P 95 (8/59): 283.
6864. The View from Our Land. Jennison, C.S. At 195 (3/55): 88.
6865. View of Earth from a Space Station. Morris, J. NY 32 (12/8/56): 175.
6866. A View of Japan. Kirkup, J. At 204 (9/59): 59.
6867. Viewpoint. Balch, B.J. LHJ 75 (10/59): 54.
6868. Viewpoints. Douglass, S. LHJ 76 (12/59): 102.
6869. The Villa. Singer, H. P 94 (8/59): 285.
6870. The Village. Tanaka, F. P 88 (5/56): 65.
6871. The Village of My Fathers. Barron, J.A. C 21 (5/56): 467-68.
6872. Village Wedding. Betjeman, J. NY 35 (7/11/59): 31.
6873. Villanelle of War. Sullivan, A.M. A 94 (10/22/55): 102.
6874. Vincent. Iris, S. P 91 (11/57): 101-2.
6875. Vintage Country. Bloom, R. P 87 (1/56): 215-16.
6876. The Violence. Jerome, J. P 88 (7/56): 236-37.
6877. The Virgin at Noon. Claudel, P. P 87 (12/55): 138-39.
6878. Virgin of Hope. Claude of Jesus, Sr. A 97 (5/25/57): 259.
6879. The Virtues of Home. De Jong, D.C. SR 42 (6/13/59): 17.
6880. Virtuous Pagan. Laing, A. N 189 (7/4/59): 16.
6881. The Virus. Groszmann, L. and Snodgrass, W. D. At 204 (11/59): 142.
6882. The Visible Moments. Squires, R. P 95 (10/59): 25-26.
6883. Vision. Lord, M.C. CC 75 (11/12/58): 1301.
6884. Vision at Franconia. Schneebaum, R. At 198 (8/56): 66.
6885. Vision at Twilight. Smith, W.J. P 87 (10/55): 6.
6886. A Vision, Caged. Dickey, W. P 90 (8/57): 291-92.
6887. The Vision of Dorinda. Bock, F. P 88 (7/56): 221.
6888. Visions. Rosen, M. A 204 (8/59): 50.
6889. The Visit. Litsey, S. GH 142 (8/56): 121.
6890. A Visit. Ponsot, M. P 91 (3/58): 354.
6891. A Visit from St. Nik. Ryskind, M. NaR 7 (8/29/59): 294.
6892. A Visit Home. Stafford, W. NR 133 (10/3/55): 22.
6893. A Visit to the Country. Ostroff, A. H 218 (6/59): 53.
6894. Visitation Day 19--. Leichty, V.E. EJ 45 (12/56): 546.
6895. The Visitor. Cousins, M. GH 142 (12/56): 8.
6896. Visitor. Lee, M.L. LHJ 75 (3/58): 183.
6897. The Visitor. Lilly, O. CC 75 (1/29/58): 131.
6898. Visitor in Eire. Small, H. SEP 231 (7/12/58): 96.
6899. Viva. Smith, W.J. NR 139 (9/22/58): 19.
6900. Voice. Kahn, H. SR 38 (12/3/55): 42.
6901. The Voice. Olson, E. P 91 (3/58): 349.
6902. The Voice in Rama. Schneider, E.F. A 97 (9/14/57): 625.
6903. Voice in the Wilderness. Sagittarius. NR 138 (5/19/58): 12.
6904. The Voice in the Wood. Kenny, H.A. SR 39 (7/1/56): 33.
6905. Voice of Experience. Richardson, N.S. LHJ 76 (3/59): 130.
6906. Voices from the Other World. Merrill, J. NY 33 (6/29/57): 26.
6907. Voices Heard in the Air. Zaturenska, M. P 95 (11/59): 104.
6908. The Voices of October. McGinley, P. SEP 231 (10/11/58): 95.
6909. Volition. Richstone, M. TH 35 (3/57): 34.
6910. Volunteer Nurse. Merchant, J. LHJ 75 (1/58): 112.
6911. Vox Humana. Gunn, T. N 184 (4/27/57): 365.
6912. The Voyage. Tremayne, P. At 199 (4/57): 51.
6913. Un Voyage a Cythere. Carroll, P. P 85 (3/55): 319-21.
6914. The Vulnerable. Galbraith, G.S. SR 38 (4/23/55): 9.
6915. Wabash Catfish. Merrill, H. SEP 229 (7/21/56): 77.
6916. Waders' Woe. Neely, L. SEP 228 (8/27/55): 56.

6917. Wage Rage. Wheeler, R. SEP 229 (5/4/57): 42.

6918. The Waist Line. Carruth, H. At 203 (5/59): 98-99.

6919. Waiting. Stepanchev, S. P 88 (6/56): 156.

6920. The Waiting. Zaturenska, M. P 95 (11/59): 105-6.

6921. Waiting for It. Swenson, M. SR 40 (11/23/57): 33.

6922. Waiting for You. Hoffman, D.G. LHJ 73 (3/56): 158.

6923. The Waiting Game. Kumin, M.W. SR 42 (3/7/59): 26.

6924. The Waking. Coxe, L.O. P 91 (1/58): 226-27.

6925. Waking City. Engle, J.D.,Jr. SEP 229 (1/12/57): 88.

6926. Waking in a Newly-Built House, Oakland. Gunn, T. P 90 (4/57): 34.

6927. The Walk Home. Whittemore, R. P 89 (11/56): 106.

6928. A Walk in Late Summer. Roethke, T. NY 33 (9/7/57): 36.

6929. A Walk on Moss. Viereck, P. P 87 (10/55): 1-5.

6930. A Walker in the Country of July. Morris, H. P 87 (2/56): 275-77.

6931. Walking All Night. Merrill, J. P 91 (2/58): 285-86.

6932. Walking North to the Dunes. Weaver, B. CC 73 (6/20/56): 746.

6933. Walking Weather. Grenville, R.H. SEP 231 (10/25/58): 102.

6934. The Wall. Enrico, H. N 188 (5/16/59): 462.

6935. The Wall. Jones, D. P 87 (11/55): 68-74.

6936. The Wall. Pierce, E.L. CC 75 (1/22/58): 103.

6937. The Wall. St.Martin, H. P 95 (11/59): 94.

6938. The Wall of Rome. Bogardus, E. YR 45 (3/56): 391-92.

6939. Walled City. Laing, D. N 187 (12/27/58): 502.

6940. The Walled Garden at Clondalkin. Sarton, M. P 85 (3/55): 344-46.

6941. The Walnut Chest. Maino, J. LHJ 73 (1/56): 118.

6942. The Walrus and the Carpenter. Jones, E.O. NaR 6 (4/11/59): 647.

6943. A Waltz in the Afternoon. Bentley, B. At 204 (8/59): 49.

6944. Wanderers. Wesley, C.C. CC 75 (4/16/58): 464.

6945. Wandering Dane. Shenton, E. SEP 230 (5/31/58): 79.

6946. Wanting Roses. Galbraith, G.S. GH 148 (3/59): 44.

6947. The War Against the Trees. Kunitz, S. N 184 (5/4/57): 395.

6948. The War Dead. Coblentz, S.A. CC 76 (12/30/59): 1523.

6949. War Diary of an Army Psychiatrist. Bauer, W.W. TH 34 (2/56): 63.

6950. The War Orphans. Sitwell, E. At 200 (11/57): 78.

6951. Wardrobe Closets. Lazarus, P. TH 36 (6/58): 61.

6952. Warm Day in Winter. Ward, M.W. SEP 227 (2/5/55): 67.

6953. Warm Sun. Kreymborg, A. P 93 (12/58): 145.

6954. Warning. Grenville, R.H. SEP 229 (3/30/57): 77.

6955. Warning. Meyer, J. H 215 (9/57): 34.

6956. Warning. Stoutenberg, A. YR 49 (9/59): 94.

6957. Warning to Haberdashers. McGinley, P. NY 33 (5/18/57): 30.

6958. A Warning to My Love. Wagoner, D. P 92 (5/58): 68.

6959. Was a Man. Booth, P. SR 41 (8/30/58): 12.

6960. Was It Florence or Venice. Norse, H. P 94 (5/59): 98-99.

6961. Was It Thus? Grenville, R.H. LHJ 72 (11/55): 203.

6962. Washington, D.C. Ciardi, J. N 183 (7/28/56): 84.

6963. Washington, 1958. Hazel, R. P 92 (8/58): 271-76.

6964. Washout. Krausz, S. SEP 227 (4/30/55): 110.

6965. Wasn't It You? Narasimhaswamy, K.R. P 93 (1/59): 266-67.

6966. Wasp and Windowscreen. Belitt, B. P 91 (10/57): 15-16.

6967. The Wasp's Nest. Rosenberg, J.L. SR 38 (9/17/55): 20.

6968. Wasted Opportunity. Hammer, P. GH 142 (7/56): 28.

6969. The Watch. Fandel, J. Co 67 (11/15/57): 169.

6970. The Watch of the Live Oaks. Schevill, J. SR 41 (3/8/58): 19.

6971. Watching Bird. Coxe, L.O. NR 135 (9/17/56): 17.

6972. Water Babies. Eisenlohr, L. SEP 231 (11/1/58): 96.

6973. Water Color. Mooney, S. NY 33 (1/11/58): 34.

6974. Water Lilies. Zilles, L.E. NY 33 (6/1/57): 87.

6975. Water Picture. Swenson, M. NY 32 (4/14/56): 109.

6976. The Water Surface. Kitahara, H. P 88 (5/56): 99.

6977. Watercolor: Life. Lilly, O. CC 75 (4/30/58): 531.

6978. Watercourse, Vermont. Earle, V. SEP 227 (4/23/55): 68.

6979. The Way and Nothing More. Hicks, J.V. H 218 (1/59): 67.

6980. The Way Good-by Happens. Balch, B.J. SEP 229 (3/2/57): 60.

6981. Wayfarers Within. Raiziss, S. Co 63 (12/9/55): 257.

6982. We Are Few. Pasternak, B. NR 140 (3/23/59): 20.

6983. We Are Not Amused. Jaffray, N.R. SEP 229 (6/15/57): 46.

6984. We Children Are All One Child. Cotter, J.F. A 100 (12/20-27/58): 365-66.

6985. We Delighted, My Friend. Sedar-Senghor, L. At 203 (4/59): 68.

6986. We Did the Best. Nathan, L. P 93 (3/59): 377.

6987. We Gathered in the Yard. Kelley, R.S. SEP 229 (8/11/56): 46.

6988. We Have a Verb 'Stood Up.' Goodman, P. P 92 (9/58): 374.

6989. We Just Have to Face It. Wheeler, R. SEP 229 (6/15/57): 46.

6990. We Keep, Here, the Record of Days. Kessler, S. SR 40 (7/20/57): 16.

6991. We Observant Human Beings. Chadwick, H. BHG 35 (2/57): 119.

6992. We Wander in Each Other's Woods. Kanfer, A. P 94 (4/59): 30.

6993. We Were not Likened to Dogs. Greenberg, U. Z. P 92 (7/58): 215-16.

6994. We Who Are Civilized Salute Ourselves. Laing, D. N 188 (1/17/59): 60.

6995. Weak in, Weak Out. Warsaw, I. SEP 227 (1/29/55): 58.

6996. Weak Resolution. Dean, E. SEP 229 (2/16/57): 73.

6997. Weapon. Usk, T. SEP 230 (6/21/58): 92.

6998. Wearing the Odd Clothes of Exile a Puerto Rican Youth Arrives in New York City and Is Laughed At. Steiner, S. P 88 (6/56): 146-47.

6999. Weary Journalist. Betjeman, J. H 213 (7/56): 69.

7000. Weather Making. Holmes, J. H 210 (5/55): 67.

7001. Weather Profit. Grenville, R.H. SEP 232 (10/24/59): 47.

7002. The Weather This Spring. Whittemore, R. P 89 (11/56): 107-8.

7003. Weather Vane. Strong, J.H. SEP 228 (4/21/56): 60.

7004. Weather-Wise. Usk, T. GH 149 (12/59): 8.

7005. The Web. Bynner, W. NR 136 (1/28/57): 16.

7006. The Web. Drake, L.B. At 201 (5/58): 65.

7007. The Web of Frost. Merrill, H. SEP 230 (11/2/57): 67.

7008. A Wedding in Harvest Time. Bomse, N. C 19 (3/55): 268.

7009. Wedding Song. Ponsot, M. P 91 (3/58): 355.

7010. Weddings and Banquets. Laing, D. N 189 (11/14/59): 346.

7011. The Weeds and the Wilderness. Drake, L.B. At 197 (5/56): 66.

7012. Weekend. Balliett, W. At 200 (8/56): 48.

7013. Weekend Tragedy. Blackwell, P.J. SEP 228 (7/30/55): 46.

7014. Weeping Springtime. Lee, A.M. SEP 231 (4/25/59): 55.

7015. The Weir. Kemp, L. H 212 (6/56): 65.

7016. The Well. Johnson, E.W. CC 72 (10/19/55): 1200.

7017. The Well Bred Children. Puner, H. and Murphy, J. H 212 (1/56): 51.

7018. The Well-House. Warren, R.P. SR 41 (11/22/58): 37.

7019. The Well-Pasted Chain. Henley, E. LHJ 73 (12/56): 98.

7020. Well-Preserved. Stevenson, C.T. SR 39 (4/28/56): 27.

7021. Well Put. Armour, R. SEP 227 (2/19/55): 54.

7022. Well, That's That. Schenck, H.,Jr. H 218 (3/59): 48.

7023. Well-Timed. McGuiggan, R.J. SEP 232 (11/14/59): 87.

7024. Well Trained. Smith, N. SEP 228 (7/23/55): 65.

7025. Wellfleet Harbor. Goodman, P. P 86 (9/55): 339-40.

7026. Wellspring. Galbraith, G.S. SEP 229 (3/2/57): 103.

7027. We're Still in the Dark. Chadwick, R. and H. BHG 35 (3/57): 197.

7028. West. Witt, H. P 91 (12/57): 178-79.

7029. The West Front, Wells Cathedral. Ackerson, J. CC 72 (8/17/55): 948.

7030. West of the Brown Missouri. Jacobs, E.L. SEP 232 (11/28/59): 118.

7031. West-Thrusting Headlands. Armknecht, R.F. SEP 232 (7/25/59): 76.

7032. Western Evening Love Song. Livingstone, G. GH 148 (1/59): 148.

7033. Western Town. Shapiro, K. NY 33 (2/15/58): 34.

7034. Whaler. Merwin, W.S. P 89 (3/57): 346.

7035. What a Bride Knows. Phillis, E. SEP 229 (11/17/56): 139.

7036. What Can Be Made from Nothing. D'Andrade, D. N 184 (6/15/57): 535.

7037. What Child Is Here? Toland, P. LHJ 72 (4/55): 112.

7038. What Comes First? Sullivan, P. WLB 29 (6/55): 793.

7039. What Did the Soldier's Wife Receive? Brecht, B. At 199 (3/57): 183.

7040. What Do Cows Think? Coatsworth, E. SR 38 (4/23/55): 36.

7041. What Do They Mean, Joint Return? Jenney, L.E. SEP 229 (4/13/57): 63.

7042. What Does Your Father Do? Bogin, G. N 185 (12/21/57): 481.

7043. What Else. Herz, B. SEP 231 (11/29/58): 64.

7044. What Happened the Day a Poet Was Appointed Postmaster. Ferlinghetti, L. N 186 (4/19/58): 351.

7045. What Happened to Hera. Nixon, J.,Jr. SR 39 (3/24/56): 14.

7046. What If You Do Shiver? Otis, A.F. SEP 230 (10/11/57): 111.

7047. What Is This Shadow? Richardson, D.L. LHJ 73 (10/56): 105.

7048. What It Is. Reynolds, T. P 93 (11/58): 97.

7049. What Life Is Worth. Stuart, J. AF 63 (4/57): 18.

7050. What My Grandmother Said When She Fed the Kingdoms of the Air. Garrigue, J. LHJ 73 (9/56): 196.

7051. What She Did in the Morning, I Wouldn't Know, She Was Seated There in the Midst of Her Resilient Symptoms Always. Moore, M. SR 39 (6/2/56): 34.

7052. What the Bones Know. Kizer, C. NR 132 (6/6/55): 21.

7053. What the Emanation of Casey Jones Said to the Medium. Smith, A.J.M. N 184 (1/12/57): 44.

7054. What the Rain Might Be. Perdue, N.F. Hn 33 (6/57): 233.

7055. What Town Survives? Lenner, E. CC 73 (12/19/56): 1477.

7056. What Was a World. Salomon, I.L. A 97 (9/14/57): 625.

7057. What You Can't Expect. Thompson, D.B. SEP 230 (7/20/57): 90.

7058. What's Sauce for the Goose.... Chadwick, R. SEP 227 (5/14/55): 113.

7059. The Wheel King. Nemerov, H. P (9/56): 387.

7060. The Wheel of Love, Like All Wheels, Comes Full Circle. Brown, H. P 90 (6/57): 137-8.

7061. The Wheel of My Life. Eisenlohr, L. SEP 231 (8/9/58): 74.

7062. Wheels. Donnelly, D. NY 33 (11/23/57): 58.

7063. Wheep No More. L., R.A. NY 33 (6/8/57): 123.

7064. When Beauty Walks the April Hills. Embury, L. LHJ 72 (4/55): 128.

7065. When Dew Dripped Silver. Mary Honora, Sr. Co 69 (10/24/58): 98.

7066. When Ducks Return. Prommel, H.H. SEP 228 (3/17/56): 136.

7067. When High School Is Out. Ginsberg, L. CH 29 (3/55): 398.

7068. When I Am Old. Magee, I. SEP 231 (11/8/58): 128.

7069. When I'm Going Well. Everson, R.G. SR 41 (11/22/58): 39.

7070. When in Disgrace with Fortune and Men's Eyes. Moss, H. C 22 (11/56): 447.

7071. When Is Bedtime? Chadwick, R. SEP 232 (10/24/59): 91.

7072. When Is Winter? Isler, B. SEP 228 (1/14/56): 58.

7073. When Lilacs Last in the Dooryard Bloom'd. Whitman, W. L 38 (6/20/55): 114.

7074. When Listening to a Lecture Preliminary to a Traffic Ticket.... Otis, A.F. SEP 231 (11/8/58): 96.

7075. When Shad Are Running. Burgess, C. NY 34 (4/12/58): 86.

7076. When the Barn Burned Down. Graves, S.B. SEP 232 (11/28/59): 75.

7077. When the Child Would Accommodate the Adult Again. Holmes, T. P 92 (4/58): 33.

7078. When the Snow Falls. Hoskins, K. P 91 (11/57): 108-9.

7079. When the Wind Blows. Slote, B. A 93 (9/24/55): 621.

7080. When We Have Gone. Coblentz, S.A. CC 73 (6/6/56): 687.

7081. When We Looked Back. Stafford, W. NY 35 (6/6/59): 150.

7082. When Ye Pray Say, "Our Father." Vannenbergh, C.W. CC 72 (7/6/55): 789.

7083. When You're Sixty. Workman, M.T. CC 72 (11/30/55): 1392.

7084. Where and No Trees. Crown, R. P 87 (12/55): 148.

7085. Where Children Have Played. Buck, B. LHJ 74 (10/57): 221.

7086. Where Is It That We Go? Hoskins, K. P 91 (11/57): 110-11.

7087. Where Tall Books Grow. Carlisle, T.J. GH 148 (5/59): 207.

7088. Where the Bodies Break. Kinnell, G. LHJ 73 (9/56): 43.

7089. Where the Plump Spider Sways to Rest. Wright, J. P 88 (4/56): 5-6.

7090. Where the Track Vanishes. Kinnell, G. P 94 (6/59): 170-73.

7091. Where There's Life, There's Soap. Wegert, E.M. TH 34 (10/56): 54.

7092. Where Thought Leaps On. Sarton, M. LHJ 75 (2/58): 140.

7093. Where You From, Mac? Jaffray, N.R. GH 142 (2/56): 44.

7094. Where Your Heart Is There Your Treasure Is Also. Hine, D. P 91 (3/58): 367.

7095. Which Came First, Obeisance or Obesity? Nash, O. NY 35 (3/21/59): 42.

7096. Which Has Speed. Siegel, E. C 20 (12/55): 540.

7097. While Shepherds Watched Their Flocks by Night. Pierce, E.L. CC 74 (12/25/57): 1535.

7098. While Watching the Movie Trapeze. Newman, P. NY 32 (8/4/56): 73.

7099. Whispered. Bandypadhyay, K.N. P 93 (1/59): 213.

7100. Whistle and the World Whistles with You. Congdon, T.B. SEP 229 (3/9/57): 100.

7101. Whistle Stop. Galler, D. P 92 (4/58): 37-8.

7102. Whistler's Mother. Jenney, L.E. LHJ 72 (9/55): 104.

7103. Whistling Boy. Quinn, J.R. SEP 230 (9/28/57): 66.

7104. White. Silkin, J. P 88 (4/56): 22.

7105. The White Christ. Carter, M.A. CC 74 (4/24/57): 515.

7106. White Citizen. Pierce, E.L. CC 74 (2/6/57): 167.

7107. White Collar. Dallas, C.H. LHJ 75 (4/58): 196.

7108. The White Crane. Jacobson, E. SR 38 (7/9/55): 25.

7109. The White Crayfish. Wallace, R.A. SR 40 (1/5/57): 28.

7110. White Egret. Thomas, R. At 198 (11/56): 72.

7111. The White Explorers. Honig, E. P 90 (6/57): 161.

7112. White Flame. Lilly, O. CC 75 (11/5/58): 1269.

7113. White Hands of Guinevere. Swann, T.B. LHJ 76 (2/59): 178.

7114. The White Moon. Sato, S. P 88 (5/56): 104.

7115. White Nights. Moynahan, J. P 94 (7/59): 236.

7116. White Poplar. Chi, L. NY 34 (3/8/58): 112.

7117. White Queen. Fuller, J. P 93 (10/58): 18.

7118. The White Rabbit. Solomon, M. P 86 (4/55): 12-3.

7119. White Sowing. Frost, F. H 213 (12/56): 66.

7120. A White Spiritual. Winters, Y. N 185 (10/5/57): 225.

7121. The Whitethroat Calls Through the May Night. Hoffman, D.G. SR 40 (5/25/57): 25.

7122. Whitsunday. Pierce, E.L. CC 73 (5/9/56): 580.

7123. Who? Kemp, L. At 200 (10/57): 192.

7124. Who Am I? Carter, M. LHJ 75 (8/59): 25.

7125. Who Am I? Reid, A. P 93 (2/59): 292-93.

7126. Who Am I to Condemn? Galbraith, G.S. SEP 239 (1/5/57): 34.

7127. Who Dat? Galbraith, G.S. SEP 229 (10/27/56): 112.

7128. Who Gives. Miller, M. N 188 (3/14/59): 232.

7129. Who Seeks Through Wastelands. Clark, L.S. CC 72 (1/19/55): 77.

7130. Who Wears the World as a Garment. Richardson, D.L. LHJ 72 (6/55): 97.

7131. Who Will Tie Your Shoe? McFarland, E. LHJ 74 (2/57): 158.

7132. Whodunit? Read, M. BHG 34 (6/56): 247.

7133. Who's Lazy? Chadwick, H. BHG 36 (12/19/58): 133.

7134. Who's Whose? Galbraith, G.S. SEP 229 (6/1/57): 83.

7135. Why Fathers Age. Rosenfield, L. SEP 230 (9/14/57): 164.

7136. Why More Women Aren't Naturalists. Neely, L. SEP 227 (5/14/55): 76.

7137. Why So Afraid? Scovel, M. CC 72 (6/8/55): 682.

7138. Why Worry? Richstone, M. SEP 228 (2/18/56): 67.

7139. Wide, Wide in the Rose's Side. Patchen, K. P 86 (5/55): 71.

7140. The Widow. Giordon, A.R. LHJ 72 (6/55): 153.

7141. The Widow. Lineaweaver, M. LHJ 74 (3/57): 236.

7142. A Widow in Wintertime. Kizer, C. P 92 (4/58): 30.

7143. The Widow of Nain. Pierce, E.L. CC 75 (6/4/58): 667.

7144. The Widows. Hall, D. SR 41 (5/17/58): 38.

7145. The Widow's Mite. Clifford, M. CC 73 (11/7/56): 1287.

7146. The Widow's Yard. Gardner, I. P 90 (9/57): 368-69.

7147. Wife. Taylor, E.S. LHJ 74 (7/57): 80.

7148. The Wife of the Superintendent of the Granaries. Hart, J.B. P 86 (8/55): 270-1.

7149. Wife to Husband. Goodman, M.W. SEP 229 (6/22/57): 86.

7150. Wife's Confession. Fowler, J. GH 149 (10/59): 8.

7151. Wild Goose. Heath, C. SEP 231 (10/11/58): 59.

7152. Wild West. Boylan, R. SR 40 (9/21/57): 34.

7153. The Wilderness. Pierce, E.L. CC 73 (3/7/56): 295.

7154. Will Success Spoil Mrs. Hunter? Bramley, W. SEP 229 (6/8/57): 46.

7155. Will Truly Yet Come. Goldberg, L. P 92 (7/58): 241.

7156. A Willow Child. Engle, P. LHJ 72 (7/55): 94.

7157. A Willow Song. Levine, R. SR 42 (12/26/59): 28.

7158. Willy-Nilly, Bacilli. Galbraith, G.S. At 203 (2/59): 104.

7159. Wind. Hughes, T. N 183 (11/10/56): 408.

7160. Wind and Fire. Merrill, H. SEP 228 (1/28/56): 105.

7161. Wind: Desert Sculptor. Carlson, V.F. SEP 229 (7/21/56): 93.

7162. The Wind in the Chimney. Mansfield, M. SEP 229 (11/3/56): 68.

7163. Wind in the North. Woodall, A.E. SEP 227 (2/5/55): 76.

7164. Wind in the West. Barker, S.O. SEP 230 (2/8/58): 80.

7165. Wind Over Cape Cod. Smythe, D. SEP 228 (5/5/56): 133.

7166. The Wind Showed Me. Mok, S. LHJ 73 (10/56): 135.

7167. Wind-Teased Sea. Long, E.E. SEP 227 (6/25/55): 98.

7168. The Windflower. Lineaweaver, M. LHJ 72 (4/55): 143.

7169. A Window, a Table, on the North. Gustafson, R. N 186 (3/29/58): 279.

7170. Window Ledge. Jacobson, E. SEP 230 (10/26/57): 82.

7171. The Window Shopper. Wheeler, R. SEP 229 (2/2/57): 40.

7172. A Windowful of London. Bevington, H. NY 32 (10/6/56): 147.

7173. The Windowpane. Char, R. P 89 (3/57): 335.

7174. Wind's Down. Landeweer, E. SEP 228 (3/10/56): 111.

7175. The Windyard. Reaney, J. P 94 (9/59): 381.

7176. The Wineshade Essence. Farber, N. SR 39 (5/5/56): 26.

7177. Winged Victory. Galbraith, G.S. SEP 230 (11/16/57): 70.

7178. Wings. Patrick, J.G. CC 76 (6/10/58): 697.

7179. Wings of the Morning. Pierce, E.L. CC 72 (8/24/55): 967.

7180. The Winner. Davison, P.H. At 201 (2/58): 61.

7181. Winter. Langland, J. NY 33 (1/11/58): 79.

7182. Winter Bouquets. Kelley, R.S. SEP 230 (1/18/58): 80.

7183. Winter by the Ironworks. Nicholson, N. SR 38 (2/19/55): 16.

7184. Winter Carpentry. Merrill, H. SEP 231 (2/28/59): 96.

7185. A Winter Come. Moss, H. NY 32 (1/5/57): 27.

7186. The Winter Crop. Merrill, H. SEP 229 (2/16/57): 109.

7187. The Winter Crow. Merrill, H. SEP 228 (2/11/56): 55.

7188. Winter Dusk. Franklin, J.M. SEP 231 (1/31/59): 43.

7189. Winter Edge. Crews, J. P 93 (12/58): 157.

7190. Winter Evening After the Theater. Everson, R.G. At 198 (12/56): 82.

7191. Winter Evening: London. Merwin, W.S. H 219 (12/59): 40.

7192. Winter Flowers. Morrison, J. SEP 228 (1/21/56): 94.

7193. Winter Grass. Muro, S. P 88 (5/56): 95.

7194. The Winter Harbor. Merrill, H. LHJ 73 (2/56): 155.

7195. Winter Has Come. Takamura, K. P 88 (5/56): 94.

7196. The Winter Heart. Merrill, H. SEP 230 (2/8/58): 57.

7197. Winter Is Icumen in. Smith, B. SR 41 (12/20/58): 28.

7198. Winter Juniper. Langland, J. N 181 (8/6/55): 121.

7199. Winter Lament. Henry, M. LHJ 75 (7/58): 12.

7200. Winter Leaves. McAllister, C. At 195 (2/55): 59.

7201. Winter Lullaby. Frost, F. A 94 (3/17/56): 664.

7202. Winter Lyrics. Trent, L. CC 75 (3/19/58): 338.

7203. Winter Memory: The Pond. Ballielt, W. SR 38 (12/3/55): 40.

7204. A Winter Morning. Amen, G.C. NY 31 (2/4/56): 30.

7205. Winter Morning in the Garden. Emans, E.V. SEP 228 (2/18/56): 99.

7206. Winter Night. Long, E.E. SEP 230 (1/11/58): 88.

7207. A Winter Night. Raha, A.V. P 93 (1/59): 212.

7208. Winter Nocturne. Facos, J. SEP 231 (1/10/59): 58.

7209. Winter Obsessed Them. Nathan, L. P 91 (3/58): 373.

7210. Winter on the Shore. Wright, P. SEP 227 (1/22/55): 77.

7211. Winter Outpost in Malaya. Palmer, L. SEP 231 (2/7/59): 91.

7212. Winter Scene. Carroll, P. NY 33 (1/25/58): 105.

7213. A Winter Scene. Whittemore, R. P 92 (9/58): 348.

7214. Winter Sleepers. Landeweer, E. SEP 228 (2/11/56): 86.

7215. Winter Stanzas for Norma. Perry, R. P 95 (12/59): 169-70.

7216. Winter: the Statue of Pomona. Bock, F. P 88 (7/56): 220.

7217. Winter Thunder. Merrill, H. SEP 231 (12/20/58): 70.

7218. Winter Traffic. Jacobs, E.L. SEP 229 (2/2/57): 79.

7219. Winter Walks. Chisholm, L.B. SEP 227 (2/26/55): 119.

7220. Winter Wonder. McBrown, G.P. NHB 18 (1/55): 92.

7221. Winter Worship. Patrick, J.G. CC 73 (2/1/56): 139.

7222. Winter's End. Brasier, V. SEP 228 (3/31/56): 63.

7223. Winter's House. Grenville, R.H. SEP 230 (1/25/58): 66.

7224. Winter's Laundry. Seager, R.W. SEP 231 (12/27/58): 47.

7225. A Winter's Song. Rosenberg, J.L. At 197 (2/56): 50.

7226. A Winter's Tale. Plath, S. NY 35 (12/12/59): 116.

7227. A Winter's Tale. Solomon, M. P 88 (8/56): 314.

7228. A Winter's Tale. Watson, B. H 214 (4/57): 64.

7229. Wire-Brier. McNeill, L. SEP 230 (8/17/57): 47.

7230. Wisdom and Ignorance. Flynn, C.E. CT 3 (8/31/59): 14.

7231. The Wisest Word. Pierce, E.L. CC 74 (8/7/57): 941.

7232. Wish. Kayko, I. LHJ 74 (11/57): 181.

7233. The Wish. Rich, A. H 215 (9/57): 57.

7234. Wistful Thinking. Warsaw, I. GH 149 (11/59): 8.

7235. The Wit. Bishop, E. NR 134 (2/13/56): 17.

7236. Witch. Fuller, J. P 93 (10/58): 16.

7237. The Witch of Endor. Nemerov, H. N 184 (3/23/57): 258.

7238. With a Branch of Acacia. Triem, E. P 89 (2/57): 275.

7239. With Apologies to Joyce Kilmer. Meyers, E. WLB 30 (4/56): 634.

7240. With Apples. Van Doren, M. At 204 (11/59): 75.

7241. With Hooks and Lines. Warsaw, I. SEP 229 (3/2/57): 40.

7242. With Jonah. Fretz, J.H. CT 4 (10/12/59): 9.

7243. With Love and No Desire. Renon, E. N 188 (6/20/59): 563.

7244. With Military Honors. Allard, B.B.N. SEP 232 (11/14/59): 60.

7245. With Muted Passion. Steiner, S. P 88 (6/56): 146-47.

7246. With Reverent Crayons. Bangham, M.D. CC 72 (1/19/55): 77.

7247. With Sympathy. Akins, Z. LHJ 72 (1/55): 127.

7248. Without a Doubt. Pritchard, G. SEP 227 (1/29/55): 109.

7249. Without Desire. Johnson, G. A 102 (10/3/59): 12.

7250. Without Parallel. Neely, L. SEP 228 (1/7/56): 77.

7251. Wit's End. Grenville, R.H. SEP 231 (4/25/59): 87.

7252. Wmffree the Sweep. Humphries, R. P 86 (6/55): 144-45.

7253. The Woman. Clower, J. P 89 (12/56): 163-65.

7254. A Woman. Williams, W.C. N 186 (5/31/58): 498.

7255. Woman and Snake. Hay, S.H. SR 38 (3/5/55): 8.

7256. Woman and Tree. Graves, R. NY 32 (6/9/56): 38.

7257. Woman at Work. Armour, R. BHG 33 (12/55): 201.

7258. Woman Clothed in the Sun. Garlick, R. A 100 (10/11/58): 45.

7259. Woman, 1955. Gilbert, P.C. GH 141 (11/55): 46.

7260. The Woman on the Rock. Milne, E. P 88 (5/56): 125-26.

7261. Woman Reading. Dudley, J.H. LHJ 73 (6/56): 38.

7262. Woman Sea Horse. Miller, M.O. P 87 (2/56): 279-80.

7263. A Woman Unconscious. Hughes, T. P 94 (8/59): 296.

7264. Woman with Child. Torres, E. P 88 (9/56): 378-79.

7265. A Woman's Prayer. Karni, Y. P 92 (7/58): 209.

7266. Women. Feldman, I. At 203 (1/59): 49.

7267. The Women. Hitchcock, A. P 88 (6/56): 143.

7268. Women in a Flowered Dress. Redgrove, P. P 94 (9/59): 372.

7269. Women's Doubles. Hatch, F.W. SEP 229 (9/1/56): 52.

7270. The Women's Jail. Waddington, M. N 184 (5/11/57): 426.

7271. Wonder Fabrics Make Me Wonder. Jennison, C.S. At 196 (12/55): 108.

7272. Wonderful Things. Judson, S. Hn 31 (4/55): 130.

7273. The Wood. Norman, C. NY 33 (11/9/57): 163.

7274. Woodchuck Rampant. Ely, G. P 92 (9/58): 370.

7275. Woodcocks Returning Northward. Tanaka, F. P 88 (5/56): 66.

7276. Wooden Darning Egg. Updike, J. H 213 (12/56): 34.

7277. The Woodpecker. Laughlin, J. N 187 (11/29/58): 411.

7278. Word and Deed. Pierce, E.L. CC 75 (10/22/58): 1203.

7279. The Word "Beautiful." Swenson, M. N 185 (9/21/57): 184.

7280. A Word for Farewell. Church, R. At 198 (9/56): 69.

7281. The Word of God. Smith, J.C. CT 1 (7/22/57): 26.

7282. The Word of Willow. Drake, L.B. At 198 (9/56): 50.

7283. Word to a Church at a Time of Grave Decision. Cully, K.B. CC 75 (1/1/58): 16.

7284. A Word to Celibate Scientists. Freeman, J.B. BHG 33 (11/55): 196.

7285. A Word to the Wise. Owens, K. LHJ 75 (12/59): 117.

7286. The Wordless Tribe. Gordon, R. H 215 (8/57): 72.

7287. The Words. Morse, S.F. P 87 (3/56): 335.

7288. Words About Women. Twiggs, D.E. SEP 232 (11/28/59): 110.

7289. Words Above a Narrow Entrance. Wagoner, D. P 92 (5/58): 67-8.

7290. Words Be Our Weapons. James, K. CC 75 (4/2/58): 407.

7291. Words Fail Me. Spring, A.T. SEP 229 (3/9/57): 49.

7292. Words for a Wallflower Waltz. Farnham, J. GH 142 (10/56): 13.

7293. Words for Hart Crane. Lowell, R. N 186 (3/22/58): 259.

7294. Words of Furthest Flight. Campbell, M.A. CC 73 (11/21/56): 1354.

7295. Words of Praise. Wheeler, R. SEP 229 (12/29/56): 57.

7296. Words Open Out Upon Grief. Duncan, R. P 91 (3/58): 383-84.

7297. Words Spoken Alone. Abse, D. NY 34 (1/10/59): 30.

7298. Words to a Budding Oddity. Lamb, M.W. LHJ 76 (5/59): 114.

7299. The Work of Thy Fingers. Clark, L.S. CC 72 (8/17/55): 948.

7300. Work Song. Sider, G. CC 76 (11/11/59): 1304.

7301. Work Surface. Raskin, A. GH 142 (9/56): 46.

7302. Workers. Workers Poet. At 204 (12/59): 94.

7303. Working on Wall Street. Swenson, M. SR 39 (6/16/56): 49.

7304. Workmen. Morris, H. P 87 (2/56): 278.

7305. The World. Appleton, S. Co 67 (2/28/58): 564.

7306. The World. Fox, I. AN 56 (1/58): 93.

7307. The World Around Us. Whittemore, R. P 89 (11/56): 108-9.

7308. The World Below the Window. Smith, W. J. P 90 (4/57): 39.

7309. The World of Mathematics. Anderson, M. NY 32 (12/22/56): 70.

7310. A World of Words. Macpherson, J. P 90 (9/57): 343.

7311. The World, the Times. Hall, D. NR 133 (11/14/55): 19.

7312. Worldly Wishes of '59. Hammer, P. SEP 231 (1/3/59): 69.

7313. Worldwide Communion. Clark, L.S. CC 73 (10/3/56): 1127.

7314. Worm. Engle, P. GH 142 (2/56): 44.

7315. Worship. Tigner, H.S. CC 76 (1/21/59): 78.

7316. The Worst of It. Chadwick, H. SEP 229 (6/8/57): 83.

7317. The Wound of Innocence. Crawford, J.,Jr. P 94 (5/59): 100.

7318. Wreath for a Bridal. Plath, S. P 89 (1/57): 231.

7319. A Wreath of Four O'Clocks. Kennedy, M. GH 149 (8/59): 150.

7320. Wreaths. Hill, G. P 90 (5/57): 80.

7321. The Wreckers Arrive. Johnson, P.P. SEP 232 (12/19/59): 74.

7322. The Writer to His Librarian Wife. Mac-Donald, L. WLB 32 (12/57): 285.

7323. Writing. Nemerov, H. NY 33 (12/14/57): 46.

7324. Written on Good Friday for My Children. Richardson, D.L. CC 74 (4/17/57): 489.

7325. Wrong Diet. Engle, J.D.,Jr. SEP 230 (9/7/57): 88.

7326. The Wrong Is Mixed. Scott, W.T. N 183 (10/13/56): 309.

7327. The Wrong Self. Weeks, J.F. At 203 (2/59): 66.

7328. Yard. Miles, J. P 92 (6/58): 139.

7329. Yards Wide and Like a Train. Malody, B.M. GH 148 (5/59): 189.

7330. The Year of Jeremiah. Fidelian, Brother. Co 69 (3/13/59): 620.

7331. The Year of the Great Freeze. Collier, M. D. LHJ 74 (10/57): 115.

7332. The Year of Zhivago. Singer, H. P 94 (8/59): 288-89.

7333. The Year Will Come. Heath, A.R. CC 74 (11/13/57): 1348.

7334. The Year Without a Santa Claus. McGinley, P. GH 142 (12/56): 94-99.

7335. Yell. Lister, R.P. At 195 (6/55): 88.

7336. Yellow Rain. Richter, H. SEP 231 (4/19/58): 78.

7337. Yellow Tom. De Jong, D.C. P 94 (9/59): 385-87.

7338. Yelp. Lewis, G. N 186 (4/26/58): 374.

7339. Yes, As a Look Springs to Its Face. Duncan, R. N 189 (10/3/59): 200.

7340. Yes, My Lord! Seifer, D. GH 149 (8/59): 53.

7341. Yesterday from My Fever. Kinnell, G. P 98 (3/56): 351.

7342. The Yewberry. Wolf, L. P 88 (4/56): 21.

7343. Yezrael. Shlonsky, A. P 92 (7/58): 221-26.

7344. Yom Kippur. Harrison, H. C 20 (10/55): 355.

7345. Yom Kippur Lamentation. Rainer, D. C 27 (2/59): 158.

7346. Yorick. Schwartz, D. NR 132 (1/31/55): 20.

7347. York State Semantic. McGonigal, M. SEP 231 (4/18/59): 114.

7348. You Can't Do That. Willson, M.W. SR 39 (11/24/56): 8.

7349. You Can't Take It With You. Ridgway, A. GH 148 (6/59): 124.

7350. You Do Not Envy Me. Graham, E. LHJ (11/56): 140.

7351. You Give the Answer. Brooks, F.L. CH 30 (11/55): 139.

7352. You Know Him. Kelley, R.S. SR 42 (12/26/59): 25.

7353. You-Me. Bewas. P 93 (1/59): 254.

7354. You Ought to Write a Book About It. Sweet, A.P. WLB 31 (11/56): 266.

7355. You Shall Be Forgotten. Galbraith, G.S. LHJ 75 (9/59): 136.

7356. You Shall Not Break a Bone of Him. Cotter, J.F. A 94 (3/3/56): 612.

7357. You Were Long Years in Leaving. LaFarge, C. SR 38 (11/19/55): 46.

7358. You Were Wearing. Koch, K. P 94 (5/59): 77.

7359. The Young. Freeman, J.T. LHJ 74 (3/57): 117.

7360. Young Again. Rosenfield, L. SEP 229 (1/19/57): 93.

7361. Young Democrat. Coffin, R.P.T. LHJ 74 (8/57): 131.

7362. Young Girl Singing. Coker, A. LHJ 73 (3/56): 130.

7363. Young Girls. Mary Maura, Sr. A 95 (7/14/56): 365.

7364. Young Girls in Spring. Howard, P. GH 142 (4/56): 164.

7365. A Young Greek, Killed in the Wars. Eberhart, R. P 85 (2/55): 274.

7366. Young Housebreaker. Anthony, E. GH 149 (10/59): 208.

7367. Young Love. Carter, M. LHJ 76 (6/59): 83.

7368. Young Mother. De Vito, E.B. SEP 229 (6/1/57): 53.

7369. The Young One. McFarland, E. LHJ 74 (4/57): 131.

7370. Young Reformers. Delattre, P.H. CC 74 (11/13/57): 1344.

7371. Young Song. Cunliffe, C. LHJ 72 (10/55): 207.

7372. Your Kisses Are So Sincere. McFarland, E. LHJ 74 (6/57): 94.

7373. Your Lead, Partner; Hope We've Read the Same Book. Nash, O. SEP 228 (4/7/56): 46.

7374. Your Smile. Burket, G.B. TH 34 (6/56): 30.

7375. Youth. Lee, A.M. SEP 232 (10/17/59): 127.

7376. Youth to Christ the King. Roseliep, R. A 94 (11/12/55): 185.

7377. The Youthful Expectations. De Jong, D.C. P 89 (2/57): 299.

7378. Zeal. Lilly, O. CC 76 (3/4/59): 250.

7379. Zealots of Yearning. Rokeah, D. C 20 (11/55): 467.

7380. Zealots of Yearning. Rokeah, D. P 92 (7/58): 245.

7381. Zenn-Cottages. Watkins, V. P 95 (10/59): 14-15.

7382. The Zero Hour. Jaffray, N.R. SEP 230 (11/30/57): 89.

7383. Zipper Suit. Anthony, E. GH 142 (5/56): 128.

7384. Zone of Silence. Stepanchev, S. SR 42 (5/16/59): 73.

7385. The Zoo. Ostroff, A. SR 39 (8/4/56): 27.

FIRST-LINE INDEX

A is for our alphabet. 6712.
A peels an **apple**, while B kneels to
  God: 5008.
About a thousand years ago: 4815.
Above finespun, unruffled sheets:
  3544.
Above my sleeping grandchild's crib I
  linger: 6368.
Above the hanging gardens she looked
  down: 6468.
Above the kneeling wood: 3196.
Above the lethal current, unalarmed:
  616.
Above the river Oise: 2671.
Above these blackened fields, distinct
  and high: 352.
Above these bleak Wyoming plains:
  7198.
Above, through lunar woods a goddess
  flies: 3563.
Abrupt as that blessing gesture you
  always made: 2064.
Absence makes the heart grow fonder:
  4610.
Abstaining from the fluted wound:
  1628.
Accept my thanks for lending me this
  time: 4935.
Accidents will happen--still in time:
  2791.
Accomodating love with something still:
  121.
According to the facts compiled:
  7071.
According to the product's claims:
  6109.
According to the silence, winter has
  arrived: 5575.
According to the time or to your
  desire: 43.
The acres that came down from his
  fathers: 5177.
Across from the Calle Primera, where
  we live facing the loud mouthed
  sea: 1304.

Across the hill and by the cedared
  brook: 404.
Across the midnight march thy stars:
  7299.
Across the open countryside: 6801.
Across the room, the full blown hair:
  1034.
Across the street from the summer house
  where I am staying: 6970.
Across the wide plateau: 5703.
Adam and Eve sat in their garden: 6453.
Addixti, Labiene, tres cinaedos:
  2149
Admire him for it? All his gifts
  contrived: 1714.
Adrift on a high: 4872.
The advantage of the line is direction:
  309.
Advent again--of soldier and of clown:
  4784.
Adventures of Tom Sawyer: 3587.
Affable, bibulous: 864.
Affix me no serrated discs: 5383.
The affluent gardener's demeanor:
  5970.
Afloat: 348.
Afoot and light-hearted I take to the
  open road: 5838.
Africa, my Africa: 69.
After a day of turmoil: 6018.
After a night of rain: 5677.
After a summer of beaches Mr. Meeching:
  1720.
After a thousand centuries the men of
  Babel have come home: 4983.
After all, you, my lady, made the first
  move: 1405.
After, at Cincinnati, the March morning
  scabs of snow: 2004.
After careful weeks of preparation:
  46.
After, each, word, he, places, a,
  comma: 4896.
After God's house burned down, they
  found the shirt: 4220.

After he had killed the dragon: 3294.
After Midnight Mass there it was cold: 1130.
After the boats are prisoners: 1984.
After the bomb burst she awoke at once: 93.
After the bronzed, heroic traveler: 3985.
After the cataracts of June, the swollen stream: 3802.
After the fretful day, when place descends: 2610.
After the laboring birth, the clean stripped hull: 3999.
After the last burst, after the poisoned light: 94.
After the long wake, when many were drunk: 388.
After the mountain peaks were pillowed in the stars: 5843.
After the murder, like parades of fools: 3972.
After the passage of the seven years: 3388.
After the rain, the snails: 5710.
After the rain, the white wool of the clouds: 98.
After the wind passed on from the battered town: 4113.
After thy father's form: 1354.
After tornado's toll, a handful dead: 926.
After winter's woeful whistling: 185.
After you pass Owl's Candle and Pick-porridge, the lane tilts: 7011.
After your soul is done to death: 7141.
The afternoon sways like an elephant: 3120.
The afternoon was an aria from Verdi: 102.
The afternoons were green and dry: 4698.
Again along the sacred paths arboreal: 17.
Again I come late to retreat: 5256.
Again the fruit, again the bough: 5979.
Again the quiet words are said: 426.
Against the pure, reflective tiles: 4017.
Against T. Veblen: 4733.
Against the cool and slanted lines: 286.
Agamemnon, proud in life: 2411.
Age two isn't height size: 4592.
Aghast I stand as I behold: 1491.
The agony of spirit: 120.
Ah how my cat Benjamin flies this midnight: 122.
Ah! Hoyland, empress of my heart: 4298.
"Ah nothin's so purty as spring," she said: 2283.
Ah, purity: 5071.
Ah, sweet youth!: 7375.
Ah, to be set and printed in: 5824.
Ah, yes, my love, I'll grant I've changed: 6044.
Ahead on the beach were bonfires: 4108.
Ai, but he hunted ill: 2700.
The air as of a world of air and line: 806.

The air grieved and the island: 676.
The air is heavy with the passing storm: 4688.
Airs of the melancholy autumn: 6054.
The aisles are blurred with winter mist: 7221.
Alas not in this temperate land: 4677.
Alas poor ghost, have you come all the way: 4833.
Alas that the strongest: 2116.
Alas, what boots it if with gifts of song: 4087.
Alas, you have put: 131.
The alchemy and mystery is this: 5274.
Alexandrina has shy eyes. Her name recalls: 134.
Alfred was a ninny: 135.
Alice, the lily maid of askalot: 7118.
Alien and stark it stands: 4081.
Alive with light the whole wood: 547.
All at once, when she was talking of something: 1827.
All clotheslines in America bannered: 6309.
All day at my window, ill and afraid: 5653.
All day, half lines or smaller parts: 5245.
All day I function happily enough: 2659.
All day long in a blaze of heat: 6140.
All day our eyes could find no resting place: 1668.
All day the monstrous dredge approaches: 868.
All down this coast the headlands fold to the ocean: 4030.
All envious of fish and fowl: 3818.
All frantic joy, all madly whirling tail: 4441.
All hail, etc., Richard Gann: 1181.
All hail to Melvil Dewey: 141.
All history is a rumble of weather making: 7000.
All I can see ahead is looking back: 1652.
"All I loved I lost," she said: 3518.
All is dust. There are but stages: 143.
All is not well with the couple animus and: 4658.
All laughing on a summer lawn: 6524.
All men leave the things they love: 2047.
All my O'Learys, bounced for love alone: 4449.
All night I lay and stared at darkness: 6700.
All night the sound had: 5118.
All of us had always said we would return: 5553.
All out of step with men, and out of line: 3022.
All precious heirlooms woven: 2535.
All right, armorer: 1495.
All said and done, a phone does much: 1537.
All season, balls have whizzed right by: 6326.
All seasons telescope before a fire: 2524.

All that: 6672.
All that morning we rowed about the
   castle: 3168.
All the good-lookin': 6130.
All the past we leave behind: 4819.
All the tumbling waste of sea: 4156.
All the wars were filed away: 4503.
All the way the art fair at Laguna:
   4638.
All the world's a library: 152.
All the world's a stage, I'll grant:
   463.
All things beautiful begin: 2151.
All things change: summer sleeps: 5749.
All things turned to Orpheus' hand:
   2409.
All those who led their spirits to re-
   joice and dance over: 6330.
All through that summer: 380.
All very old, all partially trans-
   figured: 3828.
All was as it is, before the beginning
   began, before: 3068.
All went well today in the barbers'
   college: 78.
All who attempted to find you have
   tempted you: 2202.
All women loved dance in a dying light:
   6357.
All worlds but the world miss these
   leaves: 4374.
The almanac of time hangs in the brain:
   158.
Almighty Father! Look in Mercy down:
   1182.
Almost all about her blurred. When she
   came: 674.
Almost yesterday, those gentle ladies
   stole: 3530.
Alone at the end of green allees, alone:
   6042.
Alone at the high window of the house:
   2088.
Alone with an equation in a plain room
   1603.
Along East River and theBronx: 4303;
Along how many Main Streets have I
   walked: 1754.
Aloof to progress, and its taunts:
   3641.
Already I have shed the leaves of
   youth: 494.
Already it's late summer: 1518.
Already she: 4602.
Already slow, so soon, she remarks
   funneling each word: 7264.
Although a Protestant of Niebuhr's
   crews: 4223.
Although he's able to afford: 6327.
Although I like to window-shop: 7171.
Although I'm told it's better sense
   (considering the French all all):
   1912.
Although it may not understand: 611.
Although it may seem archaic: 1739.
Although man fence a plot of earth and
   call: 4184.
Although, of course, quite well: 118.
Although on occasion, a nifty is said:
   3045.

Although our kitchen has the finest:
   3836.
Although the calendar denies bouquets:
   7192.
Although the lake held: 7066.
Although you're reluctant to face the
   day: 3427.
Although you've checked and double-
   checked: 6127.
Always after Christmas I lonely walk:
   76.
Always have these sounds been in your
   ear: 4889.
Always, he woke in those days: 3021.
Always holiness shall cling: 1257.
Always it happens when we are: 3781.
Always the big ruby sun ascends: 5412.
Always the setting forth was the
   same: 4306.
Always we have believed: 1504.
Always willing: 1528.
"Am I my brother's keeper?": 5246.
Am I the bullet: 909.
Am I the path that you must use: 4199.
An ambiguous way, at best, to ascertain:
   1916.
The ambition of Theodore Barfreeston:
   5068.
America, down through the years: 4054.
American plan: 3236.
Amid her friends my Great Aunt spoke:
   420.
Amid that Platonic statuary: 1064.
Among his birthday gifts, he found:
   7102.
Among precise people: 971.
Among the arches of the hay: 6136.
Among the lacelike leaves: 870.
Among the many faces: 4661.
Among the numerable millions: 3508.
Among the shades it is he: 5977.
Among the terrors of the trees: 1889.
Among the things that happened were
   the Christian funerals: 6863.
Amorous animation: 4680.
Anathema: 6540.
The Ancestral House talks to me: 2649.
And a lost road: 6427.
And Abraham tore: 2462.
And bells like the ringing of hounds:
   4881.
And brave to hear old ocean: 3661.
And finally, dear, I'd have you
   realize: 4339.
And he was the devil of my dreams: 1467.
And heaven widens with the skylarks
   ways: 2486.
And how the amen is seldom spoken:
   4258.
And how will Sunday find you, Son:
   468.
And if an ant returns to the hive:
   3835.
And in the northmost of the world's
   whiteness, pacing slowly: 526.
And it happens that spirit surges
   from imprisonment of bodies: 198.
And kingship, killer of Kings: 5291.
And like a snow-peak, misted in her
   nightdress: 2190.

And men, not beasts, shall be his game: 4132.

And now, lad, we have finally reached an end: 4347.

And now grown intimate with height: 6372.

And now in flight above an overcoat: 2982.

And now we come to the power of perfume, dear: 4326.

And now we too must go our separate ways: 3320.

And on the porch, across the upturned chair: 4899.

And once as it was morning and I was in the field: 4927.

And one bright morning, lad, you wake to find: 4340.

And one day, child, while homing for a ride: 4315.

And one day, child, you'll find him muttering: 4331.

And so it goes: just as the greening bud: 5493.

And so it was: 203.

And so night after night, you come to me: 3032.

And so they arrive for all the world to see: 5046.

And so they're in the village glass again: 5934.

And, son, 'tis probable thy wife will hoard: 4346.

And space becomes a lack: 1274.

And still the sun reddens: 1770.

And the path winds wild and free as we go up from Torflians: 6808.

And then of what worth beauty: 3469.

And there it stands, my stranger's work of art: 27.

And what did the soldier's wife receive?: 7039.

And when I opened my eyes and saw: 1839.

And when in his spacious courtyards Odysseus had cut down: 5262.

And which of them shall fail him first: 6873.

And who are these, here sheltered from the rain: 3528.

And who is this that sells the hot tamales: 3529.

Andrew, an understanding boy: 3162.

An angel at the door can make them sneeze: 153.

The angel said to me: "Why are you laughing?" 5428.

An angel stepping through her window said: 241.

Angel with the tired wind-burned face: 461.

Angels he'd not believe in his high hilled house: 4167.

Anger is certain: 947.

The angriness of the captives felt: 6.

Anguish is what the mind: 998.

Anniversaries and birthdays: 3847.

Anonymous as cherubs: 6746.

Another dash of vodka? Shall we say: 480.

Another great injustice done: 6767.

Another public enemy: 3356.

Another weep woman: 1924.

Ant upon ant write the text in: 501.

Anticipation falters: 6619.

Any man--God, if he had the money: 4970.

Anyone can see through your rag-picking: 3886.

Anyone in this top-floor flat: 1536.

Anything shining could transfix my eyes: 1571.

The apes yawn and adore their fleas in the sun: 3069.

Apologies are called for, but alas: 7286.

Apostle of the lottery: 3537.

Appear far up the cove at low tide: 1060.

Appetites long since back to normal: 6196.

The apple eaten to Eden's loss: 3134.

The approach is right for looking: 3234.

Approaching death: 4309.

April. Cold...: 257.

April in England: 283.

Aquilea, city of waters, you are under threat: 419.

Archangel, herald, guardian and page: 478.

Are all these stones: 1081.

"Are you Charles' mother?" she asked me: 6492.

Are you looking for us?: 4545.

Arms akimbo: 5442.

Arms wide, he races forward to enfold it: 6611.

Around a magic ring of apple pie: 3923.

Around great trees: 5024.

Around me my father built a huge care like a shipyard: 414.

Around my neck my worry: 3533.

Around old farmsteads there's a smell of mold: 1068.

Around the bend an army comes: 721.

Around the corner, up the muddy path: 3731.

Around the fireplace, pointing to the fire: 4451.

Around the house though I'm the boss: 1919.

Around their satin throats: 565.

Around us summer wrote its last farewell: 5526.

Around your planet-tilted head: 7201.

Aroused, his ire: 3575.

Arrived at my desk, it was seven forty-five: 3034.

The arrogance of ignorance: 306.

Art has become the swineherd's old blind dog: 3778.

The art of conversation: 2285.

Art of happiness: 3460.

Art thou come hither to torment us, thou: 2508.

As a cat, caught by the door opening: 896.

As a child, I feared the dark: 2126.
As a fish slips water, a hawk, air from unwavering fin and wing: 5534.
As a patron of your libraries: 887.
As a wild bird may leave untenanted: 324.
As Ali Baba in the cave of treasure: 2831.
As brooks rush headlong down their hills: 325.
As dogs will run in their dog-desperate worry: 1540.
As children grow, their needs increase: 1105.
As earth, light and grass illustrate the meadow: 7339.
As far as the shore the leaves are falling: 2906.
As florid berries to the oak, should I pin: 737.
As flowers have wars that philosophic eye: 326.
As for the furniture: 5191.
As for the liar, fear him less: 5631.
As for us, we can go on hoping: 1232.
As higher and higher the dollar inflates: 1767.
As I daily threaten 'em and beseech 'em: 3520.
As I gaze on your skin: 5496.
As I grow old, I hope I'lll grow more mellow: 3636.
As I sought in the corridors of my yesterdays: 6597.
As I view the performance: 987.
As I walked out in the streets of the morning: 5005.
As I walked whistling through the cemetery: 349.
As I wandered on the beach: 2397.
As icebergs glitter in the sun: 1838.
As if I didn't have enough to worry about: 5779.
As if I slept till Sunday of the world: 74.
As if I were Caesar back from Gaul: 5756.
As if the aimed: 3010.
As if the eye and the head: 2592.
As if the inner voice had said, Don't smile: 4794.
As if to show off his speed...: 363.
As long ago as Adam we felt: 5804.
As long as peonies unfold: 4743.
As many as there are of star and root: 1593.
As much as I wish an end to: 727.
As no one lived on Tobey's road: 4528.
As one dark grape cups all the mellowed frenzy: 3600.
As one grows older and Caesar, Hitler: 6927.
As one who lies asleep into the day: 1273.
As one who searches deserts, dune on dune: 7129.
As one who sees on its branch, in May, the rose: 1139.
As Peter loved I love, and in his fashion: 329.
As Petrarch coming with a laurel wreath: 330.

As priest and deacon the gesture make: 4720.
As rockets blast off in the race: 5897.
As salt is part of the sea: 1045.
As seventh sign, the antique heavens show: 1891.
As she proudly pilots two small girls: 7368.
As she walked by Unami: 1278.
As shopping centers swarm apace: 6185.
As sometimes, in an intricate tale, we find: 333.
As the masque went on Sehnsucht was seen to change: 6832.
As the sycamore makes one thing: 4556.
As the world goes blind...: 2365.
As Thomas was cudgel'd one day by his wife: 9.
As through a misted glass we faintly glimpse: 334.
As time goes on: 1906.
As to an unknown lover I returned: 6632.
As true as I was born into: 2466.
As we drove down the ramp from the boat: 1556.
As we expect, wheels in familiar ruts: 2352.
As we grow older it is clear: 3429.
As we stood on the edge of the crag: 112.
As you look back and wave: 4297.
Ashes are everywhere, to mock the pride: 4438.
Ask for nothing beyond this moment: 428.
Ask night how it feels to be black: 6534.
Ask not the dweller in the garden: 6834.
Asking what, asking what? All a boy's afternoon: 1402.
Asleep in violence. Through my mother's: 2200.
Assemble me then: 1078.
Assembling ways to glisten: 5482.
Assumed a verbal universe: 7310.
Astir with winds, and languid days: 4202.
At Bethlehem: 2651.
At carving chicken, turkey, ham: 3482.
At Darwin's birth Goethe and Hegel: 934.
At dawn behind a cigar: 764.
At dusk the fog-lost sea-mark on the sea: 7119.
At 8:00 A. M. I rise and shine: 5686.
At eight in the evening properly humble, I went: 6474.
At evening the falling flowers of the willow: 6976.
At every gate a guard grinds out his grief: 1606.
At first, the euphemistic "blk.": 657.
At first we sat imprisoned in the place: 1219.
At first when she began to play: 3455.

At five o'clock I saw the sergeant slouch: 396.
At five o'clock the buildings yawn: 1201.
At Givat Oz today, we stood on high Tel: 6277.
At half past four, mornings in June: 1986.
At Kimberley the sundered clay: 4613.
At last arrives: 3810.
At last the boy has laid his hands on: 2161.
At last the dawn throws the forest in relief: 92.
At late night now the piers are very still: 4413.
At mid-morning her wheelchair seems to rock: 214.
At midnight's stroke: 2677.
At Mingo Fort, the road: 3940.
At movies, how far from dear to me: 5887.
At night, alone, the animals came and shone: 224.
At night when I go to sleep: 6432.
At night, whenever I hear a Noise: 5886.
At night you see them, intermittent stars: 1941.
At our house ladies always bring: 1313.
At Ox Bow beach, the August sun a rake: 6133.
At Pennemund, V-Twos rose slowly into the air: 2232.
At sunfall, when the tide withdraws: 4813.
At the beautiful instant of gratification: 746.
At the big trumpet, we must all put on: 5305.
At the full of summer the spider swing: 3075.
At the gathered ends of rooty paths: 3024.
At the one where I: 492.
At the other end of a telescope, a long way: 2614.
At this time of poise, this permanence of maturing: 2051.
At this vast height the continents are lovely: 6865.
At times when on my couch I lean: 3668.
Atomic fallout drifting from the skies: 1846.
Atomic night was falling fast: 1789.
Attack me, Father, now: 4981.
Attacking heaven, the hawk loses his prey: 2500.
Attention with intention: 387.
Authors take note: 6020.
Autumn is a feathered cock: 729.
Autumn is noisy this fall--all clamor and clang: 6908.
Autumn swells him, an incumbent dross: 4291.
Autumn was prolonged and seemed never to want to leave us: 7332.
Autumn's onus recommences: 2444.

Awake for the night is spent: 394.
Awake, I bid your body goodbye: 2696.
Awake while others soundly sleep: 6156.
Aware that summer baked the water clear: 5668.
The awesomest spectacle: 5563.
Ay, Christ--soul wrought of: 1400.
Azure the April sky: 149.
Baby angel wings rub off: 4213.
A babe is born all of a May: 443.
The baby-sitter didn't do: 3040.
Bachelor cooking: 7023.
Back again: 669.
Back from culture, I have brought besides these views: 451.
The back road is the woods: 1253.
The backs twist with the kiss: 3174.
Backward, turn backward, o time, you old ghoul: 5463.
A badge of this weather is the yellow leaf: 2363.
Bagged for glory, then--a goat-saint calling: 2065.
Baked white from its pounding desert stretch : 1349.
Balanced on the grate we seized them back: 6179.
Balking will get: 6121.
Ball players keep such curious hours: 5079.
Bare and bleak: 5606.
The bargain counter draws a crowd: 6759.
A barn, a school, or a church: 500.
The barns like scarlet lungs are breathing in: 173.
Barred apart, but together!: 504.
The basic trouble with conjugal lives: 2227.
A basket maker, an itinerant: 506.
The bat doesn't mind: 508.
Bathed in a rosy neon glare: 6690.
Bay windows, when I was a boy: 517.
Be between us in our making love: 7009.
Be gentle, arms; be tender, lips: 42.
Be gracious! Be friendly!: 6005.
Be my friend...: 1237.
Be not afraid to pray--to pray is right: 4973.
Be not so bitter nor so cold of glance: 6526.
Be of this brightness dyed: 6149.
Be silent, ancient song: 4790.
Be still a little while, I said: 1077.
Be the lark, whose wing is sure and strong: 2763.
Be what linguist you may: 6265.
A beach of flesh above a beach of sand: 169.
Beached on my memory, once you: 4770.
The beak of dawn's rooster pecked: 379.
Bear east beyond conscience, you: 5435.
The bear has clawed my hand: 6629.
Bearded and bangled: 3608.
Bearers forever of banners: 6599.

The beast that is most fully dressed: 3435.
Beat yourself with little Lenten whips: 5751.
Beaten like an old hound: 3604.
Beautiful in the endless, black of night: 5465.
Beating his homemade wings against the sun: 2771.
Beautiful is this day that brings us home: 5955.
Beauty growing on a thorn: 954.
Beauty is never the truth: 4066.
Beauty is something the eye cannot: 582.
The beauty of earth is reality: 1618.
The beauty of small towns is that they give: 5701.
The beauty of this night: 1074.
Beauty will not be denied: 7064.
Because a stamp will bear the damp: 3322.
Because I am drunk, this Independence Night: 2154.
Because I live alone: 3381.
Because I live--and you, not--: 537.
Because Noni trespasses in the night: 538.
Because she cannot scour the kitchen tile: 3614.
Because the night was warm: 1153.
Because the warden is a cousin: 1424.
Because they belong to the genus thunder: 4075.
Because they say of you that you are: 4823.
Because we are all innkeepers, tonight: 4657.
Because you adore him: 55.
Because you would not bend: 539.
Become, you said, your self: 1787.
Bedraggled swaggerer, limp at last in mud: 1099.
The Beefburgh: 6228.
The beer at Jim and Billie's wasn't strong: 6774.
The beer that's iced is an abomination: 4448.
Beethoven, deaf, heard noble music still: 2404.
Beetles that peered from thickets of the breast: 2241.
Before Dale Carnegie began: 2967.
Before dawn a moaning dove: 3848.
Before dawn, in night's worst hours, alone: 1215.
Before he starts to wield his tape: 6233.
Before men walked: 6242.
Before the Angelicum: 5401.
Before the bush and green hay: 5409.
Before the day dawns: 6925.
Before the flood that year the rains set in: 4350.
Before the morning bay is visible: 680.
Before the smog, the bright cars, the clover-leafs: 831.
Before the sun is red: 6694.
Before this clair-obscur he recalls fire: 1785.

Before we mothernaked fall: 554.
Before your hands cease waving...: 1446.
Begin death's foe, I can't make use: 3647.
Begin with any object where: 3869.
Begin with arrangement: 1465.
Begins to emerge, the mask behind the face: 5863.
Behind a cat belled against birds: 4370.
Behind shut door, in shadowy quarantine: 1980.
Behind the bushes, under the cherry tree: 3037.
Behold a truly busy beaver: 3610.
Behold, Sakhi, the white silence, filling your eyes: 7099.
Behold the bounding ovibos: 3984.
Behold the hypochondriac: 803.
Behold, the Lord the Ruler He is come: 1726.
Behold the Social Scientist: 5745.
Behold the Yogi, who assails: 561.
Being a tourist, what I did was right: 6656.
Being an orderly soul at heart: 2440.
Being without quality: 6911.
"Belief," Grandfather Robbins: 2372.
Believing as I must that all: 5529.
The bell pursues me: 2714.
The bells all suddenly are nine: 5810.
The bells of blood are drunk, poor Mother: 217.
The bells of the door ring: 2327.
Beloved, be strong: 5505.
Beloved, we held you and swore blasphemous lies: 1009.
Below the elm, whole on that hill: 5025.
Below the planet Venus, mountain changes: 347.
Bemused, wherever you may turn: 3976.
Ben and I on dock drip circles: 3676.
Ben Jonson said he was? O I could still: 4138.
Bend the twig and trim the tree: 3925.
Bending its fury in the air: 6214.
Beneath Our Lady's wooden lobes: 1617.
Beneath the bull: 2543.
Beneath the rose mulch and the compost heap: 7214.
Beneath the trees, where hammocks blossom: 6150.
Beneath this glass bound by an ebony frame: 812.
Berserk, yet disciplined in every evil way: 5228.
Beside the cathedral: 944.
Beside the door: 2171.
Beside the sofa where I sit: 445.
Beside the very view of Notre Dame's: 4221.
Besme. You are like the tongue hidden in a dark place!: 1476.
The best are older: with the unrest time brings: 2123.
The best of life at least for me: 1517.
The best things in life may be free: 4771.
The best time to find: 2539.

Betelgeuse, Betelgeuse, what do yo do: 472.

Better on a schoolday good friends could skip: 715.

Better to trip and fall: 3373.

Between beauty and charm, there's a difference: 7288.

Between book covers secrets lie: 3664.

Between high banks of snow: 4706.

Between Red Roses and St. Clears: 5819.

Between the airbase and the radar tower: 592.

Between the dark and the daylight: 5707.

Beyond the field where crows cawed at a hawk: 6728.

Between the first and the thirty-first: 3770.

Between the frozen lake and sky: 1291.

Between the poem: 4951.

Between the upper and the nether stones: 7106.

Between their sandspit ends: 503.

Between us silence stretches for: 3844.

Between wind and sun: 2703.

Beware--Friendly Dog: 598.

Beware the horned moon, mischievous and slender: 4086.

Bewildering calm, yon tangle blade and bone: 376.

Beyond grown taller pines there's the same house: 2275.

Beyond the mountain blackness: 3882.

Beyond the river heavy morning rose: 1671.

Beyond the wharfside juke-box joints: 523.

Beyond your courteous demands: 6523.

The Bible soothes the harried soul: 6661.

The biding virtues, they do not: 602.

The big clouds look like pillows: 1091.

The big doll being broken and the sawdust fall: 232.

The big, rough farmer's quiet and subdued: 1866.

Billowing out his fiery parachute: 5240.

The birch in the lane, the cloud in its height: 6887.

Bird and hill. The eternal roll of the skyline displaces them: 2181.

The bird does not contain the song: 1235.

The bird fell like a stone, as if the night: 1681.

The bird sits on the cherry bough: 1857.

Bird song: 7170.

Bird song is flute song and a glory: 6455.

Bird wing to simian paw--life's stalwart dream: 2474.

Birds: 2072.

The birds and bees are out of date: 3056.

The birds are friendly: 1782.

The birds are still: 268.

The birds are wild with singing: 4869.

The birds in the first light twister and whistle: 3464.

Birds sing and my...: 282.

The birds still sing that sang to you: 4124.

A birthday gift: 5216.

The black bull bellowed before the sea: 788.

Black cat, cross my path: 4311.

Black eyes: 994.

Black milk of the dawn we drink it evenings: 1383.

Black robes, hoods gold scarlet purple, bright heads: 16.

Black shadow: 1543.

The black, the gnarled, nightmarish and shagreen-: 4761.

Black Venus of the dead, what sun of night: 1678.

The black wind poured the night: 3805.

The blackbird singing in the rain: 2164.

The blackfish moan like mother bereft: 3888.

The blades sway: 5178.

Blaze and blue the color of ideal water: 4285.

Bleakly, from an empty sky, the stars: 5577.

Bless Adam for a fire: 859.

Bless her, with her tomboy hands that can pitch a ball: 2043.

Bless the arms of this chair: 649.

Blessed are the blind: 731.

Blessed are you above all mothers: 530.

Blessed is she who knows the joys: 2644.

Blessings on thee, little man: 1226.

Blest are old ladies who grow straight and thin: 3672.

Blind for the lamp she's smashed and the riving tears: 4245.

The blind man sat beside his...: 797.

A blizzard in March: 656.

The blood is everything: 659.

The blood of our brothers out from the ground: 4510.

Blood's thicker than water: 5201.

Bloody Mary's venomous flames can curl: 3677.

The blossoms of the catalpa: 901.

The blow that felled him left my father's one: 3247.

Blown in a wreath of chills against the sky: 7181.

Blue-cold in a mere strip of gauze she rode: 2107.

The blue fox lifted a paw: 667.

Blue is the blood: 4675.

Blue-serged white-gloved little masters: 4536.

Blue water; upon it two possible movements: 3222.

Blue windows, blue rooftops: 4483.

The bluebells' chiming has been heard: 5698.

The boat rounded a bend and Urirostock: 4509.

Boat whistle blows like a woman crying: 677.
The boats are off the lake now: 1084.
Body's shine of sweat and the lighted trees: 5682.
Boisterous as March: 5158.
The bolting cry of crows above the wood: 678.
Bone marrow, gene and spirit I must be: 943.
The book closes. The walls suddenly fade: 904.
A book of astronomy, he announces: 1962.
Books by professors, sportsmen, artists: 7354.
Books collide: 6606.
A bore is one: 4764.
Born a dog: 3616.
Born among cattle, crucified with thieves: 1724.
Born in my month, the naked beast leaned out: 6958.
Born of love, caged in anatomy's miraculous: 620.
Borrowing trouble's as easy as pie: 2483.
Boston has a festival: 705.
Bowed negress, who aghast but light: 312.
Bowing he asks her a favor: 3062.
The boy came cooped in gold to France: 4875.
The boy leaning upon a window sees: 579.
Boy on the playground: 3245.
A boy should search through alleys now and then: 1693.
A boy sits reading his poem to me: 1461.
The boy was scarce to his father's knee: 5907.
A boy will always be hard to find: 1132.
A boy with searching eyes: 3569.
Boys like puppets dangling: 5963.
The boys were all she thought about: 7043.
Boywise once on a rickety pier: 3955.
Bracketed by a diesel switcher and five: 4204.
Brahms was very fond of children: 3545.
Braid the daisies: 801.
The branches are green that: 3503.
The bread man brought bread the other day: 2480.
Break her alembics: scatter them in the wild snow: 5614.
Breaking every law except the one: 4594.
Breakfast is served from 8 to 11: 3928.
Breasts high and open...: 5224.
The breath breaks a cold shuddered hollow: 5776.
Breath, frail talisman, bellows the sun: 5800.
Breathe! Move again! Awake! Break through: 4587.
The bridal daisies and the goldenrod: 3710.
The bridge between me and the world sometimes grows thin: 747.

The bright blue bell of the sea: 4036.
Bright-leaded walkers: 4988.
Bright town, tossed by waves of time to a kill: 4299.
A brightness never seen before: 7374.
Bring me a daisy instead of a rose: 4840.
The British puss demurely mews: 4787.
The broken-down bazaar at Antioch: 5104.
The broken pieces of our plan: 6451.
Brood: 6063.
Brother! What are you thinking?: 5758.
Brotherhood means being kind: 769.
Brown, all of the autumn, the manners of time: 771.
Brown is the road, swept smooth with showers: 495.
The Brown River, finger of a broken fist: 25.
Bubble gum under the pillow: 6393.
Buckskin men and patchwork wives: 5171.
The budget we've been keeping shows: 3949.
Build well that house, you two with eyes alight: 782.
The bulking mammoth steering: 3623.
A bumbling tippler, hour by hour: 4286.
Bump not crazy into that catalog: 872.
Burn, Spirit, burn!: 5396.
The burning heat that weighs our eyes: 3803.
A burro once, sent by express: 64.
Burrowing back and forth among: 5353.
Buses and motorcycles pour their noise: 6938.
The buses headed for Scranton travel in pairs: 798.
The bush of thorn he left: 1494.
The business life of Mr. Musial: 6752.
The busy life we lead today: 6296.
Busy now with baking bread: 3639.
But a boat is called a kayak: 1748.
But even if you go you are not there: 3115.
But for a brief: 2387.
But high above the word "love" cried: 5082.
But how can you be sure: 1428.
But I never lost faith in angels: 2746.
But I wanted power, to save me: 5258.
But the end's not yet, Amon. Who see you in disgrace: 2210.
"But there is the danger," he said, "of trying to keep": 6648.
But what did Dives do to merit Hell?: 1514.
But when and how will they arrive?: 2929.
But when they came there, no one could be found: 3895.
Buzzards in the air: 3787.
By antique mirrors blurred with memories: 2846.
By common agreement the most: 1579.
By here, where once we came: 3747.
By marriage I make evil the half brother: 816.
By the ancient castle at Kemoro: 818.
By the gray river: 4825.
By the opaque: 1362.

By the provision of God: 981.
By the road to church, Shaker Village: 5206.
By the waters of Babylon: 3741.
By the waters of Babylon we sat down to weep: 6264.
By tower call and right from talking: 4499.
By two of the ten thick thumbs: 5078.
By using intuition a woman can: 4023.
The cabin cruiser: 3660.
The cactus recalled the despairing gestures of marble: 825.
Caged fountains through the starlit summer night: 2142.
The calico cat is brown and black: 830.
Call the elephant: 1685.
Calls now for husband: 2375.
Calvin Jones, by marriage my mother's kin: 6761.
The camel is a long-legged humpbacked beast: 841.
The camion rattles onward in the rain: 2172.
A campus in summer should be like something from Tennyson: 848.
Can a man be born again? is not a new ...: 1136.
Can any sleep in peace: 3412.
Can cockcrow fix a landscape?: 7326.
"Can do! Can do!" With whir and clunk: 3184.
Can he remember when the days were brighter: 4287.
Can I be said to feel this odd sensation: 4523.
The Canada Warbler on his limb: 850.
Candid heart: 6544.
The candidates in our home town: 4915.
A candle looked up at the sky and said: 853.
This candlelight is silent as the moon: 7112.
The captive flourished like: 4934.
The car is heavy with children: 5319.
A card, a toy, a hoist: 3066.
The carpentered hen: 7276.
A carpet strewn with marbles, shells, a ball: 3479.
A carriage ran in the crevices of the skull: 2767.
The carriage waits at the door: 2766.
The carrousel has seen its better days: 2358.
Carthage and Nineveh, Babylon, Troy: 6813.
The carved St. Francis where the garden ends: 3759.
Carven Christ: 6083.
Castor and Pollux rage in the still skies: 2202.
Cat at the pane: 5221.
A cat in the sun: 1900.
The cat is eating the roses: 5391.
Cat of my winter, witless crutch: 4416.
The cat trees rotting: 5356.
Catalog cards: 1323.
Cats are not at all like people: 892.
Cats become prisoners in the snow: 6953.

The cattails shed among the reeds: 1592.
The cattle congregate: 1862.
The cedar waxwings bend the branches down: 1279.
The center of the universe: 2030.
The century's no longer new: 6609.
Certain fragrances: fresh brocade: 3889.
A certain supposition about spring: 6552.
A chalked-out game of hopscotch whites the street: 963.
Change, even when necessary and just: 4450.
The change is too complete: 925.
Change the baby; feed the cat: 2105.
Channels of happening as they run deep and deeper: 581.
The chap who keeps putting: 702.
The charcoal smoked: 458.
Charles used to watch Naomi, taking heart: 3193.
Charmed, he pokes a toe in fat brown mud: 1149.
Chastened, my dear, I humbly note: 3700.
The chest my father made I left that day: 6941.
Chicken. How shall I tell you what it is: 5000.
The chicory-mysterious hillside is down: 2386.
The Chiefs of State marched: 166.
Child at peace, a child no more: 3586.
The child-care books make frequent mention: 3060.
The child grabbed my hand and made me run with him: 2995.
Child in an Iowa dooryard: 6854.
Child, now grown, if I seem to cling: 5161.
The child of a sea change: 7094.
Child, play not: 971.
The child at winter sunset: 961.
The child came singing: 973.
The child disturbs our view. Tow-head bent, she...: 6444.
The child in disgrace, at the children's party: 6446.
Child in the house! 85.
The child of many winters came: 968.
Child of the neon age, what are you doing: 725.
Child, take your basket down: 1961.
A child who has fallen: 1194.
Childhood is when the mouth tastes earth: 977.
The children and I worked all morning to make: 2290.
Children are frightening: 3114.
Children en masse wear newer taut and 5992.
Children learn the first lesson of fear in the night: 4252.
Children of lions, you bright clouds: 1886.
Children of mine, not mine but lent: 2326.
The children sing and dance in the golden noonday: 1339.

Children, tracing patterns on the pane: 2701.

The children wade knee-deep in gold: 1363.

The children will have none of them: 6549.

The children wrapped up and skeined out and: 5730.

The chill of winter's never had my vote: 5022.

The chilling rain that drenched these parts: 7013.

Chin in, I doubt the praying mantis prays: 924.

China taught so many things to me: 2347.

Chisels, to work! 5884.

Chokecherries fill the hedgerows with a crop: 1002.

Chose from my store of Themes one Theme: 2292.

Christ called Andrew and he came: 5397.

Christ, forgive if I should break: 1145.

Christ, pity those who: 5190.

Christ, Who once wept in Galilee: 636.

Christ has sabbath work: to raise the dead: 3997.

Christmas again — with its good fellow-ship: 1027.

Christmas: and Valencia: 3467.

Christmas comes: 1350.

Christmas Day is come; let's all pre-pare for mirth: 1017.

Christmas is a feeling of giving: 5188.

Christmas is coming, it's easy to see: 6002.

Christmas is magic. Are not the mute heard...: 6895.

Christmas morning, screeching typkes: 3471.

Christmas-tree lark in a forest of bells: 3275.

Circled by trees, ringed with the faded folding chairs: 6295.

The circling shadow or the measured dial: 1033.

The city stopped: 3000.

The classic landscapes of dreams are not: 5734.

Clean and bare, slender, cold: 3300.

Clean to the bone and deeper than the bone: 1010.

A cleaning woman opened the rusty door: 1036.

Clear and high, a mountain: 2584.

"Clear as a bell!" I heard: 4288.

Cliches have come and buried him: 4500.

The cliffs parade: 814.

The climb the double flight: 1944.

Climb to the high board, heart cold and fast: 1513.

Clive, master of men, British Lord: 3514.

The clock on the dresser says 4 a. m.: 1358.

The clock shows nearly five: 6515.

The clocks begin, civicly simultaneous: 358.

Cloister and midnight lamp, what have come to?: 1588.

Close: 373.

Close by my house the trees leaf out and reach: 293.

Close friends of the water: 540.

Closer than hair, and of the air, air's bruit: 953.

The clouds seem like big fluffy pillows: 4595.

Clover grass all disappeared: 5189.

Coasting the Delta of the dead lagoons: 3438.

A cocker we have which the children adore: 4548.

The codfish: 6229.

Coffee break: 2183.

Cognizance of all we know: 1103.

Coincidence is a term we retain: 815.

The cold and gentle man: 2697.

The cold and narrow rooms at the end: 1373.

Cold dawn Harrow-on-the-Hill: 1397.

Cold I walk and cold I wander: 5787.

Cold in the night the locomotive's horn: 6924.

A cold is nothing to coddle: 5910.

Cold is the west wind: 3500.

The cold woods are fire-colored and change: 1442.

Coleridge, they say, lived in fantasy: 4838.

The colloid and the crystalloid: 5900.

Colman the Hermit: 1120.

The color of October afternoon: 1709.

The color of silence is the oyster's color: 1607.

The color of yellow: 1123.

The color red has quick teeth: 5888.

The colors of the world: 7287.

"Colors," she said, "are never so fine...": 2413.

The columbines are trampled: 1425.

Come again, Spirit!: 1753.

Come back to me at dead of night and speak to me: 6740.

Come, Capsicum, cast off thy membranous pods: 5522.

Come, don't I know that, stumbling in the dark: 6499.

Come for duty's sake (as girls do) we watch: 6890.

Come gather 'round, good gourmet: 3251.

Come here, Denise!: 1444.

Come in. Do come in. This is content-ment here--: 1208.

Come, kill our love, but let illusion live: 3992.

Come kiss me, my Mary: 3562.

Come, leaders of thought!: 847.

Come let us dance, my love: 5794.

Come, let us meditate upon the fate of a little boy who wished to be: 2957.

Come lie by the fire and hear: 5807.

Come live with me and be my love: 4691.

Come love with me and be my life: 6551.

Come out of the dark earth: 3006.

Come quickly in your small black shoes: 5793.
Come,sir, it's time though our summer was a great one: 4386.
Come try the lovely machine!: 912.
Come up unto my hill: 3004.
Come wind and glazing weather: 2390.
Coming from world's own weather through the door: 2988.
The coming of the sun is the coming of surfaces: 3896.
Coming tonight by more ways than I know: 2646.
The commerce of a schoolroom is the boyhood: 3065.
Compared to Eleanor's "Resartus.": 6263.
Comparing them to the sea: 2026.
Compassion is a virtue: 1155.
Complain about it if you will: 5411.
The complicated body: 7305.
Comrades of silence, it is time to go: 1166.
Conceived and shaped by humble shapers: 2887.
Concerning men I'll make no claims: 4185.
Condemned to life, a happier condemnation: 3292.
Conditioned to the cage, my bird: 826.
Confess, Cornelia, did the Gracchi: 5090.
Confronted with the final sunlit act: 1030.
Conservatives, the ones I know: 1192.
Consider feet--how well they end the legs: 2849.
Consider, if you will this room: 50.
Consider the banker: 259.
Consider the case of the Delalumt Pruitts: 886.
Consider the mysterious salt: 2924.
Contained in this arsenal are: 4997.
Content within your world of water: 3423.
Continuously present: 3179.
A contrapuntalist   : 3740.
Convention is a poor and crooked rule: 2295.
The conversation is slowing up: 4679.
Cornelia with an air: 3097.
The cornhusk mattress creaks: 4837.
The cost of living-up or down: 1811.
Could I believe that Death shall die: 1243.
Could it have been mine: 7125.
Count that day lost: 695.
The country girl had left her place: 5715.
Countryman, tell me if you can: 2799.
Courteous: 4635.
A courthouse in the center of the town: 5260.
The covey of quail flowed down the hill: 772.
Cowboys savvy how to cook: 1265.
Cows: 1141.
Cramped like sardines on the Queens, and sedated: 6628.

The crane, at his wits' end: 1272.
Cranky a week ago: 6445.
Create for me--: 6379.
Creation, new springing: 3239.
Crib biting: 633.
The crippled lady will forgive the boy: 6637.
The Cross against the sky: 1289.
The cross of boy with man within: 4434.
Crouched in the center of my sight: 902.
Crown of thorn: 1379.
Crows call and leaf fall: 2881.
The crude word: 3632.
The crust of snow sustains the deer: 2730.
The crying I used to hear: 4439.
Cupid is: 1310.
Curious how they all look alike: 2315.
Curls for a halo, see him come: 6177.
The current ceases, and the motor dies: 3932.
The cursive crawl, the squared-off characters: 7323.
The curtain rises on a lighted room: 2298.
The curtains belly in the walking room: 3223.
Custodian of wars, keeper of kings: 4106.
Dad takes a cold shower: 1112.
Daily we touch omniscience, come back: 1328.
Dancing in dust, dancing in sun, to you: 5847.
Danger! Danger! 2114.
Daphnis, come sit with me on the glacial: 5956.
Daring annihilation at the heart: 1281.
The dark and alien watch: 170.
The dark eyes of the girl checker are so sharp: 2838.
A dark lamp for killing insects: 6870.
Dark lightnings and loud winds and rainy spells: 5909.
The dark ones trail us over the world, we who: 2826.
The dark the darkness: 1343.
A dark woman in a straw hat: 3786.
Darkness comes early, stays late: 6435.
A darkness waits: 190.
Darling, I would like to steal time: 2035.
Darling, it frightens me!: 1348.
Daughter, when you're grown, I have no doubt you: 1882.
Daughters in the wing's boisterous roughing: 6847.
Daughters who lose their mothers early: 1353.
David sang "holy" with his harp: 132.
Dawn, in you alone there rests: 1356.
The day a man begins to state: 2340.
Day after day as the day sets: 6489.

Day after day, week after week: 5982.
The day becomes half evening, half rain: 3336.
Day before yesterday: 7107.
Day blackens out: 3384.
The day is harsher than the hellish regions: 2527.
The day; it is gauze, it is gold!: 5676.
The day may come (but not too soon): 6584.
Day, new day, burns clearer and clearer: 6135.
The day of days will surely come: 1364.
The day outdid itself in loveliness: 915.
The day the circus came I saw: 2081.
The day was a story: 1032.
Daydreaming in the weediness of growing: 717.
The days and years were coins they could not hold: 1624.
Days like this, off Jake's, the August fog: 3070.
The day's work is done: 1280.
Dead leaves, dead leaves, dead leaves: 4228.
Dead objects seem to live in the arms of the southwest wind: 660.
Dead on an island in an agate sea: 1682.
The dead rust of leaves curled up: 708.
Dear cherubs, there's a boy nearby: 2901.
Dear Cousin Nancy: 3968.
Dear Daniel, do not be afraid: 2908.
Dear fairy Godmother, hold back: 5844.
Dear gentle-hearted wife: 7322.
Dear God: 5227.
Dear God, the Wonderwright is ours: 4089.
The dear great names alive upon my shelves: 2740.
Dear lady, by all means tact: 6521.
Dear Lord: 6588.
The dear Lord Jesus was so small: 2041.
Dear Love, dear heart, when time is fled: 289.
Dear love, how of the seasons made: 3227.
Dear, on a day of dumb rain: 5120.
Dear People of China: 3832.
Dear romancer: 3690.
Dear Santa Claus: 4568.
Dear usual world you know and try to tell: 5294.
Dear water, clear water, playful in all our streams: 6095.
Dearest Wifey:Just a mention of this rather dull convention: 2498.
Dearest Theodore and Mabel: We were happy you were able: 4208.
Death is a cup: 1385.
Death that lessens and besets: 4409.
Death will come and will have your eyes: 6848.
Death's day is doomed again: 4256.
The decisive year went by: 3259.
Deck the halls with boughs of holly: 6022.

Deep as Manhattan's earth the billion-dollar: 430.
Deep bowed the branches with the snow: 807.
Deep, deep, deep into the silence I withdraw: 1418.
Deep in a dream I dwell: 774.
Deep in a stretch of silver: 4162.
Deep in the march and dappled woods: 6971.
Deep in this citadel of the peace of God: 262.
A deer ran through the dark forest: 3615.
The delicate auroras: 5570.
Delicate, minute, must be the inventory of truth: 3933.
Deliver us, please from those ponderous folk: 6983.
--delivered from a heaviness of love: 1439.
The de luxe tourist resort auto court: 4651.
Denial has a raucous voice: 2344.
Deny me every thing I want of you, beauty...: 5934.
The desert past, the shelter and the sand: 357.
Desire's a vicious separator in spite: 2936.
Desires are the tine of worldly air: 5042.
Despair is writ large on human faces: 1826.
Despite the chill, despite the snow: 5795.
Despite your manifest, alas: 1375.
The Devil: 4835.
Devil's red the cherry tree: 951.
Did someone say that there would be an end: 147.
Did you ever travel: 6602.
Dido, Sappho and Elaine: 3857.
The difference between a Cheshire cat and Norman Vincent Peale: 202.
The difficulty with all: 3181.
Diligent Janeite, happy bibliophile: 6504.
The dinner is stale, and the speaker the same: 3760.
Dinner is the cruelest time, breeding: 6918.
Dirty Christmas: 1013.
Discarding twenty million years: 5594.
Disciplining my son seems like: 2935.
Discovered in a dusty attic: 3011.
Discovery is never planned: 77.
Discrimination through pure color: 2540.
Dismayed by facts, present or past: 5019.
Distance brings proportion: 6252.
The distance spills itself, growing blue and shining: 1510.
Distorted by the rain, our garden shivers: 1559.
Distressed with human ballyhoo: 103.
Disturbed by wind that likes to tease: 7167.
Dividing my treatise in four, I will explain: 3290.

Dizzy and light with hunger, we come: 6631.
Do not be frightened: 5374.
Do not believe them: 3229.
Do not confuse this dying with the death: 3143.
Do not leave me, Lord, do not let the field lie fallow: 4984.
Do not stop playing the long thin notes, the steep sounds: 1522.
Do these walls form an egg or a tomb?: 171.
Do what thy manhood bids thee do, from none but self expect applause: 1524.
Do you: 2889.
Do you believe the concentration of beauty: 6471.
Do you know Mrs. Millard Fillmore Revere: 155.
Do you remember, as we sit in the stir-less shade: 6889.
Do you remember (One Said)and they rose from their long sleep: 6907.
Do you remember sweet Alice, Ben Bolt?: 1527.
Do you remember when we both were children: 3749.
The doctor's office waiting room: 2187.
Doctors write prescriptions: 7248.
Does God work by the committee method?: 1143.
The dog called Sesame slewed out: 6094.
The dog loved its churlish life: 3594.
The dog walks sideways on his mistress' lead: 7236.
Dogs are quite a bit like people: 1531.
Dogs that eat fish edging tidewater die: 3517.
The dogwood hurts me as I run: 1533.
Don Julio receives in a violence of roses: 1365.
Don't be misled: 285.
"Don't be so full of yourself!": 1659.
Don't go elsewhere: 3816.
Don't you love to lie and listen: 5128.
Doomed as absurd adults, we can forget: 6533.
Doomed, outdated: 4403.
A door has opened: 3265.
Dorothy: 6371.
A double flower we were: 6943.
Doubtless the leather chair in which I curled: 2992.
Dour in the parking lot: 5774.
Dove is the name of Him, and so is Flame: 5930.
The doves of my eyes rise to the sky's steel body: 1557.
Down among the rains, my dear: 6741.
Down at the docks: 1558.
Down by the water there: 2379.
Down from the north: 6642.
Down from the safe high place: 1185.
Down from the subtle grey Sorbonne and..: 5309.
Down of the hidden and the dreamless road: 2039.
Down railroad track: 2471.
Down the sky bowl rolls: 3132.

Down the track of a Philippine Island: 1703.
Down throw the sea: 1104.
Down where the dog-toothed tide: 316.
The dragons of the breast: 2561.
The dragon's Proteus: 608.
The dragons, the scale-tailed dragons have gone away: 3138.
Dream home plus Teddy bears and other odds and ends for children: 2347.
Dreams come at dawn like apple harvest: 1482.
Drenched in wet silver, pale with olive, and still: 3232.
Dressed in a costume of respectability: 5081.
The dressmaker's dummy: 1581.
Driver with your hand outflung: 837.
Drumming in warmed compartments up to town: 61.
Dry leaves are clicking somewhere over darkened pavement: 3283.
Duck, riding the reservoir waves: 4861.
Duck's-assed and leather jacketed: 1794.
Dun-colored birds, the days: 6247.
Dunes are graying that were blackest: 397.
Durer would have seen a reason for living: 2037.
Dusk is in the cat: 68.
Dust...and clay...: 1165.
Dust in the fog dropped opal and down the East River: 778.
Dusty bracken, oak, birch, pine: 4377.
Dutch treat luncheons and who owes whom how much: 6732.
Dynamo!: 6431.
Each bird is glutted: 5444.
Each day he comes burdened with worldly cares: 4615.
Each day I feed my heart on memory: 1301.
Each day I open the cupboard: 5362.
Each day the tide withdraws; chills us: 7320.
Each face repeats its former attitudes: 6088.
Each gift has its particular pain: 5636.
Each morning he arrived so grim: 3314.
Each one of us has had a sour: 6011.
Each payday I can pay my bills: 2742.
Each person has his blemish, I suppose: 4554.
Each sex has some irksome trait: 933.
Each time I watch a plywood lathe un-reel: 234.
Each time the postman cometh with: 577.
Each year as the deadline approaches: 7041.
Each year when lilac-laden spring comes round: 4182.
Eager for bushes and trees, for lattice and gate: 2225.
An ear is an asset: 590.

Early hours, the cream: 1614.
Early in April comes spring raking time: 5972.
Early in spring, against the seething hill: 2139.
Early in the morning: 1611.
Early, the stroke of dipping oars: 6974.
Early this evening, hunting for my name: 4129.
Early today the house was dim and still: 6074.
The earth: 2591.
The earth and I have come to be: 4379.
Earth and sky: 876.
Earth hates an emptiness as a woman hates...: 1619.
Earth is a tight primordial drum: 5974.
Earth is an old woman: 4284.
The earth is not an old woman: 1620.
The earth is such a solid place: 1626.
The earth is wet and running wild: 3079.
Earth, sea, and sky; the proud and patient stars: 1621.
Earth's barren face was restless everywhere: 6815.
Easy there with rope and trigger!: 1102.
The Ecco Homo on the mantel-piece: 3834.
Echoes of Orpheus' magic lyre still linger: 936.
Eerie shadows haunt the shore: 4109.
Eight iced and windy winters inter-vene: 706.
8:00 p. m. She asked her husband to be truthful: 758.
Ein oldischer frau in der shoe ben gestayen: 5288.
Either the boat shoots forward, or...: 1613.
Either to keep the thinking in: 2823.
Elder Statesmen: 1665.
The elephant never forgets: 7385.
Eleven rogues and he to judge a fool: 3960.
Ellen, Ellen, gaily smiling: 5311.
Elliptical regrets figure the nights: 707.
Embracing now this sour fast as feast: 716.
Emily: Had it been big enough to see: 1696.
Empty child of Anathoth: 7330.
Empty the sea of salt: 242.
Enclosed within its journey: 3808.
An end to Finess!: 5243.
Enemy: 5716.
The engines of the carnival, Sosthene: 5086.
English is a language than which none is sublimer: 752.
Engraved with lines of agony: 4847.
En route through space: 2690.
Ephemeral moment: 3861.
Erinna, serene in sunlight, lay on the rock: 1742.
Escape from all the sin, the dirt, the misery: 1746.

The Essenes, yes but study well the Stoics: 5405.
Essentially, this country is dry as cork is dry: 5903.
The established lovers of an elder generation: 1751.
Estivation means passing the summer in a torpid: 2712.
Etched old heads: 3261.
Eternal hilarity blooms in me: 207.
Etruscan sky of frescoes, angelic witness: 2016.
Eve is my mother, Adam my great sire: 1797.
Even after sunshine rang the crop: 2491.
Even as he recalled, the enemy: 4950.
Even as his clothes were tailored to: 3397.
Even as you went over, Neitzsche: 2279.
Even before the sky awakes: 3852.
Even I, an ancient panderer, a prophet impotent: 3087.
Even in my first fever of wrong ovations: 2940.
Even in sorrow at the feuds of man: 2905.
Even on clear nights, lead the most supple children: 2394.
Even stones are live with music: 1766.
Even the centuries divide: 237.
Even the hunters, who smile to cock: 3763.
Even the morning is formal: 3910.
Even the night resembles you: 4125.
Even the poor vulture got tired of it at last: 3240.
Even when first her face: 5775.
Even while the bright leaves: 1605.
Even wisteria, sufficiently looked at: 6199.
Evening is my sister: 4045.
Event will be the judge and will be heard: 520.
Ever since Adam: 1763.
Every day, in spring and summer: 3617.
Every day is a fresh beginning: 5637.
Every day we scatter seed: 1893.
Every gain has its loss, not every loss: 4694.
Every gentleman knows: 6493.
Every heart must keep at bay: 941.
Every time that I begin: 5753.
Every time the menu lists bleu cheese I want to order fromage blue: 2684.
Everyone clamouring: 2716.
Everything shone, everything glistened: 1650.
Ever to scourges: 1775.
Everyone makes mistakes: 7126.
Everything you do at sixty: 7083.
Except when he enters, my son: 6102.
Exiled from Eden forever: 2555.
Eximious old friendships are: 1804.
Expanding in the chill: 1115.
Expect this: 6725.
Explorers say that baseballs rise: 1690.

Exquisite sir, what blame rests in the wrinkles: 1172.
The eye closes to the horns of sleep: 4111.
The eye must leave and shape: 1815.
An eye on the grained wire: 6966.
The eye that made this knew no palor: 3981.
The eyelid has its storms: 1818.
Eyes, eyes: 1651.
Eyes glued to the highway: 5297.
Eyes on the pulpit now: 4400.
Face of the frank eyes and the gentle smile: 2188.
A face out of a cloud - Elijah Kellog, dead but looking: 5893.
A face that breathes ethereal: 586.
The faces talk: 1101.
The fact that I can't take it with me: 7316.
A falcon mewed and featly manned: 1727.
Falling from above: 424.
Falstaff stepped out in loneliness and laughed: 5495.
A family of ducks makes needle point: 4801.
Far above the shaken trees: 4760.
Far at a lonely rural station: 6456.
Far away beyond the glamor of the city and its strife: 4805.
Far be it from one lowly member to carp: 117.
Far countries of a farther land than man: 2084.
Far, far down: 1050.
Far from my mother's tear, yet near: 5014.
Far from willow-home and flow of fountains: 3534.
A far-off look is poaching in the eyes: 2233.
Far up into this sunny summery clime: 6183.
Farewell, farewell: 6531.
Farewell to beach and balmy breezes: 6644.
The farmer, in the pride of sea-won acres: 6164.
The farmer's eyes are dark; he speaks in song: 4524.
Farmers in the fields, housewives behind steamed windows: 891.
Farsighted is the town that has decreed: 785.
Farsightedly throughout the year: 5012.
Father, fist-bruises marked my cheeks and eyes: 2003.
Father, since always now the death to come: 5875.
Fear is a formal matter; after the arrow: 1888.
Fear, Orpheus, if it ever reached you: 6430.
The feather breath of love, silk of the winds: 5623.
Fed up with clinkers this: 6664.
Feel for your bad fad fall how could I fail: 6213.
The feel of April was in her bones: 279.

A feeling of freshness, moist in the air: 7133.
Feld, groes or goers, hus, doeg, dung: 5269.
A fellow and a girl who wed: 4247.
Female lakes respect the love of loons: 4932.
The female temperament: 1904.
A fence is a forbidding thing: 1909.
Ferns are white fur now, and stub her feet: 7216.
The ferrying light that crossed you: 2718.
Fetch me a man who's easy to know: 6566.
The fever has abated: 946.
A few days, and snow will come, I recall: 2805.
For friends he has; few intimates he needs: 5390.
Few groups are more boresome: 1284.
Fidget, wiggle, squirm, and jiggle! 5247.
The fields of November: 1917.
Fields where we slept: 2014.
Fierce, full jets are lowered: 4410.
Fifty, not having expected to arrive here: 3116.
The fighting nature of the intellect: 6845.
The figs on the fig tree in the yard are green: 1447.
The figures are of heroic size: 6254.
Fire had flicked a crooked tongue: 3898.
The firm circling rhythm of his arc: 3975.
A first-born child is kept so sterile: 5808.
First came the lion-rider, across the green: 1950.
First choose your hitchcock; in choosing, be wary: 2679.
The first constricted gasp: 2045.
First he must go where: 2587.
First, he's rejected: 1655.
First I must labor to earn it: 281.
First, make a letter like a monument: 694.
First membership is wonderful: 6017.
First more than fire: 6769.
The first morning of cancer he awoke: 1967.
First, only faces looking up: 340.
The first stick thrown blew leaves: 5740.
First the sand bar dipped; then winter's: 3645.
First the wine bottle broke: 1629.
First there was love: 4874.
First, we know the hangman always hangs himself: 2476.
The first whale that I saw was large as death: 3494.
A fistful of pennies unlocks the charm: 4742.
Five cents a glass. Small figures wait: 3297.
Five days a week the color flows: 5453.
Five suspects to have done the trick: 5159.

Five workmen hired here to shovel dirt: 7304.
A flaming phoenix came to rest: 4791.
Flanking the ruined wall, his last command: 1915.
Fled from the spot of Balder's burial: 6615.
Fleeing the frozen steppes of the spirit: 1879.
Flexible children tumbling in the hills: 4485.
Flickers of marshfire: 3648.
Flies cauterise as they eat dabbing the parts: 1374.
Floating his lifeless head, the river ran: 4585.
Florida rang with rain the eve of Christ's mass: 6685.
Florist, give me flowers: 4626.
The flower-bright rug and chair's brocade: 1599.
Flower in his cutaway: 743.
The fluff of feathers in the fall of snow: 2971.
Flying through the night this Lenten eve: 4740.
Fog ballooning down the street: 3077.
Fog covered all the great fleet homeward bound: 5583.
Folded hands, an illusion: 5610.
Folding money's gay and gainful: 2033.
The follies of youth and age: 5208.
Followed the bird in the long forest where it cried: 2861.
A follower of Omar through the years: 6215.
Following a dry creek without a bend: 408.
The foot of death has printed on my chest: 5596.
The footpaths dripped a flinty lying light: 2194.
For a long time now I have thought: 5502.
For a tingling of daybreaks, for a few: 3333.
For all my ills, I lie with night: 1163.
For all the cups of coffee that we poured: 3335.
For brick and mortar breed filth and crime: 3777.
For Claris it is terrible because with this he takes away: 2061.
For a little while we have lived back in: 588.
For a long time our train lay on its belly along: 101.
For a long time they merely left it there: 6940.
For a year now he has nested: 3491.
For all her subtle plans and aims: 2299.
For art he bleeds: 1717.
For every year the tree survives: 3058.
For forty days with creatures of the wild: 2138.
For forty years and more my hand has shown: 5439.

For him who early on May: 6090.
For inland he can feel an ocean rise: 5508.
For me, the naked and the nude: 4028.
For more than five thousand years: 377.
For more than once dimly down to the beach gliding: 4612.
For old acquaintance' sake: 7255.
For once arrived at the time fixed: 626.
For one or both, coverlets of peacocks: 3244.
For one who chose a hermit's life: 2432.
For others, Time may crack the whip: 1982.
For Paolo di Grazia, heaven's: 4683.
For poverty: 3246.
For sickle morn and evening star: 2070.
For six long days she's clad in jeans: 6167.
For the expectant is the glory: 7380.
For the good of both races: 1011.
For the monster's simplicity, the menacer's: 210.
For this my daily bread I give: 1248.
For this the door of sorrow has grown small: 2272.
For this the primal reed was cloven: 5330.
For this winter is thick as flannel: 6138.
For this, you really deserve contratulations: 1180.
For those who come after, that is how we named it: 865.
For those who feed on the liberal creed: 6663.
For we have seen wild geese in passage, low: 4327.
For wee baby Cheryl: 2473.
For what is foreign thanks; what English praise: 2110.
For what it serves, the center has many times: 2911.
For years I thought I knew, at the bottom of the dream: 3729.
For you the Marseillaise, Marianne!: 3658.
Fore feet, hind feet leap and land: 1242.
Foreign lands, golden strands: 2316.
A forest: 6624.
The forests rusted, and released their leaves: 3242.
Forever and ever: 6850.
Forever the eye of the sea: 1760.
Forget understanding. There will be none: 5768.
Forgive him, sea-petals: 2489.
Forgive if you can: 1322.
Forgive me for loitering in front of your pictures: 2243.
Forlorn and lost in little hells: 5705.
Formless we meet and struggle like the sea: 2869.
Fortunate lady, with rings like stars: 6098.
The fountains of fire: 5667.

Four are the corners of the earth: 3583.

Four clawed dragons, wound in muscled love: 3815.

Four feet up, under, the bruise-blue: 5702.

Four ghosts how walk the Russian forests, girls: 2145.

Four is too big for his breeches: 2143.

Four o'clock sunlight is like a bell: 5901.

Four sons only says the law: 2146.

Four walls of windows look: 277.

Fox: 2157.

A fragment of weak flesh that circles round: 4830.

Fragments: 2162.

France once more betrayed: 5339.

The frantic flicker of the vigil lights: 343.

"The freedom-loving leaders of the West.": 1317.

Freem Jenkins had just bought a donkey: 4687.

Freight trains seem beautiful to me: 2166.

Frenziedly but certain: 1369.

The friend is most obnoxious: 2661.

Friend, it is clearly morning in your mind: 145.

A friend who's kind: 1188.

The friendliest lips have little understanding: 3031.

Friends by appointment call: 5791.

Friends that for twenty years I had not met: 4437.

A frightening name, winter: 4089.

The frightful reality of things: 1502.

The fritillary: 2175.

A frog was killed: 1386.

Frogs, I hear you in the night: 5489.

From a day in the time of my own warts I recall: 780.

From across the street of the Nursing Home: 6793.

From beginning to end: 3756.

From blue to dusk and the lights came: 7169.

From cuts and bruises: 5937.

From flatness: 3871.

From her horizons that are filled: 1457.

From hill to hill: 6844.

From immaculate construction to half death: 3627.

From leaf to thorn the sunlight goes: 5352.

From loss of the old and lack of the new: 5016.

From my bank account, I sadly learn: 1762.

From my hospital window: 4219.

From one busy task to another I whirl: 1148.

From out my tomb of twenty centuries: 2783.

From risk, as women's fashions change: 949.

From roads running parallel to all this: 1707.

From rooming-house to rooming-house: 139.

From spiralling ecstatically this: 1024.

From the circle's almighty roundness: 6734.

From the flat fields of the Delta and waves of woods: 3437.

From the high order of the stars: 6308.

From the hodge porridge: 1869.

From the look of contempt in the eye: 3315.

From the Matlock Bath's half-timbered station: 3699.

From the middle of April until October: 560.

From the palace casement she looked down: 3098.

From the principality of loss: 1231.

From the rainpalace into the rain: 2193.

From the terrace where the tea is poured: 2240.

From the thick cover of unknowingness: 4457.

From the third floor, I beckon to the child: 836.

From the throne of Mary: 3444.

From the usual testing sit in old Siberia: 6818.

From the whirl of smoke: 4137.

From this island, the sea is always visible: 6128.

From walking dogs: 7191.

From where does it come, this temper display: 6251.

From your town house to your country house you look: 6821.

The frost of a new year: 4820.

Frost, the old master, etched upon my pane: 19.

The fruit in moment hangs upon: 4798.

Full of ghosts tonight, the rain echoes memories: 405.

Full 40 years, Callimachus you took: 900.

Furious birds scream for the tropic sun: 2895.

Furnace of early afternoon, light: 1469.

Futile Foster: 2803.

Future, take care of yourself: 36.

The gal who rides in front of me: 908.

Galilee speaks in the wind today: 2234.

The game of profit and loss with eyes: 952.

The garbage man goes all around the playground: 3624.

The garden held wet weather: 4884.

A garden shut, a fountain sealed: 2248.

The gardens of her mind where she most often lived: 5354.

The garden's tall white tower closed with keys: 2244.

Garments of inattention, oh mere items: 6271.

Gasping for pastorals like a displaced Daphnis: 1340.

Gateway, Grove: 5107.
Gay burly beau, his life is summer only: 1585.
Gay, guiding dashes: 6001.
A gay gust of winged things: 2973.
Gazing and gazing in the glass: 3303.
Geese: 2260.
Gentle columns, whose: 861.
A gentle master came to hers: 4222.
A gentle wind blows in the water: 2395.
Gentlemen, this serviceable bird: 4793.
Geometrical masses: 662.
The geraniums I left last night on the windowsill: 7308.
Get me a hanky, I'm going to sneeze: 5211.
Getting to be a well-liked teacher is no easy matter: 7351.
A ghostly music fills the air: 4369.
Giddyap, all my horses! : 603.
The gifts are all wrapped: 4640.
Girl: 272.
The girl lies down on the hill: 4701.
A girl must be clever to handle: 4048.
The girl smelled of vines: 1250.
The girl with green eyes: 6284.
The girls peel: 6160.
The girls, protected by gold wire from the gaze: 209.
Girls who are modest: 6085.
Girls write stories about little girls: 6270.
Give each man a book: 689.
Give her the room with the blue walls: 2451.
Give me my books: 6403.
Give me my winter land of beech and pine: 4868.
Give me the lowest place: 3577.
Give to me if you will, but out of love: 6946.
Given some fifty centuries: 1833.
Given the change to witness by my death: 2939.
Given the gift of a ring: 2097.
Glaciers leave their trail in the rolled rocks: 6978.
Gladness is for sharing: 2382.
Glance down on mortal earth immortal moon: 4614.
Glandular change provokes a vague content: 4622.
The glare goes down: 2311.
The glass is splintered in which Pico caught: 534.
Gleaming city: 1662.
Glide, glide: 5659.
Glories through the quiet stillness: 563.
Glossing these paws and planters which now are fingers--: 3638.
Gnarled, gnomelike where in rock their deep roots grope: 431.
Go back now; pause to mark: 2634.
Go fly a kite!: 7306.
Go forward, explorer: here are lands: 6302.
Go home to Wilmington: what there: 6108.
Go humbly when the sun is old: 7029.

Go ring your bells: 1635.
Go tell her that you love her: 2319.
God--: 3013.
God does not write all poems in green: 7202.
God gives us a time to wait--: 6323.
God, how I envy you these great oak roots: 3096.
God, I speak in gratitude for this: 4079.
God knows how our neighbor managed no breed: 5896.
God lives in the woods, dear, see, the fern: 1220.
God of grace and God of glory: 2324.
God of the idle heat in this glaring road: 384.
God of the sky: 3441.
God spoke space: 2265.
God when You came to our house we let you in: 2.
The God who spoke to darkness: 2325.
God, you were the handle to every door: 5395.
The gods are dying around us, the Heroes: 2870.
The gods have left Olympus hill: 6332.
God's love does not compute desert: 2797.
Going away. Yes, I'm going: 2332.
Going to bed: 5497.
Going up the river, or down, their tunnels look: 499.
Gold are the leaves that fall from the trees: 418.
The gold dome of Hartford gone: 4683.
Gold is for the mistress--silver for the maid: 1110.
The golden bell of Christmas eve: 882.
The Golden Palace where I dwell: 2337.
The golden pond crab: 6144.
Golden wings departing cast: 2006.
The goldenrod has come and gone: 1158.
Gone are the books: 5239.
Gone are the shadows: 5473.
The gone dog leaves a ghost: 3532.
Good-by to rising in the cold, bleak dawn: 6825.
Good-bye my fancy: 2342.
Goodbye and God speed you to Rotterdam: 5028.
The good Friday crowd went: 3874.
Good Morning, Love!: 2349.
"Good morning," the voice says, "Is this Harry?": 1608.
Good night. Sleep well: 3591.
Good things will happen: 331.
Good Wood: 2034.
Goodnight, unlucky three. Mice at a feast...: 3590.
Goose Pond's imaginable snow: 2354.
The gorilla: 2355.
The Government is out: 6593.
Goya-grotesque, she changes to a snake: 5711.

Grandfather's goodnight did not pass his lips: 1860.

Grandpa, admit it: 6107.

The granite angel and the cast-iron fence: 3592.

Gran'ma used to say: 835.

Grant me sweet Christ the grace to find: 2557.

Grant me the self-awareness to know honestly who I am, what I can do: 41.

Granted that what we summon is absurd: 6223.

The grape leaf and its fellow stood: 2380.

Grass channel or anodyne canal: 860.

The grass is singularly green: 2415.

Grave day the lares and penates fell: 3068.

A gravel deathbed for the king of fish: 3170.

Gray as old Time himself the cathedral stands: 1718.

The gray clouds look like: 5116.

Gray day: 5960.

Gray-eyed Columba: 1126.

The great earth shows its grain again, tossed up: 1489.

Great farmy whores, breasts bouncy more: 516.

Great obsession: 1160.

The great four-posted bed: 2336.

The greatest fear is of a change: 1887.

Green island under the waves: 4210.

A green level of lily leaves: 6577.

The green nut tree: 2220.

A green pride of green leaves: 2423.

Green Snake, when I hung you round my neck: 6600.

Green things grow discouraged: 4363.

Green, winter river flowing to the sea: 2425.

A green world, a scene of green, deep: 3801.

Greetings, friends! God rest you well: 431.

Gregorian, girls, is difficult; you must earn: 3305.

Grief comes trotting as a horse: 2437.

Grief is a dry wind: 2436.

Grief was a boulder: 3341.

Grieve, ladies, so may God keep you: 4827.

Grimly determined: 1173.

Grotesque little boy with immense head held carefully: 2001.

Grown old, long hours before its time: 6076.

Grown tired this hour of trying to concentrate: 7204.

Guard him, St. Joseph: 3442.

Guard me, oh God, from the cold wind that blows: 7265.

Guest: 2452.

A guest adept at repartee: 7234.

A gull rides on the ripples of a dream: 6928.

A Gurkha stands at the gate of sleep: 6869.

Gurney, Hampton, Cradock Newton, last: 1271.

Gus is the Cat at the Theatre Door: 2457.

The gusher-colored body of Death: 6212.

The habit of these years is constant choice: 7311.

Had fair Ophelia, gentle maid been wed: 1325.

Had fate assigned your: 172.

Had I not seen it, I could not: 7205.

Had I the shillings, pounds, and pence: 4665.

Had someone told me twenty years ago: 230.

Had the prescription read: 5382.

Had the thin golden mask hidden your face: 4021.

Had we but rivers reticence: 1648.

Hail, queen who rides the violet swell: 7258.

Hail winds, who've found your keyhole and your key!: 4188.

Hairy was here: 4098.

The half alive, the half alive: 2464.

Half! Half! The widow cries: 1307.

Half past two is a lovely age: 2465.

Half squatter, half tenant: 3642.

Halfway through the puzzle: 2128.

Halt eternal verities! Rebel: 6469.

The hammer: 157.

The hand is a laydown, an absolute snap: 3701.

The hand of God is on the man: 2471.

The hands of many Magdalenes: 3678.

Happiness is an acquisition: 2199.

Happy are those of simple ways who still bless the light: 5850.

The happy crowds are gone: 421.

A happy task, to praise this mental prince: 3408.

The harbor is full of stars: 6029.

Hard a way: 486.

Hard by the edge of earth, along the shore: 5665.

The hardest thing to imagine is: 6829.

Harlequin speaks by the moon's light: 6841.

Harry Truman: 609.

Has man the right to die and disappear: 6203.

Hatters are not hapless chaps: 2268.

Haunched like a faun, he hooed: 3780.

Have diapers (disposable): 2495.

Have dinosaurs come back again?: 2583.

Have they forgotten, quite: 3505.

Have two pretty daughters: 6613.

Have you been told?: 7334.

Have you got the moon safe?: 1446.

Have you never: 4611.

Have you noticed, dear, my hair: 4206.

Having disposed of lunchbags out the windwings: 6630.

Having enough plowshares: 777.

Having no surface of its own, the pond:

Having no worldly goods I can bestow: 3289.

Having traveled around, here's one fact I have for me: 1930.

He blunders through frustration's passageways: 5139.
He brought home to his parents: 22.
He came with music: 2506.
He comes on with a keening moan: 2281.
He counted lost each: 3817.
He cracked a word to get at the inside: 2507.
He cries pretzels in traffic jams: 7042.
He died the day before the last exam: 4498.
He does not always scold and shout: 576.
He does not remember even the recent wars: 1995.
He dragged me through the hedge: 1525.
He dreams about him like a boat: 4854.
He entered the cathedral timidly: 2974.
He excelled at Western Michigan College: 1589.
He eyes November when the hills of number: 1450.
He flies with less direction: 810.
He found a rope and picked it up: 2962.
He found the water cooling his dry lust: 4378.
He had not lived long in our town: 4097.
He had read those same words over many men: 2077.
He has driven away, and with him has gone: 1449.
He hated them all one by one but wanted to show them: 244.
He hath seen my sitting down and rising up: 6858.
He is a little horse with wings: 2029.
He is a very new boy: 4072.
He is alarmed at idea as a learned gaze: 1228.
He is an old man, bent and stooped: 6467.
He is clear gold, the delft-blue: 7337.
He is father: 6198.
He is not the wise man, who comes: 2316.
He is running like a wasp: 4912.
He is so small, and pain can be so mighty: 4977.
He is the wall of this place whose hair: 4224.
He is very unique, yes, the most only one: 1816.
He isn't malicious, he isn't evil: 3017.
He. It was on a winter's day, as cold, as clear· 6168.
He it was plowed the rows: 827.
He kneels and finds humility: 1212.
He knows! My heavenly Father surely knows: 3994.
He let down a line: 5045.
He lives where everything is heavy and tall: 959.
He longs for just one night at home: 1851.
He looked up, like a savage; nothing there: 4726.

He looks about ten: 3846.
He never lives to tell: 829.
He picked out those with run down souls: 5141.
He plants his gnarled thumb in a pot: 2428.
He quaffed, and hung the dipper by the wall: 1409.
He rides a mood swing: 4781.
He rubbed his nose against earth's darkest sky: 5932.
He sails the planets down the sky: 5385.
He sat all day: 5026.
He sat in that same chair: 2918.
He showed the skin, and thought to show the man: 3695.
He sits, his pen above: 4396.
He sleeps in three tents: 4196.
He slew his foe, but did not slay the terrors: 4628.
He splashes and wriggles and thrashes his feet: 4356.
He stood still by her bed: 2353.
He suspects that the seasons: 5543.
He tackled life with noise and vim: 40.
He thinks that saints of his own creed: 5499.
He threw his shoes away in June: 6142.
He thumbed the undistinguished morning mail: 3321.
He toiled and strove and daily dreamt of fame: 2221.
He too saw sunshine filter through the trees: 1645.
He took his wig off: 1092.
He took the universe into his room: 2987.
He tried to keep his words: 165.
He undressed his flesh: 6998.
He very rarely makes warm friends: 1225.
He waits, in a land where the daylight comes: 711.
He walked to the city from Bethany: 3822.
He was a cynic and he said to me: 1372.
He was a gardener of words: 6266.
He was a gentle soul , of valiant strength: 6548.
He was all black: 3253.
He was from Lincoln's country of common sense: 3772.
He was no good: 644.
He was not afraid: 6580.
He was out, or down, in their strange darkness: 655.
He was so anxious to please: 6803.
He wasn't the only fish in the sea: 7241.
He watched the surf beat on a single rock: 1331.
He wears his years as a mantle, warm with good deeds: 2511.
He who has never tasted the grapes of Canaan can only view...: 1994.
He who on earth was never lax: 2042.
He who sired me: 1883.
He who would present himself: 1210.

He whose cry enrolled the sea: 5578.
He wore a sport coat: 2170.
He would rip out his tongue: 789.
He writes his reference on a card: 3353.
Head gravely bent, hands spread before his face: 4328.
Hear now how Harpe's dead and...: 3458.
Hear the awkward wind in the long grass: 366.
Hearing about those winter nights: 1015.
Hearing that you would come who by my love: 2931.
The heart is almost lost in anguish and despair: 2841.
Heart is like a frozen bird: 6101.
Heat is the first ingredient: 2773.
The heated chargers of evening come rolling in on crescented city: 828.
Heave ho! Here we go!: 787.
Heaven and earth shall pass away: 1146.
The heavy sun rising: 3447.
He'd have been gentle: 1047.
He'd heard in school about the constitution: 5868.
Hegel: 4850.
"Heigh in the hevynne's figure curculere.": 2608.
Held in bondage day and night: 7346.
The Hellenic world emerges in our dream half history, half fable: 2538.
Helpless improver: 6773.
The hemlock keeps its Christmas: 6027.
Hemlocks in row, heads bowed beneath snowfall: 4655.
Henry had something on his mind: 350.
Henry James, on trips to Boston: 5286.
Henry, my distant kin: 3325.
Her agitation suddenly stops: 2141.
Her beauty was so rare: 6738.
Her birth was one day when the blunt Atlantic: 4295.
Her bold techniques: 447.
Her braids pinned high upon her head: 4193.
Her dog yapped among the running shadows: 3791.
Her face lights up in thought: 5213.
Her features were those of a Roman martyr: 6348.
Her figure was compacted from the shark: 631.
Her gifts are kindness, poise: 2362.
Her great invisible wings: 5512.
Her hands were clasped against the tumid pod: 1547.
Her husband's a crumb; he's an absolute bum: 2681.
Her letter like a caught bird, my hand: 3332.
Her name: 1758.
Her name was, I think, Alexandra: 1695.
Her voice on the wind is high and thin: 991.
Here: 2494.
Here ancient arches: 1981.
Here are no woods to wear: 4967.
Here are the feather and the song: 1892.

Here are the modern throne-rooms: 800.
Here as we kneel: 6936.
Here at the frontiers of the land: 4172.
Here at the Vespasian-Carlton, it's just one: 701.
Here at this sudden age of mine: 433.
Here by this inlet where the snow comes down: 174.
Here canvas hugs the form that love withholds: 2672.
Here Captain Nicholas Gardner lies: 4387.
Here come the parson and his wife: 867.
Here comes, with those occurrences of mind: 855.
Here distance beckons like a dusty scroll: 2579.
Here, for a certain space: 1700.
Here from this hill of many stones: 4068.
Here from this hill to which we drove: 1048.
Here he lies moulding: 1729.
Here I belong, where the wood winds blow: 2549.
Here I stand, confronted by offense: 1749.
Here in a teardrop shines the infinite: 2550.
Here in my hands I hold the Holy Book: 2737.
Here, in the drunken-depths, the mind freezes to rock: 3250.
Here in the garden, strolling slowly: 4546.
Here in the hills: 1029.
Here in the May day morning sun: 314.
Here in the stillness I: 2250.
Here in this suburb where not a single: 5732.
Here in this world of Lilliput: 3166.
Here is a country still unplowed: 1264.
Here is an open page of the secret world: 2368.
Here is how I eat a fish: 1643.
Here is the grackle, people: 1821.
Here is the place of two eternities: 5589.
...here is the stream again under the rainbow: 1790.
Here is the town of unforgiven fall: 1840.
Here it stands in humble eloquence: 905.
Here let us set a stone, here where so many died!: 6058.
Here lies seldom to be found: 1737.
Here on the farm: 3382.
Here, on this far North London height: 6999.
Here on the map we recognize Formosa: 992.
Here on their pedestals in state: 179.
Here pretty patterns fade: 5476.
Here rests his head upon the lap of earth: 1728:
Here sea sound and snow silence meet: 7210.

Here she lies in comfort blessed: 1735.
Here steered Columbus to the West: 477.
Here, take the kind with caviar: 1642.
Here teachers mold the future years: 647.
Here, the hush of silent centuries: 104.
Here the turtle: 3201.
Here, then, was summer unending: 1486.
Here where he lies, the grasses: 1731.
Here where la belle lay dreamy in bois: 4080.
Here where nothing passes: 2427.
Here where the muddy Wabash makes a slow: 6915.
Here where the sea is dead: 5462.
Here, where we pick up wind in shells: 2546.
Here wind would blow the grass out of ground: 4617.
Hermes, why still the winged sandals, hot?: 4071.
Hero, fast in your dark monument: 4314.
Heroes of another day: 2479.
Heroes of Hungary: 3744.
He's a paragon of virtue: 6780.
He's couth and sheveled and imical: 5680.
He cruised away another tankful: 6407.
He's learning to dress: 2565.
He's not allowed upon the bed: 5365.
Hey diddle diddle: 1199.
Hey, hey! Make way for the latest model: 2566.
Hibernation: 2568.
Hibou et Minou a la mer: 2569.
Hickory-dickory-dock: 6429.
Hiding his golden abdomen, the spider of the sky was at rest: 6200.
High and clear the cold star shines: 1952.
High as my star once hovered: 3128.
High on a hillside that I know: 3806.
High over Ramapo hill: 1413.
High, over the ranges, its cone in blue air as though floating: 1824.
The high-school flagpole is a jointed staff: 1998.
Higher than hills, I sat in a vague balloon: 6897.
The highest is ever the lowest found: 2317.
The highest tenor notes are a bit uncertain: 2581.
The hills forgetting snow: 5288.
Him that I love I wish to be: 1761.
The hippopatamus's face: 1198.
Horoshima was my birthplace and my death site: 6422.
His candle shines upon my head: 6045.
His candor was savage and unqualified: 4217.
His dungarees list hard to port: 7361.
His family was like Spaniards: 2401.
His father steps into the shower: 1885.
His favorite programs were 2575.
His footprints fade in narrow yesterdays: 3625.

His garden is a lovesome thing: 4055.
His helmet crest, like water hitting the headlands: 4739.
His home is as plush as you're likely to see: 606.
His lashes grow like vines upon a string: 7369.
His leg is arched about a sphere: 6742.
His life was a perpetual Lutheran Sunday: 5879.
His news lies only at the crest: 3523.
His pigeons have reached darkness: 6317.
His rage or grace as fabulous still height: 2295.
His ritual is enormous: 511.
His shoes track shreds of forest in: 874.
His thought came slowly: 4851.
His torrent sweeps the hill's shoulder: 1601.
His triumph is not yet the looked-for glory: 1135.
His voice, a bagpipe with a strain of thunder: 4671.
His was the static strength of unrung bells: 4711.
Ho! Ho! Ho! I fancy you know: 2429.
Hold it tenderly in your hand: 481.
Hold it a second, Oracle! Just contemplate: 5281.
Holding my cheek: 7114.
Holding onto myself by the hand: 4589.
Holy book!: 7281.
Home is where the windmill: 6879.
Home to the bed of youth and manhood's returns: 1471.
Home with the evening tide they came: 2617.
Homework time, no urging: 5786.
Honey in the comb is more than honey: 2624.
Honeyed with fruits: 2625.
Hope is the thing with feathers: 2631.
Hope, like a gleaming taper's light: 2629.
Hope was the mistake: 5238.
A horrid planet on its first career: 6457.
The horse bent forward: 2640.
The horse is noble: 1740.
The horses of the...: 4429.
The hostess' mother is: 3370.
Hot, graveled roads in the late afternoon of the year: 5058.
Hotei has his own hotel: 4375.
The hound-dog: 3708.
The hound of heaven: 6527.
A hound who has an active flea: 1532.
The house is quiet now: 2438.
The house is still, empty as a ghost: 1698.
House of the world is beautiful in May: 7122.
The house still stands, of course: 4398.
The house when weather-proof for man: 6038.
Housekeeping is, say many men: 1641.
The housewife face of me: 2096.
How beautiful are the...: 7309.

How beautiful is the ugliness of the city: 342.
How beautiful the early dawn is: 584.
How can I express that we are children: 4173.
How can I speak of war: 5811.
How can I tell: 6187.
How can the bird: 1755.
How constant, vigorous and brisk: 491.
How cool-kindly the road: 5360.
How cool within the fiery...: 265.
How could I call you spring?: 6562.
How could you be so happy, now some thousand years: 4207.
How dear to my heart are the scenes of my childhood: 189.
How did this hour issue from the last?: 4294.
How did you first set forth: 629.
How do we start the day on a cruise: 1366.
How does he fare...: 4763.
How does one delve the dark?: 5094.
How doth the little lazy bee: 4102.
How droll it is that we can know her only: 2361.
How everything gets tamed: 3937.
How few are missed when, after routine years: 7081.
How find a word of kindness for a gray: 3165.
How fortunate the ear: 5750.
How good it is to turn aside: 4724.
How gravely all this goes. The street lights first: 1118.
How I loved one like you when I was little: 5687.
How I went mad in the clearing: 6827.
How is it in the country paths: 3334.
How light the quiet of your hand: 5060.
How longer hold this division?: 1370.
How loudly and how surely the musician plays: 3983.
How many a genius was just a crackpot: 3476.
How many a woman has gone berserk: 2481. How many alas, are the things I've read that: 6375.
How many months did he weigh?: 2828.
How mobile is the bed on these: 5121.
How much he's my heart's delight is clear: 1551.
How much I could learn: 5034.
How much I should like to begin: 4505.
How much she must have loved her home: 3535.
How negligent they appear in this north light, our light: 4292.
How nervous I feel: 3319.
How nice being paupers at Christmas: 4714.
How nice to be able: 1493.
"How noble, wise, and great!" Less man than god: 2558.
How often, as pure virtue stood: 639.
How optimistic can we get?: 5562.
How our conceptions crack, construction fall: 113.
How poor, how paltry seems the goal: 3716.

How profoundly analytic: 4577.
How radiant each mother looks: 3696.
How rarely the causes warrant: 6275.
How rewarding to know Mr. Smith: 3965.
How shall my true love know: 6838.
How shocking her suit!: 1905.
How shall we come to him?: 442.
How should men quite sane: 2785.
How snug these scanty swimsuits get: 444.
How so lovely walks the wind: 2675.
How still the hawk: 2676.
How straight it flew, how long it flew: 5484.
How strange, the time required to see: 6766.
How the backhanders geese of you: 5182.
How the huge grief that like a hovering cloud: 2884.
How their bleak profiles grin and move: 5463.
How to describe, describe: 2098.
How to dispose of a residual hand: 6640.
How to lay down her death: 83.
How vainly open eyes amaze: 4274.
How very exquisite a quill: 3095.
How vulnerable a child can be: 1429.
How walks my love?: 2685.
How we did pay for her ballet: 3917.
How wide a shadow one small cloud will lay upon the land!: 1088.
However legendary: 1478.
Huckster's loin?: 2330.
Huddleston, a man in Africa: 5109.
Huge, from this ruinous Platonic cave: 6880.
The huge frostbank of the North: 4230.
Humbly, my feet bare, let me glide: 6174.
The hummingbird that darts and hovers: 6857.
Hummingbirds come back: 6572.
Hunched in the dark like small green gnomes: 5959.
Hungering on the gray plain of its birth: 3436.
A hunter went killing sparrows one cold day: 6436.
Hunting the springtime heath, Tammy gored by Death: 3718.
A hurricane swept in upon: 4560.
Husband stand at door of flat: 2680.
A husband works in subtle ways: 2704.
Husbands have their troubles: 4530.
Husbands wash the glasses: 2937.
Hush, little breezes, you and whispering light: 4583.
Hushaby: 3589.
Husband waves of muttering: 7128.
Hustle this moment to yourself and hold it close: 3043.
I always hope I'll read a trick: 4158.
I always know when summer's here: 927.
I am a critic: 2509.
I am a lady: 5697.
I am a lover, a pauper, and a poet: 354.

I am a Negro, an American Negro: 4828.
I am a scientist: 6635.
I am a votary: 5429.
I am afraid of high mountains: 3947.
I am an American: 3012.
I am an enthusiast myself for: 648.
I am coming into the winter season...:
1403.
I am fish: 1983.
I am fond of the late poet Sir John
Suckling: 755.
I am gentler now, who once: 2076.
I am here with my beautiful bountiful
downy womanful child: 355.
I am homesick for all different places:
3111.
I am my grave: 6846.
I am my master's eyes but not his feet:
5503.
I am Newby: 3103.
I am not yet forsaken: 216.
I am old as the hills: 6048.
I am Pattiradjawane: 6078.
I am queen: 5088.
I am silent and meek and reluctant to
speak--: 454.
I am sitting dreamy: 2148.
I am still hurt, Plin: 3323.
I am stone rolled: 4775.
I am the earthbound: 1625.
I am the green I walk; this weedy:
2419.
I am the harp: 2323.
I am the trained donkey, the one that
amazes: 3235.
I am the very model of an up-to-date:
2713.
I am the wind!: 6723.
I am tired of making these statements
about you, God: 3025.
I am young and hold no fear of laughter:
2497.
I am your double man, though first you
will: 1380.
I and the other intruders: 4323.
I approached Moses and said to him:
3915.
I beckoned North: 2695.
I being woman, this much must confess:
2717.
I believa: 344.
I believe in advertising almighty:
176.
I bequeath myself to the dirt to grow
from the grass I love: 5832.
I bought a petticoat today--uncreasable,
unsquashable: 7271.
I brought my daughter the kind of doll:
3055.
I built a windyard for the wind: 7175.
I burn and recognize imminence, the
ascending shadow: 2719.
I call on reason but to no avail: 1926.
I call up words that he may write them
down: 1441.
I called him to come in: 1768.
I came before the watercolorists: 3926.
I came through sun: 2776.
I came to this place one November day:
353.

I came to your home. I had thought I
would beg of you: 5015.
I can discern at last who grew: 6668.
I can see from your letter: 757.
I can wait a night's song until: 2113.
I cannot celebrate: 3404.
I cannot endure the sad history of my
race: 1411.
I cannot forget now at Canton we were
drinking tea together: 4768.
I cannot make my dog sit up: 4774.
I cannot recall precisely what was on
my mind: 1881.
I can't help noting that I pay: 67.
I can't imagine why the crow: 7187.
I can't quite summon up the nerve:
1956.
I can't take it with me, I know: 5628.
I carry my mood in my pocket (with
coppers and silver to anchor it):
3878.
I chop down trees with a lawn mower:
2722.
I come from the north, but where am
I going?: 2207.
I conjugated every football month:
2101.
I could not fall asleep last night:
5759.
I could wish that I had sooner waked
in hell: 5966.
I dance before my boy--long spindle
bones: 5308.
I did not hear the nameless angels:
3402.
I do not ask for moon in hand for
you: 5160.
I do not care for Rousseau: 5209.
I do not know how he can: 995.
I do not know how many leaves I see:
2668.
I do not know. I do not care: 2378.
I do not know the place where he is
lying: 5232.
I do not know what secret must: 5973.
I do not like the shape: 4151.
I do not like the sound of "additive.":
3927.
I do not need a silver plane: 2306.
I do not need to look up: 4149.
I do not see myself: 2724.
I don't want a fine architectural plan:
3622.
I do not want your love, my dear:
2986.
I don't know whether you know what's
new in juvenile literature or not:
1896.
I don't mean to carp, but I'd certainly
like: 5461.
I don't mind an evening that dissects:
1221.
I don't raise charming annuals, my
voice, or cocker spaniels: 1541.
I don't remember: 6980.
I doubt if I could love a land: 4177.
I doubt if the wind in your boots:
6052.
I dreamed I saw Lord Daniels: 2726.

I dreamed that in a city dark as
  Paris: 2727.
I dreamt the Negro, beautiful as night:
  2728.
I drink skim milk, my toast is dry:
  1898.
I drown in the drumming ploughland, I
  drag up: 2501.
I enjoy: 1910.
I explain ontology, mathematics,
  theophily: 256.
I fancied hoofbeats woke me: 1615.
I fear that I am laziest: 5954.
I fear the headless man: 3564.
I fear the man of undistinguished
  mien: 4992.
I feed the gas, I turn the wheel: 7149.
I feel myself to be a man disgraced:
  553.
I feel so gay I could ride on a feather:
  6952.
I feel when I've coped with the very
  young: 446.
I fell in love with you one summer
  night: 5855.
I felt I had met the Lord: 2729.
I fill my lungs and touch my toes:
  5544.
I find it a sinecure to compile: 6686.
I find it hard to realize: 2900.
I find it sad to think the human race
  is: 3633.
I follow from my window down: 2211.
I found a man's body on the beach: 30.
I found on a brittle card my name, my
  trade: 476.
I found this jawbone at the sea's
  edge: 5205.
I from hill country: 5892.
I gathered wild strawberries: 2731.
I get to thinking, now and then: 3856.
I give you this Bible and more to take:
  2963.
I go by touching where I have to go:
  2857.
I go there more when school is out:
  6141.
I got a fifty-yard-line seat: 3579.
I greeted the new day happily: 3792.
I grow more mellow, mellow he must
  be: 3720.
I grow old under an intensity: 3825.
I guess it is farewell to a grammati-
  cal compunction: 4266.
I had a dream and heard animals: 5250.
I had a dream once of dancing with a
  tiger: 1566.
I had a pleasant feeling: 4130.
I had a revelation once: 3497.
I had always a contempt for poets:
  269.
I had two visions. In an orange dawn:
  2707.
I hae kent magic, ferlies: 3646.
"I hate the cacti," my companion said:
  824.
I have a fondness for contrary things:
  1211.
I have a hill: 1055.

I have a little budget: 2454.
I have a little conscience: 6477.
I have a little ego that: 3993.
I have bathed, and loved one woman,
  often: 4446.
I have been through this: 6996.
I have for company myself alone: 7249.
I have forgotten you at last: 1315.
I have fought that battle in heraldic
  panels: 515.
I have four seasons in my blood: 6727.
I have gazed long at this dear book:
  4422.
I have gazed upon my shadow: 1895.
I have grown intimate with death:
  3007.
I have learned, after wandering: 3980.
I have lived in that room bigger than
  the world: 3597.
I have lost the print but in this
  negative: 4053.
I have loved loving you: 5814.
I have no field, no orchard row:
  1230.
I have, perhaps, loved overmuch: 20.
I have seen the youngest minds on my
  block spotted with measles halluci-
  nated: 7338.
I have singled out a tree: 2734.
I have strayed into the littoral zone
  with its faint light: 3474.
I hear a child inside: 6579.
I hear America singing, the varied
  carols I hear: 2735.
I hear far off a sound: 739.
I hear the busy aproned day: 72.
I hear the clerks close for the night:
  3109.
I hear the drum, the bugle song:
  2596.
I hear the golden lion rage: 1159.
I heard music in my veins that time:
  1174.
I heard the old woman who lived: 5741.
I heard the weeping of the born in
  the lap of its mother: 3486.
I had thought you distant, perfect:
  5275.
I have a friend named Mr. Sherman who
  is far from dodderin': 5600.
I have been a longtime in a strange
  country: 89.
I have believed in effort: 5012.
I have no business trespassing: 271.
I have no enemies today: 5052.
I have sat with the Indians: 5173.
I have seen a spider on a caught wasp:
  5157.
I have so much of this moon: 4157.
I hear, the old man said: 5204.
I heard a dying man: 1600.
I heard a woman soft with fat: 1876.
I heard the Diesel truck's throaty
  cry: 1647.
I heard your little song: 2665.
I hold the splendid illness of the
  strong: 5501.
I hope I never live to see the day:
  5559.
I hope that I shall never see: 7239.

I imagine them always in summer: 108.
I imagine this midnight moment's forest: 6404.
I is a singular sex: 4779.
I keep alive in Calcutta only because: 6178.
I keep a pad beside the telephone: 6279.
I keep my eye upon the ball: 3703.
I kept going home: 5348.
I killed a wounded gull at Tahoo once: 7060.
I kissed you...: 3519.
I knew a man with a terrible obsession: 4024.
I knew a good librarian: 4766.
I know a girl who sticks out her tongue: 2738.
I know a large dune rate whose first name is Joe: 1939.
I know a man whose lawn is fair: 4507.
I know a place all fennel-green and fine: 2422.
I know I brought those books all back: 3352.
I know people who enjoy going to the zoo: 4423.
I know some desert plants: 7182.
I know that plucky persons: 4351.
I know the night no longer, the terrible anonymity of death: 2739.
I know the time has come to make: 1867.
I know what every woman needs: 6964.
I know who's scratching at the door: 1807.
I lay in an agony of imagination as the wind: 4389.
I lay with my heart under me: 1038.
I left my shoes last winter in a Spain: 6304.
I let the smoke out of the windows: 1161.
I lie on my back, I lie flat on my bed: 6358.
I like old things--old tables, chairs, and stands: 4707.
I like the big screen: 3876.
I like the stubborn temper: 319.
I like this town whose streets are flung: 5333.
I like to climb: 4604.
I like to see my son when he: 3995.
I listen to the silly pop of spume: 5541.
I live as ungraciously as I'm able: 5155.
I lived one year in a small log house: 5694.
I look one way from the porch as far: 3161.
I lose myself in wonder at the cock: 5347.
I love my books--they are the quiet friends: 3362.
I love old books with covers worn and scarred: 4371.
I love the fragile beauty of your ways: 6500.

I love the laughing girls who love: 3601.
I love the roly-poly pig: 4812.
I love to see old ladies prink: 2916.
I love you. Let my testament: 6306.
I loved when I was young the outlandish 2875.
I magnify thee, Lord, to see thy light: 7315.
I make no argument, meadows are: 3711.
I may have helped but do not call me wise: 5860.
I met a half-blind Negro: 3827.
I met a monster in the wood: 3857.
I met a traveler upon an ancient road: 4516.
I met the yawning of my appetite: 4175.
I met you at our wedding, shook your hand: 1677.
I milked the cows, made butter and cheese: 2374.
I must and will forget you: 7355.
I must go down to the stacks again: 6023.
I must say I'm surprised: 1157.
I mustn't forget I'm supposed to say: 2744.
I never get mad: I get hostile: 3215.
I never go by the meadow in flag and feather: 3707.
I never knew a night so black: 2745.
I never played the Moor: 6782.
I never saw a purple cat: 5009.
I no longer have to declare myself: 3939.
I notice when the Great Producer writes: 6024.
I offer myself to everyone as his reward: 2288.
I often am inclined to think: 3427.
I often chose a mental door: 1548.
I often say to an elderly man: 4385.
I often seek, but seldom find: 5091.
I once had the honor of meeting a philosopher called McIndoe: 1426.
I once met a peddler: 4735.
I only hope you recognize: 4637.
I ought to put your cash away: 3484.
I owe you life. Would I had owed you too: 1352.
I peeked at the sea: 600.
I planned to have a border of lavender: 3271.
I plant bulbs and shrubs and trees: 4702.
I play your furies back to me at night: 2574.
I plowed all morning to the caws of crows: 6805.
I praise that ancestor of mine: 911.
I prayed and then: 1164.
I prayed the little words like children's games: 2825.
I purse my lips to whistle a tune: 7100.
I put my arms around the lilac bush: 3389.
I raise the cup on this occasion: 6608.

I read the books from A to Z--: 5093.
I recognize myself, but not by sight: 5165.
I recollect, in days gone by: 4234.
I remember how she left me standing: 4716.
I remember the lean, grape colored violets: 4883.
I remember them, man and wife, in their little car: 1259.
I remember they used to stand: 6923.
I remember violence in the old country: 6875.
I rest in His love, as a ship in a storm: 2747.
I met a lady beautiful as: 56.
I realize that today nothing is more vestigial: 6051.
I recall a movie starring Fenimore Cooper: 2112.
I said to my old teacher: 5248.
I sat down at last on a fallen log-- that bad: 4737.
I sat here as a boy: 123.
I sat upon the floor with bearded men: 4525.
I saw a gust of birds rise in a hurry of gale· 3868.
I saw a man bend to a flowing stream: 7092.
I saw a physicist the other night: 383.
I saw a white bird once: 2748.
I saw in your eyes when you lay dying: 3753.
I saw it green a year ago: 793.
I saw it light the cactus sky: 452.
I saw only the edge: 2310.
I saw out of the corner of my sight: 2008.
I saw red acres dumb beneath a stream: 6919.
I saw the boy when he was how old?: 4376.
I saw the face of my love naked: 744.
I saw the invisible: 2749.
I saw the rose and the rod: 5351.
I saw the waves dash wildly to the beach: 6463.
I saw the years: 1664.
I saw them dancing: 2259.
I saw three withered women limp across: 5017.
I saw us today in Harvard Square: 2751.
I saw you look at her, this good: 6511.
I saw you stand lonely as on a hill: 2752.
I saw you there, holding the sheaf of days: 6567.
I saw young men go marching: 3745.
I saw your shoulder swell and pitch: 1743.
I say, and may be thought absurd: 3457.
I scarcely see but feel you now at first: 2753.
I scorch sweet flowers with fiery showers: 1087.
I scrape char off a board with a dull knife: 5651.
I see a field through memory's tinted pane: 2068.

I see again your chores grow intricate: 555.
I see morning,level and shining there: 5241.
I see refracted through a prism: 2594.
I see the beasts of flooded land: 2013.
I see the lady Winter on her sleigh! 3064.
I see the ships, the plotted crash: 2046.
I see you displaced, condensed, within my dream: 1567.
I see you unable to bear: 2044.
I sell costumes, Mr. Lincoln: 1829.
I serve a Mistress, name of Art: 136.
I set my heart out in the noontime sun: 3485.
I settled in the suburbs: 5845.
I shall avoid the haunts of men: 5558.
I shall come to you, my love: 2754.
I shall discover you in those I love, like a long flash of sheet: 246.
I shall go bearded with a Latin name: 5585.
I shall go in and out now: 2204.
I shall go softly along this Sunday: 7168.
I shall never live enough: 6193.
I shall rebuild my world today: 5564.
I shall take my child where tall books grow: 7087.
I should have been delighted these to hear: 1107.
I should have been prepared that solemn morning: 3665.
 I should have gotten here at eight: 4456.
I should like to describe America to you: 3735.
I shrink from seeing people off: 2732.
I shudder at the icy blear of...: 6856.
I shut my eyes and turned round thrice: 4040.
I sidelong in this obscene world going: 2181.
I sing one for the Giantess: 1738.
I sing the Man, that grant of Science: 2559.
I sing the song of the sleeping wife: 5634.
I sit alone in a way station: 4682.
I sit and cast a tilted glance: 6800.
I sit and stare: I do not move: 2721.
I sit on the back platform of the train: 6641.
I sit on the porch, for the night is warm: 3411.
I sold my bed, I hastened west: 622.
I sometimes think I shall study to be a lama: 2755.
I speak now, dear,of dinner, plays, excursions: 4343.
I speak of that great house: 601.
I spent summer: 6158.
I splashed into a marsh: 1435.
I spy you, lone gray strand up there: 7360.
I stammer when I attempt to speak: 485.

I stamp a page of suns with the darkest: 3309.

I stand and watch them, feeling awkward and glad: 4494.

I stand high on autumn's tranquil hill: 2705.

I stand on the bridge: 4496.

I stand upon a dike at night: 2758.

I stand within this field as in a cup: 6313.

I stared at art's silk violet: 2011.

I stayed up half the night to hear that hour: 4121.

I step in the savage orders of the noon: 3189.

I still remember her standing there: 1277.

I stood above the sown and generous sea: 3890.

I stroke the backs of bare November hills: 2586.

I was a very young thing and puzzled as could be: 2808.

I take the sandy path that goes: 2503.

I take thee now to be no other: 31.

I take this twilight moment into my being: 6716.

I talked with a goat: 2321.

I tell you stop, be human, feel the cheek: 5821.

I thank my God that I am not: 4780.

I thank You, Lord, that You have not withdrawn: 566.

I think I'll study reading now: 2622.

I think of all the toughs through history: 3405.

I think of Jacob, tired, alone: 109.

I think of that poor girl in the tale: 6882.

I think of that summer place where the catalpa flowers: 6143.

I think of the young, of their dis- belief in dying: 3795.

I think of you, Joyce, and of Yeats and others who are dead: 2899.

I think on door knobs, brass and...: 1546.

I think that God tossed into spring: 1977.

I think that I shall never be: 2779.

I think that I shall never c: 6447.

I think that I shall never see: 6659.

I think that I shall never see: 5916.

I think that I shall never see: 699.

I think that I shall never see: 335.

I think the bells peal only snow to- night: 5053.

I think the birds of the city: 1052.

I think there is nothing quite so sure: 1549.

I think with my ears, the poet said, which I have firmly fused: 5652.

I thought good to write unto you my knowledge: 3867.

I thought I had heard winter in the wood: 2943.

I thought I saw him on the street: 2723.

I thought I would not write again: 3330.

I thought of a house where the stones seemed suddenly changed: 3481.

I thought the leaf an ear: 7273.

I thought there was no second Fall: 3384.

I tire of glitter and smart: 4366.

I too invoked the moon: 3885.

I took my cousin to Prettyboy Dan: 4892.

I took my light love naked in the bed: 4817.

I took the longer path to meet the colt: 6260.

I touch and recollect: 6488.

I trace my line through famous men: 456.

I transformed motion into sound: 3948.

I travel through thin jails of rain: 4709.

I turn a page and come to meet his eyes: 1318.

I turned: 3730.

I understand myself: 5516.

I used to like a quiet room: 5187.

I used to own a fatted goose: 6807.

I used to think of you and sigh: 5507.

I used to think that obstacles to love: 1596.

I wait, with those that rest: 298.

I waken in the wilderness of night: 161.

I waken to a calling: 4865.

I walk fast while the rain is falling: 779.

I walk, for walking is not for steps alone: 6386.

I walked in darkness through a twisted maze: 3237.

I walked with my love in the moonlight: 5552.

I wandered lonely as a fareless cabby: 6626.

I wander lonely in the crowds: 2765.

I wandered in a little wood, and there...: 6843.

I wandered lonely as a cloud: 2580.

I want my grave to be in a wild place: 2307.

I want to tell some Toda Tribesmen: 6601.

I want to write a sonnet stonier: 3018.

I was a mere boy in a stone-cutter's shop: 8.

I was a thousand people: 2948.

I was about to: 130.

I was afraid of the bats that swung at twilight: 823.

I was born in a land of fields: 1868.

I was born in 1895, the onliest: 6587.

I was born in the algebra night: 6240.

I was born they say on a yellow Galilee hill: 3371.

I was called at dusk: 5622.

I was mortal, like the mortal year: 6901.

I was only sixteen: 3691.

I was orbiting in space: 5902.

I was sitting in what that afternoon I thought to be: 1183.

I was sitting on a stump: 5387.
I was standan at the bar...: 3977.
I was stung by a man-of-war: 3302.
I was tempted to the grove by its
   odor: 4574.
I was the first to see the gogglehead:
   2331.
I was the swan singing upon his last
   day: 5764.
I was very tired when we arrived in
   Algeciras: 5306.
I watch each morning as the girls
   stroll past: 3821.
I watch him stumble into the place:
   4372.
I watch the sun rise seven times: 4492.
I watched rude farmers toiling east
   of Keene: 4077.
I wear my bones: 3917.
I wear them: 2312.
I went forth into the sunshine: 5054.
I went out at daybreak and stood on
   Primrose Hill: 617.
I went looking in the western foot-
   hills: 4443.
I went to school when I was little:
   6490.
I went to see the important executive:
   5182.
I will dig a well in this dry and
   bitter land: 7016.
I will feed you love: 6505.
I will find an island: 3026.
I will not look within: 4038.
I will reach into the grab-bag of
   unconscious things: 5018.
I will write a verse today: 6581.
I wince as the siren screeches, screams,
   cries: 2111.
I wish I were a child again!: 6405.
I wish I were a crocodile: 1286.
I wish it were springtime now: 2768.
I wish my problems of today: 4150.
I wish that I could understand: 2667.
I wish that someone would explain:
   1303.
I wish the world abundant cheer: 7312.
I woke but unawake, with the slow
   waking: 5494.
I wonder if, by chance: 4860.
I wonder if the student, Shakespeare,
   knew: 3131.
I wonder too in the dark: 4110.
I wonder what it looks like. Ear-
   locked men with caftans: 6871.
I wonder whether: 3920.
I wonder in the nineties just what a
   woman did: 460.
I wonder now: do any crooks: 2780.
I wondered that you treasure flowers:
   632.
"I won't! I won't!"I keep saying:
   2769.
I would call the attention of those:
   6786.
I would find it more inspiring: 5073.
I would I had a flower boy: 4829.
I would make this all as single as
   a song: 6536.
I would not gainsay if I could: 4721.

I write as one who wants to be any
   friend: 5865.
Ice-cream cones take a watchful eye:
   2774.
The icy walks which once, I used to
   slide on: 3366.
I'd find this ball game less narcotic:
   3722.
I'd gladly shovel off the walk: 3276.
The ice   that grips the silent
   stream: 512.
I'd like to be a firefly and: 2781.

I'd like to hear the bees again: 2384.
I'd like to say I found this book
   through diligent research: 4205.
I'd rather be a could be: 2782.
I'd rather carry loads of olive wood:
   4405.
I'd surely like to know: 7074.
If a child be wise: 973.
If a tree falls: 5532.
If a wife wants to have: 3154.
If any little smug remark: 6408.
If anybody is listening: 6080.
If, as they tell us, two can live:
   7027.
If Christ should come today, we would:
   5913.
If dreams were not the truth: 1576.
If each selecting holds its own blue
   choice: 4668.
If ever the door close and no wedding:
   4495.
If ever the jumbled: 6622.
If every one moved up a bit: 6116.
If from some ultimate observation
   post: 5152.
If he could see: 4419.
If he should lift his hand: 5612.
If he walks in ebb tides: 6776.
If I could be a fairy: 1836.
If I could breathe: 2790.
If I could go to Alamut: 291.
If I could hold a moment: 3715.
If I could wish upon my wedding ring:
   7232.
If I forget thee not, New York: 1316.
If I have loved you it is because:
   3565.
If I have said it once...: 6353.
If I served octopus on toast: 2720.
If I should hate that bravery of
   gaining love: 735.
If I should live to ninety-three:
   4800.
If I were only as small as a bird:
   205.
If I'd as many children: 4251.
If, in the delusion of contentment, I
   forget thee: 2912.
If it's all the same to you: 4979.
If joy could make me tremble: 4317.
If man would fly then he must wing
   his heart: 7179.
If Maxmillian and Carlotta were
   living: 3788.
If mind is pulp, heart is a waterfall:
   208.
If morning came but once: 6389.

If now but to die could be feathered and small: 1401.

If Parson Weems could never tell a lie: 950.

If pupils did their school work: 1065.

If reason would take that job: 1311.

If right is right and wrong is wrong: 4734.

If stone were stone and dead were dead: 248.

If the adage gets you down: 4816.

If the average Negro only: 3186.

If the bright bird were by me would I grieve: 2792.

If the day that April came: 2853.

If the ghost of Francisco Vasquez de Coronado: 5097.

If the stork: 6064.

If the world shrank doves to a single grain: 1636.

If there is anything of which America has a superfluity: 5302.

If there's no sun, I still can have the man: 4788.

If they show me a stone and I say stone they will say stone: 2793.

If things I give to you are small: 6494.

If this garden is a place for lovers: 4215.

If thou be rich: 5430.

If time is rushing by: 60.

If via streamlined stratoship: 1627.

If we happen to choke up on history, none too soon: 5533.

If we put the desk where the bureau is: 4553.

If we would have a brave new world: 3854.

If what heals can bless: 1129.

If you are my friend: 1942.

If you came in the half-light in the dusk: 2798.

If you can raise your head when all about you: 440.

If you dare not reality, O do not come: 6496.

If you insist, I'll make it clear: 4630.

If you save all you earn, you're a miser: 3872.

If you see it in an ad: 4442.

If you take all the gadgets: 6486.

If you take the moon in your hands: 3883.

If you take the moon in your hands: 2251.

If you telephone, she will be dead: 1679.

If you tell the librarian that the book you want: 3830.

If you want to pay me a compliment: 3164.

If you waver: 62.

If you're anxious for to shine in the pseudoegghead line: 1244.

Ignorant of the names of flowers or of birds: 5825.

Ignorant two, we glide: 4473.

Ignore the watchful sun awhile: 877.

Ignoring Rome and the Great: 6349.

I'll miss you at that quiet time: 2117.

I'll not be servant: 1414.

An ill wind is stalking: 6287.

I'm a gal who looks askance: 196.

I'm a poor book, broken down library book: 3448.

I'm all for calling: 5105.

I'm always early, I'm never late: 3628.

I'm dreaming of a car so long, so low: 3403.

I'm going to drive up: 4275.

I'm going to re-draw myself: 6939.

I'm grateful for having the truth at last: 1553.

I'm growing fonder of my staff: 2812.

I'm herdsman of a flock: 2545.

I'm home! I'm home! 2814.

I'm liberal: 6868.

I'm mad about injections: 4949.

I'm not a man that's overfond of changes: 6041.

I'm not contented with a constant round: 1691.

I'm not sure what he spoke on: 86.

I'm not so adept at schooling it: 1189.

I'm not the type to tear my hair: 6796.

I'm practically dead from lack of sleep: 5569.

I'm quick to admire: 4944.

I'm really sorry to seem abrupt: 1927.

I'm shopping for a "different" hat: 5777.

I'm sitting in the living room: 5852.

I'm sorry I ever said it: 5218.

I'm sorry, Mme Calderon: 2942.

I'm sure the Europe never had: 5551.

I'm the master of this house: 7340.

I'm thirty, no beauty and without wealth or power: 630.

I'm wary of the hostesses: 260.

I'm well aware that we are not the first: 5861.

The image of this child would be that willow: 7156.

Imagine it, a Sophocles complete: 1938.

Imagine now a deep green pool: 2093.

Imagine that the fast life of a bird: 732.

Imagining at Wellfleet: 4161.

Immense the stars are, and immense the sky: 6034.

The importance of being Adams: 34.

Impregnably enveloped in civility: 4941.

In a basement just off Saint-Michel: 4544.

In a dark meadow fenced: 2160.

In a darkened room: 327.

In a detachment cool as the giant of light: 4470.

In a dream I spoke: 2827.

In a Dutch town, a red bricked town: 2829.

In a hybernating rose sex: 7245.

In a lacquer-red pony cart, three young girls: 2304.
In a medium-priced restaurant where I go to die: 6225.
In a parlor containing a table: 2836.
In a Roman tram, where the famous Roman mob: 6360.
In a ruined Irish castle, searching for towers of vision: 6627.
In his grandmother's garden was a cake with seven candles: 5548.
In a state death: 4738.
In a teenage hangout in Maryland: 5605.
In a theater, blue-wired: 3698.
In after time, when all this dream: 2840.
In afternoon as if morning: 276.
In all the cities of this year: 3173.
In and out: 1849.
In another land (or hour) how fierce and cunning: 2698.
In Antwerp where as everywhere they blink: 4101.
In April last the Ford Foundation: 2228.
In April when raining is sunlight: 2400.
In Aragon, my mother's land: 3679.
In Athens once he had designed: 2459.
In autumn it is the stone's pull: 3230.
In August's heat I wished to be: 2810.
In autumn the great wild beast which is America: 6315.
In burnt autumn, through a trance of leaves: 2845.
In business my ideal is to get up: 3962.
In case you ask us: 5590.
In clean kept quiet a hidden voice cries out: 3293.
In clumps like grass: 437.
In daylight, even: 1249.
In doctors' waiting rooms I find: 6421.
In Drnis in Croatia, we sat on: 5704.
In dry fields Daniel walks: 2856.
In Egypt on the lion headed couch: 5917.
In favorite wedding season a demure spring bride: 1045.
In fields where lambs and lions sleep: 406.
In Florida and not Jerusalem: 2094.
In foreign ports it never fails: 2966.
In Freiburg, in Freiburg: 3932.
In gentle little village long ago: 2122.
In gray April: 3260.
In her need she brought September close: 1098.
In her now bouffant slip: 5657.
In her presence is a music: 4943.
In her splendor islanded: 2862.
In high couture the web designed over meaning: 4894.
In his face the trace of Europe: 1825.
In his firm hands he shakes the sieve of night: 1480.
In human need: 3312.

In India, the people form among the trees: 2863.
In Italy the dead have all the passion: 175.
In Kansas what is more swift to proclaim: 7101.
In Kerouac did Ginsberg sing: 583.
In late autumn the hound: 4397.
In leaf and landscape now the light: 435.
In library or distilling tower: 642.
In line of what my folks say in Montgomery: 768.
In little things, in projects planned: 1387.
In Lydia the king's unpraised: 3390.
In mercy, spare him conversation: 3900.
In Mexico St. Francis found a child: 5407.
In mid-swath stands the...: 6148.
In my breast the wound opens again: 5706.
In my childhood when I first: 5545.
In my sixties I will buy a hat: 6892.
In need of time, I thought that I: 4093.
In negligent stone the old man superintends: 314.
In nineteen-thirty-four I spent July: 4136.
In no language coming will I frighten: 2819.
In Norway is a sombre lake: 6729.
In our own image, heroes: 2456.
In our town the Lion's Club remembers: 2882.
In Paris they remember Paris was there before Christ: 3755.
Inside the pomegranite is the blue sky: 4989.
In pungent scenes: 2864.
In schools, five days for "Negro History Week.": 2488.
In sixteen hundred twenty-one: 3551.
In so much blue there is a loss of blue: 5477.
In spring the plants and animals have a dance: 1334.
In suburban gardens: 6113.
In such weather, all kind and calm, smooth as the skin of silent dreams: 3107.
In summer, beach and billows beckon: 3418.
In summer wind the elm leaves sing: 6872.
In summertime I have our tree: 1847.
In sun I sing to make the meaning clear: 967.
In testimony whereof hereunto: 4305.
In that calm provincial air: 181.
In that eternal, all things: 2709.
In that first troubling of the heart: 5096.
In that sweet, mild western air: 3766.
In that weird continent to which we go: 2893.

In the beginning: 4341.
In the beginning was the Word: 2922.
In the bleak light after the March blizzard: 792.
In the bright May, how can the startled heart: 2635.
In the canoe wilderness branches wait for winter: 5231.
In the car coming home, alone in the night: 369.
In the cold country of my youth: 2217.
In the collie-colored fields of autumn: 5755.
In the courts of evil: 5400.
In the crept hours on our street: 3950.
In the dark at first, we see things in their sleep: 2297.
In the dark of the wood. No leaf stirred: 1345.
In the days when purple was new: 2897.
In the desperate hours of fear and fumbling: 2898.
In the dim park, the gray ethereal glades: 2641.
In the distance the children are playing games: 402.
In the dolesome dark, the acid cold: 6092.
In the dour ages: 3307.
In the drapery of shadow I forgive: 2909.
In the dusk with the given phonograph: 962.
In the early morning: 3049.
In the end, though: 5653.
In the far off Himalayas: 3420.
In the forest of the Alphabet the child: 5386.
In the golden trance of air: 2693.
In the good suburb, in the bursting season: 5198.
In the gray corner, under the line: 6425.
In the green humidity of the unripe orchard: 3951.
In the hot sun and dazzle of grass: 1376.
In the house which was full of dim, in the dusty courtyard: 3241.
In the Hydrogen Age: 2905.
In the kitchen's light were our friends, with their faulty faces: 4806.
In the lake country near Mt. Fuji the Shiraito: 3941.
In the lamp that is beauty, on the farm: 2505.
In the land of turkeys in turkey weather: 1335.
In the late lafternoon, slow flouncing: 724.
In the life of this dandies of short-stops: 1479.
In the light of the sun: 7324.
In the light toxic dawns of September with the white stars in the army depots: 890.
In the manner of water winding over stone: 4748.
In the merciless daylight: 4539.

In the middle of a Southern night: 467.
In the middle of the night at least twenty deer: 1856.
In the mirror: 3681.
In the mirror the reverse image of the girl's: 4855.
In the morning I walk with gladness: 2913.
In the morning when I see her naked like cyclamen or cycles of song: 5769.
In the mountains: 2453.
In the old, arrogant way: 462.
In the pond in the park: 6975.
In the presence of roses she pauses: 651.
In the quietness: 1638.
In the reverent wind, in the religious sun: 2023.
In the riven channel torqued in its bends: 1470.
In the room of the long curtains every fold: 2218.
In the ruins of a cathedral: 7010.
In the Sarazu River Park in Karaskiki: 6771.
In the scorched summer I delight to dream: 4180.
In the silence that prolongs the span: 643.
In the slow world of dream: 3754.
In the small territory and time: 5421.
In the smart room where Lennie lies: 5692.
In the soft Finnish summer they become: 4300.
In the spring, by the big shuck-pile: 795.
In the summer solstice the women of the city: 2691.
In the sunny years of nearing darkness: 885.
In the unharnessed dark the plowman stands: 3956.
In the unsparing South: 2018.
In the wake of winter's: 2132.
In the white room is the white bed: 1669.
In the zero of the night, in the tipping hour: 275.
In wind and rain: 3799.
In the world, or behind the world: 2237.
In the year of the longest Cadillac: 6962.
In the years when I was younger: 4465.
In their silver vase her blue flowers snare and touch the sun: 1137.
In this book I see your face and in your face: 2214.
In this bright green morning: 6860.
In this country of warm weather: 3327.
In this covert where the lane's begun: 5069.
In this deeply, divinely appointed last day of our doom: 1368.
In this gay leaf: 2258.
In this green field where streams run, seven geese: 4700.
In this indifference: 614.

In this museum, locked in cases: 4569.
In this room, now--Be pleased to look--:
    6894.
In this week Saturday Review: 6026.
In those new heavens of galactic flame:
    4078.
In time it came round: 4342.
In Tombstone, Arizona, in the spring:
    1197.
In Upper Room at solemn hour: 4758.
In vain in days of chaos: 6307.
In warm rusty ships they are sent to
    places: 2167.
In waves Time ebbs away: 3934.
In which same night, this side, Horatius,
    I can see: 2414.
In winter at thunder's first echo:
    822.
In winter when I walk my two-year old:
    7219.
In winter's silk cocoon, that's where
    I've been: 1056.
In wintertime, when children go: 1108.
In Wissahickon woods one winter day:
    1932.
In woods where many rivers run: 5342.
In words?: 2670.
In wrinkled khaki pants and faded
    shirt: 5252.
In your silence, there sank like into
    deep sea: 1474.
In your prosperity I also own a penny:
    7353.
In Zululand the huts are round: 5626.
The inadequate pillow: 2972.
Incertitude my easy norm: 4388.
The incomplete music hurts the ear:
    7359.
Indeed I loved these hands and knew
    them well: 4650.
Indeed, there is a lot of fretting:
    2083.
Indian summer: 2945.
Indifference were a nobler thing:
    2305.
Inexperienced young cutthroats with
    small hands: 53.
Infallibly found out by rain: 2839.
The infant rat, all head and stumble:
    437.
The infants on the chancel stairs:
    4641.
Ink and pencil: 4858.
The inland lies, far island infinite:
    3225.
Inner eye perceives a sky: 2630.
Innocence is on the top of the world:
    5941.
An inoffensive bookplate's rare: 1786.
Inquire of the wind: 2959.
Insatiety: a variety of insecurity:
    5062.
Inside its coat of shaggy bark: 1964.
Inside my threaded ear: 1590.
Inside the porch screen and along the
    ledge: 4964.
Inside the shadow of death: 2970.
Insist, if you must, on having love:
    but seek: 6913.

Instant coffee with slightly sour cream:
    1061.
Instead of looking storeward: 1022.
Instill a dream, inspire your aides:
    5995.
Instructing pupils, I suppose: 310.
The instruments begin their sweet dis-
    course: 1170.
Intent on love, I gave: 6772.
Into a world where children shriek the
    suns: 4425.
Into an empty cube: 2235.
Into black marble we walk: 6555.
Into the annual Passover leaps: 4692.
Into the harbor now she comes: 5392.
Into this wooded place, where, since:
    5321.
Invariably dawn seeps in quiet eyes:
    6097.
Invariably do I shout: 1138.
Inventors of other worlds we wander:
    1187.
Invisible hands are now dispersing
    dew: 3378.
Invite the birth of dreams and lulla-
    bies: 5230.
Invitingly concave, bestudded, huge:
    5762.
Inward all rot and unattended pain:
    5591.
The iquitous girl often loses her
    balance: 5911.
Iron bedsteads captained his room:
    1853.
Irrelevance characterizes the behavior
    of our puppy: 3160.
Irresolute, I sit down on the bed:
    2674.
The Irresistible Intention: 3015.
Is a song of brown and red: 4225.
Is beauty unadorned adorned the most?:
    336.
Is it brushes you are selling?: 1940.
Is it enough?: 2813.
It is Mere Coincidence: 6362.
Is it three?: 1245.
Is it time now to go away?: 1393.
Is made up of reservoirs: 2482.
Is sharp, unshy: 3612.
Is the child frightened?: 7317.
Is the dark equation resolved: 21.
Is the latch fast?: 3252.
Is the spider a monster in miniature?:
Is there no modern Rameth, Bezer,
    Golan: 1046.
"Is this," she asked, " what the lower
    orders called...?": 4417.
Is time, perhaps, a gauge for earth...:
    2062.
The Island lies here waiting in the sun:
    6235.
Islands are islands though in the steady
    sea: 3029.
It comes not from your glass, but from
    your skin: 4033.
It comes to me how men in plainer years:
    2198.
It does for the time of man to walk here:
    5384.

It does not depend on music for its composition: 5849.
It does not make sense in terms of historical fact: 5422.
It does not suffice that you hew no image of me: 2189.
It doesn't look like her. It's much too new: 4945.
It falleth like a stick: 4006.
It floats on air thinned: 809.
It forms a cross, of sorts, against the sky···: 70.
It grows at the world's edge: 5472.
It happened at once and unthought of: 6061.
It has been regularly reported by every reporter: 4139.
It is a crude thing as it shapes up here: 4073.
It is a fascination we feel about ourselves: 5730.
It is a swimming drop of sun: 3881.
It is already six. From the steeple: 3704.
It is always luminous summer there: 3527.
It is an historical porch on which he sits: 1523.
It is because the sea is blue: 2408.
It is because you washed your hair that the sun: 978.
It is dark perhaps: 6714.
It is Eros, that rich artifact: 5307.
It is finished, ruat coelum, let us descend: 3127.
It is good that death lives: 2650.
It is hard going to the door: 1545.
It is hard to see what made them stay: 5299.
It is his way: 856.
It is lovely: 4267.
It is in low silence always that one errs: 425.
It is in the fear of the Lord: 6605.
It is my expectation that at the first voice of the turtle: 2800.
It is New Year's day: 582.
It is night that she is loved: her courage shines: 410.
It is noon. The church is open. I must go in: 6877.
It is not easy, poised in morning sun: 5089.
It is not its air but our own awe: 2775.
It is not necessary: 3038.
It is people at the edge who say: 5436.
It is quite definitely a place: 7251.
It is snowing. The huge world is perhaps dead: 2951.
It is sometime since I have been: 2585.
It is still raining and the yellow-green cotton fruit: 838.
It is Sunday in the laboratory: 6166.
It is swift and nimble: 509.
It is the eyes that grieve: 2348.

It is the fall of the frost in the dying season: 7225.
It is the girl I notice first of all: 3644.
It is the most enchanted spring: 1947.
It is the time when the brook behing the house fills the pool within: 1580.
It is the waiting keeps the flowers true: 4647.
It is time for plain speaking: 3039.
It is tiresome always to talk about weather: 5511.
It is true that even in the best-run state: 3973.
It is well, I think, that we began: 235.
It is what I never quite understood: 6305.
It isn't hopes: 833.
It isn't that I have to rise: 2517.
It isn't the year or the model and make: 2518.
It keeps out everything!: 6758.
It likes no wit to follow a shore crab's track: 59.
It matters not how firm the will: 4557.
It may be Stephen, breaking loaves, once said: 4272.
It never snows, but snow is on the mountain top: 5905.
It occurred to me there are no: 2388.
It seemed to give a taller sense of sky: 6883.
It seemed a fearful place to me: 7194.
It seems like only yesterday: 1992.
It seems that at keeping a secret: 6747.
It seems that the odour that the dark makes: 4591.
It seems too enormous just for a man to be: 2582.
It seems vainglorious and proud: 3465.
It shall be called your animal sorrow: 1496.
It sits in Seena's parlor like a great: 4373.
It still seems only yesterday: 4955.
It stops on a dime, but what with gas: 3989.
It takes a heap o' pluggin' t' make a classic sell: 3849.
It takes a lot of time to keep: 1031.
It took but little skill to make: 5092.
It used to be a fellow could: 3183.
It used to make us smile and coo: 5100.
It was a day like any other day: 6476.
It was a walking cane summer for the young: 4248.
It was an age of invention: 2038.
It was an angel he beckoned: 4342.
It was an autumn evening: 513.
It was an ill-appointed place: 4936.
It was as they said: 2185.
It was Chesterton who told of the Frenchman who hated the Eiffel Tower: 3721.

It was decided that the black market before the: 2219.

It was heaven-hot here, a heaven-held day: 6956.

It was in April: 6070.

It was in October, a favorite season: 1676.

It was just like any other evening: 6175.

It was many and many a year ago: 227.

It was no day to life a hand: 1989.

It was no moth: 4987.

It was no use their pleading with me: 3961.

It was not a man's way to plead: 3101.

It was not, after all, as she had feared: 1969.

It was not an afterthought: 7120.

It was only a bird-call at evening, un-identified: 4582.

It was Sunday: 5464.

It was the day for putting on the roof: 5340.

It wasn't really love: 4187.

It was so simple the way St. Michael: 2080.

It was such a night as this: 7008.

It was the field itself moving through itself: 1921.

It was the first time they had waited in: 2266.

It was the last of the parades: 3042.

It was the willow that bent in sorrow: 5809.

It was the year the IKENDICK: 470.

It was to have been: 6441.

It will be here: 3248.

It will not do Luigi: 3042.

The items at the Vendor's Stand: 3953.

It's a crowded attic, where I may find: 3750.

It's a daring thing for a girl to sign: 734.

It's a good enough life: 549.

It's a holiday morning: 368.

It's a man's world?: 7134.

It's as though: 7078.

It's hard to see this land and say: 2795.

It's lovely outdoors in the garden: 3005.

It's a struggle to live on my take-home cash: 4924.

It's been about three weeks: 138.

It's Christmas again!: 6012.

Its final stop beside the pines: 1492.

Its form speaks of gliding: 6092.

It's great to be kind and to heed each request: 6009.

It's Hallowe'en time: 6010.

It's hard, in this uncertain age: 6917.

It's hard to relax in my dirty old slacks: 2678.

Its hour has come: 7321.

Its metal boughs of leaves are bare: 6224.

It's my very painful duty: 6704.

It's no secret that the host: 1946.

It's not a landscape from too near: 6840.

It's not the gossip that's bad: 6491.

It's not the white Christmas so much I remember: 4201.

It's really no fun having nothing to do: 4929.

Its sign has weathered away: 4383.

It's something to be glad for: 2443.

It's spring! Again life focuses: 2952.

It's strange to have been so close to death: 1957.

It's the strangest chatter I ever heard: 6089.

It's tiger time in Central Park: 49.

It's time will heal and time will kill: 2402.

It's true and I yawned: 1831.

It's true that man invented cloth: 7177.

It's twenty-one twisted years since I left them: 3208.

It's very handy that a man can: 4007.

It's you who like to think: 6506.

I've a briddy bad code: 168.

I've always thought Polonius a dry: 3426.

I've done my chores: 5588.

I've gone a morning: 6733.

I've known that oak tree since its birth: 419.

I've learned this little lesson: 1488.

I've learned to babble pleasantly: 5699.

I've never known a night so cold before: 7160.

I've noted in a little book: 2430.

I've nothing good: 6419.

I've nothing good: 5255.

I've passed you several dozen times: 4479.

I've run through all the lullabies: 542.

I've seen a good school play at last: 6329.

I've sinned (peccavi!), coupling "star.": 1073.

I've this to say of him I wedded: 2516.

I've trouble getting cash together: 4749.

I've walked the streets, and this I state: 4952.

I've watered from the bottom. I've watered from the top: 71.

Ivory in her black, and all intent: 3091.

Jack, if we're nimble: 4478.

Jack lightnings strike Saint Francis' finch: 5889.

Jack Sprat would eat no fat: 1701.

Jack the Blindman, whose violin: 5546.

Jack told himself the world was pure as soap: 3067.

The Jamiesons cherish: 6737.

January not June: 2243.

Jay, the child, is crying in blue: 4401.

Jehovah came. Mica gleamed in the rock: 5629.

Jennie tossed her rolling pin: 3085.
Jeremiah Dickson was a true blue American: 986.
Jeremiah, Trident held his sway: 2231.
Jerusalem is a hill city: 3089.
A jet from the airbase wailing out of sight: 5968.
Jill owns a waggish derriere: 6209.
The Jo River flows to the land's end: 4965.
Jo, with the wind: 4014.
A job that's exciting: 6021.
Jochebed went entreating of Egypt: 3102.
Joe's got a squirt gun in the desk: 4092.
John Aubrey had a nose for news: 754.
John Hancock dressed in silks and lace: 3104.
John Otto of Brunswick, ancestor: 3105.
Johnny's healthy; Johnny's clever: 5432.
Jonas is what I shall rename the cat--: 162.
Jonquils awaken in surprise: 287.
Jose Garcia Villa: 6899.
The journey's done, we've come!...Here is the beautiful island: 6731.
Journeys of planets and sun-brilliant stars: 3171.
Joy and the soul are mates, as heart and...: 1298.
Joy is still the startle and sting: 3117.
Joyfulness of cork: 679.
Julia says she just adores the Indians: 2946.
July escapist, I hied the highways where: 3121.
July, the guillemots among them: 3221.
June comes the end of the kind year: 1914.
June is a time to lie down: 3125.
Junior brings home his marks: 4464.
Just as no one works for a living in Oscar Wilde: 4316.
Just for a yuletide joke they seized upon...: 3873.
Just in from the cold: 3136.
Just now a father took his little girl's shoes: 3148.
Just now, as I admire the leaves: 5303.
Just take a glance at our...: 2572.
Just try to keep him bedded: 5881.
Katie the whore reeled in: 3144.
Keats heard a nightingale and Shelley heard a lark: 2975.
Keats, in his maiden room, with dreams: 4897.
The kind of girl I'd like to marry: 1262.
The kind of hand I like to see: 4513.
Kind Sir: This is an old game: 3163.
The kind that I'm craving: 5683.
Kindly tell me, poor half cat: 4296.
A king: 4910.
The king, his crown, his float-above-him head, his other dandy: 3369.
The kite at the end of the string in his hand: 3176.

A kite is a victim you are sure of: 3177.
Kitty Hawk, O Kitty: 3178.
Kneeling within the holy place: 5642.
The knight from the world's end: 1569.
Knitting, they talked of Myra Moss...: 3395.
Know-how substitutes for knowledge: 5144.
Knowing not the quantity nor precise degree of my sinning: 7345.
Knowing the waves he has carved cannot float: 7161.
Knowing what even scholars have surmised: 6320.
A known room is the place for being ill: 3188.
Kool, kciD, kool: 1971.
The labor of autumn is gathering: 2492.
The lacy towers, the words so tall: 7365.
A laden ship sailed into port: 700.
Lady for whose blessed house: 4601.
A lady I know disapproves of the vulgarization: 2807.
Lady, I write to tell you: 1261.
Lady, my lady, this containment makes: 5210.
Lady, unhappy regent of the air: 3826.
Laid at your side, like the oar in the bottom: 1792.
The lake, in summer, proves a purer peace: 6930.
Lakes learn from the season: 3206.
A lamb just born: 1734.
Lament for the Makers: 862.
The lamps are lit: I gaze into the dark: 6885.
The land behind your back: 7289.
The land develops, at its end: 1095.
A land of settled government: 3219.
Landlocked, the child: 3584.
Landlocked, the water lies without a tide: 3204.
Lane borders land: 5836.
The language of bees is a dancing: 6743.
The language of flowers is to Enki known: 1722.
Language of high and laurelled Attic song: 2832.
Large as themselves the wings: 2056.
A larger world awaits us now: 4211.
The last called child has scampered in: 6180.
The last flare: 4280.
The last leaves are down, and the iron: 7240.
Last names first and first names last: 7038.
Last night a baby gargled in the throes: 7142.
Last night as I lay wrapped in quiet dark: 4123.
Last night, late: 2903.
Last night the wind blew Niagara rainbows: 5720.
Last night too soon: 6888.
The last time I saw Donald Armstrong: 4751.

The last words fell on the clovered
   grass: 5137.
Last year around the twenty-third: 5217.
Last year or twenty years ago it came:
   1042.
Last year's ice and last year's snow:
   3076.
Late Grace: 3255.
Late last night we drove through fog:
   3257.
Late scholar of my own despair: 593.
Late winter hunted in our fields: 91.
Lately by language: 4856.
The lately mockingbird white-streaking
   struck: 3262.
Laughter of children brings: 1616.
The lawn is a cool sea: 3199.
The lawn is too much with us, late and
   soon: 6417.
Lazarus shut his eyes when the white
   mice came: 5760.
Lazarus you have been touched: 5369.
Lead us, O Father, through our shadowed
   years: 137.
Leaders of the world may pose for news-
   papers: 5181.
Leaf by leaf, the days descent: 2563.
The leaf, down from the branch: 4586.
A leaf runs at my heels: 1150.
A leaf will not die straight: 2977.
Leaflight to lamplight, blind with
   so much sight: 730.
Learn to give: 4674.
--learning with age to sleep my life
   away: 3714.
Leashed by a sunbeam to the guiding
   sun: 6660.
The least of the troubles inherent in
   hashish: 6851.
The leaves are drifting from October
   trees: 5555.
The leaves fell all from the tree:
   675.
Leaves hang down jade patterns to our
   eyes: 2888.
Leaving her nest in the fall: 4057.
The leaves lie in the autumn forest:
   883.
The left side of her world is gone:
   6104.
Left to their dicing on the nobless
   hill: 6678.
A lemon popsicle of monstrous size:
   7356.
The lending library smells of glue
   and ink: 5953.
Left to his own devices: 3051.
The legend of success, the salesman's
   story: 3295.
Lend me your body, warmth: 3337.
Let fire lick at the hand: 5083.
Let go the anchors that in their iron
   shapes: 4353.
Let love consume you: 3308.
Let me be apart from you: 261.
Let me creep through the filthy aper-
   ture: 3637.
Let me get this straight my darling:
   5102.

Let me, like Horace two thousand years
   ago: 1004.
Let me not when I am old: 7068.
Let me take this acorn squash, grown
   in my garden: 6230.
Let no one say I wasn't warned: 7024.
Let no proud ritual or trumpet's blare:
   5869.
Let not my mind be blinder by more
   light: 6842.
Let not our love winter--die: 201.
Let the judgment be, the heart be
   humble: 3311.
Let the stars fade: 2369.
Let there be mountains of stillness:
   5630.
Let us assemble the medieval man:
   303.
Let us call her Mrs. Mipping, but her
   name is legion: 3046.
Let us go to a dreary little town:
   2760.
Let us forget death and the winter
   dearth: 2892.
Let us go down to the shore and look
   for shells: 2874.
Let us go softly to the bank of the
   ford: 4164.
Let us live a little longer: 1574.
Let us live, and let us love, my
   darling: 6831.
Let us praise the dull snow color of
   our dead sister: 2876.
Let us remember, here recall: 7229.
Let wild men rant of armored right:
   4281.
Let your faith be larger: 5535.
Let's go. Let's go somewhere awhile:
   3472.
Let's have just a salad: 3762.
Let's kiss in hay: 3318.
Let's not beat around the bush: 1800.
Let's sing a lay of vertebrae: 5926.
Letters exchanged between the sexes:
   5176.
Letters she left to clutter up the
   desk: 2271.
The level slope of colored sea: 3782.
The Liberal Rock-and-Rollers want a
   summit: 6157.
The liberals I chance to know: 3342.
Librarians can always fine: 704.
Librarians cried, "Alas, Alack!":
   4561.
Librarians in Reference: 2606.
Librarians who catalog: 1490.
Libraries are like churches in a
   way: 5624.
Lie closed, my lately loved, in the
   far bed: 4873.
Lie you down, dear, though the world
   is fading...: 932.
Life is more exciting for greenhorns
   than for tired-eyed old fogies: 1542.
The life is to passion: 3339.
Life offers moments of purest perfec-
   tion: 159.
Life to me is just a bowl of: 4608.
Life! What is it?: 3363.

The lifeguard sits there on his chair: 45.

Life's a wild plum in bloom: 3372.

Lift high our souls: 3374.

Light branches out to hold on to the bricks: 6937.

Light reflected through prism of glass on a glass on marble: 4519.

The light still shines in darkness: 5536.

The light was already spent when they came: 3501.

Lighten our darkness, we beseech thee, O Lord: 1347.

Light as a caravel on a bright sea: 3924.

Light, with a thousand carolings, pour down, floods down: 6388.

Lightly, lightly are plowed: 6400.

The lightning's broken fences fall: 6077.

Like a caravan of nursing camels whose humps are in the sky--: 7343.

Like a clear, concise thought: 3870.

Like a gale I was unaware: 3108.

Like a lost river running underground: 6243.

Like a naked woman sun-tanned on a South Sea island: 5848.

Like a sharp-nosed hound: 5414.

Like a singed black lark, curled in the embers: 2261.

Like a specter it rose from the mine shaft: 5898.

Like a tadpole floating north, its head highest in the bay: 2406.

Like a woman: 769.

Like acorns squirrels pelt upon a roof: 2710.

Like any other you might say: 4928.

Like any other you might say, and yet: 3150.

Like dancers poised in groups and ordered rows: 5976.

Like Diana in her summer weed: 5418.

Like flaming swords, words guard the gates of day: 4565.

Like flocks let out of fenced-in: 5587.

Like liquid shadows. The ice is thin: 5185.

Like lovers they move to this, like lovers in this trance: 3966.

Like mirrors marvelously lost in mirrors: 5890.

Like mother, like grandmother: 4662.

Like summer rain on great and small: 6007.

Like the bright noise of spring that birds compound: 1568.

Like this before you just as I am: 3387.

Like uncut pages of a book: 2571.

Like windows in that house high: 7296.

Like Winslow Homer"s Women at Croquet: 2370.

Lilacs are a brief affair: 3392.

The lilac bushes were small with winter: 1798

A lily stands in a glass: The night before: 5343.

Limbs and voices shout: 5944.

Linda swings in the April elm: 4657.

The line which we had planned to hew to: 3399.

The Lion hates my friend, the Sword: 3433.

The lion paces his motheaten skin: 1205.

Lipstick and nail polish: 3684.

The liquid jewel of the sea: 5663.

Listen, I am one of those idiot-saints who teach by unexample: 263.

Listen! The tedbird: 2578.

Listen to hidden music...: 1550.

Literature is the better part of life. To this it seems inevitably necessary: 28.

Little ballerina, stop: 5163.

A little beyond the walls of Zion of Zion, walking: 6797.

A little boy's kiss is a transient thing: 3450.

Little boys, this year of grace: 6035.

The little Christ low lies: 873.

"The little ditches of New Mexico.": 3609.

Little drops of water: 6749.

Little drops of water, great big balls of snow: 6013.

Little fingerprints attest: 1168.

Little girls are made of giggles: 2536.

Little girls with flower skirts: 1209.

Little here has changed, least of all, the gulls: 233.

The little huts demurely stand: 6820.

Little I said was very astute: 265.

Little Johnny-go-go God: 1582.

A little liking is a dangerous thing: 3463.

A little mound of earth, a granite stone: 3974.

Little sighing asservation of talk does as the orchestra tunes: 2848.

The little tray, its silver mug: 2359.

A little while some fires are high and clear: 3512.

A little white lie: 1406.

The little white lie is the balm that soothes: 2950.

Little Vidlah who mingled: 2604.

The littlest person I ever loved: 4141.

Living in lively hope: 4317.

The living room, enwrapped in slumber: 1774.

Living without wings was easy and the flesh said yes: 919.

The liz: 3480.

Loathly beast: 937.

The local school is selling flower seeds: 5413.

The locust that sings: 3488.

The lodestar climbed: 3489.

Logic merely distracts: 1830.

The London taxi is a relic: 6646.

A lonely heart needs fortitude: 2134.

Lonely is going into the light: 6932.

Long ago he had letter the sign in red: 219.

Long are the paths where a horse may take: 7032.

The long are of morning: 3364.

Long creeds are giant sharks that ride the waves: 1186.

Long, glossy caterpillar: 7279.

The long green terrace edging: 6303.

Long now with the great ships passing to the north and south: 7260.

Long sidewalks lie bleached in moonlight: 4114.

A long winter from home the gulls blew: 6557.

The longest road or trail or track: 1814.

Longing forever to gaze on the doomed city: 3536.

Look at the Forum: 5335.

Look at the man, aglistening with rain: 7243.

Look down the air--the dark sea leaping: 1096.

Look into my life: 5345.

Look out for the booby trap in the box of sand: 578.

Look where the candid sun: 6448.

The lookout watch must climb and climb: 2195.

Lord, if I dig a hole for someone else: 4511.

The Lord is my counselor, I shall not feel insecure: 5059.

Lord, keep a haven for the fearful ones: 4980.

Lord, lay your fingers on: 1083.

The Lord made clay with spittle and touched my lids: 654.

Look, oh look, oh look at her! 5020.

Lord, when you come, upon that sudden day: 6361.

Lord, who createdst man in wealth and store: 1639.

Lost among immediate creaks chirrups wrong: 2050.

The lot of a second dog is hard: 5491.

A lot of people, hearing trains: 5279.

A lot of people sit and rock: 6359.

A lot of the old folk here--all that's left: 5186.

The lot will be different if the sea cove: 2135.

Loud and querulous bird: 671.

Love begins when we have love to give: 194.

Love came like wind and sun: 756.

Love dismisses hail and: 1534.

Love, for all nights this one: 6707.

Love had a mother's hands and eyes: 1828.

Love is a fool's game; love is a prize: 5688.

Love is hidden heaven: 2532.

Love is nothing made: 3571.

Love is our periwinkle joy: 4103.

Love is the maker of mankind, I say: 3550.

Love, love, love: 2079.

Love must savor grief: 5904.

The love of beauty, nothing more or less: 323.

Love offering for the evening I hold on high: 1505.

"Love," said the blind amoeba, "smacks of pride...": 3432.

Love, to him, was a gaudy ribbon: 3281.

The loveliest things are full of mystery: 922.

A lovely day for hunting platitudes: 1361.

A lovely house it was. We all thought so...: 1875.

Lover of lettuce see: 1485.

Lover, the logs are aflaming: 6418.

Lovers have always with spirits in tune: 3549.

Love's not forever a sharp upthrust: 6297.

Lucinda in her first long dress: 3581.

Lucifer came glancing down: 3580.

Lurching in a stagecoach through the countryside: 4126.

The lute and the pear are your half sisters: 2012.

Lydia dealt in nothing duller: 3596.

Lyrical and definite: 274.

Lying against the throne-room wall: 1355.

Mabel in a hat of leaves: 6458.

Madam, we had our Modern Age at first: 5145.

Madam, your manners unman me, almost: 3198.

Madly mending ancient rips: 6220.

The maggots bred: 4484.

The magic in the Joshua tree: 4994.

The magpie philanthropist: 3231.

Make and be eaten, the poet says: 682.

Make it a prayer, they said: 7377.

Make me no lazy love: 3618.

Make room here at manger: 1012.

Make this your travel year: 6662.

"Make yourself at home.": 2615.

Malt does more than Miltown can: 6645.

Man and his wife: 5363.

Man, as unforgiving as a sharpened blade: 140.

A man-face gathered on the eyes of a child: 4035.

A man finds out, the minute he's got her: 804.

A man has so much ocean in his hide: 5466.

A man is a man is a man: 1142.

Man is but a blossom of the air held by the earth, cursed by the...: 1151.

A man is tamed for domestic life: 2656.

A man of rare persuasion: 1795.

Man stoutly labors with science and heart and soul: 7158.

Man walks, I learn, in fear of woman:

A man who was rich (that is, he had money): 4787.

The man who loves her as she is: 3282.

The man who sold his oil: 6947.
The man who sweeps the sky: 6256.
The man whose car needs gasoline:
   1953.
Man's mind: 328.
Many a new life is begot: 6855.
Many a parent's suggestion: 5456.
Many of the books I own: 6257.
Many times, oh many times: 6364.
Maple, granite, Frost the man: 6578.
The maples' fire, which: 1612.
The marble halls where cultured learn-
   ing dwells: 3348.
The marble typewriter on "wedding
   cake"...: 6859.
March is brisk and sharp: 438.
March, my lion, pet of winter's lair:
   3649.
A March of laughter smacked our hair
   askew: 6570.
March, the Apache, the insolent young
   dancer: 1339.
The mare roamed soft about the slope:
   4579.
Margaret mentioned Indians: 2947.
Maria Bautista rang the bell that
   night: 4717.
Maria habst der smallisch lamb:
   3738.
Mariner, scan this map with unbelief:
   4432.
Marked by the obeying wind which
   laughed at him: 2618.
Marthe, these old walls can no...:
3674.
Mary and Lazarus sat in sycamore shade:
   1960.
Mary bore her son in darkness: 3515.
Mary had a little lamb: 2796.
Mary had a little lamb: 3680.
Mary, you know it is not easy for us:
   6984.
Massu would go to war: 3686.
Matthew was a businessman: 2057.
May have killed the cat: 1312.
May I be one with all: 3705.
May the sun so build over whatever
   hill: 2652.
May we as parents, freely give...:
   2320.
The meal that's most delicious: 6406.
Meanwhile surely there must be some-
   thing to say: 1206.
Measured in mind, to the hammock,
   hammock to porches and horse block:
   763.
The meat in the oven is sizzling: 401.
The mediators the peacemakers, the
   compromisers, the conciliators: 3717.
Meeting the first time for many years:
   3732.
Meeting when all the world was in
   bud: 3559.
Meeting you on the street to-day:
   3736.
Melanie Rose was a wedding-cake girl:
   3739.
Mellifluous as bees, these brittle men:
   4454.
Melville had Emerson's number: 1694.

Men hate good-bys: 3316.
Men marry what they need. I marry
   you: 6553.
Men need a basic faith in man, and
   hopeful dreams to go on: 4886.
Men, ropes, horses, strain: 4917.
Men speaking to animals: 4197.
"A mere equation this," I hear you
   say: 1604.
Merrily roars the juke-box: 3733.
Merry Christmas and Bon Voyage, or
   How to Tell Santa Claus Without
   a Baedeker.": 3771.
Met at the entrance of this wood: 2024.
Mexico, the remains of no self I
   know: 5488.
The microphone glared at the stop-
   watch: 7348.
Midas watched the golden crust:
   6785.
Middle age, from forty on: 6481.
Middle age is when the side view:
   1430.
Middle age's chief defense: 4508.
The middle of a leaf he saw: 7089.
A middle-of-the roader is one: 5074.
The Midlands' a is mostly an i: 6718.
Midnight Christmas morning: 151.
The mightiest lyrist of them all:
   6181.
Milady's looks change every season:
   126.
A million unseen bubbles seeking sight:
   6684.
Millionly-whored, without wombs:
   1587.
Millions of windows, they tell us:
   923.
Mind in attic: 3751.
The mind has layer I the professor
   said: 5773.
The mind licks the bruises: 5254.
The mind pursues with bold intent:
   1744.
Mine are the names outmoded as the
   kindness of my mother: 4032.
Mine can be put so briefly that:
   1929.
The mind is a city like London: 3814.
Mine is the hand mine the cool knife:
   119.
Minnows nibble at my white feet: 4480.
The minute a wife: 6798.
Miriam, centering herself in a
   blue flower, was very close: 5929.
Mirror, mirror on the wall: 6537.
The mirroring transparencies of dark
   glass: 3829.
The mirror's law is clear--an eye for
   an eye: 6674.
Miss Brown, before these walls un-
   quote: 4198.
Miss Esther Williams: 4738.
Miss Maude came every summer Monday:
   4796.
The mistral has blown down the eye-
   glass canvas of Van Gogh: 6874.
Mistress Franklin's son: 3841.
The mists of fortune: 2137.

Mme. Bonnet is one of the best-dressed ten: 6293.
Mms. Bonnet is one of the best-dressed ten: 6293.
A modern papyrus burlesque: 1757.
Moderns, read your: 5616.
The moment that a man relaxes: 5202.
The monarch with his tetinue: 3629.
Monday it was Ricky: 6046.
"Monday's a blue day," someone said: 672.
Monday's card is wondrous droll: 4365.
Montego Bay: 875.
The month of June approaches: 4362.
The monument lies on the chest: 4430.
The moon had flooded the field with silver: 5975.
The moon I saw last night invades: 3907.
The moon is mottled: dark shadows eat: 3593.
The moon is setting in the west: 5837.
The moon says it is midnight: 7123.
The moon surveys the salt flats like a face: 3228.
Moon wafer: 1955.
A moon with Roman numerals: 1080.
Moonlight shimmered bright as dawn: 3887.
The moonlit: 4904.
The moor hen takes her brood to the stream: 4634.
The more lovely her hands look, the deeper my feeling: 1506.
The more miraculous grow the drugs: 4051.
More than affectionately old: 1903.
More than fine gold I desire: 5789.
More to be pitied than the woman in the shoe: 4146.
Morning draws near. Already water gleams: 3901.
The morning glories blow a blast: 719.
The morning it was over, I walked: 96.
Morning Mass--Tsurama, Japan: 3906.
The morning skies sway--the tangle of a great terebinth: 2212.
The morning told me, "You're alive!": 2764.
Mornings, in a stone place: 2934.
Mornings it was like a blue wind: 6433.
The morns are meeker than they were: 417.
Mortmain, the Devil's hook, black-- flaking: 2269.
Most boys and girls burst out of doors: 7067.
Most dreams have wings: 6787.
Most great men have their success: 5075.
Most of the time she is only six: 3197.
Most of us sought the involvement: 2133.
Most social life, it seems to me: 5744.
Most that I know but one: 873.
The most uncluttered spirit clings: 8635.

Most unmarried misses find summer vacation: 5485.
Mostly we get the data: 5480.
The moth, that well-known closet scourge: 3918.
Mother, do you know why I act secretive?: 5827.
A mother finds maternal fitness: 1.
The mother is a pair of wings: 5655.
Mother, Oh mother, come shake out your cloth: 5806.
Mother said to call her if the H-bomb exploded: 567.
Mother's closet: Tidy and neat: 6951.
Mothers must draw a subtle line: 3002.
Mothers of the ages past: 3931.
Mountain, old father: 4382.
The mountain quarreled: 6085.
A mountain village in Iran: 6658.
...Mounted on its triumphal chariot, Earth: 6682.
Mourning the deaths of heroes he could never forgive: 1673.
Mouse, mouse curl in your bed: 543.
Mouth down in the timothy: 2383.
The mouth of hot enchantment hovers here: 7211.
Moved by who know what memory: 3254.
Moved by you deep enough: 2073.
The moving figure writhes, and having writhed: 5370.
"The moving finger writes, and having writ...": 5912.
The moving riddle glitters: 2576.
Mr. Murple called upon his mother: 3367.
Mr. T. Williams: 320.
Mr. Toyomasu appeared on stage: 4795.
Much as he would like to make it mild: 762.
Muddy meek river. Oh, it was splendid sport: 604.
The mulberry tree: 488.
The multicolored hosts drift down the sky: 6726.
Muse, I would make a collage: 4301.
"Music hath charm," the poet said: 3355.
The music is cool and rejoices: 4469.
The must of wine and bells of prayer: 4533.
A mustang rolls in the garden: 4135.
Mustn't run across the road: 3087.
My attention the frame for a compli- cation of city roofs: 2208.
My Aunt Ella always said: 6709.
My Aunt Jenny, once queen of her cinnamon kitchen: 4810.
My back is like a kind of harp: 4459.
My bank account is small in size: 4841.
My bed rocks me gently: 392.
My bill for taxes riled me some: 7291.
My birds awaken me at break of dawn: 7049.
My black-polled birds and snow: 7050.
My body does my bidding: 6909.
My body pays the decades' toll: 2955.

My bones ascend by arsenics of sight: 6724.

My bouts with life when but a tyke: 2002.

My boy's a trader: 6639.

My brother has no need for food: 5885.

My cat jumps to the...: 6921.

My cat's a cushion plump with ease: 897.

My Cheshire friend, who: 5739.

My children, the grass is sweet: 6207.

My clean ones, in your pretty skins: 510.

My clumsy hand: 4458.

My conscience is yards wide and like a train: 7329.

My conscience pricks me, stabs me: 1190.

My cousin had four faces: 2144.

My darling will not make obeisance: 3528.

My daughter has an orthodontist: 3317.

"My daughter says, I like the way daddy holds a book": 691.

My dear and only love, I pray: 2788.

My dear sir: Forgive me if an old: 5398.

My desk is always piled with work: 496.

My dictionary defines progress as an advance toward perfection: 1128.

My English steed! my English steed! that stoodest meekly: 292.

My eyelids like twin curtains fall: 6719.

My eyes are dazzled by the white: 5723.

My eyes are shut. A weak glare from the sky: 188.

My eyes, barbarian, innocent: 6814.

My father died in Alexandria: 3996.

My father fought their war four years or so: 5854.

My Father, it is good to pray: 1781.

My father kept a speckled conch: 4501.

My father loafs and combs: 5498.

My father, looking ahead to life: 5851.

My father mounted his horse and rode away: 976.

My father was a good man: 4570.

My father was a wine importer--Pre Volstead Act. In that day: 258.

My father was born with a spade in his hand and traded it: 1670.

My father wrote a fine Italian hand: 3726.

My first true honor does indite: 3345.

My friends are those who find agreement with me: 3099.

My garden began: 5280.

My gilded runner, athlete, my sled: 2129.

My Glumdalclitch, come here and sit with me: 6695.

My Grandfather said "Stand up straight!": 4001.

My grandmother, when she was thirty-six: 5283.

My habit was to stop at noon and call: 5375.

My hair is always whistle clean: 7154.

My hand now scoops up Babylon: 5369.

My heart and soul are yours to keep: 6325.

My heart goes out in sympathy: 4824.

My heart goes out to turkeys: 2322.

My heart has loved but once...: 4004.

My heart, I grant the snow is deep: 7196.

My heart lurched at the warm: 6278.

My heart unbends to canine friends: 5619.

My heart was once a pretty booth: 1070.

My heart would be faithless: 1936.

My home is the most beautiful place: 360.

My husband thinks I'm getting stout: 7058.

My joy in watching the Late, Late Show is often marred: 5438.

My kids eat spinach: 5685.

My kids regard me as: 3462.

My kindest critic looked at me: 1817.

My language must be right: 2880.

My last defense: 525.

My life has been too much on little spires: 802.

My life, that idly swung around: 518.

My little darling looked so pale today: 3991.

My little friend: 6514.

My little Son, who looked from thoughtful eyes: 6638.

My loneliness is no lament: 3493.

My love for you is a little tin: 5373.

My love hath hid herself from me: 2242.

My love lies down tonight in an unknown country: 4008.

My love on Monday rising fair of face: 5277.

My love, put all your laces by: 3139.

My love, you are fair: 288.

My Ma sent me out one dry hot day: 3748.

My mate and I need a vacation: 39.

My mother bade me go and see: 1745.

My mother--preferring the strange to the tame: 2998.

My mother used to say: 2923.

My Mother wept, her sickness sure: 4898.

My mother, when young, scrubbed laundry in a tub: 3270.

My mother, who boasted of no degree: 3306.

My mother's beehive candlesticks: 3291.

My mother's father, crippled and seventy: 4012.

My mother's washlines terrace summer air: 2209.

My neighbor bakes fresh coffee cake: 3796.

My neighbor built a wall between: 5935.

My neighbor has a little boy: 6676.

My neighbor's house is clean and neat: 6206.

My nerves are a fright: 3365.
My New Year is unorthodox: 4676.
My nostalgia is like a butterfly!:
  4181.
My old roads now are blacktop and con-
  crete: 4632.
My own weird shadow, on the bedroom
  wall: 5554.
My patience and my bank account: 6292.
My pause refreshes no one: 2658.
My pleasure may be keen: 1162.
My rage is more than I can bear in
  silence: 4919.
My raise is due this coming week:
  5033.
My reason for rush work unfinished as
  yet: 459.
My seahorse is a tiny steed: 4016.
My son: 4018.
My son and I are visiting: 6893.
My son Jimmy, straight but small:
  2485.
My sons were May-Day willows and had
  just begun: 6902.
My soul doth magnify the Lord: 2207.
My stand is firm and resolute: 4050.
My stutter, my cough, my unfinished
  sentences: 5492.
My swollen fingers,gnarled, and
  knotted: 546.
My teen-age son and daughter: 914.
My tie is made of terylene: 2886.
My tongue is twisted up from speaking
  French: 184.
My truest treasure so traitorly taken:
  5292.
My vision of the Ford Assembly line:
  6522.
My voice is a minor one, but I must
  raise it: 2756.
My waking hunger wants its hourglass:
  683.
My wand strikes me no joy till loosened
  weeping: 6370.
My weather vane's a chimney stack:
  7003.
My wife can tell a story: 5679.
My wife has found her gloomy moods:
  5170.
My wife insists the driveway is: 4572.
My wife told me: 1305.
My wife was only fifty when she died:
  6837.
My wife's eccentric orbit: 4015.
My wife's no simpleton, no fool:
  2534.
My willing wife with loving care:
  558.
My wolfhound messenger, your work
  today: 4690.
My years of illness never mend: 1344.
Myself at the year's end, weaving the
  valley road: 1111.
A mystic in the morning half asleep:
  450.
The mystery is love by any name: 813.
Nail him to sticks: 3893.
Nailed by our axes to the snow: 1452.
The name of a fact: at home in that
  leafy world: 6414.

A narrow stream: 2121.
The natives here enjoy a delicate:
  3028.
Nature, an artist herself, gave to the
  painter: 2206.
Nature is half asleep in ponderous
  trees: 5168.
Nature repeats designs: 3159.
Naughty Sambo is cassock and lace:
  5304.
Near in mountains my heart well knows:
  4047.
Near, the upland heavens are: 2059.
A necessary evil are our black:
  6014.
Need coups d'etat in Africa give
  grounds for pained surprise?: 1484.
The needle slipped so shyly in: 3522.
The needles press us, face and hand:
  7165.
Neither: 6071.
Neither the dove nor the insufficient
  sun: 2066.
Neon throws its circus hues: 4115.
The neutralist stands on the side-
  lines: 4059.
Never again will eternity seem the
  breath: 7378.
Never boast or strut too much: 7285.
Never counsel a lovely lady gravely:
  4061.
Never from any pitcher poured that
  fluid: 1584.
Never marry a gambling man: 51.
Never, never let your pride: 4062.
Never quite old enough: 6518.
Never scoff at tales of wonder: 4063.
Never think, once married: 6086.
Never to see ghosts? Then to be:
  2277.
Never trust a bottle of ink!: 4961.
Never utter sober truth: 429.
Never will there boats set sail: 2688.
New, Britain and America have re-
  stored: 2163.
New cars are growing lower by: 3573.
New come, complete, with no precursive
  bud: 5729.
New lures with a streamer: 3894.
The new roads clamber: 1808.
New Yorkers seldom know: 1053.
"New ranch house," the ad reads: 294.
New wood of a new house: 5341.
Newborn, the pond swells the sky:
  7203.
Nice Britons greet as equals and as
  friends: 4105.
Night and day, and somberly I dress:
  7344.
Night and day we have a dream: 6710.
Night comes. Day runs for its life:
  315.
The night has a thousand eyes: 2007.
Night huddled our town: 2850.
Night in the fields: 1423.
Night is the time of dreaming: 5249.
The night is warm and birdsleep-
  beautiful: 4163.
The night lives in your skin: 3673.

Night of a sudden walks out of the sea: 4100.

The night Our Blessed Lord was born: 225.

Night-piercing, whitely illuminant: 3149.

Night tents us in: 4998.

The night sky pales: 5671.

The nightboat moving: 4026.

The nightingale has not come: 4127.

Nightlong, frogs in the pond: 2178.

Nina was a tiny girl: 5593.

Nine little children in Arkansas: 300.

Nine little niggers in Little Rock school?: 4133.

Nine months making: 4134.

Ninevah's great towers: 585.

No bars are set too close, no mesh too fine: 7059.

No beast can howl: 223.

No blacker than other in winter, but: 794.

No breast of pheasant: 988.

No clerk carries the weight: 1076.

No Deposit. No Return: 3702.

No, don't act drunk. No drunks act drunk except...: 2980.

No doubt about it now, no guessing: 1213.

No doubt the questing wild birds, never know: 5055.

No evildoer thrives unless men cower: 3169.

No flame extinguished is the hooded hawk: 3683.

No good man likes to think of his work as done: 3640.

No grass cushion here for the fogs: 1458.

No inferiority complex: 1521.

No longer casual hand to lip: 652.

No longer do I tell my woes: 2664.

No matter how carefully I have tried: 1583.

No matter what the poplars do: 917.

No message which does not touch: 4010.

No more books about safari: 692.

No, Mother! I'd not been crying, but he sprang at me seeing me: 5801.

No music but a fiddle tuned by ear: 52.

No new hot rod books today!: 4844.

No new ways to bring death on: 3213.

No, not those many snails: 5513.

No ocean wave forgives the shore: 1779.

No one has ever asked the things: 5520.

No one who has not stood and watched him go: 1438.

No one would listen: 183.

No other night bird flying: 3158.

No place to toss my hat: 1928.

No plant so dead. Each straggling vine: 5056.

No popular sport's: 6258.

No rhythmic noon plays: 1256.

No sea so silent now as this white reach: 1241.

No season: 4621.

No sense to get tense or to run from: 6236.

No snide remarks about my driving: 4750.

No sooner had the clowns got a new house built: 4895.

No storm can bleach a strong belief: 6977.

No such imaginings infect us now: 81.

No sudden magic, no swift sleight of hand: 2673.

No "ten-best names" include me: 5200.

No, there's no light in the barn down by the hill: 2956.

No tidy housewife: 1066.

No wind. A thunder of metaphor: 1788.

No wind-wakeness here: a cricket's creed: 6165.

No woman that ever bore a child: 4411.

No wonder, shaggy saint, breast-deep in Jordan's: 5415.

No words: I swallow this, as you: 4782.

No world but this for your eye: 5237.

The noble and ignoble met and paired: 4273.

Nobody has deep glimmering eyes: 3141.

Nobody knows how long ago nor where: 1780.

Nonsensical nothings is all that you're good for: 6507.

None guessed our nearness to the land of vision: 6238.

None shall intrude here. This autumnal garden: 7280.

Noon is a painted stallion: 1455.

The North Atlantic Treaty is our shield: 5322.

The noses are running at our house: 7213.

Nostalgic as a glimpse of outgrown toys: 3685.

Not a sound: 670.

Not all her day foundered between sink and stove: 5644.

Not all her passion spent, but most of it: 3413.

Not all is so simple in the yards of the houses: 4183.

Not all the seated males upon: 3415.

Not all thy tears can firm the wavering wall: 4260.

Not because of his eyes: 6703.

Not by the words he murmured low and sweetly: 5515.

Not clear to my soul: 3379.

Not daring to stay still: 7206.

Not dark of night or sodden ground: 4956.

Not entirely enviable, however envied: 3688.

Not forgetting Ko-jen, that: 3892.

Not in one of its furies, but with absent care: 5467.

Not mendacious, just gracious: 5300.

Not Nineveh, where violence took prey: 7055.

Not on the Hill: 1290.

Not only do I bite off more than I can chew: 693.

Not quite two hundred years ago: 6778.
Not simple water but the transparent blood: 4493.
Not since childhood had the dark: 6955.
Not so unsound as a path: 2639.
Not that I am strong: 7026.
Not that our enemies lift treacherous spears: 5222.
Not the calm--the clarity: 252.
Not the first man but poet who visits the moon: 5980.
Not the shy tourist, hopping up the salty steps of Rome: 13.
Not to retain: 6681.
The not too distant shore: 4195.
Not when the roses of summer: 3439.
Not with an iron will, no: 6050.
Not with mere stuttering repetition: 167.
"Not yet--not yet!" We cry but who can say: 2611.
"Nothing before something," seems to be: 4216.
Nothing can vex: 6131.
Nothing if not your breathing fastens: 740.
Nothing in the world like it. You can tell Aristotle: 6610.
Nothing is circular: 4214.
Nothing is immune: 4218.
Nothing is lost; be still; the universe is honest: 1796.
Nothing is right, nor will it ever be: 1131.
Nothing is taller than a royal palm: 3071.
Nothing of sun or sod: 2955.
Nothing that clicks in his closeted mind: 1525.
Nothing ties earth and sky together: 5964.
Nothing you say: 249.
Nothing's changed except the view: 229.
November rain's downpouring all night long: 2339.
Nothing remained: nothing, the wanton name: 228.
November has stood naked at my door: 1973.
Now alien tongues repeat Thy name: 7313.
Now and again as an air would tune the white gold: 311.
Now and for all: 3626.
Now as she catches fistfuls of sun: 2920.
Now as the flesh parts, weakened by the cold: 3299.
Now as the season approached: 4336.
Now, as the stripped tree lying in the corner: 75.
Now as the year turns toward its darkness: 2333.
Now, at the edge of the woods: 317.
Now autumn begins, and the...: 4235.
Now Bertie O. M. has informed us (Ahem! that he cannot distinguish at all): 6409.
Now bitterness and tumult stalk: 5443.

Now blessings on the afternoon: 5678.
Now, child, I speak to you with earnestness: 4338.
Now Christmas is over: 881.
Now come the day of address books: 1014.
Now credit give, my lad, where credit's due: 4330.
Now daughter, life will teach you sure as rain: 4325.
Now, daughter, we shall reverently touch: 4333.
Now, dear, as he comes nightly from the fray: 4320.
Now deep below the swells of ocean dark: 2115.
Now don't overindulge grief for your last coquette: 2632.
Now down the old, star-stubbled field of night: 6033.
Now each has climbed to the uninhabitable: 6931.
Now earth with all her colors gone: 4107.
Now every Main Street is in bloom: 1958.
Now every trivial change of style: 3954.
Now every willow leaf: 1597.
Now fall has funneled all the warmth of May: 432.
Now from quiet shore to shore: 3256.
Now girls are prettier: 6395.
Now God, being my Governor, my astonishment: 5949.
Now having closed with God and loosed my burden: 2688.
Now he is gone, but he has left these words: 3998.
Now he is gone where worms can feed: 4920.
Now I can be sure of my sleep: 571.
Now I lay me down to sleep: 4978.
Now, in distrust of silence, I lock knees: 4119.
Now, in a world where dark and light: 7314.
Now in the wake of the windy sun: 1020.
Now is the cycle broken: 1319.
Now is the moment when the Spirit stirs: 7283.
Now is the small girl's silence broken: 5582.
Now is the time of miracles when God: 6475.
Now is the time of this house and this tree: 4241.
Now it is fog, I walk: 2690.
Now it is light, now it is the calm: 4237.
Now it is time to think, I think: 3175.
Now it's time to wake from winter sleep: 47.
Now,lad, attend me closely, and believe: 4335.
Now, lad, she'll talk--and talk! upon the phone: 4334.
Now learning is entangled with the weather: 18.

Now let indoor hearths grow cold: 5961.
Now let no tarnished praise: 1966.
Now let the rivers rise and overflow: 4811.
Now let us speak of cowboys who on swift...: 7152.
Now like a symbol: 4233.
Now like the cattle byre of Augeias: 399.
Now must the mind write: 4239.
Now my muse prepare for business: 2512.
Now once again old Anselm clings to his window: 5404.
Now, one day, son, you'll see with deep amaze: 4344.
Now polished seeds of light: 6030.
Now satellites can search: 4240.
Now shall be sold the hoardings of the heart: 1251.
Now she is gone, we guess how rare: 3453.
Now side by side they stand: 4240.
Now, sometimes he'll come home a little angry: 4319.
Now, son, I speak to you of strategy: 4348.
Now, son, I teach a thing untaught by by schools: 4337.
Now stripling rivers deep with rain: 7222.
Now suddenly April: 124.
Now, swiftest month, is August: 400.
Now tempt me with no sight or whiff: 6790.
Now that arched out and cumbered with months and sun: 2447.
Now that dresses need not fit one: 3057.
Now that he's left the room: 6789.
Now that I have insight what has happened to outsight?: 3061.
Now that new shoes have been given to me: 4654.
Now that our hero has come back to us: 4490.
Now that the world grows small, and jet-bouane cars!: 3094.
Now that we bide the death of winter: 5796.
Now that you are gone and sorrow: 5285.
Now the spectral moon: 975.
Now the tide is coming in, each long, low, hastening wave in the cove: 4891.
Now the time is come that you must: 4058.
Now the wild cherries are red: 5172.
Now there are gold reflections on the water: 2925.
Now things get turned around: 4392.
Now, this will happen, daughter, late or soon: 4345.
Now those spruces, tiny trees: 6043.
Now through the lady's darkened glass: 4731.
Now time runs all one way: 218.
Now we all read condensations: 4312.
Now when I came, still anxious for my kin: 2619.
Now when I have thrust my body: 6565.

Now when waters press in force: 4242.
Now when you sit in your accustomed place: 7143.
Now, wrangling bells discipline the day: 2099.
Now white and gray as memory of gulls: 1894.
Now will I sing to my Mother: 4598.
Now winter's flowers fill the air: 5725.
Now you have said goodby, and I may rest: 4243.
Now you must wake: 6501.
Nowadays I observe, poetry is chiefly lyrical: 5771.
Nowadays, little girls: 4887.
Nude bodies like peeled logs: 5870.
Numb, stiff, broken by no sleep: 4122.
A number of loves consumed his April heat: 6849.
The numismatist enjoys with professional passion: 2410.
The nurse was gone and the door was closed: 1666.
"O"Antiphons vocal again on my tongue: 4253.
O Captain! my Captain! Your fearsome trip is done: 4254.
O constant moon: 3285.
O darkly in the summer's eye: 4257.
O Doves, dismember me!: 1555.
O Dr. Albert Schweitzer, this is very sad to find!: 6903.
O Father hear our prayer! 4593.
O frail and ancient lady of the portrait: 2267.
O God most graciously thou walkest here: 4975.
O hardly out of hate: 3666.
O he who lends: 690.
O Holy Spirit come!: 2859.
O how often I have thought of those tears: 1395.
O it is beautiful, beautiful: 7036.
O it used to be such a pleasure: 4259.
O Love in your empty bed: 1538.
O let me learn to write in such a way: 1156.
O love the little wood doves call and call: 395.
O lovey with the blue blue eyes: 664.
O my love, the earth unfolding us: 5950.
O never, never take his love for granted: 4065.
O Nirvana: 4930.
O now the drenched land wakes: 4262.
O passer-by, remember these two friends: 2877.
O Pearl and breasted world: 4263.
O she is as lovely--often as every day: 4264.
O sister of the shadow: 1976.
O sleep, it is a gentle thing: 541.
O sleep, it is a soft and gentle thing: 4128.
O small St. Agnes, dressed in gold: 4993.
O thou sweet dumb-bell: 6563.

O Thou who givest food and stars: 2928.
O Thou who has made of one blood all nations of: 4982.
O to fall easily, easily, easily in Love: 3555.
O wad some Pow'r the giftie gie us: 6003.
O, we were penitent enough, God knows: 4027.
O weave the fir!: 1951.
O what a physical effect it has on me: 2866.
O when in San Francisco do as natives do: 5445.
O where lies that land: 1472.
O writer of ecstatic prose: 6585.
O you Dr. Ycas, you!: 635.
The object is not worthy, not even you: 6259.
Obscure, the unpromised land: 1806.
Observed from age to age: 5327.
Obviously profound, four pastured horses: 6084.
The ocean is a housewife scouring beaches all her life: 4278.
October, and an early snow: 1974.
October turns the woodland to a muse: 6650.
October's: 4282.
The odor of corruption killed: 439.
Of a sudden the heavens exploded with the Star!: 5871.
Of all mamma-saving tricks: 6392.
Of all recessions that affect: 3502.
Of all sad fates: 4070.
Of all that tribe the young must do: 2302.
Of all the immortality concoctors: 6547.
Of all, the loveliest lore is love-longing: 5831.
Of all the many things which give love rise: 4308.
Of all the sounds enchanting, clear: 6112.
Of all the world's noises: 2519.
Of all who like to blow their horns: 2636.
Of all with whom I correspond: 5261.
Of bricks...Who built it? Like some crazy balloon: 4605.
Of conversations that may be: 6250.
Of course I saw the Muses: 2750.
Of course, we must die: 2442.
Of deprivation, dusks, and of the blood: 2191.
Of early spring flowers: 2127.
Of Europe I sing, her railroads and theatres: 4013.
Of every condiment and herb: 6460.
Of gold and bread on which he banqueted: 832.
Of horizontal light, of long blue shade: 6170.
Of living creatures most I prize: 811.
Of people running down the street: 4803.
Of singing nothing now: 3793.
Of such formal will: 2026.
Of such pure gold was Helen's hair: 5287.

Of tact I have a smattering: 5041.
Of teaching Thoreau was not too fond: 6268.
Of the flesh that lately shone: 466.
Of the garden of Odouis, Lydia, I love: 4304.
Of various errors, my gamut agony: 4531.
Off on her first heels M'linda goes: 127.
Often I saw, as on my balcony: 1008.
Oh, a wonderful land is Grand Opera Land: 2371.
Oh, and I set my course of air: 6912.
Oh! Carry on, Mr. Bowditch!: 3346.
"Oh, dear," said a book: 697.
Oh, do not grieve that they go: 1193.
Oh, for a camera technique to capture: 6484.
Oh, for the madcap adventures of youth!: 4489.
Oh, for those carefree days when I: 3210.
Oh, Friday night is here again: 610.
Oh, had I known it once for all: 2770.
Oh, how they come, the channering rains come down: 6356.
Oh how this sullen, careless world: 2784.
Oh, how we dread the month of Feb: 3877.
Oh, hush, my dear, and let them go: 290.
Oh, how they persecute my attempts at working!: 5597.
Oh, I am far from wishing: 254.
Oh, I could buy mink in the latest fashion: 3656.
Oh, I do love to watch you shave: 6568.
Oh, I rode right through childhood: 4361.
Oh, if there's a coalbin: 3969.
Oh, it's worth the hectic riot: 6569.
Oh, let the bell ring now!: 6443.
"Oh, Library Lady, may I have your attention?": 3351.
Oh, little body, do not die: 965.
Oh, look!: 1224.
Oh, Mistress Springtime, shame! shame!: 7014.
Oh, once on a time I knew all the answers: 5166.
Oh pupil mine of dryad grace: 6269.
Oh, swifter my key in the mailbox would be: 4145.
Oh, sweet chariot, swung low: 4908.
Oh thank you for giving me the chance: 6310.
Oh that horse I see so high: 2287.
Oh that men should learn how to wage...: 7290.
Oh! that the desert were my dwelling place: 4364.
Oh the sumac died: 5770.
Oh there was a babee: 5295.
Oh, these stones that I cannot give voice to: 5132.
Oh, think of the Historian: 2593.

Oh, to be in England: 3926.
Oh, to be in England, now that April's there: 6016.
Oh, to be Orville Prescott: 6616.
Oh, what befell the classic clan: 6836.
Oh, what does the roseman answer: 709.
Oh, who can hear the fall-out?: 3585.
Oh, who will tie your shoe...: 7131.
Oh, why is he painted with iodine?: 1841.
Oh, will wear my silver ring: 465.
Oh yes, I know I had been blind too long: 5169.
Oil a dream and make it work: 5952.
Oily to bed and oily to rise: 5581.
Okaru is weeping: 4368.
Old birches, full of autumn, sound--: 1044.
Old Ella Mason keeps cats, eleven at last count: 1689.
The old family crashed; closeted skeletons: 4845.
Old friends are best of all, and yet: 4471.
Old ghosts have my blood: 5763.
Old John Knox: 4699.
The old man with the snow-white beard: 2490.
Old man like, they feel, is done, is numb: 3943.
An old man's flamingo-colored kite: 5519.
Old men discourse upon wise topics here: 5004.
Old men, forgotten, mumbling, all alone: 66.
Old men now dead instructed us in this: 211.
The old nightshade: 570.
Old Noah heard their cries: 4160.
Old one, I'm drunk with the voice: 3725.
The old story went that the cajoling hag: 2461.
Old stone wall, old apple tree: 6689.
The old, the mad, the blind have: 536.
Old timers, even had forgotten why: 3090.
Old winter's dusk dogs, loosed near night: 7188.
The old woman village, wrapped in a quilt: 7207.
Older than Eden's planting, older than elves: 7282.
Olympus fades, the Greeks and Roman: 3288.
Oman dives deep and deeper for his pearls: 4421.
On an empty stage, out of space: 808.
On an old shore, the vulgar ocean rolls: 3635.
On beachheads of the hills: 1609.
On Boston Common a red star: 7226.
On Christmas Day the good Lord willin': 5486.

On climbing a mountain: 6784.
On Commonwealth, on Marlborough: 6274.
On December fifth: 3009.
On grocery box tops: 514.
On hands and kness upon the green: 1269.
On her vinestump haunches she: 899.
On house-cleaning days they head for the doors: 4321.
On late evaluation, I would say my education: 38.
On Malheur's searing lots the honored toad: 1805.
On Memorial Day, the first spring: 3524.
On my way through the park: 958.
On our television aerial: 7277.
On our temperature side we have a series of songs in us: 5077.
On roads beyond the camp the heat wave struck me: 2904.
On Saturday still there is Sunday: 6687.
On Sundays light, and a respect for law: 5539.
On Sundays now the house is still: 4302.
On that day of summer, blue and gold: 4866.
On that first day new Adam saw the world: 5565.
On the first day of Spring I am wakened by blackbirds: 5417.
On the August-beaten pavement: 3495.
On the axis of my sleep: 3912.
On the bank the wash-stick is beating out time: 4772.
On the beachfront: 5948.
On the coast of my choice there are two rainfalls: 5119.
On the empty seas destroyer writers its name: 4725.
On the fifteenth day God walked: 1463.
On the first night: 7115.
On the forgotten siding: 6249.
On the glebe: 2537.
On the goose green, on the street, softly as snow: 7183.
On the hoof or dead, a satyr weighs: 1094.
On the jetty, our fingers shading: 2894.
On the leafless winter vine: 4859.
On the morning of noise: 4878.
On the road: 5378.
On the scrawled wall: 4518.
On the sheep-cropped summit, under hot sun: 893.
On the subject of natural human re-action I would say: 4009.
On the summer's end edge: 5509.
On the unbreathing sides of hills: 5981.
On the wild plateau: 2821.
On this day I was born: 4642.
On this day they break bread: 4526.
On this dull day: 2932.
On this night: 5289.

On this wall, in this town, in their own state: 4527.
On valley highways sun still shines: 3935.
On what a strangely varied trail: 6550.
Once a child who did not know: 200.
Once a young shepherd went off to despoil: 6434.
Once bombs of shout were emptied down the stair: 4249.
Once, dreaming of eternal fire: 4428.
Once home, I pat each purpling bruise: 4095.
Once I had 1000 roses: 14.
Once I knew love as the wind: 5574.
Once I saw a grown man fall from a tree: 1382.
Once in Japan as I was traveling Nikko: 2201.
Once in late summer I had a fine lover: 1563.
Once more the father rides with his child through the forest: 6114.
Once my evenings were large as a: 2660.
Once the sea has hated you, once ever: 930.
Once there was a fair young damsel and she early went, from an inferiority complex, out of her wits: 5136.
Once there was a pawnbroker who got stuck with a batch of unredeemed slots: 453.
Once there was a wealthy bachelor named Mr. Leaper: 2478.
Once upon a golden day: 150.
Once upon a summer, loved braided hair: 4538.
Once we went gladly to that place of vague: 6390.
One blenches to think how the Lord was chided: 4424.
One blueberry morning in Maine: 1223.
One by one, they slip away: 398.
One can forget amid the sunlight's burnish: 6438.
One dawn: 1041.
One day he awoke: 2599.
One day of wind and rushing skies: 5936.
One day the nouns were clustered in the street: 4757.
One day when spring rain fell heavily: 621.
One eerie night when the moon was bright: 2276.
One evening when I took a stroll: 3790.
One fact eccentric I often muse on: 703.
One feels the handsome old poet: 4433.
One flame came at me, from the outer runs: 4543.
One for the baby: 5940.
One for the money: 7098.
One golden leaf on a twig is clinging: 6377.
One kind of teacher is the bhikku, the Buddhist monk: 6265.
One last good-by! One final "Yes, sir!": 5027.

One lesson I have learned to my sorrow: 5641.
One life, one time to loose the spirit in: 2961.
One little word that extends far, too far: 5450.
One man, one worm, one butterfly, one stone: 4540.
One morning when I went downtown: 3904.
One moves ultimately from hatreds: 6319.
One night from the stern I thought, as I watched: 728.
One night in the lilting leaf: 4870.
A one-night world of fairy lights and music: 15.
One o'clock, two o'clock: 1306.
One pink azalea in an earthen pot: 5029.
One power controls our cans and can'ts: 2514.
One prays for enough silence: 2173.
One star-tipped morning the blizzard is still: 3938.
One step: 4555.
One summer day a blackbird sang: 2869.
One thing I am certain of: 58.
One thing about us: 4099.
One thing always amazes me: 2484.
One time I was invited to see Croce: 3542.
One understands your sort of sun: 482.
Only a handful of weeks ago: 3203.
Only a month or two gone by: 4270.
Only a moment ago: 2179.
Only a single cooling plant: 7242.
Only in the dream that is like sleep: 4567.
Only in water could your name be writ: 3431.
Only light and shades of light: 32.
The only place I know where time stands still: 4391.
Only that one maple tree: 3504.
Only the cynic scoffed: "I'll fool that man: 1466.
Only the horizon fire is bright outside: 6680.
Only the living have need for flowers: 6355.
Only when there is no sound: 2930.
Open to love at springtide: 4563.
Open your window, my love: 5530.
The opening of sunrise: 2914.
Ophelia on the threshold of the season: 4395.
Opportunity knocked: 6237.
...or the satyrs, a: 5433.
Oranges three, lemons two: 4575.
The orchard is in flower: 3310.
Orchards, we linger here because: 2049.
Order attends us in these elder days: 4384.
"Organized knowledge in story and picture.": 2192.
Originally our decor: 4755.
The orphans in the bird-storm flitter: 7079.
Orpheus played upon his lyre: 4566.
Other have seen men die: 4468.

Others will enter the gates of the ferry: 4412.
Others will give you gifts: 2284.
Our boat was slow, moving between islands, in a peaceful sea: 2620.
Our bus pulls up; cold eyes inspect each face: 6452.
Our children toy with food at lunch: 3712.
Our city plans for green escape: 2786.
Our clothes were a mess: 2933.
Our den's the room we all relax in: 4597.
Our doormat, dear: 5207.
Our earliest games delight us still: 6972.
Our earth is but a small star: 4976.
Our first family trees, though: 940.
Our garden plot requires no toil: 3059.
Our home is modern: 4474.
Our house had wings for children: 1802.
Our house is alive with electrical tension: 1359.
Our Lady of the Word, calyx and caul: 4600.
Our lives are keyed to fear and grim despairing: 767.
Our lives, we mourn, are like the mists that pass: 3842.
Our lung grows languid in the trudge of note: 6109.
Our medicine cabinets loaded with stuff: 5381.
Our memory is a song: 7300.
Our neighbors have manifold charms and graces: 4268.
Our neighbors' zeal is keener: 2417.
Our new church building will be the best in the community: 3445.
Our prayers have searched his gray horizon for signs: 4705.
Our screen door has one weakness: 634.
Our song! We heard its short refrain: 6623.
Our sun-born schools have reared in Ocean Stream: 761.
Our traffic regulations say: 2757.
Our tables all wear nicks and dents: 1436.
Our talk is brusque and full of spunk: 7347.
Our tall sons move with eagerness and pride: 6503.
Our teen-age daughter flops and falls: 24.
Our visits, friend: 6621.
Our yard now has a children's gym: 1134.
The OUT basket's: 3990.
Out in the country where we live: 1408.
Out in the sun a maplehead takes three: 738.
Out of a war of wits, when folly of words: 4606.
Out of my brother's yellow trousers, my black trousers: 1850.

Out of the bosom of the air: 5724.
Out of the depths have I cried, O Lord: 5661.
Out of the dusky rose of sky: 7108.
Out of the filing cabinet of true steel: 1296.
Out of the hottest night yet, the morning: 4623.
Out of the husk I come to curse the rain: 781.
Out of the sea store: 5149.
Out of the solitude: 5175.
Out of the woods of night: 5965.
Out of these thin, thin cups I drink pale tea: 685.
Out on the tormented midnight sea: 4876.
Out past the pier's splintered arm: 5650.
An outgrown shoe, hand waving good-by: 6385.
Outside a verandah gives upon a court: 4332.
Outside in the light of the neon sun: 4909.
Outside, the green rain of a willow: 7157.
Outside the shutters, a gigantic palm: 6654.
Over against the north side of the town: 4633.
Over the marsh and swamp and pond: 4736.
Over the city beneficent drugs conspire: 6886.
Over the coffee cups he tells: 80.
Over the forest stones: 1776.
Over the hills with somersaults: 3653.
Over the seaworthy cavalry: 3385.
Over the slopes by pine and river: 981.
Over there, where a wall: 4168.
Over these blunted, these tormented hills: 3140.
Over what freshets of light on April mornings: 3543.
Over your five bodies: 2403.
Over your mother's grave: 204.
Overnight, the flowering of the castor beans: 2195.
Owls that cry in the night: 2628.
Oxford to London, 1884: 2837.
A pact or not a pact--that is the question: 805.
Pain is ever: 4644.
Painted and pale the weather: 2702.
The Painted Lady is a small African: 4645.
Painter, poet, runner, thrower of the disk: 4940.
The palace clocks are stiff as coats of mail: 3167.
Pale darts still quivering, crocuses: 4877.
Pale yellow and the sunlight make her hair: 4529.
Palmist, you waste your time upon my hand: 6485.
The Pandavas divided Droupadi: 4534.
The panorama of your heart: 4652.

The parade starts: 2270.
Paradise is a grove: 4664.
A paradoxical chase is this we stage: 4667.
Parents of little boys, explore: 5458.
Parents always get wrought up: 4843.
Paris sky: 4670.
The park tonight is black without a moon: 5070.
Paroled from age, I run like song: 4673.
Parked hard against the cornfield slant: 2433.
The part-time nudists on south beach: 594.
Partly a man's, partly a river's daughter: 5312.
A passenger between his daily selves: 182.
A passerby being fair about sacrifice: 957.
Passing along the wharves: 6735.
Past eighty, but never in eighty years: 1483.
Past Romney and past Tankerton: 5481.
The past sends images to beach: 3414.
A pastor must be truly great, but in humility: 4703.
Past twelve. The mats in the mosque have been rolled up: 4116.
A patchwork of littleness is known about his life: 5542.
Paterson has grown older: 2196.
The pathos of his century marks his face: 3613.
The patience of parents: 6657.
The patron isn't always wrong: 3357.
The patterned fields are full of cows: 4710.
Paul the Apostle cast a chilly eye on: 5625.
Peace is the must that all men would share: 4722.
Peanut butter thickly spread: 6109.
Pearl Avenue runs past the high-shool lot: 1784.
The pedagog who cannot keep: 3266.
Peering above: 4277.
The pelican's voracity: 612.
Pellucid as the tune from a violin: 3689.
Penciled etchings on the sand: 1456.
The pendulum sun swung: 4124.
The Pentagon maintains the reign in Spain: 5199.
The penultimate voyage accomplished and the world: 869.
People always depart, always say good-bye: 4462.
People always stand and talk: 4745.
People are continually shocking me: 4276.
People are destinations in our adventure: 4744.
People are putting up storm windows now: 6075.
People read for hours and hours: 362.
People used to vote for Congressman Hoke Smith: 3106.

People who are not inclined: 3044.
People who live in New York are simply New Yorkers: 7093.
Perception, a life tool: 4747.
Percussive, furious, this wind: 3840.
Perfection is, as saints attest: 1195.
Perhaps as much the driven as the driver: 1321.
Perhaps it's sin: 7150.
Perhaps this valley too leads into the head of long-ago days: 2367.
Perilous at twilight: 6643.
Permanent beauty stands: 1667.
Perpetual motion never found?: 7284.
Perpetual wonder that this is I: 413.
The person who is on the stout side: 2682.
Persons among the flapping clothes: 7328.
Peter Brueghel, the elder, painted: 775.
Petals of fingers: 1948.
Peter, this epode of tears that follows chagrin: 2092.
Petrarch watched a plague: 5030.
Philip Melanchton: 5592.
Philosophy write subscript 1: 4785.
A phosphorescent flash in the rational garden: 2694.
Pick up your sprawling self my love! 5765.
Piecemeal, the ruck of fall: 3406.
Pigeons on the roof: 6839.
Pile no stones here! Set up no altar!: 5219.
Piling: 3192.
Pillowed on cloudy drifts of air: 1512.
Pine and pine, you grow: 2213.
A pink primrose from the plant he knows: 6765.
The pipes thump in the still house: 3862.
Pirate or traveller, the open sea: 4933.
Pitter, patter goes the rain: 7054.
Place is the focus. What is the language...?: 2854.
Plain Jane? If Jane is plain: 3072.
The plate-glass barrier: 2833.
Platoons of dogma raid our zone: 2868.
The player was neither king nor clown: 2106.
The player who is hurt or sick: 681.
Please render your decision: 1908.
Please use the towels: 5772.
Please, Valentine, don't be among the scoffers: 3620.
The plot is deviously spun: 3971.
A plow's broad swipe: 239.
Pluck and pull: 2627.
Pluck the flowering branch from: 5856.
Plucking at handy plenty in their dreams: 3218.
The poem is written, we have come too late: 4034.
A poet doesn't speak in paradigms: 1285.

The poet is a man who feigns: 415.
The poet is dead: 1391.
The poet is dead--and who will sing for him?: 5272.
The poet, like the lion, needs: 5675.
The poet saw a pillar towering in the sky amid the fires of hell: 1443.
Poetry is certainly: 3172.
Poets are always in search of just the right word: 6082.
The poets are weary and the wind is weak: 5524.
Poets make pets of pretty, docile words: 5002.
Poised on the brink of dream Ilie: 5670.
Poisoned by spite, he pricked his friend with blows: 5257.
Police or fire? We've been in bed because: 5643.
Political-science note: 4918.
The pomegranate: 6227.
The pond circled upon: 4921.
Pond country, and when willows in their pools: 4174.
The pond is full of frogs that come: 1082.
A pondering frog looks: 1144.
Poor Keats had died again in my mind that day: 88.
Posies from a Second Childhood: 4948.
The possibles we dare: 3570.
A poster can be a wondrous sight: 6004.
Power lies in my hand: 5599.
A pox on Mr. Pitney, plague on Bowes: 4783.
Praise God for "Busy work.": 4609.
Praise we the gods of sound: 4971.
Praises to those who can wait: 7379.
Prayer asking that I may prove worthwhile today: 4972.
Prefer the cherry when the fruit hangs thick: 6770.
Prepare the ground when April buds have burst: 4832.
Presently, at our touch, the teacup stirred: 6906.
Presto, pronto! Two boys, two horses: 723.
Pride is the seal, the massive stone: 6614.
A pride of lions, a pod of whales: 938.
The princess was baptised inside a shell: 5673.
Prince Lucifer, now cast beyond the moat: 4946.
The princes, ranged like daggers round the throne: 339.
The princess never knew her gentle mother: 3083.
The principal part of the python--: 5010.
Prisoners behind the blank, contiguous bars: 653.
Prithee, think not that pages: 4631.
The prodigal is home again: 6945.
The prof is kind and cheerful: 6234.
The pronoun is a word that I: 3133.

Promiscuous lovers: 5023.
The prophet is without honor till the year: 5510.
A prophet you declare?: 879.
Proud are the men of Lebanon: 6757.
Provide transportation: 2981.
The psalmist, singing wide your praises: 3264.
Psychoanalysis makes me tremble: 5061.
Psychologists list the traumatic terrors: 6039.
Pulpiteers will censure: 2398.
Pure rains, awaited women: 7173.
The purest eye can pierce: 1661.
The purple violet: 4831.
Pussy cat, pussy cat: 5899.
Put me into the breach with every rolling stone: 5076.
Put off the deference that this sea compels: 524.
Put out the light and watch the lightning dance: 2633.
Put your manuscript away, Horace said: 436.
A quality inheres in Congo light: 3376.
The quarter killed...: 4293.
Que buen: 3538.
Quicker than silver: 4250.
The quickest movement of the quickest bird: 6618.
Quickly, boy, get a bowl of wine: 187.
Quickly, in loving praise: 7147.
The quiet hour when we have put the good-looking dinner: 3498.
The quiet mention of God's name: 3761.
Quiet she stands with searching, sightless eyes: 2286.
The quilt that covers all of us, to date: 5101.
The quirking wheels slide him under: 5108.
Quite a tricky thing to do: 696.
Quite rightly, we remained among the living: 6197.
Quite suddenly, unexpected by all: 1711.
The radio begins to sing: 3899.
Radioactive vultures will plunge through ashes: 3086.
Racing the great, green-gloved fire we reach: 6110.
"Raftery I am," he said: 5113.
The rails wait: 305.
Rain: 5133.
Rain, all night, laps the holly: 2603.
Rain comes and goes: 2424.
Rain comes in various sizes: 5117.
The rain has come and gone: 5123.
The rain was falling sullenly: 1769.
Rare is the man who can march through a grocer: 6176.
The rain has passed: 618.
The rain has stopped: 4959.
Rain keeps the golfer off the course: 5115.
A rain-like costume: 5127.
Rain on the roofing slate: 5129.
The rain rains out out of the fall: 5816.

Rain stains and jelly smears: 5986.
The rainbow looks like different colored
    flowers: 5130.
A rainstorm falls on this northern land:
    6660.
Rainy, sore at the whole town: 4968.
Ran waving a branch of Acacia: 7238.
Raphael Archangel runs strange ways:
    5135.
The rare old woman feeding chickadees:
    5253.
Rarely a rose that seems as celebrant:
    356.
Ravening through the persistent bric-
    a-brac: 4502.
A raw-boned and an ignorant man: 5399.
Rawboned lank warrior of the single
    eye: 3243.
The raying fog we walked through wasn't
    thought: 5142.
Read and consider well earth, air and
    seas--: 3820.
The reason I'm a budget-hater: 1554.
The reason my thoughts are inexpress-
    ible's: 2725.
Read now the gland pronunciation:
    2475.
Reading of Laura, as the trains: 7261.
The reason you are apt to see: 6241.
A rebel of the absolute: 5156.
The Red Army fears not the trials of a
    distant march: 3499.
A red flag of warning flies in the
    maple tree: 1868.
Red in the face: 444.
Red wraps our children in the snow:
    1124.
The red yewberry in the tangled copse:
    7342.
Redemptive fingers of the goddess turn:
    1632.
Reduces to helpless chastity: 5604.
Regard the roach: 5193.
The regular spooks are off tonight:
    2468.
The regulations of this world are like
    a hand: 4580.
Rehearsals for death have always
    troubled me: 6520.
Rejoice rejoice that the taken seed:
    1167.
Relieved by prayers or years from such
    erratic...: 6186.
Religion may be fashioned by a man:
    6748.
Reluctantly he plods the scales: 714.
Reluctantly I walk, with many a look:
    6806.
Remarkable benefits often accrue: 575.
Remember me?: 5380.
Remember our children in November?:
    1870.
Remember, son, the things that you
    were told: 3422.
Remember summer, for the summer is
    dead: 6137.
Remember that we are dust: 840.
Remember - warned the speaker: 3845.
Remember when they used to talk: 2607.

Remember when we chatted: 6123.
Remembering maps we think the road
    unchanged: 5267.
Remembering the past: 7052.
Remnants of sunlight shift in the dark
    air: 4990.
Repeat--and Present: 5226.
The reprobate purses the virtuous
    woman: 6416.
Researchers want help, that's why:
    6019.
Respect all surfaces: 2855.
Rest, leper-flamed: 5006.
Restless on whose bosom do we dream:
    4862.
Retrogressive, these shell-backed
    cars: 7274.
Returning to the theater alone: 4166.
Returns like a leopard: 6853.
Revealed in a twist of chance: 3560.
Revelation's not so much: 1329.
Review the ancients and their ilk:
    4152.
Reviewing me without undue elation:
    999.
Rexroth and Patchen and Fearing--
    their mothers: 3147.
Reynolds' palette was, for flesh:
    3734.
A rhinoceros was running: 5285.
Rhyme-linked: 1072.
A ribbon is floating in the air: 4431.
The rich bees live in a five-story
    house: 548.
The riches of my life shall never
    fail: 5293.
Riding a wave of birdsong, onward the
    sun came: 6132.
Right: 5184.
Right from the lines: 3588.
Right now is when a lot of yak'll:
    2484.
The right of way of this road: 821.
Rimbaud: On his muse: 5298.
Ring out, ring out, security Bell:
    3123.
Ring the bells!: 4627.
Ripe were the grapes and olive tree:
    6087.
Risen in a...: 624.
Rising straight in the air above this
    earth: 3190.
The rising sun: 5037.
The river once was farthest boundary:
    5314.
A river runs Havana brown and bronze:
    3819.
The river swanly in its swanhood
    flowed: 5316.
The river was blowing scarves: 6777.
Rivers are not patient in duress:
    5317.
The river's freshness sailed from un-
    known sources: 1565.
Rivers should start in rocks too
    steep to climb: 3202.
The road that has newly been opened
    here: 4090.
A Robin and a Nightingale: 1021.

The rock shed blood: 817.
Roll away the stone from my heart!:
   1633.
The rose and the body of the rose:
   5350.
The rotted sun-weary shacks sit on the
   land: 7266.
A rotten log with ferns at base: 5355.
The rough wall with a stripe of sun:
   5357.
A roaring company that festive night:
   1341.
Rockaby, Cheryl: 1326.
Rocks with lichen on: 4863.
Romance was always at her fingertips:
   3343.
The roofs get in the way: 1054.
Rooms were fragrant long ago: 2027.
Rooster strutting in your sheen: 6760.
The rope that binds this child about:
   2643.
The rose fades: 4871.
The roseate Judas trees: 2711.
Rotted the fence of the old corral:
   1591.
Rouged, daubed: 5196.
The rough wall with a stripe of sun:
   2396.
Round and around on the glockenspiel:
   627.
Round and round: 4408.
Round the huge, darkened circle of the
   stalls: 2809.
Roundling: 5359.
Rub his wrists. He never dreamt: 1880.
Rubbing her mouth along my mouth, she
   lost: 1686.
The rug knew that Mr. M had died:
   3963.
Ruined fruit was hanging gold: 7331.
Rumbling: 2238.
Run, run, run: 2247.
Run seaward, launch upon the air, and
   sound your desolate cry: 2564.
Run to her foliage arms: 5234.
The runner who has always won: 125.
Running and standing still at once:
   4648.
Rush-hour traffic: 2824.
Russia and America circle each other:
   7263.
Russian proverbs say: 4178.
The Russian said it was no dream:
   3286.
The sable flock comes down: 4289.
Sadness is a timid bird: 613.
Safe from the touch of sun, of rust:
   302.
Safely and sanely: 6795.
Said Descartes, "I extoll.": 1071.
Said ethnologist, Dr. J. Loring:
   5455.
Said Swingli to Muntzer: 2683.
Said the curator to easy dying: 1477.
Said the physicist mounting his
   bicycle: 7022.
Sailboat, your secret with what dove-
   and-serpent: 5393.
Sailors who had: 6202.
Sails on the Nile: 834.

St. Agnes' eve and Keats is long since
   dead: 5338.
Saint Jerome and his lion: 3301.
St. Martin's summer's ended and the
   trees: 1333.
St. Simeon, I came to join your rule:
   5446.
Sainted women: 1432.
Saints out of stone, or is it at last
   saints: 5410.
The salt with which I have taken
   love: 5242.
Salute her, you green thumbs and
   muddy knees: 4960.
Salute, my soles!: 5270.
Salute the mirror's candid stare:
   2313.
Samantha hardly favored Annie Laurie:
   1276.
The same blows which floored him,
   hurled him at once far: 5669.
The same level look through clear,
   gray eyes: 1351.
A sampan with a tilted scull: 5812.
The sand around the ironwood: 591.
Sankey was moody, and Sunday, he
   ranted like Saturday night: 5031.
Saunterer on this autumn track: 599.
The savage flutes of disaster: 5434.
Savage now with hunger at midwinter:
   1394.
Save for a lusterless honing-stone
   of moon: 4418.
Say the soft bird's name, but do not
   be surprised: 2445.
Say to the mild melancholy of re-
   gret: 332.
A scandal burned at both ends gives
   a blaze: 769.
The scarecrow in our garden scares:
   5440.
Scarred and weathered fences: 665.
Scatter back, skim forth: 4414.
Schooner, most gracious craft, O
   swift: 3217.
Science is my Shepherd: 6713.
The scientists' work on human
   nutrition: 2420.
Scrubbed till his freckles shine like
   coins: 5451.
Sculptors have stuffed these walls
   with splendor: 2391.
Sea and sky: 5464.
The sea comes up, and the sun goes
   over: 6461.
The sea gulls in their splendor bow
   and miss the whirling air and dive
   and die: 5469.
The sea is always there: 7086.
The sea is the long clock spacing
   its tripped waves: 3496.
A seacoast late at night and a wheel
   of wind: 95.
Seadive for hidden wisdom of pearl:
   4729.
Seagulls are flinging: 1712.
The season of chilling rain and storm
   is here: 5766.
The seasons: 1030.

Seaweed in its looking-glass lagoon: 3742.

The second-grade play was a grand success: 5452.

The secular view is no longer in flower: 5500.

See here His Holy Face: 5596.

See how the brown kelp wither in air: 3220.

See how they love me: 5846.

See it, the beautiful ball: 461.

See me crouching: 2239.

See now how goes it with the...: 3329.

See the reference librarian and the joys that: 5180.

The seeds are sowed: 5613.

Seeing it in the French astonishes: 5761.

Seek not the laurel: 2109.

Seem like a tower walking streets of sky: 1884.

The self-containing world of adolescence: 4037.

The self-infliced screw: 5406.

Send flowers, dear friends: send: 5517.

Senses bud to peoples recognizing: 2976.

Seneschals of the soft, still smoky morning: 3081.

A sensible woman turned to poetry: 2318.

A separate place between the thought and felt: 1238.

September rain falls on the house: 5540.

Serene, I fold my hands and wait: 5601. Serpents: 7307.

Set down the mortars, line them up neatly: 5289.

Set not thy heart on things: 7349.

The seven-branched candelabra glowed: 1570.

Seven miles to north upon his throne: 2910.

Several layers of heavenly soba...: 2926.

A shaded room, an easy chair are often: 5990.

The shadow of the apple fell across her dream: 5416.

Shadows gather as daylight dims: 5813.

Shadows in the air: such phantoms: 5556.

Shadows shaped like rabbits and the mottlings: 5823.

A shaft of moonlight falls in silver folds: 4461.

Shaggy and heavily natural, they stand: 2642.

Shake out the ruffle, turn and go: 6502.

Shake the gourds: 29.

Shake your fist of brain: 2053.

Shakespeare, contemplating time: 3724.

Shall we die together on the mountain: 5437.

Shapes of summer haunt the autumn wood: 434.

The sharper the tongue: 6997.

She, a stone-breaker: 6057.

She always had a pleasant face: 1732.

She always wanted a house to cherish: 2222.

She began to blow away, and put her soft: 3833.

She calmly talked of love as if were: 1100.

She came in maddened ways, dank hair: 2759.

She can't find her earrings: 4190.

She cools love's fever: 7262.

She could lie in bed and see: 6812.

She could not love my shaggy, satyr self: 1462.

She counts you the list of her calories through: 367.

She creams the butter with her hands: 186.

She did not speak of Mab, nor recout: 2376.

She died away from home: 491.

She does not fuss about her clothes: 948.

She doesn't deserve a husband like you: 5523.

She dreamed of a knight in bright armor: 5372.

She dwelt among the untrodden ways: 1697.

She embarked: 4003.

She feeds the new doll when it frets: 2301.

She feels so restless and forlorn: 3293.

She feels so sorry for herself: 4629.

She followed her man: 5203.

She found a drawing made of me when young: 4935.

She gave me her eglantine: 1657.

She grieves in her apple-bough bed: 4719.

She has a sundial memory: 6669.

She has a warm and generous heart: 2264.

She has gone across the road: 2350.

She has the immaculate look of the new: 993.

She held the slimy worm, but couldn't bear it: 2289.

She is asleep: Yet is her hand awake: 5568.

She is a tidy housewife: 1873.

She is a house that welcomes many in: 2091.

She is so special she is almost unique: 3419.

She may not have the eyesight: 4686.

She misses him when early sunlight pours: 1865.

She moves among the shadows every day: 528.

She never could be his, too much required: 4590.

She only took one parking spot: 5063.

She packs two six guns wears a Western belt: 1266.

She reads the grocery ads en masse: 4019.

She said, half sighing, "Where these houses...": 4082.
She sat red distances away: 2595.
She should have died hereafter: 3603.
She should have had...I said, and there I: 90.
She sickened. We could tell: 5603.
She sits at an evening window spinning wool: 5927.
She sits by the loom through the sun-long day: 1934.
She skimmed the yellow water like a moth: 4002.
She stands upon a corner of our city: 3349.
She that was a queen stood here: 844.
She vows to give up all save you: 3669.
She walked along the street with cat-like grace: 4381.
She wants a sonnet from me, instantly!: 5873.
She was a woman: 6910.
She was an island, lying in a sea: 3023.
She was chubby: 3454.
She was not beautiful, the water showed: 5866.
She went her way, and never knew: 7145.
She who weighs pearls, who plays lutes: 1920.
She works the stairs, like a beetle caught in flowers: 7268.
Shells, husks, the wandering: 5301.
The shelves are full of type: 4848.
She's in the forward echelon: 498.
She's lovely in her evening gown: 493.
Shiloh's seed shall not be sewn: 5579.
The shingles streamed out like a mane: 7174.
The ship is gliding, the ship is journeying: 6056.
Ship-launched at last: 3268.
A shirted stick, a lean, lopsided torso: 5441.
Shocking crisp tinfoil from two chocolate bars: 2958.
A shoestring knot's: 2152.
Short man as leader, chest of cere-mony, stalking: 5268.
The short shadow: 222.
Shorts on tennis courts are quite: 7269.
Should a panther: 4653.
Should every creature be as I have been: 5580.
Should flowers, jewelry, perfume be: 4999.
Should the shade of Plato: 4467.
Should vision of the Godhead dim?: 7246.
Shrewd husbands rejoice that examples are ample: 1656.
Shrill-voiced and demanding: 3561.
Shuffling dice to win His robe: 2236.
Shun the vindictive word: 1257.
Sickness heals the world: 2852.
A side of sunbeam: 5114.
The sign post says three miles to town: 6979.

A sign that I have always seen: 7021.
The signatures: 6151.
The signs that read: 5878.
Silence: 4792.
Silence and aura. An ancient Yemenite 2314.
Silence comes down the street to us in the shape: 1475.
Silence is a great blue bell: 1000.
Silence, like white, is composed of a thousand colors: 5617.
Silence spoke with your voice: 5618.
The silent couples now re-enter town: 1710.
Silent, dispassionate, the night-long snow: 3340.
Silently He hung: 5621.
Silk's being made to look like linen: 6221.
Since flight is faith: 7178.
Since that wood has turned to stone: 1177.
Since certainty's the mother of repose: 3274.
Since Eden's dawn they'd wandered--man and child: 6944.
Since essays lean too much on reason: 4271.
Since I am mistress of my fate: 5003.
Since my stalwart son has grown: 3129.
Since of your kind so few: 375.
Sincerity: 5523.
Sing a song of mores!: 253.
Sing a song of six o'clock: 1773.
Sing, Coyote, on some far hill: 1267.
Singing he went, and...: 2590.
Singing sounds have turned to words: 2100.
Singing, they stand here, row on row: 1560.
The sins of man, transmitted into spouts: 2253.
Sir, as one royal personage to an-other: 5087.
Sir Lancelot was bad cess to his women: 7006.
Sister Adorata wiped her brow: 1708.
Sisterly: 5649.
Sit upon the floor with your back against: 889.
Sit you there on Lithostrotos, paved-in-stone: 562.
The site relives its tender monotone: 365.
Sitting at my knee shawled with the fire: 5640.
Sitting between the sea and the buildings: 4646.
Sitting here in my house: 6111.
Sitting in silence for an hour: 1207.
Sitting in them is relaxing: 3574.
Sitting with backs to the engine: 457.
Six foot four, with eyes of blue: 5639.
Six frail tomato plants looking half alive: 2613.
Six weeks I loved you; was by fever racked: 1214.

Sixteen for dinner, and she was: 5895.

Skaters upon thin ice: 645.

The skimmerand ideal? Na, but think: 6266.

The skinny stem above the sun-baked sand: 6756.

Skoal to the social anthropologist: 5095.

The skull of the old man wears a...: 686.

The sky bears heavily down upon this ochre: 297.

The sky being blue the air being sweet: 3036.

A sky calm, deserted, now noon-stunned: 378.

The sky hung idiot blue all windy day: 5666.

The sky is a bucket of stars tonight: 605.

The sky line is hazed with blue: 6715.

Sky over me: 3911.

The sky ran down in rain all night: 1844.

The sky stainless flawed by one gull: 3226.

The sky was a brazen gong: 2530.

The sky was darkened but for two rent clouds: 5320.

Slanting sunlight: 3360.

Slap. Clap: 5367.

The sleek creek: 3576.

Sleep is the ax, I've heard men say: 5195.

Sleep while the wings of: 2036.

Sleep would not come against those ritual bells: 6754.

Sleeping by the stump-fire, ashes in: 2405.

Sleepwalker, slave of wind, what is your name?: 2458.

Sliced and chilled: 4085.

A slight-boned animal, young: 5690.

Slow feathered fowl a peacock dragged his tail: 4728.

A small and perfect universe, each form: 5721.

Small as vulnerable as a bird: 6804.

The small astonished angels said: Who can that be?: 3957.

The small birds swirl around: 5689.

Small careful fingers, tracing these: 6369.

The small deep country which he made of songs: 1389.

Small master-builder, nigh invisible: 6519.

Small shifting knives of hundred-- broken sun: 3807.

Small sin: 4732.

Smaller size: 1487.

A smell of dried flounder broiling: 4041.

The smiling of women and motion: 308.

Smooth and swift their passing: 4684.

Smooth as a custard: 2020.

The snails have made a garden of green lace: 87.

"Snails lead slow idyllic lives...": 7146.

Snow fell as for Wencelas: 5324.

Snow had become scarce: 7245.

The snow is blue: 5727.

Snow is falling, falling snow: 5722.

Snow is meant for Heaven--where they wear: 5718.

The snow is the blood of these poor Dead... they have no other: 6950.

Snow is, today, the mind's remained: 658.

The snow lies patched on our enduring hills: 5728.

Snow, Mozartian profundity: 7228.

Snow on the gray crest of Mount Hermon wakes: 199.

The snow revives in the apple trees: 7090.

A snowflake by itself is frail: 1200.

Snows on the mountaintop: 1451.

So be it. Spiteful! Triumph in your spite: 3475.

So fair, so beautiful, so young: 1578.

So, having lost first and best love: 6508.

So innocent the scene, I feel I see it: 3205.

So it may be clear and inconceivable: 6963.

So, last night was spent at the Counters: 2407.

So little to write to one so far away: 3324.

So many altars: 854.

So many times I have felt them come, Lord: 5408.

So might we mourn for flowers: 2385.

So much biography is incipient in the present moment: 3410.

So much I've known of life, like towering music: 5742.

So much sun on the war, suddenly there is so much brilliance: 773.

So much to learn: 4808.

So populous the region: 2941.

So scrape the snow from off the wood: 3459.

So short a time ago this page of printing: 722.

So, standing on the bridge: 5313.

So, too, I think, did Mary late of night: 6697.

So turn to sky that does not drop a shadow: 382.

So very small the Christ-child was: 6040.

So we brought home the little tree: 6320.

So we set signs over the world to say: 568.

So, you are in Paris: 3326.

The soft crumbling of the wind and rain: 264.

Soft ferns of autumn awareness: 1777.

Soft lullaby of quiet cloud: 2329.

Soft, velvet grass erases all the scar: 2082.

The softer the better: 5752.

The softest day of Spring is Spring: 1169.

A softly lighted window in the air: 3880.
A soldier with no zest for fighting: 5883.
A soldier with no zest for living: 5882.
Solid as houses: 3191.
A solitary crow: 7212.
The solitary dooryard oak: 6195.
Some city parks, I think, are too austere: 3386.
Some day as we are sitting at our dinner: 6770.
Some days you can ignore the outer weather: 661.
Some folks enjoy winter: 2733.
Some forgotten Rhineland morning: 1342.
Some forty thousand feet above the trees: 1357.
Some girls are perfect little ladies: 1834.
Some labyrinths curl round like a sea shell: 2891.
Some mornings when I board the Broadway train: 6543.
Some of the bumbling keys are: 4436.
Some of you may know, others perhaps can guess: 304.
Some people are in favor of compromising, while others to compromise are loath: 6081.
Some people invest in real estate: 888.
Some pioneers, among the birds: 4818.
Some shapes cannot be seen in the glass: 2600.
Some shepherds see: 641.
Some silent, others full of talk: 5606.
Some sing when they've been given: 3879.
Some sod-cart dropped a weed: 5290.
Some things I simply can't resist: 6541.
Some things I would (if I could) steal: 483.
Some truths, like murder, stand: 2978.
Some women have a recipe: 6620.
Some women wear their clothes with an air: 1871.
Some years ago I first hunted on Sauvies Island: 5424.
Someday I shall return to an...: 1699.
Someday my hand shall tame your savage veins: 2229.
Someday not long hence: 3212.
Someday, when I am alone in your office: 2075.
Somehow the Chinese know that more than birds: 996.
Somehow the ropes that held its wonder swayed: 4236.
Somehow they dragged the charred wood from the pit: 7076.
Somehow to find a still spot in the noise: 1813.
Someone had made an error in the books: 3451.

Someone has idly set a record turning: 2834.
Someone watched the corn in the field. I thought it was: 3008.
Somer is icumen in: 5632.
Something any kid'll love: 750.
Something he sees: 712.
Something in me is lavender and lace: 7259.
Something of how the home bee at dusk: 5894.
Something once beautiful as a wave: 4535.
Something there is that doesn't like at all: 3063.
Something to do with catching Kelly smile: 3851.
Something was in the air of the chilly day: 5778.
Something's been added!: 3547.
Sometime past twelve as I locked up: 1384.
Sometimes a pet just won't stay home: 5994.
Sometimes, at Matins, jets rip up the sky: 929.
Sometimes I find it fun to: 5278.
Sometimes I have recognized: 6161.
Sometimes I think my nose will be: 4179.
Sometimes I think the sternest trial descends: 193.
Sometimes when: 4581.
Sometimes with nothing to do but to give ear: 4154.
Somewhere along the limped line: 6171.
Somewhere is peace: 4723.
The song of the Divine needs many ears: 5835.
The song of winds and running waves: 6823.
The song you sang you will not sing again: 3483.
The sonnets in the Pierian solitude: 3082.
Soon we'll be: 6047.
The sort of girl I like to see: 4420.
Sotis, Sothis, Sith, Venus, Venus, Mercury be near: 5197.
Soul, drink your fill!: 4244.
The soul soaring on indefinable: 5792.
Soul, the wanderer, fetch it out: 2180.
A sound like that of a meadowlark: 3709.
The sound of Calvary: 1288.
Sound of 'frigerator door: 7132.
Sound of wingbeat, murmur of running springs: 3296.
The sound of the reaper is gone from the field: 2991.
Sounds sum and summon the remembering of summers: 6145.
The sour note's sounded in love's sweet song: 776.
South in Tallahassee's bleakest reach: 6201.
South of Hiroshima, where the craggy coast of the Inland Sea: 6210.

Southward the gulls grow dovelike: 3155.
Space keeps us, time forgives us: 6603.
Space, vacant of wind and the sweep of
    silence: 1275.
Sparrow over the snow, O soft-shoe
    dander: 6437.
Speak carefully to my stofe and sink:
    4064.
"Speak it in Yiddish," I kept hearing:
    4477.
Speak of the conquest of outer space:
    4549.
Speak softly, Heart, nor cry aloud:
    2818.
Speak softly this morning: 6592.
Speak them slowly, space them so:
    2052.
The speaker who upsets me: 489.
Speaking out of a clear sky: 6683.
Speech in an orchard: 5920.
Speed, we say of our time; racing my
    writing word: 5921.
The spirit of the marshes stands: 7110.
Spring has betrayed me once again this
    year!: 6705.
Spring wheat sleeps green beneath this
    white: 7224.
Squirrelfaced Shelley is suddenly lit
    up: 4797.
The spider expects the cold of winter:
    5923.
The spider sits in his spider bed:
    3922.
A spider spun the dark from leaf to
    fence: 5924.
Spiders in your fragile web: 7007.
A spill of rain has damped the clean,
    boxed sand: 966.
Spinning her net of space: 4885.
Spinsters always write of sex: 412.
Spirits united to-day and tomorrow
    dispersed: 5282.
Splendid the grass he ran upon: 3331.
Splender of 70-year old: 2896.
Spoiled by all my tyrants, and whomped
    to bed: 5938.
Spontaneous bottle out of which: 5939.
Spring birds wing to the feeding tray:
    1577.
A spring-breath sighing by: 5743.
Spring comes and autumn goes:
    5908.
Spring is a juice: 5646.
Spring is strong and virtuous: 5638.
Spring is your season. Where you
    are...: 5244.
Spring lingered late inside this rim
    of hills: 3126.
Spring, my Father's youngest daughter:
    6191.
Spring shows: 3015.
Spring, the sweet Spring, is the
    year's pleasant king: 866.
Spring wheat sleeps green beneath
    this white: 573.
The spring's first freighter: 4176.
Staff should have a helping hand:
    5985.
Stale is the air, and vacant is the
    room: 4532.

Stalemated their armies stood, with
    tottering banners: 5729.
Stand up, Lord, in the boat: 4689.
...standing alone by the sea: 6900.
Standing beside the grave: 3728.
Standing on top of the hay: 3769.
A star: 3797.
A star hit in the hills behind our
    house: 6028.
Starfish, crayfish, sea-: 1204.
Staring at the east: 5259.
The stars: 4044.
Stars for the sake of whom I know
    not: 1089.
The stars of wonder swing across the
    streets: 2060.
The startled mind within the mind:
    6478.
Startled to life: 6586.
The state of Minnesota is a wonder:
    2108.
The state of the union, the devalued
    dollar: 6006.
Statistic, mechanically issuing out
    of the mimeograph: 3619.
Statistics prove this bit of lore:
    6991.
The statue of Balenciage was
    dripping into other statues: 1399.
Stay me, Constable, on the stone
    bridge: 531.
Stenographers must have bothe will...:
    4203.
Step softly in this gold and crimson
    wood: 2162.
Stepping on air in slippered toes:
    1922.
Steve is Davy Crockett: 3452.
Still abandoned to her travels: 1872.
The still explosions on the rocks:
    5560.
Still half drunk, after a night at
    cards: 1367.
Still in the cold blue silence by:
    7208.
Still shafts, substantial light: 6103.
Stilted as scarecrows, sickly, sickly:
    2652.
Stirring porch pots up with green-
    figured: 346.
Stone, a pebble, pounded: 7048.
A stone axe among others: 3979.
Stone by stone I pile: 3662.
The stone-faced clock listens through
    her eyeglass: 1079.
A stone placed inside before baking:
    1069.
The stone without edges has not been
    mined: 6553.
The Stony Lonesome cattle: 6060.
The stories have all burned out like
    fires: 5038.
The storm began to prove the world will
    end: 6065.
A storm is brewing somewhere: 2990.
The storm-swallow nests where the land
    fails: 6072.
Storm that prevailed against the gold:
    5818.

Stout, ungainly beetle, parting early mist: 5449.
Straight down, the noon was boarding up the trees: 5377.
Straight runs the road to Chartres, and sharply flutes: 1p18.
The strange perfume of the milkweed: 23.
The strange road passing Hawley: 1007.
Strange under land trees: 3776.
Strange Western town at the round edge of night: 7033.
Stranger, ignore yon loud bassoon: 6324.
Strangers in the mob of our resemblances: 6994.
The stream divided for a space: 6248.
Streets creak with cold, and deepening snow: 5251.
Streets opening like wounds: 1500.
Streets where the moral man: 3746.
The strength of your waiting knew me: 1330.
The strings of my guitar are e: 4821.
The strip of cloud flings: 5586.
Strong are the thews of old contentment: 6294.
The strong white hand, the voice: 4576.
The strongest ties are the weakest ones: 1721.
Struggle makes its own strice sense: 33.
The students, puzzled that a gal would stew: 3831.
Studillac, Fuick, Chevrolash, Chrysoto: 2645.
Stunned by the Consecrated Frown of this Child: 5162.
Style is the water out of Homer: 2245.
Success is a test where it may be said: 1337.
Successful men look much alike: 7057.
Such folly of margins that may retaliate: 313.
Such means to simplify our lives we've known: 114.
Such privilege was his to stay bewitched: 970.
The sudden morning startled us with light: 7056.
Suddenly all of the dead were dancing: 2860.
Suddenly all the clocks stopped ticking: 1390.
Suddenly in summer: 6125.
Suddenly, one summer morning: 2999.
Suddenly there on the paper air: 1564.
The suit was a steal at $22.50: 497.
Summer clothes are scanty, yes: 7301.
Summer grows old, cold-blooded mother: 2177.
Summer knowledge is not the winter's truth: 6139.
A summer night: 2499.
Summer was hot and dry: 243.
Summon the Pinkertons! Call out the guards!: 3525.
Summoned to desolation by the dawn: 3902.

The sun: 5525.
The sun: 2304.
The sun and the moon: 1320.
The sun at noon: 6794.
The sun came roaring round: 6173.
The sun has no appetite. In the forbidden park: 4969.
The sun is not in love with me: 3030.
Sun makes a gold path on the sea: 5471.
Sun over all and air over all and clover: 3768.
The sun passes: 6810.
The sun said: "Stop, and see me 'round." How could I?: 178.
The sun shines west: 6822.
Sun suit, bonnet, shovel, Paul: 3823.
The sun that climbed my wall made a slow music: 6318.
Sunday drivers are those: 3278.
The Sunday endless on the wide bank: 385.
Sunlight the tall women may never have seen: 985.
The sun's a slovenly char: 6328.
Sunset, a flock of waiting sheep: 5106.
Suppose an angel slipped down on a rope: 5103.
Suppose the peeling seasons crack:
Suppose your house was entered by some silly stranger who: 7366.
Surely the morning was made: 1360.
Surely the slash of birds: 3599.
Surely we knew our darkling shore:
Surely you folks must know about me: 2815.
Surely that moan is not the thing: 2032.
Surely the rain, surely the pine: 4552.
Surmise: 6188.
Susan started school today: 6091.
A swamp with nakedness, pulled to a consummate of of body: 6159.
A swan among goslings: 6245.
A swan's dive's one that I eschew: 2573.
Swearing his age and festering leg: 1837.
Sweet beast, I have gone prowling: 5797.
Sweet influences keep the planet sweet: 5.
Sweet process, rose-blue: 5506.
Sweet William's breath: 6208.
The sweet wind climbed with a laggard pace: 3391.
The sweetest pear-shaped tones were once: 4084.
Swift be my passing, like a falling star: 6027.
Swim little king-fish. Leap small salmon: 863.
Sy at first but quick: 5266.
The sycamore stood tall as Time: 6216.
The table overflows. We thank Thee, God: 5820.
Tail swinging like a walking stick to lop: 82.
Take a pot with water in it: 4091.
Take all you have, the Bible says...: 1520.

The tale is different if even a single breath: 5584.
Taken from the women for the chorus: 5475.
The tale of the black man's grim journey: 6539.
The tales they tale of McGee, McGrew: 4765.
Talk to me if you will, my dear: 2801.
Tall are the mountains of Christmas: 6244.
Tall Atlas, Jupiter, Hercules, Thor: 1433.
Tall cities flamed in the sun along their seafront: 5479.
Tamperer vainly tidying up the stream: 1756.
A tangible shape of water, earth and air: 2223.
A tarrying moon still drips the redness of her blood: 3798.
A taut tone scrapes a scarred mute: 441.
Tear-shaped and colored like the moon: 6957.
Tears of ages: 448.
The technician pulled out all the comrade's teeth: 4506.
The telephone line goes cold: 1863.
Tell fables, Lamp, oh honey: 3216.
"Tell me a story," you said: 6283.
Tell me all things: 6169.
Tell me not that there is no purpose: 5826.
Tell me the wind is but a whimper--: 6282.
Tell tell me poetry doesn't pay: 1552.
Tell that neighbor girl: 1935.
Tell young stranger on the stairs: 2806.
The tellers of myths and folk tales had it right: 3865.
The temple of the animals has fallen into disrepair: 6289.
The temples of God, the stalwart: 416.
Tempted by a taunting Devil: 3675.
The ten-branched truth and the real lie: 6464.
Ten cuckolds slain without confession: 1539.
Ten thousand times ten thousand miles away: 736.
Ten years ago our courtship had become: 3557.
Ten years ago, who chased me madly at the Mutter fair?: 6965.
Ten years and more I have walked since I finished school: 1511.
Ten years of age and intent upon a tea-brown burn: 6688.
The tendency to brood and fret: 7138.
A tender goddess came of a south wind: 5122.
The tennis court is fenced with a tall: 7015.
Teresa, the cook, was biscuit-colored: 6300.
Thames, mortal hubris beggars us: 1890.

Than a choice of subject: 945.
Thank You for the availability of You: 6311.
Thanksgiving, Lord, for all the shining thing: 6316.
That beauty's only skin deep: 6184.
That coarse and unmelodious song: 6792.
That day everything went wrong: 4905.
That dim shattering character of nerves: 2334.
That evening we met on Prospero's strand: 333.
That great, meaningless poem! It races...: 2871.
That I did not walk into the waves that day: 2954.
That is dawn, that light in the west: 391.
That keeping up with building trends: 2655.
That man's subconscious mind is constituted: 4310.
That March had a neck like an animal: 221.
That matter, Lord, we talked about so very long: 4986.
That morning, when I heard the news, I went into the street: 596.
That's the queer life, said the chair: 920.
That "Once" she dropped her red pegnoir: 533.
That park, full of social meaning: 2960.
That plump girl in the second row: 5431.
That poplar tree is ten years old: 7116.
That princeling bland with dapper smiles for daylit danger: 2552.
That raise the improbable to an art: 1535.
That sea we see of surfaces: 6213.
That she does me a favor to: 5693.
That she is dead is terrible: 1381.
That she's redheaded assogms": 3860.
That short-sleeved man: 3860.
That Sunday morning, at half past ten: 469.
That was the Sunday everybody was good: 1468.
That was the summer I didn't sleep at all: 4169.
That way the moonflower and the sunflower this: 6677.
That which is beatific about: 550.
That which you are: 7124.
That windless hour of dawn when madness wakes: 390.
That year winter never came at all: 745.
That yellow circle is the sun: 322.
That's a detestable thing you did!: 1417.
That's a sore point. I was wounded there: 640.
That's being told by someone else: 1999.

That's enough, I said to the morning dove: 4212.
Their faces, safe as an interior: 3794.
Their growing-up point: 4481.
Their stares of stark astonishment: 2548.
Their wheel broke down, their kingdom's turning wheel: 6482.
Then all the listening cries of nature cried out Danger: 4857.
Then felt I like some spotter of the skies: 4453.
Then let this present act: 5183.
Then the visionary lady: 5919.
Then, there are folks who talk and talk: 3358.
Then what are they coming to take me to?: 5656.
Then when love needs you do you lean away: 2648.
There are children ringing bells tonight: 142.
There are days when living: 6129.
There are designs in curtains that can kill: 2010.
There are enchanting remedies, they say: 4504.
There are kisses to remember: 3407.
There are no friends like: 3052.
There are other worlds than ours: 6337.
There are places which my heart: 6338.
There are several attitudes toward a poem: 4512.
There are skirts with sequin clusters: 148.
There are some quiet crossings in his city: 6973.
There are such; I have seen them: 6119.
There are taboos here it would be wise to consider: 372.
There are tears to being woman: 2125.
There are the aeon and the age: 3863.
There are the spires of chimney pots: 7172.
There are times when I despair of my brains: 2811.
There are too many waterfalls here: 5098.
There as usual, she stood: 100.
There at Auschwitz, far from the Vistula: 411.
There goes my child: 6339.
There goes the piper: 4822.
There in Bologna eight saints are lodged: 3383.
There is a chant that goes with skipping rope: 5664.
There is a lady in our town: 3430.
There is a line dragging down: 3398.
There is a little bird that comes and cries: 6720.
There is a panther stalks me down: 5072.
There is a point past which the contemplation: 3088.
There is a rain: 7336.
There is a region stranger far: 559.
There is a shore line on the edge of sleep: 1653.

There is a silence where children have played: 7085.
There is a silent question: 3737.
There is a valiant look about new: 4076.
There is a woman in our town: 7254.
There is another country to the north: 6692.
There is no dew tonight: 6343.
There is no noise as the stairs turn: 3779.
There is no road in the wilderness: 7153.
There is snow. Beneath its preoccupation: 7227.
There is some lost Nicaea: 1035.
There is something: 5064.
There is a spite in me: 6411.
There is a sun every head--: 2547.
There is a time for coffee and the wine: 2147.
There is a time when a man should stand: 6341.
There is a time when only the hall lights glisten: 551.
There is a weeping in the palace, the king is weeping: 295.
There is an ancient forest, its giant trees: 2022.
There is an inner patterning of mind: 3152.
There is an instant of rest for the heavy driving heart: 2944.
There is but one for whom I make this song: 6342.
There is his torso to take apart: 3687.
There is in man a deeper weave: 2692.
There is much to be said for the portrait painted in winter: 4938.
There is no island here: 895.
There is no luxury in accomplishment: 6118.
There is no man but one: 4147.
There is no nourishment in verbs: 4522.
There is no one alive so lean: 5842.
There is no reason for the things I know: 1222.
There is no reason in it: 1453.
There is no stillness: 6055.
There is no time now for words: 4475.
There is nothing no nothing like it: 2541.
There is something the matter: 180.
There is the famous Babel Tower: 6634.
There is very little poetry about war: 6949.
There isn't a lady now alive: 2515.
There may be some guile in the man with a smile: 2623.
There must be language to reconstruct that country: 3539.
There must be so many souls washing: 5478.
There once was an owl perched on a shed: 6345.
There seemed the two of us within the dream: 6986.

There she stands as though we'd pre-arranged: 4463.
There the gold falls...: 4578.
There the three maidens are standing: 318.
There was a cow that said moo: 4171.
There was a happy secret in her eyes: 7367.
There was a little elvish man: 3634.
There was a morning to remember well: 3122.
There was a rat: 1822.
There was a squint-eyed holy-man who shoved: 251.
There was a young farmer named Stout: 2357.
There was no printing press in Homer's day: 5633.
There was once a guy: 5615.
There were many people on the island: 2169.
There were no trumpets blaring on the hill: 4083.
There were three: 1239.
There were three small pegs: 6426.
There where transported, partial Greece: 107.
There will be endless moors to tramp: 5457.
There ye gang, ye daft: 2360.
There you lie dead. You were...: 7140.
There'll Come a day!: 6346.
There's a doctor in our family: 1529.
There's a high white count in what I call my sporting blood: 1913.
There's a race of men that don't fit in: 3757.
There's a stone deer in the garden and two or three nude: 2019.
There's a thin wild song on the tele-phone wire: 2119.
There's more than beauty here: 5220.
There's an Alsop on the Tribune: 4914.
There's just ourselves: 913.
There's no arrangement: 791.
There's no goodbye to heat, for melted tar: 6153.
There's quite a barbecue next door: 5708.
There's so much to be known, and so much to be done...: 1171.
There's this to say: 8153.
The thermometer dipped at night in: 403.
These acres ripple in the sun: 4636.
These are for burning: 688.
These are no strolling bear cub's prints: 6096.
These are the elements tamed from the Void: 3113.
These are the scents I have known today: 4752.
These are those who: 5047.
These autos, a nice class: 5942.
These chill communiques that haunt the page: 2605.
These friends of yours are hard to understand: 6350.
These horned islands that the possing seas: 6866.

These leaves, so deeply and so lately green: 1122.
These locks on doors have brought me happiness: 3487.
These lovers have wandered away from each other into: 6351.
These rolling hills lie down at night: 1254.
These shameful eyes can only flinch and blear: 6299.
These streets are so forsaken I would say: 907.
These Sunday things remind me of you, sweet: 6354.
These things I find too strenuous: 2531.
These trucks invade my sleep like an enraged truth: 6691.
These warmer afternoons, we've found: 1561.
These winds of Martinmas have stripped the trees: 4229.
These words of violence are not my own: 5877.
Theseus: Was he an old, bald King of Athens: 2562.
They all have weary, weary mouths: 215.
They all set out to shoot the mocking birds: 7370.
They all spoke softly about her: 3195.
They are all navigable now, the great oceans of the void: 1067.
They are building a wall around you: 6934.
They are yours for the picking: 1268.
They arranged what was left and put it away: 1725.
They buried the soldiers where they fell: 374.
They call to pass the time with Giovanni: 2294.
They came, the rangers of the other side, those unknown: 3001.
They cannot read or write or spell: 5035.
They come unwilling: 6032.
They cross the frontier as their names cross your pages: 4074.
They did not know the story of the cross: 2830.
They died to save the world and they prevailed: 6948.
They don't always cook like: 1140.
They fain in labor for the while idea: 7111.
They have become no legend: 3526.
They have numbered all my limbs: 3510.
They have the right to smile, being parents of the good life: 4746.
They left him hanging for the deed: 4537.
They lie dressed right in uniform: 2058.
They live together in peace, the sparrow, the wren: 4060.
They lynched Him too, you know: 6402.
They made her a grave too cold and damp: 474.
They now predict a hurricane: 6073.

They nudged "who's that"?: 1820.
They pay him court, the weekly clan: 4708.
They said it was the year of the locusts: 5550.
They said, "Leave your castle in the sand...": 969.
They said that Guinevere had hands like foam: 7113.
They say in that far land all flowers wither: 5048.
They say in town, a spectre has been seen: 2762.
They say that winter is cold: 3500.
They searched the attic and came down: 2601.
They seemed this morning on their way to work: 3839.
They sing: 851.
They sit with colanders on their knees: 2418.
They stalk the streets in bold, opaque: 4777.
They stumbled to their hill of sacrifice: 2153.
They threaten us with war: 6538.
They took the tinsel down from the tree: 7220.
They wave their arms: 2435.
They were like sofa-cushions: 7051.
They were passing impetuously: 4906.
They were small waves: 2921.
They were spraying 7-up and moth-juice: 490.
They who impelled by loneliness at end: 2089.
They who sit in luxury's lap: 6788.
They worked, not for eight hours a day: 1791.
They would birch me, then church me: 1692.
They wove into their hair the marguerites: 6722.
They'd charge a bit less, of course, in the off season: 3958.
They'd known her long who chose her epitaph: 3936.
They're apt to blither at things that slither: 7136.
They're so meticulous: 5194.
They're still devoted and adoring: 4096.
They're using jeeps to turn the cane 3084.
They've built a perfect replica: 3706.
They've come to an untimely end: 928.
Thin as April then and leafed to please: 4834.
Thin as memory to a bloodhound's nose: 6363.
A thin layer of gray hair, broad forehead: 2920.
A thin layer of gray hair, broad forehead: 2902.
The thin new paint is on the walls: 5803.
Thin shoulder swung to debonair: 1598.

The thing called success: 6764.
The thing he sees: 718.
The thing that cannot be spoken: 1832.
The thing to do is to try for that sweet skin: 903.
Things change the morning of the birthday: 4440.
Things disappear. The ball that flew: 3531.
The things for which I always get: 3033.
Things that were lumped "too numerous to mention.": 1864.
Think no more of me: 5757.
Think of this, that man is the enemy of man: 6365.
Thinking causes shrinking: 5389.
Thinking of summer in these days of fall: 4769.
Thinking of the capsized harbor: 3238.
Thirty today, I saw: 628.
This age of civil strife is not an age for poetry: 4907.
This Aztec mask moved through the August vineyard: 3785.
This back yard: 2249.
This bibliophile we'd like to put: 3359.
This castle of your being I will name desert: 5150.
This chair I trusted, lass, and I looted the leaves: 296.
This Christmas, Pete's fourteen and he has told: 376.
This coast's not: 4200.
This crow, my love, black bird: 5531.
This cypress was a cypress: 3671.
This dainty writing box with inlaid pearl: 7292.
This day brings pandemonium: 3719.
This dream budded bright with leaves around the edges: 1573.
This dream of yours! Time melts. And all the pages: 5013.
This dying bridge of a hundred thousand ants: 884.
This fine long multitudinous unending sound: 5125.
This garden is outlandish: 7270.
This garden is the summer's soul at ease: 6378.
This 'gator, alchemist of learned "chops.": 2736.
This holler guy who we are following: 2602.
This holy night in open forum: 4355.
This hot, acacia wilderness of noon: 1672.
This house has been far out at see all night: 7159.
This house is lovely, yes, but it is new: 6512.
This I saw on St. Ives Acres: 6115.
This idiot had suffered his own faults: 4104.
This, if you please: 7250.
This is a birth conceived before: 4005.
This is a book that thrilled not once but twice: 6449.

This is a boy: 1972.
This is a country where there are no mountains: 3909.
This is a day of little shining showers: 6779.
This is a day when good men die from windows: 1392.
This is a little town you'll never know: 796.
This is a man with an old face, always old: 1062.
This is a narrative dirge about: 4039.
This is a quiet country: 2278.
This is a snow scene on rice paper: 5731.
This is a very tall river: 3837.
This is a water-colored time of year: 287.
This is about the stillness in moving things: 5376.
This is an immaculate land: 3773.
This is it: 3118.
This is it: by the pungent smell from the flocks: 5947.
This is my prayer, and has been from my youth: 1421.
This is my time of attention: 1059.
This is remembered when the hairs drop out: 6381.
This is the age: 5140.
This is the beauty that catches a man: 6382.
This is the case of a high-school land: 849.
This is the day of all the days: 3919.
This is my son and hers who bore the weight: 5874.
This is the day when on the hills of noon: 3866.
This is the era of the positive negative: 5782.
This is the first big snowfall of the year: 1975.
This is the first rain of spring: 1970.
This is the Gaeltacht where they fled--: 5264.
This is the grass your feet are planted on: 5379.
This is the hour: 2647.
This is the lad who brought the branch: 5713.
This is the land of my father's cross: 6898.
This is the month of autumn charity: 4283.
This is the month we are aware of grasses: 5527.
This is the nut-brown time of year: 4290.
This is the one morning of the year: 1809.
This is the place. I dreamed when Oklahoma: 1835.
This is the place that time has long forgot: 6383.
This is the place where summer comes to sleep: 748.
This is the point where all arguments fail: 7091.

This is the season the great crystal-line flocks: 3651.
This is the smooth maroon horse-chest-nut that fell: 5709.
This is the springtime of my year: 7037.
This is the summer season, golden fruit hangs full and mellow: 1371.
This is the sun you knew and loved of old: 6384.
This is the sun's high exultation: 6134.
This is the tale of Quintius Quip: 1314.
This is the theory of relativity: 1602.
This is the time of year: 301.
This is the trail: 3809.
This is the waiting time, lonely with love: 48.
This is the way: 6154.
This is the way it starts, you know: 3838.
This isn't a spring: 5971.
This lady, curled like a shell: 5571.
This lifelike toy a small boy: 5518.
This light is loss backward; delight by hurt and bias gained: 3652.
This little winding road by day and night: 455.
This lonely figure of not much fun: 10.
This lonely following in the old town: 3409.
This magic glass: 6280.
This man, this poet, said: 5906.
This matter, wife, is troubling me: 2570.
This may be the last; time is out on the old river: 4514.
This may seem strange: 2381.
This moment will not fit: 5654.
This morning, counting my assorted selves: 7327.
This morning, daughters, as we play: 115.
This morning in the shadows there was frost: 1843.
This morning, overpowered: 3477.
This morning, rolling through a cloud: 1121.
This morning, somewhere in the mass: 3843.
This morning we were witness to: 4660.
This morning we were witness to: 4660.
This moth caught in the room tonight: 3598.
This mound the sea side lifts of growing red: 2523.
This must be done in narrative form: 6736.
This nun the flaming lance could sanc-tify: 6301.
This part of ocean, this far-traveled swell: 6391.
This placard wouldn't be posted: 4958.
This plump and handsome rat: 5983.
This porthole overlooks a sea: 572.

This question and difficulty is con-
founding me: 2274.
This radio says that snow: 2118.
This red lopsided heart: 990.
This rubble of stained glass: 1675.
This sky is unmistakable: 504.
This soap ad shows for no clear reason
birds: 2817.
This song is for the angels: 880.
This Spring, being what it is this
year: 5611.
This star is only an augury of the
morning: 197.
This suits my mood: 4112.
This sunday in late February: 1234.
This table? Oh, it's nothing much--:
3130.
This tenth one was a diver, the thin
blade--: 6298.
This the faith our Lord embraced: 7082.
This, then, is all: 5627.
This, then, is the child's wish: 1464.
This toddling daughter seems to be:
2878.
This tooth, which came early to re-
place the childhood one: 6811.
This town fits me like a glove--:
2616.
This train: sleek, sure, no long-
lost local, brake-bound: 2176.
This valentine is just to tell: 519.
This was a day that nature put to-
gether: 4704.
This was our mother: 4966.
This was the adopted: 2883.
This was the color of coolness: 5951.
This was the end and yet, another start:
3767.
This way in the green garden: 4358.
This whole matter of the national
economy is exquisitely simple: 4189.
This winter--another winter--: 4069.
This yonder death: 6380.
This youth carries in his palm or
pocket: 726.
The thistle blossoms and the thorn:
6751.
Those abysses of silence where roses
grew...: 6398.
Those children who were born with coats
of light: 982.
Those eyes shifting the scenery: 5089.
Those Fulbright..: 6442.
Those three men walking down that
slope toward dawn: 3946.
Those were the days: 2351.
Those who will be compelled to dance:
1498.
Those words footloose and fancy-free:
1503.
Thou art so small: 1154.
Thou fair-hair'd angel of the evening:
6589.
Thou sayest chivalry: 3182.
Thou shalt have trouble trying me:
6401.
Though children provide family weather:
1854.
Though constant practice and teacher
skills: 786.

Though death will trap you in the end:
6509.
Though doors are quite handy: 5783.
Though English Church and State: 4762.
Though Eve must have wept for Eden's
loss: 6667.
Though grass is not: 6420.
Though gypsy feet may carry me: 3490.
Though I admit without reservations
that if children take tobacco,
liquor, or opium: 3988.
Though I am sick: 3553.
Though I now live here: 1716.
Though I smolder with secret passions:
2216.
Though I'm first to agree: 3572.
Though I'm overly sleepy these morn-
ings: 1299.
Though I've taken my legal deductions:
2662.
Though John McClellan (Arkansas) is
apt to use the lash: 3764.
Though love is done, I'm glad to say:
3558.
Though man's bemoaned, no: 4639.
Though many a person: 6037.
Though marriages may be made in heaven:
1459.
Though more than beast, these poets
boast of their unhuman minds: 3758.
Though my wallet is thick: 3506.
Though people approve of the...:
3930.
Though Peter was the first Pope: 5328.
Though rather fond of quizzes: 6701.
Though silken-fragile is the rose:
6914.
Though soft and pliable, you do not
crumple: 484.
Though sound has ceased: 765.
Though temper outbursts often seem:
6288.
Though tools are made for fixing
things: 1933.
Though traitor angels ply the subtlest
art: 7376.
Though traveler or passer-by: 5323.
Though we before the summer is done:
2965.
Though well acquainted, Mind and
Heart: 4656.
Though you are there tonight and I
am here: 2522.
Though you were once the hand that
teemed: 6559.
Thoughtlessly homing in a rainy twi-
light: 1705.
The thoughts came to him like long
lines of freight: 5853.
A thousand years have come and gone:
1778.
Threat of death draws F. B. I.: 4900.
Three counties, white and green:
280.
Three deaths: the squirrel, the
partridge, and the dove: 6232.
A three-pound pickax of steel: 7302.
Thrice happy am I in His love: 6673.
Three thousand miles and nearly half a
year: 3267.

The three tricornes beat up against the gale: 5747.

Three there be - and only three: 6231.

Three years I lolled in that country of the girls: 4354.

Through a dark screen with many a green-stemmed bough: 240.

Through fruitless years: 4.

Through leaf-waves lapping warm up against the sky: 1572.

Through massive oak blows the wind: 5931.

Through my window: 906.

Through seasons elegant or rude: 5164.

Through the birch's whited boughs: 7063.

Through the clear: 5958.

Through the jungles: 3347.

Through the night, the dark morning hours: 5891.

Through the sea, a chill: 3273.

Through these two mirrors, or holes in the face: 1106.

Through woods Madame Une Telle, a trifle ill: 422.

Thrown backward first, head over heels in the wind: 6565.

Thrusting through the wall of dark-ness: 2005.

A thumb and a forefinger on the eyes: 2055.

Thump. Thump. The door: 1544.

The thunders crashed: 1240.

Thus, on a summer evening, how the light: 1460.

Thy mercies, Lord, a multitude: 3970.

Thy speaking of Him, Mother, flings: 4402.

The thylacine, long thought to be ex-tinct: 4380.

Tick-a-lock rock-a-bye: 989.

The tide is rising under the beached boat: 6462.

Tide of those tractions that are modern life: 63.

Tidy by nature, I make it my chore: 5978.

Tight-socketed in space, the watch: 4922.

Tile be green tile: 749.

Till thinking had worn out my enter-prise: 5967.

Timbers heaving to heaven we sailed at seven: 1270.

Time breathes upon your hair and stains it silver: 3556.

The time came: 6470.

Time is thy loyal subject, Lord: 6466.

Time, linger here, here stay: 4426.

Time need not hurry you: you had seasons: 3119.

The time of year has grown indifferent: 5784.

Time sighs for dust and ever as she sighs: 6366.

Time to put food on to cook: 1993.

Time was, we said; and once upon a time: 6333.

Time was I used to knock on wood: 3694.

Time was when death: 6480.

Time-weathered arm against time-weathered timed: 3631.

The time when 31 seems old: 6276.

They will not wait for us: 6194.

Tinged leaves lie: 2872.

Tinkle, tonkle, tinkle, ting: 842.

A tiny cover: 5696.

Tired? Let go!: 4695.

Tired, yes, I am tired: 2131.

The tireless clover climbs the drapery: 4488.

'Tis fine to read of Daniel Boone, and Madeline and Ben: 1202.

To a scientist: 6516.

To anglers galore: 1990.

To ask forgiveness is not easy: 337.

To aid a memory that's a mess: 2496.

To all of you our greetings hearty: 5487.

To be a man most surely pass off: 6412.

To be in so few years translated from: 2009.

To be in want and one's last pittance wring: 1752.

To be struck by a taxicab: 2666.

To be unlike most people: 7298.

To beg your Valentine were to be-stow: 6830.

To begin as the riven: 6535.

To congregate below the street: 1037.

To disappear is proper in a country: 73.

To "do it yourself": 6699.

To do our work we need know how: 5996.

To eat and run is not polite: 6595.

To find all virtues: 5521.

To find her hidden talents she: 5276.

To forget self and all, forget fore-most: 6546.

To go to bed I have to be: 5828.

To jitterbug with effervescence: 2626.

To keep awake, Sun Ching: 5447.

To know despair: 1006.

To know that marriages come quickly, observe, consult the young: 742.

To learn this expedient took me too long: 4562.

To look down one thousand feet: 3511.

To love one woman, or to sit: 7256.

To love one's fellow man: 2528.

To make a husband squirm inside: 1176.

To me lying hear sleep, at the pale edge: 3657.

To most, the impossible dream, the face: 4323.

To my grateful eye: 1378.

To my regret the silhouette: 6322.

To one who had lost his armband...: 1388.

To other's tone: 236.

To own nothing, but to be: 7297.

To pass inhuman barriers: 5364.

To pay as you go: 3035.

To reason with an adolescent boy: 710.
To reckon height I lie along your side: 3713.
To see my small son: 7.
To see myself as others see me: 7127.
To sing the unsung hero is: 2865.
To stop at the window of a shop: 3853.
To tell lowbrow from high brow: 3053.
To the cheese, a mouse: 3611.
To the cleaners with his trousers: 720.
To the end of time mankind will hold: 1016.
To the four waters of this blood: 5263.
To the list of history's greats: 2467.
To them who prate of sense of humor: 6607.
To think of Troy now Lent is down: 5876.
To this earth, whereon the winds are cold: 473.
To understand is to be misunderstood: 1247.
To whom the bass pay homage: 507.
To win her favor try: 2588.
To writers of humor this offers a hint: 1764.
To write upon the sand, to write on cliffs: 733.
To you, Fletcher, from my dark house asleep: 4542.
To your clean hands I now commend: 6591.
Today I looked with clearer eyes and saw: 1759.
Today I stood and watched an opening leaf: 3279.
Today is not tomorrow: 6617.
Today is so Swiss, that if I had for-gotten: 2389.
Today is the day of beer and skittles: 4265.
Today is the occasion for the mouthing of obliquities and platitudes: 2086.
Today makes 20 days: 5834.
Today on a sandy road: 4435.
Today, or maybe yesterday, the minnows returned: 5962.
Today the Congo is a glass wherein: 1179.
Today we picked flowers in spite of the snow: 4672.
Today we set this post to point the line: 3401.
Today when buying eggs, I find: 4191.
Today you need me. Now you ask: 6673.
Together we braid flowers: 4678.
Together we whittled a stick of sunny: 6636.
Togetherness, the watchword of the age: 2399.
Tomorrow wears so wide a pocket: 4849.
Tonight I am a stricken thing: 6799.
Tonight I lit the first fire of the season: 4551.
Tonight I looked into your thousandth book: 2140.

Tonight is the night all children seek: 4457.
Too grave for speech in a bleak and lonely silence: 3074.
Too late I met you and too soon I gave: 3552.
Too many couples: 4155.
Too many folk: 4117.
Too many hearts come like too fluid noses: 1093.
Too old to play with paper-dolls: 2844.
Too proud to die, broken and blind he died: 1674.
Too sheerly bone and beautiful, those ankles: 684.
The toothbrush lies in its case: 4165.
The tortoise, introverted wight: 2556.
Touching in sleep, my only speech: 4120.
Towards morning the sun stalked within the forest: 3020.
The towers of Ilium are low: 6649.
The toys of childhood for a heritage: 4836.
The toys which they'll squabble and scream over: 5043.
Tracing Picasso's flashbulb line: 3284.
The tragic man stares at the sun: 1090.
A train, an April rain and thou: 1147.
The traits of the too-eager beaver: 1715.
Trapped like an idiot in a wilderness of feeling: 3540.
Travelers who came that day to Pisa's Baptistry: 1646.
Travelling the well-known road: 1051.
Treachery, unfaith, loose-slippered untruth: 11.
A tree can be a forest when: 2416.
A tree is a crow's castle: 1293.
A tree of gulls towers: 1631.
The tree of heaven, ailanthus, grows like weed: 6665.
Tree of her name, I bother the muted bells: 4713.
Trees and grass stand all right: 2455.
Trees are like clumsy giants: 2280.
The trees in clouds of November mist: 1622.
Trees, mountains, rocks: 535.
The trembling words: 1702.
Tremendous eyes and trembly chin: 7135.
The tribes of Limbo, Travelers re-port: 3394.
The triumphant papers came, out of the past: 4466.
True, we are thrown on earth like babes, and see: 557.
Truly, people are a forest: 6652.
Trumpet and drum, the old soldier said: 4407.
Trust, if insured: 3368.
"Trust in the future! It will right all wrongs!": 6693.
Trusting neither clothes nor wit: 7253.
The truth I do not stretch or shove: 1902.

Try, with a proverb: 5448.
Trying to speak to a woman vacuuming: 54.
Tsokadze leans unknowingly: 6696.
A tub's a place to brood: 2637.
Tucked away in musty nooks: 2927.
Tuesday when you opened your eyes your: 2197.
Tumbling among its stones: 3194.
The tune at first is odd, though still familiar: 2487.
Turin beneath, on the green banks of the Po: 381.
The Turk's-cap like lily unfolds his flowers: 615.
Turmoil is over: 5329.
Turn from high road, right to: 5318.
Turn inward on the brain: 7053.
Turn. In spring-up green freshed: 5143.
Turn like a top, spin on your dusty axis: 2979.
Turn, river giving the land the length of young: 5712.
Turn, turn: 164.
Turning over old earth: 1184.
The turning-point is morning: 4991.
The turtles I've coped with!: 4773.
"Twas the night before Christmas: 2789.
'Twas the night before Christmas, when all through the house: 6706.
Twenty little maidens: 6155.
Twice a year: 156.
Two aerial tigers: 6967.
Two birds flying East, hit the night: 1445.
Two flocks I see: 2366.
Two girls there are: within the house: 6739.
Two go down and one come back: 5841.
Two guardian angels awaited us, motionless in darkness: 2449.
Two little rabbits-- the tale's for kids of four: 6594.
Two lovers walking in a lovers' garden: 6929.
Two never-ever-will-be lovers each: 3697.
Two swimmers of a summer sea: 2103.
Two things I saw on the way to the office: 3280.
Two virtues ride, by stallion, by nag: 1396.
The typewriter-bird with the pitch-fork beak: 6752.
U. S.-- officials and employees: 37.
The ugly duckling pleases you and me: 6755.
Ultimately we come to love the dead: 6473.
The unaccustomed speaker speaks: 5915.
Uncertainly he takes his place: 1963.
The uncles live on: Augustus, Geoffrey: 6763.
Under Nikko-Zan the Mountains: 4131.
Under the bluegreen surface of the se: 3513.
Under the bright sea lies the coral reef: 1229.
Under the bulb the stun: 3952.
Under the cedar tree: 5039.
Under the day's crust a half-eaten child: 4807.
Under the dusty, the lace-dimmed windows: 1420.
Under the heave of a far-off storm: 663.
Under the maples at moonrise--: 2879.
Under the plaster cast of my presence: 3812.
Under the slow heron: 5557.
Under the sullen of this Surrey fall: 6717.
Under the tree of life: 5830.
Under the white-starred bough: 6961.
Under this other arch: 449.
Under your polar star: 4261.
The undertaker's come to take our measure: 6891.
An unexpected holiday: 5044.
Unfair, a lie. The baby was not gray: 1327.
Unfit for worship, still I learned each prayer: 2168.
The universe is godly vast: 6702.
Unknown are the heroes: 1663.
Unmediterranean: 5126.
Unprayed-for, undivined, and bodiless: 6525.
Unravel the tangled thoughts of thirty years: 3207.
Untenanted, my heart, for now a day: 6819.
Up and down the small streets: 7144.
Up and down the steps: 589.
Up early, out of a dream: 3903.
Up flies the window shade!: 6730.
Up from some tile-towered slumber: 7180.
Up from the dark green valleys creep: 1049.
Up half a dozen hills I've sworn in vain: 3400.
Up in the elevator went the nuns: 6273.
Up the mountain highway scenes: 1855.
Uplifted birds who into burning skies...: 6920.
Upon a lake, His eye, the image of a bird: 270.
Upon the ancient manuscripts of night: 3783.
Upside down and hindside to: 3361.
Vacations are over: 6147.
Vachel, you visioned Congo through a haze: 5151.
A vagrant wisp of hydrogen that turns: 5943.
"Valentine.": 6828.
The valedictorian's mouth was a manufactory of little white flags: 2364.
Valley, meadow and hill lie frigid and white: 7218.
The valves of silence clap: 255.
Vanished the summers when we: 105.
The various members of the hierarchy move: 3905.
Various objects appeared on the floor: 6261.

A vase: 7189.

The vast and patient love which lies:
6571.

Very high: 5007.

Vestal of the verb, her style she held:
1116.

Vexing the heart, old scenes returned:
3492.

Veysey's store was a country store:
1255.

The views I express seem: 3314.

The vigor and majest of the air: 3380.

The Villa Jernyngham belonged by inheritance to the Dampiers: 2017.

The virginal, living and beautiful today: 6861.

A virus crouched upon the terrace:
6881.

Visibly here the tide: 7025.

Vitelli rides west toward Fano, the
morning sun: 1398.

The vixen, trembling in desire: 26.

The voice of the church and the voice
of the wind: 1178.

Voices protected from the dead summon
us: 7105.

Voluptuous angels hummed today in
Jerusalem: 4693.

The voyager, trader, pioneer have past:
5785.

"Wait for me," said spring: 597.

Wait Kate! You skate at such a rate:
6554.

"Wait. Let me think a minute.": 7235.

Waiting for when the sun an hour or
less: 2890.

Waiting for you, I warm my...: 6922.

Wakes wet; is promptly toileted: 4564.

Waking outside his Babylonian binge:
6423.

Walk, ghost, no more in the long
corridor: 939.

Walking a woodland in the spring:
2687.

Walking before the cathedral, its
pinnacle struck in my being: 552.

Walking by day or night: 1623.

Walking out in the late March midnight: 6397.

Walking the wood's edge, but outside
the wood: 6336.

Walking to the Museum: 687.

The Walrus and the Carpenter: 6942.

War shears the buds from the Constant
Vine: 2439.

A war to save civilization, civilization you say?: 6574.

The ware shinobu hairdo identifies
girls as maikos: 2021.

Warm is the house of the woods: 2654.

Warm sun, cold river, mist: 6109.

Was Delilah there in Dagon's court:
1437.

Was it Florence or Venice: 6960.

Was it for the love of language I:
1719.

Was it the moon, the rip full moon:
6833.

Was there ever a wader: 6916.

Washington sends Santa out: 5423.

Wasp and Windowscreen: 6966.

Watch and cool Northern girl: 6172.

Watch him. He has for clubbing:
fists, wrists, knees, heels, head:
4472.

Watch it son!: 5922.

Watching you walk head down: 3913.

Watching your near anonymous hand:
5236.

Watchman, what of the night? What of
the hour: 1203.

Water dripping: the insatiable voice:
4888.

Water drooped from nowhere and was
lazy: 1706.

Water must ripple: 4460.

Waters and earth once more parted:
99.

The water's fingers shift, by sand
and sand: 5946.

Wave-borne no more nor landlocked
yet: 4390.

Waves knit over fish: 857.

Waving sad fins: 7193.

The waxy petals of magnolia: 4042.

Way out they are riding, it is an
old: 2544.

We all need criticism: 5997.

We are a nation of Jews; of Jews, I
repeat: 3157.

We are adrift on a broad ocean that
has no shores: 5112.

We are betrayed by what is false:
220.

We are indeed afraid of monsters we
create: 3859.

We are few. Perhaps three: 6982.

We are much of oxen, some of beaver:
997.

We are not alone but with ourselves
in loneliness: 6852.

We are not loud. Our women dress in
black: 5336.

We are the last that there are any-
where: 2063.

We are the pottery: 4963.

We are toothless hags: 1877.

We are two countries girded for the
war: 2120.

We awaited the child: 619.

We brought up twigs and branches to
the fire: 1943.

We built a tree house above a glen:
6666.

We call to mind those dear old friends:
490.

We cannot meet, two citadels of
stone: 6721.

We check them, we shelve them, we
stamp them: 3350.

We climbed, from the burning plain:
3944.

We climbed together up to our mountain cabin: 4452.

We deceive ourselves, with names:
1454.

We delighted, my friend, in an
African presence: 6985.

We did not choose each other, you and
I: 5859.

We do not build these ships any more: 7034.

We do not speak to one another in poems: 2885.

We don't give Modern Medicine the attention it deserves: 4842.

We don't know the ins and outs?: 6935.

We don't send our tyke: 3468.

We drove ovah convoy: 3478.

We follow a solid river: 3789.

We follow our schedules, take care of: 6000.

We gathered in the yard and watched: 6987.

We get along well with our neighbors: 4143.

We give them vitamins and stuff: 3146.

We glimpse the Day through mortal dark: 5361.

We had, at midnight,flicked the outside light: 6625.

We had expected a long siege, and when: 846.

We had it, we had it--the violet hour: 5504.

We had the great tree cut: 2263.

We hauled the old hose up the cellular stairs: 2069.

We have a Policeman and I used to call him Cop: 4913.

We have a verb "stood up" it means: 6988.

We have climbed the mountain: 2551.

We have departed from those lovely lands: 4599.

We have here a concept quizzical, the modern metaphysical: 2160.

We have looked through the world for our mother: 7199.

We have ordered a boy: 4995.

We have put memory to every use but one--: 6120.

We have three lanes and you have three lanes: 595.

We have the handsomest minister: 3443.

We hear the lisping salt-sea drip: 5394.

We keep, here, the records of days: 6990.

We kept the silence as we knew we should: 3811.

We lay on the grass and gazed down and heard: 133.

We lay small Jesus to sleep in the snow: 2851.

We left the party and the literati: 1005.

We live here in each other's laps: 5700.

We live in a constellation: 3124.

We live in the time of the colossal upright oblong: 956.

We look at the map. She asks about names: 3643.

We look in friend's eyes: 5402.

We lounged at the window watching: 4893.

We love our books and rightly so: 6015.

We may be tops, A-1, the best: 5999.

We meant well, travelling with flair: 6655.

We must do our work: 2341.

We purchased a nice old house in the hills: 6864.

We rush headlong to meet the dawn's embrace: 2343.

We said good-by: 4427.

We sat in the Cambridge orchard drinking tea: 2915.

We see a cross before: 5049.

We see too much of time and place: 2040.

We seldom if ever: 6192.

We set our candle upon the window sill: 852.

We shall be far away when raspberries bear: 5138.

We shall remember the wheat, stalk in the greenness of her youth: 5214.

We spent many nights in building: 2412.

We spoke of the Equinox: 475.

We stayed too long with the red candles: 284.

We stoop for flowers: 5798.

We struck straight up the bluff by dark and tilted: 6876.

We Sunday strode--I in leather: 5225.

We sweep all pathways clean in search of meaning: 1287.

We too have filled our inns too full: 4094.

We used to wash his hands for him: 4669.

We walk her underneath a great wave: 4406.

We walk the hill: 1119.

We walked through the...: 5326.

We walked together once: 1683.

We walked without a word: 97.

We wander at each other's fields: 6993.

We went to gather beach plums: 522.

We were betrothed in the falling year: 5597.

We were both born: 1404.

We were like lovers lying: 7244.

We were lucky today; the sun rose: 393.

We were not even out of sight of land: 5474.

We were not likened to dogs among the Gentiles--by them a dog: 6994.

We were not there to see, yet know: 6561.

We were our enemy in the image of our fear: 3014.

We were related by the flesh: 5001.

We were safe and sane then, I: 2155.

We were strolling in the wood: 5459.

We were thankful to have last January ...: 4925.

We were the instrument: 2794.

We were three women: 5880.

We were wary all summer: 7088.

We who cannot stand too long a day: 5595.

We who come after: 6472.

We who have loved today we bring: 2345.

We who must act as handmaidens: 3978.

We who waited on her bed: 2873.
We will remember you at Mass: 2054.
We will whirl our souls at your...: 980.
We woke in dark and rushed to work: 4696.
Weak in wits and muddled now with light: 4487.
Wearing some kind of iron hat armed to the teeth with: 5337.
Weary of winter too inert for spring: 6374.
Weary, the surgeon drops his knife, his skillful fingers: 1440.
The weather this spring has been rotten; I don't know: 7002.
The weather wept, and all the trees bent down: 4864.
Weaving and interweaving: 1987.
We'd like to remember with our regards: 871.
Wee by as I remember, yet the same: 3050.
Wee Willie Winkie: 3858.
The weekly undoing of the house: 4776.
Weep bloody tears, my eyes, such as never flowed from you: 5602.
Welcome me, if you will: 2078.
The Welfare State in Britain, making citizens secure: 1848.
A well earned pat upon the back: 5988.
Well, God is love: 5065.
Well met beside the attitudes of water: 4879.
Well said young man, well said! You made your case: 1427.
Well up beyond the tropostrata: 4754.
Went to the barnlot, and I saw: 1978.
Went up after the rare thing of love: 1649.
Were he composer he would surely write: 4947.
We're building a building: 1114.
We're from the city, and the birch trees knew it: 2450.
We're locked in the pillory of repentance: 5040.
We're now at the season: 1026.
We're showering our friends and neighbors: 6189.
West, in the windy Indies of her mind: 7028.
West of the brown Missouri, many things change: 7030.
West-thrusting headlands just at sunset hold: 7031.
The Western Powers are now agreed: 4153.
Westward from Vancouver where: 7384.
We've had a goodly share of snow: 163.
We've laid no love by for rainy days: 4814.
We've made the move to North Suburbia: 4789.
What a little boy is told: 6205.
What!: 1508.
What a pity the great Fidel Castro: 3016.

What a pother of words we weave around: 7005.
What about measure, I learnt: 4753.
What are the dreams within his white old head: 6781.
What are we waiting for: 1810.
What are you?: 3344.
What are you wearing? "Snow.": 5802.
What baffled every male alive: 4049.
What battle could you fight with zest: 2090.
What beggar, tinker, or sow-gelder: 4942.
What blue is that dwells within this gem?: 5425.
What bothers me more: 4142.
What can I give to you that you may keep?: 2291.
What can weather: 12.
What can you do with an apple: 273.
What carloads of words we heaped and tossed: 1217.
What creature of the Mesozoic seas--: 384.
What day was it she slid: 625.
What did I bring from across the sea?: 4681.
What do cows think: 7040.
What do I think of you now: 4148.
What does love look like?: 5561.
What does she remember?: 6867.
What does your wife say when you come home?: 6528.
What else is it: 3473.
What gathering beneath the sun: 5066.
What glistening, finny brood is this?: 4756.
What glories would we? Motions of the soul?: 5223.
What great colossus or leviathan: 3942.
What happened there, it was not much: 7018.
What happened to that Bavarian pear: 6053.
What happy appellations, these: 4043.
What has a crow to do with this May Morning: 1294.
What has taken you, rose tree, endlessly to sway, under: 4541.
What have we stars to stammer as we pass: 1473.
What have you brought back from that clear and sea-rinsed day: 5331.
What horrid sight is this I see: 6415.
What I like moth: 5684.
What I remember is: the sun: 5780.
What is now?: 4232.
What is the ploughman heard to say: 2521.
What if the right to sue were older: 3272.
What if, through uplands, tongues of Pentecost: 4482.
What is all this fingering about?: 1516.
What is everything really but brown?: 770.

What is it that we need, demand: 299.
What is it that you see? Or think you
    see?: 6745.
What is Italian? It is the language
    spoken: 3047.
What is man, that mindful of him: 6352.
What is poetry? Who knows?: 4903.
What is the difference between that
    day: 4916.
What is the mirror saying with its
    O?: 5346.
What is the tribute I shall pay: 3567.
What is this shadow that I greet: 7047.
What ladies at conventions wear: 1216.
What lifts the heron leaning: 5737.
What makes me stop, what's in me
    bullet-struck: 4804.
What makes the sun to rise and shine:
    250.
What man has greater rapture known:
    3650.
What man there be whom: 5576.
What mornings to the west: 7096.
What movement?: 1949.
What music can you hear?: 4882.
What my parents thought and said:
    2224.
What nettles me most: 4445.
What, old mole?: 2441.
What pages I've stripped: 1075.
What partial dark, inverting on the
    sea: 2403.
What pillows of red coral hold their
    heads: 1586.
What pledge of honour: 7381.
What rendered you: 4046.
What rhymes with hope?: 1799.
What says UNESCO's Board: 2156.
What secret force is in this river?:
    7075.
What shakes the eye but the unvisible?:
    1410.
What shall be said was left them past
    their theatres : 4022.
What shall I do with her poems: 2257.
What shall Presto do for prettle
    prattle: 6211.
What shall we say of friendship: 4455.
What sort of bosses make: 3663.
What surely was the emperor of spiders:
    3156.
What the sad and passionate gay player
    of Avon avowed: 2235.
What they loved, what their brushes
    proudly caressed: 2000.
What thirst for knowledge brought you
    here?: 6529.
What though green leaves only witness:
    7318.
What was her beauty in our first
    estate: 5566.
What was it to have seen: 2473.
What was not meant to hear: 5332.
What was the blond child building:
    783.
What was unimportant: 1730.
What was that blinding off-color: 646.
What we enjoyed was the yogi's secret:
    5265.

What were the things that our fathers
    said?: 177.
What will we do for loving...: 918.
What will you name the Lincoln child:
    3396.
What would you have us do, complacent
    ones: 4588.
Whatever bed he slept in, from his
    sides: 1519.
Whatever his own eyes troubles to
    make clear: 3263.
Whatever may be going through our
    heads: 5427.
Whatever residue of pride adhere: 3916.
Whatever spectacle the crowd came
    for: 2150.
Whatever the somber day might have
    held for us: 6031.
What's in a nursery as brisk and as
    light: 2293.
What's left of the sunset's water
    blood: 7303.
What's sweeter than at the end of a
    summer's day: 6312.
Wheels are works of wit: 7062.
The wheels of thought spin in my
    mind: 7325.
When a city undergoes disaster, it
    moves as a mass: 6440.
When a gal goes on a diet: 5681.
When a girl is seventeen: 5549.
When a man dies and is lowered into the
    ground: 6439.
When a patron approaches don't dash
    and...: 5991.
When a picnic is in progress on a
    day that breeds romance: 238.
When a question has you up a tree:
    5987.
When a woman looks wistful: 2589.
When Adam's rib arose and stood:
    741.
When all her hairdo, facial and: 3891.
When all night from the tree the
    emerald toad: 423.
When all the animals have fled into
    your eyes: 1332.
When Archimedes hauled his engine
    high: 1968.
Where are those friends?: 2174.
When ashes in the courtyard sat and
    birds: 5857.
When autumn whips the varying winds:
    226.
When big things are being done: 607.
When bitter blows the winter blast:
    1297.
When blessed Lord had opened up the
    cave: 1634.
When brandy burns in the air: 1793.
When bright Orion has declined: 5872.
When, careful steel circling the
    satin leaf: 4826.
When children are cross: 1772.
When children are small: 4517.
When Christ: 1040.
When coldly winter woods drain twi-
    light through: 3752.
When contemplating moving: 7046.

When country hills are soft with snow: 1001.

When daughters play at dressing up: 5714.

When David painted my aunt's perfect child: 4447.

When death has chastened me: 195.

When dew dripped silver from each peach-blown bough: 7065.

When does a baby suddenly: 1783.

When drawing up a list: 502.

When each day comes before us like a knight: 6596.

When Easter morning on its silver feet: 5672.

When ebbing tides have left their strands: 521.

When Elizabeth fell in love: 3425.

When evening noises scare my wife: 2513.

When farmhouses stand stark beneath the moon: 1418.

When first I came to Colchis Bay: 1750.

When frost moves fast and gardens lose their ground: 7185.

When God sleeps does not the Beloved sleep: 4643.

When God throws down his sudden, daring glove: 6190.

When he tags along behind: 6413.

When he's been deaf to an assortment: 2520.

When I: 4718.

When I am ill, birds fly: 1803.

When I am in a crowd: 4586.

When I am reading Junior tales: 2743.

When I am tired and wary give me rest: 5233.

When I at youth's expiry: 541.

When I attempt to cheer some friend: 6995.

When I awake (he said) I shall be lonely: 564.

When I, besieged, distrust my indigent's prayer: 2985.

When I boast of pretty girls I've known: 2303.

When I came back from my last dream: 129.

When I come home from work at close of day: 6117.

When I consider the time you spend: 3967.

When I depart this life, I fear: 3287.

When I employ statistics: 1907.

When I hasten homewards after the morning bath in the river: 2657.

When I have been dead for several years: 4911.

When I opened the door that morning: 5215.

When I see a book, I am instantly struck: 2308.

When I see how high it is: 5738.

When I shall lose my heart's last beat and go: 5867.

When I struggled out from your final hold: 1434.

When I was a child I broke: 6025.

When I was a tot at Granny's knee: 267.

When I was a young girl: 4415.

When I was born, I was rather young: 7335.

When I was coasting on the hill: 2392.

When I was filled with youthful pride: 2136.

When I was five, and distant from immense: 4000.

When I was little, when: 4926.

When I was on night line: 1658.

When I was very young, I saw these things and they were the whole world: 916.

When I was young: 2867.

When I was young, there were: 6267.

When I wear a zipper suit: 7383.

When I went to bed last night: 7272.

When I would let the dishes go: 6809.

When ice at last has come across the pond: 2772.

When ills seem distant puffs of smoke: 1509.

When I'm an old codger I'll sit by the fire: 819.

When I'm an old lady, thin as a whistle: 7362.

When I'm in the North: 2835.

When I'm making cookies or mixing cake: 2949.

When I'm out of cash and full of shame: 7070.

When in summer everything is light: 5131.

When in the hour of last night thoughts: 6290.

When, in the mask of night, there shone that cut: 3224.

When it comes to the lasting name of one: 1236.

When it first appeared: 4476.

When it is snowing, I like to imagine things: 5717.

When it is truly the moon that he sees: 3595.

When I've been reading: 6604.

When Janice says, "Know something?": 3185.

When Jesu was a little boy: 3092.

When Jesus rose on Easter morn: 2761.

When lilacs last in the dooryard bloom'd: 7073.

When little boys: 3449.

When love came calling yesterday: 6896.

When lovely woman stoops: 3180.

When man is marked for fame, you'll find: 6968.

When mankind lays the age of time to sleep: 2328.

When man's weekend excursions start: 1133.

When married folks: 7072.

When Mary came laden: 1023.

When Mary sat by the cool trees: 3137.

When meadows melt: 5815.
When measles arrived, rosy-red,
    efflorescent: 4192.
When Moses came down from the mountain
    and the cloud: 1687.
When Moses in Horeb struck the rock:
    4444.
When Mother in sheer exasperation:
    4520.
When Mous, my kitten, walks across the
    scales: 1233.
When my grandfather, small and neat:
    4404.
When my uncle came for supper twice a
    year: 4020.
When my years stood at just a score:
    6059.
When news: 2715.
When night falls: 3080.
When now I'm going well: 7069.
When one has taken a child: 44.
When patrons have a slip of tongue:
    5989.
When peaks discard their frigid mien:
    5419.
When people watch me take my pill:
    3693.
When psalms surprise me with their
    music: 5057.
When saints, sitting after dinner:
    515.
When scrub-oak leaves turn autumn
    brown: 1422.
Where sea gulls, holyghosting rainbow,
    ran: 2777.
When she was young her skirt swung
    wide: 673.
When shall I see the islands of my
    ancestors?: 5084.
When she, laughing, plastered a snow-
    ball on me: 2526.
When Sisyphus was pushing the stone
    up the mountain: 6222.
When, sleepless, at the crawling clock
    you blink: 7382.
When smashing bottles on railroad
    tracks: 6340.
When starlight breaks like a surf
    down the dark sky: 6255.
When summer, clover, cologne: 3654.
When summer no swerver at all: 1085.
When swordfish leap from dust: 5349.
When tears have dropped like autumn
    rain: 6100.
When teen-age chatter seems to be:
    3621.
When telling me how I can get there:
    1640.
When the birds are all atwitter:
    5993.
When the child would accomodate the
    adult again: 7077.
When the chrome clouds break: 5547.
When the colossus of the will's
    dominion: 2460.
When the Continental Congress drew a
    bill to cope with treason: 4269.
When the couple passed me on the
    walk: 5790.
When the cuckoo: 3548.

When the dark dawn humped off to die:
    3456.
When the first bird had spoken: 3897.
When the first leaf moved: 1501.
When the fires of youth were burning
    bright: 3249.
When the first vague years, the
    years of questions and toys: 574.
When the hero of the threshold enters
    our lives and our houses: 2560.
When the immortal blond basketball
    player: 5296.
When the last Pullman of the day
    pulls into Grand Canyon: 6862.
When the lean Wolf Moon climbs from
    underground: 3078.
When the letter came: 4394.
When the little ones: 3142.
When the long book of earthly life
    is done: 371.
When the long root, the tensile stem
    disturb: 1610.
When the love is old: 389.
When the Marxists and the Eggheads
    and the Planners: 3774.
When the noise of the room reaches
    low shouting pitch: 5998.
When the nurse held you up to the
    glass wall: 1801.
When the play--The Tempest--ended,
    they resumed: 7190.
When the Pulitzers showered on some
    dope: 7293.
When the rain makes afternoon come
    grey: 479.
When the tools are put in their places
    the day's: 5403.
When the white wind whistles: 5805.
When the wild winds sweep: 698.
When the world had turned two hours
    after midnight: 894.
When they came near: 4031.
When they understood he would go on
    a journey: 3112.
When time and space are shattered in
    oblivion: 4194.
When toasts are made at banquets:
    7295.
When true love broke my heart in
    half: 858.
When twilight dimmed the beach: 5334.
When ugliness meant so little: 5647.
When Uncle Devereux died: 1594.
When unto us was born a son: 7017.
When warm and strangeing moonlight:
    4852.
When was I scalloped with leaves:
    245.
When was opened the window: 1152.
When we at length: 6791.
When we have become too old, too old:
    4685.
When we have talked and there's no
    more to say: 361.
When we move on to greener fields:
    6008.
When we shut the house in Indian
    Summer: 7012.
When we were young: 6744.
When we were young we used: 7371.

When will he come? The Jew keeps waiting: 1704.
When windows of my workshop: 7184.
When, with your hair combed up for the first time: 1965.
When women of a sudden cry: 6272.
When you are old and beautiful: 364.
When you borrowed me among the uncouth knight: 6246.
When you come, as you soon must, to the streets of our city: 57.
When you go in the Pearly Gate: 3135.
When you have pitied enough: 6633.
When you have touched your evening lamps: 1530.
When you remember all the bother: 5271.
When you rose in your dirndle skirt: 3303.
When you stood smiling under a roof of leaves: 427.
When you think how big their feet are in black rubber: 1988.
When young I was smugly convinced: 3151.
When young, she never did pay much attention: 4649.
When your husband puts a job off: 6182.
When you're sure there's a lot: 2226.
When you've got a thing to say: 65.
Whenas in crinolines she goes: 4778.
Whenever she stands there, feet apart: 1996.
Whenever I take Marquand: 3964.
Whenever we see a home marked model: 2612.
When you come to the end of a hectic day: 5984.
Whenever a fellow: 4246.
Whenever Mr. Edwards spake: 6334.
Whenever poetry saw me: 3667.
Whenever wings: 6878.
Where and no trees: 7084.
Where apples sweet: 5833.
Where are my long hills?: 4559.
Where are the lips, the breast, the thigh: 1497.
Where are the stars of our rich balconies: 2104.
Where are those words that once: 6204.
Where can you match the mighty music: 4349.
Where, cast away, I wake from numb surprise: 3655.
Where chilly robins hurdle now: 5325.
Where the cities end...: 6647.
Where cold infiltrates and the partridge whirs: 4226.
Where Europe and America build their arches: 6367.
Where everything's listed: 1925.
Where grey Land's End repels the sky: 471.
Where he rows the dark: 527.
Where he stood in boots in water to his calves: 1985.
Where in the emerald evening the hills change color: 6262.
Where is for this Within a Without?: 2989.
Where is she going: 106.

Where is the bell the horn: 1595.
Where is the hound: 1931.
Where is the speaker to compare: 370.
Where is your England now, cock robin: 1654.
Where is your lady: 5674.
Where Lackawanna's tracks graze our backyards: 3200.
Where Moses' plashy rod would fail: 3824.
Where mountain marshland met a hill: 845.
Where now was joy expectant: 4558.
Where Saud's caravan has rested: 4140.
Where shall he put his eyes: 3211.
Where snow-encrusted poplars lift: 3800.
Where the antipodes' palmy Tuamotu are: 1300.
Where the light has no horizons we lie: 1819.
Where the light's bells ring: 5315.
Where the room may be, I do not know: 1911.
Where the slopes turn cliff: 359.
Where were we in that afternoon?: 231.
Where were you, little pumpkin head: 4880.
Wherever a man stands still: 1292.
Whether blue grains shall stay, as they are: 668.
Whether in prayer God changes my mind: 247.
Whether it's deasil cancrizans, or widdishins: 6670.
While diesels smudge the vineyards on the hills: 1097.
While foothills pull their blankets of gray cloud: 2577.
While in the race: 4618.
While my head hangs down the shampoo tray: 3470.
While on the high bridge-wing I stand: 1448.
While people hunt for what can satisfy their wants: 5573.
While some to the purple: 5635.
While the class waited: 4996.
While the pine-caught sun distills its blue: 321.
While the teleprinters click: 1308.
While Wag sniffs the dirt her friends have about: 2356.
Whirl, whorl, or wharve!: 5179.
A whirlpool of whiteness: 5726.
The white cat, my friends, the cat of our master the eminent savant: 1562.
The White Christ stands alone in cypress trees: 7105.
The white crayfish lives in a cave: 7109.
White curtains, clean, this side of dark-framed windows: 955.
White diamond fretwork shimmers in the trees: 84.
White flare of stone in the sun: 3375.
A white-hot midday in the Snake Park: 2919.

White in the shallow winter sun: 5470.
A white moth in the bay bush, power 228: 799.
A white moth floats in the night: 799.
White scalloped paws of kitten waves: 1901.
White without being washed--: 5767.
The whitethroat calls through the May night: 7121.
Who am I to contend with thee?: 3100.
Who are you?: 5154.
Who are you? Do you love me? What do you mean?: 1218.
Who bear a child: 4846.
Who builds a fence: 6396.
Who can see or hear them for the leaves?: 979.
Who can tell: 4029.
Who dips a spoon in, knows this ordinary jam: 4209.
Who does not like a luggard rook's high: 1127.
Who does not sit in the seat of the scoffer: 650.
Who feeds his neighbor's starving cat: 6905.
Who gives us such winter: 2282.
Who has a feeling she will come one day: 7117.
Who holds my book and turns the page? 5149.
Who is it fathoms what you mean?: 5754.
Who is the wizard of the world: 7130.
Who is this sea: 124.
Who is this sentry standing at the gate?: 3415.
Who is this skinny girl I've seen: 1086.
Who knows for sure what fails, when faint praise falls: 1175.
Who laughs at ghosts: 6954.
Who lived in the greenhouse when I was very small: 2421.
Who remembers how far the discus was thrown?: 4620.
Who says they're difficult to keep? 6399.
Who says you're like one of the dog days?: 111.
Who seeks too far afield: 6321.
Who smiles to see the summer go?: 7001.
Who steals my purse steals: 3743.
Who to the state of lawful marriage brings: 3258.
Who was it whispered beside the tree: 6904.
Who was not threatened, never quailed: 6099.
Who was St. Valentine? The legends say: 6826.
Who watches blue fire: 666.
Who wears a button nose: 960.
Who will settle the Cyprus crisis: 1324.
Who would have thought it mattered so?: 6049.
Who would recall this pool, away from paths: 1481.
Who'd ever think the Whitneys: 6331.

Whoever, by whatever stride or luck: 2802.
Whoever said that love is blind: 1309.
Whoever she is, you will always know her: 7215.
Whoever works a storm to windward: 942.
Whoever you are, this poem is clearly about you: 2254.
Whole days are city minutes if you measure: 1252.
Who'll break the tough glebe now?: 6612.
Whom do I give my neat little volume: 6424.
"Whom does he love?" the goddess cried: 5080.
Whose eyes were watching me I do not know: 5609.
Whose fist delivered me this blow: 2820.
Whose heart cries Peace shall have no peace at all: 1302.
Whose woods these are I think I know: 2338.
Why am I so afraid: 7137.
Why and how?: 6768.
Why, dear wife, can't you take on trust: 5153.
Why do our dandelions, common with gold: 4397.
Why do people have to say: 5051.
Why do people say: 5050.
Why do we turn in our beds: 2186.
Why do you linger so long at the window: 5366.
Why do you not transform: 6510.
Why do you play such dreary music: 5110.
Why do you stare down that way: 4901.
Why do you wake this valley?: 3145.
Why does communism spread: 5514.
Why does one song of the many songs, cling in the listening mind: 4607.
Why ever name the word again: 5310.
Why, if, my lady, you could pick and choose: 4799.
Why, in God's name, we put you in the ground: 2346.
Why it's called "cold cash.": 2273.
Why must decision ever leave: 79.
Why must you come: 4393.
Why should we praise them, or revere: 110.
Why should you bite your fingernails? What have they done to you?: 5567.
Why this predilection, pretty lady: 3606.
Why, twenty-seven years after you died: 6582.
Why was a radio sinful? Lord knows. But it was: 5111.
"Why was she lost?" my darling said aloud: 212.
Why was she sung and played: 1688.
Why was the city so sunk in sleep?: 6495.
The wick burns down the length: 5662.
Wide, wide in the rose's side: 7139.
The widow's house, the penury: 5866.
Wife, I summoned you from time past: 6146.

The willow shining: 3187.
Willow-tassels grow in tremors of the spring wind: 2964.
Willows rushing over, windfed, whispered: 4802.
The wind: 3110.
The wind at dawn was a lonely bird: 7164.
The wind blows the grasses the way of its will: 1765.
A wind came roaring up today: 3269.
Wind droops. Sloop stops: 6253.
The wind fell and the frozen night: 7186.
Wind from the sea, shadows tall against a visit: 4616.
The wind goes keening through the dark: 4231.
The wind has hollowed me: 5067.
The wind has whetted itself on the edge of the frozen moon: 7163.
The wind imports a flash of heaven: 6981.
Wind in the eaves of the old house, wind over Russia: 6483.
The wind knocked at the door: 160.
The wind showed me how to love: 7166.
Wind like twenty lions: 3434.
The wind that howls, the snow that swirls outside: 1771.
The wind that once brought birth: 4159.
Wind? This is no wind: 5645.
The wind was on your side: 638.
The window, a wide pane in the bar: 6926.
Window-gazing, at one time or another: 2553.
The winds and rains were quite moderate during the spring: 1196.
The window is covered: 2215.
The window kept sealed, bars with locks, the drape: 6653.
The wind's complaining in the chimney: 7162.
The wind's in the willows: 386.
The winds of summer are disposed: 6152.
The winds that winnowed the rain are spent: 6066.
A windy day in a wooden house: 4279.
Wine in this cloudy north could change the still: 2597.
The wing instinctive: 3461.
Winged seeds are flying: 910.
Winged walls, as majesty!: 1125.
Winter Aconite: 1923.
Winter, and the swarthy look of noon: 7200.
Winter, and through the snow: 6884.
Winter has come: 7195.
Winter, I said, is skinflint mean: 2493.
Winter is icumen in: 7197.
Winter, in rigid dress, moves to my window: 2953.
The winter is dismal to some people, but--: 3507.
Winter is here?: 154.
Winter is ice-time; wind is rising: 3019.

Winter is not beautiful: 1845.
Winter is sparkling: 3682.
Winter keeps a tidy house: 7223.
Winter obsessed them with the thoughts of white: 7209.
The winter owl banked just in time to pass: 4307.
The winter owl banked just in time to pass: 3546.
Winter will be feasts and fires in the shut houses: 1842.
The winter window gathers all outside: 4025.
Winter's the time: 7004.
Winters when we set out traps offshore: 3027.
The wintry winds of Christmas: 1019.
Wisdom goes looking for a light: 7230.
The Wise Men had been watching too: 7097.
The wisest word, the longest song of all: 7231.
The witch doctors, I have it on authority of intuition: 2567.
The witch of the Gulf Stream shapes fat kine: 6067.
With a husband and a wife sharing: 1515.
With a mirror: 5344.
With altogether winning ways: 345.
With banked fire to mark the occasion: 1852.
With baton twirling: 5691.
With beasts and gods above, the wall is bright: 983.
With block and tackle of golden clouds: 4118.
With crude oil flooding into new: 4367.
With dabs of that and bits of this: 2638.
With daffodil and crocus: 1227.
With daily devotions to neutralist nations: 6816.
With excess: 1058.
With fingers crossed, she can't resist: 1874.
With four-year footsteps plowing deep: 4767.
With hands like faded aspen leaves: 2025.
With its contempt for all calamities: 1057.
With jeweled bark and marcelled bite: 4923.
With jewels flashing on his head: 4727.
With magic the silver fingered moon: 2525.
With nothing to brag about but the size of their hearts: 192.
With my ready wit: 5388.
With peepers winding marshy ducks: 3003.
With piebald wig askew: 1043.
With retina blurred and eyeballs aching: 6281.
With science daily gaining speed: 5454.
With shirt wide open at the collar: 1431.

With sinews fashioned for as swift a
  leap: 1499.
With some of our friends and some of
  our loves: 2470.
With sparrows curses on her head:
  898.
With the dishes mouldering in neon:
  5817.
With their lithe, long, strong legs:
  790.
With thread and needle she outlined a
  bear: 2377.
With vibrant tones church bells announce
  the hours: 3775.
With violet pencils: 7044.
With vitamins from A to D: 2938.
With what devoted tender toil: 5608.
With what do I compare our meeting,
  my darling?: 4974.
With white frost gone: 6106.
With whomsoever I share the spring:
  5788.
With wildflowers bedded in his mind:
  1680.
Within a green enclosure: 3813.
Within a quad of aging brick: 2787.
Within my solitude I long: 2996.
Within myself I walk the hidden wave:
  1637.
Within the quick of justice shall she
  stand: 3765.
Within the recession: 7148.
Within the thorax it is dark: 2968.
A Wivern Gules for Mr. Jones, a Bor-
  dure and a Bend Per Fess: 128.
Wmffree the Sweep was mad as a mink:
  7252.
A woeful silence, following in our
  wash: 4352.
Woke: 3908.
Woken, I lay in the arms of my own
  warmth and listened: 1979.
The women anciently famed in Israel:
  7237.
A woman can tell: 6817.
A woman has, of course, to be: 2984.
A woman made of wire: 5799.
The woman on the mountain kept her
  fictive ocean: 6347.
The woman smiling in the sun: 2071.
A woman stands alone upon the shore:
  3864.
A woman's dressing table's quite:
  7257.
A woman's loyalty begins at three:
  3578.
"Woman's place is in the home.":
  1507.
Women and gods require impossible:
  7045.
Women and men may dance on greens:
  5840.
Women are, beyond a doubt: 6989.
Women are more irritable: 5229.
Women are superficial in their choices:
  1283.
Women, like car: 4624.
Women of journeys, always you send
  the picture: 4954.

The women snipped the sea down flat:
  4853.
Women waiting for their husbands: 7267.
Women wear silence well: 2255.
Women who have made a stern choice:
  5620.
Women, women: 1997.
"A wonderful old woman," someone said:
  7020.
Wooden staff, the time has come: 3214.
A woodland bell kept ringing by: 6454.
A woodpecker in the zoology room of a
  girls' schol: 1109.
Woodrow Wilson, addressing the masses:
  5918.
The woods lie cool: 5273.
Wool, you need wool in this weather:
  5358.
The Word: 7294.
The word moves a bit of air: 5928.
The Word of God was spoken, chanted
  to: 6428.
Words fall: 5719.
The words mean little: I love you--I
  care--: 5839.
The words of friend and friend: 4697.
Work and a town on every side: 6651.
Work with a will: 5957.
Working the orchard: 1954.
A workman likes his tools to have
  left their marks: 2842.
World, a little longer wait: 2997.
The world and everything in it: 1660.
The world gathers itself away from her:
  3521.
The world is a stream, one says, all
  things are one: 3850.
The world is dark on many sides: 4547.
The world is full of mostly invisible
  things: 6542.
The world is so full: 6291.
The world would certainly abound: 2983.
Worlds away what other praise: 2085.
The worn scythe hangs in the box-elder
  tree: 2373.
Worry, waiting, wondering: 2300.
Would He have bid you "Walk!": 6576.
Would you be wise? Then do these many
  things: 2087.
Wouldn't know the lark?: 3440.
The wreaths of four-o'clocks, silken
  red: 7319.
Wriest of uncles, and most remote:
  6762.
Writing is made on stone, on leather
  and on clay: 3093.
Wrongs of this crisis will not be ab-
  solved: 1991.
Wrought by the odd desire for perma-
  nence: 6394.
Xochimilco flower float: 3784.
Ye call me Master and obey me not:
  6459.
Ye think it was the end?: 4584.
Year after year upon St. Felix!:
  4713.
The year is round around me now: 2426.
The year lies open and unmarked before us:
  1063.

Year on rounded year: 5748.
The year pours into my wheelbarrow: 2252.
The year that weeping I was born: 1684.
The year was river-thrated, with stare of legend: 3921.
The year will come, and still will be: 7333.
Yearlong, the subterranean stream: 1028.
The years have built and whittled at these dunes: 191.
Years in the field: 2609.
The years of school as short as any dream: 1899.
Years hence perhaps some one of you who sits: 6802.
Years slip under the keel: 3692.
Yelled Corporal Punishment at Private Reasons: 1723.
A yellow-headed, gold-hammered, sun-flower-lanterned: 3945.
The yellow legs and beak: 2502.
The yellow river and the violet hills: 2015.
Yellow Yellow Yellow: you are the child's: 1897.
Yes before my window many times: 5648.
Yes, in the janitor's place: 3073.
Yes, that's true, he slipped away: 5167.
Yes, there is his mother: 4957.
Yesterday from my fever: 7341.
Yesterday, gray peals of light: 1741.
Yesterday, with Ovid's course: 2158.
Yet dancers: 2293.
Yet sometimes I would sweep the floor: 5781.
Yoke word with deed, and drive an equal apair: 7278.
You always see the same side of the moon: 3804.
You an' me, bister, been giraffes: 6530.
You are of pine yourself, stick-like in Maine: 5212.
You are still the man of the sling and the stone: 3630.
You are the Lago, the Lucerne: 7233.
You are too light, blond, to bear much hardship: 6200.
You are wonderful: 3277.
You ask me about the tide: 961.
You asked me to write of angels: 1377.
You believe you have an antidote: 1191.
You bend, great plane tree, and offer yourself stripped: 6598.
You blow yourself to a handsome watch: 4962.
You built him strong, O God, but not to strong: 1644.
You called me a name on such and such a day: 2102.
You came from Orleans. You brought with you: 935.
You can go farther: 1407.
You come to me tonight with perfect clearness: 3554.

You crawl on my neck and in buzzing you revel: 2028.
You died. I know you died: 4666.
You forgot that you had invited your-selves: 1738.
You get used to these lean hills: 4324.
You had to come to earth to learn it, Lord: 2510.
You have, in a sense...: 6675.
You have shown me much: 6575.
You hear me well: and yet you try: 843.
You know him: Certainly know him: 7352.
You laugh? Strong flattens a greenish tower: 206.
You learned Lear's Nonsens Rhymes by heart, not rote: 4839.
You live on the plains: 7350.
You look up nine authorities: 3354.
You loved the morning always and its blue: 4902.
You, Mark Chagall, should be able to tell us: 341.
You might as well string up: 1736.
You might prefer a pasture spring: 6708.
You must have met the lady: 4603.
You pick one up along the shore: 5572.
You resemble great Apollo: 1415.
You said, "Imagine black velvet and you will sleep.:: 2130.
You say "This Scene's where we came in: 1713.
You see, I am quite alone: 4939.
You see, I have known you a long time: 2048.
You see, shore-hugging is neither surety: 2031.
You see these halted days of: 5945.
You shall not always sit in sunlight, watching: 6126.
You shock to shame, my poor prudential soul: 6558.
You should have died dear: 56.
You should know that the landscape is: 3566.
You small ones, breathing softly in the night: 3723.
You smile, quite confident my praise is right: 5284.
You spoke my name and you smiled at me: 3041.
You spoke of islands, where the fishing boats: 5914.
You stand alone in an emptied house: 6783.
You stand encircled: 1346.
You stay there: 2822.
You take me at the full, a held flood: 2203.
You that wander so disconsolate: 529.
You there in your world: 6495.
You think you'll just touch up the edge: 4759.
You thrust your gift into our hands and "Here.": 1025.
You took my fingers, terrified: 5426.

You turn the household upside down: 4359.

You wait? So I. We wait the capering clown: 6969.

You want my pledge that I will seal: 4486.

You want to look into my heart: 3509.

You wanted roses: 4809.

You waterhead: 2706.

You, well-meaning friend: 1260.

You were the shape of green in your glass: 6775.

You were twelve and I was eight: 5420.

You were wearing your Edgar Allan Poe printed cotton blouse: 7358.

You who have been so long alone: 1918.

"You who have no money," says the Scripture: 4170.

You who mend simple fuses by magic: 3466.

You who have sat disconsolate: 6410.

You whose vision lies deep within: 6564.

You will awake each morning: 7247.

You will go away some time: 4625.

You won't return from the front: 1859.

You work for an hour on snowsuits: 5733.

You wrote, "I walked up to your...": 3328.

You'd be sitting pretty, with nothing in the world to trouble you: 7095.

You'd better not trust it, kitten: 6583.

You'd be surprised at all we plan: 6346.

You'd think a rabbit would at least: 1113.

You'd think to hear his rapture ring: 5174.

You'll find me quite content to condone: 2448.

You'll rank as quite a hit amon: 5148.

Young girls are columbines, or mountain mint: 7363.

Young girls in strawberry skirts: 5483.

The young girls pass--a twittering: 7364.

Young ladies like dating: 4313.

A young man's fancy makes its bow: 1412.

The young man's fancy turns, in springs: 2542.

Young mother with a child on either side: 3417.

Young newlyweds today can get: 5371.

Your afternoon sleep after our Protean anger into: 580.

Your bed: 338.

Your belly button, little man: 2843.

Your body may be a sack: 1336.

Your dog is the kind with a bottom-less tummy: 3421.

Your eyelash is a shade: 3377.

Your eyes glancing like praises leave us arias of sparkle: 4715.

Your eyes which see this remnant shell of hope: 3.

Your face more than others' faces: 3568.

Your gown tonight reminds me: 2669.

Your guests who enter: 6824.

Your kisses are so sincere: 7372.

Your lead, Partner; hope we've read the same book: 7373.

Your lines, dear sir, are rather: 2183.

Your living on my seeing falls: 146.

Your love has made me grave: 4573.

Your rice-bowl is empty, little brother: 921.

Your stories of the shrunken sea's abandon: 6517.

Your well-meant good advice is farm: 6219.

"Your wife," the doctor said: 3959.

You're a tiny study in sheer frustra-tion: 6498.

You're always interrupting, though you know it isn't right: 3054.

You're dedicated to parenthood: 5537.

You're grown up when you find that with: 2446.

You're through--now walking up and down: 116.

Yours was a cycle quicklier run: 759.

You've dreamed of the day when your stripling lad: 4890.

You've heard of Frederick Douglas?: 2165.

A zig-zag bee, and zzz-ing, came: 545.

Zipped into a frivolous dress: 35.

AUTHOR INDEX

ABBE, GEORGE: The Animal, 221; Blueberry Girl, 676; The Bridge, 746;
Children Sliding, 984; A Fat Man Dies,
1876; Forbidden Flight, 2115; The
Handcar, 2471; Horizon Thong, 2634;
The Icehouse, 2776; The Nourishment
of Memory, 4222; Pizzicato, 4825.

ABDOUGH, TANIYOUS: Dr. Choumayyil's
Cat, 1562.

ABEL, LIONEL: Afterward..., 109; On
Man Considered as an Instrument for
Hurting; 4472.

ABRAHAMS, ROBERT D.: The Half Alive,
2464.

ABRAHAMS, WILLIAM: Nobody Here But Us,
4161; Tapestry Figures, 6255.

ABRAMS, CAL: The Hoofer, 2626.

ABSE, DANNIE: Abandoned, 2;
Anniversary, 229; Inscription on the
Flyleaf of a Bible, 2963; On Hearing
the Monologue of a Deaf Poet, 4462;
Poem and Message, 4876; Words Spoken
Alone, 7297.

ACKERSON, JOHN: Departure, Off the
Congo, 1448; The Murmuring Fountains,
Rome, 3976; Rubbish Heap by the
Euphrates, 5369; Sunrise, the Bishop's
Palace, 6174; Through Tears in
Antioch, 6452; The West Front Wells
Cathedral, 7029.

ACRET, JAMES: For My Mother, 2086.

ADAMS, FRANKLIN P.: Antipiscatorial,
254.

ADAMS, JOHN QUINCY: A Congressman's
Prayer, 1182.

ADAMS, MYRTLE REYNOLDS: Moon Road,
3884, Part-Time Calendar, 4676.

ADCOCK, JOE: The Single Man, 5639.

ADIB, ALBERT: The Rebel, 5154.

ADLER, LUCILE: The Hunter, 2697;
The Reservoir, 5241; Sisterly, 5649.

ADRIAN, VONNA HICKS: Bride in Eden,
741; In a Hospital Nursery, 2833;
Parable for April, 4657.

AIKEN, CONRAD: The Phoenix and the
Garden, 4792; Triptych, 6677.

AKINS, ZOE: A Rhyme Without a Moral,
5287; La Terrace Dans La Pluie, 6303;
Variation, 6838; With Sympathy, 7247.

ALBRIGHT, ROGER L.: Bittersweet, 638.

ALISJAHBANA, S. TAKDIR: Meeting, 3728.

ALKUS, MARY: Card Trick, 871; Double
Trouble, 1554; Headwork, 2516; It's
in the Bag, 3057; Model for a New
World, 3854; New Year's Resolution
Made the Week Before Christmas, 4095;
Seasonal Disturbance, 5485; Summer
Sequel, 6147.

ALLARD, BESSIE BUTLER NEWSON: With
Military Honors, 7244.

ALLEMAN, EMILY CAREY: Never Take His
Love for Granted, 4065; The School
Play, 5452.

ALLEN, EDWARD J.: Murder Within the
Law, 3974.

ALLER, CATHERINE: E = mc^2, 1602.

ALTERMAN, NATHAN: From 'Nude Fire,
2194; From The Ten Plagues of Egypt,
2210.

AMEN, GROVER C.: A Winter Morning,
7204.

AMES, BERNICE: Even So the Adolescent,
1765; Roman Candle, 5334.

AMES, EVELYN: Because I Live, 537.

AMIHAI, YEHUDA: Autobiography in the
Year 1952, 414; The Mediators, the
Peacemakers, 3717; Now When the
Waters Press in Force, 4242; Poem,
4851; Sonnet, 5853; Sonnet, 5854.

AMMA, BALAMANI: The Housewife, 2657.

AMMONS, A. R.: Close-Up, 1081; Grassy
Sound, 2388; Joshua Tree, 3110.

ANDERSON, MAXWELL: The World of
Mathematics, 7309.

ANDERSON, WANDA: Three Poems, 6432.

ANDREWS: GRACE CLYDE: Of Course Not!,
4311.

ANDREWS, MIRIAM: Dragonfly Dream,
1563; A Farewell, 1858.

ANGOFF, CHARLES: It Is Not Necessary,
30388; Nothing Is Immune, 4218.

ANONYMOUS, DISCREET Q.: Apologies to
W. S. Gilbert and Most Directors of
Libraries, 267.

ANTHONY, EDWARD: He's Learning to Dress, 2565; Homework, 2622; I Know a Girl, 2738; I Mustn't Forget, 2744; I Won't!--Or Will I?, 2769; It's 'Cause You Get Excited, 3054; Lines to a Boy Regarding His Dog, 3421; Our Stairs, 4604; Policeman Song, 4913; Remember?, 5211; She Has a Way of Putting Things, 5567; The Strangest Chatter, 6089; Young Housebreaker, 7366; Zipper Suit, 7383.

ANTHONY MARIE, SISTER: Surprise Defeated, 6191.

ANTOLINI, MARGARET FISHBACK: In the Pink, 2916; Oh, Baby!, 4359.

ANWAR, CHAIRIL: Paradise, 4662; Story for a Girl, Dien Tamaela, 6078.

ANZAI, FUYUE: Spain--III, 5903.

APIN, RIVAI: Between Two Worlds, 596.

APPEL, WALTER: Gentlemen Never Go Bareheaded, 2268; Sidewalk Superintendents, 5606.

APPLETON, SALLY: Singing, 5636; The Song of a Stone, 5829; To St. John the Evangelist; 6580; The World, 7305.

ARDAYNE, JULIA COLLINS: I, Too, Shall Sing, 2763; Sleep, 5670; To a Groundhog, 6501.

ARMKNECHT, RICHARD F.: Beware-- Friendly Dog, 598; Crow's Nest, 1295; The Faithful Lover, 1838; Gracious Lady, 2362; High Place, Southwest, 2579; It's All in the Raising, 3053; It's Impolite to Change the Subject, 3056; Knock for Luck, 3183; Lines Which Will Probably Go Unappreciated, 3429; Newlyweds, 4096; Night Shift, 4117; On Making Friends, 4471; Skin Divers, 5663; Strategy at Six, 6091; Sudden Knowing, 6123; Third Generation, 6368; Three-Year-Old, 6445; Unhappy Landings, 6787; West-Thrusting Headlands, 7031.

ARMOUR, RICHARD: Acrobat, 24; Advice from a Hoarse Husband, 54; Back to Nature, 456; Boy Meets Bath, 720; Brief Description of Hoarded String, 751; Center of Gravity, 914; Comment on Cows, 1141; Conscience Struck, 1190; Conservatives, 1192; Convalescent, 1213; Curious, 1313; Double Talk, 1553; Feeling Low, 1898; Feline Felicity, 1900; Fifth Wheel, 1919; Folding Money, 2033; A Friend Indeed, 2170; Height of Affection, 2534; Home Thoughts, 2615; Husbands Are Like That, 2704; Ice-Cream Cones, 2774; Incomplete Dishwasher, 2937; Instructions for Chaperons at a Teen-age Party, 2981; Kitchen Sink, 3175; Let's Get This Straight, 3317; Little Girl Skipping, 3457; Loafer, 3482; Meal Timing, 3712; Mother Tongue, 3926; The Neutralist, 4059; New Technique, 4093; (cont'd)

Note on Stenographers, 4203; Occupied, 4277; On His Marks, 4464; On the Grass, 4507; On the Run, 4517; Our Den, 4597; Overhaul, 4624; Perfect Passenger, 4750; The Perpetual Painter, 4759; Portrait of an Enthusiast, 4944; Rain, 5115; Scarecrow, 5440; Shine on, Little Wife, 5581; Slip Cover, 5683; Slow Motion, 5685; Song of the Frightened Motorist, 5836; Space Age Schooling, 5897; Squeaking Through, 5982; Study Habits, 6109; Tears May Be Idle, But Women Aren't, 6262; Thoughts While Waiting, 6421; Top Secret, 6620; Trader, Second Generation, 6639; Travelling Companions, 6661; The Trouble with Sunday Is Monday, 6687; Well Put, 7021; Woman at Work, 7257.

ARMSTRONG, PAUL: Backlog, 459; Chemiseration, 949; Surgical Thoughts, 6187.

ARNOLD, LYN: In Concert, 2848.

ARNOLD, VANN: Summer Winds, 6152.

ASHBERY, JOHN: Abstentions, 13; And You Know, 209; Death Paints a Picture, 1399; Grand Abacus, 2367; The Idiot, 2784; Our Youth, 4605; The Painter, 4646; The Pied Piper, 4807.

ASHBY, DOROTHY: Librarian's Charade, 3345.

ASHER, ELISE: Sickbed, 5604.

ASHMAN, RICHARD: The Crematory, 1279.

ASKUE, RUSSELL PETTIS: The Arrogance of Ignorance, 306; Head of the House, 2513.

ASTIER, MARY: The Passing of the Days, 4684.

ATHERTON, JOHN: I Wander Lonely in the Crowd, 2654; On Inheriting an Empty House at Coney Island, 4466; Open Saturdays, 4569; Penny Arcade, 4741; Recollections of Gulliver: The Inquiring Reporter in Lilliput, 5167; Tank Town, 6249; Threes, 6447.

AUCOURT, JOAN: Charms, 941; On an Irreparable Piano, 4436.

AUDEN, W.H.: First Things First, 1979; Limbo Culture, 3394; On Installing an American Kitchen in Lower Austria, 4467; Streams, 6095; Time Is our Choice of How to Love and Why, 6472.

AUSLANDER, JOSEPH: Memo to the Hungarian Patriots, 3744.

AUSTIN, DEBORAH: Morning-O, 3908; Paradise, 4663.

AUXIER, SYLVIA: Spring Sounds, 5974.

AVERITT, ELEANOR: Child's Voice, 991; Just Before Dawn, 3132; November Day, 4227; Out of Sight, 4609.

AVERY, LEE: Freight Trains, 2166; I Can't Win, 2720; Not So Big, 4191.

AVISON, MARGARET: All Fool's Eve, 139; Prelude, 4991; Rich Boys' Birthday Through a Window, 5290; Stray Dog, Near Ecully, 6094.

AVRETT, ROBERT: Librarian, 3343.

AWAD, JOSEPH: Ash Wednesday, 343.

B, M. A.: To A. L., 6504.

BAGG, ROBERT: Confetti for a Red Haired Bride, 1175; 'Laine, 3200; Penelope, 4739; The Risen Eyelid, 5306; Sonnet by the Lakeside, 5866;

BAILEY, ANTHONY: The Green and the Black, 2413; A Map of Europe: Some Paintings by Vermeer, 3644.

BAIRD, MAURA: Facets, 1828; For the Defense, 2105.

BAKER, D. W.: Recital, 5162.

BALCH, BETTY JANE: Companions, 1149; The Guest, 2451; Indian Summer Day, 2945; Poem for an Afternoon, 4883; Short Short Story, 5593; SOS, 5881; Viewpoint, 6867; The Way Good-by Happens.

BALCH, EMILY: Miss Balch's Letter to China, 3832.

BALDWIN, LEE M.: Inner Fire, 2955; Strength Beyond the Day of Storm, 6100.

BALLIETT, WHITNEY: East River, 1631; Equinox, 1741; The Gift, 2282; Weekend, 7012; Winter Memory: The Pond, 7203.

BANDEIRA, MANUEL: The Cactus, 825; Mozart in Heaven, 3957.

BANDYPADHYAY, KARUNA NIDHAN: Whispered, 7099.

BANGHAM, MARY DICKERSON: Betrayed, 587; Cities of Refuge, 1046; The Indians, 2946; Oblation, 4272; With Reverent Crayons, 7246.

BANGS, JOHN KENDRICK: I Never Knew a Night So Black, 2745; Philosophy, 4788.

BANNING, EVELYN I.: A Librarian in Today's School, 3344.

BANNON, MARCELLA M.: None the Wiser, 4169.

BARBEE, FRANCES M.: The God Who Spoke to Darkness, 2325.

BARKER, EDNA L. S.: Son of the Prairie, 5785; Talking Books for the Blind, 6243; Time, the White Fox, 6478.

BARKER, ERIC: Abandoned Orchard, 4; In Easy Dark, 2857; In Memory of Dylan Thomas; 2874; The Land of Cockayne, 3218; The Mask, 3681; Mirage, 3824; Once Beautiful as a Wave, 4535; The Rock Pool, 5331; Summer Tourists, 6151.

BARKER, GEORGE: Domestic Poem, 1538; The Dove of the Seas, 1555; Heroes and Worms; 2561; Narcissus and the Star, 4038; O Pearl and Breasted World, 4263; The Rose and the Rod, 5351; Swansong of the Hyena; 6204.

BARKER, MARY LUCRETIA: Legacy, 3288.

BARKER, S. OMAR: Burned Forests, 793; Carlsbad Caverns; 877; Cow Country, 1264; Cowboy Cookin', 1265; Critical Situation, 1284; The Deer Come Down, 1422; The Everlasting Surge, 1779; Feminine Figure, 1906; Hidden Rage, 2571; Honest, Anyhow, 2623; The Human Weave; 2692; Liberals on the Loose, 3342; Look at Prosperity, 3506; (cont'd)

Mementos, 3743; The Moth, 3918; Pessimist's Plaint, 4771; Popular Pastime, 4929; Ski Run for Beginners, 5660; Timely Warning, 6481; Wind in the West, 7164.

BARKINS, ELIZABETH: To My Parents, 6571.

BARNES: KATE: Look Alikes, 3503; The Old Woman's Song, 4415; Pastoral, 4700; Song of a Thorn Tree, 5830; Summer Entombed, 6137.

BARNSTONE, WILLIS: The Devil of My Dreams, 1467.

BARO, GENE: Across the Valley, 26; Figures of Farewell, 1924; The Ladder, 3194; Saints, 5410; The Secondary Players, 5495; Under the Boughs, 6770.

BARRETT, ALFRED: For a Golden Jubilarian, 2047.

BARRON, JEROME A.: The Village of My Fathers, 6871.

BARTLETT, ELIZABETH: As You Make It, 338; A Measure of Reason, 3715; Mexican Profile, 3787.

BARTLETT, FRANK: Serenity Is Not Enough, 5532.

BASCH, HUGO F.: Moaning Dove, 3848.

BASTONE, JOHN: On Viewing an Empty Classroon Early in the Morning, 4532.

BATCHELDER, ANN: On A Dial, 4426; To a Certain Person, 6494.

BATHGATE, JOHN: Not Too Distant Shore, 4195.

BAT-MIRIAM, YAHEVED: The Distance Spills Itself, 1510; Like This Before You Just As I Am, 3387.

BAUER, GRACIA LOWELL: Sanctuary, 5419.

BAUER, W. W.: War Diary of an Army Psychiatrist, 6949.

BAXTER, JOE: I'm Just an In-Between, 2815.

BEACH, JOSEPH WARREN: All My Knowing, 146, Early Morning, 1613.

BECK, VICTOR E.: In Flames of Fire, 2859.

BEHN, HARRY: Song to Cloud, 5847.

BELITT, BEN: Andaluz, I-IV, 210; Battle-Piece, 515; A Stand of Pine, 6026; Wasp and Windowscreen, 6966.

BELL, CHARLES G.: The Catalpa, 901; Dialectic of Love, 1471; Dusk of May, 1597; From 'Delta Return', 2188; Liquidation Sale, 3437; Of Water Come to Water, 4350; Song of Our Season, 5833.

BELLOWS, SILENCE BUCK: Pup at a Parade, 5066.

BELOOF, ROBERT: An Easter Riddle Song, 1636.

BELVIN, WILLIAM: A BLIND MAN'S BLUFF, 655; A Christening, 1009; Satan on Economics, 5430.

BEMELMANS, LUDWIG: Madeline's Christmas, 3605.

BENDER, BERTHA B.: Our Brother's Keeper, 4593.

BENDRE, D. R.: The Secret, 5496.

BENEK, MORRIS: On Beauty, 4439.

BENELEY, NELSON: The Eye, 1815.

BENET, LAURA: Screech Owl, 5459; The Stricken Heart, 6101.

BENET, STEPHEN VINCENT: Prayer for a Better World, 4976.

BENN, GOTTFRIED: Fragments, 2162.

BENNETT, ESTER WOLLAM: I Light My Candle from Their Torches, 2740.

BENNETT, JOSEPH: Earthly Love, 1628.

BENNETT, PAUL L.: Spring, 5944.

BENNETT, PENELOPE AGNES: Queen's Summer Song, 5088.

BENON, ERIKA: Al' Aube, 3265.

BENTLEY, BETH SINGER: Aspects of Venus, 347; The Frozen Lake, 2217; A Waltz in the Afternoon, 6943.

BENTLEY, ERIC: And Smile, Smile, Smile, 202; Progress, 5031; The Secular View, 5500; To the Librarians of Montgomery, Alabama, 6594.

BENTLEY, GARTH: Jennie Missed Me, 3085; Serenade, 5530.

BERG, STEPHEN: The Gypsy Moth, 2458; The Room, 5343.

BERIGAN, BUNNY: The B-Hive, 441.

BERKELEY, DAVID S.: A Brighter Hellas, 761.

BERKOWITZ, ROBERT: The Searchers, 5480.

BERNARD, OLIVER: At Hearne, 361; For What Is Foreign, 2110; If the Bright Bird, 2792; Pavane, 4718.

BERNARD, SID: Policy Statement, 4914.

BERNHART, VIRGIE: Gethsemane, 2272; The Stranger, 6087.

BERNING, HELEN DARBY: Daughter of a Son, 1351.

BERRIGAN, DANIEL, Abraham, 7; Domes, 1535; Elegy, 1667; Flowers, 2026; Landscapes There Are, 3233; Loneliness, 3492; More Like the Sea, 3893; Parable, 4655; Saint John Baptist, 5402; Snowman, 5736; Stars Almost Escape Us, 6032.

BERRY, VIRGINIA: The Garden Enclosed, 2244.

BERRY, WENDELL: Diagon, 1470; Elegy, 1668; Rain Crow, 5124; Serenade in Black, 5531.

BERRYMAN, JOHN: Note to Wang Wei, 4207; A Sympathy, A Welcome, 6218.

BESCH, ROBERT: Magi and Manger, 3608.

BESTON, ELIZABETH COASTSWORTH: Finder, Please Return to Henry Thoreau, 1931.

BETJEMAN, JOHN: A Child Ill, 965; In the Public Gardens, 2917; Matlock Bath, 3699; The Olympic Girl, 4420; Seaside Golf, 5484; Village Wedding, 6872; Weary Journalist, 6999.

BEUM, ROBERT: Anniversary Birds, 233; Chanty, 930; The Cholthoi Panel, 1003; The Exhibition, 1801; Six A.M., 5653; Sonnet XXI, 5865.

BEVINGTON, HELEN: The Elizabethan Maid, 1688; Midsummer Night, 3804; The Teacher; 6265; A Windowful of London, 7172.

BEWAS: You - Me, 7353.

BEYER, WILLIAM: Rural Night, 5378.

BIEL, NICHOLAS: The Old Order, 4404.

BING, JOHN: The Cross, 1287.

BIRNBAUM, HENRY: A Family Group, 1858; Orizons, 4581; A Sense of Hugging To Oneself, 5520.

BIRNEY, EARLE: Canada: Case History, 849; Elles-Mereland, 1690.

BISHOP, ELIZABETH: The Armadillo - Brazil, 301; Manuelzinho, 3642; Questions of Travel, 5098; Sestina, 5540; The Shampoo, 5560; Squatter's Children, 5981; The Wit, 7235.

BISHOP, MORRIS: City Science, 1053; Do Good Works, Up to Twenty Per Cent of Adjusted Gross Income, 1520; Hark, Hark, the Bark, 2484; Old Folks at the Home, 4385; Somebody's Been Parking in My Parking Space, 5774; Something Should Be Done About the Muses, 5779; Sometimes I Feel Like a Left-Handed Neutron, 5782; Thoughts on Rereading 'Don Juan', 6416; Thunder on the Left, 6457.

BLACK, SUSAN M.: If Harold Ross Had His Way, 2789.

BLACKBURN, PAUL: At the Crossroad, 373; Cancion de Las Siete Doncellas, 851; Cortaron Tres Arboles, 1239; Good Morning, Love!, 2349; Light, 3375; The Lottery, 3538; The Routine, 5362; Signal, 5611; Sirvente, 5646; Song of the Ants, 5834; Song of the Hesitations; 5837; Suerte, 6126.

BLACKWELDER, DIANA C.: To Love and to Cherish, 6556.

BLACKWELL, HARRIET GRAY: Ana Making Cheese Straws, 186; Butterfly, 809; Fox, 2157; Green Eulogy, 2416; Honey, 2624; In Lieu of a Press Agent, 2865; New House, 4081; Rainy Season, 5133; Reverse Allure, 5279.

BLACKWELL, P. J.: Christmas Problem: 1026; Circus, 1042; Dividing Lanes, 1515; Effective Footwork, 1656; Energy Likes Company, 1715; Expensive Victory, 1812; Have I Forgotten Anything?, 2496; Lines to a Goldfish, 3423; Moody Music, 3879; No Previous Experience Necessary, 4150; Present Tension, 4999; Surface Tension, 6185; Sympathy, Please!, 6219; Tailor-Made, 6233; Tantalizing Morsel, 6250; Unaccustomed As I Am, 6759; Weekend Tragedy, 7013.

BLAGDEN R.: Rat Race, 5140.

BLAKE, WILLIAM: To The Evening Star, 6589.

BLANCHARD, EDITH: Bridegroom, 743; Notes on the Cap-Pistol Set, 4213.

BLEVINS, HOWARD: The Rain, 5116.

BLOOM, ROBERT: Vintage Country, 6875.

BLUM, MORGAN: For a Friend Who Died Along, 2045.

BLY, ROBERT: The Storm Swallow, 6072.

BOCK, FREDERICK: Aubade: The Desert, 397; For the Queen of Franklin High, 2107; A Full Heart, 2225; The Heart on the Sand, 2523; In Memory of Pfc. R. N., 2875; The Moonlight, 3886; 'No Storms Trouble This Part of the Key', 4154; The Picnic of Othello, 4802; (continued)

BOCK, FREDERICK (cont'd): A Return from the Wars!, 5260; The Sparrows on Christmas Morning, 5909; The Vision of Dorinda, 6887; Winter: the Statue of Pomona, 7216.

BODE, CARL: And the Virgin, 206.

BOGAN, LOUISE: March Twilight, 3652; The Meeting, 3279; St Christopher, 5399.

BOGARDUS, EDGAR: Le Puritain et la Putain, 5070; The Wall of Rome, 6938.

BOGGS, W. ARTHUR: Life's Race, 3373; Modern Science; 3859.

BOGIN, GEORGE: What Does Your Father Do?, 7042.

BOHM, ELIZABETH: Alone, 160; Autumn Beach, 421; Boy in a Museum, 717; Ocean Voyage, 4279; Sea Place, 5476.

BOKUDO: Sweetly on the Ear Falls the Sound of the Sea, 6210.

BOLES, FABENS: To One I Love, 6575.

BOLTON, BILL: Letdown, 3313.

BOMSE, NUCHIM: A Wedding in Harvest Time, 7008.

BONALUTO, LUCILLE M.: But Doctor--, 803; Museum Musing, 3980.

BONNEFOY, YVES: Real Name, 5150.

BOOTH, PHILIP: Adam, 31; Barred Islands, 503; Chart 1203, 942; Convoy, 1223; The Countershadow, 1249; Ego, 1658; Forgive Me Nothing, 2125; Good Friday: 1954, 2344; Great Farm, 2400; Green Song, 2426; Gresham's Law, 2433; The Islanders, 3027; Jake's Wharf, 3070; Letter from a Distant Land, 3325; The Margin, 3655; The Seiners, 5509; Shag, 5557; These Men, 6352; The Total Calm, 6625; Was a Man, 6959.

BORDEN, DAVID: The Triumph of Death, 6680.

BOSE, BUDDHADEVA: Versatility, 6849.

BOULTENHOUSE, CHARLES: Elegy, 1669.

BOWEN, DONNA: Return of the Lover, 5263.

BOWER, HELEN FRAZEE: He Came with Music, 2506.

BOWIE, BEVERLEY M.: Arkansas, 299.

BOWSER, ISADORA WHITLEY: Request for a Little Miracle, 5232.

BOYLAN, ROBERT: Crusoe, 1300; Wild West, 7152.

BOYLE, KAY: Dreams Dreamed, 1577; The New Emigration, 4074; A Poem of Gratitude, 5891; Spring, 5945.

BOYLE, ROSALIE: Rivers Are not Patient in Duress, 5317.

BOYNTON, SUE C.: Past All Understanding, 4697.

BOYSON, EMIL: The Child, 958.

BRACKEN, PEG: Lines for an Educated Spaniel, 3411; Of Highways and Byways, 4315; Of Reefs and Marital Waters, 4325; Of Scents and Sensibility; 4326; Of Matters Marital and Martial, 4319; Of Matters Small and Great, 4320; Of the Bride and the Bargain, 4330; (cont'd)

Of the Budget and the Shining Chariot, 4331; Of the Hammer and Its Habitat, 4333; Of the Husband and the Telephone Belle, 4334; Of the Husband, the Wife, and the Inner Ear, 4335; Of the Lady and the Household Law, 4337; Of the Male and the Status Quo, 4338; Of the Man and the Plan, 4339; Of the Monday Mood and the Man, 4340; Of the Tortoise and the Hare, 4343; Of the Vine Which Clingeth, 4344; Of the Warrior Upon His Shield, 4345; Of the Wife and Haute Cuisine, 4346; Of the Wife and the Big Picture, 4347; Of the Wife, the Hyacinth, the Loaf of Bread, 4346.

BRACKER, MILTON: Atomic Submarine, 384.

BRADBURY, BIANCA: June Hot Spell, 3126; Mate, to the Skipper, 3692.

BRADEY, BERTON: Fundamental Flaw, 2227.

BRADFORD, BENJAMIN: Litany of the Apathetic, 3443; Litany on an Edifice, 3445.

BRADLEY, SAM: Only Begotten Son, 4565; Philistines in Hired Rooms, 4784.

BRADY, CHARLES A.: Soeurs de Charite: March 1956, 5747.

BRALEY, BARTON: Step Lively, Please, 6048; Take the Rap, 6237.

BRAMLEY, WILLIAM: The One-Room Apartment, 4553; Will Success Spoil Mrs. Hunter?, 7154.

BRAND, MILLEN: Brown, 770; Country Girl in April, 1253; Creek Song, 1278; Hunting Song, 2700.

BRANDON, WILLIAM: Room for Rent, 5345.

BRASIER, VIRGINIA: Apricot in a City Courtyard, 277; Before Good Night, 551; Concerning the Guest Towel, 1168; The Glassy Look, 2313; Invitation to Dalliance; 3005; Low Chairs: Beware!, 3574; The Mendicants, 3759; No Little Problems, 4146; Poor Parents' Almanac, 4925; A Pot of Geraniums, 4960; Poetent Fluid, 4961; Tall Little Girl, 6245; Winter's End, 7222.

BRAUN, RICHARD EMIL: Islanders, 3028.

BRECHT, BERTOLT: Ballad of the World's Kindness, 473; What Did the Soldiers' Wife Receive?, 7039.

BRENNAN, FRANCIS: Lament for Heroes, 3212.

BRENNAN, JOSEPH PAYNE: The Splintered Streets, 5936.

BRENNEMAN, JEAN: A Prayer, 4972.

BRIDGMAN, BETTY: Fifth Child, 1918.

BRIGGS, OLGA HAMPEL: Mistress Franklin's Son, 3841.

BRILEY, ALICE: Future Homestead, 2229.

BRINNIN, JOHN MALCOLM: Ich Am of Irlaunde, 2777; News from the Islands, 4100; Song for Strangers in Wales, 5819.

BRISCO, PATRICIA: Continuity, 1209.

BRITTAIN, ROBERT: Fairlight, 1835.

BROCH, HERMANN: From 'Die Schuldlosen', 2189.

BRONK, WILLIAM: Midsummer, 3801.

BROOKS, ELEANOR: Miracle in the Back Yard, 3823.

BROOKS, FRED L.: You Give the Answer, 7351.

BROOKS, GENE: A Survey of the Italian Cinema, 6192.

BROOKS, GWENDOLYN: The Bean Eaters, 525; The Explorer, 1813; For Clarice, 2061.

BROOKS, HALLIE BEACHEM: Personnel Problems, 4766.

BROTHERSON, ROBERT: Footnote on Saintliness, 2039.

BROUGHTON, JAMES: Beyond Her Depth, 600; Birthday Card, 629; The Gravity of Spilt Milk, 2393.

BROWN, BRUCE M.: Line Suggested by a Picture of a Tibetan Library, 3420.

BROWN, D. C.: The Mirroring Transparencies, 3829.

BROWN, DOROTHY: Convention Wives, 1216.

BROWN, HARRY: The Drowned, 1586; Ode 3, 4295; Two Unrelated Facts, 6743; The Wheel of Love, Like All Wheels, Comes Full Circle, 7060.

BROWN, JULIAN: Rued Awakening, 5372.

BROWN, LORAINE: Too Polite for My Own Good, 6619.

BROWN, LOURENA RENTON: Candle Star, 853.

BROWN, SPENCER: The Blind Lead the Blind, 653; Boatyard in Spring, 680.

BRUCE, CHARLES: Boy and Pool, 712; Something You'd Say, 5780.

BRULKAR, MARY: The Third Continent, 6367.

BRYAN, BETTY: Morning Mass-Tsuruma, Japan, 3906.

BRYAN, RICHARD: Evergreen, Northwest, 1777; On Playing Games with the Children, 4481; Signs of the Times, 5616.

BRYANT, ANN: To A Misguided Maiden, 6508.

BUCHANAN, PEGASUS: Advice, 51; Embryo Tycoon, 1693; I Didn't Catch the Face, 2723.

BUCHWALD, EMILIE BIX: A Cabin Summer, 823; Song, 5787.

BUCK, BYRON: Where Children Have Played, 7085.

BULKELEY, MORGAN: Chores with Robert Frost, 1005; November Anniversary, 4226.

BUNNER, FREDA NEWTON: Crying in the Wilderness, 1302; Hunger, 2695.

BURFORD, WILLIAM: The Ambassadors, 170; Clay God, 1069; The Days of Love, 1370; El Dorado, 1662; Face of the Earth, 1824; John Brown's Bodies, 3103; Law of Motion, 3273; The Poet's Brain, 4910; The Sea Lavender, 5472; Sea and Sky, 5464; South Harpswell, 5893; The Space Balloon, 5898.

BURGER, OTIS KIDWELL: Convalescent, 1214; The Invasion, 2999; Rain Before Noon, 5123; Sonnet, 5855.

BURGESS, CHARLES: When Shad Are Running, 7075.

BURGUNDER, ROSE: The Eve of Bergunder, 1760.

BURKE, KENNETH: Big Claus and Little Claus, 603; Case History, 885; A Citizen Looks at the Female Figure on an Ancient Jar, 1047; A Letter from the Center, 3329; An Old Liberal Looks to the New Year, 1953, 4392; .

BURKET GAIL BROOK: Protest, 5050; Protest, 5051; Responsibility, 5246; The Sectarian, 5499; Shared Joy, 5565; Your Smile, 7374.

BURNS, JOHN: Ahab on His Wedding Night, 124.

BURNS, MARY G. G.: Piano Lesson, 4796.

BURNS, ROBERT GRANT: Butterfly, 810; Candy for a Little Mexican Boy, 856.

BURR, GRAY: A Glance at the Album, 2310; Lunar Tune, 3593; Meadow Remembered, 3710.

BURR, HUGH: Barbershops; 492.

BURROWAY, JAN: Song, 5788.

BURROWES: ELISABETH: Misunderstanding, 3844; Refusal, 5190; Return from Bethlehem, 5258; Verse for Christmas, 6850.

BURROWS, E. G.: A Change in the Weather, 926; Emigree, 1695; From Music to Mire; 2193; Landfall, 3221; Landscape with Bo Tree, 3231; Nineteen Seventeen, 4135; Saybrook Point, 5435; The Sound of Love, 5889; Uncles, 6763.

BURTON, RICHARD: Do What They Manhood Bids Thee Do, 1524.

BUTLER, DIANA: Pregnant Woman, 4990.

BYNNER, WITTER: An Autumn Walk, 433; Descending Landscape, 1451; Garden, 2239; Inscriptions on Chinese Paintings, 2964; Journey, 3111; The Lark, 3239; The Web, 7005.

BYRON, EVA: The Sea and the Secret, 5465.

BYRON, GEORGE GORDON NOEL BYRON: Oh! That the Desert Were My Dwelling Place, 4364.

CAEDMON, SISTER: Retreat Poems, 5256.

CAEIRO, ALBERTO: Discontinuous Poems, 1502; The Herdsman, 2545.

CALKINS, THOMAS V.: Desegregation, 1454; Living Power, 3478; Miracle, 3820.

CAMP, JAMES: Pascal in the Schoolroom: A Rephrasing, 4680.

CAMPBELL, MARY ALDEN: Words of Furthest Flight, 7294.

CAMPBELL, ROY: Don Juan Tenorio and the Man of Stone, 1539; Liscot's Horses, 3438; The Old Horsebreaker, 4388; To Frederic Mistral (Neven), 6547.

CANADY, JEANNE W.: Least Likely to Succeed, 3282; Tulsa Speaks to Baltimore, 6698.

CANE, MELVILLE: Alpine View, 166; Color, 1122; The Cosmos, 1240; Crickets, 1280; Meadow Incident, 3708; Peepers, 4736; The Plausible, 4835.

CANTWELL, EDLYN: Song of a Girl, 5826; Sonnet, 5856.

CAPETANAKIS, DEMETRIOS: The Isles of Greece, 3030.

CARDARELLI, VINCENZO: Dawn, 1356.

CARDOZO, NANCY: Of Space and Time, 4327.

CARKE, HILARY: A Charm to Be Whispered, 939.

CARLETON, SARA KING: New Look, 4083; No Matter What Disguise You Work, 4148; Souvenir, 5895; Tryst, 6694.

CARLILE, JOYCE: The Postman, 4956.

CARLISLE, IRENE: Biology, I Love You, 610.

CARLISLE, THOMAS JOHN: For Whom the Siren Screams, 2111; The Grass, the Flowers, and the Word of God, 2385; Holiday House, 2601; A Light to Bring Us Safe, 3381; Seeing-Eye Dog, 5503; Teacher, 6266; Thriller, 6450; Where Tall Books Grow, 7087.

CARLSON, VADA: Wind: Desert Sculptor, 7161.

CARMI, T.: She Is Asleep, 5568.

CARNICELLI, THOMAS: Separation, 5525.

CARPENTER, MARGARET HALEY: September Afternoon, 5526.

CARRIER, CONSTANCE: Black Water and Bright Air, 645; An Elegy Long After, 1682; Notes for a Poem, 4210; Quand Meme, 5083; The Tanager, 6247; Terra Nova, 6302; Transformation Scene, 6648.

CARRIER, WARREN: Green I Walk, 2419.

CARROLL, PAUL: The Cigar Store Indian's Gift to the Puritans, 1039; Quomodo Sola Sedet Curtas, 5104; Still Life: Tankard Sun, and Avocado Plant, 6053; Un Voyage a Cythere, 6913; Winter Scene, 7212.

CARRUTH, HAYDEN: Anxiety, 257; The Asylum, 353; Bedrock, 541; The Birth of Venus, 623; A Canon for Two Voices, 857; Depression, 1450; The Fat Lady, 1875; Flagpole, 1998; The Hindu Painter Prepares to Paint, 2587; I Also Love Thee Proserpine: A Romantic Elegy, 2711; Keraunograph, 3149; The Key, 3150; Mondican, 3869; Museum Piece, 3981; November: Indian Summer, 4230; Pavan for a Young Duchess at Christmastide, 4715; Return to Love, 5266; Sinai, 5629; Sparrows, 5908; Spring Raking, 5972; The Street, 6097; Under the Long Wind, 6772; The Waist Line, 6918.

CARSON, ARTHUR: Bullfighter Story, 780.

CARTER, ALBERT HOWARD: Advent, 46; Critique for Our Times, 1285; For Christmas and the New Year, 2060; This Is Only the End, 6380.

CARTER, MANFRED A.: Flood, 2013; Horizon Organ, 2633; A Line Dragging Down, 3398; One Flame, 4543; Soft Whips, 5751; Spray of Stars, 5943; Trivialities of God, 6684; The White Christ, 7105.

CARTER, MARY: Loneliness, 3493; Who Am I, 7124; Young Love, 7367.

CARTER, ROBERT A: The Minstrel in Search of a Legend, 3819.

CARTER, RUTH H.: Dilemma, 1490; Exercise in Rime, 1800; Homage, 2606.

CASEY, KATE: In Poems, 2885; Ode, 4293.

CASSIN, MAXINE: Rescue Party, 5240.

CASSITY, TURNER: Astrology, 352; Chronology, 1033; The Coast at Grand Isle, 1095; Earrings for the Virgin, 1617; Haitian Endymion, 2463; Lotteria, Lotteria, 3537; The Lumber Baron, 3592, The Mounted Bell, 3948; Out of the Pit, 4613; The Quarter, 5086.

CASTLE, HELEN: To My Hostess at a Party, 6566.

CASWELL, OZZIE: Faster! Faster!, 1872; Uriah Heep Rides Again, 6816.

CATHERON, LORRAINE: Processional, 5024.

CATHLIN, SISTER MARY: Behold Your King, 562.

CATON, PAUL W.: The Radical, 5109.

CAVAFY, CONSTANTINE: Aristobulus, 295; Portrait of a Jew, 4940.

CELAN, PAUL: Death Fugue, 1383.

CHADBOURNE, M.: An Act of Her Own, 27; Nantucket, 4034; Never the Truth, 4066.

CHADWICK, HAL: April 15th Complaint, 281; Best Time of Day, 584; Brief Definition of a Sunday Nap, 750; Chronic Necessities, 1031; Confidential to Wives, 1176; Definition Arrived at While Looking in a Mirro, 1430; The Difference Between A Little Boy and His Dad, 1487; Different Substance, 1488; Fishing Line, 1990; Gone to Pot, 2340; Helpful Hint on Keeping Friends, 2539; How to Reduce, 2682; If You Believe the Commercials, 2796; Incident at High Chair, 2933; Just a Hobby, 3130; Key to Accomplishment, 3153; Lazy...Me?, 3276; Life Begins at Forty?, 3366; Longer Faces, 3502; Marked Man, 3663; Modern Conveniences, 3856; My Thrifty Wife, 4019; Neat Feat, 4048; Number One, 4246; On the Other Hand, 4513; On Trying to Stay a Bachelor, 4530; One Little Difference, 4548; Opposite Opinions, 4572; Quit Kidding, Dear!, 5102; Slightly Frustrating; Sure-Fire Self-Starter, 6182; Tittle-Tattle, 6491; We Observant Human Beings, 6991; Who's Lazy?, 7133; The Worst of It, 7316.

CHADWICK, RUTH: It's a Constant Battle!, 3051; Solved the Hard Way, 5765; Somewhat Shaken, 5783; That's Going Too Far, 6325; Thoughts of an Envious Housewife, 6412; What's Sauce for the Goose...., 7058; We're Still in the Dark, 7027; When Is Bedtime?, 7071.

CHAFFEE, ELEANOR ALLETTA: Child on a Beach, 969; The Day Begins, 1360; Letter to a Country Cousin, 3334; Memorial Day, 3745; Rueful Reflection, 5373; Unsubstantial Ghost, 6803.

CHAKRAVARTY, AMIYA: The Traveler, 6658.

CHAMBERLIN, ENOLA: The Desert, 1455.

CHANDLER, DAVID: Chartres: July 1955, 944; Havre de Grace, 2499.

CHANG, DIANA: Four Views in Praise of Reality, 2151; Lines for an Anniversary, 3409; On Seeing My Great-Aunt in a Funeral Parlor, 4491.

CHANG, KIRANGCHI C.: Garden of My Childhood, 2247.

CHAPIN, CAROL EARLE: Highway Construction, 2583.

CHAPIN, KATHERINE GARRISON: Butter-flies, 808; Child and the Tide, 961; Late Song, 3259; Oxfordshire Song, 4634; Portrait in Winter, 4938; The Savage Flutes, 5434; Summer Cape Song, 6135.

CHAR, RENE: Anoukis and Later Jeanne, 246; Companions in the Garden, 1151; Coral, 1228; The Inventors, 3001; One and the Other, 4541; Put on Guard, 5077; The Slapped Adolescent, 5669; Les Transparents, 6651; The Windowpane, 7173.

CHATTERTON: THOMAS: Ode to Miss Hoyland, 4298.

CHE, SHEN: In a Textile Factory, 2838;

CHI, LI: Black Eyes, 642; White Poplar, 7116.

CHIN-TRAI, PU: Plucking the Stars, 4848.

CHISHOLM, JEAN B.: Winter Walks, 7219.

CHRISTOPHER, JOHN: Meeting, 3730.

CHU, TAO: Consolation to the Returning Fighters Against the Floods, 1196.

CHURCH, RICHARD: Choosing the Site, 1004; A Word for Farewell, 7280.

CIARDI, JOHN: Abundance, 14; An Antarctic Hymn, 251; Ballad of the Ikendick, 470; Breakfast in Bed in the Hospital, 738; Bufo, Vulgaris, 780; A Dialogue in the Stoneworks, 1477; A Dream, 1566; Elegy, 1670; For Bernard De Voto, 2055; For Ezra Pound, 2065; George Gordon of Gight, 2269; Memory of Paris, 3755; Naples, 4035; Of History, Fiction, Language, 4316; On Looking East to the Sea Without a Sunset Behind Me, 4470; On the Birth of Jeffrey to William and Barbara Harding, 4495; The One Dull Thing You Did Was to Die, Fletcher, 4542; A Praise to Good Poets in a Bad Age, 4970; The Principal Part of a Python, 5010; Rain, 5117; A Requiem for Hungary, 5238; S. P. Q. R. -- A Letter from Rome, 5384; A Sermon, 5534; Snowy Heron, 5737; Some Figures for Who I Am, 5768; A Sonnet for Robert Frost But Not About Him, 5868; Stopped Suddenly That He Is Beautiful, 6061; There Was Once an Owl, 6344; Thoughts on Looking into a Thicket, 6414; A Thousandth Poem to Dylan Thomas, 6423; To Judith, 6553; To Lucasta, About That War, 6557; Washington, D. C., 6962.

CLANCY, JOSEPH P.: Encounter, 1705; Lourdes: A Poem, 3540; A Poem for Elizabeth; 4885.

CLAPP, DUDLEY: A Benison on C. S. Jennison, 577.

CLARK, DAVID RIDGLEY: Old Chapel: A Poem in Favor of the World, 4374; Pinnacle, 4817.

CLARK, DUNCAN C.: "The Seventeen-Year Locusts, 5550.

CLARK, JOHN ABBOT: On Not Knowing What Lies About Us, 4476; Pecuniary Aren't We?, 4733.

CLARK, LESLIE SAVAGE: Anno Domini, 237; Christmas Card List, 1014; Country Well Curb, 1257; Defenseless, 1429; Delilah, 1437; For Earth Alone, 2062; For Gift of Sky, 2070; Immanence, 2818; Inasmuch, 2928; Jezebel, 3098; Lot's Wife, 3535; Measurements, 3716; The New Year, 4094; Not as a Stranger, 4184; Rachel, 5106; Scarred Earth, 5443; Seek Ye, 5505; Star Flight, 6027; Stature, 6040; Tree of Knowledge, 6667; Who Seeks Through Wastelands, 7129; The Work of Thy Fingers, 7299; Worldwide Communion, 7313.

CLARK, NEIL M.: Adventure, 49; Midnight, 3797.

CLAUDE OF JESUS, SISTER: Our Lady of Advent, 4598; Virgin of Hope, 6878.

CLAUDEL, PAUL: Dec. 25, 1886, 1405; Dialogue from La Ville, 1476; From the Art Poetique, 2201; From the Magnificat, 2207; Heat of the Sun, 2527; The Infant Jesus of Prague, 2951; Parable of Animus and Anima, 4658; Saint Joseph, 5403; The Virgin at Noon, 6877.

CLIFFORD, MARJORY: The Widow's Mite, 7145.

CLOWER, JEAN: Beauty and the Beast, 533; The Birth of Athena, 622; Corpus Mundi, 1233; Night Sounds, 4119; Principles of Flight, 5011; Stance, 6025; The Woman, 7253.

COATSWORTH, ELIZABETH: And the Time Were May, 205; The Birds Begin to Gather, 615; But What Was Beauty?, 807; I Wish It Were April, 2768; Look Alikes, 3504; Look Alikes: By the Shore, 3505; Mary Tudor's Song, 3679; Song, 5789; To a Marie Laurencin Girl, 6507; What Do Cows Think, 7040.

COBLENTZ, STANLEY A.: The Ancient Quest, 193.

COBLENTZ, STANTON A.: Age of Miracles, 114; The All-Forgiving, 140; As Sometimes in a Tale, 333; At the Book's Ending, 371; Birds on a Telegraph Wire, 616; Business Offices, 800; From Sun-God to Mushroom Cloud, 2198; Fruition, 2221; Here in a Teardrop, 2550; Hero, 2558; Hydrogen Age, 2707; I Saw the Invisible, 2749; In a Day of Menaced Freedom, 2826; In Perspective, 2884; In That Weird, 2893; In the Hydrogen Age, 2905; Ishmaelites, 3022; Isolation, 3031; Jet-Age Dilemma, 3094; The King of Evil, 3169; A Materialist Pictures Man, 3695; Missing, 3835; (cont'd)

COBLENTZ, STANTON A (cont'd): Mists, 3842; The Motor and the Man, 3932; The New Heavens, 4078; On an Old Album, 4437; The One and the Many, 4540; Out of Many Songs, 4607; Oversight, 4628; Playthings, 4836; Reappraisal, 5152; Renegades, 5222; Retribution, 5257; Sage, 5390; Self-Portraiture, 5515; Shadows, 5554; So Much I've Known of Life; 5742; Trust in the Future, 6693; The War Dead, 6948; When We Have Gone, 7080.

COCHRANE, PHYSLLIS G.: Through a Glass, Brightly, 6451.

COCTEAU, JEAN: Fortune, 2135.

COE, A. C.: Variation on a Theme, 6839.

COFFIN, ROBERT P. Tristram: A Hummingbird, 2693; New Coin, 4072; Troy in Green, 6689; Young Democrat, 7361.

COGLEY, JOHN: Season's Greetings, 5486.

COHEN, LEONARD: A Kite is a Victim, 3177.

COHEN, YAKOV: Tirzah, 6489.

COKER, ADOLAIDE: Young Girl Singing, 7362.

COLBY, WILLIAM H.:   Repentance, 5227.

COLE, BILL: Hey, Hey! Make Way for the Latest Model, 2560.

COLE, CATHY: The Dance of Spring, 1334.

COLE, WILLIAM: Alma Mater, Forget Me, 156.

COLEMAN, ELLIOTT: The Garden of Delights, 2246; Joyce's Grave, 3118.

COLERIDGE, H.: Prayer, 4973.

COLES, CHRISTIE LUND: Come Summer, 1132; From the Garden, 2204.

COLLIER, MARGARET D.: Every Summer's Children, 1780; Retired Missionary, 5253; The Year of the Great Freeze, 7331.

COLLINS, BESSIE F.: Amusement Park, 185; Grab Bag, 2358; A Kind Word for Winter, 3165; Letter from Verona, 3330; The New Houses, 4082; Stray, 6092.

COLLINS, IVAN J.: Charge and Countercharge, 933; How Dare They Make My Mountain a Molehill?, 2664; It Works Both Ways, 3044; Out of My Reach, 4608; Shopping Fatigue, 5588; Softie, 5753; Spring Confession, 5954; Strange Species, 6085.

COLLINS, MARGARET GRAHAME: Animated Leaves, 226; Braggadocio, 729; Desert Doubles, 1456; Farm Widow, 1865; Flowers and Spice, 2027; Kind Design, 3159.

COLUM, PADRAIC: After Speaking of One Who Died a Long Time Ago, 90; The Basket-Maker, 506; The Book of Kells, 694; Raftery, 5113.

COLT, BYRON: Castra, 890.

COLVIN, FRANCES: Red and Brown, 5171; Rooftrees, 5341.

CONE, LOUIS O.: Between Worlds, 597.

CONGDON, A. KIRBY: Disciple, 1501

CONGDON, TOM: A Gobbler's Lament for Gobblers, 2322; Halloween Do-It-Yourself, 2468; In Answer to Your Question, Son...., 2843; Marriage's First Paradox, 3669; Monsterama Movies and Me, 3876; New Teacher, First Day of School, 4092; Redeemable in Full, 5176; Revenge, 5278; Shape of Things to Come, 5563; Survivors, 6195; Whistle and the World Whistles With You, 7100.

CONKLIN, BARBARA SHOOK: Boat Whistle Blues, 677; Dream's End, 1578; The Forsaken, 2131; How Walks My Love?, 2685; Lucinda, 3581; To a Gentle Lover, 6500; Until You Came, 6804.

CONRAD, SHERMAN: A Beethoven Dance, 549.

CONSTANT, BARBARA B.: Mama Turns the Tables, 3621.

CONSTANTINE, JULIE: Backward Glance, 460.

CONSTANTINOFF, RICHARD: Sonnet, 5857.

CONWAY, MARGARET DEVEREAUX: L'Horloge, 2635; Our Lady of the Migrant, 4599.

COOKE, ROBERT: Manger Scene, 3637.

COOLIDGE, SUSAN: Singing Voices, 5637.

COOPER, BILLY B.: Salesmanship, 5413.

COOPER, JANE: The Builder of Houses, 783; The Innkeeper's Story, 2956; Morning on the St. John's, 3909.

COOPER, JOHN C.: Enigma, 1721; In the Midst of Life I Petition Thee, 2912; Job, 3100; One Thing Is Sure the Heaven's Declare, 4557; Soul Searching, 5882; Soul Searching, 5883; A Thought, 6402; Uncreated Love, 6768.

CORDAN, WOLFGANG: Cain, 827.

CORKE, HILARY: After the Bomb, 93; After the Rain, 98; Chair, Dog, and Clock, 920; The Dark the Darkness, 1343; Fan-Piece, 1857; The Frontier, 2213; It Is a Wind Where All Was Still, 3036; Poem at Equinox, 4877; Speech in an Orchard, 5920; The Tristram Picnic, 6679.

CORMAN, CID: After Reading Keats' Letters, 88.

CORTES, DON: The Bulganin Boat Song, 787.

COSBEY, ROBERT C.: Ground Mole, 2441.

COTTER, JAMES F.: All the Rivers of Eden, 151; And Mary Sang, 199; Blind Child, 651; A Child at Play, 963; Child of Light; 967; Conversation with a Child, 1220; Dance, Dance, 1333; Desire Not the Night, 1461; A Dialog of Stars, 1473; Fireflies, 1941; The First Communion, 1954; For Joan of Arc, 2080; The Girl at Play, 2298; Hands, 2473; Jubilee, 3119; Kingdom of Daylight, 3171; Moment Of Incarnation, 3864; The Morning, 3895; No Man but One, 4147; Paulinus of Nola, 4712; The Road from Emmaus, 5320; The Shroud of Turin, 5596; Song for the Widow of Naim, 5822; We Children Are All One Child, 6984; You Shall not Break a Bond of Him, 7356.

COUGLIN, PAUL: A Sung Sonnet, 6171.

COUNSELMAN, MARY ELIZABETH: Boy, Reading, 722; The Passionate (Union) Shepherd to His Love, 4691; Tribute to My Mother, 6669.

COURT, ATTELIA BOWNE: Four Poems, 2148.

COUSENS, MILDRED: Spring Tide, 5975.

COUSINS, MARGARET: The Visitor, 6895.

COX, MIRIAM S.: Unsaid..., 6799.

COXE, LOUIS O.: After The Burst, 94; America to Hungary, 1956, 174; Arbor Vitae, 293; Autumn Numphal, 429; Between the Airbase and the Radar Tower, 592; The Bush, 799; Elegy, 1671; End of the Road, 1709; Fall of Leaf, 1844; Field Marshall, Retired, 1915; For My Son's Birthday, 2088; From the Window Down, 2211; Hero's Winter, 2563; The Hostage, 2643; The Last Hero, 3243; Lent, 3299; The Mythmakers, 4025; Prodigal Son, 5025; Spring Near the Airbase, 5968; A Study of History, 6109; The Waking, 6924; Watching Bird, 6971.

CRAIG, E.C.: Sneak Thief.

CRAIG, ROSE BETTY: Autumn, 416.

CRANE, CAROL L.: Two O'Clock Talk, 6730.

CRAVEN, MARGARET: First Grader in Library, 1962.

CRAWFORD, JACK, JR.: A Breast Humming, 739; Empty House, 1698; Goddess of the Doorbell, 2327; Sleepwalkers, 5676; The Wound of Innocence, 7317.

CREEKMORE, HUBERT: The Excavator, 1787.

CREELEY, ROBERT: The Door (I), 1544; The Door (II), 1545; A Gift of Great Value, 2287; Going to Bed, 2334; The Herd, 2544; The Hill, 2585; My Love, 4006; The Names, 4031; The Rain, 5118; Sing Song, 5634.

CREGEEN, SHEILA: Confusion, 1178; Two Moons, 6729.

CRESSON, ABIGAIL: The Calico Cat, 830; Cheerful Company, 948; Our Mutual Friend, 4603; The Patina of Memories, 4707.

CREWS, JUDSON: The Artist, 318; Excelsior, 1788; The Lovers, 3560; Matadora, 3690; The River, 5310; Sole the Fabled Dim Recess, 5760; Winter Edge, 7189.

CRITES, STEPHEN: Shepherds at Advent, 5577; Sonnet of the Shepherds, 5871.

CROOK, KILE: August, 400.

CROUSE, MIRIAM LEFEVRE: After Spring 91.

CROWN, RACHEL: Boy with Snake, 726; My Father's Benediction, 3998; To a Scientist Friend, 6517; Where and No Trees, 7084.

CRUMPET, PETER: Fund-amentalism, 2228.

CULBERT, ANNE C.: Question, 5092.

CULLY, KENDIG BRUBAKER: Committees in Heaven?, 1143; Darkness Needing Light, 1347; Deeper Than Knowledge, 1421; Eros and Agape, 1744; For Music, 2084; Moment in Time, 3863; (cont'd)

One Light, One Love, 4547; Reply to Demonic Assault, 5228; Valentine for One Loved, 6830; Word to a Church at a Time of Grave Decision, 7283.

CUMIN, MAXINE W.: The Quest, 5091.

CUMMINGS, E.E.: Christmas Poem, 1024.

CUNEY, WARING: I Dreamed I Saw Lord Daniels, 2726.

CUNLIFFE, CORINNA: Fortitude, 2134; Summer Chapel, 6136; Sunrise, 6173; There Are Places, 6338; Young Song, 7371.

CUNNINGHAM, DONALD J.: Gloria in Excelsis, 2317.

CUOMO, GEORGE: On Reading Shakespeare Near a Window, 4485; On the Death of a Student Hopelessly Failing My Course, 4498; Somebody Has to Teach Them Their ZYX's, 5773; Soundings, 5891.

CURNOW, ALLEN: He Cracked a Word, 2507; To Forget Self and All, 6546.

CUTLER, BRUCE: At Acatitlan, 356; The Creation, 1274; A Hymn to the Creator, 2709.

CUTLER, GLADYS B.: The Aim's the Same, 126.

D, H.: Do You Remember?, 1526; In Time of Gold, 2925; The Moon in Your Hands, 3883; Nails for Petals, 4027; Regents of the Night, 5197; The Revelation, 5274; Sometimes and After, 5781.

DAERR, MARIE: Lemonade Stand, 3297.

DAHLBERG, EDWARD: Five Poems, 1994.

DAICHES, DAVID: Historical Footnote, 2594; To Kate, Skating Better Than Her Date, 6554.

DALE, ESTHER: Sonnet, 5858.

DALLAS, CONSTANCE H.: White Collar, 7107.

DANA, DORIS: Death Unmourned, 1400; Grief, 2436.

DANA, ROBERT PATRICK: For Sister Mary Apolline, 2099; My Glass Brother, 4000.

D'ANDRADE, DIANE: On a Portrait of Wallace Stevens, 4433; What Can Be Made from Nothing, 7036.

DANNER, MARGARET: Best Loved of Africa, 582; The Painted Lady, 4645.

DARCY, LOUISE: Leaf, 3279; Surplus, 6189 To a Real-Estate Agent, 6512.

DARCY, M.M.: To an Atomic Scientist, 6528.

DAS, JIBANANDA: Twenty Years After, 6714.

DATTA, SUDHINDRANATH: Camel-Bird, 843.

DAVIDSON, GUSTAV: Cliche, 1073.

DAVIDSON, JOHN F.: Emancipated, 1692, End of Vacation, 1712; Lines for Holy Week, 3412; O Death Where is Thy Sting, 4256; To a Fellow Shipmate, 6496.

DAVIDSON, LOIS: Prayer of an Aged Man, 4985.

DAVIDSON, LOREN K.: The Iron Gate, 3013; Strange Christ, 6083.

DAVIS, F. MARK: On the Late Hungarian Massacre, 4510.

DAVID, O.L., JR.: The Library, 3347.

DAVID, SAMUEL: Night Music for Old Men, 4111.

DAVISON, PETER H.: The Site of Last Night's Fire, 5651; The Winner, 7180.

DAWSON, ELIZA LOUISA: Food, Shelter, and Clothing Slumber Song, 2036; House of the Warm Woods, 2654.

DEAN, ABNER: October, 4282.

DEAN, ELMA: In Defense of a Green Christmas, 2851; On Boarding the Dog, 4441; Weak Resolution, 6996.

DEBEE, RAJLUKSHMEE: The House, 2649.

DECAVALLES, ANDONIS: A Greek Trireme, 2412; Time of Judgement, 6474; Tragedia Minima.

DEFORD, SARA: Simplicity, 5627; The Spring, 5946; Turn on the Light, 6700.

DEJONG, DAVID CORNEL: Adagio: On a Summer's Beach, 30; April in the Country, 284; Do Re Me of Young Watching and Waiting, 1523; Do You Remember?, 1527; The Doings of Love, 1534; Eglantine: A Souvenir, 1657; I Never Lost Faith in Angels, 2746; In a Dutch Town, 2829; The Janitor's Face, 3073; Master, 3687; Old Men Observing Small Boy Crying, 4401; Pavan on a Beach, 4716; Postmortem of a Solon: State Level, 4957; Preparing for a Love Nest on the Plains, 4997; The Smallness and Strangeness, 5704; Song of a Little Experience, 5827; There Is a Railroad Track, 6340; Travel Log, 6655; The Virtues of Home, 6879; Yellow Tom, 7337; The Youthful Expectations, 7377.

DEKAY, ORMONDE, JR.: Poet Cornered, 4900; Sonnet, 5859; Tap Nap, 6253;

DELAMARE, WALTER: Daughter to Mother, 1352.

DELATTRE, PIERRE HENRI: Apocalyptic, 264; Bach at a Funeral Service, 448; Beat, 529; Chapel, 931; Compassion, 1154; The Cycles, 1320; Eachaton, 1606; First Communion, 1955; Fission, 1991; Jeremiad, 3086; Jongleur de Dieu; 3108; Noah, 4159; Repose, 5230; Ruach, 5368; Sentry, 5524; Shoal, 5586; Sniper, 5716; Young Reformers, 7370.

DELEEUW, CATEAU: Conviction, 1222;

DELL, GEORGE F.: Clay, 1068; Country Auction, 1251; For My Son: Twenty, 2087.

DELONGCHAMPS, JOANNE: Between the City Gates and the Sea, 593; Blind, I Speak to the Cigarette, 652.

DENNEY, REUEL: Closing the Resport, 1085; Fixer of Midnight, and Other Portraits, 1996; The Snake River in August, 5712.

DERWOOD, GENE: Camel, 839; Shelter, 5573; Third Madrigal, 6370.

DEUTSCH, BABETTE: Barges on the Hudson, 499; A Carol Out of Season, 881; Disasters of War: Goya at the Museum, 1500; Earliness at the Cape, 1607; Feeding the Chickens, 1897;

July Day, 3120; N. Y. Tanka, 4026; Seascape, 5482; Small Colored Boy in the Subway, 5690; Suspension, 6200; Unearthy Toy, 6777.

DEVER, JOSEPH: Father Lord, R. I. P., 1879.

DEVITO, ETHEL BARNETT: Beach Baubles, 521; Conversational Taboo, 1221; Death of a Good Neighbor, 1387; Female Fashion kxpert, 1904; Girl in Love, 2299; Girl with a Diamond, 2300; Grown-Up Note, 2446; Happy Ending, 2479; Horn Blower, 2636; Hostess Who's the Toastess of the Town, 2644; Medical School Red-Letter Day, 3719; Moment of Truth, 3865; New Look in Divas, 4034; Personal Glossary, 4764; Synthetic Age, 6221; Young Mother, 7368.

DEWHURST, S.H.: Pursuit of Happiness, 5073.

DICKER, HAROLD: Bird Song, 614; Bridges, 749; The Failure of the Mask, 1833; Seven-tenths Cloud, 5547; The Sword, 6214; Upper Bay, 6810.

DICKEY, JAMES: The Angel of the Maze, 214; Below the Lighthouse, 571; Dover: Believing in Kings, 1556; The Enclosure, 1703; The Father's Body, 1885; The First Morning of Cancer, 1967; The Game, 2237; The Landfall, 3222; Orpheus Before Hades, 4586; The Other, 4589; The Performance, 4751; The Signs, 5612; The Sprinter's Sleep, 5977; The String, 6102.

DICKEY, WILLIAM H.: For Easter Island or Another Island, 2063; Last Classic Scene, 3240; Of the Festivity, 4332; Oxford 16 October 1555, 4633; Quae Lucis Miseris Tam Dira Cupido? Dicam, 5082; Teaching Swift to Young Ladies, 6271; A Vision, Caged, 6886.

DICKINSON, EMILY: Autumn, 417; Hope Is the Thing with Feathers, 2631.

DICKINSON, PETER: Advice to Commuters, 61.

DIGIOVANNI, NORMAN THOMAS: In the Morning You Always Come Back, 2914; The Night You Slept, 4125; Nocturne of the Dead Adolescent, 4164; The Paupers, 4714; Verra la Morte, 6848.

DIOP, DAVID: Africa, 69.

DISHER, NORMAN: Poem for a Child Who Slept too Long, 4880.

DOCKRY, MARGARET MCANDREW: Deep Hour, 1418.

DODGE, HARRY G.: Growing, 2443.

DODSON, SPURGEON, Sheepshape, 5569.

DOHERTY, KEVIN F.: The Burial, 792; Dark Mirror, 1342; The New Ordained, 4088.

DOMOFF, JUDITY: Quick Change, 5100.

DONALDSON, STANLEY: The Bees, 548; The Hurt of Autumn, 2702.

DONNELLY, DOROTHY: Alexandrina, 134; Charm, 936; Chinese Baby Asleep, 993; Constellation of the Tree, 1203; Drawing of a Little Girl by a Little Boy, 1564; For Peter Who Cried Because He Could Not Catch the Moth, 2092 (con'd)

DONNELLY, DOROTHY (cont'd): Girandole, 2297; Greek Coins, 2410, People, 4744; Perennial Landscape, 4748; Snowflakes, 5735; Trio in a Mirror, 6674; Wheels, 7062.

DONNELLY, MARGARET: Grandmother, 2374.

DORHEIM, RINA NAMEN: Foreboding, 2117.

DOUGLASS, SUZANNE: Artistic Appreciation, 322; Authority, 412; Dawn Patrol, 1358; Even in Eden, 1763; The Life of the Party, 3370; On the Tip of the Tongue, 4522; Positive Thinking, 4949; Theatrical Review, 6329; Traveler's Song at Twilight, 6659; Viewpoints, 6868.

DOYLE, CHARLES: My Love Lies Down Tonight, 4008.

DOYLE, MARION: Christmas Questions, 1027; The Everlasting Light, 1778; The Gift, 2283.

DRAKE, CAROL CHRISTOPHER: Immigrant, 2819.

DRAKE, LEAH BODINE: The Convent Bell, 1215; Drone, 1585; Flemish Artists, Fifteenth Century; 2000; The Hellenic World, 2538; The Web, 7006; The Weeds and the Wilderness, 7011; The Word of Willow, 7282.

DREWRY, CARLETON: Autumn on the Skyline Drive, 431; A Consolation, 1193; The Outer Banks, 4617.

DREYER, CORA WILCOX: Rocky Mountain Town, 5333.

DROUET, MINOU: Paris Sky, 4670; The Sandcastle, 5420.

DRUMMOND DE ANDRADE, DRUMMOND: Childhood, 976.

DUDEK, LOUIS: The Cage, 826.

DUDLEY, JEAN HOGAN: As Peter Loved, 329; Woman Reading, 7261.

DUFAULT, PETER KANE: Ash Can, 342; Black Jess, 644; Crow, 1293; Gielgud Reading Lear, 2281; Glimpse of Three Children on a Picnic, 2315; Good Night to a Little Girl, 2350; Jet-Vapor Trail, 3095; A Letter for Allhallows, 3323; Long, Darwin, and Others, 3497; Piper, 4822; Route, 5360.

DUFFY, DENNIS: Counsel to Budding Aesthetes, 1244.

DUGAN, ALAN: The Branches of Water or Desire; Landfall, 3223; Portrait, 4934; A Pretty Girl, 5001.

DUGAN, MAIDA MASON, The Little Book's Story, 3448.

DUKE, THEODORE: Sweater, 6205.

DUNBAR, VIRGINIA ESTERLY: If You Came, 2798; Song of the Stars, 5840.

DUNCAN, LOLA: Farmer by the Sea, 1868.

DUNCAN, ROBERT: August Sun, 407; Bone Dance, 686; Brought to Love, 769; Food for Fire, Food for Thought, 2034; Metamorphosis, 3779; A Morning Letter, 3905; Out of the Black, 4611; Re--, 5143; Returning to Roots of First Feeling; 5269; A Ride to the Sea, 5296; A Storm of White, 6071; The Temple of the Animals, 6289; There's Too Much Sea on the Big Sur, 6347; To Vow, 6605; (cont'd)

Under Ground, 6769; Words Open Out Upon Grief; 7296; Yes, as a Look Springs to Its Face, 7339.

DUNN, MARY BERNICE: Apology to Poets, 269; Christmas Presents from a Little Girl, 1025.

DUNSANY, LORD: Dirge for a Performing Lion, 1499.

DURYEE, MARY BALLARD: The Blue Saint of Brecon, 673; Cottontail in Snow, 1242.

EARLE, VIRGINIA: Deya (Mallorca), 1469; Eden, Afterward; Snails, 5710; Watercourse, Vermont; 6978.

EASTMAN, FRED: This I Ask of Poetry, 6379.

EATON, BURNHAM: To Tabitha, 6583.

EATON, CHARLES EDWARD: The Bride Is a Motive of Melody, 742; October's Man of Gold, 4291; Sea Trauma, 5477; Such Force as Blinds the Giant, 6120.

EATON, WALTER H.: Song of the Passionate Psychologist to His Beloved, 5839.

EBERHART, RICHARD: Anima, 220; Attitudes, 388; The Blue Grains, 668; Clam Diggers, 1060; Fortune's Mist, 2137; Futures, 2231; The Garden God, 2245; The Hard Structure of the World, 2482; Hoot Owls, 2628; In After Time, 2840; Late Summer, 3261, Light from Above, 3380; Love Among the Ruins, 3542; Only in the Dream, 4567; Riches, 5293; A Soldier Rejects His Time Addressing His Contemporaries, 5757; The Spider, 5923; Sportive Accolade, 5941; Spring Mountain Climb, 5967; The Still Spirit, 6054; Sunday in October, 6164; A Testament, 6305; Throwing the Apple, 6453; Thrush Song at Dawn, 6455; To Bill Williams, 6536; To Helen, with a Playbill, 6551; True North, 6692; Vast Light, 6845; A Young Greek, Killed in the Wars, 7365.

EBRIGHT, FREDERICK: After Ice Storm, 84; Berceuse, 578; Bus Journey, 796; Masquerade Night, 3685; Old Wharves, 4413; Philatelist's Prayer at Twilight, 4783.

ECKHARDT, A. ROY: Between Christmas and Good Friday, 588; Compassion, 1155; Faces, 1826; Kenossis 1955, 3148.

ECKMAN, FREDERICK: After Work, 100; Old Man, Phantom Dog, 4397; The Sign, 5610.

EDELMAN, KATHERINE: After Decision, 79; Answered, 249; Garment of Grace, 2255; Telescope, 6280.

EDEY, MARION: October Fly, 4287.

EDWARDS, BRUCE: Reflection on the Innate Fairness of Words, 5184.

EFF, JOHANNES: Asiatic Flew, 344; The Barracuda, 502; The Bat, 508; Call of the Jungfrau, 833; The Elephant, 1685; The Final View of Henry Two, 1927; For Whom the Times Chimes, 2112; The Geese, 2260; The Gorilla, 2355; Idiot's Delight, 2785' The Lizard, 3480; My Malenkovy Baby, 4009; (cont'd)

EFF, JOHANNES (cont'd): The Sloth, 5685; The Stork, 6064; The Tiger, 6465.

EICH, GUNTER: Think of This, 6365.

EISENLOHR, LAURENCE: Along About March, 163; Anyone for Nothing, 260; Bedtime, 542; Birthday Roses, 632; Bracketeer, 727; Conspiracy, 1199; The Enchanted Cottage, 1701; End of the Weekend, 1710; The Food of Love, 2035; Heat Raves on the Airways, 2529; It Figures, 3033; It's Too Darn Quiet!, 3060; Line of Trucks, 3400; A Matter of Distribution, 3701; Oh, My Aching Baccalaureate, 4362; On Opening a Wedding Invitation, 4478; P. S. to a Letter of Recommendation, 4637; Progress, 5032; Styled for the Future, 6109; Sunday Afternoon, 6163; Thoughtful Junior, 6407; Return Mail, 5261; The Unhappy Farmer, 6786; Water Babies, 6972; The Wheel of My Life; 7061.

EKULKAR, MARY: Street Song, 6098.

ELDRIDGE, JESSIE CANNON: To a Blue-Jeaned Heart, 6492.

ELIOT, THOMAS STEARNS: Gus: The Theatre Cat, 2457; Possum Agonistes, 4951.

ELLERT, MARGARET MCKEEVER: High Note, 2578; Moan from the Doghouse, 3847; My Car, 3989.

ELLIOT, GEORGE: Poem, 4852.

ELLIOT, MARGARET: Unspoken Words, 6802.

ELLIS, CAROLYN: Angler Emeritus, 219; Beatitude for Steven, 530; Credo, 1277; Inland Angler, 2955; More Research, Please, 3894; A Professor Goes Fishing, 5026; Rapunzel! Rapunzel!, 5136; Spring Magic, 5964; Spring Observation, 5970; This Thing Called Spring, 6395; Upon Reflection, 6809.

ELLIS, E.K.: Hugh Latimer, 2687.

ELLIS, SIDELLE: A Book, 689.

ELLYSON, LOUISE: In a Manner of Speaking, 2835.

ELMER, FRANKLIN D., JR.: Candle-lighter, 854; Lord of Darkness, 3515; Sermon for Today, 5535; Sermon of Our Century, 5536; Tall Are the Mountains of Christmas, 6244.

ELMER, IRENE: Purely Nominal, 5068.

ELY, EFFIE SMITH: Alike to Thee, 137;

ELY, GLADYS: Eximious Old Friendships Are, 1804; The Lane, 3234; Moral Spontaneity: A Love Poem, 3889; Woodchuck Rampant, 7274.

ELYTIS, ODYSSEUS: I Know the Night No Longer, 2739.

EMANS, ELAINE V.: In Defense of Living in the North, 2853; Note With a Jar of Jam, 4209; Postscript to Rain, 4959; Soft Sounds, 5750; To My Husband, Hanging a Calendar, 6567; Winter Morning in the Garden, 7205.

EMBIROKOS, ANDREAS: Daybreak, 1369.

EMBURY, LUCY: When Beauty Walks the April Hills, 7064.

EMERSON, RALPH WALDO: Not Gold, But Only Man Can Make, 4186; Singing Voices, 5638.

EMMONS, DICK: The Advantage of Me, 45; Bare Trap, 493; Change of Hearts, 928' Fall's Alarm, 1847; The Grass, Alas, 2384; Having a Miserable Time (Glad You're Here!), 2498; Hidden Lost or Right Where It Belongs?, 2570; Home Groan, 2612; It Isn't a Job: It's a Position, 3040; Matter of (Golf) Course, 3703; Note to Weekend Guests, 4208; Recovery Discovery; Sore Point, 5878; Sound Approach, 5886; Surface Reflection.

EMMONS, HELEN: Grid Gripe, 2434.

ENGEN, EDNA: Lullaby for a Baby Bookworm, 3587.

ENGELS, JOHN: The Old Duke, 4378;

ENGLE, JOHN D., JR.: Bars and the Bear, 504; Brown Moment, 772; Correction, 1235; Request for Quiet, 5233; Thanks, 6311; Waking City, 6925; Wrong Diet, 7325.

ENGLE, PAUL: Amagansett Beach, 169; A Christmas Child, 1015; Colette, 1116; Cowboys, 1266; A Dedication, 1413; Don't Go, 1540; A Gift of Song, 2289; I'm Home, 2814; Map, 3643; An Old Palestinian Donkey, 4405; On This Wall, in This Town, in Their Own State, 4527; River Daughter, 5312; Sick, 5603; The Sound of Green, 5888; The Sound of Red, 5890; To Be a Child, 6533; To Praise a Man, 6578; A Willow Child, 7156; Worm, 7314.

ENGLISH, ISOBEL: Advice to a Convalescent, 56.

ENGONOPOULOS, NIKOS: Poetry 1948, 4907.

ENRICO, HAROLD: Auschwitz, 411; Man of My Time, 3630; The Wall, 6934.

ENRIGHT, ELIZABETH: Nursery, 1956.

ENZENSBERGER, HANS MAGNUS: Cultivate Your Garden, 1368.

ERBA, LUCIANO: The Inattentive, 2929; Land and Sea, 2929.

ERICSON, ALLEN: St. Valentine's Day, 5409.

EVANS, ABBIE HUSTON: On the Curve-Edge, 4497.

EVANS, VIRGINIA MORAN: Letter to a Former Neighbor, 3335; Lines on a Bus to the Young Matron Across the Aisle, 3417; Snapshot in a Teacher's Album 5713.

EVERSON, LANDIS: Famine, 1856; The Last Marriage, 3244; These Friends of Yours, 6350.

EVERSON, R.G.: After Evening Milking, 82; Cold-Weather Love, 1115; Delayed Fuse, 1435; Forgotten Light, 2126; Looking for Firewood, 3512; The Strange Horses, 6084; When I'm Going Well, 7069; Winter Evening After the Theater, 7190.

EVERWINE, PETER: Designs on a Point of View.

EWING, ANNEMARIE: Never Scoff, 4063; Now You Have Said Good-Bye, 4243.

F, H. P.: The Marriage of Mankind, 3668; Perils of Modern Living, 4754.

FABSTEIN, W. E.: Green Light, 2420.

FACOS, JAMES: After the Quarrel, 97; Psalm of Love, 5060; Rendezvous, 5220; Reveille, 5273; The River Belle, 5311; Winter Nocturne, 7208.

FADIMAN, CLIFTON: Biographical, 609; Clerihews, 1071; Clerihewsful, 1072; Poe-Tatory, 4850; Sartorial, 5429; Spectacular, 5918.

FAIRBAIRN, DES: Instrument Approach, 2982.

FAIRBION, DOROTHY: Sweetheart in Jeans, 6209.

FAIRCHILD, ROSEANN: Snowed Under, 5733; Triple Threat, 6676.

FALL, DONALD: College Walk, Postwar, 1119.

FANDEL, JOHN: After All, 74; The Bee, 545; Chant at Aquidneck: Pars Verna, 929; Editions of a Poet, 1655; The Flowering, 2023; Husbandry, 2703; Indians, 2947; Legend, 3294; Monday's Vision, 3868; Storm, 6065; The Watch, 6969.

FARBER, NORMA: The Grasses Are Cut Down, 2386; Make Me No Lazy Love, 3618; The Smooth Maroon Horse-Chestnut, 5709; The Wineshade Essence, 7176.

FARJEON, ELEANOR: First Gathering, 1961; Poetry, 4903.

FARNASH, HUGH: The Madonna of the Ill-Favored, 3606.

FARNHAM, JESSIE: Argument for Attics, 294; Formula for Sleep, 2130; Legacy in Brass, 3291; Words for a Wallflower Waltz, 7292.

FARRAR, JOHN: Nostalgia, 4180.

FASEL, IDA: A Housewife's Time, 2660; Prayer for a New Daughter, 4979.

FAST, NATHAN: A New System of Water Purification, 4091.

FAUBION, DOROTHY: Boy in Clover, 719; Child, Adopted, 960; Long August, 3495; Old Orange Trees, 4403.

FAWCETT, BRUCE: Kathleen Ferrier (1912-1953), 3143.

FEIGHNY, GERALDINE F.: Proud Steps, 5054.

FEIN, RICHARD: On Equality, 4450.

FEINE, VIRGINIA B.: Ex Libris, 1786; Foyer Trap, 2160; No Letter Today, 4145.

FEINSTEIN, HERBERT: The Dark Wood, 1344; Elegy on a Personal Pronoun, 1683; Psychoemantics, 5062.

FELDMAN, IRVING: Adam, 32; The Apotheosis of Alexander, 270; Broadway Harlequin, 764; A Curse, 1316; The Death of Vitellozzo Vitelli, 1398; From a Wandering Jew, 2181; Loss, 3521; Reading Rousset's 'L'Univers Concentrationnaire', 5149; The Saint, 5395; The Tourists in Spain, 6631; Women, 7266.

FENNELL, ROBERT E.: Harriet's Train Again, 2488.

FERLINGHETTI, LAWRENCE: An Autumn in a Word, 424; Rooks, 5342; What Happened the Day a Poet Was Appointed Postmaster, 7044.

FERRIL, HORNSBY: The Train Butcher, 6641.

FERRY, ASA J.: A Prayer for the United Nations, 4983.

FICHMAN, YAKOV: Midnight, 3798.

FIDELIAN, BROTHER: The Year of Jeremiah, 7330.

FIELD, ALIDA: Book Gluttony, 693.

FIELDING, WILLIAM K.: To Mrs. Lindbergh, 6561.

FIEDLER, LESLIE A.: Four Midrashim for Passover, 2146; I Change Time and Think of Margaret; 2721; I Force Myself to Watch the Scenery, 2730; I Wake But It Is Always the Wrong Time, 2764; The Lion, 3433.

FINKEL, DONALD: The Day of the Dead, 1365; The Great Wave: Hokusai, 2408; The Imbecile, 2816; Loss of Hearing, 3523; Two Steps of a Lame Man, 6742.

FINKS, JESSIE WHITESIDE: A Prenatal Prayer, 4995.

FISCALINI, JANET: Diana, 1481.

FISHER, LENORE EVERSOLE: Event, 1774; Ex-Baby, 1783.

FISHER, VIRGINIA: Spirit Sons, Spirit Lovers, 5929.

FITZELL, LINCOLN: O'Clock, 4281; Song for a Guitar, 5807.

FITZGERALD, GERALD: Death and the Maiden, 1381; Three Orpheus Songs, 6430.

FITZGERALD, JOHN E.: Rev. Alfred J. Barrett, S.J., 5272.

FITZGERALD, ROBERT: Jesu, Joy of Man's Desiring, 3091; Metaphysical, 3782.

FITZSIMMONS, THOMAS: Checkmate, 947.

FLATTO, ELIE: A Jeremiad, 3087.

FLAUMENHAFT, A. S.: Afternoon in the Animal Kingdom, 103; American Valhalla, 179; Oliver Would Twist, 4419; Teacher Comes of Age, 6267.

FLEISCHER, LAWRENCE: Regard the Roach, 5193.

FLEMING, HAROLD: An Atmosphere, 382; Elocution at Thirty, 1691; The Farm, 1860; The Hour Before the Coming of the Night, 2648; The Lens Grinder, 3293; Rainbow, Rainbow ..., 5131; Sure of What the Birds Know, 6183.

FLEMING, SEUMAS: Tranquilizers, 6645.

FLEXNER, HORTENSE: Messenger, 3776.

FLINT, LARRY: Build Well That House, 782.

FLYNN, CLARENCE EDWIN: Stage Settings, 6024; Wisdom and Ignorance, 7230.

FORD, EDSEL: Consolation, 1194; Inseparable, 2966; March Scene (With Applause), 3650; A Sly Fox Waiting, 5688; The Tree House, 6666.

FORT, CAROLINE L.: On Torrance Beach, 4529.

FOSDICK, HARRY EMERSON: God of Grace and God of Glory, 2324.

FOSS, SAM WALTER: The Head Librarian, 2512; The Reference Librarian, 5180.

FOSTER, RICHARD: Apocalypse, 262.

FOWLER, ELSIE MELCHERT: To My Young Daughter, 6573

FOWLER, JOYCE: Wife's Confession, 7150.

FOX, IDA: Kline and Stein, 3179; The World, 7306.

FRANCE, W. B.: Now and Then, 4234.

FRANCIS, L. V.: Daddy's Turn, 1326; Handle with Care, 2472.

FRANCIS, MARILYN: The Edge of Sleep, 1653.

FRANCIS, ROBERT: Boy Riding Forward Backward, 723; Sailboat, Your Secret, 5393; A Tribute to W. H. Auden and His Vocabulary, 6670.

FRANKENBERG, LLOYD: O Little Town, 4261; A Refusal to Mourn, Etc., 5192.

FRANKLIN, GENE: The Trap, 6652.

FRANKLIN, JESSIE MERLE: Country Hills, 1254; Lady in Waiting, 3197; Little Girl at the Piano, 3455; Spring-Cleaning Notes, 5952; Winter Dusk, 7188.

FRAZEE-BOWER, HELEN: Decision, 1409; I Hold the Book, 2737; I Rest in His Love, 2747; This Is to Walk, 6386; To a Husband on Father's Day, 6503.

FREEDMAN, C. P.: Not to be Stilled, 4194; Uncounted, 6766.

FREEMAN, A. D.: Boy with a Basket Ball, 724; Caretaker, 874; Cat Nap, 897; Meeting, 3731; The Old Dowser, 4377; Old Granary Burying Ground, 4387; TV Tree, 6224.

FREEMAN, BLANCHE K.: Mañana, 3636.

FREEMAN, JAMES DILLET: Aim, 125; Go Tell Her That You Love Her, 2319; June, 3125; Snow Flowers, 5725; Strength, 6099; This Christmas Pete's Fourteen, 6376.

FREEMAN, JEAN TODD: Bell Song, 569; The Dreamers, 1574; For Wendy, 2109; In the Desperate Hours, 2898; Inland, 2954; Island Song, 3026; My Dream Was Real, 3992; Or Turn to Stone, 4573; Proserpine, 5048; Robin's Secret, 5326; Telephone, 6278; The Young, 7359.

FREEMAN, JOE B.: A Word to Celibate Scientists, 7284.

FREEMAN, JOSEPH: Earth, Sea, and Sky: 1919, 1621; In Memoriam: 1954, 2868.

FRENEAU, I. D.: April in Vermont, 285; Cliff Idyll, 1074; A Discovery, 1503; Redbird in the South, 5174; School Bus, 5449; Tenth Anniversary, 6297; Vacated Camps, 6820.

FRETZ, J. HERBERT: One Thing Thou Lackest, 4558.

FREZZA, LUCIANA: Seascape, 5483; The Two Cousins, 6722.

FRIAR, KIMON: In Childhood's Chair, 2846.

FRIEDRICH, GERHARD: April Night, 286; Aubade, 390; August Moon, 404; Autumnals, 435; Day unto Day, 1368; Love Song, 3554; Nocturne, 4163; O for the Child, 4258; This Garden, 6378.

FRIEND, ROBERT: Exorcism, 1807; In the Orchard, 2915; Pygmalion, 5080; The Riddle, 5294.

FRIMET, HILLEL: In the Morning, 2913.

FROST, FRANCES: Busy Child, 801; Cat and the Autumn Stars, 894; Child Running, 972; Earth Walker, 1623; Ipswich Ballad, 3009; January Night, 3078; Mortal, 3914; Night Shift, 4118; Sea Mark, 5473; White Sowing, 7119; Winter Lullaby, 7201.

FROST, ROBERT: The Great Event is Science, the Great Misgiving, the Fear of God, Is That the Meaning of It Shall Be Lost, 2398; Kitty Hawk, 3178; Of a Winter Evening, 4307.

FROST, TRACEY: I'd Like To Be a Firefly, 2781.

FRUMKIN, GENE: The Hawk and the Lizard, 2500; An Inquiry Into the Ultimate Loneliness, 2960; Lament for an Old Pressman, 3211; The Salesman, 5412;

FULLER, ETHEL ROMIG: Little Song, 3469; Shoppers at a Clearance Sale, 5587.

FULLER, JOHN: In a Railway Compartment, 2837; Jealous, 3083; Sleeping, 5673; White Queen, 7117; Witch, 7236.

FUNK, MARY RUTH: The Telephone Pad, 6279.

FURLONG, WALTRINA: The Sling of Vision, 5682.

FUSSELL, EDWIN: Black Cross, 640.

GABLER, CAROL M.: On Getting to Work at 8:10 A.M., 4456.

GAERTNER, JOHANNES: Committees, 1142.

GAINES, CHARLES: Lost Heritage: II COMMENTARY 22, 3529.

GAKAK, V. K.: On Womanhood, 4534.

GALBRAITH, GEORGIE STARBUCK: As a Wild Bird, 325; As Brooks Rush Headlong, 325; At No Loss for Words, 367; Au 'Voir, 389; The Bargain, 497; Bedtime Rhyme, 543; The Biggest Thing, 607; Brighten the Corner, 760; By Coincidence, 815; Cash Reserve, 888; The Citadel, 1045; Conspicuous Variation, 1198; Contemplative Blossom, 1207; Conversation, 1217; The Cynic, 1322; Dangerous Inflation, 1337; Date Line: December 26, 1350; Dear Departing Guests, 1378; Designing Woman, 1459; Displaced Person, 1507; Double Deficiency, 1551; Easy Does It...Or Does It?, 1641; The Egotist, 1660; The Fair Sex, 1834; Fall Guy, 1841; The Famale of the Beaches, 1905; Fire with Fire, 1940; Flattery, 1999; Force-Fed, 2116; Frozen Assets, 2216; Getting the Drift, 2273; Give Kindness Grandly, 2305; Hard Lines on a Soft Touch, 2481; A Heap of Difference, 2518; Heartlight, 2525; Heavy, Heavy, But Not Too Heavy, 2533; The Hermit, 2556; Hero of the Yellow Pages, 2559; Hint to Anybody's Husband, 2589; Inexpensive Remedy, 2950; Introvert's Lament, 2996; Irritant Incarnate, 3017; Jane, 3072; Just His Dish, 3134; Lines with a High Moral Tone, 3430; Little Elegy, 3453; (continued)

GALBRAITH, GEORGIE STARBUCK: (cont'd)
Little Homely, 3460; Little Pitchers,
3468; Lives of Great Mean All Remind
Us, 3476; Losing Phase, 3520; The
Lost Stone, 3533; Love Will Distract
Me No More, 3558; Low-Cost Holocaust,
3575; Magnetic Attractions, 3611;
The Man in the Aisle Seat, 3628;
Marginal Note on a Milk Bill; 3656;
The Mud-Pie Set, 3969; My Correspon-
dence, 3990; Mysterious Gift; 4023
Neat Trick, 4049; Neck and Neck,
4051; Never Let Your Pride, 4062;
The Night Wind, 4124; No Ifs, Ands,
or Buts, 4142; Now: A Definition;
4232; Now Autumn, 4235; Of Mops and
Men, 4321; Old Tears in Galilee,
4411; On a Certain Spinster, 4424;
On Having Meant Well, 4458; On
Refusing Secrets, 4486; On the High
Cost of Primroses, 4508; Opinions,
4571; Out of Sight, 4610; Package
Deal, 4639; Paradox Retained, 4667;
Poem Found in a Grass Catcher, 4890;
Political-Science Note, 4918; Post-
script to a No Visitors Sign, 4958;
Prompt Pardon, 5040; The Rebel, 5155;
Recollection of a Very Young Oracle,
5166; Relatively Speaking, 5201;
Remarkable Mutation, 5208; Residue,
5242; Rest Period, 5247; The Rose Is
Both, 5353; Rude Awakening, 5371;
A Seizure of Couplets, 5510; Send
Flowers, Dear Friends, 5517;
Serpent's Teeth, 5537; Seventeen,
5549; Singin' the Blues, 5635;
Slightly Souciant Song, 5680; Slow
Starter, 5686; So Many Children,
5741; Sound Defects, 5887; Spoon-
Feeding Rhyme, 5940; Spring Nocturne,
5969; Statistical Blank, 6039;
Summary of the Situation, 6131;
Summary of the Man, Situation at Any
Summer Resort, 6130; A Summer's Tale,
6155; Superman, 6176; Teen-Age
Defense, 6275; This Morning, 6389;
Time Off for Bad Behavior, 6477; To
a Mouse, 6509; To a Too, Too Gracious
Hostess, 6521; Treason with Reason,
6664; Value, 6834; The Vulnerable,
6914; Wanting Roses, 6946; Well-
spring, 7026; Who Am I to Condemn?,
7126; Who Dat?, 7127; Who's Whose?,
7134; Willy-Nilly, Bacilli, 7158;
Winged Victory, 7177; You Shall Be
Forgotten, 7355.
GALE, VI: The Old Fishstation, 4383
The Spit, 5933.
GALL, ANGELA: First-Born, 1947; For
Father, 2068.
GALLER, DAVID: The Anesthetic, 188;
Ascendance, 339; The Beetle, 550;
The Carousel, 883; The Crossroads,
1292; The Execrators, 1794; Fields
of Flowers, 1916; For Blake's Angels,
2056; For Robert Graves, 2098; The
Graces of Autumn, 2361; The Great
Vox: A Dumb Show, 2407; In the
Maze, 2911; The Interview, 2992;
Jericho, 3088; Joseph, 3109;
The Little Candy Store, 3451; The
Long Walk, 3501; The Mockery, 3851;
Night Letter, 4110; Outdoors One
Makes Most Strange, My Lady, 4616;
Scenario, 5444; The Siren of the
Kitchen, 5644; Snow Scene, 5730; The
Trap, 6653; Whistle Stop, 7101.
GARCIA LORCA, FREDERICO: Ode to Walt
Whitman, 4303.
GARDENER, WILLIAM: Cacti, 824.
GARDNER, ISABELLA: At a Summer Hotel,
355; Canzonetta, 863; Here Is a Candle
to Light You to Bed...., 2552; Math-
ematics of Encounter, 3697; Summer
Remembered, 6145; The Widow's Yard,
7146.
GARLICK, RAYMOND: Woman Clothed in the
Sun, 7258.
GARRIGUE, JEAN: Another Third, 245;
Catch What You Can, 903; The Chess
Dance, 952; Declamation After the
Three Bears, 1411; Dialog in the Dark
Tower, 1472; A Figure for J. V. Meer,
1920; For the Circuit of the Orpheum
and the Isis, 2104; In Burnt Autumn,
2845; Incantatory Poem, 2931; Night
Talk, 4121; Notation, 4197; Notes
From Underground, 4212; One Third of
a Dream, 4559; Soliloquy in Cemetery
of Per Lachaise, 5763; This Swallow's
Empire, 6394; What My Grandmother
Said When She Fed the Kingdoms of the
Air, 7050.
GASKILL, MARGARET: Question Heir, 5093.
GASS, W. H.: Lament for Our Failure to
Improve Ancient Skills, 3213.
GATES, CLARA: Give Me a Book for
Traveling, 2306; Similarity, 5624.
GEIGER, DON: Aunt Mabel, 410.
GELLER, ARTHUR: In My Beginnings, 2880.
GEMMELL, JEAN: City Late, 1051.
GERKLE, WILLIAM F.: Not Quite a Poem
on Togetherness in the Witherness,
4189.
GERLACH, L. F.: 48 B. C., 2139.
GHISELIN, BREWSTER: In Search of Man,
2891.
GIBBONS, ANN: Calling Heaven, Line 2,
Ring 4, 835.
GIBBS, B. R.: An English Cathedral,
1718; Sea Gulls on an English Cliff,
5470; Stillness, 6055.
GIBBS, BARBARA: California, an Ode,
831; Demeter, 1442; The Engines Never
Quite Die Away, 1716; The Fountain,
2141; The Gardener Outside a College
Window, 2252; Lion, 3434; The Meeting-
Place of the Colors, 3734; Petition
to This Room, to Allow One to Work,
4776; Pianists, 4795.
GIBBS, ELISE: Birthday Gift, 630; Four,
2143; To a Second Child, 6518.
GIBBS, ROZALIE: A Change in the
Weather, 927.
GIBSON, DOUGLAS: Cocktail Party, 1100;
My Father and My Son, 3995.
GIBSON, WALKER: Advice to Travelers,
64; Fear of Falling, 1889; Focus,
2030; The Great Healer, 2402.
GIBSON, WILLIAM: Apology for No Poems,
268; Lullaby, 3583.

GILBERT, PAULA COFFEY: Four O'Clock, 2147; Woman, 1955, 7259.

GILBOA, AMIR: Against the Wind, 112; Birth, 618; Evening of Whirlwind, 1770; If They Show Me a Stone and I Say Stone, 2793; Issac, 3020; The Lock of Weeping, 3486; Moses, 3915; On a Recollected Road, 4435; Song Yet Song, 5850; Their Past Laughter Will Strike Them, 6330.

GILL, BRENDAN: Bad Dream, 462.

GILL, JOHN J.: Comparison of Flowers, 1153.

GILL, MARY: Georges Roualt: Processions, 2270.

GILLIS, WILLIAM E.: The Month of February, 3877.

GILMAN, MILTON: Poem, 4853.

GINSBERG, LOUIS: Autumn Leaves, 426; Bird Feeding Young, 611; Concert, 1170; G. I.'s in Classroom, 2233; Little Boys, 3449; Morning in Spring, 3904; Now a Satellite, 4233; Now Satellites, 4239; The Peddler, 4735; The Quarrel of the Mountain with the Wood, 5085; School, 5448; Spring Song, 5973; When High School Is Out, 7067.

GIORDAN, ALMA ROBERTS: As We Forgive--, 337; Litany for a Man-Child, 3442; Never as Men, 4060; The Widow, 7140.

GISNET, AHARON: The Tel at Givat Oz, 6277.

GIULIANI, ALFREDO: I Burn and Recognize Imminence, 2719; The Lame Heart, 3207.

GLAZE, ANDREW: A Cut of Copernicus, 1318; The Political Prophet, 4916; Suwanee River, 6201.

GLAZIER, LYLE: The Fisher, 1986.

GLEASON, HAROLD WILLARD: Creature of Custom, 1276; Distaff, 1509; The Leveler, 3340; Limited Vista, 3395; Once Over, Weekly, 4536; Short Cut, 5590; Song for Halloween, 5813; Stay of Sentence, 6043.

GLEASON, MARIAN: Charmed Circle, 940; History Revisited, 2596; Jerusalem, Vermont, 3090; Materia Medica, 3693; Small Talker, 5699.

GNASH, O.: The Cynical Librarian, 1323.

GODDARD, H. C.: The Feather and the Song, 1892.

GODLEY, MARGARET: All the World's a Library, 152.

GOGARTY, OLIVER ST. JOHN: Free Will, 2164; The Supreme Crown, 6181; Then and Now, 6332.

GOHN, GERALDINE EVERETT: Apron Strings, 290.

GOLD, ARTHUR RALPH: For Pop, 2094.

GOLDBERG, LEAH: Dialogue, 1474; From 'On the Flowering', 2195; On This Day, 4526; Remembrance of Beginnings of Things, 5214; Will Truly Yet Come, 7155; Facsimile, 1829

GOLDEN, LEE: Facsimile, 1829; Lovers, 3561; The Self-Appointed, 5512.

GOLDIN, JUDAH: Deep Deep, 1416; Inside the Shadow, 2970.

GOLDSMITH, O.: Hope, 2629.

GOLFFING, FRANCIS: The Arizona Desert, Filmed, 297; The Cross, 1288; Drinking at Dusk, 1584; Dry Gold, 1590; New Hampshire Eclogue, 4077; Ode to the Memory of Paul Wightman, Painter, 4301; On Prescience, 4482; The Sibyl, 5598; Smitten with Too Much Foresight, I Resigned, 6513; To a Recent Believer, 6513; The Tomb of Stephane Mallarme, 6615.

GOODMAN, MAE WINKLER: Blue Jay, 671; Day in Gold, 1363; Earthbound, 1625; Kindergarten, 3166; Miracle, 3821; Retort While Shoveling Snow, 5255; Sapphires, 5425; Thoughts While Cutting Grass, 6419; Wife to Husband, 7149.

GOODMAN, PAUL: Ballade to Venus, 483; The Car Barn Under Coogan's Bluff, 870; The Great Black Hound Upstairs--, 2396; Lavender, 3271; Long Lines, 3498; My Daughter Very Ill, 3991; No, 4137; On the Lake, 4509; The Past, 4694; A Rough Wall, 5357; Song, 5790; Two-Poems on the Way, 6735; We Have a Verb 'Stood Up', 6988; Wellfleet Harbor, 7025.

GOODMAN, RYAH TUMARKIN: Silence Spoke with Your Voice, 5618.

GOODREAU, WILLIAM J.: The Quiz, 5103.

GOODWELL, ROBERT: Stack, 6023.

GORDON, DON: The Blow Lands, 660; The Middle Passage, 3795; The State, 6038.

GORDON, ROBERT: Mr. Moto, I Presume, 3964; One Way Out, 4561; Rhyme for April, 5286; The Wordless Tribe, 7286.

GORDON, WALTER M.: Justus ut Palma, 3137.

GORMAN, FRANCIE: The Cuckoo Clock, 1306.

GOTTLIEB, SAUL: Father to Son, 1881.

GOTTLIER, H. J.: Inside Athens, 2967.

GRABISCH, PAUL L.: Doorway Delay, 1549.

GRACE, WILLIAM J.: Being, 563; Pearl of Great Price, 4729; Spiritual Journey, 5931; This Light, 6388.

GRAHAM, CHARLES: The Picture is Turned Toward the Wall, 4805.

GRAHAM, ELIZABETH: Alas! Farewell, 131; Alliance, 154; Always Room for One More, 168; Anniversary Eve, 235; A Curious Song, 1315; For I Have Known Your Love, 2076; Girls in a Pony Cart, 2304; If You Are a Stranger Here, 2795; In Reply to Your Query, 2889; Oh, I Rode Right Through Childhood, 4361; A Philosophic Thought Based on Income, 4787; Release, 5203; Silhouette, 5622; Sundial, 6169; To a Child Seen Skipping, 6495; You Do Not Envy Me, 7350.

GRAHAM, JAMES, MARQUIS OF MONTROSE: If...?, 2788.

GRAHAM, RACHEL: March Wind, 3653.

GRAHAM, W. S.: The Constructed Space, 1206.

GRAVES, MILDRED HATCH: Skating by Moonlight, 5659.

GRAVES, ROBERT: Around the Mountain, 304; Augeias and I, 399; Bitter Thoughts on Receiving a Slice of Cordelia's Wedding Cake, 637; Catkind, 906; A Bouquet from a Fellow-Roseman, 709; The Enlisted Man, 1723; Established Lovers, 1751; The Fever, 1911; Fingers in the Nesting Box, 1936; Flight Report 2009; Here Live Your Life Out, 2553; Heroes in Their Prime, 2562; Joan and Darby, 3099; The Naked and the Nude, 4028; Nothing, 4214; Old World Design, 4417; The Outsider, 4622; Plea to Boys and Girls, 4839; The Second-Fated, 5492; To a Caricaturist, Who Got Me Wrong, 6493; Woman and Tree, 7256.

GRAVES, SARA BRIDGE: The Back Road, 455; Future Partners, 2230; Manning an Observation Post in a Remote Area in Maine, 3639; When the Barn Burned Down, 7076.

GRAY, ELMER LESLIE: The Message of the Bells, 3775.

GRAY, EVA: Peace and Prayer, 4724.

GRAY, THOMAS: Epitaph, 1728.

GRAYBEAL, MARIE: Poem, 4854.

GRAYER, ROSALIE: The B Minor Mass, 442.

GREBANIER, BERNARD D.: In the Manger, Christmas Day, 2910.

GREEN, F. PRATT: Back to the Engine, 457; A Little Ode, 3466; Return to Earth, 5265.

GREENBERG, ELIEZER: In the Gray Light, 2902.

GREENBERG, URI ZUI: We Were Not Likened to Dogs, 6993.

GREENE, CHARLES SAMUEL: In a Great Library, 2831.

GREENE, JEAN CORWIN: The Most, 3917.

GREENE, ROBERT: Samela, 5418.

GREENSLET, FERRIS: Tempora Mutantur, 6291.

GREENWOOD, ROBERT: Line for My Grandmother's Death, 3413.

GREER, SCOTT: Danse Macabre, 1338; Human Interest Story, 2691; Noon Fire, 4172.

GREET, ANNE HYDE: Spring Eclogue, 5956.

GREGOR, ARTHUR: Late Last Night, 3257; The Mist from Tree to Tree, 3839; A Mode of Hangings, 3853; Song Without Words, 5849.

GREGORY, HORACE: Dottusimi Signori: Giacomo Leopardi, 1550.

GREIG, MICHAEL: Friends of My Bones, 2174.

GRENIER, MILDRED BROMLEY: Forecast Colder, 2119.

GRENVILLE, R. H.: Aging Process, 118; Bird of Prey, 613; Blue Monday, 672; Brief Note to a Creditor, 757; Child Singing, 973; Circus Clown, 1043; Class of '58, 1063; Clatter, 1066; Colchis Bay, 1105; Consolation, 1195; Crow, 1294; Crude Reply to a Classic Question, 1297; Crying Shame, 1303; Domestic Dilemma, 1537; Essentials, 1750; Expanding North, 1808; First Quarrel, 1969; First Wrist Watch, 1982; Five-Year-Old, 1995; Hasty Judgment, 2493; Heat Storm, 2530; Homesteader, 2621; Late Frost, 3254; Leap-Year Lyric, 3281; Love Gift, 3547; Man on the Bridge, 3631; A Matter of Discipline, 3700; Memory, 3750; Mother of the Bride, 3924; Neighbor's Garden, 4055; No Laughing Matter, 4144; October Escapade, 4286; October Morning, 4288; Once Upon a Summer, 4538; Patchwork Weather, 4704; Prairie Song, 4967; Prize Hen, 5020; Salmon Run, 5414; Scarecrow in a Winter Field, 5441; Small World, 5703; Sneak Preview, 5714; Speaking as a Parent, 5912; Suppertime, 6180; The Sycamore, 6216; Tell Me a Story, 6283; To Complicate Matters, 6541; To the Author of a Travel Ad, 6585; Told by a Gypsy, 6613; Two Birds, 6720; Vanishing American, 6836; Walking Weather, 6933; Warning, 6954; Was It Thus?, 6961; Weather Profit, 7001; Winter's House, 7223; Wit's End, 7251.

GRIFFIN, HOWARD: Ex-GI at the Show of Berlin Paintings, 1785.

GRIFFITH, E. V.: Farm Wife Dead, 1866; Line Post West, 3401; Untimely Crows, 6805.

GRIFFITH, HALL M.: Prayer for a Child in a Hospital, 4977.

GRIMM, EDWARD: Site, 5650.

GROOM, I. SUTHERLAND: The First Friends' Meeting, 1960.

GROSS, HARVEY: Mahler, 3613.

GROSSMAN, ALLEN: I Am in Babylon Dying, 2714; Norma, 4173; Pain, 4643; Pompeii, 4919; The Secret Religionist, 5498; Trucks, 6691.

GROSSMAN, MARSHA: I Like Pink, 2741.

GROSZMANN, LORE: To a Nightingale, 6510; The Virus, 6881.

GROUND, YVONNE: Ode to a Half Persian Cat, 4296.

GROVER, KATHRYN AINSWORTH: Answer at Easter, 248; Days of the Sun, 1371.

GUENTHER, CHARLES: Midsummer Night, 3805.

GUHA, NARESH: Supernatural, 6178.

GUILLEN, JORGE: The Horses, 2642.

GUNN, THOM: The Annihiliation of Nothing, 228; Autumn Chapter in a Novel, 422; Black Jackets, 643; The Corridor, 1238; During an Absence, 1596; High Fidelity, 2574; Human Condition, 2689; In Santa Maria del Popolo, 2890; Legal Reform, 3292; Lines for a Book, 3405; Merlin in the Cave: He Speculates Without a Book, 3767; A Plan of Self Subjection, 4830; The Unsettled Motorcyclist's Vision of His Death, 6801; Vox Humana, 6911; Waking in a Newly-Built House, Oakland, 6926.

GUNTERT, JEAN: Lines to Elizabeth, 3425.

GURI, HAYIM: Song and Me, 5801; The Spring, 5947.

GUSTAFSON, RALPH: The Election, 1664; Fort Tryon Park, 2133; Her Love As a North, 2541; In the Time of Fall, 2921; A Window, a Table, on the North, 7169.

GUTHRIE, RAMON: The Clown: He Dances in the Clearing by Night, 1092; The Clown's Report on Satyrs, 1094; Europa, 1758; Ezra Pound in Paris and Elsewhere, 1820; To and On Other Intellectual Poets on Reading That the U.S.A.R. Had Sent a Team of Scientists to Africa to Learn Why Giraffes Do Not Black Out, 6530.

HAAG, JOHN: The Child of Many Winters, 968; The Recluse, 5164.

HABER, LEO: Albert Einstein on the Violin, 132; Confessions of Zilpah, 1174; The Khazar Poet, 3157; My Father Died in Alexandria, 3996.

HACKETT, ELOISE WADE: To a Small Spider, 6519.

HAGELSTANGE, RUDOLF: All Is Dust, 143; Memento, 3741.

HAGER, WESLEY H.: A Prayer of Gratitude, 4986.

HAGIWARA, KYOJIRO: The Family, 1850; I Will Suffer from What My Father Suffered From, 2767; Death of a Frog, 1386; A Dish of Skylarks, 1505; Littoral Zone, 3474; The New Road of Koide, 4090; Song Without a Name, 5848; Tortoise, 6624.

HAINES, JACK A.: His--or Ours?, 2591.

HALACY, D. S., JR.: Form 1040 Blues, 2128; Lyricist, 3572.

HALE, OLIVER: Fires, 1943; 42nd Street Library, 2140; John Hancock, 3104.

HALE, ROBERT BEVERLY: Denise, 1444.

HALL, CAROL: An Old Woman's Words to Her Young Cat, 4416; To a Woman Seen Eating the Evening Paper, 6523.

HALL, DONALD: Amos, 183; Bamboo, 487; Caribbean, 875; Christ Church Meadows, Oxford, 1008; A Friend Revisited, 2171; I Chop Down Trees, 2722; In Memory of Augusta Hall, 2873; Iuvenes Dum Sumus, 3062; Jack and the Other Jack, 3007; Jamaica, 3071; The Kiss, 3174; Lycanthropy Revisited, 3595; Matter of Fact, 3702; Merrimack County, 3769; The Morning Porches, 3910; Mr. and Mrs. Billings, 3959; 1934, 4136; A Novelist, 4223; Now Side by Side, 4240; On a Horse Carved in Wood, 4429; Religious Articles, 5206; Remarks on the Occasion of Love, 5210; A Set of Seasons, 5543; The Shudder, 5596; The Starlings, 6031; T. R., 6223; These Faces, 6349; To Break a Mirror, 6537; Transcontinent, 6647; The Umbrella, 6758; The Widows, 7144; The World, the Times, 7311.

HALL, FRANCES: Retort, 5254.

HALL, JAMES B.: Grandmother, 2375.

HALLOCK, KATIE: Pick Me Green, 4800.

HALPERN, MARTIN: My Mother's Father, 4012.

HAMBURGE, MICHAEL: Instead of a Journey, 2979.

HAMEIRI, AVIGDOR: Passover in Jerusalem, 4693.

HAMILTON, HORACE: Complin, 1163; On Her Third New Year, 4463.

HAMILTON, RUTH HULBERT: Song for a Fifth Child, 5806.

HAMIZAH, AMIR: Prayer, 4974.

HAMMER, PHILENE: Air-Borne Missy, 127; All That Glitter Is Not Me, 148; And I Say the Hell with It, 196; A Case of Premeditated Compatability, 886; Cooling System, 1226; Fat Chance, 1874; Four-Year-Old Fingers, 2152; From Bed to Worse, 2187; How to Love Friends and Influence Nobody, 2681; Infernal Equinox, 2952; Late Marriage, 3258; Little Traditionalist, 3471; Morning Becomes Electric, 3899; My Love Is a Many-Splintered Thing, 4007; On First Looking at the Chap's Homer, 4453; The Parade, 4660; Petticoat Convention, 4777; Poem for Men Only, 4886; *S, 5383; Saturday's Child, 5432; Sing Kukla, 5632; Suburbia, 6115; Suggestion from the Subject, 6127; The Taciturn Type, 6231; Thoughts While Cutting Grass, 6420; Torch Song, 6623; Unreasonable Facsimile, 6796; Wasted Opportunity, 6968; Wordly Wishes of '59, 7312.

HAN, U THIEU: The Beda Flower, 540.

HANES, HELEN ROWE: The Clock, 1076.

HANES, LEIGH: Invitation, 3003.

HANFORD, JAMES HOLLY: Harvard Revisited, 2490; Poet on Horseback, 4901.

HANSEN, CHADWICK: For the State of Minnesota, 2108.

HANSEN, JOSEPH: Ballad of the Red Giants, 472; Good Friday--Burying a Jay, 2346.

HANSON, PAULINE: And Everywhere Ghost, 194; From As Far As Once, 2185; So Beautiful Is the Tree of Night, 5738.

HARDY, ELIZABETH STANTON: Echo, 1646; Transmutation, 6650.

HARDY, JOHN EDWARD: Louisiana Foxhunt, 3539.

HARDY, THOMAS: The Unplanted Primrose, 6765.

HARE, WINIFRED: Christmas Eve at Chartres, 1018; Coast Flight, 1096.

HARING, PHYLLIS: Oman the Diver, 4421.

HARKNESS, GEORGIA: To Galen Fisher, 6548.

HARPER, JANET: Old Man, 4394.

HARRINGTON, HELEN: Byroad, 821; Child on a Streetcar, 971; Created, 1273; Farm at Evening, 1861; Spellbound, 5922; There Is a Time, 6341; This Is the Way, 6385; Time of Miracles, 6475; Toddler Free, 6611.

HARRIS, JOEL CHANDLER: Advice to Writers for the Daily Press, 65.

HARRISON, HOWARD: Encore, 1704; Yom Kippur, 7344.

HART, HOWARD: Elegy for Sally, 1679.

HART, JOHN BARKLEY: The Wife of the Superintendent of the Granaries, 7148.

HART, MARY ALICE: Hearth Fire, 2524.

HART, RICHARD L.: The Returner, 5268.

HARTICH, ALICE: Rewards in the First Grade, 5284.

HARTLEY, ROLAND ENGLISH: Autobiography, 413; Cloud Above the Land, 1088, Grand Canyon, 2368; Moon Dawn, 3882.

HARVEY, MOLLY G.: Affairs No Longer Foreign, 67.

HASSMER, WARREN: Cloud of an Ancient Rage, 1089; A Darkening Threshold, 1346.

HATCH, FRANCIS W.: Dead Reckoning, 1375; Women's Doubles, 7269.

HAVARD, PAULINE: Conspirators, 1200; Small Towns, 5701; Upstairs Window, 6812.

HAWES, EDITH BENEDICT: The Little Girl, 3454.

HAY, JOHN: An American Summer, 178; Digging a Neighbor's Grave, 1489; Order, 4580.

HAY, SARA HENDERSON: The Devil Shamed, 1468; In the Lions' Den, 2908; The Parting, 4677; Woman and Snake, 7255.

HAYDEN, ROBERT L.: To the Lover, 6596.

HAZEL, ROBERT: Washington, 1958.

HAZEN, BARBARA SHOOK: April Song, 288; Snow Flurry at Midnight, 5626; Soft Song for Autumn, 5749; To a Young Girl, 6524.

HAZO, SAMUEL J.: Mary to the Dead Christ, 3678; Paul Before Agrippa, 4711; Teresa de Cepeda, 6301; Tryptych, 6678.

HEAFIELD, KENNETH: August Rain, 2740; The Hand of God, 2470; One Step, 4555; Prayer at a Place of Learning, 4975; Snow Crystal, 5721; Trinity, 6672.

HEARST, JAMES: Autumn Love, 427; Grandfather's Farm, 2373; Moment Toward Spring, 3866; Success, 6117; The Unprotected, 6794.

HEATH, A. R.: Escapist, 1746; They Year Will Come, 7333.

HEATH, CURTIS: Benevolent Boss, 576; First Leaf, 1964; Fitting Comment, 1992; Junior Partner, 3129; Leading the Parade, 3278; Steadfast, 6044; The Uses of Intuition, 6817; Wild Goose, 7151.

HEATHERLEY, RUTH HOLLEY: Two Weeks in August, 6749.

HECHT, ROGER: The Difference, 1486; The Laws; 3274; Man at a Window, 3626; Summer's End, 6153.

HEDDEN, MARK: Ochre Yellow, 4280; Regards the Changes, 5196.

HEISSENFUTTEL, ERNEST G.: A Stone for Ravensbrueck, 6058.

HELFER, HAROLD: Signs of the Times, 5605.

HELLER, CLARENCE EDWARD: City Life, 1052; Mother, 3919.

HEMLEY, CECIL: In the Birdhouse, 2895.

HEMPHILL, GEORGE: A Dream of Birds, 1568; Old Gentlemen Rising, 4386.

HEMSCHEMEYER, JUDITH: The Roofers, 5340.

HENLEY, ELIZABETH: The Birthday Cake Glockenspiel, 627; For Certain Idaho Babies, 2059; Grace After Meals, 2359; The Laying Away of Ornament, 3275; The Little Dark One, 3452; The Puritan Conflict, 5063; To the First-Grade Teacher, 6591; Twelfth Night, the Casele, 6707; The Well-Pasted Chain, 7019.

HENRITZY, SARA MUDGE: Interval Before Autumn, 2991.

HENRY, JANET: Dining Out, 1493; Lines to Four Small Children, 3425; Mamma's Dream House, 3622; Necessary Evil, 4050; This Side of Sanity, 6392; This Side of Sanity, 6393.

HENRY, JOSEPHINE: Pedagogic Logic, 4734.

HENRY, MARGARET: Winter Lament, 7199.

HERBERT, GEORGE: Easter Wings, 1639.

HERINGMAN, BERNARD: Anomalous Oyster, 242.

HERSCHBERGER, RUTH: The Big Buck and hte Little Buck, 602; Boating at Yaddo, 678; Meditation, 3720; Sibling Hostility, 5597; Thou Shalt Have Trouble Trying Me, 6401.

HERZ, BOB: Advice to Husbands, 62; What Else, 7043.

HESS, M. WHITCOMB: All the Blue April, 149; Bonfire, 688; Redbird: Late Winter, 5175; Testament of Wonder, 6308.

HETZNECKER, WILLIAM: Hydrocephalus, 2706.

HEYMANN, JOHN PORTER: The Dead at Rest Standishtown and Settler's Harbor, 1373.

HICKS, JOHN V.: Early One Morning, 1615; First Call, 1949; Shepherd Song, 5576; The Way and Nothing More, 6979.

HICKS, JOSEPHINE COUCH: Primitive Art, 5009.

HICKY, DANIEL WHITEHEAD: Butterfly Collection, 812; Cotton Fields by Moonlight, 1241; February Landscape, 1894; Home With the Evening Tide, 2617; Letter from a Deep-South Village, 3324; Marsh Night, 3671; Sailboat at Sunset, 5392; A Thanksgiving Prayer, 6316.

HIGHET, GILBERT: Horace to Tibullus, 2632.

HILBERRY, CONRAD: Agnus Dei, 119; Carol: to a Child, 882; Diver, 1513; First Reader, 1971; Hell-Driver, 2537.

HILL, GEOFFREY: Wreaths, 7320.

HILLYER, ROBERT: Academic Spring, 18; Assembling the Family, 349; Eppur Si Muove?, 1739; The Eternal Return, 1754; The Gregarious Age, 2432; The Marauders, 3647; Marooned, 3665; One Kind of Colloquy, 4546; Proteus, 5052; (continued)

HILLYER, ROBERT (cont'd): Rough Winds Do Shake the Darling Buds of May, 5358; The Scar, 5439; Seven Times One Are Seven, 5548; The Victim, 6857.

HINE, DARYL: After the Agony in the Garden, 92; Where Your Heart Is There Your Treasure Is Also, 7094.

HIRSHMAN, ROSE: Kaleidoscopic, 3139; Soft Hope, 5748.

HIS MAJESTY THE EMPEROR OF JAPAN: An Imperial Tanka, 2821.

HITCHCOCK, ANNE: Cata, 907; Chinese Poetry, 997; The Women, 7267.

HITE, W. G.: Signs, 5613.

HITZIZ, WILLIAM M.: Time and Space, 6469.

HODES, AUBREY: A Jew Walks in Westminster Abbey, 3096; Leaving Haifa, 3284.

HODES, ELIZABETH J.: Complaint at the Library, 1157.

HOFFMAN, DANIEL G.: A Celebration, 911; Heraldry, 2543; In the Beginning, 2894; It Is Time for Plain Speaking, 3039; There Is But One, 6342; Waiting for You, 6922; The Whitethroat Calls Through the May Night, 7121.

HOLLANDER, JOHN: Aristotle to Phyllis, 296; Autumn in Another State, 425; The Great Bear, 2394; Heat of Snow, 2526; The Jewels and the Gracchi, 3097; A Lion Named Passion, 3436; The Observatory, 4274; Off Marblehead, 4352; A Theory of Waves, 6335.

HOLLERER, WALTER: The Face of the Fisherman, 1825.

HOLLOWAY, RICHARD: Material Change, 3694.

HOLMES, DORIS: Belladona, 570.

HOLMES, JOHN: Bless, 649; The Chance, 924; Death in the Back Yard, 1384; Eleventh Commandment, 1687; The Expectation, 1809; Grass, 2383; Lady Is a Lady, 3198; On a Cage of Mice, 4423; Poetry Defined, 4905; Weather Making, 7000.

HOLMES, THEODORE: The Dressing of a Young Girl, 1580; J., 3065; On Becoming of Age, 4440; A Single Man at the Fire, 5640; When the Child Would Accommodate the Adult Again, 7077.

HONIG, EDWIN: Advice from a Comic Book, 53; Averages: A Pantomime, 437; By Auto and Camera in Navajo Country, 814; Do You Know Him?, 1525; The Gazabos, 2259; Poetry and Pedantry, 4904; The White Explorers, 7111.

HOOPER, PATRICIA: The Homecoming, 2618; Suburban, 6110.

HOPE, WELLBORN: The Great River and Small, 2405.

HOPKINS, FRANCES: Hibernation, 2568; Recess Ended, 5158.

HOPKINS, GERARD MANLEY: Persephone, 4760.

HORIGUCHI, DAIGAKU: I Do not See Myself, 2724; A Rain-Like Costume, 5127.

HORNER, JOYCE: From the North, 2207; The Meadow, 3707.

HOSKINS, KATHERINE: The Dutchman's-Pipe Vine, 1598; Eve's Eden, 1782 Last Resource, 3246; Nuit Blanche, 4245; Responsibilities, 5245; To Apollo Musagetes, 6531; To Live at All, 6555; When the Snow Falls, 7078; Where Is It That We Go?, 7086.

HOUGH, ELLIS JONES: Meditation, 3721.

HOUGHTON, FIRMAN A.: New Bethlehem, Pa., 4068.

HOUSTON, DORA LAURENCE: Fences, 1909.

HOWARD, FRANCES MINTURN: Picture in Rain, 4804.

HOWARD, PAULINE: Young Girls in Spring, 7364.

HOWARD, RICHARD: Agreement with Sir Charles Sedley, 121; Landed: A Valentine, 3220; The Return from Nontauk, 5259.

HOWARD, SARAH: Flight of Finches, 2006; Memento Mori, 3742.

HOWE, M. A. DE WOLFE: From an Editor, 2183; Look to It, Then, My Soul!, 3508; The Passenger, 4682; Thanksgiving in May, 6314.

HOWES, BARBARA: City Afternoon, 1050; Death of a Vermont Farm Woman, 1393; Delivery Room, 1440; Early Supper, 1616; The Gallery, 2235; Lignum Vitae, 3383; A Lullaby, 3584; Midwinter Flight, 3808; Mistral, 3840; On Falling Asleep in a Mountain Cabin, 4452; Port of Call, 4931; Portrait of the Boy as Artist, 4847; Sirocco, 5645; To W. H. Auden on His Fiftieth Birthday, 6606; Tramontana, 6642; The Triumph of Pride, 6681; The Triumph of Time, 6682; The Triumph of Truth, 6683.

HUBERT, ANDRAS MAGYAR: Budapest: November 1, 1956, 779.

HUBLER, RICHARD G.: Orchard, 4578.

HUDSON, DEALT: On the Death of an Ordinary Person, 4500.

HUFF, ROBERT: Catamount, 902; Children of Light, 982; Colonel Johnson's Ride, 1121; Emily Dickinson and Patanjah Examine a New Soul, 1696; King Salmon, 3170; Minstrel, 3818.

HUG, ROBERT A.: The Library, 3348.

HUGHES, D. J.: Hokusai, 2599; Kokoro, 3189.

HUGHES, DOROTHY: Storm Memory, 6070; Flight Landing at Night, 2005.

HUGHES, LANGSTON: Brotherly Love, 768.

HUGHES, TED: The Ancient Heroes and the Pilot, 192; Bawdry Embraced, 516; Bullfrog, 790; The Casualty, 891; Cat and Mouse, 893; Dick Straightup, 1483; The Drowned Woman, 1587; The Hag, 2461; The Hawk in the Storm, 2501; Historian, 2592; Incompatabilities, 2936; The Jaguar, 3069; Lupercalia, 3594; (continued)

HUGHES, TED (cont'd): The Martyrdom of
    Bishop Terrar, 3677; Of Cats, 4310;
    Relic, 5205; Roarers in a Ring, 5324;
    The Thought-Fox, 6404; To Paint a
    Water-Lily, 6577; Wind, 7159; A
    Woman Unconscious, 7263.
HUGO, RICHARD F.: Skykmoish River
    Running, 5668.
HUHN, JUSTI: Relative, 5200.
HULL, ORA MAY: Anger of the Bull,
    217; By Marriage I Make Evil, 816;
    Edith Cavell, 1654; The Great Lakes,
    2403; I Believe in Your Country,
    2718; A Seated Figure, 5488.
HUMPHRIES, ROLFE: Among the Paeligni,
    181; The Angels, 215; For a Word-
    farer, 2052; A Green Pride, 2423;
    The Lament of Llywarch Hen, 3214;
    Merioneth, Wales, 3766; Oak, 4267;
    Portrait of a Poet, 4942; Rain in
    Jackson Heights, 5125; A Song for
    Mardi Gras, 5814; Valentine from a
    Young Gentleman of Verona, 6831;
    Wmffre the Sweep, 7252.
HUNTER, ELIZABETH W.: Hands to Match
    the Mind, 2474.
HUNTER, KRISTIN: Graven Images, 2390.
HUNTER, NANCY: I, Being Woman, 2717.
HUNTER, RICHARD E.: Hymn for the
    Church Dilettante, 2708.
HUNTIERS, KEITH: Atomic Institute,
    383.
HUNTRESS, KEITH: Storm in the Midlands,
    6069.
HURD, PEARL STRACHAN: Nudge, 4244.
HURIANEK, VLASTA: Thoughts on Summer
    Reading, 6417.
HURSHMAN, ROSE: Requiem, 5234.
HUSS, AVRAHAM: The Green Refrain,
    2424.
HUTCHINSON, ROBERT: Boy in Church,
    718; Night Speech, 4120.
HUWS, DAN: Family Evening, 1852; The
    Fox, 2158.
HYMES, DELL: Penalty, 4738.
IGNATOW, DAVID: And Step, 204; I
    Felt, 2729; I Stand Upon a Dike,
    2758; Job's Anger, 3101; The Mountain
    Is Stripped, 3939; Mr. Mammon, 3961;
    Mr. Mammon, 3962; The News Photo,
    4104; Obsolete, 4275; The Orange
    Picker, 4574; A Semblance, 5516.
IQBAL, MOHAMMED: Sicily, 4602.
IRELAND, THELMA: Fastidity or Phobia,
    1873; Storm Warning, 6073.
IRIS, SCHARMEL: Before the Cathedral,
    552; How Shall I Sing Again, 2671;
    Vincent, 6874.
IRVINE, JOHN: Night, 4107.
ISLER, BETTY: Anniversary, 230; Boy
    at Piano, 714; Children's Menu, 988;
    Citrus Country, 1048; Citrus Harvest,
    1049; Coquette, 1227; Date Town,
    1349; Driftwood Arrangement, 1583;
    First Hair Cut, 1963; Midmorning
    Snack, 3796; Mockingbird's Reveille,
    3852; Night Patterns, 4114; On
    Moving Into a New House, 4474;
    Revelation, 5275; Steppingstone,
    6049; School Peformance, 5451 (cont'd)

Summer Overhead, 6142; To a Passing
    Young Man, 6511; When Is Winter?,
    7072.
ISSA: Under the Cherry Blossom Trees
    There Are No Real Strangers, 6771.
IWAI: Sannousuke: Fruit, 2219.
J., H.: Portrait of a Philadelphian,
    4941.
JACOBS, CATHERINE HAYDON: Thoughts in
    a Doubting Time, 6410.
JACOBS, ELIJAH L.: Grandmother's
    Granddaughter, 2378; High-School
    Choir, 2581; In an Old Blacksmith
    Shop, 2842; Loyalty, 3578; A Man's
    Length Shadow, 3640; The Night of
    the Tornado, 4113; October Robbers,
    4289; One Small Quirk, 4554; Some-
    thing in the Day, 5778; West of the
    Brown Missouri, 7030; Winter Traffic,
    7218.
JACOBS, FLORENCE B.: Bethlehem Was
    Small, 585; Fulfillment, 2222; The
    Generations, 2263; Post-Vacation
    Pibroch, 4953.
JACOBSEN, JOSEPHINE: The Animal Inside
    the Animal, 222; The Animals, 224;
    Deaf-Mutes at a Ball Game, 1376;
    The Four Faces of My Cousin, 2144;
    Hunter, Immobile, 2698; Landscape
    Finally with Figure, 3226; Mr.
    Tantripp's Day, 3966; Poems for My
    Cousin, 4892; Radiated Man, 5108;
    Tropic of Advent, 6685; Variations
    on a Theme, 6841.
JACOBSON, ETHEL: Apple Time, 273; The
    Awakened, 438; Blue Grosbeaks, 669;
    Coyote Night, 1267; Cro-co-dile,
    1286; Deer in the Garden, 1425;
    Equine Lines, 1740; Heart Cry, 2521;
    Hunters of the Dusk, 2699; Marsh at
    Night, 3670; Menu Maneuvers, 3762;
    Moonlight Dance, 3887; Mountain
    Homestead, 3938; Mustn't, 3987; One
    on a Hearth, 4551; Public Nuisance,
    5063; Rendezvous, 5221; Rover
    Recumbent, 5365; Safe, 5389; Scare-
    crow Trees, 5442; Shadow Dancer,
    Sierras, 5607; Starstruck, 6035;
    Steady Girl, 6046; Tanglewood Island,
    6248; The White Crane, 7108; Window
    Ledge, 7170.
JAFFRAY, NORMAN R.: The Academician,
    19; All Joking Aside, 144; But Honey,
    It Wasn't Like That!, 804; Count
    Twenty, 1257; Courtship Unencumbered,
    1262; Criteria, 1283; Fatherly Advice,
    1882; Her Side, 2542; I'd Just Like
    to Know, 2780; It Works Both Ways,
    3045; Let's Stop at the Next Gas
    Station, 3319; Love 'Em--and Leave
    'Em, 3545; Masquerade, 3684; The
    Mayflower Sails Again, 3706; My
    Satellite, 4015; Notes for a Valedic-
    tory Address, 4211; Proof of My Tact,
    5041; Reluctant Host, 5207; Remorse,
    5218; Sink of Iniquity, 5641; Spurred
    to Action, 5978; Thirty Years in the
    Wrong Profession, 6375; Those New
    Year's Resolutions, 6399; Thoughts on
    Opening Someone Else's Medicine
    Cabinet, 6415; (continued)

JAFFRAY, NORMAN R. (cont'd): The Tip-Off, 6485; Urban Archaeology, 6813; We Are Not Amused, 6983; Where You From, Mac?, 7093; The Zero Hour, 7382.

JAMIESON, JOHN: Alternatives, 167.

JAMMES, FRANCIS: Il Va Neiger, 2805; L'Ane Savant, 3235; Quand Verrai-- Je Les Iles..., 5084.

JANES, KELLY: Anselmic, 247; As in a Mirror, Dimly, 328; Component, 1164; Counterpoint, 1247; Pharisaic, 4780; St. Paul in Arabia, 5405; Words Be Our Weapons, 7290.

JANKE, DOROTHY: Please, Father / The Neighbors Will Hear You/ , 4843.

JANSON, ELLEN: One Place, 4552.

JARRELL, RANDALL: Children Selecting Books in a Library, 983.

JEANS, MARYLU TERRAL: Home for Christmas, 2611.

JELLEMA, ROD: The First Easter: Two Views,

JENKINS, BETH HENRY: Achievement Report--First Grade, 22.

JENKINS, DONALD: The Nameless Ocean, 4030; Night at the Ocean: A Walk, 4108.

JENKINS, OLIVER: Lost Country, 3527.

JENNEY, LOUISE EVE: The Errand, 1745; The Three Little Pegs, 6426; What Do They Mean, Joint Return?, 7041; Whistler's Mother, 7102.

JENNINGS, ELIZABETH: Disguises, 1504; The Painter, 4647; The Roman Forum, 5335; Sister of Charity, 5648; Strangers, 6088.

JENNINGS, LESLIE NELSON: This Other Sleep, 6390.

JENNISON, C. S.: Address to the Senior Class, 38; Adieu to That Trip for Two, 39; Battle of the Box Tops, 514; Don't Let Suburbia Disturbia, 1541; Evening Song for Mothers, 1773; Few Objections Concerning Elections, 1912; Few Things Unnerve Me Like People Who Serve Me, 1913; How To Be Charming Though Farming, 2678; It's Easy to Please a Child, 3055; I've Had a Superfluity of Yankee Ingenuity, 3063; Life at a Premium, 3365; Modern Mother Goose, 3858; Mother's Needlework, 3930; New Show Defiance Toward A Kitchen Appliance, 4064; Please Don't Mention Another Tension, 4842; The View From Our Land, 6864; Wonder Fabrics Made Me Wonder, 7271.

JENNISON, ELIZABETH: The Pride of Life, 5004.

JEROME, JUDSON: Aubade, 391; Child's Game, 989; Deer Hunt, 1424; Flight by Instruments, 2004; Imitation of Nature, 2817; Instructions for Acting: Drunk Scene, 2980; Love, the First Decade, 3557; Negative, 4053; Philander Musing, 4782; The Violence, 6876.

JILAVERI, MANSUKKLAL: To My Child, 6562.

JOHNSON, ANN S.: Part-Time Aristocrat, 4675.

JOHNSON, CAROL: Eclogue for Rachel, 1648; The Feast of Stephen, 1890; Gloss on a Text from the Mansions.

JOHNSON, COLLEEN HYNES: Pinch of Sage, 4816.

JOHNSON, EDITH WARNER: The Well, 7016.

JOHNSON, GEOFFREY: Building Estate, 785; January, 3074; The Portrait, 4935; Without Desire, 7249.

JOHNSON, GEORGIA DOUGLAS: Arkansas Children, 300; Share My World, 5564; To Carter G. Woodson--Historian, 6539.

JOHNSON, HILDEGARDE WALLS: A Scot Dreams of Heaven, 5457.

JOHNSON, LOUIS: Age of Discovery, 113; Nimrod, 4132; The Quick and the Dead, 5099.

JOHNSON, PEARL PATTERSON: The Wreckers Arrive, 7321.

JOHNSON, VICTORIA BLANDIN: Vacation Treasure, 6823.

JOHNSON, W. R.: The Cabin Builders, 822; Hunting Tale, 2701; Signs for Travelers, 5614.

JOHNSON, WINIFRED M.: Child in a Sandbox, 966.

JOHNSTON, GEORGE: Eating Fish, 1643; Ice at Last, 2772; Kind Offices, 3162; Life from a Goldfish Bowl, 3367.

JONES, CULLEN: The Defense Rests, 1427.

JONES, DAVID: The Wall, 6935.

JONES, ELLIS O.: Give Us Another Slice, 2309; Ignis Fabuous (Addressed to our Secretary of State, wherever he may be), 2803; The Walrus and the Carpenter, 6942.

JONES, FRANKLIN P.: Put It This Way, 5074; Put It This Way, 5075.

JONES, HOWARD MUMFORD: The Anthropologist, 253; The Historian, 2593; Meditations on the Humanities, 3724; The Philosopher, 4785; The Psychoanalyst, 5061; The Social Scientist, 5745.

JONES, INA HEROLD: Oh, Uncouth Lover!, 4366.

JONES, M. E.: Death and Resurrection, 1379.

JONES, T. H.: The Pride of the Morning, 5005.

JOOST, NICHOLAS: Some Unsung Poems, 5771.

JOSEPHS, LAURENCE: The Garden, 2240; A Mirror, a Window, a Pool, 3828; Roses for My Grandmother, 5354.

JOSHI, UMASHANKAR: The Death of a Poet, 1391.

JUDSON, STEPHANIE: Wonderful Things, 7272.

JUSTICE, DONALD: Beyond the Hunting Woods, 601; A Birthday Candle, 628; From Bad Dreams, 2186; Here in Katmandu, 2551; Love's Map, 3568; The Poet at Seven, 4899; The Snowfall, 5734; (continued)

JUSTICE, DONALD (cont'd): Sonnet to My Father, 5875; Southern Gothic, 5894; Speaking of Islands, 5914; Variations on a Neo-Classic Theme, 6840.

JUSTICE, LOUISE: Memories, 3748.

K, E. F.: Fire Island Walking Song, 1939.

KABIR, HUMAYUN: Prisoners, 5015.

KADOW, AUGUST: Key West, 3155.

KAHN, HANNAH: All the Leaves That Fall, 150; And One Small Leaf, 200; Appointment, 274; Conformer, 1177; Counterpoint, 1248; Cycle, 1319; The Gathered Crumbs, 2257; Grieving House, 2438; Legacy, 3289; Letter, 3320; Sequence, 5529; Sheltered by Your Light, 5574; Tardy Spring, 6256; To a Lost Child, 6505; To Be Black, To Be Lost, 6534; Twilight, 6715; Voice, 6900.

KAISER, WALTER: Love's Island, 3566.

KANEKO, MITSUHARU: Demons and a Poet, 1443.

KANFER, ALLEN: Advice for a Wedding, 52; Fear Is a Formal Matter, 1888; The Giraffe, 2295; Goodman Up for Election, 2352; Jacob, 3068; Like Two Old Theologians, 3388; The Lonely Fugitive, 3494; Moses, 3916; A Mountain Standing Strong, 3943; Never Counsel a Lovely Lady, 4061; The Trigger Man, 6671; The Ugly Duckling, 6755; We Wander in Each Other's Woods, 6992.

KAPLAN, ELAINE TOBY: Sunset on the 5:10, 6175.

KAPLAN, HAROLD: Survival, 6193.

KAPLAN, MILTON: Hotel Room, 2674; My Son, 4018.

KARANDIKAR, VINDA: Early Morning,

KARNI, YEHUDA: Put Me Into the Breach, 5076; A Woman's Prayer, 7265.

KARNS, HARRY: Living Room at Nine P.M., 3479.

KASER, DAVID: Twenty-Six Brief Lectures on the History of Printing, 6712.

KATZ, MENKE: At a Patched Window, 354; Names of Michalishek, 4032.

KATZ, ROBERT L.: An Administrator's Prayer for the New Year, 41.

KAVAFIS, CONSTANTINE: Expecting the Barbarians, 1810.

KAY, ELLEN DE YOUNG: Eve Beyond Eve, 1759; Song, 5791; Sonnet, 5860; Tiresias' Lament, 6488.

KAYKO, INGEBORG: Wish, 7232.

KAZANTZAKIS, NIKOS: The Return of Odysseus, 5262.

KEARNS, BEN S.: Money, 3871.

KEEGAN, MARTHA: Two Sides of a Street, 6737.

KEITH, JOSEPH JOEL: Chosen Roads, 1007; Eternal South, 1755; New Home, 4079; Old Man at Desk, 4396; The Release, 5204; Summer's Refrain, 6154.

KELLER, MARTHA: American Primitive, 177; The Foal of Medusa, 2029.

KELLEY, REEVE SPENCER: Back Again From Yucca Flats, 452; The Fish That Got to Stay, 1984; Got Wise, 2357; The Insects, 2965; Like Proud Women, 3386; Little Hearth Song, 3459; The Magical Harvest, 3609; Meadows and Mesas, 3711; The Mesa Land, 3773; Of Peaks and Parables, 4324; Red and White Television, 5173; Reverse Harvest, 5280; Spring on the Desert, 5971; This Isn't Spring, 6387; To a Man Gazing at a Girl Gazing at an Ocean, 6506; An Ungodly Appetite, 6784; We Gathered in the Yard, 6987; Winter Bouquets, 7182; You Know Him, 7352.

KELLOGG, KAY: Form 1040, 2127.

KELLY, MARTY: The Old Chair, 4373.

KEMP, LYSANDER: Footnote, 2037; The Vacation, 6821; The Weir; 7015; Who?, 7123.

KEMP, ROY Z.: Trinity, 6673.

KEMPHER, RUTH M: Arriving 6:25, 305.

KENNEDY, MARY: Afternoon in the Thirties, 105; The Silent Woman, 5620; A Wreath of Four-O'Clocks, 7319.

KENNEDY, X. J.: On A Child Who Lived One Minutes, 4425.

KENNY, HERBERT: On the Eighth Day, 4506; The Scholars, 5447; The Voice in the Wood, 6904.

KENNY, NICK: Family Doctor, 1851.

KENSETH, ARNOLD: Death and Resurrection, 1380.

KERNAN, F. G.: Cold Proposition, 1112; Two-Way Revelation, 6747.

KESSLER, EDWARD: Art for Art, 308; Home, 2609.

KESSLER, SYDNEY: Letter from America, 3326.

KESSLER, JASCHA: People in Vogue, 4746; Requiem for an Abstract Artist, 5237; Routine Assignment, 5364; To J. B., 6552; Advertisement, 50; At the Border, 372; Ratio, 5141; Reminder, 5215; Since We Shall Die, One Night, with the Radio On, 5630; Sister, 5647; We Keep, Here, the Records of Days, 6990.

KILKEARY, GERTRUDE: African Violet, 71; High Altitude, 2573; House Plans, 2655.

KIME, HAROLD C.: Book Reviewers Lament, 695.

KING, FRANCIS: The Fear, 1887.

KINNELL, GALWAY: Across the Brown River, 25; Ah Moon, 123; Alewives Pool, 133; Braemar, 728; Canada Warbler, 850; The Descent, 1452; Earth-Sparrow, 1622; In a Parlor Containing a Table, 2836; Lilacs, 3391; Peer Gynt, 4737; Seven Streams of Nevis, 5546; Where the Bodies Break, 7088; Where the Track Vanishes, 7090; Yesterday from My Fever, 7341.

KINNICK, B. JO: To a Son in Boot Camp, 6520.

KINSEY, RALPH L.: Sonnet for the Good Warrior, 5869.

KIPLING, RUDYARD: Cold Iron, 1110.

KIRSTEIN, LINCOLN: Memorial Window: 1946-56, 3747.

KIRKUP, JAMES: Sendai Sequence, 5519; A View of Japan, 6866.

KIRRUP, G. SANKARA: The Moment, 3861.

KISSLER, JANET S.: The Last Time, 3248.

KITAGAWA, FUYUKIKP: Festival, 1910; A Horse and a Landscape, 2640.

KITAHARA, HAKUSHU: Okaru and Kampei, 4368; The Water Surface, 6976.

KITASONO, KATUE: Poetry Going Out, 4906.

KIZER, CAROLYN: Complex Animal, 1161; The Death of a Public Servant, 1392; The Great Blue Heron, 2397; The Intruder, 2998; Love Song, 3555; A Muse of Wather, 3978; Plaint of the Poet in an Ignorant Age, 4829; The Ungrateful Garden, 6785; What the Bones Know, 7052; A Widow in Wintertime, 7142.

KLINE, LLOYD W.: Have You Ever Known Children Watching an Old-Time Movie?, 2497; Just Before Class, 3131; Make Mine People, 3619.

KLITZKE, LEWIS W.: Library Memories, 3360.

KLOPP, JUDY: The Two Faces of the Wind, 6723.

KNIGHT, JOHN A.: The Library, 3349.

KNOEPFLE, JOHN: Keelboatman's Horn, 3145; Little Harpe's Head, 3458; On the Passing of a Sternwheel Tow, 4514; Time's Out, 6482.

KNOWLTON, ROBERT A.: Air for a Plastic Hautboy, 128; Mountain Passage, 3940.

KOBER, ARTHUR: Scance Macabre, 5438.

KOCH, KENNETH: Down at the Docks, 1558; Gigue, 2293; The Horse, 2639; In Love with You, 3487; Locks, 3487; Meeting You at the Piers, 3735; Permanently, 4757; Pregnancy, 4989; Thank You, 6310; Thanksgiving, 6312; You Were Wearing, 7358.

KOEHLER, G. STANLEY: A Blue Day, 663; Encounter at Salerno, 1707; Man Overboard, 3632; New Construction, 4073; Off New London, 4353; Peace and the Pacific, 4725.

KOGURE, KATSUHIKO: The Face, 1823; It was a face I did not know, I could not recognize, 1823.

KONDO, AZUMA: Afternoon, 101; The Country, 1250; Poem, 4855.

KOPPES, M. CHRYSOSTOM SISTER: Christmas Lullaby, 1023.

KOSHLAND, MIRIAM: Cuckold Contented, 1305; Spite, 5934.

KOSKI, GEORGE: The Syncretist, 6220.

KOVAL, ALEXANDER: The Elect and the Damned, 1663.

KOZMENUIK, NICK: Head Wind, 2515.

KRAFT, VIRGIL A.: Children of God, 981; Inaudibles, 2930; The Irresistible Intention, 3015; To the Unnamed Lake, 6602.

KRAMER, ARTHUR: Step by Step, 6047.

KRAUSZ, SIBYL: Auld Lang Syne, 409; Evening Song, 1772; On Second Thought, 4489; Right on My Toes, 5297; Washout, 6964.

KREISER, MILDRED: Bitter the Cup, 636; Seen Some Years Later, 5507.

KREMER, BARBARA GRAYBEAL: Even the Ivy Isn't Free Any More, 1767.

KREYMBORG, ALFRED: As If, 327; Correspondence, 1236; December Tenth, 1404; Long View, 3500; The School of Life, 5450; Song, 5792; Warm Sun, 6953.

KRIEGER, ROBERT: Child on a Pullman, 970; The Delay, 1434; Flowering Antler, 2024; Homecoming, 2619; A Now Famous Escape, 4236.

KROLL, ERNEST: Armored Car, 302; Church Supper, 1037; Crab Grass, 1269; Diner, 1492; Emerson, 1694; Figures in a Garden, 1923; From American Panels, 2183; Marine, 3660; Passing East of Hartford, 4683; Summer, 6132; The Thrush Returns to Find a Subdivision, 6454.

KROLOW, KARL: Shadows in the Air, 5556.

KRUSE, RHODA: All Hail!, 141; Book Reviews, 696.

KUMIN, MAXINE W.: Between Them and Portugal, 594; The Bite, 633; The First Rain of Spring, 1970; Grocery List, 2440; Growing Daughters, 2444; Halfway, 2466; Horoscope, 2637; Lines on a Half-Painted House, 3418; The Moment Clearly, 3862; Rehabilitation Center, 5198; The Rites, 5307; The Waiting Game, 6923.

KUNITZ, STANLEY: The Approach to Thebes, 275; As Flowers Are, 326; The Choice of Weapons, 999; The Call Will Come to Order, 1064; The Dark and the Fair, 1341; Foreign Affairs, 2120; Goose Pond, 2354; Off Point Lotus, 4354; A Spark of Laurel, 5906; The Thief, 6360; The War Against the Trees, 6947.

KUNZ, MARGARET: Fairy May, 1836.

L, R. A.: Wheep No More, 7063.

LA BOMBARD, JOAN: The Child Whose Name Is Love, 975; If We Were Water Voice, 2794; O Darkly in the Summer's Eye, 4255; The Sibyl, 5599.

LA FARGE, CHRISTOPHER: You Were Long Years in Leaving..., 7357.

LA FOLLETTE, MELVIN WALKER: Lake Beaver, 3202; Portage, 4932.

LAING, ALEXANDER: Iron Mirror, 3014; Know-How, 3184; Virtuous Pagan, 6880.

LAING, DILYS: And Goe the Fooles Among, 195; Anti-Poem, 255; Aubade, 392; Don't Tread on Us, 1543; Easter, 1632; I Attend a Reception for a Visiting Celebrity, 2716; Ignis Dominae, 2802; Let Them Ask Their Husbands, 3312; Lost Stolen Strayed, 3532; The Pure Passion, 5067; Return to Strangeness, 5267; The Sacred Wood, 5386; Six Picassos, 5635; (continued)

LAING, DILYS (cont'd): Song After
    Seven Glasses of Picasso, 5799;
    Walled City, 6939; We Who Are
    Civilized Salute Ourselves, 6994;
    Weddings and Banquets, 7010.
LAL, P.: The Chinese Doll, 994.
LAMB, ELIZABETH SEARLE: Space Travel,
    5902.
LAMB, GEORGIE STARBUCK: Mary's Lamb,
    3680.
LAMB, MARY WRIGHT: Amiss, 180; Aubade,
    393; A Lyric for Lovers, 3601; Martha
    Jane, 3673; Nests, 4057; Sonnet,
    5861; Vacancy, 6819; Words to a
    Budding Oddity, 7298.
LAMDAN, YITZHAK: In the Hot Wind,
    2904; Israel, 3032.
LAMPORT, FELICIA: Cook's Detour, 1224;
    A Knee-Length Trapeze, 3180; Orbit,
    4577; Speakable Bacle, 5911; Spinal
    Discord, 5926; Thyme Gallops Withal,
    6460; Vice Verses, 6855.
LANCE, CYNTHIA: Giants, 2280.
LANDAU, BETH MARIE: Nonsense Rhyme,
    4171.
LANDEWEER, ELIZABETH: Baby Sitter,
    445; Beach Site, 523; Big Dipper,
    1408, Deceptive Sounds, 1408; Dog
    With Flea, 1532; Duck Blind, 1592;
    First Birthday, 1946; First Swallow,
    1978; Forsythia, 2132; Girl with a
    New Doll, 2301; Greenhouse Grandpa,
    2428; Killdeer Crying, 3158; Lights
    Off-Light's On, 3382; Mexican Holiday,
    3784; Mountain Saddle, 3942; Oil
    Tanker, 4367; Oyster Farm, 4636;
    Peacock, 4727; Rain Talk, 5129;
    Range Calf, 5134; Rotten Log, 5355;
    Sea Born, 5466; Small Drum Majorette,
    5691; Spring Frogs, 5959; Streamside
    Spoor, 6096; Supermarket Rider, 6177;
    Truck Stop by Night, 6690; Two-Year-
    Old Talker, 6750; Wind's Down, 7174;
    Winter Sleepers, 7214.
LANDERS, DENNIS: The Rainbow, 5130.
LANG, DANIEL: The Usual Cloud, 6818.
LANG, V. R.: Death of Another Swan--
    Miami, 1394; From Poems to Preserve
    the Year at Home, 2197; I Too Have
    Lived in Arcadia, 2762; Pique-Dame,
    4823; Poem, 4856; Poem, 4857.
LANGLAND, JOSEPH: Choice, 998; Ever-
    green, 1776; Henri Matisse, 2541;
    The Honeybees, 2625; A Love for God,
    3546; A Madrigal: For Judith, 3607;
    Naples, 4036; Noah's Ark, 4160;
    Recollections of Octobers, 5168;
    Rock, 5327; Split Root, 5937; Winter,
    7181; Winter Juniper, 7198.
LANGTON, DAN: On the Poet William
    Carlos Williams, 4515.
LAPE, FRED: Cow at Her Own Drinking
    Fountain, 1263; Of Mrs. Bird Bishop
    and the Beyond, 4322; Twentieth
    Century Pastoral: Cow at Her Own
    Drinking Fountain, 6708; Twentieth
    Century Pastoral: Croquet, 6709;
    Twentieth Century Pastoral: The
    Simple Life, 6710; Twentieth Century
    Pastoral: Summer, 6711.

LARRAUD, VALERY: The Death of
    Atahuallpa, 1395; The Gift of Oneself,
    2288; My Muse, 4013; Poet's Wish,
    4911.
LARSSON, RAYMOND E. F.: The First Carol,
    1951.
LARUE, DON: On Buying By Mail, 4442.
LATHAN, JEAN: O for the Boy, 4257.
LATTIMORE, RICHMOND: Rise and Shine,
    5305; The Academic Overture, 16;
    After Christmas, 75; Anniversary,
    231; Arms and the Man, 303; Details
    from the Nativity Scene, 1465;
    Epigraphical Note, 1725; Green and
    White, 2414; Landscape with Story,
    3232; Leilah, 3296; Marginals, 3657;
    New Homes, 4080; North China and the
    Children, 4174; Note on the Land N,
    4204; The Pillow and the Book, 4815;
    The Roman Soldier, 5337; Sea Changes,
    5467; Three Greek Virgins, 6425.
LAUGHLIN, J.: How Fortunate, 2666; The
    Woodpecker, 7277.
LAURENCE, RUTH: The In-Betweener, 2844.
LAWSON, DOUGLAS E.: Abandoned Home, 3;
    To My Friend Who Reads Braille, 6564.
LAZARUS, AROLD L.: Objective-Tester,
    4271.
LAZARUS, HARRY: Nothing But the Truth,
    4217.
LAZARUS, PHILIP: Biting Remarks, 634;
    The Good Old Days, 2351; Heat Wave,
    2531; Political Agreement, 4915;
    Reminder From the Recipient, 5216;
    Wardrobe Closets, 6951.
LEE, AUDREY M.: Love's Messages, 3569;
    Weeping Springtime, 7014; Youth, 7375.
LEE, CHARLES: Aspiration, 348; The
    Broken Music Box, 765; Earth's
    Passion, 1630; Election-Year Commen-
    tary, 1665; Memory, 3751; The River
    From the Bridge, 5313.
LEE, MARJORIE LEDERER: Behold the Yogi,
    561; Boy on Bike, 721; Clearance,
    1070; For Steven at Three, 2100;
    Of All the Many Things Which Give
    Love Rise, 4308; Ragout Robert, 5114;
    Suburban Song, 6112; Thoughts on the
    Christmas Vacation, 6418; Vicious
    Cycle, 6856; Visitor, 6896.
LEET, PAULINE M: Ah How My Cat Benja-
    min, 122.
LEGER, ALEXIS: See PERSE, SAINT-JOHN.
LEGG, LOUISA: My Seahorse, 4016.
LEGLER, PHILIP: Landscape for a Wife,
    3227; On the Death of a Test Pilot:
    A Footnote, 4499.
LEHMANN, WILHELM: After the Second
    Flood, 99.
LEHON, ANNA: Litany of the Matrons,
    3444.
LEIBRAND, ESTHER: Annual Garden, 239;
    City Woman, 1055.
LEICHTY, V. E.: Visitation Day 19--,
    6894.
LEMON, RICHARD: Campaign Song, 847;
    Congratulations, Commiserations and
    So Forth, 1181; The Curious Case of
    the Tongue Which Would Not Wag, 1314;
    The Last Words of the President of
    the Gourmet Society, 3251; (cont'd)

LEMON, RICHARD (cont'd): On Passing a
    Small Place on Fifth Avenue Where a
    Building Once Was, 4479.
LENNEN, ELINOR: Christmas Symbol, 1028;
    Environment, and More, 1724; On Ash
    Wednesday, 4438; Past Misunderstand-
    ing, 4697; What Town Survives?, 7055.
LERNER, MAX: Cairo, 828.
LEVANT, HOWARD: Connection in October,
    1184; The Pious Squire Regrets His
    Year's Sins of Lust, 4820; Pleasures
    of the Imagination, 4845.
LEVERTOV, DENISE: Bread, 737; The
    Communion, 1144; The Departure, 1445;
    A Happening, 2477; On the Edge, 4505;
    A Ring of Changes, 5301; The Room,
    5344; The Sage, 5391; Seems Like We
    Must Be Somewhere Else, 5506; A
    Straw Swam Under the Christmas Tree,
    6093; To the Snake, 6600.
LEVIANT, CURT: The LP Catalog: An
    Appreciation, 3191.
LEVINE, NORMAN: Crabbing, 1270.
LEVINE, PHILIP: Mad Day in March,
    3604; Night Thoughts Over a Sick
    Child, 4122; Rotting Trees, 5356;
    Summer, 6133; The Toys, 6637.
LEVINE, RICHARD: Pacific 101: The
    Ranch by the Sea, 4638.
LEVINE, ROSALIND: Coming of the Bridal
    Wind, 1137; From the Pomegranite,
    2209; Natural History, 4042; Rain,
    5119; Space Design, 5901; Three Songs
    at Midsummer, 6437; A Willow Song,
    7157.
LE VINSON, FRANCES H.: Little Boys
    Kisses, 3450.
LEVY, NEWMAN: Grand Opera Land, 2371;
    Tutee, 6704.
LEWARS, JERRIE SQUIER: Ecce Homo,
    1644.
LEWIN, RALPH A.: Les Choise--Neige,
    1001.
LEWIS, C. DAY: A Meeting, 3732.
LEWIS, GROVER: Yelp, 7338.
L'HEUREUX, JOHN: Cassandra, 889;
    Flowering Sudden, 2025; Requiem for a
    Nun, 5236; Therese, 6348; Tyburn,
    6751.
LIDDELL, BETTIE CASSIE: At Summer's
    End, 369; For None But the Lonely,
    2089; Note to My Husband, 4206.
LIEBERMAN, ELIAS: Advice to a Strong
    Man with Weak Knees, 58; The Great
    of Heart, 2404; Hint to a Young Man
    Getting Nowhere, 2588; Notation in
    Haste, 4198; Old Autograph Album,
    4369; Skipping Rope, 5664.
LIEBERMAN, LAURENCE: Eucalyptus Dance,
    1757; Housewife, 2658; Life Insurance,
    3368.
LILLY, OTHELIA: And This Is Hallelujah,
    207; And Thomas Knows, 208; Carpenter-
    Wise, 884; Conscience, 1186; Easter
    Sea, 1637; Even Stones, 1766; For an
    Agnostic, 2053; How Silently, 2672;
    In Heaven All Were Dancing, 2860;
    Let Me Whirl Suns, 3309; Master
    Musician, 3689; Michelangelo's Moses,
    3789; Mid-Autumn Evening, 3790;

Park Orator, 4671; Paroled, 4673;
    Rooted, 5349; Sediment, 5501; The
    Seer, 5508; Song Eden, 5804; The Song
    of Then, 5843; Tendons, 6294; The
    Visitor, 6897; Watercolor: Life,
    6977; White Flame, 7112; Zeal, 7378.
LINCOLN, ANNE: Housewife to Husband,
    Sliding Scale, 5678.
LINDBERGH, ANNE MORROW: Bare Tree,
    494; Dogwood, 1533; Even--, 1761;
    Mid-Summer, 3802; Two Citadels, 6721.
LINDEMAN, JACK: August 1, 401; August
    2, 402; August 5, 403.
LINEAWEAVER, MARION: Acquired Taste,
    23; Be Constant, My Love, 518; A
    Charm of Goldfinches, A Writhe of
    Worms, 938; Give Me My Name, 2307; In
    the Heart of a Shell, 2903; Let No
    Tree Wither, 3310; Letter from Home,
    3328; The Lilac Bush, 3389; Star
    Shower, 6029; Storm Warning, 6074;
    To Grownups Bearing Gifts, 6549; The
    Windflower, 7168.
LINDEMAN, JACK: Letter Man, 3331.
LINDSAY, MABEL: The Multitude of His
    Mercies, 3970.
LIOTTA, JAMES: Libris Meis, 3362; On a
    Book, 4422; The Outcast, 4615;
    Portraits in a Library, 4937; Thought,
    6403.
LIPTON, LAWRENCE: Moon Song for a Night
    in May, 3885; The Questioner, 5096.
LISTER, R. P.: The Amphitheatre--
    Arles, 184; Angels at Breakfast, 216;
    Bone China, 685; The Bridge, 747;
    Brown Study, 774; Captain Bud, 867;
    Dawn in Kensington Gardens, 1357;
    Defenestration, 1426; Gargoyles, 2253;
    The Golden Palace, 2337; Green as the
    Rice at Humpty Doo, 2415; I Sometimes
    Think, 2755; The Musician, 3983; The
    Musk Ox and the Musk, 3984; The Old
    Familiar Faces, 4381; On a Horse and
    a Goat, 4428; On Drinking English
    Beer, 4448; On Having the Backache,
    4459; On His Robust and Slatternly
    Muse, 4465; On Listening to Music
    with Two Minds, 4469; On Seeing the
    Sun Rise Seven Times, 4492; On the
    Unreality of Toothache, 4523; On the
    Youth of England Corrupted by Coffee,
    4525; The Patterned Fields, 4710;
    Pick and Choose, 4799; Pipe and
    Strings, 4821; Relaxation, 5202; A
    Revolution of Grandmothers, 5283;
    Shakuhachi and Samisen, 5558; The
    Stars and I, 6034; Toast to 2000,
    6609; Turpentine, 6702; Yell, 7335.
LITSEY, SARAH: The Visit, 6889.
LITTLE, KATHARINE DAY: The Nameless
    Color, 4029; The Third Poet, 6371.
LIVINGSTONE, GEORGE: Western Evening
    Love Song, 7032.
LLOYD, DONALD: The Raft, 5112
LOCKE, EDWARD: A Note on Hart Crane,
    4202; A Summer Rowing, 6146.
LOCKHART, MARJORIE LEE: Cards, Cards,
    Cards, 872.
LOEHLIN, JOHN: Cathay, 904.
LOESER, KATINKA: Fall of Snow, 1845;
    Sound and Echo, 5885.

LOGAN, JOHN: The Death of Southwell, 1397; Lines at the Death of a Child, 3404; Lines for a Young Wanderer in Mexico, 3409; Lines to His Son on Reaching Adolescence, 3426; Monologue for the Good Friday Christ, 3874; On a Prize Crucifix by a Student Sculptor, 4434; The Preparation, 4996; Reflection on the Date of a Book: October 26, 5183; St. Philip and the Martyrs of Japan, 5407.

LOGUE, CHRISTOPHER: Rules, 5374.

LOHF, KENNETH A.: Picasso at Vallauris, 4798.

LONG, ELIZABETH-ELLEN: Bejeweled Callers, 565; Cat on the Walk, 898; Mountain Afternoon, 3935; Navaho Woman at Day's End, 4045; Nosegay, 4179; October, 4283; Old Men in Church, 4400; Spite Fence, 5935; Storm Worry, 6076; Summertime Insomniac, 6156; Tucking Him In, 6697; Wind-Teased Sea, 7167; Winter Night, 7206.

LONGCHAMPS, JOANNE DE: Color in the Cold, 1124; Delivered from a Heaviness of Love, 1439; Idyll, 2786.

LONGFELLOW, ELIZABETH BRYANS: Black and White, 639.

LONGFELLOW, HENRY WADSWORTH: Snow-Flakes, 5724.

LONGFELLOW, ISABELLE BRYANS: Christmas List, 1022; Hope, 2630; October, 4284; Old Summer, 4410; Tip to Treasure, 6486.

LORD, MAY CARLETON: Vision, 6883.

LORING, HERBERT R.: Leap, 3280.

LOUCHHEIM, KATIE: Love's Worth, 3571.

LOUGEE, DAVID: Charade, 932; Mountain View, 3946.

LOVE, ADELAIDE: Cry of the Heart, 1301; November Night, 4231; Regardless, 5195.

LOWELL, ROBERT: Dunbarton, 1594; Words for Hart Crane, 7293.

LOWENFELS, WALTER: The Avant Garde, 436; Hart Crane, 2489; Spring, 5948; To Certain Poets, 6540.

LOYAL, GEORGIA: The Pax, 4720.

LUCY, SEAN: The Drifting Man, 1582; The Moving Man, 3956.

LUKACS, J. A.: The French in Cyprus, 1956, 2167.

LUND, DORIS HEROLD: Pet Aversion, 4773.

LUND, MARY GRAHAM: Insomnia, 2972.

LYNCH, BRENDA: The Clouds of Spring, 1091.

LYNCH, JOHN A.: In Dry Fields Daniel Walks, 2856; On Waking in Rome, 4533; Saint Martin's Infirmary, 5404.

M. DAVIDA, SISTER: Contentment, 1208; The New Grass, 4076.

M. DOLORES, SISTER: The End of a Perfect Lesson, 1708.

M. MAURA, SISTER: Picnic, 4801; Young Girls, 7363.

M. PAULINUS, SISTER: However Casually You May Go, 2686; Latter Day Psalm, 3264.

M. THERESE, SISTER: De Angelis, 1377.

MACAFEE, HELEN: Lines Found Under a Blotter, 3415.

MACAULAY, J. C.: My Father, 3994.

MACCAIG, NORMAN: Beach Talk, 524.

MACCOLLOM, JEAN: In Spring, 2892.

MACDIARMID, HUGH: In the Fall, 2899; Lo! A Child is Born, 3481; Reflections in a Slum, 5186; To Nearly Everybody, 6574.

MACDONALD, LACHLAN: The Writer to His Librarian Wife, 7322.

MACDONALD, WILSON: Galilee, 2234.

MACGILLIVRAY, ARTHUR: Old Man's Song, 4399.

MACINNES, MAIRIA: A Cold Day on the Marx-Engles Platz, East Berlin, 1106.

MACINNIS, HELEN PAULSEN: Taiwan, Western Outpost, 6235.

MACK, RACHEL: Auction at the Hillside Farm, 398; Contrary Things, 1211; Small Log House, 5694; Song of the Suburbs, 5841; Valleys of the Night, 6833.

MACKAYE, PERCY: In the Same Club Chair, 2918.

MACKINSTRY, ELIZABETH: Artist's Testimony, 323; The Man Who Hid His Own Front Door, 3634.

MACLEISH, ARCHIBALD: Poem for a Festival of Art at the Boston Public Gardens, 4882.

MACLEOD, NORMAN: Lament, 3208; Occasional Intelligence by Radar, 4276.

MACLOW, JACKSON: Canticle in October, 860.

MACNEISE, LOUIS: Canto XVIII, 862.

MACNEIL, MARY ANN: Grandmother, 2376; In Our Town, 2882.

MACPHERSON, JAY: The Ark, 298; The Beauty of Job's Daughters, 536; A Garden Shut, 2248; Inside the Angel, 2969; Like Adamant, 3384; The Old Man, 4395; A World of Words, 7310.

MADDOW, BEN: Elegy Upon a Certificate of Birth, 1684.

MAGARET, HELENE: Christmas, 1012; For Businessmen Only, 2057; The Rock, 5328; Saint Andrew, 5397.

MAGEE, IRENE: Cupid Reappraised, 1309; The Gullible Budget, 2454; Knightly Behavior, 3182; Night Plight of an Urbanite, 4115; When I Am Old, 7068.

MAGUIRE, C. E.: Nonprofit, 4170.

MAINO, JEANNETTE GOULD: The Tourist's Complaint to God: Yellowstone Park, 6629; The Walnut chest, 6941.

MALCOLM, DONALD: The Ruby Yacht of Paramount, 5370.

MALODY, BONNIE MAY: Compensation, 1156; Memory, 3752; Yards Wide and Like a Train, 7329.

MANDELBAUM, ALLEN: From the Ardent Forest, 2200.

MANHEIM, MARTHA: Social Analysis, 5744; Two A. M., 6719.

MANIFOLD, J. S.: Sonnet on Nightmares, 5872.

MANKER, DON: Pigs in Clover, 4814.

MANN, ISABEL ROOME: Cytherea's Isle, 1325.

MCFARLAND, ELIZABETH (cont'd): Gifted, 2290; Going Away, 2332; Have Baby, Will Travel, 2495; How Fair, 2665; If I Could Breathe, 2790; The Insatiate, 2961; The Kate, 3141; A Little Liking, 3463; Lovers, 3562; Lullaby for a Rainy Day, 3589; My Only Jo, 4014; Nursery Rhyme, 4251; Old Song, 4408; Song, 5793; Sweet Grass, 6207, Riddle Song for Tad, 5295; Time for a Little Serious Talk Along Lines, 6471; Two Voices, 6744; Who Will Tie Your Shoe?, 7131; The Young One, 7369; Your Kisses Are So Sincere, 7372.

MCFAHEY, JEANNE: Ballad, 466; Refusal for Heaven, 5191.

MCGHEE, MARCIA: Earth, 1618.

MCGINLEY, PATRICIA DUFF: Five P. M., 1993; Head of the House, 2514; On Returning, 4488.

MCGINLEY, PHYLLIS: Attention: Book-of-the-Month Club, 386; Bootless Speculations, 703; A Christmas Legend, 1021; Colman the Hermit, 1120; Columbia the Abbot, 1126; Girl's Eye View of Relatives, 2302; How the Beasts Keep Christmas, 2677; How to Start a War, 2683; Journey Toward Evening, 3116; The Landscape of Love, 3229; A Little Night Music, 3465; Love Letter for the 24th of November, 3551; Martin Luther, 3675; My Six Toothbrushes, 4017; Office Party, 4355; Sugar and Spice, 4357; The Pastor and the Lady, 4699; Rock-and-Roll Session, 5330; Saint Francis Borgia, or a Refutation for Heredity, 5400; Short History of a Peace-Lover, 5592; A Simple Explanation of Certain Epistles, 5625; Speaking of Television, 5916; The Theology of Jonathan Edwards, 6334; A Tour of English Cathedrals in the Summer (or Rainy Season), 6626; The Voices of October, 6908; Warning to Haberdashers, 6957; The Year Without a Santa Claus, 7334.

MCGONIGAL, MEMORY: Drugstore Bookstand, 1588; For a Daughter, Learning to Sew, 2043; York State Semantic, 7347.

MCGOVERN, MARGARET: Dream of Liverpool, England, 1571; Faith of My Father, 1837.

MCGRANE, JULIA: I, 2710.

MCGRATH, C. J., JR.: Nests are Made to Fly From, 4058.

MCGRATH, JOHN J.: Here Lovely, 2554.

MCGRATH, THOMAS: Same Old Jazz, 5417.

MCGUIGGAN, RICHARD J.: Well-Timed, 7023.

MCGUIRE, JOHN V.: Holy Innocents 1956, 2605.

MCILNAY, R. D.: The Ancient Dark, 190.

MCINERY, RALPH: In a Wet Season, 2839.

MCKAY, CRAIG C.: Vessels, 6852.

MCKEE, GLADYS: Lullaby for Monday Night, 3588; Night of Fog, 4112; October Wisdom, 4290; Poem for Pigtails, 4887; Song for a Second Child, 5808; Spring Cellar, 5951.

MCKEEHAN, VIRGINIA: The Snow, 5717.

MCNEILL, LOUISE: April Testament, 289; Caw-Cus, 910 ; Cornucopia, 1230; Earthling, 1628; Gravity, 2392; In October, 2881; The Invisible Line, 3002; The Pledge, 4846; Wire-Brier, 7229.

MEIRELES, CECILIA: The Birth, 619.

MEISSNER, W. W.: On the Road to Bethlehem, 4516.

MELLICHAMP, LESLIE: Epitaph, 1729.

MELO NETO, JONO CABRALDE: The Poem, 4858.

MENASHE, SAMUEL: Paradise, 4664; A Poem, 4859; Someone Walked Over My Grave, 5776; Three Poems, 6433.

MERCHANT, JANE: Another Summer, 243; Belated Thanks, 566; Blowing Weather, 661; Certified, 917; Cherry-Pie Paradox, 950; Each Winter, 1605; For Falling Asleep, 2067; For Pleasant Dreams, 2093; The Generous Heart, 2264; Grandfather's Belief, 2372; Handy Rule of Thumb, 2475; How Many Leaves?, 2668; Individual, 2948; Intelligence Test, 2984; Jeeped Molasses, 3084; Known Room, 3188; The Loser, 3518; Meetings, 3737; Midsummer Invitation, 3803; Morning Care of Husbands, 3900; On Hearing Certain Words, 4460; Report Retort, 5229; Retired, 5251; The Shell, 5570; Sigh of a Gardener's Wife, 5608; Smells, 5705; Spring Freeze, 5958; Star Time, 6030; Suited, 6129; Uncamouflaged, 6760; Unembarrassed, 6779; Unjust Desserts, 6790; Values, 6835; Volunteer Nurse, 6910.

MEREDITH, WILLIAM: Ablutions, 5; Bachelor, 450; A Botanical Trope, 707; The Fish-Vendor, 1985; Godchildren, 2326; Notre Dame de Chartres, 4220; On Falling Asleep by Firelight, 4451; Pastoral, 4701.

MERGARD, JEAN CARPENTER: Day After Labor Day, 1359; Maid Servise, 3614; Perspective, 4767; Reciprocal, 5160.

MERKER, KARL KIMBER: Poem for Con, 4884.

MERRIAM, EVE: The Esquimaux Have No Word for Divorce, 1748; Lullaby, 3585.

MERRILL, HERBERT: Acceptance, 20; Alone Awake, 161; April, 278; By the Fire, 819; Closed Shop, 1082; Closing the Cabin, 1084; Cold Reception, 1113; Complaint Department, 1158; Crossing the Ice, 1291; Deep-Rooted, 1419; The Defense Rests, 1428; Disturbing the Peace, 1512; The Fragile Time, 2161; In the Garden, 2900; Involuntary, 3007; July Fourth Memory, 3122; Lake Change, 3203; Late Lake, 3256; Launching Platform, 3269; Man-Versus Housekeeping, 3633; Midnight Zero, 3800; Midsummer-Night Christmas, 3806; Misty Meeting, 3843; Morning After Storm, 3898; The Night Watch, 4123; No Thanks, Dear, 4156; A Northern View, 4177; Objection, 4270; Old Earth, 4379; Old Jubal, 4391; Recital, 5163; Requiem, 5235; (cont'd)

MANSFIELD, MADGE ACTION: At Eventide, 360.

MANSFIELD, MARGERY: Blizzard in March, 656; Daughters Who Lose Their Mothers, 1353; Pioneers, 4818; The Wind in the Chimney, 7162.

MARIS STELLA, SISTER: The Animals' Carol, 225; Carol for the Christmas Angels, 880; Raphael Archangel, 5135; Tree at Guadalupe Church, Santa Fe, 6665.

MARKLE, MARIE: Doctor, 1528; Doctor in the House, 1529.

MARLEY, FAYE JOHANNES: A Listening Prayer, 3441; To an Agnostic, 6527.

MARSH, CORINNA: A Flower at Five, 2020.

MARSHALL, CHARLES BURTON: A Great Fall, 2399.

MARSHALL, LENORE G.: Gogglehead, 2331; Respite, 5244.

MARTAUGH, IRBY AMBERG: Ascension, 340.

MARTIN, PATRICIA: I'll Always Love You, 2806.

MARTIN, PETE: The Constant Merchandising Manger to His Love, 1201.

MARTINEK, JOSEPH: Desert Soliloquy, 1458.

MARUYAMA, KAORU: A Distant View of the School, 1511; A Rhinoceros and a Lion, 5285.

MARX, ANNE: Checkers, 946; Mother Told Me So, 3925.

MARY ADA, SISTER: For A Child's Book of Courtesy, 2041.

MARY AQUIN, SISTER: The Human Condition, 2690.

MARY FAITH, SISTER: Chicago, 955; For an April Day, 2054; November, 4225; Songs for the Fourth Commandment, 5851.

MARY GILBERT, SISTER: Diary Of Dreams, 1482; The Same Old Cracked Tune, 5416; Skid Row, 5661; Thirty-Fifth Spring, 6374.

MARY HONORA, SISTER: Dissemblers, 1508; Monks at Recreation: 13th Century, 3873; O'Antiphons, 4253; When Dew Dripped Silver, 7065.

MARY IGNATIA, SISTER: Gift, 2284.

MARY IMMACULATA, SISTER: By Any Name, 813; Grapes from Thorns, 2382; Our Lady of the Word, 4600.

MARY JEREMY, SISTER, Ever to Scourges, 1775; Pavana in Avila, 4717; The Professor's Farewell, 5028; Richard Rolle's Lament for the Passion, 5292.

MARY MADELEINE SOPHIE, SISTER: Reflections on a Guernsey, 5189.

MARY MADELEVA, SISTER: Parables, 4657.

MARY OF OUR LADY OF CHARITY: Easter Vigil, 1638.

MARY ST. VIRGINIA, SISTER: Bach in Sacred Heart Chapel, 449.

MARY TIMOTHY, SISTER: How Shall I Measure You?, 2670.

MARZ, ROY: The Blind Man, 654; The Blue Tablecloth, 674; Boy Buried on Sunday, 715; The Children, 978;

The Children, 978; The Island-Maker, 3025; The Legacy, 3290; Life of the Virgin, 3371; The Paulownia Tree, 4713; The Poem's Words, 4894; Targets, 6259.

MASEFIELD, JOHN: In Memory of Two Friends, 2877; The Shipwreck, 5583.

MASTERS, EDGAR LEE: Clarence Darrow, 1062.

MASTERS, MARCIA: The Graveyard at Genoa, 2391; Impressions of My Father, 2823; Mansion at Sundown, 3641; The Memory, 3753; Rainfall on The Puritans, 5132.

MASTIN, FLORENCE RIPLEY: Lady Day, 3196; The Listener, 3439.

MATRAN, KHALIL: Memories of Childhood, 3749.

MATTHEWS, ALICE CLEAR: Ballet Slippers, 484; City View, 1054.

MATTHEWS, T. S.: Conversation English, 1218; Moods, 3878.

MAURA, SISTER M.: Any Summer Afternoon, 258.

MAY, JAMES BOYER: Forbidden Equation, 2114.

MAYES, RICHARD I.: To a Used Auto Parts Dealer, 6522.

MAYHALL, JANE: Matinee, 3698; Summer Pond Romance, 6144.

MAYO, E. L.: The Factory, 1832; Icarus, 2771; Snow Scene, 5731; The Third Tower, 6373; Twinkling, 6717.

MCALLISTER, CLAIRE: Budapest, 778; Winter Leaves, 7200.

MCBROWN, GERTRUDE PARTHENIA: The Hush of Autumn, 2705; Nature's Carolers, 4044; Winter Wonder, 7220.

MCCANDLESS, J. H.: Variations on a Theme by John Donne, 6842.

MCCARTHY, LEONARD: Advent: Nunc Est Hora..., 47; All Hallows Eve, 142; Boy in a Monastery, 716; Come Home, 1130; On Re-Reading Hawthorne, 4487; Penitential Sonnet, 4740; Romantic Lament, 5338; Shadowbrook Revisited, 5553; To Seek A Child, 6581.

MCCARTHY, MARY WEDEMEYER: Nursery Rhyme, 4250.

MCCLINTIC, WINONA: The Solipsist, 5764.

MCCLURE, MIKE: 2 for Theodore Roethke, 6724.

MCCORD, DAVID: Ballade at Eight Bells, 475; Ballade for the Birds, 476; New Chitons for Old Gods, 4071.

MCCOWAN, LINDA: The Man, 3624.

MCCOY, CHARLES S.: Resurrection, 5249.

MCCRANE, JULIA: Angle, 218.

MCCULLOCH, W. F.: The Forest and the Town, 2122.

MCDONNELL, THOMAS P.: After Christmas, 76; Christmas Harvest, 1020; Incident at Calvary, 2932; Lucifer in Anytown, 3580; Song for Mid-August, 5815.

MCFARLAND, ELIZABETH: Ballad, 465; The Bath, 510; Beach Plums, 522; The Beggar's Manuscript, 556; The Blue-Eyed Daisy, 664; Correspondence, 1237; Enclosed, 1702; (continued)

MERRILL, HERBERT: The Robin Tree,
5325; The Rooster and the Sun, 5347;
Salamander, 5411; Second Chorus, 5489;
Sky Cottage, 5665; The Sleepers and
the Sun, 5672; Snow Fire, 5723; Stars
and a Frog, 6033; Status Quo, 6041;
A Stony Field, 6059; Stubborn, 6107;
The Summer Lake, 6140; Sundown, 6170;
Thanksgiving Cup, 6313; Time to Go
In, 6479; Two-Legged Year, 6727;
Unwilling Travels, 6806; The Unwise
Goose, 6807; Wabash Catfish, 6915;
The Web of Frost, 7007; Wind and Fire,
7160; Winter Carpentry, 7184; The
Winter Crew, 7187; The Winter Crop,
7186; The Winter Harbor, 7194; The
Winter Heart, 7196; Winter Thunder,
7217.

MERRILL, JAMES: At Manallapuram, 365;
For a Second Marriage, 2049; Italian
Lesson, 3048; Laboratory Poem, 3193;
Mirror, 3825; Salome, 5415; A
Valentine in Crayons, 6832; Voices
from the Other World, 6906; Walking
All Night, 6931.

MERRITT, VIRGINIA: Via Southern Iowa,
6854.

MERTON, THOMAS: A Prelude: For the
Feast of St. Agnes, 4993; Sincerity,
5631.

MERWIN, W. S.: After Some Years, 89;
After the Flood, 96; Bear, 526; Bell
Buoy, 568; Birds Waking, 617; Birth-
day, 626; Bucolic, 777; Burning
Mountain, 794; Burning the Cat, 795;
Camel, 840; Campaign Note, 846; Cape
Dread, 865; Corps de Ballet, 1232;
Deception Island, 1407; The Eyes of
the Drowned, 1819; Faces and Land-
scapes, 1827; The Fishermen, 1988;
Fog, 2031; Foghorn, 2032; The Highway,
2582; The Iceberg, 2775; In the Light
of Autumn, 2906; Is uar geimred;
atracht gaeth, 3019; John Otto, 3105;
Lost Voices, 3534; The Master, 3688;
Mercy, 3763; Odysseus, 4306; The
Other Tree, 4591; Plaint for the
Death of Guillen Peraza, 4827; Pro-
logue at Midnight, 5038; Rimer, Penna,
5299; Saint Sebastian, 5408; Sea
Monster, 5474; Sea Wife, 5473; Ship-
wreck, 5584; Small Woman on Swallow
Street, 5702; Song in a Cloud of
Hands, 5823; Summer Song, 6149; The
Survivors, 6196; Thorn Leaves in
March, 6397; Tobacco, 6610; Uncle
Cal, 6761; Uncle Hess, 6762; Under
the Old One, 6773; Whaler, 7034;
Winter Evening: London, 7191.

MEYER, JOHN: Warning, 6955.

MEYERS, ESTER: With Apologies to Joyce
Kilmer, 7239.

MEZEY, ROBERT: Against Seasons, 110;
If I Should Die Before I Wake, 2791;
It Is June, This Jesting Heat, 3037.

MIDDLETON, CHRISTOPHER: Aesthetics for
Benetto Gulgo, 66; The Suspense,
6199.

MIDDLETON, COSETTE: The Breach, 736;
Downpour, 1559; It Looks Like a

Beautiful Day, 3041; Variations on a
Voice, 6844.

MILBRATH, MARY MARGARET: Admonition,
42; Brave Valentine, 734; Lines for
a Little Man, 3407; Please, Dear.
Soon Dear!..., 4840; Song Before
Bedlam, 5803.

MILES, JOSEPHINE: Belief, 567; Berg,
581; Care, 873; Conjure, 1183; Dialogue, 1475; Dream, 1567; Increment,
2941; Iowa and the West, 3008;
Italian, 3047; Location, 3485;
Sysyphus, 6222; Three Stages, 6440;
To Time, 6603; View, 6862; Yard,
7328.

MILES, LILLIAN E.: Dry Water Hole,
1591.

MILLER, DEREK: A Poem, 4860.

MILLER, HARRY ALBERT: The Cathedral,
905; Inspiration, 2974.

MILLER, MARY OWENS: Woman Sea Horse,
7262.

MILLER, MAUDE BARNES: Adoption, 44.

MILLER, MAX: Who Gives, 7128.

MILLS, BARRISS: Renoir Girl, 5224.

MILNE, EWART: Could I Believe, 1243
The Gifts of the Oracle, 2292; The
Woman on the Rock, 7260.

MINCK, GRACE STILLMAN: Just in Case,
3135.

MINER, VIRGINIA SCOTT: Blue Heron,
670; Fun at the Dentist's, 2226;
Heirlooms, 2535; Home Town, 2616;
Lilacs Are a Brief Affair, 3392;
Mothers of the Ages Past, 3931;
Passed by Customs, 4681; Shipboard
Dance, 5582; Start of School, 6036.

MITCHEL, HELEN: Grandmother, 2377;
School's in, School's Out, 5453.

MOFFITT, JOHN: Betrayal, 586; Morning
Song, 3911; Morning Stroll, 3913;
Second Coming, 5490; Song for a Bad
Night, 5805; Spring Gray, 5960;
Surmise, 6188; To Emily Dickinson,
6544; Tranced, 6643.

MOHANTY, G. P.: The Doves of My Eyes,
1557; The New Muse, 4087.

MOK, SUSAN: For You, 2113; Invitation,
3004; May I Be One, 3705; The Wind
Showed Me, 7166.

MOLLOY, RUTH BRANNING: On Educational
Toys, 4449.

MOLTON, WARREN LANE: The Church in
Search Thereof, 1035; The Fourth Day,
2153; Intercessor, 2985; Towards
Gethsemane, 6633.

MONTAGUE, JAMES L.: Chokecherries,
1002; Fall Morning, 1843.

MONTAGUE, JOHN: Nursery Story: Modern
Version, 4252.

MONTALE, EUGENIO: Boats on the Marne,
679; A Letter Not Written, 3333; The
Mediterranean, 3725; On the Scrawled
Wall, 4518.

MONTGOMERY, JOHN: Temples in the Dark,
6290.

MONTGOMERY, MARION: First Cold Snap,
1952; The Run: A Parable for Tired
Teachers, 5375.

MOODY, MINNIE HITE: Boy with a Kerosene
Lamp, 725; (continued)

MOODY, MINNIE HITE (cont'd): In Loving
    Evidence, 2867; Iron Bedstead, 3011;
    Roadside Phone Booth, 5323.
MOONEY, ALFRED LELAND: The English
    Teacher, 1719.
MONNEY, STEPHEN: Water Color, 6973.
MOORE, CLEMENT: 'Twas the Night Before
    Christmas, 6706.
MOORE, MARIANNE: Blessed Is the Man,
    650; Boston, 705; Combat Cultural,
    1127; Leonardo Da Vinci's, 3301;
    Melchior Vulpius, 3740; No Better
    Than a Withered Daffodil; 4138.
MOORE, MERRILL: Deaconing Is an
    Honorable Profession, 1372; In China
    I Learned About Gardens, 2847; Things
    Like This I Do Not Understand, 6362;
    Time Makes All People Necrophiliacs,
    6473; What She Did in the Morning,
    I Wouldn't Know, She Was Seated There
    in the Midst of Her Resilient Symp-
    toms Always, 7051.
MOORE, RICHARD: A Deep Discussion,
    1417; In Memory of an Over-Ambitious
    Poem, 2871; In Praise of Newspaper
    Verse, 2887; Leaves at Night, 3283.
MOORE, ROSALIE: Boy and Parade, 711;
    Joy and the Presence of Snakes, 3117;
    Latin Lecturer, 3263; Life of a King,
    3369; The Manicure, 3638; Poem for a
    Commencement, 4881; Richard in
    England, 5291.
MOORE, RUTH: Vernal Equinox, 6847.
MOORE, THOMAS: A Ballad--The Lake of
    the Dismal Swamp, 474.
MOORHEAD, JAMES KEITH: Determination,
    1466; Surprise, 6190.
MORABADI, JIGAR: Ghazal, 2274.
MORAES, DOM: Being Married, 564;
    Kanheri Caves, 3140.
MORAN, MOORE: Rimbaud: On His Muse,
    5298; That Breakfast, 6317.
MORELAND, G. B.: The Case of the
    Helping Hand, 887.
MORELJONO, JOKE: In Alien Land, 2841.
MORGAN, FREDERICK: Epitaph, 1730;
    Epitaph, 1731; Poem, 4861; Primary
    Notion, 5007.
MORGAN, JAMES: Lesson in Bone-Song,
    3305.
MORGAN, LOLA S.: Because You Would not
    Bend, 539.
MORRAH, DAVE: Mein Grossfader's Mamma
    Goosen, 3738; Rhymers Mein Grossfader
    Made: Ein Oldischer Frau, 5288.
MORRIS, HERBERT: Blood, 658; Bone,
    684; The Brahms, 730; Breath, 740;
    The Clown's Heart, 1093; The Cyclist,
    1321; For That Unjourneyed Man and
    Visioned Sea, 2103; Hotel de Dieu,
    2646; The Medium, 3726; The Morning
    Moon, 3907; Myself and Thou from
    Theatres of the Night, 4022; The
    North of Wales, 4175; Les Parapluies:
    Renoir, 4668; Prothalamium, 5053; A
    Shirt-Silk from Havana, 5585; Soleil,
    5761; The Task, 6260; Terrain, 6304;
    A Walker in the Country of July,
    6930; Workmen, 7304.
MORRIS, JACKSON: View of Earth from a
    Space Station, 6865.

MORRIS, JOHN N.: For Captain Walter
    Phillips, U. S. M. C., 2058; Nikko
    Kekko, Beautiful Nikko, 4131; An Old
    Man's August, 4398; Over Grave
    Flowers, 4623.
MORRIS, MORT: Gift of Gab, 2285.
MORRIS, VINICIUS DE: Blue and White,
    662.
MORRISON, JANE: The Pastel Girls,
    4698; Winter Flowers, 7192.
MORSE, SAMUEL FRENCH: Coming Down,
    1135; Edgar, Solus, 1652; Elegy in a
    Dream, 1681; The Enemy, 1714; Foot-
    note to a Revolution, 2040; In the
    Line Storm, 2907; A Kind Of View,
    3161; Links in a Chain, 3432; Looking
    Out to Sea, 3513; The Peaceable King-
    dom, 4726; A Periphrasis, 4756, The
    Poet Who Lived with His Words, 4902;
    The Sleeping Gipsy, 5675; Then, Now,
    Hereafter, 6333; Two Voices in a Cave,
    6745; The Words, 7287.
MORTIMER, JOHN: News Item: Science
    Now Reveals Busy Bee Really Lazy,
    4102.
MORTON, DAVID: Obscure Incident, 4273;
    Therapy, 6336; Thrifty Lover, 6448.
MOSES, W. R.: Big Dam, 604; Grackle
    Days, 2363.
MOSS, HOWARD: Against That Time, If
    Ever That Time Come, 111; Boiling
    Eggs, 683; Dreams, 1575; The Dumb
    Show, 1593; Florida, 2018; If You Can,
    2799; King Midas, 3167; Light and
    Dark, 3377; Local Places, 3483; A
    Marriage, 3666; On the Difficulty of
    Obtaining Potions, 4504; On the Site
    of the Old Lafayette, 4519; A Problem
    in Morals, 5023; Rain, 5120; Shall I
    Compare Thee to a Summer's Day, 5559;
    Skin and Bone, 5662; Small Elegy,
    5692; A Song Stricken from the Records,
    5844; A Song To Be Set to Music, 5846;
    A Swimmer in the Air, 6213; Tourists,
    6628; When in Disgrace with Fortune
    and Men's Eyes, 7070; A Winter Come,
    7185.
MOSS, STANLEY: The Hangman, 2476; A
    Spanish Landscape, 5905.
MOTONARI: In the Blossoms of a Village
    the City Is Lost, 2896.
MOTTRAM, ERIC: The Cat Sat on the Mat,
    899.
MOUNTS, CHARLES EUGENE: Remembrance for
    Rosemary, 5213.
MOYNAHAN, JULIAN: The Graduation
    Exercise Recollected, 2364; White
    Nights, 7115.
MUELLER, LISEL: Afterthoughts on the
    Lovers, 108; The Bride's Complaint,
    744; In the Thriving Season, 2920;
    In Memory of Anton Webern, Dead
    September 15, 1945, 2872; Nine Months
    Making, 4134; The Queen of Sheba Says
    Farewell, 5087; Sans Souci, 5422;
    Sunlight and Shadow, 6172.
MUIR, E. A.: Before Your Third, 555.
MUIR, EDWIN: The Tower, 6634; The Two
    Sisters, 6738.
MULDOON, ENA: An Arabian Valentine, 291.

MULDOON, ROBERT J.: A Psalm for the Magi, 5058.

MULLINS, TERENCE Y.: Braille, 731; The Busy Man, 802; Cinquain: Easter Morning, 1041; A Contrite Heart, 1212; Pecadillo, 4732; The Prospect, 5049; The Sinner, 5642; Two Ways, 6748.

MUMFORD, OLIVE: The Constant Reviewer, 1202.

MUNDELL, WILLIAM D.: The Deer Come Down, 1423; The Empty House, 1699; On Tobey's Road, 4528; The Passing Remark, 4687.

MURANO, SHIRO: Pole Vault, 4912.

MURO, SAISEI: Winter Grass, 7193.

MURPHY, WILLIAM J.: In Conclusion, 2849; Inside Story, 2968.

MURRAY, PHILIP: Charm for the Tooth-Ache, 937; Firefly: A Japanese Romance, 1942; A Little Book of Hours, 3447; L'Ogre a L' Estime, 4358; Song Against Sorrow, 5800; A Song of Love-Longing, 5831; Song of the Thin Man, 5842.

MUYOSHI, TATSUJI: Nostalgia, 4181.

MYERS, E. LUCAS: Ballade of the Early Seas, 479; Journey in the Tessellated Corn, 3113.

MYHRE, SARAH PARKER: Deception, 1406.

NABOKOV, VLADIMER: The Ballad of Longwood Glen, 469; Rain, 5121.

NADER, ADRIAN: Flesh Can Say Loudly, 2001.

NAKANO, SHIGEHARU: Good-By Before Dawn, 2341.

NALL, BINK: The Rented Garden, 5225.

NAPIER, JOHN T.: A Letter to V. R. Lang, 3338.

NARASIMHASWAMY, K. R.: Wasn't It You?, 6965.

NARDI, MARCIA: Meeting You on the Street Today, 3736; New From Our Town, 4097.

NASH, ARNOLD: A Prayer for the South, 4982.

NASH, MELISSA: Beauty-Blind, 535.

NASH, OGDEN: Alias and Melisande; or, Gammon Me Once, Gammon Me Twice, You Can Count Gammoning Me Thrice, 136 All's Noel That Ends Noel, or Incompatability Is the Spice of Christmas, 155; Anybody for Money?, 259; The Back of Mine Hand to Mine Host, 453; Baltimore, 485; Behind the Umpires' Backs the Stars Relax, 560; The Body Builder, 681; A Brief Guide to Rhyming; or, How Be the Little Busy Doth?, 752; Brief Lives in Not So Brief-I, 753; Brief Lives in Not So Brief-II, 754; Brief Lives in Not So Brief-III, 755; The Buses Headed for Scranton, 798; Capercaille, Ave Atque Vaille, 866; Come, Come, Kerouac! My Generation Is Beater Than Yours, 1128; A Day on a Cruise, 1366; The Diamond Dude, 1479; Don't Look Now, But There's Something Behind the Curtain, 1542; Dreams, 1576; The Drummer Boy, 1589; Fee Fi Ho Hum, No Wonder Baby Sucks His Thumb, 1896; Fellow-Creatures, Tray and Outre, 1902; The Happy Christmas Hop of Mr. Leaper, 2478; Holler Guy, 2602; How to Harass a Hitchcock, 2679; How to Harry a Husband, 2680; How to Tell a Kitchen from a Cuisine: Take a Quick Look at Ours, 2684; I Always Say There's No Place Like New York in Summer, or, That Cottage Small by a Waterfall Was Snapped up Last February, 2712; I Spy, or, the Depravity of Privacy, 2756; I'll Eat My Split-Level Turkey in the Breezeway, 2807; I'm Glad You Asked That Question, Because It Shows You in Your True Colors, 2811; It Would Have Been Quicker to Walk, 3046; The Magician; 3610; Merry Christmas and Bon Voyage, or How to Tell Santa Claus Without a Baedeker, 3771; The Mother Tongue, 3927; Ms. Found Under a Servette in a Lovely Home, 3968; Nature Walks, 4043; No Conformity, to Enormity!, 4139; Oafishness Sells Good, Like an Advertisement Should, 4266; Paradise for Sale, 4665; Posies from a Second Childhood, 4948; A Potted Watch Never Boils, 4962; The Puzzler, 5079; Rapunzel, Rapunzel, Let's Down Our Hair, 5137; The Ring in Grandfather's Nose, 5300; Ring Out the Old, Ring in the New, But Don't Get Caught in Between, 5302; Scrooge Rides Again, 5463; The Shad, 5551; Sic Semper Mr. Sherman's Temper, 5600; Sticks and Stones May Break My Bones, But Names Will Break My Heart, 6051; The Strange Case of the Blight That Failed, 6080; The Strange Case of the Lucrative Compromise, 6081; The Strange Casement of the Poetic Apothecary, 6082; The Pizza, 6226; Table Talk, 6227; Table Talk, 6228; Table Talk, 6229; That's Funny, Wasn't It?, 6324; Transatlantic Transports, 6646; The Trouble with Shakespeare, You Remember Him, 6686; The Tycoon, 6752; Which Came First, Obeisance or Obesity?, 7095; Your Lead, Partner; Hope We've Read the Same Book, 7373.

NASH, VERNON: I'd Cancel His Poetic License, 2779.

NATHAN, LEONARD: Between Town and City, 595; Birthday Observance, 631; Children Defy the Winter King, 980; Edelweiss, 1649; Figure in the Distance, 1921; The Green Lodger, 2421; Homage to the King's Choir, 2608; Looking Down, 3511; A Mexican in Passing, 3785; Movement in the Peach Orchard, 3951; The Sky Hung Idiot Blue, 5666; We Did the Best, 6986; Winter Obsessed Them, 7209.

NATHAN, NORMAN: Aged Eight and Three, 115; Past Midwinter, 4696; Small Protection, 5696.

NATHAN, ROBERT: On the State of Art, 4521.

NATIONEK, HANS: Everywhere, 1781; Last Wisdom, 3249.

NATSUME, SOSEKI: How Cooly Refreshing, 2663; Inquire of the Wind, 2959.

NEAME, ALAN: An Academic Occasion, 15; Conservation Piece, 1957, 1191; Correcting, 1234; Medical College: Levant, 3718; Meeting, 3733; Night Scene, 4116; Riposte, 5304; Thursday Afternoon, 6458.

NECKER, ROBERT: Sunday, 6162.

NEELY, ARIMENTHA: Look Within My Heart, 3509.

NEELY, LUCY: Family Scenes, 1855.

NEELY, LUKE: After-Dinner Speaker, 80; Bad Script, 463; Bargain Hunter, 498; Father of Twins, 1880; Meditation, 3722; The Overlooked Anniversary, 4626; Parade, 4661; Parents' Progress, 4669; Post-Blizzard Report, 4952; Rioting for a Fall, 5303; Summer Slumber, 6148; Summer Suspense, 6150; Thought of an Icebox Raider, 6406; Wader's Woe, 6916; Why More Women Aren't Naturalists, 7136; Without Parallel, 7250.

NELSON, TRUDI: Delayed Reaction, 1436; A Little Knowledge Is a Dwindling Thing, 3462; Package Deal, 4640.

NEMEROV, HOWARD: Absent-Minded Professor, 10; Art Song, 316; The Battenkill in Winter, 512; Boom, 701; A Clock Without Hands, 1080; Cloud-Seeding, 1090; The Dancer's Reply, 1336; A Day on the Big Branch, 1367; Death and the Maiden, 1382; Elegy for a Nature Poet, 1678; Forecast, 2118; The Fourth of July, 2154; Going Away, 2333; Holding the Mirror Up to Nature, 2600; Lore, 3516; The Mapmaker on His Art, 3646; A Mobile of Carved Wooden Fish, 3850; The Murder of William Remington, 3973; The Old Solders' Home, 4407; On Certain Wits, 4444; Painting a Mountain Stream, 4648; A Picture, 4803; Political Reflection, 4917; A Primer of the Daily Round, 5008; Reactionary History, 5145; Runes, 5376; Sandpipers, 5421; Sarabande, 5427; Shells, 5572; A Speckled Stone Mirror, 5917; The Statutes in the Public Gardens, 6042; Steps for a Dancer, 6050; Storm Windows, 6075; Sunderland, 6168; To David, About His Education, 6542; The Wheel King, 7059; The Witch of Eudor, 7237; Writing, 7323.

NEVILLE, HELEN: The Portrait of Gertrude Stein, 4945.

NEWBOLD, FRANCIS: Empty House, 1700; On a Gray Afternoon, 4427; The Roving Eye, 5366.

NEWMAN, PRESTON: While Watching the Movie Trapeze, 7098.

NEWMEYER, MARTHA F.: Simultaneous Departure, 5628.

NEWTON, VERNON: The Sparrowmaker, 5907.

NICHOLL, LOUISE TOWNSEND: Bright Gravity, 759; Broader the Lawn in

Those Summers, 763; The Cruse, 1298; Death Wish, 1401; The Grape Leaf, 2380; Interior Day, 2988; Key Pattern, 3152; Lines Written After Reading Keats Whose Name Is Writ in Water, 3431; Plainsong, 4826; Second Wonder, 5494.

NICHOLS, DOUGLAS: Landscape Near Salt Lake, 3228; A Merry Heart, 3772; Postcard Harlequin, 4954; Remembering John Marin, 5212.

NICHOLS, ELMER H.: Gambling for His Seamless Robe, 2236.

NICHOLSON, NORMAN: On My Thirty-Fifth Birthday, 4475; Winter by the Ironworks, 7183.

NICKERSON, LOUISE A.: Feline Sea, 1901.

NICKERSON, VESTA: Heritage of Words, 2555; Old Houseboats, 4390.

NICOLAS, CLAIRE: Italian Market, 3049; Thanksgiving on Long Island, 6315.

NIMS, JOHN FREDERICK: Florence, 2015; Isaiah's Coal, 3021; Of the Annunciation, 4329; Of the Most Holy Trinity, 4341; Of the Nativity, 4342; Three Poems of St. John of the Cross, 6434.

NIRALA: The Stone-Breaker, 6057.

NISHIWAKI, JUNZABURO: Rain, 5122; The Sun, 6158.

NISSENSON, CAROL ANN: The Forest, 2121.

NIXON, JOHN: April Bus to Richmond, 280.

NIXON, JOHN, JR.: I As Charles IX, 2715; Khan of the Sunflowers, 3156; A Niche for the Architect, 4106; On Taking a Shower, 4493; What Happened to Hera, 7045.

NOLL, BINK: Martinis at the Schneiders, 3676.

NORMAN, CHARLES: Footnote, 2038; Spring Morning, 5965; The Wood, 7273;

NORSE, HAROLD: Florence, 2016; Monet's Venice, 3871; Roman Ghetto, 5336; Victor Emanuel Monument (Rome), 6859; Was It Florence or Venice?, 6960.

NORTH, ELIZABETH: Survival, 6194.

NORTH, JESSICA NELSON: So Disappear, 5739.

NORTON, ALBERT C.: Freedom's Morning Star, 2165.

NOYES, ALFRED: Ballade of the Peace Conferences, 480; The Grand Canyon, 2369; Thoughts and the Billiard Balls, 6409.

OAKES, NORMAN E.: At the Shore, 380.

OBEAR, EMILY HANSON: To Edwin Arlington Robinson, 6543.

O'CONNELL, REGINA: Victimae Paschali Laudes, 6858.

O'CONNELL, ROBERT: In the World-Crowded Corner of a Stall, 2922; Peter the Rock, 4775.

O'CONNOR, FRANK: The Hermitage, 2557.

O'DOHERTY, BRIAN: Katie, 3144; Poem, 4862; Poems from a Hospital, 4893.

OERKE, ANDREW: Harvest, 2491; Hawk on the Roadside, 2502; I Gathered, 2731.

OGA, TAKU: Soldiers, 5758.

OGILVIE, JOHN: Encounter, 1706.
O'GORMAN, NED: An Afternoon with a Poet, 107; An Art of Poetry, 309; Because Noni Trespassed in the Night, 538; The Blood, 659; Childhood, 977; L'Annunciazione: From Bellini, 241; The Complaint of a Young Priest, 1159; A Description of the Sea for Lina Lenzi Who Has Never Seen It, 1453; A Dirge, 1496; Easter Among Four Children, 1634; For Ezra Pound, 2066; Great Grandfather, Clamdiggers, and Homer, 2401; In Memory of Sister Virgilia of the Sacred Heart, 2876; A Movement of Peoples, 3952; Myth, 4024; On David's Portrait of a Grand-niece, 4447; A Poem About a Prince, 4875; Reading Dante With Ionians, 5146; The Resurrection of Animals, 5250; The Rose and the Body of the Rose, 5350; A Song foe the Passionate, 5821; The Spring, 5949; The Summer, 6134; The Sunbathers, 6159; The Thoughts of a Scholarly Shepherd, 6411; To My Father, 6563; This Will Be the Song, 6675; Two Homilies, 6725; Two Poems on Larger Topics, 6734.

O'HARA, FRANK: About Courbet, 6; Cambridge, 838; The Eyelid Has Its Storms, 1818; For James Dean, 2078; Got Janice and Kenneth to Voyage, 2079; Now It Is Light..., 4237; On a Mountain, 4431; On Rachmaninoff's Birthday, 4483; On Seeing Larry Rivers' Washington Crossing the Delaware at the Museum of Modern Art, 4490; Poem, 4863; Radio, 5110.

O'KEARNEY, JOHN: Ides of March, 2783.
OLIVIER, REGINE: Adolescence, 43.
OLSON, CHARLES: Christmas, 1013.
OLSON, ELDER: Directions to the Armorer, 1495; The Exegesis, 1796; For the Demolition of a Theater, 2106; In Defense of Superficiality, 2855; Knight, with Umbrella, 3181; The Last Entries in the Journal, 3242; A Valentine for Marianne Moore, 6829; The Voice, 6901.

OLSON, TED: Text for Grandma Moses, 6309.
ONITSURA: Mountain River--And Even the Stones Sing Poems to the Blossoms, 3941.
OPPENHEIMER, J. L.: April Fool, 282.
ORLOVITZ, GIL: Art of the Sonnet: VI, 311; Art of the Sonnet: IX, 312; Art of the Sonnet, XXIX, 313; Art of the Sonnet: LV, 314; Art of the Sonnet: LVI, 315; Lyric, 3599.

ORR, CAREY: Pierrot to Columbine, 4809.
OSBORNE, ANN: Prayer for a Litter Girl, 4978.
OSTRANDER, GILMAN M.: The Social Structure of Early Massachusetts, 5746.
OSTROFF, ANTHONY: Dirge, 1497; Elegy, 1672; Lake Allen: Summer, 1954; 3201; Letter from Berkeley, 3327; A Visit to the Country, 6893;

The Zoo, 7385.
OTE, TAKUJI: Blue Fox, 667.
OTIS, ARTHUR FREDERIC: After-Luncheon Speaker, 86; Big Wheel, 606; Bird of Paradox, 612; Fly in My Car, 2028; I Don't Decry Hi-Fi, But--, 2725; Lucky Lady, 3582; No Sugar, 4155; Pay-Off, 4721; People Are So Inconsistent, 4745; Regarding the Ash-Tray Attitude of a Certain Hostess, 5194; There'll Come A Day!, 6346; To Wit, 6607; What If You Do Shiver?, 7046, When Listening to a Lecture Preliminary to a Traffic Ticket..., 7074.

OVERMYER, BARBARA HAN: Doxology in Suburbia, 1560.
OWEN, GUY: The Phoenix Too Frequent, 4793; Teachers All, 6263; Teacher's Pet, 6269.
OWEN, JIMMY: The Christmas Tree, 1029.
OWEN, KAY: A Word to the Wise, 7285.
OZICK, CYNTHIA: Apocalypse, 263.
PACK, ROBERT: Candles of the Heart, 855, The Creation, 1275; The Fall, 1839, The Monster Who Loved the Hero, 3875, Ode for a Windy Afternoon, 4294, The Other Lives, 4590; Poem for You, 4889; The Success.

PACKARD, A. APPLETON: Narcissus, 4037.
PADDACK, MURRAY: Orthodoxy, 4588.
PADGAONKAR, MANGESH: The Rock, 5329.
PAGE, P. K.: After Rain, 87; Giovanni and the Indians, 2294.
PALAMAS, KOSTIS: Two Octaves, 6731.
PALEN, JENNIE M.: January Fog, 3077.
PALMER, HARRISON: I Too Arose, 2761.
PALMER, LUCILE: Winter Outpost in Malaya, 7211.
PANIGRAHI, KALANDI CHARAON: My Message, 4010.
PAPATZOUIS, TAKIS: Before the First Opening, 553.
PARDUE, IDA M.: Roundling, 5359.
PARKER, BONNIE ELIZABETH: Afternoon in the Library, 104.
PARKER, DUANE HOWARD: A Note, 4199.
PARKINSON, THOMAS: Praise for a Tom Cat, 4968.
PARONE, EDWARD: Last Words for a Sunken Ship, 3250.
PARRISH, M. M.: Advice to Be Ignored, 60; Baby Sitting Grandma, 446; Cliptomaniac, 1075; Feminine Figuring, 1907; Hand and Glove, 2469; Labor-Saving System, 3192; Thoughts After Stating I Hadn't Time to Serve on a Certain Committee, 6408; To the First-Born, 6590.
PARRY, MARIAN: Daguerreotype, 1327.
PASLEY, LOIS F.: Reflections of a Busy Mother, 5187.
PASTERNAK, BORIS: Darling, It Frightens Me!, 1348; Definition of Creative Art, 1431; The High Malady, 2576; I Would Go Home, 2770; The Miracle, 3822; Oh, Had I Known It Once for All, 4360; The Passing Storm, 4688; Sailing Away; 5394; Snow Falls, 5722; A Testament from Lieutenant Schmidt, 6307; (cont'd)

PASTERNAK, BORIS (cont'd): Thrushes,
    6456; To a Friend, 6499; We Are Few,
    6982.
PATCHEN, KENNETH: First Came the Lion-
    Rider, 1950; The Great Birds, 2395;
    O Now the Drenched Land Wakes, 4262;
    O She Is As Lovely--Often, 4264;
    Poemscapes, 4895; Wide, Wide in the
    Rose's Side, 7139.
PATHAN, PERVIN: Dedication to Elvis
    Presley, 1415.
PATMORE, COVENTRY: The Toys, 6638.
PATRICE, ANN: Ameliorating Possibility,
    172.
PATRICK, JOHNSTONE G.: Blest Crib!
    Blest Cross!, 641; Christmas Greeting,
    1019; Closing Prayer, 1083; The Cross
    in the Cup, 1290; Easter Carol, 1635;
    Ecce Homo, 1645; God and Man, 2323;
    Good Friday, 1955, 2345; The House
    of Bread, 2651; The Lodestar, 3489;
    Nazareth, 4046; Prayer for Peace,
    4981; So Near Is God, 5743; Unlikely
    Clay, 6791; Wings, 7178; Winter
    Worship, 7221.
PATSTONE, ARTHUR J.: A Perpetual
    Memory, 4758.
PATTERSON, EMMA L.: Valedictory of a
    Retiring Teacher, 6825.
PAUSCH, EMILY: Morning, 3896.
PAYNE, ANNE BLACKWELL: How Slow Spring
    Is!, 2673.
PAZ, OCTAVIO: In Her Splendor Islanded,
    2862.
PE, U WIN: Tavoy Evening, 6262.
PECK, JOHN: Awful Thought, 439.
PEDRICK, JEAN: Hey, Who Put This
    Hoofprint on the Counterpane?, 2567;
    If You Have an Appointment for April,
    Break It, 2800; It's Your Ego, But
    It's My Id, 3061.
PEEL, DORIS: I Have Singled Out a Tree,
    2734; Three-Year Old, 6446.
PELL, JAY: A Tale of Isogonic Far Ago,
    6240.
PELLOWE, WILLIAM C. S.: The Camel
    Bells of Jericho, 842.
PENNINGTON, PENNY: The Brute!, 776;
    Mental Note Made at the Annual
    Banquet, 3760.
PENNINGTON, STUART: Comment in Re
    Girls Who Look Good Enough to Eat,
    1140.
PENNY, LUCRETIA: Mountain Burial,
    3936; One More Chore, 4549.
PEPLER, LOLA J.: On Friendship, 4455.
PERDUE, NAOMI F.: What the Rain Might
    Be, 7054.
PERKINS, DAVID: Incorrigibles, 2940;
    Instance of the Leaf, 2977.
PERREAU-SAUSSINE, RICHARD: For Helen
    Keller, 2071.
PERRINGS, MYRA: Lincoln's Tailor,
    3397; A River to Cross, 5314.
PERRY, RONALD: Adagio for Jazz, 29;
    Cat Cay, 895; Chaconne, 918; The
    Chinese Horse, 995; From Letter to
    J. M., 2191; The Giraffe, 2296; Land-
    scape: Ragged Key, 3230; Pavane,
    4719; The Shellpicker, 5571; Sonnet

XI, 5863; Sonnet XIII, 5864; Suite
    for Wind Instruments, 6128; Vientiane
    Journal, 6860; Winter Stanzas for
    Norma, 7215.
PERSE, SAINT JOHN: Excerpt from Sea-
    marks, 1792; Sea of Baal, sea of
    mammon..., 5475; Seamarks, 5479.
PESSIN, CARMEN: On Hallowe'en, 4457.
PESSOA, FERNANDO: Auto-psychography,
    415; Odes, 4304.
PETERS, HERMAN J.: The Septic Pencil,
    5528.
PETERSON, RUTH DELONG: Barefoot Road,
    495.
PETITE, IRVING: Autumn Diet, 423; To
    My Son, Who Is Grown and Gone, 6572.
PETRIE, PAUL: Backward Psalm, 461;
    Bridge Park, 748; The Church of San
    Antonio de La Florida, 1036; Departure,
    1446; Elegy for an Unrelated Cousin,
    1677; Fall, 1840; Fathers and Sons,
    1884; In Defense of Colds, 2852;
    Launched, 3268; Loss, 3522; Mother
    into Child, 3923; Rites in October,
    5308; Snow, 5718; Superseded Love
    Letters, 6179; Valentine, 6827.
PFEIFFER, ERIC: Undine, 6775.
PHILBRICK, CHARLES: Moontide Low, 3888;
    No Daughter of Mine, 4141; Put-Out,
    5078.
PHILLIPS, ESTA: The Tides of Emotion,
    6463.
PHILLIS, ELEANOR: What a Bride Knows,
    7035.
PIERCE, EDITH LOVEJOY: Along the Shore,
    164; American Prayer, 176; Be Still,
    520; The Beginning of Wisdom, 557;
    Come Soon, Come Now, 1131; Communion
    Meditation, 1146; The Coral Reef,
    1229; Delinquent Son, 1438; The
    Diamond Hunter, 1480; Dives and
    Lazarus, 1514; Do Not Stop Playing,
    1522; Flight of the Wild Geese, 2008;
    For Helen Keller, 2072; Forty Days,
    2138; Gather Up the Fragments, 2256;
    Good Friday, 2343; He Descended into
    Hell, 2508; He Was Despised and
    Rejected, 2510; Horse and Donkey,
    2641; In a Gallery of Oriental Art,
    2830; Jesus Wrote with His Finger on
    the Ground, 3093; Journey to the Holy
    Land, 3115; The Lake Eternal, 3204;
    Masked Man, 3683; My Father is Working
    Still and I Am Working, 3997; O
    Jerusalem, Jerusalem, 4260; Pageant,
    4641; Portrait of Lucifer, 4946;
    Prayer, for the Useless Days, 4984;
    Snow, 5719; Sputnik, 5979; Strontium
    90, 6105; They Uncovered the Roof,
    6358; A Thief in the Night, 6361; The
    Tide is Rising, 6462; Time, 6466;
    Time of Visitation, 6476; The Tomb,
    6614; Traveler's Tale, 6660; The Wall,
    6936; While Shepherds Watched Their
    Flocks by Night, 7097; White Citizen,
    7106; Whitsunday, 7122; The Widow of
    Nain, 7143; The Wilderness, 7153;
    Wings of the Morning, 7179; The
    Wisest Word, 7231; Word and Deed,
    7278.

PIEROTTI, DANIEL L.: My Lord and My Heart, 4005.

PIERREAU-SAUSSINE, RICHARD: Swimmer Emerging, 6212.

PILLIN, WILLIAM: The Ascensions, 341; Beasts, 528; Berceuse, 579; Holy Beggars, 2604; In a Dream I Spoke, 2827; Nocturne with Ghosts, 4166; On Hearing Frederick Play the Apassionata, 4461; Prelude, 4992.

PINKERFIELD-AMIR, ANDA: Hagar, 2462.

PINKNEY, DOROTHY COWLES: Fisherman on a Foggy Day, 1989.

PITCHFORD, KENNETH: Motto for an Uncompleted Monument, 3934; 104 Boulevard Saint-Germain, 4544.

PITTS, DUDLEY: Four Poems of Martial, 2149.

PLATH, SYLVIA: The Bull of Benclylaw, 788; Circus in Three Rings, 1044; The Death of Myth-Making, 1396; Departure, 1447; Dream with Clam-Diggers, 1573; Ella Mason and her Eleven Cats, 1689; Epitaph for Fire and Water, 1736; Frog Autumn, 2177; A Lesson in Vengeance, 3307; Metamorphosis, 3780; Mussel Hunter at Rock Harbor, 3986; On the Decline of Oracles, 4501; On the Difficulty of Conjuring up a Dryad, 4502; Pursuit, 5072; Second Winter, 5493; The Snowman on the Moor, 5729; Sow, 5896; Strumpet Song, 6106; Temper of Time, 6288; Two Sisters of Persephone, 6739; A Winter's Tale, 7226; Wreath for a Bridal, 7318.

PLATT, JOHN RADER: First Physicist, 1968.

PLOMER, WILLIAM: In the Snake Park, 2919.

PLUNKETT, PATRICK MARY: Lydia, 3596.

PLUTZIK, HYAM: And in the Fifty-First Year of That Century, While My Brother Cried in the Trench, While My Enemy Glared from the Cave, 197; The Bass, 507; Beware, Saunterer, of this Deperado, a Mr. Bones, a Bad Actor, 599; Consolations, 1197; For T. S. E. Only, 2102; A New Explanation of the Quietude and Talkativeness of Trees, 4075; Of Objects Considered as Fortresses in a Baleful Space, 4323; To the Painter Paul Klee, 6597.

POE, EDGAR ALLAN: Annabel Lee, 227.

POGUE, DORIS E.: On, Shade and Lemonade, 4363; Unhappy Surprise, 6788.

POLIKOFF, BARBARA GARLAND: Phobia Suburbia, 4789.

POMEROY, RALPH: In the Days When Purple Was New, 2897; Islands, 3029; Kite Flying, 3176; Lakes Learn from the Season, 3206; Love Poem II, 3552; The Novelist at Home in New Jersey, 4224; October, 4285; Out of the Window into Moonlight, 4614; Patrol, 4709; Resolution, 5243; Row, 5367; Silence, 5617.

PONSOT, MARIE: Absentee Landlordism, 11; Adam, Afterward, 33; Anniversary, 232; Anti-Romantic, 256; Berceuse, 580; Conception, 1167; Continuity, 1210; For a Still-Born Child, 2050; For Elizabeth Bleecker Averell, D. 20 June 1957, 2064; For My Brother: Other Systems Must Exist, 2085; Growth, 2447; Private and Profane, 5016; Ritournelle, Paris 1948; A Visit, 6890; Wedding Song, 7009.

PORTER, FAIRFIELD: Great Spruce Head Island, 2406; The Island in the Evening, 3024; The Pyromaniac, 5081.

PORTER, KATHERINE ANNE: November in Windham, 4229.

POSNER, DAVID LOUIS: By Saint Callixtus' Tomb, 817; Doctor Johnson, 1530; The Garden, 2241; Lecture to the Geophysical Society, 3286; Lesson in Anatomy, 3304; The Mirror, 3826; Phoenix, 4790; Song for an Unknown Battle, 5812; Song for Music, 5816; Suburban Sunday, 6114.

POSTER, WILLIAM S.: For His Father, 2075; G. I. Reprise, 2232.

POTTER, MIRIAM: Afternoon Moon, 106; Table Tree, 6230.

POWELL, DIANA KEARNY: Melanie Rose, 3739; Mountains and Lowlands, 3947.

POWER, JAMES W.: Calling the Turn, 837; I Must Have Dozed Off, 2743; Inconsistency, 2938; Milestone, 3810.

POWERS, JESSICA: Epiphany of Prayer, 1726; A Meadow Moreover, 3709; The Spirit's Name, 5930; Take Thy Only Son, 6238.

PRASAD, JAYSHANKAR: Aubade, 394.

PRATT, WILLIAM W.: Annual Complaint, 238; Extra Mileage, 1814; It's My Turn to Snooze in the Hammock, 3059; Make Room for Me, 3620; Poor Me!, 4924.

PRITAM, AMRITA: Pledge, 4847.

PRITCHARD, GLENN: Without a Doubt, 7248.

PROMMEL, HELEN HOWLAND: When Ducks Return, 7066.

PUDNEY, JOHN: Stiles, 6052.

PUGH, SHIRLEY SHAPIRO: Flickerphobia, 2002; No Way Out, 4158.

PUNEKY, CLAIRE: Teens, 6276.

PUNER, HELEN: The Well Bred Children, 7017.

PUSTILNIK, JACK: This Is the Beauty, 6382.

PUTNAM, JESSIE CANNON: Love Sick, 3553.

QUASIMODO, SALVATORE: Insomnia, 2973.

QUENTIN, AMES ROWE: Alone in the House, 162; Gardener, 2250; Song of a Person of Puritan Extraction, 5828; The Swallowed Man, 6202.

QUINN, CARL: First Mass, 1966.

QUINN, JOHN ROBERT: April, 279; Artesian Spring, 317; Bay Windows, 517; The Clock, 1077; Lesson in Philosophy, 3306; New Moon, 4085; Peonies, 4743; Whistling Boy, 7103.

R, W. A.: Irreverent Thought, 3016.

RACHEL: Let the Judgment Be, 3311.

RAGO, HENRY: Attending, 385; (cont'd)

RAGO, HENRY (cont'd): A Celebration, 912; The Knowledge of Light, 3187; Latch Fast, Cargo Down, 3252; The Letter: Morning, 3332; A Sky of Late Summer, 5667.

RAHA, ASOKE VIJAY: A Winter Night, 7207.

RAINER, D.: The Captain of Sand Dredge, 868; Cuban Woman Confronts the Sea, 1304; January Thaw, 3079; Pertinent to My Heart, 4770; Spring and Fall, 5950; Yom Kippur Lamentation, 7345.

RAIZISS, SONA: Conscience, 1187; Fathers, 1883; Marine Mood, 3661; Real, False, Cultured, 5146; Wayfarers' Within, 6981.

RAJAN, B.: Damayanti, 1330.

RALTRAY, DAVID: Anacreontic, 187.

RANK, MARY O.: Ambiguity, 171; To My Husband, Shaving, 6568.

RANKO: Dreams Pass Before My Sight As Blossoms Fall, 1579.

RAO, K. RAGHAVENDRA: The Journey to Golgotha, 3114.

RASKIN, ANITA: Anniversary Song, 236; Cold Facts, 1108; Commuter's Sentence, 1147; Declaration of Dependence, 1412; Courteous Counter-Attack, 1260; Man of Authority, 3629; News from the Home Front, 4099; No Purple Bovine Have I Spied (Nor Any Other Shade, Beside), 4152; Scrap Mettle, 5458; To My Neighbor, 6569; Topic Zone, 6621; Work Surface, 7301.

RASKIN, SELMA: The Baby, 444; Feathered Etiquette, 1893; First Day at the Beach, 1956; The Phase That Fazes, 4781; Two Plus Two Equals Furor, 6732.

RATLIFF, HENRY, JR.: Child, Play Not in the Sand, 972; The Prophet, 5045; Store Thyself, 6063.

RAUTH, MARY THRO: Farm Sale, 1864; Note in November, 4201.

RAWLINS, WINIFRED: Behind Science, 559; Claustrophobia, 1067; The Dance, 1331; I Saw You Stand Lonely..., 2752; The Journey, 3112; Portrait of a High Court Judge, 4939.

RAY, DAVID: For Issac Rosenfeld, 2077.

RAY, LILA: A Day In Early Winter, 1362.

RAYAPROL, SRINIVAS: Three Love Poems, 6427.

RAYNOR, OWEN: Baltimore Summer, 486.

RAZAF, ANDY: Brotherhood, 766; Know Thyself, 3186; The Negro Speaks, 4054.

READ, MARGARET: Whodunit?, 7132.

REANEY, JAMES: A Cellar Song, 913; The Windyard, 7175.

REDGROVE, PETER: Dead Bird, 1374; From Feeding-Pieces, 2190; Old House, 4389; Woman in a Flowered Dress, 7268.

REDIVIVUS, MAX JACOB: Taylor-Made, 6263.

REDMAN, BEN RAY: Episcopal Confession, 1727; Minotaur, 3817.

REDMAN, PEGGY DOWST: For a New Friend, 2048; Love's Legacy, 3567; Problem in June, 5022.

REED, SARAH REBECCA: The Catalog Is Only Secondarily a Reference Tool, 900.

REID, ALASTAIR: Calenture, 829; Cat - Faith, 896; Curiosity, 1312; For Ring-Givers, 2097; Frog Dream, 2178; Ghosts, 2277; Growing, Flying, Happening, 2445; A Harmony, with Stars, 2487; A Lesson for Beautiful Women, 3303; Living in Time, 3477; A Morning in Spain, 3903; A Note from the Coast, 4200; Outlook, Uncertain, 4621; The Rain in Spain, 5126; Small Sad Song, 5697; Three Stages of Spring, 6441; Who Am I?, 7125.

REINERT, DONALD E.: Borrowing Bookworms, 704; Epitaph to an Old Book, 1737; The Markers, 3664; Summer Library Visits, 6141; Tardy Tales, 6257.

REINGOLD, NAHAMI KRUPP: Letter to My Husband from a Distant City, 3337.

RENNERT, MAGGIE: Among the Traffic Dead, 182; Nancy Revisited, 4033; Pieta, 4810.

RENON, ERIKA: Lullaby to Myself, 3591; Of Joy, 4318; There Goes My Child, 6339; There Is No Dew Tonight, 6343; With Love and No Desire, 7243.

REX, CHARLES GORDON: Sonnet to a Newborn Son, 5874.

REXROTH, KENNETH: Marthe, 3674; The Mill of Death, 3812; Seven Poems for Marthe, My Wife, 5545.

REYNOLDS, TIM: What It Is, 7048.

REZNIKOFF, CHARLES: A Group of Verse, 2442.

RICH, ADRIENNE CECILE: At Majority, 364; At the Jewish New Year, 377; A Ball Is for Throwing, 464; David's Boyhood, 1355; The Diamond Cutters, 1478; Exodus, 1806; From Morning-Glory to Petersburg, 2192; Hadrian's Villa, 2460; The Loser, 3519; Lullaby, 3586; A Mark of Resistance, 3662; The Middle-Aged, 3794; Moving Inland, 3954; A Piece of Happiness, 4806; Rural Reflections, 5379; The Survivors, 6197; Travail et Joie, 6654; A Tryst in Borobdingnag, 6695; The Wish, 7233.

RICHARDS, I. A.: Fellow Feeling, 1903; Not No, 4188.

RICHARDSON, DOROTHY LEE: December, 1403; Finders Keepers, 1932; For One Impatient to Know All, 2090; For One Who Has Lost a Son, 2091; He Wears His Years..., 2511; If You Will, 2801; Indian Summer, 2943; Let Love Consume, 3308; Passion, 4689; The Prophets, 5047; S. S. Tungus--Midnight, 5385; Saint, 5396; St. Paul of the Epistles, 5406; Show us the Father and it sufficeth us, 5595; The Things We Never Had Remain, 6364; Venture, 6846; What Is This Shadow?, 7047; Who Wears the World as a Garment, 7130; Written on Good Friday for My Children, 7324.

RICHARDSON, NELLIE S.: Voice of Experience, 6905.

RICHMAN, FRANCES BRAGAN: Double Entry, 1552; Guess I'll Get Used To It, 2450; Stony Lonesome, 6060.

RICHSTONE, DAVID: Reasonable Answer to a Reasonable Question, 5153.

RICHSTONE, MAY: Added Problem, 35; Agenda, 117; Ask Any Aunt, 345; Bringing Up Parents, 762; Children's Hospital, 987; Companion, 1148; Compliment, 1162; Conscience, 1188; Family Lineup, 1854; Fashion Picture, 1871; Goal, 2320; Half Past Two, 2465; Kind Word, 3164; Lament for a Lost Morning, 3209; Maternity Ward, 3696; Meet the Mrs., 3727; Mother Views a Holiday, 3928; A Mother's Brand of Logic, 3929; On the Spot, 4520; Period, 4755; Petticoat Fever, 4778; The Price of Leisure, 5003; Quota, 5105; Reciprocal, 5161; Routine, 5363; Scorned, 5456; Sentiments, 5523; Size 6, 5657; Something Different, 5777; Strangely Familiar, 6086; Such Is Life, 6121; Tantrum, 6251; Topsy-Turvy, 6622; Volition, 6909; Why Worry?, 7138.

RICHTER, HARVENA CONRAD: Early Maples, 1612; Green Girls, 2418; Hills of My Youth, 2586; March Snowfall, 3651; Outer Doubt, 4618; The Tipplers, 6487; Yellow Rain, 7336.

RICKEYSER, MURIEL: Speed, We Say, 5921.

RIDDLE, M.: Oyez!, 4635; Proletarian Pastorales, 5037; Song of a Denatured Man, 5825.

RIDGLEY, DAVID: Grapes, 2381.

RIDGWAY, AGNES: You Can't Take It with You, 7349.

RIDLAND, JOHN M.: One Volume Soiled, 4560; Soldier on Leave, 5756.

RIDLER, ANNE: Leaving Ringshall: A Quodlibet, 3285; News of the World, 4103.

RIGGS, DIONIA COFFIN: First Snow, 1973; Raspberry Canes, 5138.

RIGOTTI, CLARICE J.: 3:35, 6443.

RILKE, RAINER MARIA: ...From the Book of Hours, 2202; The Interior of Roses, 2989.

RINGSTAND, MURIEL E.: Answers Please, 250; Book Shelf, 697; Books, 698; Books on Exhibit, 700; Library Lady, 3351; Library Period, 3361; Requiem to the Remains of Library Books, 5239.

RIORDAN, AVIS: Midnight Train, 3799.

RITTELL, HELEN: Brief Summary of the Events Leading Up to the Explosion, 758; Earthling Aged Ten, 1627; Fashion Note for March 21, 1870; Of Such Is the Kingdom, 4328; Query: To Cornelia, 5090.

RITTER, DIANNE: Our Clouds, 4595.

RIZZARDI, ALFREDO: Boulevards in Autumn, 708; Constellations, 1204; Noname Road, 4168; Portovenere, 4933.

ROBBINS, BLANCHE BERSON: A Challenge to Teachers, 923.

ROBBINS, MARTIN: Spring is a Looping-Free Time, 5963.

ROBERTS, DOROTHY: After A Visit, 73.

ROBERTSON, GLADYS VONDV: It Won't Be Yours Again, 3043.

ROBERTSON, PATRICIA ANNE: Autumn, 418.

ROBIN, RALPH: In a Drugstore, 2828; Such, 6119; Tam Speaks, 6246.

ROBSON, ERNEST M.: Inside the Snow, 2971; Silk of the Winds, 5623.

ROCHE, LORETTA: No Progress, Please, 4151.

ROCHE, PAUL: Midsummer Thames, 3807.

ROCKWELL, MARGARET: Moments in America: First Letter from New Albion, 3867.

RODITI, EDOUARD: A Private World, 5019.

ROETHKE, THEODORE: The Cantankerous One, 858; The Decision, 1410; Dirge, 1498; The Dying Man, 1600; The Early Flower, 1610; I'm Here, 2813; Love's Progress, 3570; Memory, 3754; Poem, 4864; The Renewal, 5223; Saturday Eight O'Clock, 5431; The Shimmer of Evil, 5580; The Slug, 5687; The Small, 5689; They Sing, 6357; A Walk in Late Summer, 6928.

ROKEAH, DAVID: Zealots of Yearning, 7380.

ROLLAND, JOHN: Spiritually Lost, 5932.

ROMINE, RAY: How Are You, George?, 2661; Silent Partner, 5619.

RONALSON, JOHN MOTT: Full Circle, 2223.

RONSARD, PIERRE DE: Comme on Voit Sur la Branche, 1139; Estre Indigent, 1752; Je Faisois ces Sonnets, 3082.

ROOT, MERRILL E.: The Only Granite, 4566; Red and White, 5172.

RORKE, MARGARET: Sunday Segment, 6167.

RORTY, JAMES: Cold Journey, 1111; Return of the Native, 5264.

ROSE, ELINOR K.: Left at the Lift, 3287.

ROSELIEP, RAYMOND: All Mornings Brief, 145; As Petrarch Coming, 330; Canticle, 859; For Students Away at Christmas, 2101; The Linen Bands, 3402; The Misogynists, 3831; Outline of a Lecture for Seniors Too Actively Engaged in Athletics, 4620; Priest to Certain Penitents, 5066; Student Marginal on a Professor's Death, 6109; The Tenth Station of the Cross, 6299; Testament, 6306; Youth to Christ the King, 7376.

ROSEN, MALINKA: Visions, 6888.

ROSEN, STANLEY: At Milton's Imagined Cave, 366.

ROSENBERG, HAROLD: Situation of the Artist, 5652.

ROSENBERG, JAMES L.: Bee Stings Cure Arthritus, 546; Hummingbird, 2694; Moving Lights, 3955; The Wasp's Nest, 6967; A Winter's Song, 7225.

ROSENFIELD, LOYD: Clothes Tree, 1086; Comet Crossing Ahead, 1133; Coming Attraction, 1134; Eat Every Crumb, Chum, 1642; Endless Exit, 1713; Feminine Privilege, 1908; First Come First Serviced, 1953; Here I Am!, 2548; I Hate to Say Good-By, 2732; Indian Summer, 2942; (continued)

ROSENFIELD, LOYD (cont'd): Languages
I Never Mastered: H telese, 3236;
Low and Behold!, 3573; Loyalty Does
Pay, 3579; Missing Invention, 3836;
More Essential Than Lanolin, 3891;
Movies More Fattening Than Ever,
3953; The Smoke's on You, 5708; To
the Lifeless of the Party, 6595;
Uncover Charge, 6767; Why Fathers
Age, 7135; Young Again, 7360.
ROSENTEUR, PHYLLIS I.: Divine Decline,
1517; Song to a Sacroiliac, 5845.
ROSENTHAL, M. L.: Memorial Inscrip-
tions, 3746; Resume, 5248; The
Reviewer to Himself, 5281; Souls Like
Chisels, 5884; The Tenth One, 6298;
To the Shades of Old Time Revolution-
aires, 6599.
ROSENTHAL, ROBERT A.: Elegy, 1673; The
Menagerie Goes for a Walk, 3753.
ROSKOLENKO, HARRY: I Stole the Mad
Woman's Love, the Mad Woman Said,
2759.
ROSS, GERALDINE: Lincoln Christening,
3396; Mid-November, 3792; Third-Grade
Thanksgiving Project: Pilgrim Cut-
Outs, 6369.
ROSS, LEWIS TENNEY: Pastoral, 4702.
ROSS, NANCY WILSON: Late Spring, 3260.
ROSSETTI, CHRISTINA GEORGINA: The
Lowest Place, 3577.
ROTH, CECIL, JR.: Jochebed Mourns for
Moses, 3102.
ROTHBERG, LEAH: Storm and After, 6066.
ROTHENBERG, JEROME: Fate, 1877.
ROTHENBERG, REBECCA: Beauty, 532;
Time, 6467.
ROTTMAN, BETTY COOK: Nostalgia, 4182.
ROWLAND, STANLEY, JR.: The End of the
World, 1711; Speaking Jesuswise, 5913.
ROWSE, A. L.: Soren Kierkegaard, 5879.
ROYSTER, SALIBELLE: Progressive Educa-
tion, 5034.
RUBENSTEIN, ROBERTA: Falsehood, 1849;
Frost, 2215.
RUBIN, LARRY: The Exile, 1802; First
Reader, 1972; The Lesson, 3302.
RUBIN, MAUDE: After Long Waiting, 85;
A Fine Small Blanket, 1934; High
Morning, 2577; The Lantern, 3237;
Small-Town Folks, 5700.
RUDD, LESTER CLARK: The Happy House-
wife, 2480.
RUDOLPH, LILLIAN: The Ugly Duckling,
6756.
RUKEYSER, MURIEL: After the Death of
Her Mother, 95; The Birth of Venus,
624; Body of Waking, 682; Children,
the Sandbar, 985; Flood Valley, 2014;
Haying Before Storm, 2504; Hero
Speech, 2560; King's Mountain, 3173;
Mother Gordon's Round, 3921.
RUSSELL, BETH DUVALL: Span of Life,
5904.
RUSSELL, FRANCIS: High Finance in the
Suburbs, 2575.
RUSSELL, PETER: In Memoriam--Wyndham
Lewis, 2870; Mots Justes, 3933; A
Mountain Stream, 3944.
RUSSELL, SIDNEY RUSSELL: Murder a la
Mode, 3971.

RUSSO, LOLA INGRES: The Apple Eaters,
272; Screech Owl, 5460.
RUSSO, PAUL GIA: Agonia, 120; Cross
Against the Sky, 1289; Our Common
Humanity, 4596.
RUTLEDGE, ARCHIBALD: Source, 5892;
Toilers, 6612.
RYSKIND, ALLAN HOUSE: Professor X:
Composite Portrait, 5027; Summit
Time, and the Giving Is Easy, 6157.
RYSKIN, MORRIE: Apologia Pro Vita Sua,
266; Hall of Fame, 2467; Inspiration,
2975; July 4, 1984: Ode Written in
Newspeak, 3123; Mercy Is Its Own
Reward, 3764; The Mess of Pottage,
3774; Obiter Dicta, 4268; Orbiter
Dicta on the Inside Story, 4269; Open
Letter to Santa, 4568; Progressive
School: Fourth Grade, 5035; Sybarite's
Philosophy, 6215; Theme with Varia-
tions, 6331; Ultimatum, 6757; A Visit
from St. Nik, 6891.
SABA, UMBERTO: The Goat, 2321.
SABE, KEN: April in England, 283.
SACK, JOHN: Emotions Recollected in
Late Cenozoic Tranquility, 1697.
SAGITTARIUS: The Adamses, 34; An Arab's
Appeal to His Steed, 292; Awkward
Attitude, 440; The Battle of Bonn,
513; Be My Valentine, 519; But Soft...,
805; China Is an Island, 992; The
Cloud, 1087; Curtains, 1317; Cyprus
Calling, 1324; Dictator's Democracy,
1484; Excelsior, 1789; False Alarm,
1848; The Fourth R, 2156; Frankly
Speaking, 2163; Marianne, 3658;
Massu S' En Va T' En Guerre!, 3686;
Nevermore, 4067; Nice People, 4105;
Nine Little Niggers, 4133; No Date in
the Desert, 4140; No Secrets, 4153;
O Captain! My Captain!, 4254; Persona
Non Grata, 4762; The Reign in Spain,
5199; Road to Spaakistan, 5322; La
Ronde, 5339; Santa Without Strings,
5423; Self-Criticism, 5514; To the
Guillotine, 6593; Travelogue, 6662;
Treacherous Liberals, 6663; Voice in
the Wilderness, 6903.
ST. JOHN OF THE CROSS: Of Hunger for
the Coming, 4317; Of the Incarnation,
4336.
ST. MARTIN, HARDIE: Snow, 5720; The
Wall, 6937.
ST. SIMON, SISTER: Late Grace, 3255.
SALINGER, HERMAN: Cocktails, 1101; In
Laws and Lust, 2864.
SALOMON, I. L.: Saint Francis in the
Square, 5401; What Was a World, 7056.
SALY, JOHN: Mycene, 4021.
SAMPLEY, ARTHUR M.: The Long Clock,
3496.
SANDBURG, CARL: Chicago Dynamic, 956.
SANDBURG, HELGA: He Speaks a Critic
Speaks, 2509.
SANDEEN, ERNEST: L'Apres-Midi d'Un
Homme, 276; Bus to Marienlund, 797;
Child, 959; Crison on the Hill, 1282;
Death of a Maker, 1389; The Improve-
ment of Prayer, 2825; Last Things,
3247; (continued)

SANDEEN, ERNEST: News Item: Chimpan-
   zee Escapes from Zoo in Antwerp, 4101;
   On the Adoption: An Anniversary,
   4494; Pater Noster in Winter, 4705;
   Surgery Ward, Dec. 8, 6186; Toy Wind-
   mill, 6636.
SANSONE, EMILY: Reflection on Christ-
   mas, 5188.
SANZENBACH, PAUL: To the Bird, 6586.
SARABHAI, BHARATI: No Time for Remorse,
   4157.
SAROYAN, SONYA: Lament of the Wife of
   a Psychoanalyst, 3215.
SARTON, MAY: After Four Years, 83; All
   Souls, 147; The Beech Wood, 547;
   Binding the Dragon, 608; Conversation
   in Black and White, 1219; Green Song,
   2427; In Time Like Air, 2924; Invo-
   cation, 3006; Metamorphosis, 3781;
   My Father's Death, 3999; A Pair of
   Hands, 4650; Song, 5794; Spring Day,
   5955; The Walled Garden at Clondal-
   kin, 6940; Where Thought Leaps On,
   7092.
SATO, SATORU: Japan That Sank Under the
   Sea, 3080; The Moon, 3880; On the
   Bridge, 4496; Our Maidservant, 4602;
   The White Moon, 7114.
SATYARTHI, DEVENDRA: The Earth Is Not
   an Old Woman, 1620.
SAUNDERS, JOSEPHINE: The Sensible
   Voyage, 5521.
SAUNDERS, KATHERINE: April Snow, 287;
   Barely Visible, 496; Pig, 4812.
SAVAGE, FRANCES HIGGINSON: Apple-
   Blossom Vandal, 271; Brief Love, 756;
   Fisherman's Love Song, 1987; Love
   Song for Middle Age, 3556; New Moon,
   4086.
SAWYER, DONALD J.: Inspired Race, 2976.
SCHENCK, HILBERT, JR.: The Scientific
   Viewpoint, 5455; Well, That's That,
   7022.
SCHENKER, DONALD: Nocturnal Aerial Act,
   4162.
SCHEVILL, JAMES: The Cherry Tree in a
   Storm, 951; Love in a Grotto; or, The
   Scorpion's Courtship, 3548; The Nose
   of Gogol, 4178; The Old Blind Man in
   Spring, 4370; A Plea for Alias, 4838;
   The Tourist on the Towers of Vision,
   1957, 6627; The Watch of the Live
   Oaks, 6970.
SCHIERLOH, SAMUEL: Night Creek, 4109.
SCHIFF, LEONARD K.: Animal Reaction,
   223; Building Problem, 786; Crush
   Hour, 1299; Dishpan Dirge, 1506;
   Door Knobs, 1546; Even, 1762; Expense
   Amount, 1811; Finale, 1928; Heat Rave,
   2528; Let's Face It, 3314; Mrs.
   Tortoise and Mr. Hare, 3967; One Way
   Out, 4562; Overwrought, 4630; Rx,
   5381; Television Transfer, 6281.
SCHLITZER, STEPHEN: At Son-Up, 368;
   At the Banquet, 370; Banquet Bore,
   489; Executive, 1795; Filing Cabinet,
   1925; Financially Speaking, 1930;
   Heard and Not Seen, 2519; It's a
   Pleasure!, 3052; Keeping Up with the
   Youngsters, 3146; Lines to Myself at

6:30 a.m., 3427; New Car in the Family,
   4070; No Interference, 4143; Not Ready
   to Go Yet, 4190; Party Spirit, 4679;
   Property Rights, 5043; Repeat--and
   Present, 5226; Slim Chance, 5681;
   Unobserved, 6764.
SCHLUNEGER, FRANCES ELEANORE: Marta,
   for Example, 3672; Sonnet for a Good
   Shepherd, 5867.
SCHMIDT, AUGUSTO FREDERICO: The
   Guardian Angels, 2449.
SCHMIDT, WILLIAM J.: Damascus Road,
   1329.
SCHNEEBAUM, RALPH: Vision at Franconia,
   6884.
SCHNEIDER, E. F.: Et Renovabis Faciem
   Terrae, 1753; A Prophecy for Pedes-
   trians, 5044; Stratagems and Spoils,
   6090; The Voice in Rama, 6902.
SCHNEIDER, PATRICIA V.: Song for an
   American, 5811.
SCHOEBERLEIN, MARION: The Hayloft,
   2505; New Bread, 4069; These Sunday
   Things, 6354.
SCHOFIELD, DOROTHY HUNT: Lady with
   Trowel and Basket, 3199.
SCHOFIELD, DOROTHY WEST: Thaw, 6328.
SCHOLES, KENNETH: Uber Nacht, 6754.
SCHOLSSER, J. JEROME: To Teach or Not
   to Teach, 6584.
SCHREIBER, ADAM: A Pastor's Sermon to
   Himself, 4703.
SCHULBERG, LUCILLE: Color Chart, 1123;
   Not Love, 4187.
SCHULZ, HAROLD A.: Cinquain, 1040.
SCHWARTZ, DELMORE: Abraham, 8; The
   Children's Innocent and Infinite
   Window, 987; The Choir and Music of
   Solitude and Silence, 1000; Cupid's
   Chant, 1310; The Dread and the Fear
   of the Mind and Others, 1565; Gold
   Morning, Sweet Prince, 2335; The
   Innocence and Windows of Children and
   Childhood, 2957; The Kingdom of
   Poetry, 3172; A Little Morning Music,
   3464; The Mind Is an Ancient and
   Famous Capital, 3814; Mountain Summer,
   3945; Poem, 4865; Poem, 4866; Poem,
   4867; A Popular Score, 4930; The
   River Was the Emblem of All Beauty:
   All, 5316; Sarah, 5428; Sonnet, 5862;
   Spiders, 5925; Summer Knowledge,
   6139; Swift, 6211; Yorick, 7346.
SCHWARTZ, SELWYN S.: Birth, 620.
SCOLLARD, CLINTON: A Rain Song, 5128.
SCOTT, SOPHIA: Life, 3363.
SCOTT, TOM: Ithaka, 3050; Orpheus,
   4584; Telmachos, 6286.
SCOTT, WINFIELD TOWNLEY: Alas!, 130;
   Between Ironwood and the Sea, 591;
   The Blue Tree, 675; Come Green Again,
   1129; Exercise in Aesthetics, 1797;
   Friday So Soon, 2169; The Ghost, 2275;
   Into the Wind, 2995; Love and a
   Season, 3543; Merrill's Brook, 3768;
   Paging Mr. Paterson, 4642; Questions
   for Us and Coronado, 5097; Summer
   Place, 6143; Two Lives and Others,
   6728; Unfurnished Room, 6783; The
   Wrong Is Mixed, 7326.

SCOVEL, MYRA: God's Music, 2329; Pity God, 4824; Why So Afraid?, 7137.

SCRUTTON, K. T.: The Exegete, 1798. Song, 5795; Song, 5796; Twain for Spring, 6705.

SEABURG, CARL: Genesis, 2265.

SEAGER, RALPH W.: Beneath This White, 573; Danseur Apache, 1339; The Letter, 3321; Owed to the Country Road, 4632; Sight Unseen, 5609; Winter's Laundry, 7224.

SEARS, GEORGIA: Messmuk, 3777.

SECRIST, MARGARET: Margaret Was Stranger, 3654; Not So Sure, 4193.

SEDAR-SENGHOR, LEOPOLD: We Delighted, My Friend, 6985.

SEFERIS, GEORGE: Calligraphy, 834; The King of Asine, 3168; The Smiles of the Statues, 5706.

SEG, KIM DANG: A Company of Mine Is Nature, 1152.

SEIFER, DANNY: Inactive File, 2927; Legal Separation, 3293; Progress in Poverty, 5033; Temporary Permanent, 6292; Unrest Home, 6798; Yes, My Lord!, 7340.

SELBY, S. A.: Symbolism, or Moby Dick Has Eaten of the Grapes of Wrath, and the Children's Teeth Are Set on Edge, 6217.

SELLERS, ROSE Z.: The Reactionary, 5144.

SENGE, MOTOMARO: Secret, 5497.

SERVICE, ROBERT: The Men That Don't Fit In, 3757.

SEUSS, DR.: Signs of Civilization, 5615.

SEXTON, ANNE: The Farmer's Wife, 1869; Kind Sir: These Woods, 3163; The Lost Ingredient, 3530; The Road Back, 5319; Sunbathers, 6160.

SHAFFER, THOMAS: Unseen Beauty, 6800.

SHAH, RAJENDRA: Last Day, 3241.

SHAKESPEARE, WILLIAM: Macbeth, on Being Told the Queen Is Dead, 3603.

SHALOM, SHIN: Not All Is So Simple, 4183; The Stoker, 6056.

SHAPIRO, HARVEY: The Destructive Will, 1464; A Dream of Life, 1570; Feast of the Ram's Horn, 1891; From a Sermon on the Five Afflictions, 2179; Lines for the Ancient Scribes, 3414; Mountain Fire, Thornbush, 3937; The Prophet Announces, 5046; Spirit of Rabbi Nachman, 5928; Travel Piece, 6656.

SHAPIRO, JOE: Evening Picture, 1771.

SHAPIRO, KARL: Book Burial, 691; Calling the Child, 836; The Crucifix in the Filing Cabinet, 1296; The First Time, 1980; In India, 2863; The Olive Tree, 4418; 151st Psalm, 4545; Photographs of the Poets, 4794; Teasing the Nuns, 6273; Western Town, 7033.

SHARP, HAROLD S.: Library Lament, 3352; Library Lament, 3353; Library Lament, 3354; Library Lament, 3355; Library Lament, 3356; Library Lament, 3357; Library Lament, 3358;

Library Lament, 3359.

SHARP, L. B.: Lift High Our Souls, 3374.

SHAW, ELMER W.: Anniversary Challenge, 234.

SHAW, GEORGE BERNARD: Lines for a One Hundredth Birthday, 3408.

SHAW, LUCI DECK: Steadfast Fever, 6045.

SHENTON, EDWARD: Hulks, 2688; The Passing of Time, 4685; Wandering Dane, 6945.

SHERWIN, JUDITH JOHNSON: They Gave Him Vinegar to Drink, 6356.

SHIFFERT, EDITH: Earthquakes, Kona, Hawaii, 1629; A Plant of High Altitudes, 4831.

SHIMAZAKI, TOSON: By the Ancient Castle at Komoro, 818; First Love, 1965.

SHIMONI, DAVID: And It Happens That Spirit, 198; The Flower Pot, 2022; Gleanings, 2314.

SCHLONSKY, AVRAHAM: From 'Toil, 2212; Jerusalem Is a Hill City, 3089; Yezrael, 7343.

SHNEUR, ZALMAN: The Fruited Month, 2220; Poppies, 4927; Up Goethe's Path, 6808.

SHOOK, BARBARA: And Say We Are not Lost, 201; August Song, 406; I Shall Come to You, 2754; Suddenly April, 6124; Suddenly in Summer, 6125; Tell Me, 6282; There Are Other Lands, 6337.

SHORES, WINIFRED M.: Books, 699.

SHORT, DONNA: The Library, 3350.

SHOTWELL, J. T.: Christmas Day in the Morning, 1016.

SHUSETSU: First Birds--Like the Eyes of a Girl Hidden, 1945.

SHYER, LEE FANTA: Tranquilizer for Mother, 6644.

SIDEN, WILLIAM: The Toast, 6608.

SIDER, GERALD: Work Song, 7300.

SIEGEL, ELI: Which Has Speed, 7096.

SIKELIANOS, ANGELOS: Unrecorded, 6797.

SILKIN, JOHN: For a Deaf Girl, 2044; To Michael Riviere, for His Second Son, Thomas, 6559; White, 7104.

SIMON, DINA: Spring Morning, 5966.

SIMON, JOHN: A Day for Hunting, 1361.

SIMPSON, LOUIS: America, 173; An American in the Thieves' Marker, 175; A Dream of Governors, 1569; Early in the Morning, 1611; Flight to Cytherea, 2010; The Goodnight, 2353; I Dreamed in a City Dark as Paris, 2727; It Was the Last of the Parades, 3042; The Legend of Success, the Salesman's Story, 3295; The Lover's Ghost, 3564; Sleeping Beauty, 5674.

SIMPSON, R. A.: Civil War House: England, 1057.

SINGER, HELEN: Blast Off, 648; The Brave Names, 733; From an Exotic Country, 2184; A Good Man's Dying, 2348; Graubunden: Cape Ann, 2389; Lives in Spite, 3475; Old Rome, 4406; (continued)

SINGER, HELEN: Painting of a Courtesan on a Roof, at Venice, 4649; The Presence of Their Honor, 4998; To Stella, Who Would Be 77, 6582; To the Todas, 6601; The View at Thome, 6863; The Villa, 6869; The Year of Zhivago, 7332.

SINGER, SARAH: The Patriarch, 4708.

SINGLETON, MARGARET EVELYN: Bride's Winter, 745; The Door That Won't Close, 1548; English Assignment: Poem, 1717; First Flight, 1959; In Miniature, 2878; The Lever, 3341; Route, 5361; Spring Hearth, 5961.

SINISGALLI, LEONARDO: I Saw the Muses, 2750.

SITWELL, EDITH: Elegy for Dylan Thomas, 1678; Praise We Great Men, 4971; The War Orphans, 6950.

SITWELL, OSBERT: Florence: At the villa Jernyngham, 2017; Il Capitano, the Fencing Master, 2804; Major Cameron and Miss Cairns, 3617; Milordo inglese, 3813; Spring Comes to the Lending Library, 5953; Teresa, 6300.

SKINNER, KNUTE: Undergraduate Notes, 6774.

SLAVITT, DAVID R.: Earth Hates an Emptiness, 1619; Orpheus, 4585.

SLEMP, JOHN C.: Fallout, 1846.

SLOAN, JACOB: Apologia Pro Vita Nostra, 265; Death of a Librarian, 1388; The Lost Children, 3526.

SLOAT, CAROLYN: First Snowfall, 1975.

SLOTE, BERNICE: When the Wind Blows, 7079.

SMALL, HELEN: Catty Commuter, 908.

SMITH, A.J.M.: The Important Personages, 2822; A Narrow Squeak, 4040; On Knowing Nothing, 4468; Le Vierge, le Vivace et le Bel Aujourd'hui, 6861; Variations on a Theme of Cavalcanti, 6843; What the Emanation of Casey Jones Said to the Medium, 7053.

SMITH, BETTY L.: Overshoe Exchange, 4627.

SMITH, BEULAH FENDERSON: First-Born, 1948; Gifts, 2291; Second Dog, 5491; Susan's First Walk, 6198.

SMITH, BRADFORD: Winter Is Icumen In, 7197.

SMITH, CHARLES EDWARD: Fritz Gulda Takes the 'A' Train, 2176; I Hear America Swinging, 2736.

SMITH, FRANK: The Jokesmith, 3106.

SMITH, H. AUSTIN: African Prophecy, 70; Congo, 1179; Friends, 2172; Light, 3376; Reality, 5151.

SMITH, J. JEAN: After a Night Vigil with a Sick Child, 72; The Conqueror, 1185.

SMITH, JOE CARSON: Chosen and Appointed Path, 1006; The Word of God, 7281.

SMITH, LAURENCE C.: Baby Spoon, 447; Hieroglyphics, 2572; Not for Babes, 4185; Preferred Treatment, 4988; Travel Trials, 6657.

SMITH, NORMA: Epitaph, 1732; Profit and Loss, 5029; Well Trained, 7024.

SMITH, OSWALD J.: The Day of Days, 1364.

SMITH, ROBERT PAUL: Certain Things, 916.

SMITH, SYDNEY GOODSIR: Cokkils, 1104; The Grace O God and the Meth Drinker, 2360; Granton, 2379; The Jungfrau in Season Bricht wi Eternal Whiteness Is Natheless Raped by the Buits O a Cloud O Witness, 3127; Maraeld, 3646; The Muse in Rose Street, 3977.

SMITH, WILLIAM JAY: At the Tombs of the House of Savoy, 381; Butterfly, 811; Camel, 841; Cat, 892; Dog, 1531; The Dressmaker's Workroom, 1581; Flight of the One-Eyed Bat, 2007; Gossips, 2356; A Green Place, 2422; In Memoriam Wallace Stevens, 2869; Interior, 2987; Letter, 3322; Lion, 3435; Love Birds, 3544; The Lovers, 3563; Mr. Smith (With Nods to Mr. Lear and Mr. Eliot, 3965; A Parable, 4656; Poet, 4896; Pompes Funebres, 4920; A Room in the Villa, 5346; The Ten, 6293; Three-Syllable Sonnet, 6442; The Typewriter Bird, 6753; Vision at Twilight, 6885; Viva, 6899; The World Below the Window, 7308.

SMYTHE, DANIEL: Desert Quail, 1457; Early Clearing of Fog, 1609; Fox Barking Late, 2159; Meteor Shower, 3783; Wind Over Cape Cod, 7165.

SNELL, TED: Old Books, 4371.

SNODGRASS, W. D.: Lying Awake, 3598; Song, 5797.

SOBILOFF, HY: The Clock Hart, 1079; A Notice to My Emotions, 4219.

SO-IN: Flower Is My Proper Name--Watch the Dancing Sleeves of My Twirling Kimono, 2021.

SOLES, MARY: Two Poems, 6733.

SOLLIS, LIBBY: Oh, Tidings of Comfort and Joy, 4365.

SOLOMON, LOUIS B.: Univac to Univac, 6789.

SOLOMON, MARVIN: A Beautiful Day at Jerusalem's Mills, 531; Children and Leaves, 979; The Chinese Kite, 996; The Fourth of July, 2155; Jays in the Wood, 3081; Last One In, 3245; The Mondrian, 3870; The Persimmon Tree, 4761; The Poodle, 4923; The White Rabbit, 7118; A Winter's Tale, 7227.

SOLOVAY, JACOB C.: Art of Teaching, 310; Ballade to a Book Borrower, 481; Bedtime Story, 544; Book Borrower, 690; Classroom Heaven, 1065; Comma Il Faut, 1138; Epitaph for a Librarian, 1735; For a Congressman's Tombstone, 2042; Just Between You and I, 3133; Laugh and Learn, 3266; Nightmare in the Color Red, 4128; On a Literary Censor, 4430; T'Ain't No Taint, 6234; 'Tis Folly and 'Tis Wise, 6490; To a Reluctant Student, 6514; To a Youth Afraid, 6526.

SOLUM, SJANNA: Central Park Spring, 915; Ego, 1659; Sleep at Dawn, 5671; To an Insect Entombed in a Tome, 6529.

SORRENTINO, GILBERT: Brown Mountain, 773; Little Oranges, 3467.
SOULE, JEAN CONDER: Inevitable, 2949.
SOUSTER, RAYMOND: Just in From the Cold, 3136; November, Early, 4228; One A.M.: Bleury and Mayor, 4539.
SPACKS, BARRY B.: Degrees of Charity, 1432.
SPARK, MURIEL: Domestic Dawn, 1536.
SPARSHOTT, FRANCIS: Gannets' Bath, 2238; Seasalter, 5481.
SPEAR, GRACE B.: Merry Christmas, 3770; Stack Cracks, 5984; Stack Cracks, 5985; Stack Cracks, 5986; Stack Cracks, 5987; Stack Cracks, 5988; Stack Cracks, 5989; Stack Cracks, 5990; Stack Cracks, 5991; Stack Cracks, 5992; Stack Cracks, 5993; Stack Cracks, 5994; Stack Cracks, 5995; Stack Cracks, 5996; Stack Cracks, 5997; Stack Cracks, 5998; Stack Cracks, 5999; Stack Cracks, 6000; Stack Cracks, 6001; Stack Cracks, 6002; Stack Cracks, 6003; Stack Cracks, 6004; Stack Cracks, 6005; Stack Cracks, 6006; Stack Cracks, 6007; Stack Cracks, 6008; Stack Cracks, 6009; Stack Cracks, 6010; Stack Cracks, 6011; Stack Cracks, 6012; Stack Cracks, 6013; Stack Cracks, 6014; Stack Cracks, 6015; Stack Cracks, 6016; Stack Cracks, 6017; Stack Cracks, 6018; Stack Cracks, 6019; Stack Cracks, 6020; Stack Cracks, 6021; Stack Cracks, 6022.
SPEER, CLARA AIKEN: As to Beauty, 336; Perfumes, 4752; Road Through Forest, 5321.
SPEISER, MILTON: E:mc^2, 1603.
SPENCER, BESSIE SAUNDERS: Orphan Bride, 4583.
SPINGARN, LAWRENCE P.: Coast Route: California, 1097; Hobbema and the Casks, 2597.
SPRING, ARCHER T.: Dozer's Dilemma, 1561; Line of Most Resistance, 3399; Reminder in September, 5217; Speaking of Speakers, 5915; Words Fail Me, 7291.
SQUIRES, PAUL: The Gentle Yes, 2267.
SQUIRES, RADCLIFFE: Clara Bodfish, 1061; The Forms of Blindness, 2129; The Graiae, 2365; Letter to an American, 3336; Self as an Eye, 5513; Sunday in the Laboratory, 6166; The Visible Moments, 6882.
STAFFORD, WILLIAM: As Pippa Lilted, 331; At Earle Birney's School, 359; At the Custer Monument, 374; At the Old Place, 379; Augustine, 408; The Bravery of Love, 735; Chickens and Weasel Killed, 957; The Farm on the Great Plain, 1863; From the Gradual Grass, 2205; In Dear Detail, By Ideal Light, 2850; Lore, 3517; The Lyf So Short...., 3597; The Move to California, 3950; On Penitencia Creek, 4480; Our City Is Guarded by Automatic Rockets, 4594;

Overhearing, 4625; Reflection, 5181; Representing Far Places, 5231; Sanvies Island, 5424; Sayings from the Northern Ice, 5436; Shepherd, 5575; Spring Interest, 5962; The Star in the Hills, 6028; Strokes, 6104; Things We Did That Meant Something, 6363; A Visit Home, 6892.
STALLMAN, R. W.: The Figurehead, 1922.
STANDISH, JEAN SEWELL: An Eye for an Eye, 1817.
STANFORD, ANN: Lost Objects, 3531; The Measure, 3713.
STANLEY, IRENE: Here I Belong, 2549; Prairie Mother, 4966.
STARBUCK, GEORGE: Aspects of Spring in Greater Boston, 346; Autumn on Cape Cod, 430; Bone Thoughts on a Dry Day: Chicago, 687; Civil Defender, 1056; Cold War Bulletin from the Cultural Front, 1114; Constitutional, 1205; Fable for Blackboard, 1821; Fable for Flipped Lid, 1822; Ghosts of the Missionaries, 2278; Housebroke, 2656; On First Looking in on Blodgett's Keat's Chapman's Homer, 4454; On Reading a Collection of Essays on Baudelaire, 4484; Prognosis, 5030; Sixth September, 5656; Technologies, 6274; Tourists from the City, 6630; Tourists from the City, 6630; Unfriendly Witness, 6782.
STEBBING, FRANK: That Which Is Found in Straw, 6321.
STEEGMULLER, FRANCIS: Le Hibou et la Poussiquette, 2569.
STEEL, NANCY: The Sad Dragon, 5387.
STEELE, ROY V.: Unfair Competition, 6780.
STEFANILE, FELIX: The Afternoon As an Aria, 102; Brown, All of the Autumn, 771; Egotist, 1661; A Late Elegy for a Baseball Player, 3253; An Old Bootblack in the Cafeteria, 4372; A Poem for S--, 4888; The Poet (after 'L' Ultima Rinunzia' of Gindo Gozzano, 1883-1916), 4898; Sea Gulls, 5468; Services, 5539; Spoiled by All My Tyrants, 5938; That Miser, Fear, 6318.
STEFANSKI, SANDRA: Note to a Librarian, 4205.
STEIN, EUGENIA GERLACH: Lines to a Christmas Angel, 3422.
STEIN, GLORIA: Death of a Nun, 1390; Old Nun Recalls God, 4401.
STEINER, STAN: The Ph. D. Learns About Love, 4779; The Pond, 4921; Wearing the Odd Clothes of Exile a Puerto Rican Youth Arrives in New York City and Is Laughed At, 6998.
STEINMAN, D. B.: As Through a Misted Glass, 334.
STEPANCHEV, STEPHEN: The Artist, 319; The Artist and the Nude, 321; Desiring Other Selves, 1462; Didactic Poem, 1485; Flight and Return, 2003; A Flirting Hat, 2011; A History, 2595; The Minister of Finance, 3815; A Rebel, 5156; Skaters, 5658; (cont'd)

STEPANCHEV, STEPHEN (cont'd): Snow
Storm, 5732; Unmelodious Song, 6792;
Waiting, 6919; Zone of Silence, 7384.
STEPHENS, ALAN: Urban Moral, 6814.
STERLING, GEORGE: Swan Song, 6203.
STERN, M. PHILIP: The Analyst's
Lament, 189.
STEVENS, GEORGE: Men of Letters, 3756.
STEVENS, WALLACE: Adagia, 28; Banjo
Boomer, 488; Dance of the Macabre
Mice, 1335; From the Adagia, 2199;
July Mountain, 3124; The Man Whose
Pharynx Was Bad, 3635; Somnambulism,
5784.
STEVENSON, CANDACE T.: Music Box,
3982; Well-Preserved, 7020.
STEWART, ALBERT: His Going, 2590;
Near, in Mountains, 4047.
STEWART, CHRISTINE WARREN: Global
Strands, 2316.
STEWART, DESMOND: Vi Connolly's Spring
Song, 6853.
STEWART, MARGERY S.: Guest, 2452;
Katherine, 3142; Sea in October,
5471; Son Studying, 5786.
STEWART, MARION: Boor But Honest, 702;
Hardly Worth It, 2483; Not So Measly,
4192.
STOCK, ROBERT: Ballade to Be Read in
the Medici Gardens, 482; The Irritated
Office, 3018; Revelation According to
the Beloved, 5277; That the Sestina
Is What It Is Despite What It Is Not,
6320.
STOCKDALE, ALICE BOYD: At, 1; A Child's
Valentine, 990; The First Spring,
1977; Ouch!, 4592; 6 P.M.!, 5654;
To a First-Grade Desk, 4697.
STOKELY, JAMES: Blackboard Jungle,
646; Christian Patriots, Inc., 1011;
Code of Honor, 1102; Iron Curtain,
3012; The Mate, 3691; Mirror, 3827;
Odessa Gal, 4305; Reed Jarnagin,
5177.
STOLOROW, HARRIET R.: The High Price
of Daffodils, 2580.
STONE, HENRY: Hark, Hark, the Lark,
2485.
STONE, RUTH: As Real As Life, 332;
Confession, 1172; Home Movie, 2614;
In a Liberarl Arts Building, 2834;
In the Madness of Age, 2909; Juve-
niles, 3138; Laundry, 3270; Of Heroes,
4314; Orchard, 4579; Private Panto-
mime, 5018.
STONE, WALTER: Couple, 1259; On the
Welsh Marches, 4524.
STORK, CHARLES WHARTON: The Ancient
Dunes, 191.
STOUTENBURG, ADRIEN: Affinities, 68;
The Allergic, 153; Assembly Line,
350; The Bear Who Came to Dinner,
527; Cicada, 1038; Clairvoyance,
1059; Companions, 1150; Invasion,
3000; Plaza de Toros, Iowa, 4837;
Stormy Reception, 6077; Warning,
6956.
STOW, RANDOLPH: Dream of the Pastoral
Poet, 1572.
STRACHEN, ELSIE MCKINNON: Country

Town at Night, 1256; A Little to the
Left, Please, 3470; They Are for the
Living, 6355.
STRAND, MARK: See Too the Morning Come,
5502.
STREET, RUTH: It Happened One Friday,
3034.
STREIT, CLARENCE: Gay Leaf, 2258.
STRICKHAUSEN, HARRY: The Frozen Lake,
2218; Gemini, 2262.
STROBEL, MARION: Loft, 3491.
STRONG, JULIA HURD: Postlude to Men-
delssohn, 4955; Weather Vane, 7003.
STROUP, WILLIAM H.: The Complete Cycle
of Government Social Planning, 1160.
STUART, ALPHA MELL: To a Scientist,
6516.
STUART, GEORGE C.: To the Easter Dead,
6588.
STUART, JESSE: Earth Was Their Banker,
1624; For MHS, 2082; The Gone, 2339;
Green River, 2425; The Heart Flies
Home, 2522; Light and Shadow, 3378;
Poem, 4868; Shadows, 5555; The Snow
Lies Patched, 5728; This Is the
Place, 6383; Two Leaves, 6726;
Unforgotten, 6781; Urgent Spring,
6815; What Life Is Worth, 7049.
STURGES, GLORIA M.: All at sea, See,
C, Si, Ci, (C), /C_/, 138; Nothing
Before Something, 4216.
SUBBARAO, NANDURI, Enki, 1722.
SULLIVAN, A. M.: Question of Light,
5094; Storm at Dingle, 6067; Villa-
nelle of War, 6873.
SULLIVAN, DANIEL: A Ballad of Holy
Week, 468; Inconstancies, 2939;
Nigrei Sum, Sed Formosa, 4130.
SULLIVAN, FRANK: Greetings, Friends!,
2429.
SULLIVAN, PEGGY: What Comes First?,
7038.
SULLIVAN, WILLIAM: Lenten Chant, 3300.
SULLIVAN, X. X.: After Columbus, 77.
SUMMERS, HOLLIS: Advice to Another
Man's Son, 59; Coming of Air Age,
1136; Concerning Weather, 1169;
Mexico Picnic, October 31, 3788; On
Completing His Hundredth Year, 4440;
Valentine, 6828.
SUPERVIELLE, JULES: Comrades of
Silence, 1166; Fauna of the Sky,
1886; This Part of Ocean, 6391.
SUTHERLAND, WALTER: Owed to a Book-
binder, 4631.
SUTIN, HELEN GORN: February Second,
1895.
SWAN, JON: Chagall's Ebony Horse, 919;
A Courtly Poem, 1261; The Cure, 1311;
Homecoming, 2620; In Her Song She Is
Alone, 2861; Jonah and the Whale,
3107; The Magpie, 3612; Reunion
Recollected, 5271.
SWANN, THOMAS BURNETT: The Ivory
Wanderer, 3064; White Hands of
Guinevere, 7113.
SWARD, ROBERT S.: Aloud, 165; Barbecue,
490; The House, 2650; Miss Elderli
Dora Des Moines, - One March, 3833;
Mr. Middlegreene, Etc, 3963.

SWARTZ, ROBERTA TEALE: Easter, 1633; The Property of Saint Jerome, 5042.

SWEENEY, FRANCIS: Mestrovic, 3778.

SWEET, ARTHUR P.: Condensation, 1171; Misfiled, 3830; Pierian Thirst, 4808; SIC Transit Goria Mundi!, 5601; You Ought to Write a Book About It, 7354

SWENSON, MAY: Almanac, 157; Cause and Effect, 909; A Fixture, 1997; From the Office Window, 2208; Frontis-piece, 2214; Iris, at the Piano, 3010; A Lake Scene, 3205; Landing on the Moon, 3224; News from the Cabin, 4098; The Poplar's Shadow, 4926; The Shape of Death, 5561; Squirrel, 5983; Sunday in the Country, 6165; The Tide at Long Point, 6461; The Time Came, 6470; Waiting for It, 6921; Water Picture, 6975; The Word Beautiful, 7279; Working on Wall Street, 7303.

SWIFT, JONATHAN: Abroad and at Home, 9.

SWIFT, MARY JANE: Personals, 4765; Season's Greetings, Etc., 5487; Service Rendered, 5538.

SYKES, VELMA WEST: Modern Farm Boy, 3846.

SYLVESTER, WILLIAM: An Essay Upon Excess, 1749; Sestina at the Sea, 5541.

TADLOCK, MAX: Eye-Filling Notes Blown Abroad by a Rather Large Wind During a Public Speech, 1816; Mnemesis, 3845.

TAGLIABUE, JOHN: The Divine Dancers, 1516; The Fact Is the Sweetest Dream That Labor Knows: Robert Frost, 1831; In Various Alleys Zig Zagging with Dilapidated and Sometimes Squeaking Bicycles Does not the Buddha Spirit Surpise Us?, 2926; Mexican Poems, 3786; An Old Chinese Zen Traveller Often Depicted in Sumi-E Carrying a Large Dim White Bag Like a Light Cloud, 4375; The Sea Gulls..., 5469; Sleepy Standing in the Sunny Windy Kokubunji Station, 5677; Some Poems, 5769; These Lovers Have Wandered..., 6351; Those Abysses of Silence..., 6398.

TAGORE, RABINDRANATH: I Will Not Let You Go, 2766.

TAKAHASHI, SHINKICHI: Birth, 621.

TAKAMURA, KOTARO: Winter has Come, 7195.

TAKENAKA, IKU: At Lyons, 363.

TALMAN, TOM: The Back of My Mind to You!, 454; Barberous, 491; Financial Autobiography, 1929; Full Circle, 2224; Gridiron Heroics, 2435; Healthy, Wealthy and Grumpy, 2517; Hors D' Oeuvres, 2638; How Come?, 2662; Interest-Bearing, 2986; Let's Face It, 3315; Lost and Sound, 3525; The Prior Buyer, 5012; Setting-Up Exercises, 5544; Somebody Has To, 5772; Take It Queasy, 6236.

TANAKA, FUYUJI: By the Marsh, 820; The Cold Glass Door, 1109; Evening Land-scape, One Day in Winter, 1769; Native Village, 4041; A Small Mountain Town, 5695; The Village, 6870; Wood-cocks Returning Northward, 7275.

TANIKAWA, SHUNTARO: Museum, 3979.

TATE, VERNON D.: Death Is a Cup, 1385.

TAYLOR, ALEXANDER: Autumn Song, 432; Child at Dusk, 962; First Apartment, 1944.

TAYLOR, EVA SPARKS: Wife, 7147.

TAYLOR, JOHN RENWICK: God's Dimension, 2328.

TAYLOR, K.P.A.: The Road, 5318.

TAYLOR, MAURIE: Easy Directions, 1640.

TAYLOR, MYKIA: Scrod Is Sliced God, 5461.

TAYLOR, SARAH WINGATE: Our Lady, Patron of Arts, 4601.

TEMPLIN, E. H.: First Touch of Spring in the Plaza Mayor, Madrid, 1981.

TENNEY, JANE HERRICK: Charter Member, 943.

TENNYSON, ALFRED, LORD: A Land of Settled Government, 3219.

TERRY, JOHN: Teach Us to Pray, 6264.

THATCHER, MARTA K.: Uneasy Lies..., 6778.

THOMAS, ANN: Recovery, 5169.

THOMAS, CALVIN, JR.: For a Girl Killed at Sea, 2046.

THOMAS, DOROTHY: Potting the Plants, 4964.

THOMAS, DYLAN: The Almanac of Time, 158; Before We Mothernaked Fall, 554; Elegy, 1674; Out of a War of Wits, 4606; Shiloh's Seed, 5579; This Is Remembered, 6381.

THOMAS, MARTHA BANNING: Military Funeral, 3811; Reunion, 5270; Small Tale of Summer, 5698.

THOMAS, ROSEMARY: Dylan Thomas, 1914-1953, 1601; Lost and Found, 3524; White Egret, 7110.

THOMPSON, CLAIRE AVEN: Song for Thanks-giving, 5820.

THOMPSON, DOROTHY BROWN: Address to the Fates, 36; Law and the New Order, 3272; Recipe for Mystery Writing, 5159; September Grasses, 5527; To a Fly in a Glass-Dome Car, 6498; Vaca-tioning Housewife, 6824; What You Can't Expect, 7057.

THOMPSON, ELLEN TERRARO: Thoughts of an Expectant Mother, 6323.

THOMPSON, JOHN BEAUCHAMP: Carillon, 876; Chiaroscuro, 954; Lot's Wife, 3536.

THOMSON, MARGARET: March, My Lion, 3649.

THORLEY, WILFRID: A Carol, 878; The Garden, 2242; Jesu's Toy, 3092.

THORNTON, LALIA MITCHELL: Fountains, 2142.

THORNTON, M. B.: Electrencephalograph--Hyperventilation, 1666; Excerpt from Narcissus--A Parallel of Art, 1791; Paradise Regained, 4666; Poem, 4869; Rebirth, 5157; Root, 5348; These Sons of Loveless Women, 6353.

THORNTON, WILLIE: Ballade of a Tropical Cruise, 477.

THORPE, BERENICE: How My True Love Proposed to Me, 2669.

THORSON, SARAH WINFREE: Backyard
Barbecue, 458; First Fashion, 1958.
TIEMPO, EDITH L.: Mid-Morning for
Sheba, 3791; The Pestle, 4772.
TIGNER, HUGH STEVENSON: Morning, 3897;
Worship, 7315.
TOBIN, JAMES EDWARD: Ballade of a
Voice Crying, 478; Question of Sur-
vival, 3095.
TODD, RUTHVEN: An Autumn Wood, 434;
Captain Slocum in West Tisbury for
W.M.T., 869; The Farm, Early Morning,
1862; The Geese, 2261; The Hawk's
Victim, 2503; Laugharne Churchyard in
1954, 3267; A Pertinent Observation,
4769; Pruning Vines, 5056; A Sestina
for Georges De La Tour, 5542; Trout
Files, 6688; An Upper Left Central,
Insisor, 6811.
TODRIN, BORIS: I Thought I'd Tell You,
2760.
TOLAND, POLLY: I Scarcely See But Feel
You Now at First, 2753; What Child
Is Here?, 7037.
TOMLINSON, CHARLES: Antecedents, 252;
At Delft, 358; Autumn, 419; Beauty
and the Beast, 534; Chateau de Muzot,
945; Civilities of Lamplight, 1058;
Cradock Newton, 1271; Glass Grain,
2311; How Still the Hawk, 2676; Icos,
2778; In Defence of Metaphysics, 2854;
The Mausoleum, 3704; More Foreign
Cities, 3892; Ponte Veneziano, 4922;
Reeds, 5178; Reflections, 5185; White,
a Shingled Path, 2778.
TONGUE, MARGARET: Noel, 4167.
TORRES, EMMANUEL: Woman with Child,
7264.
TOUSTER, SAUL: Charles Peguy, 935;
Personae, 4763; The Poet, 4897.
TOVATT, ANTHONY: Life and Literature,
3364.
TOWNSEND, EMILY: Fish, 1983.
TOWNSEND, OLIVE E.: The Accounting, 21.
TRAAD, MICHEL: Fingers, 1935; Tell That
Neighbor Girl, 6284.
TRACY, PAUL E.: Existentialist, 1805.
TRAIL, JOY: Old Love, 4393.
TREADWELL, SALLY: That's My Daughter,
6326.
TREMAYNE, P.: Deep South Kensington,
1420; Illusion, 2809; Love Is the
Maker of Mankind..., 3550; This Is
the Sun You Know and Loved of Old,
6384; The Voyage, 6912.
TRENT, LUCIA: Brotherly Eden, 767;
Challenge, 921; Grim Pruner, 2439;
Panorama, 4652; Peace, 4722; Somber
Wonder, 5766; Twilight Moment, 6716;
Winter Lyrics, 7202.
TRIEM, EVE: Here Are Roses, 2547; The
Lamp, and Heliodora, 3216; Not Yet
the New Adam, 4196; With a Branch of
Acacia, 7238.
TROSPER, GLADYS: Librarian's Nightmare,
3346.
TROTT, ROSEMARY CLIFFORD: The Blue
Fire of April, 666.
TSE-TUNG, MAO: Kunlun, 3190; The Long
March, 3499; Loushan Pass, 3541;

Pertaiho, 4768; To Mr. Lui Ya-tzu,
6660.
TURNBULL, AGNES SLIGH: Illumination,
2808
TURNER, ALBERTA T.: To Prue, Below
Sleep, 6579.
TURNER, ALVA N.: Unmolested Beauty,
6793.
TURNER, D. G.: Diminishing Returns,
1491.
TURNER, ETHEL D.: A Little, If Not
Much, 3461.
TURNER, ETHEL E.: Blue-Eyed Grass,
665.
TURNOY, BETTY: The Possibility, 4950;
Query, 5089.
TUTTLE, STELLA WESTON: Song For Sep-
tember, 5809.
TWIGGS, D. E.: Thought in a Dentist's
Waiting Room, 6405.
TYLER, PARKER: Advice to Lovers as
Dancers, 63; Baroque Epigram, 501;
But Ultamaro: Secretly, 806; Chez
Cythera, 953; From A Summer Sequence,
2180; Prismatic Psyche, 5013; Three
Sonnets on Works of Art, 6438.
TYLER, ROBERT L.: OAA Check, 4265.
TZE-CHIANG, CHAO: Farewell to My
Soldier-Friend, 1859; Pounding the
Clothes, 4965.
ULMAN, RUTH: Ode to a Retiring Editor,
4297.
UNGARETTI, GIUSEPPE: First Song, 1976.
UNRUH, STANLEY: Silently He Hung, 5621.
UNTERMEYER, LOUIS: Orpheus with His
Lute, 4587.
UPDIKE, JOHN: Bendix, 572; A Bitter
Life, 635; Blked, 657; Caligula's
Dream, 832; Capacity, 864; Deities
and Beasts, 1433; Ex-Basketball
Player, 1784; The Fritillary, 2175;
Glasses, 2312; Idyll, 2787; In Praise
of $(C_{10}H_9O_5)X$, 2886; Jack, 3066;
Kenneths, 3147; Mobile of Birds,
3849; The Moderate, 3855; A Modest
Mound of Bones, 3860; Mr. High-Mind,
3960; Old Faces of '56, 4380; The
One'Year-Old, 4564; Philological,
4785; Planting a Mailbox, 4832;
Publius Vergilius Maro, the Madison
Avenue Hick, 5064; Quilt, 5101; A
Rack of Paperbacks, 5107; Reel, 5179;
Scenic, 5445; The Sensualist, 5522;
The Simple Life, 5626; Solid Comfort,
5762; Song in American Type, 5824;
Sonic Boom, 5852; Suburban Madrigal,
6111; Tao in the Yankee Stadium
Bleachers, 6252; Tome-Thoughts From
the Times, 6616; Tsokadze of Altitude,
6696; Wooden Darning Egg, 7276.
URDANG, CONSTANCE: Anecdote in the
Parque Espana, 211; Birth of Venus,
625; For Jonathan, 2081; Four Unro-
mantic Portraits, 2150; The Gun-
fighters, 2456.
USK, THOMAS: Almost Bliss, 159; Assist,
351; Between Friends, 590; Conscience,
1189; The Fact Is, 1830; Greetings
(Belated), 2430; Grudge, 2448;
Hearing Aid, 2520; (continued)

USK, THOMAS (cont'd): Inclined to Be
   Lenient, 2935; Junior Grows Wise,
   3128; Key to His Confidence, 3154;
   Mournful Numbers, 3949; On Closer
   Inspection, 4445; Small Favor, 5693;
   Spring Fever, 5957; Spartan, 5910;
   Target, 6258; Timing, 6484; Turn of
   the Screw, 6699; Weapon, 6997;
   Weather-Wise, 7004.
U TAM' SI, TCHICAYA: Excerpt from
   Debout, 1790.
VAIL, BARNABAS: Nothing, 4215.
VALERY, PAUL: Canticle of the Columns,
   861; The Spinner, 5927; To the Plane
   Tree, 6598.
VAN ALLEN, GEORGE R.: Annunciation,
   240; Song of the Divine, 5835.
VANCE, ELEANOR GRAHAM: Home, 2610;
   Such Precious Things, 6122.
VANCE, THOMAS: The Maiden Shrouded as
   a Deer, 3615; Morning Song, 3912; On
   the Difficulty of Justice, 4503; The
   Prisoner of War Returns Through the
   Underground, 5014; The Stroke of
   Noon, 6103; The Instant in the Eye,
   2978.
VAN DOREN, MARK: And So It Was, 203;
   The Child at Winter Sunset, 964;
   Country Boredom, 1252; Departure:
   September, 1449; Dunce's Song, 1595;
   The Fields of November, 1917; If You
   But Dreamed It, 2797; Incinerator,
   2934; Little Trip, 3472; Once the
   Wind, 4537; Sweet William's Breath,
   6208; Time Was When Death, 6480; Too
   Old to Read, 6618; With Apples, 7240.
VAN DUYN, MONA: A Kind of Music, 3160;
   A Serious Case, 5533; Three Valen-
   tines to the Wide World, 6444.
VAN HISE, ALICE: Attention with Inten-
   tion, 387; Cognizance of All We Know,
   1103; Pain, 4644; Perception, 4747;
   The Softer the Batter..., 5752.
VAN HORN, RUTH G.: Influenza, 2953;
   Rx for Joyce Cary, 5382.
VAN KEUREN, W. G.: Remarks from the
   Man on the Stein End at the Second
   Carry, 5209.
VANNENBERGH, C. W.: When Ye Pray,
   Say, Our Father, 7082.
VAN SLYKE, BEREN: The Flooded Yard,
   2069; The Path to the Barn, 4706.
VAN VALEN, LEIGH: The Toxicologist,
   6635.
VAZAKAS, BYRON: Grand Concert by the
   Lake, 2370; The Innocents, 2958;
   Like Country Gardens and the
   Shepherd's Hey, 3385; Missa Solemnis,
   3834.
VEENENDAAL, CORNELIA: Looking at the
   X rays Taken, 3510.
VEGA, LOPE DE: Sonnet Right Off the
   Bat, 5873.
VELTON, WILLIAM: Autumn and After,
   420.
VESELY, RUTH SEYMOUR: Home Groan,
   2613; Passing Reflection, 4686;
   Retired Colonel, 5252.
VICTOR, FLORENCE: Friday Night
   Cantata, 2168; My Uncle's Books,

4020; The Need for Candles, 4052; On
   Not Knowing Yiddish, 4477; Vanity,
   6837.
VIERECK, PETER: Benediction, 574;
   Etruria, 1756; Lyric, 3600; A Pas-
   sionate Commissar to His Love, 4690;
   A Walk on Moss, 6929.
VIRDEN, HELEN: Lodestone, 3490.
VLIET, R. G.: That Sense As in the
   Tragedies, 6319.
WADDING, LUKE: Christmas Day is Come,
   1017.
WADDINGTON, MIRIAM: Exchange, 1793;
   The Orator, 4576; The Women's Jail,
   7270.
WADE, EVELYN AMUEDO: Offspring
   Cleaning, 4356.
WAGONER, DAVID: After Consulting My
   Yellow Pages, 78; The Crisis, 1281;
   Elegy for a Distant Relative, 1675;
   Elegy for Simon Corl, Botanist, 1680;
   Epitaph, 1733; Lines for a Dangerous
   Day, 3406; Lullaby Through the Side
   of the Mouth, 3590; The Man from the
   Top of the Mind, 3627; The Migration,
   3809; Murder Mystery, 3972; The
   Recognition, 5165; Song at the End
   of Winter, 5802; The Teaching Load,
   6270; To My Friend Whose Parachute
   Did not Open, 6565; A Warning to My
   Love, 6958; Words Above a Narrow
   Entrance, 7289.
WAIN, JOHN: Anecdote of 2 A.M., 212.
WALDMAN, SUSIE: Golf Widows' Lament,
   2338.
WALKER, CATHERINE TOMISON: Candle in
   the Wind, 852.
WALKER, FAYE CHILCOTE: Heirlooms,
   2536.
WALL, MARY B.: Of Digests, 4312.
WALLACE, ROBERT A.: Christoforo
   Colombo, 1030; The Garden Snail, 2249;
   January, 3075; The Mammoth, 3623; A
   Problem in History, 5021; The White
   Crayfish, 7109.
WALSH, CHAD: A Barn, a School, or a
   Church, 500; Divorce, 1519; Ode to
   the Finnish Dead at Hietaniemi
   Heroe's Cemetery, Helsinki, 4300.
WALSH, F. O.: Vacation, 6822.
WALSH, PETER B.: I Dreamt the Negro,
   Beautiful as Night, 2728.
WALTER, EUGENE: The Locust, 3488.
WALTON, EDA LOU: At Bay, 357; Clock
   and Three Candles, 1078; Epitaph,
   1734; First Snow, 1974; Golden
   Anniversary, 2336; Harvest, 2492; In
   Passage Tropical, 2883; Mid Winter,
   3793; Now must the Mind Write, 4238;
   An Old Song, 4409; Portrait, 4936;
   Precarious Serene, 4987; Rock Wren,
   5332; The Third Stair, 6372; Those
   Whom Death Leaves, 6400.
WALUJATI: Parting, 4678.
WANGSGAARD, EVA WILLES: Camera Piece,
   845; Life's a Wild-Plum Tree, 3372;
   This Edge of Autumn, 6377.
WARD, LYLA BLAKE: Look, Ma--No Leaves,
   3507; A Sweeping Victory, 6206.
WARD, MARIE ERWIN: Door Marked
   Maternity, 1547.

WARD, MAY WILLIAMS: How Guess, 2667; Indian Summer, 2944; Mississippi, 3837; Old Woman on a Fine Day, 4414; Warm Day in Winter, 6952.

WARD, WILLIAM ALLEN: Communion, 1145.

WARFEL, HERBERT: Do-It-Myself-Analysis, 1521.

WARING, ROBERT L.: Shovel Dionsaur, 5594.

WARREN, JAMES E., JR.: The House of the Seven Gables, 2652.

WARREN, ROBERT PENN: Debate: Question, Quarry, Dream, 1402; Garland for You, 2254; Holly and Hickory, 2603; In Moonlight Somewhere, They Are Singing, 2879; Nocturne: Traveling Salesman in a Hotel Bedroom, 4165; Ornithology in a World of Flux, 4582; Promises, 5039; Three Nursery Rhymes, 6429; The Well-House, 7018.

WARSAW, IRENE: Adjustment, 40; Advice From Lovelorn, 55; Benefit Performance, 575; Cool Comment, 1225; Even in Your Doggerel, 1764; Give Me That Book, Worm, 2308; Green-Eyed View, 2417; Local Showers, 3484; My Ego, 3993; Northern River Port, 4176; The Shape of Things, 5562; Tale of Two Shortages, 6241; To the Girls, 6592; Weak in, Weak Out, 6995; Wistful Thinking, 7234; With Hooks and Lines, 7241.

WARWICK, DOLORES: Advent Song, 48; Christening, 1010; Genesis Revisited, 2266; Three Masses of Christmas, 6428.

WATERMAN, WILLIAM: Ballad for Montgomery, 467.

WATKINS, AILEEN E.: Please Mr. Felson, 4844.

WATKINS, VERNON: Ballad of the Mermaid of Zennor, 471; Camelot, 844; The Colosseum, 1125; The Coronation, 1231; The Crane, 1272; Dedication, 1414; Demands of the Muse, 1441; Erinna and the Waters, 1742; The Forge of the Solstice, 2123; The Mask of Winter, 3682; Ode to Swansea, 4299; Revisited Waters, 5282; Taliesin and the Mockers, 6242; The Tributary Seasons, 6668; Zennor, 7381.

WATSON, BARBARA: A Winter's Tale, 7228.

WATSON, ROBERT W.: Odalisque, 4292.

WATT, W. W.: Academic Procession, 17; Behavior That Gives Who Away? or Whom?, 558; Homage to Don Marquis, 2607; Penny Wise and Found Foolish, 4742.

WAUGAMAN, CHARLES: A Carol for Palm Sunday, 879; To One Who Walks Only on Boards and Wheels, 576.

WEALES, GERALD: The Best Minds of What Bloody Generation, 583; The Greek Drama in Translation, 2411; On the Occasion of the First Edition of Mr. T. S. Eliot's The Cultivation of Christmas Trees, 4512.

WEAVER, BENNETT: Mercy's Dark Shadow, 3765; Remorse in Our Time, 5219; Shore Line, 5589; Thinner Sun, 6366; Walking North to the Dunes, 6932.

WEBB, MARY HAYDN: Chrysalis, 1034.

WEEKS, JANICE FARRAR: The Wrong Self, 7237.

WEGERT, ETHEL M.: Where There's Life, There's Soap, 7091.

WEINSTEIN, ALLYN: My Grandmother's Province, 4003.

WEINSTEIN, ARNOLD: Epithalamium, 1738; From the Greek, 2206; In the Garden, 2901; Lady Dancing in the Street, 3195.

WEISMILLER, EDWARD: College Town, 1118; Old Father Mountain, 4382; Short History, 5591.

WEISS, IRVING I.: Soiree, 5754.

WEISS, NEIL: The Ageing Athlete, 116; Cuckoo Clock, 1307; Friends, 2173; From The Fantast in the City, 2203; Grief, 2437; Gulls, 2455; Heaven, 2532; The Hike, 2584; The Hunt, 2696; Laocoon and the Bomb, 3238; Letter Written Standing in a Train, 3339; Lily, 3393; Mother at Poker, 3920; The New Overcoat, 4089; Ruth, 5380; Song for My Dead Grandmother, 5817.

WEISS, SANFORD: Poem, 4870.

WEISS, T.: Absolutely Roomy, 12; The Change, 925; The Fire at Alexandria, 1938; The Giant Yea, 2279; Godspeed, 2330; The Greater Music, 2409; The Little Winter Gardens, 3473; One Sundry Thing, 4556; The Shield, 5578; So He Was Sung, 5740; The Telltale Moment, 6285; To Forget Me, 6545; A Trip Through Yucatan, 6675.

WELCH, MARIE DE L.: Hark, Hark, the Lark, 2486; Minor Realism for a Major Poet, 3816.

WELLS, ANNA MARY: To Helen, Being Weaned, 6550.

WELLS, MARIE: To Begin as the Rivers, 6535.

WELTY, EUDORA: A Flock of Guinea Hens Seen from a Car, 2012.

WERNER, HELEN CARRAHER: Prayer for Cowards, 4980.

WESLEY, CECIL COBB: The Pocket, 4849. Wanderers, 6944.

WESTGATE, HAZEL: ...As Tidy Does, 335.

WESTON, MILDRED: Hat Bar, 2494.

WHEELER, PAUL MOWBRAY: Challenge, 922.

WHEELER, RICHARD: Confession Concerning My Troubles With the Straight-and-Narrow Path, 1173; Fine Fix, 1933; Fortune and I, 2136; I Live Quietly, 2742; I Stand and Wait, 2757; Intellectual Observation, 2983; It Hardly Pays, 3035; Key Note, 3151; Lament for a Shining Past, 3210; Lines in Which I Try to Modify a View Hold by Many Women, 3416; Love in a New Light, 3549; Nuptial Knot, 4247; Of Girls and Beaux, 4313; Off Key, 4351; Perennial Problem, 4749; Pet Theory, 4774; Please Don't Ask Me for a Loan, 4841; Ready Remark, 5148; Scientific Fact, 5454; Sports Cars, 5942; Starting Point, 6037; Temper Truth, 6288; Tense Situation, 6296; (cont'd)

WHEELER, RICHARD (cont'd): That's the Way It Goes, 6327; They're All in the Same Boat, 6359; Turning Point, 6701; Wage Rage, 6917; We Just Have to Face It, 6989; The Window Shopper, 7171; Words of Praise, 7295.

WHEELOCK, JOHN HALL: Aubade, 395; The Dark Wood, 1345; The Divine Insect, 1518; The Gardener, 2251; Herring-Gull, 2564; Morning Draws Near, 3901; The Timid Future, 6483; The Two Societies, 6740.

WHELDON, JAMES: One Word for Four Seasons, 4563.

WHITBREAD, THOMAS: A Student, Departing for Christmas Vacation, to Himself, 6108; For a Twenty-Fifth Birthday, 2051.

WHITE, CLAIRE NICOLAS: Interlude; Low Tide, 3576.

WHITE, E. B.: The Feet of the Mayor of Clay, 1899; Lines, 3403; A Listener's Guide to the Birds, 3440; The Misstep, 3838; A Table for One, 6225; The Tennis, 6295.

WHITE, ETHEL FAIRFIELD: Sprinkler System, 5976.

WHITE, GLENN: Apartness, 261; Sayonara, 5437.

WHITE, HAL SAUNDERS: Peace, 4723; Sunbright on a City Way, 6161.

WHITE, JOAN: Nurse at the White Cove, 4248; Tied Intangibles, 6464.

WHITE, LUE ETTA: To the Bureau of the Census, 6587.

WHITE, PARK JERAULD: E=mc^2, 1604; Gift of God, 2286.

WHITE, SHELDON: The Girls I Remember, 2303; Sad-Libber, 5388; Send Six Box Tops, 5518; That's Funny, I Used to Take a 38, 6322; Thoughts on a Motorcycle Policeman, 6413; Three Phases of a Small Boy Helping With the Chores, 6431.

WHITMAN, RUTH: The Phoenix, 4791; Song for A Vigil, 5810; Touro Synagogue, 6632.

WHITMAN, WALT: Good-Bye, My Fancy, 2342; I Hear America Singing, 2735; Old War-Dreams, 4412; Out of The Cradle Endlessly Rocking, 4612; Pioneers! O Pioneers!, 4819; Song of Myself, 5832; Song of the Open Road, 5838; When Lilacs Last in the Dooryard Bloom'd, 7073.

WHITT, MILLICENT WARD: Bout, 710; Echo, 1647; Soldier, 5755; Unquiet Fourth, 6795.

WHITTEMORE, REED: An Address to the Holder of Some High Government Office, 37; Alfred Lord Tennyson, 135; Another, 244; A Campus in Summer, 848; Charles Darwin, 934; An Early Call, 1608; An English Teacher, 1720; A Few Ways of Pulling Apart a Poem, 1914; A Floridian Museum of Art, 2019; Lord Clive, 3514; Mr. and Mrs., 3958; The Palms, 4651; The Popular Magazines, 4928; A Projection, 5036; Purity, 5071; The Radio Under the

Bed, 5111; The Self and the Weather, 5511; Sputnik, 5980; A Storm from the East, 6068; A Tale of a Poem and a Squash, 6239; Three Poems to Jackson, 6435; Three Sonnets to Time, 6439; Two Ruthless Pieces, 6736; The Walk Home, 6927; The Weather This Spring, 7002; A Winter Scene, 7213; The World Around Us, 7307.

WIGGAM, LIONEL: Eden, 1650.

WILBUR, NANCY GARBETT: Ode to the New Tenant on the Top Floor, 4302.

WILBUR, RICHARD: Advice to a Prophet, 57; Fall in Corrales, 1842; A Grasshopper, 2387; Lover of Puppets, 3559; She, 5566; Someone Taling to Himself, 5775; Two Voices in a Meadow, 6746.

WILKINSON, MARJORIE: To Mary of Bethany, 6558.

WILLIAMS, WILLIAM CARLOS: The Artist, 320; A Brueghel Nativity, 775; From Paterson V, 2196; The Measure, 3714; Of Asphodel, 4309; Poem, 4871; Puerto Rico Song, 5065; The Satyrs, 5433; Some Simple Measures in the American Idiom and the Variable Foot, 5770; Sonnet in Search of an Author, 5870; Tapestries at the Cloisters, 6254; The Turtle, 6703; A Woman, 7254.

WILLIS, PAULINE: Plaint of a Darker Brother, 4828.

WILLIS, STANLEY DUTTON: Between Classes, 589.

WILLSON, MABEL WINTER: You Can't Do That, 7348.

WILSON, CHARLOTTE A.: Poem 4872.

WILSON, D. C.: The Hour and the Arrow, 2647.

WINCHESTER, CHARLES W.: Provision, 5055.

WINSLOW, ANN GOODWIN: Hadrian's Lullaby, 2459; Platform Before the Castle, 4833; Scrolls, 5462; Sing, O Goddess, the Wrath, 5633.

WINSOR, FREDERICK: The Space-Child's Mother Goose, 5899.

WINSTON, WENDY JULIET: The Ocean, 4278.

WINTERS, YVOR: A White Spiritual, 7120.

WIRT, SHERWOOD ELIOT: On the Ninth Psalm, 4511.

WISE, MIRIAM L.: Song for September, 5818.

WITT, HAROLD: Back, 451; Botanical Garden, 706; The Cock of Confidence, 1099; Daphnis, 1340; Here, 2546; In Redwoods, 2888; July Escapist, 3121; The Lately Mockingbird, 3262; Night-coach from Salzburg, 4126; Notre Dame Perfected by Reflection, 4221; On Various Errors, 4531; Peacock, 4728; Piazza Di Spagna, 26, 4797; The Platonist Sees Snakes at an Ideal Moment, 4834; A Rat of Rabit, 5139; The Raying Fog, 5142; Snake, 5711; A Spider, 5924; Spontaneous Bottle, 5939; West, 7028.

WOLCOTT, KATHARYN: Blackboard Room, 647.

WOLF, LEONARD: The Bather, 511; (cont'd)

WOLF, LEONARD (cont'd): Congratulations, 1180; The Exile, 1803; For Mrs. Cadwallader, 2083; Ice Cream, 2773; In Those Days, 2923; My Grandfather's Rules for Holy Living, 4001; My Mother, 4011; O! It Used To Be Such A Pleasure, 4259; On Carley Ridge, 4443; Passover, 4692; The Peasant, 4730; A Praise for the Sun, 4969; St. Basil to the Elder Harmatius, 5398; Siren, 5643; The Tailor, 6232; The Yewberry, 7342.

WOLF, MICHAEL: Daily We Touch Omniscience, 1328.

WOLFE, THOMAS: Of Time and the River, 4349.

WOLKING, EXTA WILLIAMS: Mother Hubbard's Cupboard, 3922.

WOOD, ALLYN: A Coat for My Mother, 1098.

WOOD, J. P.: Know Something, 3185; Old Clothes, 4376; Tomorrow, 6617.

WOOD, MARGARETTE A.: The Psalm of Comfort, 5059.

WOOD, NATHAN R.: In a Greek New Testament, 2832.

WOODALL, ALLEN E.: Wind in the North, 7163.

WOODRUM, LON: Pottery, 4963.

WOODRUM, LOU: Man, 3625.

WOODS, CARL: The Snow is Blue, 5727.

WOODS, JOHN: How So Lovely Walks the Wind, 2675; The Map of Water, 3645; Poem, 4873; Poem at Thirty, 4878; Poem by Water, 4879; Running a Temperature, 5377; Two Songs for Lute, 6741.

WOOLLEY, IVY HOUTZ: I Hate Winter, 2733.

WOOTEN, PAUL: January Afternoon, 3076.

WORKMAN, MIMS THORNBURGH: No Need, 4149; Par, 4654; Reflection, 5182; When You're Sixty, 7083.

WRENN, PHILIP W.: Narrative Dirge for Wind Instruments, 4039.

WRIGHT, ALBERTE: It's Later Than I Think, 3058.

WRIGHT, CELESTE TURNER: On a Philosophical System, 4432.

WRIGHT, DAVID: At the Death of Roy Campbell, 375; At the Kaiser's Villa, 378; A House of Friends, 2652.

WRIGHT, JAMES: The Alarm, 129; At the Executed Murderer's Grave, 376; Aubade at the Zama Replacement Depot, 396; The Cold Divinities, 1107; David, 1354; Directions Out of a Dream, 1494; Eleutheria, 1686; Erinna to Sappho, 1743; Evening, 1768; The Farmer, 1867; For Her Who Carried My Child, 2073; A Gesture by a Lady with an Assumed Name, 2271; A Little Girl on Her Way to School, 3456; The Morality of Poetry, 3890; Morning Hymn to a Dark Girl, 3902; The Murderer, 3975; My Grandmother's Ghost, 4002; Night-Pieces, 4129; On Minding One's Own Business, 4473; A Presentation of Two Birds to My Son, 5000; The Private Meeting Place, 5017; Sappho's Child,

5426; To a Hostess Saying Goodnight, 6502; To a Salesgirl Weary of Artificial Holiday Trees, 6515; To a Young Girl on a Premature Spring Day, 6525; To My Older Brother, 6570; Where the Plump Spider Sways to Rest, 7089.

WRIGHT, JAMES ABELL: Old Folks at Home, 4384.

WRIGHT, PHYLLIS: I'm Dreaming of a White Daisy, 2810; Winter on the Shore, 7210.

WUEBKER, KAE: Parlor Travels, 4672.

WUN, U.: Some Burmese Riddle Verses, 5767.

WURDEMANN, AUDREY: Meditation at Midnight, 3723.

WYLIE, ELINOR: Pretty Words, 5002.

WYLIE, PAMELA C.: Poem, 4874.

WYLIE, PHILIP: Stopping to Write a Friend on a Thick Night, 6062.

YAMANOGUCHI, BAKU: Marriage, 3667; Tatami Floor, 6261.

YBORRA, THOMAS J., JR.: Versicle, 6851.

YELLEM, SAMUEL: Exercise in Pessism, 1799.

YONEDA, EISAKU: A Thousand Paper Cranes, 6422.

YORK, ESTHER BALDWIN: The Ghost With Curly Hair, 2276.

YOSANO, AKIKO: I Saw a White Bird Once, 2748; The Nightingale Has not Come, 4127.

YOUNG, ANNE: Ophelia Sings Under Observation, 4570; Portrait of Alethea, a Quakeress, 4943; Song, 5798.

YOUNG, JOANNE: Good-Gracious Living, 2347.

YOUNG, NACELLA: Impasse, 2820.

YOUNG, STANLEY: Mutiny with Bounty, Considered Reflections on TV, Without Color, 3988.

YOUNG, VIRGINIA G.: I Am an Up-to-Date Librarian, 2713.

YUDKIN, MRS. SAMUEL: Book Buyer's Plea, 692.

ZACKS, HENNA AROND: Let's Face It, 3316; Subway Frustration, 6116.

ZATURENSKA, MARYA: Four Ghosts, 2145; The Garden, 2243; Pieta, 4811; The River Voyagers, 5315; Time and Atlantis, 6468; Voices Heard in the Air, 6907; The Waiting, 6920.

ZAW, U KHIN, TR.: Rice Pounding Songs, 5289.

ZAWADSKY, PATIENCE: Revelation, 5276.

ZELDIS, CHAYYM: Seek Haven, 5504.

ZIEGLER, EDWARD K.: The 23rd Psalm (Materialist's Version), 6713.

ZILLES, LUKE: The Bat, 509; Bunch of Wild Flowers, 791; Crab Apples, 1268; The Hooked Rug, 2627; Landscape, 3225; Let's Kiss, 3318; The Moon, 3881; Water Lilies, 6974.

ZIMMERMAN, ELEANOR HOLBROOK: The Boy and the Watch, 713; My Heart Has Loved but Once, 3004; Oversupplied, 4629; Soldier's Mother, 5759; Thorn and Weed, 6396; To Timothy, 6604.

ZIMSKIND, NATHANIEL: Suburban Spring, 6113.

ZITNER, S. P.: The Hot-Rods Ride at
    Dusk, 2645; Light Bulb: Lares, 3379;
    The Rose and the Sun, 5352; To C,
    with Two Lines from Eluard, 6538.
ZLOTNIK, HAROLD: Autumn Moment, 428;
    Chronicle, 1032; Grammar on a Clear
    Day, 2366; Island, 3023.
ZUKOFSKY, CELIA: Three From Gaius
    Valerius Catullus, 6424.
ZUKOFSKY, LOUIS: The Guests, 2453;
    Peri Poietikes, 4753; Two, 6718.
ZWEIG, PAUL L.: The Dance, 1332.
ZYLSTRA, MILDRED: Final Arbiter, 1926;
    Sonnets for the Space Age, 5877.

SUBJECT INDEX

ABRAHAM: 7, Berrigan; 8, Schwartz.
ABRAMS, CAL: 2626, Abrams.
ABSENT LOVERS: 4610, Galbraith.
ABSENT-MINDEDNESS: 10, Nemerov; 3847,
    Ellert.
ABSENTEES: 11, Ponsot.
ABUNDANCE: 14, Ciardi.
ACACIA: 7238, Triem.
ACADEMIC PROCESSIONS: 16, Lattimore.
ACCENTS: 2835, Ellyson.
ACCEPTANCE: 20, Merrill.
ACHIEVEMENT: 22, Jenkins.
ACTORS: 5438, Kober; 5495, Baro.
ADAM: 31, Booth; 32, Feldman, 33,
    Ponsot; 1797, Scrutton; 2266,
    Warwick; 2555, Nickerson; 3384,
    Macpherson; 4196, Triem; 6453,
    Eberhart.
ADAMANT: 3384, Macpherson.
ADCOCK: 5639, Adcock.
ADENAUER, KONRAD: 513, Sagittarius.
ADJUSTMENTS: 40, Warsaw.
ADMINISTRATORS: 41, Katz.
ADOLESCENCE: 43, Olivier; 710, Whitt;
    3426, Logan; 4948, Nash; 6276,
    Puneky.
ADOLESCENT GIRLS: 5549, Galbraith.
ADOLESCENTS: 1765, Ames; 2479,
    De Vito; 3621, Constant; 4815,
    Lattimore; 5669, Char; 6774, Skinner.
ADOPTED CHILDREN: 960, Faubion.
ADOPTIONS: 44, Miller.
ADULTS: 6533, Engle.
ADVENT: 46, Carter; 47, McCarthy;
    48, Warwick; 4784, Bradley; 5577,
    Crites.
ADVERTISEMENTS: 2796, Chadwick; 6585,
    Grenville.
ADVERTISING: 176, Pierce.
ADVICE: 59, Summers; 7285, Owens.
ADVICE TO DAUGHTERS: 1882, Jaffray.
AESTHETES: 1244, Duffy.
AESTHETICS: 1798, Scott; 66,
    Middleton.
AFRICA: 69, Diop; 70, Smith; 582,
    Danner; 6985, Sedar-Senghor.

AFRICAN SONGS: 1305, Koshland; 5880,
    Koshland; 5934, Koshland.
AFRICANOS: 6985, Sedar-Senghor.
AFTER-DINNER SPEECHES: 80, Neely.
AFTERNOONS: 102, Stefanile; 1050,
    Howes; 4069, Schoeberlein; 4294, Pack;
    5678, Lincoln.
AFTERNOONS IN THE MOUNTAINS: 3935,
    Long.
AGAMEMNON: 4021, Saly.
AGAPE: 1744, Cully.
AGE: 2511, Richardson; 2909, Stone;
    2925, D; 3062, Hall; 3826, Merrill;
    3995, Gibson; 4358, Murry; 4386,
    Hemphill; 4938, Chapin; 6861, Smith;
    7020, Stevenson; 7083, Workman.
AGE TWO: 4592, Stockdale.
AGENDAS: 117, Richstone.
AGING: 494, Lindbergh; 2196, Williams;
    2451, Balch; 2812, Saxe; 3058, Wright;
    3597, Stafford; 3636, Freeman; 3943,
    Kanfer; 4265, Tyler; 4384, Wright;
    4414, Ward; 4642, Scott; 4685,
    Shenton; 4800, Hallock; 6618,
    Van Doren; 7068, Magee.
AGING PROCESS: 118, Grenville.
AGNES, ST.: 4993, Merton.
AGNOSTICS: 2053, Lilly; 6527, Marley.
AGONY: 120, Russo.
AGREEMENT: 3099, Graves.
AHAB: 124, Burns.
AIR: 806, Tyler; 2037, Kemp.
AIR AND WATER: 645, Carrier.
AIR TRAVEL: 1136, Summers; 2004,
    Jerome; 2009, Graves.
AIRBASES: 592, Coxe.
AIRPLANES: 2005, Hughes; 2009, Graves;
    2982, Fairbairn.
AIRPLANE FLIGHTS: 3808, Howes.
AISLE SEATS: 3628, Galbraith.
ALEWIVES: 133, Kinnell.
ALEXANDER THE GREAT: 270, Feldman.
ALGEBRA: 6240, Pell.
ALIASES: 4838, Schevill.
ALIENS: 2841, Moreljono.
ALICE IN WONDERLAND: 7118, Solomon.

ALL: 5316, Schwartz.
ALL SOULS' EVE: 3323, Dufault.
ALLEGORIES: 1417, Moore.
ALLERGIES: 154, Stoutenburg.
ALLEYS: 2926, Tagliabue.
ALLURES: 5279, Blackwell.
ALMA MATERS: 156, Cole.
ALONE: 160, Bohm; 677, Conklin; 7249, Johnson.
ALTAR: 6936, Pierce.
ALTERNATIVES: 167, Jamieson.
ALUMNI DUES: 156, Cole.
AMBASSADORS: 170, Burford.
AMBITION: 6059, Merrill.
AMERICA: 173, Simpson; 2735, Whitman; 3326, Kessler; 3735, Koch; 4054, Razaf.
AMERICAN INDUSTRY: 5302, Nash.
AMERICANS: 3012, Stokely; 3336, Squires; 5811, Schneider; 6601, Singer.
AMOS: 183, Hall; 5045, Ratliff.
AMPHITHEATRES: 184, Lister.
ANDALUSIA: 210, Belitt.
ANALYSTS: 189, Stern.
ANCESTORS: 911, Hoffman; 3105, Merwin; 5084, Jammes.
ANCESTRY: 456, Armour; 2649, Debee.
ANCIENT JARS: 1047, Burke.
ANDREW, ST.: 5397, Magaret.
ANGELS: 214, Dickey; 215, Humphries; 461, Petrie; 1377, Therese; 2746, De Jong; 2969, Macpherson; 5103, Goodreau.
ANGER: 3101, Ignatow; 5218, Jaffray.
ANGLERS: 1990, Chadwick.
ANIMALS: 222, Jacobsen, 224, Jacobsen; 225, Maris Stella; 4197, Garrigue; 5250, O'Gorman; 6289, Duncan.
ANKLES: 684, Morris
ANNABEL LEE: 227, Poe.
ANNIVERSARIES: 229, Abse; 231, Lattimore; 235, Graham; 236, Raskin; 3410, Chang; 4626, Neely; 6297, Freneau.
ANNUNCIATION: 240, Van Allen; 241, O'Gorman; 4329, Nims.
ANSELM: 5404, Lynch.
ANSWERS: 249, Edelman; 250, Ringstad; 5166, Galbraith.
ANTECEDENTS: 252; Tomlinson.
ANTHROPOLOGISTS: 253, Jones.
ANTIOCH: 6452, Ackerson.
ANTIPHONS: 4253, Mary Honora.
ANTIQUES: 4442, La Rue.
ANTLERS: 732, Dugan; 2024, Krieger.
ANTS: 501, Tyler; 884, Lilly; 5834, Blackburn.
ANXIETY: 257, Carruth.
ANXIOUS PARENTS: 1358, Douglass.
APARTMENTS: 1944, Taylor; 4553, Bramley.
APATHY: 3443, Bradford.
APOCALYPSE: 263, Ozick; 5036, Whittemore.
APPARITIONS: 4397, Eckman.
APPETITES: 6784, Kelley.
APPLE-BLOSSOMS: 271, Savage, 2751, Der Hovanessian.
APPLES: 272, Russo; 273, Jacobson; 6453, Eberhart; 7240, Van Doren.

APPOINTMENTS: 2800, Pedrick.
APRICOT TREES: 277, Brasier.
APRIL: 124, Shook; 149, Hess; 278, Merrill; 279, Quinn; 280, Nixon; 284, De Jong; 285, Freneau; 288, Hazen; 289, McNeill; 666, Trott; 1253, Brand; 2054, Faith; 2768, Coatsworth; 2800, Pedrick; 4657, Adrian; 7037, Toland; 7064, Embury.
ARBORS: 7176, Farber.
ARCADIA: 2762, Lang.
ARIAS: 102, Stefanile.
ARISTOBULUS: 295, Cavafy.
ARISTOTLE: 1285, Carter.
ARIZONA DESERT: 297, Golffing.
ARJUNA: 6849, Bose.
ARK: 298, Macpherson.
ARKANSAS: 299, Bowie.
ARMORED CARS: 302, Kroll.
ARMORERS: 1495, Olson.
ARMS AID: 4568, Ryskind.
ARMSTRONG, DONALD: 4751, Dickey.
ARMY VETERANS: 5252, Vesely.
ARRAN, SCOTLAND: 4200, Reid.
ARROGANCE: 306, Askue.
ART: 308, Kessler; 3778, Sweeney; 4521. Nathan; 6438, Tyler.
ART, ORIENTAL: 2830, Pierce.
ART, PRESCHOOL: 5009, Hicks.
ARTHRITUS: 546, Rosenberg.
ARTISTS: 318, Crews; 319, 321, Stepanchev; 323, MacKinstry; 2000, Drake; 2587, Carruth; 3491, Strobel; 3734, Gibbs; 4947, Howes; 4647, Jennings; 5237, Kessler; 5652, Rosenberg; 6053, Carroll; 6324, Nash.
ARTS: 4601, Taylor.
ASCENSION: 340, Martaugh; 341, Pillin.
ASH CANS: 342, Dufault.
ASH WEDNESDAY: 343, Awad.
ASINE, KING OF: 3168, Seferis.
ASPIRATIONS: 348, Lee.
ASSEMBLY LINES: 3184, Laing.
ASSHUR: 1463, Dana.
ASTERISKS: 5383, Hammer.
ASTROLOGY: 352, Cassity.
ASYLUMS: 353, Carruth.
ATAHUALLPA: 1395, Larraud.
ATHENA: 622, Clower.
ATHLETES: 116, Weiss; 3331, Lindeman.
ATHLETICS: 4620, Roseliep.
ATLANTIS: 6468, Zaturenska.
ATMOSPHERE: 382, Fleming.
ATTENDING: 385, Rago.
ATTENTION: 387, Van Hise.
ATTICS: 294, Farnham; 2601, Carlisle; 3751, Lee.
ATTITUDES: 388, Eberhart; 440, Sagittarius.
ATTRACTIONS: 3611, Galbraith.
AUBREY, JOHN, 1626-1697: 753, 754, Nash.
AUCTIONS: 398, Mack; 1251, Dell.
AUDEN, WYSTAN HUGH: 6606, Howes; 6670, Francis.
AUGEIAS: 399, Graves.
AUGUST: 400, Crook; 401, 402, 403, Lindeman; 3070, Booth; 3495, Faubion; 4398, Morris; 5815, McDonnell; 6749, Heatherley.

AUGUSTINE, ST.:   408, Stafford.
AUNTS: 410, Geiger; 6080, Nash.
AUSCHWITZ: 411, Enrico.
AUTHORITIES: 412, Douglass.
AUTHORITY: 3629, Raskin.
AUTHORS: 1938, Weiss; 3756, Stevens;
   6020, Spear; 6585, Grenville.
AUTOBIOGRAPHIES: 413, Hartley.
AUTOGRAPH ALBUMS: 4369, Lieberman.
AUTOMOBILE DRIVERS: 3278, Heath; 3974,
   Allen; 7149, Goodman.
AUTOMOBILE NOISES: 2519, Schlitzer.
AUTOMOBILE PARTS: 6522, Mayes.
AUTOMOBILE TRAFFIC: 2824, Herz.
AUTOMOBILES: 350, Stoutenburg; 814,
   Honig; 1259, Stone; 2518, Galbraith;
   2566, Cole; 3573, Rosenfield; 3810,
   Power; 3989, Ellert; 4070, Schlitzer;
   4275, Ignatow; 4756, Morse; 4908,
   Poetry on Wheels; 7274, Ely.
AUTUMN: 416, Craig; 417, Dickinson;
   418, Robertson; 419, Tomlinson; 423,
   Petite; 424, Ferlinghetti; 425,
   Hollander; 428, Zlotnik; 429, Coxe;
   883, Galler; 1161, Kizer; 2162,
   Merrill; 2177, Plath; 2361, Galler;
   2522, Stuart; 2702, Donaldson; 2705,
   McBrown; 2845, Garrigue; 2906,
   Merwin; 4235, Galbraith
AUTUMN AND LOVE: 427, Hearst.
AUTUMN BEACHES: 421, Bohm; 430,
   Starbuck.
AUTUMN, END OF: 420, Velton; 6377,
   Wangsgaard.
AUTUMN EVENINGS: 3790, Lilly.
AUTUMN SONGS: 432, Taylor; 5749,
   Hazen; 5833, Bell.
AUTUMN SKYLINE DRIVE: 431, Drewry.
AUTUMN WALKS: 433, Bynner.
AUTUMN WOODS: 434, Todd; 547, Sarton.
AVERELL, ELIZABETH BLEECKER: 2064,
   Ponsot.
AWAKENING: 394, Prasad.
BAAL: 5475, Perse.
BABEL: 4983, Ferry; 6634, Muir.
BABIES: 85, Rubin; 444, Raskin; 447,
   Smith; 993, Donnelly, 1326, Francis;
   1783, Fisher; 1947, Gall; 1948,
   Smith; 2059, Henley; 2472, Francis;
   2495, McFarland; 3525, Talman; 4134,
   Mueller; 4359, Antolini; 5371,
   Galbraith; 5703, Grenville; 5940,
   Galbraith.
BABY GIRLS: 948, Cresson; 1351,
   Berning.
BABY SITTERS: 445, Landeweer.
BABYLON: 5369, Ackerson.
BACH, JOHANN SEBASTIAN, 1685-1750:   442,
   Grayer; 448, Delattre.
BACK, JOHANN SEBASTIAN: 449, Mary St.
   Virginia; 3091, Fitzgerald.
BACHELORS: 450, Meredith; 1503,
   Freneau; 4530, Chadwick; 5922,
   Harrington; 6155, Galbraith; 7023,
   McGuiggan.
BACILLI: 7158, Galbraith.
BACKACHES: 4459, Lister.
BACKYARDS: 3823, Brooks.
BALDNESS: 2516, Alkus.
BALLERINAS: 320, Williams.

BALLET: 484, Matthews; 1232, Merwin;
   3917, Greene.
BALLS: 464, Rich.
BALTIMORE, MARYLAND: 485, Nash.
BAMBOO: 487, Hall.
BANK ACCOUNTS: 1762, Schiff.
BANQUET SPEAKERS: 370, Schlitzer.
BANQUETS: 3760, Pennington.
BAPTISM: 2683, McGinley.
BARBARIANS: 1810, Kavafis.
BARBECUE: 490, Sward.
BARBERS: 491, Talman.
BARBERSHOPS: 492, Burr.
BARDS: 5253, Collier.
BARGAIN COUNTERS: 6759, Blackwell.
BARGAINS: 497, Galbraith.
BARGES: 499, Deutsch.
BARNS: 500, Walsh; 7076, Graves.
BARRACUDAS: 502, Eff.
BARRETT, REV. ALFRED J., S.J.: 5272,
   Fitzgerald.
BARS: 3977, Smith.
BASEBALL: 4453, Hammer; 5078,
   Philbrick; 6326, Treadwell.
BASEBALL GAMES: 3722, Neely.
BASEBALL PLAYERS: 560, 681, 1479,
   1589, 2602, Nash; 2626, Abrams;
   3106, Smith; 3253, Stefanile; 3610,
   5079, Nash; 5639, Adcock; 6752; Nash.
BASKET MAKERS: 506, Colum.
BASKETBALL: 724, Freeman.
BASKETBALL PLAYERS: 5296, Duncan.
BASS: 507, Plutzik.
BATHERS: 511, Wolf.
BATHROOMS: 4277, Armour.
BATHS: 510, McFarland; 720, Armour;
   2637, Kumin.
BATS: 508, Eff; 509, Zilles; 2007,
   Smith; 2699, Jacobson.
BATTLES: 5812, Posner.
BAUDELAIRE, PIERRE CHARLES, 1821-1867:
   4484, Starbuck.
BAY WINDOWS: 517, Quinn.
BAYS: 6810, Dicker.
BEACHES: 30, Dejong; 169, Engle; 421,
   Bohm; 521, de Vito; 523, Landeweer;
   524, Maccaig; 594, Kumin; 969,
   Chaffee; 1375, Hatch; 1956, Raskin;
   2546, Witt; 2903, Lineaweaver; 4529,
   Fort; 4612, Whitman; 4716, De Jong.
BEARS: 504, Engle; 526, Merwin; 527,
   Stoutenburg; 2394, Hollander.
BEAUS: 1585, Drake.
BEAUTIFUL: 7279, Swenson.
BEAUTY: 336, Speer; 532, Rothenberg;
   534, Tomlinson; 535, Nash; 536,
   MacPherson; 807, Coatsworth; 3030,
   Capetanakis; 3469, Fuller; 4066,
   Chadbourne; 4439, Benek; 5766, Trent;
   6382, Pustilnik; 6800, Shaffer, 7064,
   Embury.
BEAUTY AIDS: 3891, Rosenfield.
BEDA FLOWER: 540, Han.
BEDS: 338, Bartlett.
BEDSTEADS: 3011, Moody.
BEDTIME: 551, Brasier; 2334, Creeley;
   2552, Gardner; 7071, Chadwick.
BEECH TREES: 547, Sarton.
BEER: 4448, Lister.
BEES: 545, Fandel; 548, Donaldson;
   3000, Stoutenbert; 4102, Mortimer.

BEETHOVEN, LUDWIG VAN: 549, Conrad.
BEETLES: 550, Galler; 6114, Posner.
BEGGARS: 365, Merrill; 556, McFarland; 2604, Pillin.
BEGINNINGS: 2880, Geller; 5214, Goldberg.
BEING: 563, Grace; 2782, Good H.; 6171, Coughlin; 7006, Bynner.
BELIEF: 265, Sloan; 567, Miles; 1243, Milne; 2372, Merchant; 6977, Lilly.
BELIEFS: 6332, Gogarty.
BELIEVERS: 6513, Golffing.
BELLADONNA: 570, Holmes.
BELLS: 569, Freeman; 3948, Cassity; 4881, Moore; 6126, Blackburn.
BELONGING: 2549, Stanley.
BENEDICTIONS: 574, Viereck; 3998, Crown.
BEREAVED: 7143, Pierce.
BERRY PICKING: 5609, Seager.
BETHLEHEM: 585, Jacobs; 4261, Frankenberg; 4516, Meissner.
BETRAYED: 587, Bangham.
BHIKKUS: 6265, Bevington.
BIBLE: 2737, Frazee-Bower; 2963, Abse; 7281, Smith.
BICYCLES: 721, Lee.
BIGOTRY: 6761, Merwin.
BILLBOARDS: 5615, Seuss.
BILLIARD BALLS: 6409, Noyes.
BILLS: 7021, Armour.
BIRD CAGES: 826, Dudek.
BIRD CALLS: 4582, Warren.
BIRD FEEDING: 611, Ginsberg; 7050, Garrigue.
BIRD KNOWLEDGE: 6183, Fleming.
BIRD SONGS: 6455, Eberhart.
BIRDHOUSES: 2895, Hemley.
BIRDS: 268, Gibson; 565, Long; 616, Coblentz; 1857, Corke; 2180, Tyler; 2395, Patchen; 2477, Levertov; 2667, Ward; 2792, Bernard; 3221, Burrows; 3759, Brasier; 4060, Giordan; 4124, Galbraith; 4818, Mansfield; 4869, Thornton; 5007, Morgan; 5444, Galler; 6586, Sanzenbach; 6920, Zaturenska; 7079, Slote.
BIRDS AND ETIQUETTE: 1893, Raskin.
BIRDS AND SPRING: 1977, Stockdale.
BIRDS AS GIFTS: 5000, Wright.
BIRDS AS WATCHERS: 6971, Coxe.
BIRDS, DEAD: 1374, Redgrove.
BIRDS FLYING SOUTH: 1755, Keith.
BIRDS, GATHERING OF: 615, Coatsworth.
BIRDS, GUIDES TO: 3440, White.
BIRDS IN MAY: 205, Coatsworth.
BIRDS IN WINTER: 4307, Frost
BIRDS' NESTS: 7366, Anthony.
BIRDS' SINGING: 617, Merwin
BIRDS SINGING: 3464, Schwartz.
BIRTH: 618, Gilboa; 620, Schwartz; 621, Takahashi; 629, Broughton; 1801, Beum; 2073, Wright; 2920, Mueller; 7260, Milne; 7335, Lister.
BIRTH CERTIFICATES: 1684, Maddow.
BIRTHDAY CANDLES: 628, Justice.
BIRTHDAY CARDS: 629, Broughton.
BIRTHDAY GIFTS: 630, Gibbs; 5216, Lazarus.
BIRTHDAYS: 626, Merwin; 627, Henley;

631, Nathan; 632, Eisenlohr; 795, Merwin; 1404, Kreymborg; 2051, Whitbread; 4440, Holmes; 4475, Nicholson; 4878, Woods; 5290, Avison; 5548, Hillyer; 5895, Carleton.
BIRTHS: 619, Meireles; 4495, Ciardi.
BISHOPS: 6174, Ackerson.
BITTERNESS: 5443, Clark.
BITTERSWEET: 638, Albright.
BLACK GIRL: 486, Raynor.
BLACK HISTORIANS: 6539, Johnson.
BLACK WOMEN: 4305, Stokely.
BLACKBIRDS: 5417, McGrath.
BLACKS: 646, Stokely; 768, Hughes; 1011, 1102, 3827, Stokely; 4130, Sullivan; 5177, Stokely; 5690, Deutsch.
BLACKSMITH SHOPS: 2842, Jacobs.
BLAKE, WILLIAM: 2056, Galler.
BLAME: 6258, Usk.
BLANKETS: 1934, Rubin.
BLESSINGS: 649, Holmes.
BLIND: 2286, White; 5113, Colum; 6564, Lawson.
BLINDMEN: 5546, Kinnell.
BLINDNESS: 651, Cotter; 654, Marz; 655, Belvin; 797, Sandeen; 2129, Squires; 4370, Schevill; 5169, Thomas.
BLIZZARDS: 656, Mansfield.
BLOOD: 119, Hilberry; 658, Morris; 659, O'Gorman; 4493, Nixon.
BLOSSOMS: 274, Kahn.
BLUE: 662, Morris; 5425, Goodman.
BLUE JAYS: 671, Goodman; 2346, Hansen.
BLUEBERRY PICKERS: 676, Abbe.
BLURS: 6911, Gunn.
BOARDING DOGS: 4441, Dean.
BOAT WHISTLES: 677, Conklin.
BOATING: 678, Herschberger; 4473, Wright; 5315, Zaturenska.
BOATS: 679, Montale; 2688, Shenton; 2894, Hoffman; 4514, Knoepfle; 5848, Hagiwara; 6482, Knoepfle.
BODIES: 7088, Kinnell.
BODY: 2955, Baldwin.
BOMBS: 93, Corke; 3238, Weiss.
BONDAGE: 7346, Schwartz.
BONE CHINA: 685, Lister.
BONES: 3860, Updike; 5662, Moss; 7052, Kizer.
BOOK BUYER: 692, Yudkin.
BOOK CLUBS: 386, McGinley.
BOOK EXHIBITS: 700, Ringstad.
BOOK MARKS: 3664, Reinert.
BOOK OF KELLS: 694, Colum.
BOOK REVIEWERS: 695, Kime; 696, Kruse; 1202, Mumford.
BOOK SHELVES: 697, Ringstad.
BOOK WORMS: 2308, Warsaw.
BOOKBINDING: 4631, Sutherland.
BOOKKEEPING: 3451, Galler.
BOOKPLATES: 1786, Feine.
BOOKS: 689, Ellis; 691, Shapiro; 698, Ringstad; 699, Shores; 774, Lister, 1737, Reinert; 2306, Gates; 3362, Liotta; 3448, Dugan; 4020, Victor; 4371, Snell; 4422, Liotta; 4560, Ridland; 5183, Logan; 6257, Reinert; 6403, Liotta; 6450, Carlisle; 6529, Solum, 6616, Updike.

BOOKSTANDS: 1588, McGonigal.
BOOKWORMS: 704, Reinert; 3587, Engen.
BOORS: 702, Stewart.
BOOTBLACKS: 4372, Stefanile.
BOOTS: 12, Weiss.
BORDELLOS: 2822, Smith.
BOREDOM: 6327, Wheeler.
BORGIA, SAINT FRANCIS: 5400, McGinley.
BORROWING: 590, Usk.
BOSCH, HIERONYMUS: 2246, Coleman.
BOSTON FINE ARTS FESTIVAL: 705, Moore.
BOSTON, MASSACHUSETTS: 346, Starbuck.
BOSTON PUBLIC GARDENS: 4882, MacLeish.
BOTANISTS: 1680, Wagoner.
BOTTLES: 5939, Witt.
BOULEVARDS: 708, Rizzardi.
BOX TOPS: 514, Jennison; 5518, White.
BOY FRIENDS: 6780, Steele.
BOYHOOD: 3065, Holmes.
BOYS: 713, Zimmerman; 1132, Coles;
    1226, Hammer; 2100, Lee; 2636,
    de Vito; 3128, Usk; 3245, Solomon;
    3449, Ginsberg; 3629, Raskin; 3650,
    Ford; 4072, Coffin; 4536, Gleason;
    5295, McFarland; 5881, Balch; 6035,
    Jacobson; 6073, Ireland; 6142, Isler;
    6205, Duke; 6407, Eisenlohr; 6676,
    Fairchild; 7301, Raskin.
BOYS AND NATURE: 719, Faubion.
BOYS AND SCHOOL: 5451, Isler.
BRAGGARTS: 192, Hughes.
BRAGGING: 729, Collins.
BRAHMS, JOHANNES, 1833-1897: 730,
    Morris.
BRAILLE: 731, Mullins; 6564, Lawson.
BREAD: 737, Levertov; 4526, Goldberg.
BREAD OF LIFE: 4272, Bangham.
BREAKFAST: 216, Lister; 738, Ciardi;
    4155, Otis.
BREATH: 740, Morris; 6208, Van Doren.
BREATHING: 2790, McFarland.
BREMEN TOWN MUSICIANS: 4293, Casey.
BRIDES: 742, Eaton; 745, Singleton;
    1137, Levine; 1175, Bagg; 1945,
    Shusetsu; 3924, Grenville; 4330,
    Bracken; 4583, Spencer; 7035,
    Phillis.
BRIDGES: 746, Abbe; 747, Lister; 749,
    Dicker; 3631, Grenville; 4496, Sato.
BROBDINGNAG: 6695, Rich.
BROOKS: 3768, Scott.
BROTHELS: 820, Tanaka.
BROTHERHOOD: 766, Razaf; 2976, Sawyer;
    4105, Sagittarius; 4654, Workman;
    5246, Burket; 7179, Pierce.
BROTHERS: 2085, Ponsot; 4000, Dana;
    6570, Wright.
BROWN: 770, Brand; 771, Stefanile.
BROWN, JOHN, 1800-1859: 3103,
    Burford.
BRUEGHEL, PETER: 775, Williams.
BUCKSKIN MEN: 5171, Colvin.
BUDAPEST: 778, McCallister; 779,
    Hubert; 4991, Avison.
BUDGETS: 1554, Alkus; 2454, Magee;
    3949, Usk.
BUILDINGS: 785, Johnson; 4479, Lemon.
BULGANIN, NIKOLAI ALEKSANDROVICH, 1895-:
    787, Cortes.
BULLETS: 909, Swenson.

BULLFIGHTERS: 789, Carson.
BULLFROGS: 790, Hughes.
BULLS: 217, Hull; 788, Plath.
BUOYS: 568, Merwin.
BURDENS: 2687, Ellis.
BURIALS: 792, Doherty; 6769, Duncan;
    3936, Penny.
BURNING AIRCRAFT: 891, Hughes.
BUS TRIPS: 280, Nixon.
BUSES: 798, Nash.
BUSHES: 799, Coxe.
BUSINESS: 3962, Ignatow; 4473, Wright.
BUSINESS OFFICES: 800, Coblentz.
BUSINESSES: 3958, Whittemore.
BUSINESSMEN: 2057, Magaret.
BUTTERFLIES: 808, Chapin; 809,
    Blackwell; 810, Burns; 811, Smith;
    4645; Danner.
BUTTERFLY COLLECTIONS: 812, Hicky.
BYRON, LORD, GEORGE GORDON, 1788-1824:
    2269, Ciardi.
CABIN CRUISERS: 3660, Kroll.
CABINS: 822, Johnson; 823, Buchwald;
    1084, Merrill; 4098, Swenson.
CACTI: 824, Gardener; 825, Bandeira.
CAESAR, JULIUS: 2783, O'Kearney.
CAIN: 827, Cordan.
CAIRO: 828, Lerner.
CALA DEYA: 1469, Earle.
CALENDARS: 4676, Adams.
CALIFORNIA: 831, Gibbs; 3950, Stafford.
CALIGULA: 832, Updike.
CALLIGRAPHY: 834, Seferis.
CALLIXTUS I, SAINT, 217-222: 817,
    Posner.
CALORIE COUNTERS: 367, Galbraith.
CALORIES: 3980, Bonaluto.
CALVARY: 1288, Golffing; 2932,
    McDonnell.
CAMBRIDGE UNIVERSITY: 838, O'Hara.
CAMEL BELLS: 842, Pellowe.
CAMELOT: 844, Watkins.
CAMELS: 839, Derwood; 840, Merwin;
    841, Smith.
CAMERAS: 814, Honig; 6127, Hammer;
    6484, Usk.
CAMPAIGN SONGS: 847, Lemon.
CAMPAIGNS: 846, Merwin.
CAMPBELL, ROY: 375, Wright.
CAMPS: 6820, Freneau.
CANADA: 849, Birney.
CANCER: 1967, Dickey.
CANDLELIGHT: 7112, Lilly.
CANDLELIGHTERS: 854, Elmer.
CANDLES: 852, Walker; 853, Brown; 854,
    Elmer; 855, Pack; 4052, Victor.
CANDLESTICKS: 3291, Farnham.
CANE MILLS: 3084, Merchant.
CANTICLES: 859, Roseliep.
CAPACITY: 864, Updike.
CAPE COD: 430, Starbuck; 7165, Smythe.
CAPITALISM: 4506, Kenny.
CAPTIVES: 4934, Dugan.
CAR BARNS: 870, Goodman.
CARD CATALOGS: 872, Lockhart.
CARDS: 1367, Nemerov.
CARE: 873, Miles.
CAREFREE: 4378, Engels.
CARETAKERS: 874, Freeman.
CARGO TRUCKS: 1855, Neely.

CARGOS: 3252, Rago.
CARIBBEAN: 875, Hall.
CARICATURISTS: 6493, Graves.
CARILLONS: 876, Thompson.
CARING: 6052, Pudney.
CARNIVALS: 5086, Cassity.
CARROUSELS: 185, Collins.
CARTOGRAPHERS: 3646, Nemerov.
CARVING MEAT: 3482, Armour.
CARY, JOYCE: 5382, Van Horn.
CASSANDRA: 889, L'Heureux.
CASTLES: 818, Shimazaki.
CASTOR BEANS: 2195, Goldberg.
CASTRO, FIDEL: 3016, R.
CASUALTIES: 891, Hughes.
CAT NAPS: 897, Freeman.
CAT TAILS: 1435, Everson.
CATALPA TREES: 901, Bell.
CATFISH: 6915: Merrill.
CATHAY: 904, Loehlin.
CATHEDRALS: 552, Iris; 905, Miller;
   1718, Gibbs; 6626, McGinley; 7010,
   Laing.
CATS: 68, Stoutenberg; 122, Leet;
   162, Quentin; 795, Merwin; 892,
   Smith; 894, Frost; 898, Long; 899,
   Mottram; 906, Graves; 907, Hitchcock;
   1562, Abdough; 1689, Plath; 1900,
   Armour; 1901, Nickerson; 4310,
   Hughes; 4416, Hall; 5391, Levertov;
   5739, North; 6905, Richardson; 6921,
   Swenson.
CATS, CALICO: 830, Cresson.
CATS, PERSIAN: 4296, Ground.
CATS, THEATRE: 2457, Eliot.
CATS, TOM: 4968, Parkinson; 7337,
   DeJong.
CATULLUS, GAIUS VALERIUS: 1072,
   Fadiman; 6424, Zukofsky.
CAUSE: 909, Swenson.
CAUTION: 578, Ebright.
CAVELL, EDITH: 1654, Hull.
CAVES: 3140, Moraes.
CELEBRITIES: 2716, Laing.
CELIBACY: 7284, Freeman.
CELLARS: 913, Reaney; 5951, McKee.
CEMETERIES: 1594, Lowell; 1728, Gray;
   2391, Masters; 3592, Cassity; 3921,
   Rukeyser; 4387, Freeman; 5763,
   Garrigue.
CENSORSHIP: 4430, Solovay.
CENTERS: 4586, Dickey.
CHAIRS: 920, Corke; 2846, Friar;
   2918, MacKaye; 3574, Brosier; 4373,
   Kelly; 5762, Updike.
CHALLENGES: 6190, Moorhead.
CHANGE: 4450, Fein; 5196, Hedden;
   5267, Laing; 5301, Levertov.
CHANGES: 925, Weiss; 1504, Jennings.
CHANNELS: 1470, Berry.
CHAOS: 6307, Pasternak.
CHAPELS: 931, Delattre; 4374, Clark;
   6136, Cunliffe.
CHAPERONS: 2981, Armour.
CHARACTER: 4732, Mullins.
CHARADES: 932, Lougee.
CHARITY: 1432, Spacks; 5648,
   Jennings.
CHARLES IX: 2715, Nixon.
CHARM: 936, Donnelly.

CHARTRES CATHEDRAL: 944, Chandler;
   1018, Hare.
CHASING: 6965, Narasimhaswamy.
CHATEAU DE MUZOT: 945, Tomlinson.
CHATTER: 6089, Anthony.
CHECKERS: 946, Marx.
CHECK MATES: 947, Fitzsimmons.
CHECKS: 6767, Rosenfield.
CHEER: 6995, Warsaw.
CHERRIES: 5172, Root; 6770, Baro.
CHERRY TREES: 951, Schevill; 1579,
   Ranko; 2896, Motonari; 6771, Issa.
CHESTS: 6941, Maino.
CHICAGO: 955, Mary Faith; 956,
   Sandburg.
CHICKENS: 476, McCord; 957, Stafford;
   1897, Deutsch.
CHIEFS OF STATE: 166, Cane.
CHILD: 801, Frost; 836, Shapiro; 958,
   Boyson; 962, Taylor; 964, Van Doren;
   967, Cotter; 969, Chaffee; 2465,
   Richstone; 3055, Jennison; 4258,
   Friedrich; 4880, Disher; 5432,
   Hammer; 6339, Renon; 7077, Holmes;
   7156, Engle; 7369, McFarland.
CHILD - FIFTH: 1918, Bridgman.
CHILD - FIVE YEAR OLDS: 2020, Marsh.
CHILD REARING: 1750, Grenville; 5590,
   Gleason.
CHILD - SECOND: 5809, McKee; 6518,
   Gibbs.
CHILD TRAINING: 7017, Puner.
CHILD BIRTH: 3481, MacDiarmid.
CHILDHOOD: 976, Drummond de Andrade;
   977, O'Gorman; 2247, Chang; 2948,
   Merchant; 2957, Schwartz; 3749,
   Matran; 4361, Graham; 4538,
   Grenville; 5497, Senge; 5696, Nathan;
   7176, Farber.
CHILDREN: 380, Oakes; 863, Gardner;
   982, Huff; 986, Schwartz; 1194,
   Ford; 1427, Jones; 2230, Graves;
   2769, Anthony; 2815, Baxter; 2949,
   Soule; 2983, Wheeler; 2990, White;
   3051, Chadwick; 3060, Eisenlohr;
   3162, Johnston; 3185, Wood; 3293,
   Seifer; 3425, Henry; 3505,
   Coatsworth; 3520, Galbraith; 3545,
   Jaffray; 3576, White; 3987, Jacobson;
   4063, Ewing; 4517, Armour; 4672,
   Wuebker; 5090, Rittell; 5537,
   Galbraith; 5733, Fairchild; 5741,
   Galbraith; 5783, Chadwick; 5793,
   McFarland; 5978, Jaffray; 6613,
   Grenville.
CHILDREN AND DEATH: 4425, Kennedy.
CHILDREN AND ENERGY: 1715, Blackwell.
CHILDREN AND GOSSIP: 3468, Galbraith.
CHILDREN AND LOVE: 975, La Bombard.
CHILDREN AND MONEY: 888, Galbraith.
CHILDREN AND PARENTS: 290, Gohn; 6562,
   Jilaveri.
CHILDREN AND REST: 5247, Galbraith.
CHILDREN AND SLEEP: 6579, Turner.
CHILDREN AT HOME: 2814, Engle.
CHILDREN AT PLAY: 963, Cotter; 984,
   Abbe; 3452, Henley; 4464, Armour;
   4481, Bryan; 6495, Graham; 7085,
   Buck.
CHILDREN, BLIND: 651, Cotter.

CHILDREN -- DEATH AND FUTURE STATE: 3404, Logan.
CHILDREN DRESSING: 2565, Anthony.
CHILDREN -- EIGHT-YEAR-OLDS: 115, Nathan.
CHILDREN -- FIVE-YEAR-OLDS: 1995, Grenville.
CHILDREN -- FOUR-YEAR-OLDS: 2152, Hammer.
CHILDREN - GOD'S GIFT: 2729, Ignatow.
CHILDREN GROWING UP: 1436, Nelson.
CHILDREN, LOST: 6505, Kahn.
CHILDREN -- ONE-YEAR-OLDS: 4564, Updike.
CHILDREN RUNNING: 973, Frost.
CHILDREN -- THREE-YEAR-OLDS: 6445, Armknecht; 6446, Peel.
CHILDREN WALKING: 6198, Smith.
CHILDREN'S ART: 322, Douglass; 1564, Donnelly.
CHILDREN'S BOOKS: 2743, Power; 3138, Stone.
CHILDREN'S CLOTHES: 1870, Rittell.
CHILDREN'S GAMES: 989, Jerome; 5664, Lieberman.
CHILDREN'S GYMS: 1134, Rosenfield.
CHILDREN'S HOSPITALS: 7356, Cotter.
CHILDREN'S LITERATURE: 1896, Nash.
CHILDREN'S MANNERS: 3056, Armknecht; 7017, Puner.
CHILDREN'S MENUS: 988, Isler.
CHILDREN'S TOYS: 2347, Young; 6638, Patmore.
CHILDREN'S VOICES: 991, Averitt.
CHIMNEY SWEEPS: 7252, Humphries.
CHIMPANZEES: 4101, Sandeen.
CHINA: 992, Sagittarius; 2847, Moore; 3832, Balch; 4174, Lattimore; 4768, Tse-Tung.
CHINESE ART: 2964, Bynner; 5884, Rosenthal.
CHOICES: 998, Langland; 1283, Jaffray; 5016, Ponsot.
CHOIRS: 2581, Jacobs; 2608, Nathan;
CHOKECHERRIES: 1002, Montague.
CHOOSING: 5627, De Ford.
CHORES: 555, Muir; 575, Warsaw; 6431, White.
CHOU EN LAI: 344, Eff.
CHRISTENINGS: 1009, Belvin; 1010, Warwick.
CHRISTMAS: 75, Lattimore; 76, McDonnell; 151, Cotter; 1012, Magaret; 1013, Olson; 1020, McDonnell; 1024, Cummings; 2478, Nash; 2651, Patrick; 2807, Nash; 2851, Dean; 3605, Bemelmans; 4167, Tongue; 4258, Fredrich; 5324, Hughes; 6244, Elmer; 6581, McCarthy; 6685, Jacobsen; 6707, Henley; 6850, Burrows; 6984, Cotter.
CHRISTMAS AND CHILDREN: 1026, Blackwell.
CHRISTMAS AND HOME: 1130, McCarthy.
CHRISTMAS AND LIBRARIES: 6002, 6012, 6022, Spear.
CHRISTMAS AND STUDENTS: 2101, Roseliep.
CHRISTMAS AND TOYS: 6376, Freeman.
CHRISTMAS ANGELS: 3422, Stein.

CHRISTMAS AT HOME: 2611, Jeans.
CHRISTMAS CARDS: 1014, Clark.
CHRISTMAS CAROLS: 880, Maris Stella; 1951, Larsson.
CHRISTMAS DAY: 1016, Shotwell; 1017, Wadding; 2910, Grebanier; 1405, Claudel.
CHRISTMAS, DAY AFTER: 1350, Galbraith.
CHRISTMAS GIFTS: 1025, Dunn.
CHRISTMAS GREETINGS: 1019, Patrick; 2431, Sullivan; 3770, Spear; 4365, Sollis; 5486, Cogley; 5487, Swift.
CHRISTMAS IN BOSTON: 7226, Plath.
CHRISTMAS LEGENDS: 1021, 2677, McGinley.
CHRISTMAS MASSES: 6428, Warwick.
CHRISTMAS MORNING: 5909, Bock.
CHRISTMAS PAGEANTS: 4641, Pierce.
CHRISTMAS PARTIES: 4355, McGinley.
CHRISTMAS - POETRY: 6706, Moore.
CHRISTMAS QUESTIONS: 1027, Doyle.
CHRISTMAS REFLECTIONS: 5188, Sansone.
CHRISTMAS REMINDERS: 4201, Rauth.
CHRISTMAS SHOPPING: 1022, Longfellow; 5217, Spring.
CHRISTMAS SONGS: 5829, Appleton.
CHRISTMAS SYMBOL: 1028, Lennen.
CHRISTMAS TREES: 1029, Owen; 3275, Henley; 3806, Merrill; 6515, Wright.
CHRISTMAS VACATIONS: 6418, Lee.
CHRYSALIDES: 1034, Webb.
CHURCH: 718, Hutchinson; 4400, Long.
CHURCH BELLS: 3775, Gray.
CHURCH BUILDINGS: 3443, Bradford.
CHURCH SERVICES: 5539, Stephanile.
CHURCH SUPPERS: 1037, Kroll.
CHURCHES: 3699, Betjeman; 1036, Petrie.
CHURCHYARDS: 3267, Todd.
CIGAR STORES: 1039, Carroll.
CIGARETTES: 652, De Longchamps; 4142, Galbraith.
CIRCUMCISION, FEAST OF: 4717, Mary Jeremy.
CIRCUSES: 1042, Blackwell; 2081, Urdang; 5298, Moran.
CITADELS: 6721, Lindbergh.
CITIES: 342, Dufault; 595, Nathan; 1052, Heller; 1662, Burford; 2203, Weiss; 2691, Greer; 2786, Longchamps; 3892, Tomlinson; 4566, Root; 5479, Perse; 6925, Engle.
CITRUS: 1048, 1049, Isler.
CITY GATES: 593, De Longchamps.
CITY PARKS: 3386, Kelley.
CIVILIZATION: 660, Gordon; 6574, MacDiarmid.
CIVILIZED: 6994, Laing.
CLAIRVOYANCE: 1059, Stoutenburg.
CLAM DIGGERS: 1060, Eberhart; 1573, Plath.
CLASSROOMS: 4532, Bastone.
CLAUSTROPHOBIA: 1067, Rawlins.
CLAY, KENTUCKY: 1899, W.
CLEARANCE SALES: 5587, Fuller.
CLERGYMEN: 5304, Neame.
CLERTHEWS: 1071, Fadiman.
CLICHES: 1073, Davidson.
CLIMBING: 2551, Justice.
CLIPPING PAPERS, ETC: 1075, Parrish.

CLIVE, ROBERT, BARON CLIVE OF PLASSEY,
  1725-1774: 3514, Whittemore.
CLOCKS: 920, Corke; 1077, Quinn;
  1078, Walton; 1079, Sobiloff; 1080,
  Nemerov; 1307, Weiss; 1903, Richards.
CLOTHES: 1086, Rosenfield; 6998,
  Steiner.
CLOTHES CLOSETS: 1515, Blackwell;
  6951, Lazarus.
CLOTHES LINES: 2209, Levine; 3791,
  Tiempo; 7328, Miles.
CLOUDS: 1087, Sagittarius; 1091,
  Lynch; 1886, Supervielle; 4375,
  Tagliabue; 4595, Ritter; 5547,
  Dicker; 5847, Behn.
CLOWNS: 1043, Grenville; 1092,
  Guthrie; 1093, Morris; 4895,
  Patchen; 6969, Fandel.
COASTING: 2392, McNeill.
COASTS: 3474, Hagiwara.
COATS: 1098, Wood; 4089, Weiss.
COCKCROW: 7326, Scott.
COCKROACHES: 5193, Fleischer.
COCKTAILS: 1101, Salinger.
CODFISH: 6229, Nash.
CO-EXISTENCE: 519, Sagittarius.
COFFEE BREAKS: 2183, Kroll.
COFFEE HOUSES: 1530, Posner.
COGNIZANCE: 1103, Van Hise.
COINCIDENCES: 6362, Moore.
COINS: 2410, Donnelly.
COLD: 3500, Kreymborg.
COLD WAR: 1114, Starbuck.
COLD-WEATHER: 1115, Everson.
COLDS: 2852, Petrie; 5910, Usk.
COLETTE, SIDONIE GABRIELLE, 1873-1954:
  1116, Engle.
COLLEGE LIFE: 1767, Kremer.
COLLEGE PRESIDENTS: 6263, Redivivus.
COLLEGE TOWNS: 1118, Weismiller.
COLLOQUIES: 4546, Hillyer.
COLORS: 1123, Schulberg; 1124,
  Longchamps; 2413, Bailey; 4029,
  Little; 5888, Engle.
COLOSSEUM: 1125, Watkins.
COLUMBA, ST.: 1126, McGinley.
COLUMBUS, CHRISTOPHER: 904, Loehlin.
COLUMBUS, CHRISTOPHER, 1446?-1502:
  1030, Wallace.
COLUMNS: 861, Valery.
COME: 3006, Sarton.
COMIC BOOKS: 53, Honig.
COMMANDMENTS: 5851, Mary Faith.
COMMAS: 4896, Smith.
COMMITTEES: 1142, Gaertner; 1143,
  Cully; 3153, Chadwick; 6408,
  Parrish.
COMMUNION: 1145, Ward; 1146, Pierce;
  1954, Cotter; 1955, Delattre.
COMMUNISM: 4506, Kenny; 5514,
  Sagittarius.
COMMUTERS: 61, Dickinson; 908, Small;
  1147, Raskin.
COMPASSION: 1154, Delattre; 1155,
  Eckhardt; 1533, Lindbergh; 3412,
  Davidson.
COMPATABILITY: 886, Hammer.
COMPLAINTS: 1158, Merrill.
COMPLIMENTS: 1162, 3164,
  Richstone.

COMPREHENSION: 2202, Rilke.
COMPROMISES: 6081, Nash.
COMPUTERS: 6789, Solomon.
CONCENTRATION CAMPS: 1383, Celan.
CONCEPTION: 1167, Ponsot; 1879,
  Dever.
CONCERTS: 2370, Vazakas; 2848, Arnold.
CONDENSATIONS OF BOOKS: 1171, Sweet;
  4312, Wall.
CONDIMENTS: 5522, Updike; 6460,
  Lamport.
CONFESSIONS: 1172, Stone; 1173,
  Wheeler; 1727, Redman; 5954, Collins.
CONFIDANTES: 6964, Krausz.
CONFIDENCE: 1099, Witt.
CONFORMITY: 1177, Kahn.
CONFUSION: 1178, Cregeen.
CONGO: 1179, 3376, 5151, Smith.
CONGRATULATIONS: 1180, Wolf.
CONJURATION: 1183, Miles.
CONNOLLY, VI: 6853, Stewart.
CONSCIENCE: 1186, Lilly; 1187,
  Raiziss; 1189, Usk; 1190, Armour;
  6477, Galbraith; 7329, Malody.
CONSCIENCES: 639, Longfellow.
CONSERVATIVES: 1192, Armour.
CONSTANCY: 518, Lineaweaver.
CONSTELLATIONS: 1204, Rizzardi.
CONSTRUCTION: 4073, Koehler.
CONTEMPLATION: 1207, Galbraith.
CONTENTMENT: 1208, M. Davida; 6294,
  Lilly.
CONTINENTS: 6367, Brulkar.
CONTRADICTIONS: 220, Eberhart.
CONTRARY THINGS: 1211, Mack.
CONVALESCENTS: 56, English; 1213,
  Armour.
CONVENTIONS: 1216, Brown; 2498,
  Emmons.
CONVERSATION: 1218, Matthews; 2285,
  Morris; 3028, Braun; 5699, Gleason.
CONVERSATIONS: 1219, Sarton; 1220,
  Cotter; 1221, De Vito; 3056,
  Armknecht; 5790, Goodman; 6250,
  Blackwell.
CONVICTION: 1222, De Leeuw.
COOKERY: 4346, Bracken.
COOKING: 3680, Lamb.
COOKS: 186, Blackwell; 1140,
  Pennington; 1224, Lamport; 5644,
  Galler; 6300, Sitwell.
COPERNICUS: 1318, Glaze.
CORAL: 1228, Char; 1229, Pierce.
CORN: 3008, Miles; 3113, Myers.
CORONADO, FRANCISCO VASQUEZ de: 5097,
  Scott.
CORONATIONS: 1231, Watkins.
CORRALS: 1591, Miles.
CORRESPONDENCE: 1236, Kreymborg; 5261,
  Eisenlohr.
CORRIDORS: 1238, Gunn.
COSMOS: 1240, Cane.
COST OF LIVING: 1811, Schiff.
COSTUMES: 1829, Golden.
COTTON FIELDS: 1241, Hicky.
COUGARS: 902, Huff.
COUNSELING: 4061, Kanfer.
COUNTING: 5897, Armour.
COUNTRIES: 2718, Hull.
COUNTRY STORES: 1255, Thomson.

COURAGE: 1637, Lilly; 2324, Fosdick,
  2404, Lieberman.
COURBET, GUSTAVE, 1819-1877: 6,
  O'Hara.
COURTESY: 2041, Mary Ada.
COURTHOUSES: 5260, Rock.
COURTING: 3282, Canady.
COURTLINESS: 1261, Swan.
COURTNEY, CLINT: 3610, Nash.
COURTSHIP: 1262, Jaffray; 2588,
  Lieberman; 3277, Good H.
COUSINS: 1677, Petrie; 4892,
  Jacobsen; 6722, Frezza.
COVERS: 5683, Armour.
COWARDS: 4980, Werner.
COWBOYS: 1265, Barker; 1266, Engle.
COWERING: 3169, Coblentz.
COWS: 1263, Lape; 4171, Landau; 5189,
  M. M. Sophie; 6067, Sullivan; 7040
  Coatsworth.
CRAB APPLES: 1268, Zilles; 1269,
  Kroll.
CRABBING: 1270, Levine.
CRADLES: 4612, Whitman.
CRANE, HART: 2489, Lowenfels; 4202,
  Loche; 7293, Lowell.
CRANES: 1272, Watkins; 7108,
  Jacobson.
CRAYFISH: 7109, Wallace.
CRAZY: 5933, Gale.
CREATION: 1273, Harrington; 1274,
  Cutler; 1275, Pack; 3239, Bynner;
  5843, Lilly.
CRECHES: 2882, MacNeil.
CREDIT CARDS: 3506, Barker.
CREEDS: 5499, Burket; 5535, Elmer.
CREEKS: 1278, Brand; 4109, Schierloh.
CREMATION: 341, Pillin.
CREMATORIES: 1279, Ashman.
CRICKETS: 1280, Cane.
CRIME: 53, Honig.
CRISES: 1281, Wagoner.
CRITICISM: 5997, Spear.
CRITICS: 1817, Standish; 2509,
  Sandburg; 4577, Lamport; 5281,
  Rosenthal.
CROCODILES: 1286, Jacobson.
CROOKS: 2780, Jaffray.
CROQUET: 6709.
CROSS: 70, Smith; 1287, Bing; 1289,
  Russo; 1637, Lilly; 2317, Cunningham;
  2830, Pierce; 7300, Sider.
CROSSROADS: 373, Blackburn.
CROWDS: 2765, Atherton; 4596, Russo.
CROWS: 910, McNeill; 1293, Dufault;
  1294, Grenville; 5531, Berry; 6805,
  Griffith; 7187, Merrill.
CROW'S NEST: 1295, Armknecht.
CRUCIFIXES: 1296, Shapiro; 4434,
  Logan.
CRUCIFIXION: 1203, Donnelly; 1282,
  Sandeen; 1290, Patrick; 1379, Jones;
  2236, Nichols; 2508, 2510, Pierce,
  5049, Mullins; 5621, Unruh; 6678,
  Hazo.
CRUISERS: 3660, Kroll.
CRUISES: 1366, Nash.
CRYING: 4401, De Jong; 5801, Guri.
CUCKOLDS: 1305, Koshland.
CUCKOO CLOCKS: 1306, Gorman.

CULTS: 6458, Neame.
CULTURE: 1127, Moore.
CUPID: 187, Rattray; 1310, Schwartz.
CURES: 1311, Swan.
CURIOSITY: 1312, Reid.
CURTAINS: 1317, Sagittarius; 3223,
  Dugan.
CURVE-EDGES: 4497, Evans.
CUSTER, GEORGE ARMSTRONG, 1836-1876:
  374, Stafford.
CUSTOMS: 4681, Miner.
CUTTING WOOD: 4589, Dickey.
CYCLES: 1319, Kahn.
CYCLISTS: 1321, Morris.
CYNICS: 1322, Galbraith; 1372, Moore.
CYPRUS: 1324, Sagittarius; 2167,
  Lukacs.
DAFFODILS: 2580, Stolorow.
DAGUERREOTYPES: 1327, Parry.
DAILY BREAD: 1248, Kahn.
DAISIES: 2810, Wright.
DALLIANCE: 3005, Brasier.
DAMNED, THE: 1663, Koval.
DAMS: 604, Moses.
DANCE: 1332, Zweig.
DANCERS: 63, Tyler; 1336, Nemerov;
  1516, Tagliabue; 1757, Lieberman;
  2293, Koch; 3195, Weinstein; 4715,
  Carruth; 5127, Horiguchi; 6050,
  Nemerov.
DANCES: 686, Duncan; 1338, Greer; 1656,
  Blackwell; 2407, Galler; 5582, Miner;
  7292, Farnham.
DANCING: 1331, Rawlins; 1333, Cotter;
  1566, Ciardi; 2860, Lilly; 3195,
  Weinstein; 4536, Gleason.
DANCING CLASSES: 2230, Graves.
DANCING IN HEAVEN: 2860, Lilly.
DANGEROUS DAY: 3406, Wagoner.
DANIEL: 2098, Hay.
DANIELS, LORD: 2726, Cuney.
DANTE: 5145, O'Gorman.
DAPHNIS: 1340, Witt.
DARK: 6885, Smith.
DARKNESS: 190, McIlnay; 1343, Corke;
  1347, Cully; 2857, Barker; 3515,
  Elmer; 4591, Merwin; 5141, Kessler;
  5536, Elmer; 6955, Meyer.
DARNING EGGS: 7276, Updike.
DARROW, CLARENCE: 1062, Masters.
DARWIN, CHARLES, 1809-1882: 934,
  Whittemore.
DATING: 4048, Chadwick; 4313, Wheeler;
  6046, Jacobson; 6988, Goodman.
DAUGHTERS: 1352, de la Mare; 1904,
  de Vito; 2878, Singleton; 4169,
  Bannon; 4250, McCarthy; 4325,
  Bracken; 4463, Hamilton; 5312, Engle;
  6573, Fowler.
DAUGHTERS WITHOUT MOTHERS: 1353,
  Mansfield.
DAVID: 1354, Wright; 1355, Rich.
DAWN: 276, Sandeen; 390, Friedrich;
  391, Jerome; 557, Coblentz; 1356,
  Cardarelli; 1360, Chaffee; 1536,
  Spark; 3132, Averitt; 3265, Benon;
  6097, Carruth; 7133, Chadwick.
DAY: 4040, Smith.
DAY DREAMS: 5786, Stewart.
DAY BREAK: 1362, Embirokos.

DAYLIGHT: 2988, Nicholl; 3171,
  Cotter.
DAYS: 663, Koehler; 1032, Zlotnik;
  3966, Jacobsen; 4684, Astier.
DAYTIME: 2988, Nicholl.
DEACONS: 1372, Moore.
DEAD, THE: 1373, Heymann; 5099,
  Johnson.
DEAD BODIES: 4854, Graybeal.
DEAD BOY: 3718, Neame.
DEAF-MUTES: 1376, Jacobsen.
DEAFNESS: 1384, Holmes; 2044, Silkin;
  3523, Finkel; 4462, Abse.
DEATH: 83, Sarton; 195, Laing; 1384,
  Holmes; 1385, Tate; 1392, Kizer;
  1866, Griffith; 1976, Ungaretti;
  2328, Taylor; 2442, Reznikoff; 2511,
  Richardson; 2893, Coblentz; 3213,
  Gass; 3528, Gaines; 3728,
  Alisjahbana; 3812, Rexroth; 3959,
  Hall; 4097, Nardi; 4141, Philbrick;
  4240, Hall; 4256, Davidson; 4447,
  O'Gorman; 4500, Hudson; 4738, Hymes;
  4809, Orr; 5215, Kessler; 5305,
  Lattimore; 5368, Delattre; 5561,
  Swenson; 5596, Hall; 5857, 5859,
  Constantinoff; 6480, Van Doren;
  6848, di Giovanni; 7080, Coblentz.
DEATH AND DYING: 2348, Singer.
DEATH AND LOVE: 1439, Longchamps.
DEATH AND MUSIC: 442, Grayer.
DEATH AT SEA: 2046, Thomas.
DEATH, BITTERNESS OF: 636, Kreiser.
DEATH - CHILDREN: 965, Betjeman.
DEATH, DREAMS OF: 4872, Wilson.
DEATH - GRANDMOTHERS: 3413, Greenwood.
DEATH - NEIGHBORS: 1387, de Vito.
DEATH - NUNS: 1390, Stein.
DEATH - POETS: 1391, Joshi.
DEATH, SHADOW OF: 2970, Goldin.
DEATH SIGNS: 5612, Dickey.
DEATH, SONG OF: 4409, Walton.
DEATH - SONS: 2091, Richardson.
DEATH, VISION OF: 6801, Gunn.
DEATH WISH: 1401, Nicholl.
DEATH - WIVES: 3227, Legler.
DEATH'S TRIUMPH: 6680, Borden.
DECATUR, ALABAMA: 2014, Rukeyser.
DECEMBER: 1403, Richardson; 4826,
  Nicholl.
DECISIONS: 79, Edelman; 1410, Roethke.
DECOR: 4755, Richstone.
DEEDS: 7080, Coblentz; 7278, Pierce.
DEER: 1413, Engle; 1423, Mundell;
  2730, Fiedler; 3615, Vance.
DEER HUNTS: 1424, Jerome.
DEFEAT: 4291, Eaton.
DEFENESTRATION: 1426, Lister.
DEFENSELESS: 1429, Clark.
DEGREES, HONORARY: 3016, R.
DEITIES: 1433, Updike.
DE LA TOUR, GEORGES: 5542, Todd.
DELAYS: 1434, Krieger.
DELILAH: 1437, Clark.
DELINQUENCY: 1438, Pierce.
DELIVERY ROOMS: 1440, Howes.
DEMETER: 1442, Gibbs.
DEMOCRATS: 7361, Coffin.
DEMONS: 1443, Kaneko.
DEMOSTHENES: 2967, Gottlieb.

DENS: 4597, Armour.
DENTISTS: 2226, Miner; 6405, Twiggs.
DEPARTURES: 1445, Levertov; 1447,
  Plath; 1448, Ackerson; 1449,
  Van Doren; 4625, Stafford.
DEPOSITS: 3702, Hall.
DEPRESSION: 1450, Carruth; 3437, Bell.
DEPRIVATION: 2191, Perry.
DESCENT: 1452, Kinnell.
DESEGREGATION: 1454, Calkins.
DESERT WIND: 7161, Carlson.
DESERTS: 397, Bock; 1455, Chamberlin;
  1456, Collins; 1458, Martinek.
DESIGNS: 1460, Everwine; 5901, Levine.
DESIRE: 1462, Stepanchev; 2936,
  Hughes; 7249, Johnson.
DESKS: 496, Saunders; 5693, Usk.
DESPAIR: 613, Grenville; 1416, Goldin;
  1826, Eckhardt; 4611, Duncan.
DESSERTS: 6790, Merchant.
DESTINY: 4360, Pasternak; 5083,
  Carrier.
DESTRUCTION: 2905, Coblentz; 6365,
  Eich.
DETAIL: 2850, Stafford.
DETECTIVE STORIES: 3964, Gordon.
DETERMINATION: 1466, Moorhead.
DEVIL: 1468, Hay; 4835, Cane; 5228,
  Cully.
DE VOTO, BERNARD: 2055, Ciardi.
DEW: 3378, Stuart; 6343, Renon; 7065,
  Mary Honora.
DIABETES: 2286, White.
DIALOGUES: 1472, Garrigue; 1474,
  Goldberg; 6677, Aiken.
DIAMOND CUTTERS: 1478, Rich.
DIAMOND HUNTERS: 1480, Pierce.
DIANA: 1481, Fiscalini.
DIARIES: 1482, Mary Gilbert.
DICKINSON, EMILY, 1830-1886:   1404,
  Kreymborg; 1696, Huff; 6188, 6544,
  Moffitt.
DICTATORS: 1484, Sagittarius.
DIDACTICISM: 1485, Stepanchev.
DIETING: 1874, Hammer; 1898, Armour;
  5681, Schlitzer.
DIETS: 1895, Sutin; 2340, Chadwick;
  7058, Chadwick.
DIFFERENCE: 1486, Hecht.
DIKES: 2758, Ignatow.
DINERS: 1492, Kroll.
DINING: 1493, Henry.
DINNER: 3498, Goodman.
DIRECTIONS: 1640, Taylor.
DIRGES: 1496, O'Gorman; 1497, Ostroff;
  1498, Roethke; 4039, Wrenn.
DISAPPEARANCES: 3531, Stanford.
DISASTER: 5434, Chapin; 6440, Miles.
DISCIPLINE: 2935, Usk; 3700, Grenville.
DISCIPLINING CHILDREN: 5753, Collins.
DISCOVERIES: 77, Sullivan; 113,
  Johnson; 246, Char.
DISCUSSION: 1417, Moore.
DISGRACE: 553, Papatzonis.
DISGUISES: 4148, Carleton.
DISH WASHING: 1506, Schiff; 5641,
  Jaffray.
DISHWASHERS: 2937, Armour.
DISSEMBLERS: 1508, Mary Honora.
DISTANCE: 1510, Bat-Miriam.

DISTRIBUTION: 3701, Eisenlohr.
DIVERS: 1513, 2537, Hilberry; 4421, Haring; 6298, Rosenthal.
DIVES: 1514, Pierce.
DIVING: 2573, Kilkeary.
DIVINITIES: 1107, Wright.
DIVORCE: 1748, Merriam.
DO-IT-YOURSELF: 886, Hammer; 6699, Usk.
DOBY, LARRY: 681, Nash.
DOCKS: 1558, Koch.
DOCTORS OF PHILOSOPHY: 4779, Steiner.
DOCTORS' WAITING ROOMS: 2187, Hammer.
DOGGEREL: 1764, Warsaw.
DOGS: 920, Corke; 1444, Hale; 1531, Smith; 3160, Van Duyn; 3411, Bracken; 3421, Anthony; 3616, Good H; 4123, Merrill; 4548, Chadwick; 4750, Armour; 5066, Bellows; 5365, Jacobson; 5491, Smith; 5619, Romine; 5867, Schluneger; 6094, Avison; 6945, Shenton.
DOLLS: 232, Ponsot; 994, Lal; 2301, Landeweer; 3525, Talman.
DOMES: 1535, Berrigan; 2184, Singer.
DONEGAL: 5264, Rorty.
DONKEYS: 2641, Pierce; 4687, Mundell.
DONNE, JOHN, 1573-1631: 6842, McCandless;
DOOM: 1368, Friedrich; 6464, White.
DOOR KNOBS: 1546, Schiff.
DOORBELLS: 2327, Crawford.
DOORMATS: 5207, Jaffray.
DOORS: 1544, 1545, Creeley; 5783, Chadwick; 5982, Armour.
DOUBT: 5787, Buchwald.
DOUGLASS, FREDERICK, 1817?-1895: 2165, Norton.
DOVES: 1555, Barker; 1557, Mohanty; 3848, Basch.
DOZERS: 1561, Spring.
DRAGONS: 608, Saron; 5387, Steel.
DRAMA, GREEK: 2411, Weales.
DREAMERS: 1574, Freeman.
DREAMING: 129, Wright; 334, Steinman; 462, Gill; 712, Bruce; 774, Lister; 1467, Barnstone; 1494, Wright; 1523, De Jong; 1573, Plath; 1577, Boyle; 1593, Moss; 2186, Justice; 2727, Simpson; 2797, Van Doren; 2827, Pillin; 4322, Lape.
DREAMS: 1566, Ciardi; 1567, Miles; 1575, Moss; 1576, Nash; 1578, Conklin; 1831, Jagliabue; 2093, Merchant; 2148, Court; 2840, Eberhart; 2923, Wolf; 2955, Baldwin; 3218, Barker; 3245, Solomon; 3527, Jenkins; 4567, Eberhart; 5013, Tyler; 5019, Rodite; 5171, Colvin; 5781, D; 5842, Murray; 6321, Stebbing; 6781, Stuart; 6787, Armknecht; 6986, Nathan.
DREAMS, REALITY OF: 3992, Freeman.
DREDGES: 868, Rainer.
DRESS UP: 5100, Domoff.
DRESS-UP: 3684, Jaffray.
DRESSES: 35, Richstone; 3057, Alkus.
DRESSING: 1580, Holmes; 3967, Schiff.
DRESSMAKERS: 1581, Smith.
DRIFTWOOD: 1583, Isler.

DRINKERS: 2360, Smith.
DRINKING: 885, Burke.
DRIVERS: 707, Meredith.
DRIVERS' SIGNALS: 837, Power.
DRIVEWAYS: 4572, Chadwick.
DROWNED: 30, Dejong; 1586, Brown; 1819, Merwin; 4164, di Giovanni.
DROWNED WOMAN: 1587, Hughes.
DRUGS: 4051, Galbraith.
DRUGSTORES: 6601, Singer.
DRUNKEDNESS: 1367, Nemerov.
DRUNKS: 2980, Jerome.
DRYADS: 4502, Plath.
DUCKS: 7066, Prommel.
DULLES, JOHN FOSTER: 1072, Fadiman; 2803, Jones.
DUNCES: 1595, Van Doren.
DUNES: 191, Stork.
DUSK: 2699, Jacobson.
DUST: 143, Hagelstange.
DUTCH TREATS: 6732, Raskin.
DYING: 1382, Nemerov; 1393, Howes; 1600, Roethke; 2714, Grossman; 6357, Roethke; 7332, Singer.
EARLINESS: 1607, Deutsch.
EARRINGS: 1617, Cassity.
EARTH: 1618, McGhee; 1620, Satyarthi; 1623, Frost; 1624, Stuart; 1626, McNeill; 1824, Burford, 4284, Longfellow; 4379, Merrill; 6308, Hess; 6865, Morris.
EARTHBOUND: 671, Goodman.
EARTHQUAKES: 1629, Shiffert.
EAST BERLIN: 1106, MacInnes.
EAST RIVER: 1631, Balliett.
EASTER: 569, Freeman; 641, Patrick; 1041, Mullins; 1632, Laing; 1633, Swartz; 1634, O'Gorman; 1635, Patrick; 1636, Beloof; 1638, America; 1639, Herbert; 1957, Jellema; 2761, Palmer; 3895, Cotter; 5672, Merrill; 6588, Stuart; 6858, O'Connell.
EATING: 272, Russo; 1199, Eisenlohr; 1643, Johnston; 2204, Coles.
ECCE HOMO: 1645, Patrick.
ECHO AND SOUND: 5885, Loeser.
ECHOES: 6844, Middleton.
ECONOMIC ASSISTANCE: 1191, Neame.
ECONOMICS: 5430, Belvin.
EDEN: 5804, Lilly.
EDEN, GARDEN OF: 1651, Earle.
EDIBLE PLANTS: 196, Hammer.
EDITORS: 4297, Ulman, De Paul.
EDMAN, IRWIN, 1896-1954: 2868, Freeman.
EDUCATION: 38, Jennison; 5897, Armour.
EDUCATION, HIGHER: 4975, Heafield.
EDUCATION OF CHILDREN: 5093, Gaskill.
EDUCATION OF WOMEN: 6271, Dickey.
EDWARDS, JONATHAN, 1703-1758: 6334, McGinley.
EGGS: 683, Moss; 4191, Avery.
EGLANTINE: 1657, Dejong.
EGO: 1659, Solum.
EGOS: 1658, Booth; 3061, Pedrick; 3993, Warsaw.
EGOTISTS: 1660, Galbraith; 1661, Stefanile.
EGRETS: 7110, Thomas.
ELECT, THE: 1663, Koval.
ELECTION YEAR: 1665, Lee.

ELECTIONS: 1664, Gustafson; 1912, Jennison; 2352, Kanfer.

ELECTRICITY: 3899, Hammer.

ELECTROENCEPHALOGRAPH: 1666, Thornton.

ELEGIES: 1667, Berrigan; 1669, Boultenhouse; 1670, Ciardi; 1671, Coxe; 1673, Rosenthal; 1675, Wagoner; 1681, Morse; 3253, Stefanile; 5692, Moss.

ELEPHANTS: 1685, Eff.

ELEVATORS: 3287, Rose.

ELIOT, THOMAS STEARNS: 2102, Plutzik; 4512, Weales; 5286, Gordon.

ELIZABETHAN MAIDENS: 1688, Bevington.

ELLESMERELAND: 1690, Birney.

ELOCUTION: 1691, Fleming.

EMANUEL, VICTOR: 6859, Norse.

EMERSON, RALPH WALDO, 1803-1882: 1694, Kroll.

EMIGRES: 1695, Burrows.

EMMAUS ROAD: 5320, Cotter.

EMOTIONS: 1873, Ireland; 4219, Sobilofy; 6463, Phillips.

EMPERORS: 2663, Natsume.

EMTINESS: 1619, Slavitt; 6783, Scott.

ENCOUNTERS: 1705, Clancy; 3697, Gardner.

END: 6380, Carter.

ENDS: 5243, Pomeroy.

ENDYMION: 2463, Cassity.

ENEMIES: 1714, Morse; 2107, Bock; 4950, Turnoy; 5716, Delattre.

ENERGY: 1715, Blackwell; 6241, Warsaw.

ENGINES: 1716, Gibbs.

ENGLAND: 6016, Spear.

ENGLISH LANGUAGE: 3926, Armour; 4266, Nash.

ENGLISH TEACHERS: 1234, Naeame; 1720, Whittemore.

ENLISTED MEN: 1723, Graves.

ENORMITY: 4139, Nash.

ENTERTAINERS: 1491, Turner.

ENTERTAINMENT: 50, Kessler.

ENTHUSIASM: 4944, Armour; 5882, Cooper.

ENTRANCES: 7289, Wagoner.

ENVY: 7350, Graham.

EPIGRAMS: 3045, Jaffray.

EPIPHANY: 1726, Powers.

EPITAPHS: 7036, Plath; 1729, Mellichamp; 1731, Morgan; 1733, Wagoner; 1734, Walton; 2042, Solovay.

EQUALITY: 5868, Ciardi.

EQUATIONS: 1603, Speiser; 1604, White.

EQUINOX: 1741, Balliett.

EROS: 1744, Cully.

ERRORS: 4531, Witt.

ESCAPES: 4236, Krieger.

ESCHATOLOGY: 1606, Delattre.

ETCETERA: 1181, Lemon.

ETERNAL LIFE: 371, Coblentz.

ETERNITY: 2443, Dodge; 2550, Coblentz; 3508, Howe; 4218, Angoff; 4673, Lilly; 5589, Weaver; 5752, Van Hise; 6063, Ratliff; 7378, Lilly.

ETIQUETTE: 2475, Merchant.

ETRURIA: 1756, Viereck.

EUROPA: 1758, Guthrie.

EUROPE: 2841, Moreljono; 4013, Larraud.

EURYDICE: 4769, Todd.

EVANGELISTS: 5031, Bentley; 6923, Kumin.

EVE: 1759, Kay; 1782, Hoskins; 1797, Scrutton; 2266, Warwick; 2555, Nickerson; 5416, Mary Gilbert; 6453, Eberhart; 6667, Clark.

EVENING: 4045, Long.

EVENING GOWNS: 493, Emmons.

EVENINGS: 6262, Pe.

EVERGREENS: 1776; Langland; 1777, Bryan.

EVIL: 2826, Coblentz; 3683, Pierce.

EVILDOERS: 3169, Coblentz.

EXCELSIOR: 1788, Crews.

EXCHANGE: 1793, Waddington.

EXCUSES: 3276, Chadwick; 5248, Rosenthal.

EXECUTIVES: 5182, Workman.

EXILES: 1892, Rubin; 1803, Wolf.

EXISTENCE: 2274, Morabadi.

EXISTENTIALISM: 1805, Tracy.

EXPECTATIONS: 1809; Holmes; 7377, De Jong.

EXPERIENCE: 1070, Lee.

EXPLORATIONS: 255, Laing.

EXPLORERS: 1813, Brooks; 3867, Rockwell; 7111, Honig.

EXTINCT ANIMALS: 4380, Updike.

EYE LASHES: 7369, McFarland.

EYELIDS: 5306, Bagg; 1818, O'Hara.

EYES: 755, Nash; 1815, Beneley; 4274, Hollander; 5089, Turnoy; 5513, Squires.

FABLES: 1821, Starbuck.

FACES: 586, Moffitt; 1827, Merwin; 2144, Jacobsen; 2188, Bell; 3568, Justice; 4539, Souster.

FACTORIES: 1832, Mayo.

FACULTY CLUBS: 253, 2593, 4785, 5745, Jones.

FAILURE: 4498, Cuomo.

FAILURE IN COLLEGE: 4498, Cuomo.

FAIN, FERRIS: 5079, Nash.

FAIRIES: 1836, Kunz.

FAIRY GODMOTHERS: 5844, Moss.

FAIRY TALES: 5137, Ellis; 6604, Zimmerman.

FAITH: 854, Elmer; 896, Reid; 1145, Ward; 1837, McGovern; 2692, Barker; 3237, Rubin; 4195, Bathgate; 4652, Trent; 6194, North; 6358, 6476, Pierce; 6842, McCandless; 7178, Patrick.

FALL: 435, Friedrich; 554, Thomas; 729, Collins; 862, MacNeice; 1839, Pack; 1840, Petrie; 1842, Wilbur; 1843, Montague; 2363, Moses; 2899, MacDiarmid; 5950, Rainer; 6794, Hearst; 6717, Mayo.

FALL-OUT: 3585, Merriam.

FALLING, FEAR OF: 1889, Gibson.

FALLOUT: 1846, Slemp.

FAME: 2109, Freeman; 2221, Coblentz; 2641, Pierce; 6968, Hammer.

FAMILIAR FACES: 4381, Lister.

FAMILIES: 349, Hillyer; 1850, Hagiwara; 1852, Huws; 1853, Birnbaum; 1854, Richstone; 1918, Bridgman; 4708, Singer.

FAMILY RESEMBLANCES: 2446, De Vito.

FAMINE: 1856, Everson.

FANCY: 2342, Whitman.

FANTASY: 208, Lilly; 5114, Lee.
FAR PLACES: 5231, Stafford.
FAREWELLS: 131, Graham; 1859, Tze-
   Chiang; 1924, Baro; 2006, Howard;
   2732, Rosenfield; 5028, Mary Jeremy;
   6531, Hoskins; 6980, Balch; 7280,
   Church.
FARM SALES: 1864, Rauth.
FARMERS: 1868, Duncan; 6786,
   Eisenlohr; 1867, Wright.
FARMERS' WIVES: 1865, Collins; 1866,
   Griffith.
FARMING: 2357, Kelley; 2678, Jennison;
   6612, Rutledge.
FARMS: 1860, Fleming; 1861,
   Harrington; 1862, Todd; 1863,
   Stafford; 2373, Hearst; 2400, Booth;
   4665, Nash.
FARMSTEADS: 1068, Dell.
FASHIONS: 126, Cutler; 949, Armstrong;
   1958, Thorson; 4234, France.
FAT WOMEN: 1875, Carruth.
FATE: 1877, Rothenberg.
FATHER-DAUGHTER RELATIONSHIPS: 2353,
   Simpson.
FATHERS: 965, Betjeman; 1326, Francis;
   1670, Ciardi; 1837, McGovern; 1881,
   Gottlieb; 1883, Raiziss; 1884,
   Petrie; 1885, Dickey; 1919, Armour;
   2003, Stepanchev; 2068, Gall; 2075,
   Poster; 2094, Gold; 2353, Simpson;
   2485, Stone; 2769, Anthony; 2823,
   Masters; 3129, Heath; 3247, Sandeen;
   3996, Haber; 3999, Sarton; 4376,
   Wood; 4570, Young; 5000, Wright;
   5654, Stockdale; 5854, Amihai; 5857,
   Constantinoff; 5875, Justice; 6393,
   Henry; 6563, O'Gorman; 6638,
   Patmore; 7042, Bogin; 7352, Kelley.
FATHER'S DAY: 6503, Frazee-Bower.
FATHERS AND SONS: 1487, Chadwick.
FAULKNER, WILLIAM, 1897-1962: 3446,
   Fadiman.
FAULT-FINDING: 1260, Raskin.
FAULTS: 172, Patrice.
FAUNS: 6489, Cohen.
FEAR: 1888, Kanfer; 1913, Jennison;
   2898, Freeman; 3014, Laing; 4195,
   Bathgate; 4628, Coblentz; 5505,
   Clark; 5386, Laing; 6038, Gordon;
   6318, Stefanile; 7137, Scovel.
FEARS: 1887, King.
FEATHERS: 316, Nemerov; 1892, Goddard.
FEBRUARY: 3877, Gillis.
FEELING: 5269, Duncan.
FEET: 2849, Murphy.
FENCES: 1909, Houston; 6396,
   Zimmerman.
FENCING: 2787, Updike.
FENWICK, LADY ALICE: 5435, Burrows.
FERRAR, ROBERT: 3777, Hughes.
FERRIER, KATHLEEN: 3143, Fawcett.
FESTIVALS: 1910, Kitagawa.
FESTIVITIES: 4332, Dickey.
FEVER: 829, Reid; 1911, Graves; 7341,
   Kinnell.
FEW: 6982, Pasternak.
FICTION: 4316, Ciardi.
FIELD MARSHALS: 1915, Coxe.
FIELDS: 1921, Nathan.

FIGUREHEADS: 1922, Stallman.
FIGURES: 1920, Garrigue.
FILES: 2927, Seifer.
FILING: 3192, Parrish.
FILING CABINETS: 1925, Schlitzer.
FINANCE, PERSONAL: 1929, Talman.
FINDERS: 1932, Richardson.
FINGERPRINTS: 2572, Smith.
FINGERS: 1935, Traad.
FINNISH DEAD: 4300, Walsh.
FIRE: 1736, Plath; 2194, Alterman;
   2802, Laing; 5396, Richardson.
FIREFLIES: 1941, Cotter; 2781, Frost.
FIREPLACES: 7160, Merrill.
FIRES: 1943, Hale; 5038, Merwin; 5651,
   Davison.
FIREWOOD: 1774, Fisher.
FIRST-BORN: 6590, Parrish
FIRST FAMILIES: 940, Gleason.
FISH: 507, Plutzik; 857, Carruth;
   1643, Johnston; 3888, Philbrick;
   5551, Nash.
FISHER, GALEN, 1873-1955: 6548,
   Harkness.
FISHERMEN: 219, Ellis; 1825, Hollerer;
   1986, Glazier; 1987, Savage; 1988,
   Merwin; 1989, Pinkney; 2617, Hicky;
   3894, Ellis; 7024, Smith; 7241,
   Warsaw.
FISHING: 254, Adams; 2955, Ellis; 6096,
   Landeweer; 6688, Todd.
FISHSTATIONS: 4383, Gale.
FISH VENDORS: 1985, Meredith.
FLAGPOLES: 1998, Carruth.
FLAME: 2323, Patrick; 4543, Carter.
FLATTERY: 1999, Galbraith.
FLEAS: 1532, Landweer.
FLESH: 466, McGahey; 4830, Gunn.
FLIES: 2028, Otis; 4287, Edey; 5611,
   Blackburn.
FLIGHT: 5011, Clower.
FLIGHTS: 2115, Abbe.
FLIRTATION: 5485, Alkus.
FLOODS: 96, Merwin; 99, Lehmann; 1196,
   Chu; 2013, Carter.
FLOORS: 6261, Yamanoguchi.
FLORENCE, ITALY: 2015, Nims; 2016,
   Norse; 6960, Norse.
FLORIDA: 2018, Moss.
FLOWER POTS: 2022, Shimon.
FLOWERS: 146, Beach; 326, Kunitz; 1153,
   Gill; 1722, Subbarao; 1736, Plath;
   1916, Galler; 2022, Shimoni; 2026,
   Berrigan; 3003, Hanes; 5517,
   Galbraith; 5798, Young; 6143, Scott;
   6756, Rudolph; 7168, Lineaweaver;
   7192, Morrison.
FLUTES: 266, Ryskind; 5434, Chapin.
FOG: 1609, Smythe; 2031, Merwin; 3077,
   Palen; 3257, Gregor; 5142, Witt.
FOGHORNS: 1647, Whitt; 2032, Merwin.
FOLK TALES: 3865, De Vito.
FOLLOWING: 981, Kraft.
FOOD: 2034, Duncan; 2420, Fabstein;
   6226, Nash.
FOOTBALL: 2434, Emmons.
FOOTBALL GAMES: 3579, Rosenfield.
FORD, HENRY, 1863-1947: 350,
   Stoutenburg.
FORD FOUNDATION: 6331, Ryskind.

FOREBEARS: 349, Hillyer.
FOREIGN: 2110, Bernard.
FOREIGN AFFAIRS: 67, Harvey; 2120,
  Kunitz.
FOREIGN AID: 2228, Crumpet; 2309,
  Jones; 5423, Sagittarius; 6757,
  Ryskind.
FOREIGN CUSTOMS: 89, Merwin.
FOREIGN RELATIONS: 344, Eff; 2163,
  Sagittarius.
FORENAMES: 3147, Updike.
FORESIGHT: 4482, Golffing.
FORESTS: 234, Shaw; 793, Barker;
  2121, Nissenson; 2122, McCulloch;
  2200, Mandelbaum; 3242, Olson.
FORGETTING: 1814, Pratt; 3535, Clark;
  7355, Galbraith.
FORGIVENESS: 337, Giordan; 1432,
  Spacks; 2912, Cooper; 4805, Graham;
  5257, Coblentz; 5443, Clark; 5642,
  Mullins; 6100, Baldwin; 6135, Chapin.
FORGIVING: 140, Coblentz.
FORMOSA: 6465, Eff.
FORSYTHIA: 2132, Landeweer.
FORT TRYON PARK: 2133, Gustafson.
FORTRESSES: 4323, Plutzik.
FORTUNE: 2137, Eberhart; 2136,
  Wheeler; 2135, Cocteau.
FOUNTAINS: 2141, Gibbs; 2142,
  Thornton; 3976, Ackerson.
FOUR-YEAR-OLDS: 2143, Gibbs.
FOURTH OF JULY: 2154, Nemerov; 3122,
  Merrill; 3123, Ryskind.
FOXES: 667, Ote; 2157, Blackwell;
  2158, Huws; 2159, Smythe.
FOXHUNTS: 3539, Hardy.
FOYERS: 2160; Feine.
FRAGMENTS: 2162, Benn; 2258, Pierce.
FRANCIS OF ASSISI, ST.:   3108,
  Delattre.
FREDERICK THE GREAT: 5422, Mueller.
FREE: 1761, Lindbergh.
FREE WILL: 2164, Gogarty.
FREEDOM: 177, Keller; 1692, Davidson;
  3213, Tennyson.
FREEDOM OF CHOICE: 4780, Janes.
FREEZING WEATHER: 7331, Collier.
FRETTING: 2083, Wolf.
FRIENDS: 409, Krausz; 1225, Warsaw;
  1260, Raskin; 1446, Petrie; 2048,
  Redman; 2116, Galbraith; 2170,
  Armour; 2171, Hall; 2173, Weis; 2174,
  Greig; 2652, Wright; 2661, Romine;
  2877, Masefield; 3052, Schlitzer;
  4471, Armknecht; 4630, Schiff; 4697,
  Lennen; 5222, Coblentz; 5275, Isler;
  5865, Perry; 6350, Everson; 6499,
  Pasternak; 6613, Grenville; 6964,
  Krausz.
FRIENDSHIP: 1804, Ely; 2172, Smith;
  4455, Pepler.
FRIEZES: 1003, Beum.
FRITILLARIES: 2175, Updike.
FROGS: 1144, Levertov; 1386, Hagiwara;
  2178, Reid; 4996, Logan; 5489, Merrill;
  5959, Landeweer.
FRONTISPIECE: 2214, Swenson.
FROST: 2215, Rubenstein.
FROST, ROBERT, 1874-:   1005, Bulkeley;
6062, Wylie; 6573, Engle.

FROWNS: 2623, Barker.
FROZEN LAKES: 2218, Strickhausen.
FRUIT: 2219, Iwai.
FRUSTRATION: 6498, Thompson.
FUGUES: 1383, Celan.
FULBRIGHT FELLOWS: 6442, Smith.
FUNERALS: 388, Eberhart; 448, Delattre,
  715, Marz; 1365, Finkel; 4623, Morris;
  4920, Smith; 6891, Ryskind;
FUSSES AND MARRIAGE: 4099, Raskin.
FUTURE: 2231, Eberhart; 6483, Wheelock;
  6693, Coblentz.
GABRIEL: 478, Tobin.
GADGETS: 4836, Coblentz.
GALILEE: 2234, MacDonald; 6087,
  Bernhardt.
GALLERIES: 2235, Howes.
GALLI-CURCI, AMELITA: 3828, Josephs.
GAMES: 2237, Dickey.
GANNETS: 2238, Sparshott.
GARBAGE MEN: 3624, McCowan.
GARDEN OF EDEN: , Nickerson.
GARDEN OF GETHSEMANE: 92, Hine.
GARDENERS: 2250, Quentin; 2252,
  Gibbs; 5970, Ellis.
GARDENERS' WIVES: 5608, Merchant.
GARDENS: 239, Leibrand; 1308,
  Enzensberger; 1425, Jacobson; 1780,
  Collier; 1923, Kroll; 2204, Coles;
  2239, Bynner; 2241, Posner; 2242,
  Thorley; 2243, Zaturenska; 2244,
  Berry; 2248, Macpherson; 2613, Vesely;
  2847, Moore; 2901, Weinstein; 3473,
  Weiss; 4215, Vail; 4884, Merker;
  5225, Nall; 5280, Kelley; 6042,
  Nemerov; 6113, Zimskind; 6378,
  Friedrich; 6785, Kizer; 6940, Sarton.
GARDENS OF NEIGHBORS: 4055, Grenville.
GARGOYLES: 2253, Lister.
GAZABOS: 2259, Honig.
GAZING: 6506, Kelley.
GEESE: 2008, Pierce; 2260, Eff; 2261,
  Todd; 4700, Barnes; 6807, Merrill;
  7151, Heath.
GEISHAS: 2021, So-In.
GEMINI: 2262, Strickhausen.
GENERATIONS: 583, Weales.
GEOPHYSICS: 3286, Posner.
GERANIUMS: 4960, Brasier; 7308, Smith.
GETHSEMANE: 2272, Bernhardt; 6633,
  Molton.
GHOSTS: 194, Hanson; 2145, Zaturenska;
  2275, Scott; 2276, York; 2277, Reid;
  4002, Wright; 4166, Pillin; 4833,
  Winslow; 6803, Chaffee; 6954,
  Grenville.
GIANTESSES: 1738, Wagoner.
GIANTS: 472, Hansen.
GIELGUD, SIR JOHN, 1904-:   2281,
  Dufault.
GIFTED: 2290, McFarland.
GIFTS: 2282, Balliett; 2284, Mary
  Ignatia; 2288, Larraud; 2291, Smith;
  4640, Nelson; 6549, Lineaweaver.
GIFTS FOR WIVES: 4348, Bracken; 4999,
  Blackwell.
GIN: 4033, Rennert.
GIFAFFES: 2295, Kanfer; 2296, Perry;
  6530, Guthrie.
GIRLS: 1209, Brisco; 1253, Brand; (cont'd)

GIRLS (cont'd):1580, Holmes, 1834,
    Galbraith; 2303, White; 2536, Walker;
    2844, Laurence; 3456, Wright; 3581,
    Conklin; 3614, Mergard; 3684,
    Jaffray; 3739, Powell; 4014,
    McFarland; 4193, Secrist; 4357,
    McGinley; 5001, Dugan; 5100, Domoff;
    6284, Traad; 6492, Eldridge; 5311,
    Facos; 7043, Herz; 7156, Engle;
    7363, M. Maura.
GIRLS AND ATHLETICS: 4420, Betjeman.
GIRLS AND PLAYING: 2298, Cotter.
GIRLS AND SCHOOLS: 2738, Anthony.
GIRLS AND SINGING: 7362, Coker.
GIRLS AND GROWING UP: 3197, Franklin.
GIRLS IN LOVE: 2542, Jaffray.
GIVAT OZ: 6277, Gisnet.
GIVING: 4674, Good H; 5190, Burrowes;
    6157, Ryskind; 6946, Galbraith;
    7128, Miller; 7145, Clifford.
GLADNESS: 2382, Mary Immaculata.
GLASS: 2311, Tomlinson.
GLEANINGS: 2314, Shimoni.
GLITTER: 148, Hammer.
GLOBES: 2316, Stewart.
GLOCKENSPIELS: 627, Henley.
GLOVES: 2469, Parrish.
GOALS: 125, Freeman; 4093, Armour;
    5883, Cooper.
GOATS: 2321, Saba; 4428, Lister.
GOD: 2, Abse; 21, Townsend; 1164,
    James; 1247, Janes; 1342, Doherty;
    1926, Zylstra; 1991, Delattre;
    2223, Ronalson; 2591, Haines; 2729,
    Ignatow; 3546, Langland; 3554,
    Friedrich; 5059, Wood; 5390, Coblentz
    5595, Richardson; 5835, Van Allen;
    5843, Lilly; 6024, Flynn, 6308, Hess.
GOD AND DARKNESS: 2325, Barbee.
GOD AND EASTER: 248, Grover.
GOD AND FEAR: 7137, Scovel.
GOD AND GENESIS: 2265, Seaburg.
GOD AND LIGHT: 3376, Smith.
GOD AND MAN: 802, Mullins; 2323,
    Patrick.
GOD AND SCIENCE: 6516, Stuart.
GOD AND TRIVIALITIES: 6684, Carter.
GOD THE CREATOR: 2709, Cutler.
GODCHILDREN: 2326, Meredith.
GODDESSES: 1742, Watkins.
GODS: 1069, Burford; 4071, McCord;
    7045, Nixon.
GOD'S GIFT: 2286, White.
GOD'S HAND: 2470, Heafield.
GOD'S LOVE: 2946, Bangham.
GOD'S NAME: 3761, Strachan.
GOD'S NEARNESS: 5743, Patrick.
GOD'S WORD: 3093, Pierce.
GOD'S WORK: 7299, Clark.
GOETHE, JOHANN WOLFGANG VON, 1749-1832:
    6808, Shneour.
GOGGLEHEAD: 2331, Marshall.
GOGOL, NIKOLAI: 4178.
GOING: 2590; Stewart; 2766, Tagore.
GOLD: 1590, Golffing.
GOLDFISH: 3423, Blackwell.
GOLF: 5484, Betjeman.
GOLFERS: 2338, Waldman.
GOLGOTHA: 3114, Rao.

GOOD-BYE: 1378, Galbraith; 1549,
    Grabisch.
GOOD FRIDAY: 588, Eckhardt; 2343,
    Pierce; 2344, Booth; 2345, Patrick;
    2346, Hansen; 3874, Logan; 7324,
    Richardson.
GOOD INTENTIONS: 4458, Galbraith.
GOODNIGHT: 2350, Dufault.
GORILLAS: 2355, Eff.
GOSSIP: 3395, Gleason; 6491, Chadwick.
GOSSIPERS: 2356, Smith.
GOURMETS: 3251, Lemon.
GOVERNMENT: 3219, Tennyson.
GOVERNMENT PLANNING: 1160, Stroup.
GRACE: 3255, St. Simon.
GRACES: 2359, Henley.
GRADUATION: 15, Neame.; 2364,
    Moynahan; 3248, Kissler; 4211,
    Jaffray.
GRAFFITI: 4518, Montale.
GRAIAE: 2365, Squires.
GRANARIES: 7148, Hart.
GRAND CANYON: 2369, Noyes
GRAND ISLE: 1095.
GRANDCHILDREN: 6368, Armknecth.
GRANDAUGHTERS: 2378, Jacobs.
GRANDFATHERS: 2373, Hearst; 2401,
    O'Gorman; 4837, Stoutenberg; 5300,
    Nash; 6107, Merrill.
GRANDMOTHERS: 610, Carlisle; 835,
    Gibbons; 2374, Donnelly; 2375,
    Hall; 446, Parrish; 2376, MacNeil;
    2377, Mitchel; 2378, Jacobs; 3413,
    Greenwood; 4003, Weinstein; 5283,
    Lister.
GRANDPARENTS: 4001, Wolf; 5354,
    Josephs; 5817, Weiss.
GRAPES: 2381, Ridgley.
GRASS: 665, Turner; 1269, Kroll; 2383,
    Holmes; 2384, Emmons; 2386, Farber;
    2415, Lister; 4076, M. Davida; 5379,
    Rich; 6207, McFarland.
GRASSHOPPERS: 2387, Wilbur.
GRATITUDE: 566, Merchant; 4891, Boyle;
    4986, Hager; 6310, Koch.
GRAVE FLOWERS: 4623, Morris.
GRAVES: 1489, Hay; 2307, Lineaweaver;
    3118, Coleman; 5516, Ignatow; 5776;
    Menashe.
GRAVES, ROBERT: 2098, Galler.
GRAVITY: 759, Nicholl.
GRAY HAIR: 4206, Liddell; 7360,
    Rosenfield.
GRAZIA, GIOVANNI DI PAOLO DI, C. 1402-
    1482: 4663, Austin.
GREAT BRITAIN: 1848, Sagittarius.
GREAT DEPRESSION: 4136, Hall; 6892,
    Stafford.
GREAT LAKES: 2403, Hull.
GREAT MEN: 4971, Sitwell.
GREATNESS: 4186, Emerson.
GREED: 1186, Lilly.
GREEK LANGUAGE: 2832, Wood.
GREEKS: 7365, Eberhart.
GREEN: 6775, Pfeiffer.
GREEN PLACES: 2422, Smith.
GREENE, ROBERT, 1560-1592: 5418,
    Greene.
GREENHORNS: 1542, Nash.
GREENHOUSES: 2421, Nathan; 2428,
    Landeweer.

GREETINGS: 1699, Mundell; 2430, Usk; 2661, Romine.
GREGORIAN MUSIC: 3305, Morgan.
GRIDIRON: 2435, Talman.
GRIEF: 90, Colum; 1193, Drewry; 2436, Dana; 2437, Weiss; 2438, Kahn; 2671, Iris; 3341, Singleton; 4245, Hoskins; 4368, Kitahara; 5517, Galbraith; 7016, Johnson; 7296, Duncan.
GROCERY LISTS: 2440, Kumin.
GROSBEAKS: 669, Jacobson.
GROUND MOLES: 2441, Cosbey.
GROUNDHOGS: 6501, Ardayne; 3708, Cane.
GROWING: 2443, Dodge; 2445, Reid.
GROWING UP: 4193, Secrist; 6573, Fowler.
GRUDGES: 2448, Usk.
GUARANTEES: 3033, Eisenlohr.
GUARDIAN ANGELS: 2449, Schmidt.
GUARDS: 6914, Galbraith.
GUEST TOWELS: 5772, Talman.
GUESTS: 168, Graham; 1378, Galbraith; 2451; Balch; 2453, Zukofsky; 4208, Emmons; 7234, Warsaw.
GUGGENHEIM FELLOWS: 6442, Smith; 6593, Sagittarius.
GUILT: 2972, Lund.
GUINEVERE: 7113, Swann.
GUITARS: 4821, Lister; 5807, Fitzell.
GULLIVER: 5167, Atherton.
GULLS: 283, Beum; 363, Takenaka; 728, Kinnell; 2455, Weiss; 5468, Stefanile; 5933, Gale.
GUNFIGHTERS: 2456, Urdang.
GURKHAS: 648, 6869, Singer.
GYPSY MOTHS: 2458, Berg.
HABERDASHERS: 6957, McGinley.
HABIT: 5139, Witt.
HADRIAN: 2459, Winslow; 2460, Rich.
HAGAR: 2462, Pinkerfeld-Amir.
HAGS: 2461, Hughes.
HAIFA, PALESTINE: 3284, Hodes.
HAIRCUTS: 1963, Isler.
HAIRLINES: 3502, Chadwick.
HALF-BROTHERS: 816, Hull.
HALF-SISTERS: 816, Hull.
HALL, AUGUSTA: 2873, Hall.
HALL OF FAME: 179, Flaumenhaft.
HALLOWEEN: 139, Avison; 142, McCarthy; 2468, Congdon; 4457, Pessin; 5813, Gleason; 6010, Spear.
HALLUCINATIONS: 7338, Lewis.
HAMBURGERS: 988, Isler; 6228, Nash.
HAMMOCKS: 3059, Pratt.
HANCOCK, JOHN, 1737-1793: 3104, Hale.
HAND-CARS: 2471, Abbe.
HANDICAPPED: 2001, Nader.
HANDS: 1506, Schiff; 2025, L'Heureux; 2473, Cotter; 2474, Hunter; 4650, Sarton; 5823, Merwin.
HANGINGS: 4537, Van Doren.
HANGMEN: 2476, Moss.
HAPPENING: 581, Miles.
HAPPINESS: 207, Lilly; 324, Galbraith; 2164, Gogarty; 2199, Stevens; 3460, Galbraith; 3736, Nardi; 5073, Dewhurst; 6181, Gogarty.
HARBORS: 4110, Galler; 7025, Goodman; 7194, Merrill.

HARLEQUINS: 764, Feldman; 4954, Nichols.
HARPS: 2323, Patrick.
HARVEST TIME: 1230, McNeill.
HARVESTS: 2491, Oerke; 2492, Walton.
HASHISH: 6851, Yborra.
HAT BARS: 2494, Weston.
HATRED: 529, Delattre; 1730, Morgan; 2078, O'Hara; 3838, White; 6319, Vliet; 6873, Sullivan.
HATS: 1928, Schiff; 2011, Stepanchev; 2268, Appel; 2515, Kozmenuik; 5777, Richstone.
HATTERS: 2268, Appel.
HAVRE DE GRACE, MARYLAND: 2499, Chandler.
HAWKS: 2500, Frumkin; 2501, Hughes; 2502, Oerke; 2676, Tomlinson.
HAWTHORNE, NATHANIEL: 2652, Warren; 4487, McCarthy.
HAYING: 2504, Rukeyser.
HAYLOFTS: 2505, Schoeberlein.
HEALING: 1129, Scott.
HEARING: 843, Datta; 2520, Usk.
HEART: 2525, Galbraith; 3485, Miles.
HEARTHS: 2524, Hart; 4551, Jacobson.
HEARTS: 1298, Nicholl; 2225, Bock; 4861, Morgan; 6101, Benet; 4656, Smith; 6321, Stebbing.
HEAT: 2529, Eisenlohr.
HEAT WAVES: 2531, Lazarus; 2904, Lamdan.
HEAVEN: 372, Kessler; 2532, Weiss; 5191, McGahey; 6188, Moffitt.
HEEP, URIAH: 6816, Caswell.
HEGEL, GEORG WILHELM FRIEDRICH, 1770-1831: 4850, Fadiman.
HEIRLOOMS: 2535, Miner.
HELIODORA: 3216, Triem.
HELL: 5092, Culbert.
HELLAS: 761, Berkeley.
HELLENISM: 2538, Drake.
HENS: 5020, Grenville.
HERALDRY: 2543, Hoffman.
HERBS: 6460, Lamport.
HERDS: 2544, Creeley.
HERDSMEN: 2545, Caeiro.
HEREDITY: 5400, McGinley.
HERITAGE: 3529, Gaines.
HERMITS: 1120, McGinley; 2556, Galbraith.
HEROES: 2558, Coblentz; 2560, Rukeyser; 2561, Barker; 2562, Graves; 2865, Blackwell; 3181, Olson; 3212, Brennan; 4106, Nixon; 4314, Stone; 6078, Anwar.
HERONS: 670, Miner; 2397, Kizer; 5737, Ciardi.
HERRING-GULLS: 2564, Wheelock.
HESITATION: 5837, Blackburn.
HIBERNATION: 7214, Landeweer.
HIGHBROWS: 3053, Armknecht.
HIGH FIDELITY: 2574, Gunn; 2725, Otis.
HIGH FINANCE: 2575, Russell.
HIGHWAYS: 1097, Spingarn; 1349, Isler; 2582, Merwin; 2583, Chapin.
HIKES: 2584, Weiss.
HILL COUNTRY: 5892, Rutledge.
HILLS: 1254, Franklin; 2585, Creeley.
HIPPOPOTAMUSES: 1198, Galbraith.
HIROSHIMA: 6422, Yoneda.

HISTORIANS: 2501, Hughes; 2593, Jones.

HISTORY: 1064, Kunitz; 4316, Ciardi; 5145, Nemerov; 5533, Van Duyn; 5591, Weismiller; 6109, Coxe.

HIT-AND-RUN: 4810, Rennert.

HOBBIES: 3130, Chadwick.

HOGS: 5896, Plath.

HOLES: 4511, Wirt.

HOLINESS: 251, Ciardi.

HOLY COMMUNION: 4758, Patstone; 7313, Clark.

HOLY LAND: 3115, Pierce.

HOLY SPIRIT: 1753, Schneider; 2859, Beck; 5930, Powers; 4341, Nims.

HOLY WEEK: 468, Sullivan; 3412, Davidson.

HOME: 360, Mansfield; 2197, Lang; 2337, Lister; 2347, Young; 2609, Kessler; 2610, Vance; 2615, Armour; 2654, Dawson; 2770, Pasternak; 2814, Engle; 3328, Lineaweaver; 3535, Clark; 5348, Thornton; 6108, Whitbread; 6110, Hooper; 6879, De Jong.

HOME REPAIRS: 6664, Galbraith.

HOMECOMING: 2618, Hooper; 2619, Krieger; 2620, Swan.

HOMER. ODYSSEY: 5262, Kazantzakis.

HOMES: 3, Lawson; 3622, Henry; 3862, Kumin; 3930, Jennison; 4079, Keith; 4080, Lattimore; 4474, Isler; 4488, McGinley; 6622, Richstone; 7061, Eisenlohr.

HOMESTEADS: 2229, Briley; 3939, Jacobson.

HOMESTEADERS: 2621, Grenville.

HOMEWORK: 2622, Anthony; 3462, Nelson.

HOMILIES: 6725, O'Gorman.

HONEY: 2624, Blackwell.

HONEYBEES: 2625, Langland.

HONEYMOONS: 2169, Scott.

HOOFBEATS: 1615, Hicks.

HOOKED RUGS: 2627, Zilles.

HOPE: 553, Papatzonis; 1148, Richstone; 1712, Davidson; 2629, Goldsmith, 2630, Longfellow; 2631, Dickinson; 3389, Lineaweaver; 3490, Virden; 4788, Bangs; 5748, Hirshman; 6451, Cochrane; 6878, Claude of Jesus; 7379, Rokeah.

HOPPER, HEDDA: 5429, Fadiman.

HORACE: 2414, Lattimore.

HORIZONS: 2634, Abbe.

HORNS: 2636, de Vito.

HORS D'OEUVRES: 1642, Rosenfield; 2638, Talman.

HORSE-CHESTNUTS: 5709; Farber.

HORSE THIEVES: 2962, Good H.

HORSEBACK RIDERS: 723, Francis.

HORSES: 633, Kumin; 919, Swan; 995, Perry; 1740, Jacobson; 2287, Creeley; 2639, Koch; 2640, Kitagawa; 2641, Pierce; 2642, Guillen; 3438, Campbell; 4428, Lister; 4429, Hall; 6084, Everson.

HOSPITAL NURSERIES: 2833, Adrian.

HOSPITALS: 738, Ciardi; 4893, O'Doherty; 6186, Sandeen.

HOSTAGES: 2643, Coxe.

HOSTESSES: 260, Eisenlohr; 2644, de Vito; 3370, Douglass; 5194, Otis; 6502, Wright.

HOT RODS: 2645, Zitner.

HOTELS: 453, Nash; 3236, Rosenfield; 2646, Morris; 2674, Kaplan.

HOTHEADED: 2216, Galbraith.

HOURS: 3447, Murray.

HOUSE CLEANING: 223, Schiff.

HOUSE PAINTING: 3418, Kumin.

HOUSE PLANS: 2655, Kilkeary.

HOUSE WRECKERS: 7321, Johnson.

HOUSEBOATS: 4390, Nickerson.

HOUSEBREAKERS: 7366, Anthony.

HOUSECLEANING: 4321, Galbraith.

HOUSEKEEPING: 3633, Merrill; 6206, Ward.

HOUSES: 782, Flint; 783, Cooper; 1057, Simpson; 1698, Crawford; 1700, Newbold; 2612, Emmons; 2650, Sward; 4081, Blackwell; 4183, Shalom; 4389, Redgrove; 4528, Mundell; 5341, Colvin; 5866, Beum; 5894, Justice; 6512, Dary; 6864, Jennison; 6926, Gunn.

HOUSES AND DEATH: 2650, Sward.

HOUSEWIVES: 835, Gibbons; 1641, Galbraith; 1772, Kraus; 1873, Ireland; 2096, Fitz; 2105, Baird; 2481, Galbraith; 2658, Lieberman; 2657, Amma; 2660, Fasel; 4609, Averitt; 6412, Chadwick; 6824, Thompson.

HUCKSTERS: 2330, Weiss.

HUMAN FIGURES: 5562, Warsaw.

HUMANITIES: 3724, Jones.

HUMANITY: 1411, Garrigue; 2690, Mary Aquin.

HUMANS: 6991, Chadwick.

HUMILITY: 1212, Mullins; 3577, Rossetti.

HUMMING: 739, Crawford.

HUMMINGBIRDS: 2693, Coffin; 2694, Rosenberg.

HUNGARIAN MASSACRE: 4510, Davis.

HUNGARY: 174, Coxe; 2605, McGuire; 3744, Auslander; 5238, Ciardi.

HUNGER: 921, Trent; 2695, Bunner.

HUNTERS: 2697, Adler; 2698, Jacobsen; 6232, Wolf.

HUNTING: 2696, Weiss; 2700, Brand; 2701, Johnson; 3975, Wright.

HUNTING WOODS: 601, Justice.

HURRICANES: 6073, Ireland.

HUSBANDRY: 2703, Fandel.

HUSBANDS: 62, Herz; 1176, Chadwick; 1538, Barker; 2513, Askue; 2534, Armour; 2559, Galbraith; 2570, Emmons, Douglass; 2656, Starbuck; 2680, Nash; 2704, Armour; 2720, Avery; 2937, Armour; 4319, 4334; 4338, 4343, 4345, 4347, Bracken; 5160, Mergard; 6112, Lee; 6182, Chadwick; 6664, Galbraith.

HUSSITE SCHISM: 2594, Daiches.

HYDROCEPHELUS: 2706, Hetznecker.

HYENAS: 6204, Barker.

HYMNS: 2708, Hunter.

HYPERVENTILATION: 1666, Thornton.

HYPOCONDRIACS: 803, Bonaluto; 867, Lister.

ICARUS: 2771, Mayo

ICE: 968, Haag; 1291, Merrill; 2772, Johnston; 3076, Wooten; 5185, Tomlinson.
ICE-CREAM CONES: 2774, Armour.
ICE CREAM: 2773, Wolf.
ICE SKATING: 2069, Van Slyke.
ICE STORMS: 84, Ebright.
ICEBERGS: 2775, Merwin.
ICEHOUSES: 2776, Abbe.
ID: 3061, Pedrick.
IDENTITY: 2674, Kaplan; 7125, Reid.
IDEOLOGIES: 4506, Kenny.
IDIOTS: 2784, Ashbery; 2785, Eff.
IDLENESS: 4146, Brasier.
IGNORANCE: 306, Askue.
ILL-FAVORED: 3606, Farnash.
ILLEGITMACY: 4173, Grossman.
ILLNESS: 72, Smith; 946, Marx; 965, Betjeman; 1517, Rosenteur; 3991, Goodman; 5604, Asher.
ILLUSIONS: 2809, Tremayne; 5610, Eckman.
IMAGES: 222, Jacobsen; 2390, Hunter.
IMAGINATION: 2864, Salinger; 3627, Wagoner; 4845, Levant.
IBECILES: 2816, Finkel.
IMMIGRANTS: 354, Katz; 2819, Drake.
IMMINENCE: 2719, Giulaini.
IMMORTALITY: 954, Thompson; 5046, Shapiro; 6547, Campbell; 6944, Wesley.
IMPOSSIBLE: 5799, Laing.
INATTENTIVENESS: 2929, Erba.
INCARNATION: 3864, Cotter; 4336, St. John of the Cross.
INCINERATORS: 2934, Van Doren.
INCOME: 4924, Pratt.
INCOME TAX: 281, Chadwick; 727, Eisenlohr; 1520, Bishop; 2127, Kellogg; 2128, Halacy; 2662, Talman; 7041, Jenney.
INCOMPATABILITY: 155, Nash.
INCONSTANCIES: 2939, Sullivan.
INCORRIGIBLES: 2940, Perkins.
INDEPENDENCE DAY: 2155, Solomon.
INDIA: 2294, Page; 2863, Shapiro.
INDIAN SUMMERS: 2943, Richardson; 2945, Balch; 4230, Carruth.
INDIANS: 2946, Bangham; 2947, Fandel.
INDIANS, NORTH AMERICAN: 5173, Kelley; 6312, Koch.
INDIANS OF MEXICO: 2942, Rosenfield.
INDIFFERENCE: 614, Dicker.
INDIGENCE: 1752, Ronsard.
INDIVIDUALITY: 2948, Merchant.
INDIVIDUALS: 2689, Gunn.
INEBRIATE: 3780, Plath.
INEQUALITY: 4862, O'Doherty.
INFANTS: 4356, Wade.
INFLUENCE: 2001, Nader.
INFUENZA: 2953, Van Horn.
INHERITANCE: 2902, Greenberg; 4466, Atherton.
INNER SELF: 4618, Richter.
INNOCENCE: 5941, Eberhart; 7317, Crawford.
INNOCENTS: 2958, Vazakas.
INSATIATE: 2961, McFarland.
INSATIETY: 5062, Feinstein.
INSECTS: 781, Houghton; 1518, Wheelock; 2965, Kelley; 6529, Solum

INSECURITY: 5062, Feinstein.
INSOMNIA: 2130, Farnham; 2972, Lund; 2973, Quasimodo; 5569, Dodson; 6156, Long; 6700, De Ford; 6719, Manheim; 6754, Scholes.
INSPIRATION: 1717, Singleton.
INSURANCE: 3365, Jennison.
INTEGRATION: 4133, Sagittarius.
INTEGRITY: 3387, Bat-Miriam.
INTELLIGENCE: 2984, Merchant.
INTELLIGIBLE: 2183, Howe.
INTERIORS: 2987, Smith.
INTERRUPTIONS: 3054, Anthony.
INTERSTELLAR TRAVEL: 1133, Rosenfield.
INTERVIEWS: 2992, Galler.
INTROVERTS: 2996, Galbraith.
INTUITION: 4023, Galbraith; 6817, Heath.
INVASIONS: 2999, Burger.
INVENTORS: 3001, Char.
INVESTMENTS: 888, Galbraith.
INVISIBLE: 2749, Coblentz.
INVITATIONS: 3004, Mok.
IPSWITCH: 3009, Frost.
IRELAND: 2777, Brinnin; 5919, Montague; 6898, Small.
IRISH ELECTIONS: 5919, Montague.
IRON: 1110, Kipling.
IRONWOOD: 591, Scott.
IRRIGATION: 7302, Atlantic.
IRRITANTS: 3017, Galbraith.
ISAAC: 3020, Gilboa.
ISAIAH: 3021, Nims.
ISHMAELITES: 3022, Coblentz.
ISLANDS: 503, Booth; 2063, Dickey; 2406, 3024, Porter; 3026, Freeman; 3027, Booth; 3029, Pomeroy; 4100, Brinnin; 6248, Jacobson.
ISRAEL: 3032, Lamdan; 7343, Shlonsky.
ITALIAN LANGUAGE: 3047, Miles; 3048, Merrill.
ITALIAN MOVIES: 6192, Brooks.
ITALY: 175, Simpson.
ITHACA: 3050, Scott.
JACKETS: 643, Gunn.
JACOB: 109, Abel; 3068, Kanfer; 5106, Clark.
JAGUARS: 3069, Hughes.
JAM: 4200, Emans.
JAMAICA: 3071, Hall.
JAMES, HENRY: 5286, Gordon.
JANITORS: 3073, De Jong.
JANUARY: 3074, Johnson; 3075, Wallace.
JAPAN: 1579, Ranko; 1945, Shusetsu; 2021, So-In; 6210, Bokudo; 6771, Issa; 6866, Kirkup.
JAWBONES: 5205, Hughes.
JAYS: 3081, Solomon.
JAZZ: 29, Perry.
JEALOUSY: 3083, Fuller.
JEHOVAH: 5629, Carruth.
JEREMIAH: 7330, Fidelian.
JERICHO: 3088, Galler.
JEROME, ST.: 5042, Swartz.
JERUSALEM: 3089, Shlonsky.
JERUSALEM, VERMONT: 3090, Gleason.
JESUS CHRIST: 151, Cotter; 237, Clark; 333, Coblentz; 356, Cutler; 1006, Smith; 1131, Pierce; 1257, Clark; 1724, Lennen; 2023, Fanel; 2672, Lilly; 3895, Cotter; (continued)

JESUS CHRIST (cont'd): 4005, Pierotti;
4147, Cotter; 4170, Maguire; 4194,
Freedman; 4543, Carter; 4641, Pierce;
4963, Woodrum; 5049, Mullins; 5505,
Clark; 5913, Rowland; 6090,
Schneider; 6402, Cooper; 6576,
Waugaman; 6981, Raiziss.
JESUS CHRIST - ANIMALS: 225, Maris
Stella; 2641, Pierce.
JESUS CHRIST - ART: 2830, Pierce.
JESUS CHRIST - BETHLEHEM: 4516,
Meissner.
JESUS CHRIST - BETRAYAL: 587, Bangham.
JESUS CHRIST - BREAD: 2651, Patrick.
JESUS CHRIST - CANDLELIGHTER: 854,
Elmer.
JESUS CHRIST - CANTICLES: 859,
Roseliep.
JESUS CHRIST - CAROLS: 878, Thorley.
JESUS CHRIST - CHILDREN: 2041, Mary
Ada; 6984, Cotter.
JESUS CHRIST - CHRISTMAS: 1015,
Engle.
JESUS CHRIST - CRUCIFIXION: 1287,
Bing; 1290, Patrick; 3678, Hazo;
5621, Unruh; 6356, Sherwin.
JESUS CHRIST - GALILEE: 2234,
MacDonald.
JESUS CHRIST - GETHSEMANE: 6633,
Molton.
JESUS CHRIST - GOOD FRIDAY: 2343,
Pierce.
JESUS CHRIST - HANDS: 2473, Cotter.
JESUS CHRIST - HOLY WEEK: 468,
Sullivan.
JESUS CHRIST - INFANT: 2951, Claudel.
JESUS CHRIST - INTERCESSION: 2985,
Molton.
JESUS CHRIST - LIGHT: 1778, Doyle.
JESUS CHRIST - LOVE: 2747, Frazee-
Bower; 4547, Cully; 6768, Cooper.
JESUS CHRIST - MIRACLES: 3822,.
JESUS CHRIST - NEED: 4149, Workman.
JESUS CHRIST - PASSION: 4689,
Richardson; 5292, M. Jeremy.
JESUS CHRIST - REJECTION: 2510,
Pierce.
JESUS CHRIST - SON OF GOD: 3997,
Pierce; 4565, Bradley; 6238, Powers.
JESUS CHRIST - STATURE: 6040, Clark.
JESUS CHRIST - STRANGER: 6083,
Davidson; 6087, Bernhardt.
JESUS CHRIST - TEMPTATION: 2138,
Pierce.
JESUS CHRIST - TOYS: 3092, Thorley.
JESUS CHRIST - TRINITY: 6673, Kemp.
JESUS CHRIST - UNDERSTANDING: 4697,
Boynton.
JESUS CHRIST - WILDERNESS: 7153,
Pierce.
JET AGE: 3094, Coblentz.
JEWELS: 3097, Hollander.
JEWS: 1980, Shapiro; 2181, Feldman;
3109, Galler; 3526, Sloan; 4012,
Halpern; 4443, Wolf; 4860, Miller;
4940, Cavafy; 5147, 5149, Feldman;
5336, Norse; 6871, Barron; 6994,
Greenberg.
JEZEBEL: 3098, Clark.
JOAN OF ARC: 2080, Cotter

JOB: 536, MacPherson; 3100, Cooper;
3101, Ignatow.
JOHN OF THE CROSS, ST.: 6434, Nims;
JOHN THE BAPTIST: 3249, Nationek;
5402, Berrigan.
JOHN THE EVANGELIST, SAINT: 6580,
Appleton.
JOHNSON, SAMUEL: 1530, Posner.
JOHNSON, SAMUEL, 1709-1784: 5429,
Fadiman.
JOKES: 6619, Brown; 6983, Jaffray.
JONAH: 3107, Swan; 6202, Quentin;
7242, Fretz.
JONES, CASEY: 7053, Smith.
JONSON, BEN, 1573?-1637: 4138, Moore.
JORDAN: 292, Sagittarius.
JOURNALISTS: 6999, Betjeman.
JOURNEYS: 1111, Rorty; 2979, Hamburge;
3111, Bynner; 3112, Rawlins.
JOY: 205, Coatsworth; 1298, Nicholl;
3117, Moore; 4318, Renon; 5565,
Burket.
JOY, SHARING OF: 3044, Collins.
JOYCE, JAMES: 3118, Coleman.
JUDAISM: 4404, Biel.
JUDAS ISCARIOT: 4411, Galbraith.
JUDGES: 4939, Rawling.
JUDGMENT: 520, Pierce; 3311, Rachel;
3765, Weaver; 6474, DeCavalles.
JUKEBOXES: 3733, Neame.
JULY: 3120, Deutsch; 5411, Merrill.
JUNE: 3037, Mezey; 3125, Freeman;
3126, Bradbury.
JUNIPERS: 7198, Langland.
JUNK YARDS: 2433, Booth; 6647, Hall.
JURIES: 3960, Updike.
JUSTICE: 4503, Vance.
KEATS, JOHN: 4454, Starbuck; 4897,
Touster; 5338, McCarthy.
KEATS, JOHN, 1795-1821: 3431, Nicholl;
4797, Witt.
KEELBOATS: 3145, Knoepfle.
KELLER, HELEN: 2071, Perreau-Saussine;
2072, Pierce.
KELLOGG, ELIJAH: 5893, Burford.
KENOSSIS: 3148, Eckhardt.
KENSINGTON GARDENS: 1357, Lister.
KENTUCKY: 6383, Stuart.
KEROSENE LAMPS: 725, Moody.
KEY WEST, FLORIDA: 3155, Kadow.
KEYS: 3150, Carruth.
KHAZARS: 3157, Haber.
KIERKEGAARD, SOREN: 5879, Rowse.
KILLDEER: 3158, Landweer.
KILMER, JOYCE: 2779, Nash.
KIMBERLEY MINE: 4613, Cassity.
KINDERGARTEN: 3166, Goodman.
KINDNESS: 473, Brecht; 2305,
Galbraith; 3162, Johnston.
KINGDOMS: 4726, Morse.
KINGS: 339, Galler; 1556, Dickey;
2270, Gill; 3369, Moore; 5291,
Moore; 6778, Thatcher.
KISSES: 3407, Milbrath; 3318, Zilles;
3450, Le Vinson; 5176, Congdon;
6344, Good H; 7372, McFarland.
KITCHEN APPLIANCES: 4064, Jennison.
KITCHEN SINKS: 3175, Armour.
KITCHENS: 2684, Nash; 3836, Rosenfield;
4467, Auden.

KITES: 996, Solomon; 3176, Pomeroy; 3177, Cohen; 5964, Ellis.
KITTENS: 1233, Clower; 1245, Parent's Magazine; 6583, Eaton.
KITTY HAWK, N. C.: 2398, 3178, Frost.
KLEE, PAUL: 6597, Plutzik.
KNEEL: 6936, Pierce.
KNIGHTS: 6246, Robin.
KNOWING: 4468, Smith.
KNOWLEDGE: 2090, Richardson.
KNOX, JOHN, 1515?-1572: 4699, McGinley.
KRUSHCHEV, NIKITA: 6891, Ryskind.
KUNLUN: 3190, Tse-tung.
LABOR UNIONS: 3764, 4269, Ryskind.
LABORATORIES: 3193, Merrill, 6166, Squires.
LACKAWANNA: 3200, Bagg.
LADDERS: 3194, Baro.
LADIES: 2362, Armknecht; 4061, Kanfer.
LADIES' HATS: 758, Rittell.
LAFARGE, FATHER JOHN, S.J.: 2047, Barrett.
LAKE ALLEN: 3201, Ostroff.
LAKES: 2217, Bentley; 3203, Merrill; 3205, Swenson; 3206, Pomeroy; 4932, La Follett; 5863, Bagg; 6140, Merrill; 6602, Kraft.
LAMBETH CONFERENCE IN ENGLAND: 4762, Sagittarius.
LAME MAN: 6742, Finkel.
LAMENTS: 3208,
LAMPLIGHT: 1058, Tomlinson.
LAMPS: 3216, Triem; 6885, Smith.
LANCELOT, SIR: 7005, Drake.
LAND: 1409, Frazee-Bower; 3217, Erba; 4262, Patchen.
LANDSCAPES: 895, Perry; 1451, Bynner; 1827, Merwin; 2640, Kitagawa; 3225, Zilles; 3226, Jacobsen; 3230, Perry; 3232, Lattimore; 3233, Berrigan; 4748, Donnelly; 5905, Moss; 6840, Justice.
LANES: 3234, Ely.
LANG: 3338, Napier.
LANGUAGE: 1314, Lemon; 4316, Ciardi; 4856, Lang; 6285, Weiss.
LANGUAGES: 2818, Drake; 3028, Braun; 6743, Brown.
LAPINS: 6058, Heissenfuttel.
LARKS: 3239, Bynner.
LAST DAY: 3241, Shah.
LATCHES: 3252, Rago.
LATE SHOWS: 5438, Kober.
LATIMER, HUGH: 2688, Ellis.
LATIN TEACHERS: 3263, Moore.
LAUGHTER: 2359, Henley; 2497, Kline; 3266, Solovay; 3601, Lamb; 6330, Gilboa.
LAUNDRY: 1108, Raskin; 3269, Merrill; 3270, Stone; 4965, Tze-Chiang.
LAURELS: 5906, Kunitz.
LAURENSIN, MARIE: 6507, Coatsworth.
LAVENDER: 3271, Goodman.
LAW: 3272, Thompson; 3274, Hecht.
LAWNS: 763, Nicholl; 2417, Warsaw; 3199, Schofield; 4507, Armour; 6420, Hammer.
LAWRENCE, D. H.: 7381, Watkins.
LAZARUS: 1514, Pierce; 5368, Delattre.

LAZINESS: 7133, Chadwick.
LEADERS: 2058, Morris.
LEADERSHIP: 5996, Spear.
LEAP YEAR: 3281.
LEARNING: 18, Hillyer; 6490, Solovay; 4808, Sweet; 7083, Workman.
LEAVES: 979, Solomon; 547, Sarton; 1122, Cane, 1150, Stoutenberg; 1844, Coxe; 1964, Heath; 2258, Streit; 2380, Nicholl; 2668, Merchant; 2959, Natsume; 2977, Perkins; 3279, Darcy; 3283, Moore; 4228, Souster; 5303, Neely; 5740, Weiss; 6397, Merwin; 6726, Stuart; 7200, McAllister; 7371, Cunliffe.
LEAVING: 4984, Pierce; 7357, La Farge.
LEGACIES: 3290, Marz.
LEGAL REFORM: 3292, Gunn.
LEMONADE: 3297, Daerr.
LEMONS: 4575, Krolow.
LENS GRINDERS: 3298, Fleming.
LENT: 3299, Coxe; 3300, Sullivan; 4438, Lennen; 5876, Johnson.
LEONARDO DA VINCI: 3301, Moore.
LETTERS: 1237, McFarland; 2666, Laughlin; 3321, Seager; 3322, Smith; 3324, Hicky; 3325, Booth; 3327, Ostroff; 3328, Lineaweaver; 3332, Rago; 3333, Montale; 3905, Duncan; 4145, Feine.
LEVITATION: 5265, Green.
LEWIS, FULTON: 6215, Ryskind.
LEWIS, WYNDHAM: 2870, Russell.
LIBERAL ARTS: 2834, Stone.
LIBERALS: 3342, Barker; 4392, Burke; 5184, Edwards; 6663, Sagittarius.
LIBERTY BELL: 3123, Ryskind.
LIBRARIANS: 267, Anonymous; 1323, Gnash; 1388, Sloan; 1490, Carter; 1735, Solovay; 2512, Foss; 2606, Carter; 2713, Young; 3034, Street; 3343, Avrett; 3344, Banning; 3345, Ashby; 3346, Trosper; 3351, Ringstad; 3419, Wilson Lib Bull; 4205, Stefanski; 5180, Foss; 5987, 5991, 5992, 5995, 5999, 6005, 6009, 6015, 6018, 6019, 6021, Spear; 7322, MacDonald.
LIBRARIES: 104, Parker; 138, Sturges; 141, Kruse; 152, Godley; 481, 690, Solovay; 693, Field; 704, Reinert; 983, Jarrell; 1157, Hodges; 1800, Carter; 1938, Weiss; 2140, Hale; 2740, Bennett; 2831, Greene; 3347, Davis; 3348, Hug; 3349, Knight; 3350, Short; 3357, Sharp; 3360, Klitzbe; 3361, Ringstad; 3830, Sweet; 4561, Gordon; 4615, Liotta; 5239, Ringstad; 5616, Bryan; 5624, Gates; 6141, Reinert; 7038, Sullivan; 7087, Carlisle.
LIBRARIES - FILING RULES: 4216, Sturges.
LIBRARIES, LENDING: 5953, Sitwell.
LIBRARIES - PORTRAITS: 4937, Liotta.
LIBRARIES - TIBET: 3420, Brown.
LIBRARY CATALOGS: 900, Reed.
LIBRARY JARGON: 5144, Sellers.
LIBRARY PATRONS: 887, Moreland; 3352, 3353, 3354, 3355, 3356, 3358, 3359, Sharp; 5538, Swift.

LIES: 1406, Myhre; 1721, Cooper; 1849, Rubenstein; 2950, Galbraith; 6464, White.

LIFE: 193, Coblentz; 494, Lindbergh; 635, Updike; 1331, Rawlins; 1570, Shapiro; 2286, White; 2323, Patrick; 3363, Scott; 3365, Jennison; 3373, Boggs; 3842, Coblentz; 4244, Hurd; 4596, Russo; 4608, Collins; 4846, McNeill; 5141, Kessler; 5152, 5742, Coblentz; 5904, Russell; 6121, Richstone; 6660, Pierce; 6731, Palamas.

LIFE - END OF: 371, Coblentz.

LIFE INSURANCE: 3368, Lieberman.

LIFE'S WORTH: 7049, Stuart.

LIFEGUARDS: 45, Emmons.

LIGHT: 94, Coxe; 579, Pillin; 2126, Everson; 3187, Rago; 3309, Lilly; 3375, Blackburn; 3380, Eberhart; 4237, O'Hara; 5094, Sullivan; 5141, Kessler; 5535, Elmer; 6388, Grace; 6700, De Ford.

LIGHT AND DARK: 3377, Moss.

LIGHT BULBS: 3379, Zitner.

LIGHTHOUSES: 571, Dickey.

LIGHTNING: 6069, Huntress.

LIGHTS: 3382, Landeweer; 3955, Rosenberg; 7169, Gustafson.

LILACS: 3391, Kinnell, 3392, Miner; 7073, Whitman.

LILIES: 3393, Weiss.

LIMBO: 3394, Auden.

LINCOLN, ABRAHAM, 1809-1865: 1829, Golden; 3396, Ross; 3397, Perrings.

LINDBERGH, ANNE MORROW, 1907-: 6561, Fielding.

LINDSAY, VACHEL, 1879-1931: 5151, Smith.

LINES OF RESISTANCE: 3399, Spring.

LION-RIDERS: 1950, Patchen.

LIONS: 1205, Starbuck; 1499, Dunsany; 3433, Fiedler; 3435, Smith; 3436, Hollander; 5285, Maruyama.

LISTENERS: 3439, Mastin.

LISTENING: 5148, Wheeler.

LITERARY CRITICS: 6062, Wylie.

LITERARY GUILD SELECTIONS: 1181, Lemon.

LITERATURE: 28, Stevens.

LITTLE ROCK, ARKANSAS: 300, Johnson; 4133, Sagittarius.

LIVERPOOL, ENGLAND: 1571, McGovern.

LIVING: 537, Ames; 2742, Wheeler; 3124, Stevens; 3255, St. Simon; 3289, Kahn; 3500, Kreymborg; 5155, Galbraith; 5450, Kreymborg; 5627, De Ford; 6100, Baldwin; 6129, Merchant; 6193, Kaplan; 6737, Keegan.

LIVING ROOMS: 3479, Karns.

LIZARDS: 2500, Frumkin; 3480, Eff.

LOANS: 4841, Wheeler.

LOCKS: 3487, Koch.

LOCUSTS: 3488, Walter; 5550, Clark.

LODESTARS: 3489, Patrick.

LODESTONE: 3490, Virden.

LOG HOUSES: 5694, Mack.

LOGIC: 1830, Usk.

LOGS: 5355, Landeweer.

LONDON: 7172, Bevington.

LONELINESS: 1522, Pierce; 2089, Liddell; 2134, Cunliffe; 2960, Frumkin; 3492, Berrigan; 3493, Carter; 6060, Richman; 6161, White; 6852, McKay.

LONG LIFE: 4667, Galbraith.

LOOKING BACK: 1652, Morse.

LORE: 3517, Stafford.

LOSERS: 3518, Merchant.

LOSS: 3521, Feldman; 3522, Petrie.

LOSSES: 4694, Goodman.

LOST: 1796, Olson.

LOST AND FOUND: 3524, Thomas.

LOST LOVE: 939, Carke.

LOT: 3536, Thompson.

LOTTERIES: 3537, Cassity; 3538, Blackburn.

LOTUS EATERS: 4354, Kunitz.

LOURDES: 3540, Clancy.

LOUSHAN PASS: 3541, Tse-tung.

LOVE: 147, Sarton; 161, Merrill; 201, Shook; 261, White; 296, Hollander; 325, Galbraith; 393, Lamb; 395, Wheelock; 642, Chi; 664, McFarland; 735, Stafford; 736, Middleton; 756, Savage; 769, Duncan; 884, Lilly; 918, Perry; 954, Thompson; 975, La Bombard; 1061, Squires; 1074, Freneau; 1105, Grenville; 1214, Burger; 1341, Kunitz; 1370, Burford; 1428, Merrill; 1540, Engle; 1699, Mundell; 1702, McFarland; 1753, Schneider; 1761, Lindbergh; 1942, Murray; 1965, Shimazaki; 2035, Eisenlohr; 2061, Brooks; 2076, Graham; 2185, Hanson; 2257, Kahn; 2264, Merchant; 2265, Seaburg; 2290, McFarland; 2299, de Vito; 2522, Stuart; 2541, Gustafson; 2632, Highet; 2721, Fiedler; 2745, Bangs; 2754, Shook; 2759, Roskolenko; 2798, Dunbar; 2806, Martin; 2866, Koch; 2931, Garrigue; 2976, Sawyer; 2986, Talman; 3004, Mok; 3041, Middleton; 3139, Hirshman; 3141, McFarland; 3249, Nationek; 3304, Posner; 3308, Richardson; 3341, Singleton; 3432, Morse; 3463, McFarland; 3518, Merchant; 3519, Rich; 3543, Scott; 3547, Grenville; 3549, Wheeler; 3550, Tremayne; 3557, Jerome; 3565, Stafford; 3566, Kaiser; 3674, Rexroth; 3827, Posner; 4004, Zimmerman; 4006, Creeley; 4008, Doyle; 4053, Jerome; 4083, Carleton; 4103, Ridler; 4156, Merrill; 4161, Abrahams; 4187, Schulberg; 4243, Ewing; 4308, Lee; 4393, Trail; 4427, Newbold; 4547, Cully; 4552, Janson; 4573, Freeman; 4590, Pack; 4690, Viereck; 4701, Meredith; 4809, Orr; 4814, Manker; 4817, Clark; 4840, Milbraith; 4889, Pack; 5013, Mounts; 5057, Merton; 5060, Facos; 5080, Friend; 5153, Richstone; 5203, Graham; 5204, Keith; 5242; Galbraith; 5277, Stock; 5420, Drouet; 5507, Kreiser; 5559, Moss; 5688, Ford; 5950, Rainer; 6045, Shaw; 6119, Robin; 6123, Armknecht; (cont'd)

LOVE (cont'd): 6168, Nemerov; 6259,
Marz; 6304, Morris; 6306, Roseliep;
6337, Shook; 6342, Hoffman; 6401,
Herschberger; 6494, Batchelder;
6508, Bryant; 6511, Isler; 6545,
Weiss; 6551, Eberhart; 6553, Ciardi;
6575, Boles; 6707, Henley; 6772,
Carruth; 6804, Conklin; 6819, Lamb;
6896, Lee; 6913, Carroll; 6961,
Grenville; 7067, Ginsberg; 7070,
Moss; 7243, Renon; 7244, Allard.
LOVE, ABSENCE OF: 1596, Gunn.
LOVE AND BEAUTY: 533, Clower.
LOVE AND CUPID: 1309, Magee.
LOVE AND DISTRACTION: 3558, Galbraith.
LOVE AND MARRIAGE: 742, Eaton; 6556,
Blackwelder.
LOVE BIRDS: 3544, Smith.
LOVE, BROTHERLY: 768, Hughes.
LOVE, COMPLICATIONS OF: 6541,
Grenville.
LOVE, CYCLE OF: 7060, Brown;
LOVE, DIALECTIC OF: 1471, Bell.
LOVE - DREAMS: 1563, Andrews; 1578,
Conklin; 3992, Freeman.
LOVE, EARTHLY: 1628, Bennett.
LOVE - FACETS: 1828, Baird.
LOVE - HIDDEN: 2571, Barker.
LOVE, LANDSCAPE OF: 3229, McGinley.
LOVE, LEGACY OF: 3567, Redman.
LOVE LETTERS: 3329, Burke; 3330,
Collins; 6179, Petrie.
LOVE LONGING: 5831, Murry.
LOVE - MOTHERS: 2073, Wright.
LOVE NESTS: 4997, De Jong.
LOVE OF MAN AND WOMAN: 2113, Mok.
LOVE POEMS: 3425, Guntert, 3552,
Pomeroy; 3600, Viereck; 3889, Ely;
4298, Chatterton; 4873, Woods;
4874, Wylie; 4885, Clancy; 6427,
Rayaprol.
LOVE, PROGRESS OF: 3570, Roethke.
LOVE, REFLECTIONS OF: 5373, Chaffee.
LOVE, REMEMBRANCES OF: 1527, De Jong.
LOVE, SAFETY OF: 3381, Carlisle.
LOVE, SHELTERED BY: 5574, Kahn.
LOVE SONGS: 465, McFarland; 474,
Moore; 1315, Graham; 3555, Kizer;
4634, Chapin; 5680, Galbraith; 5794,
Sarton; 5810, Whitman; 5826,
Cantwell; 5846, Moss; 6792,
Stepanchev; 7032, Livingstone.
LOVE SONNETS: 5855, Burger; 5856,
Cantwell; 5858, de Kay; 5861, Lamb.
LOVE, SOUND OF: 5889, Burrows.
LOVE, STEADFASTNESS OF: 6044, Heath.
LOVE TAKEN FOR GRANTED: 4065,
Alleman.
LOVE - VARIATIONS: 6838, Akins.
LOVE, WORTH OF: 3571, Louchheim.
LOVE, YOUNG: 7367, Carter.
LOVELINESS: 2554, McGrath;; 4264,
Patchen; 6828, Summers.
LOVELORN: 55, Warsaw.
LOVEMAKING: 3553, Putnam.
LOVEMAN, AMY: 6504, B.
LOVERS: 108, Mueller; 776,
Pennington; 1686, Wright; 1751,
Graves; 1838, Armknecht; 3562,
McFarland; 3563, Smith; 3601, Lamb;

3875, Pack; 4366, Jones; 4719, Perry;
5263, Bowen; 5929, Fisher; 6351,
Tagliabue; 6500, Conklin; 6596,
Hayden; 6613, Grenville; 6623,
Hammer; 6929, Viereck.
LOVERS, ADVICE TO: 63, Tyler.
LOVERS' QUARRELS: 580, Ponsot.
LOVE'S POWER: 1534, De Jong.
LOVE'S RETURN: 5266, Carruth.
LOWBROWS: 3053, Armknecht.
LOWER CLASSES: 4417, Graves.
LOYALTY: 3578, Jacobs.
LUCIFER: 3580, McDonnell; 4946,
Pierce.
LUCK: 3183, Armknecht.
LULLABIES: 542, Eisenlohr; 579,
Pillin; 1023, M. Chrysostom Koppes;
2036, Dawson; 2459, Winslow; 3583,
Gibson; 3584, Howes; 3586, Rich;
3589, McFarland; 3590, Wagoner;
3591, Renon; 7201, Frost.
LUPERCALIA: 3594, Hughes.
LUST: 4820, Levant.
LUTES: 6741, Woods.
LUTHER, MARTIN, 1483-1546: 3675,
McGinley.
LUXURY: 6788, Pogue.
LYDIA: 3596, Plunkett.
LYNCHING: 6402, Cooper.
LYSIDICE: 1725, Lattimore
MACHINES: 912, Rago.
MCNAMARA, PAT: 3764, Ryskind.
MADNESS: 1381, Fitzgerald; 2759,
Roskolendo.
MADONNAS: 3606, Farnash.
MADRIGALS: 6370, Derwood.
MAGI: 3608, Besch; 5058, Muldoon.
MAGNIFICANT: 2207, Claudel.
MAGNOLIAS: 4042, Levine.
MAGPIES: 3612, Swan.
MAHLER, GUSTAV, 1860-1911: 3613,
Gross.
MAIDSERVANTS: 4602, Sato.
MAIL BOXES: 5054, Feighny.
MAIL ORDERS: 4442, La Rue.
MAINE: 3659, Booth.
MAJORETTES: 5691, Landeweer.
MAKE BELIEVE: 3654, Secrist.
MAKE-UP: 7257, Armour.
MAKER: 1389, Sandeen.
MALAYA: 7211, Palmer.
MALENKOV, GEORGI MAXIMILIANKOVICH,
1901-: 4009, Eff.
MALLARME, STEPHANIE, 1842-1898: 6615,
Golffing.
MAMMON: 3961, Ignatow; 5475, Perse.
MAMMOTHS: 3623, Wallace.
MAN: 328, Janes; 1151, Char; 1639,
Herbert; 2752, Rawlins; 2891,
Ghiselin; 3625, Woodrum; 3626, Hecht;
3630, Enrico; 3683, Pierce; 3695,
Coblentz; 3893, Berrigan; 4472,
Abel; 4992, Pillin; 5181, Stafford;
6365, Eich; 6776, Steiner; 6791,
Patrick; 6914, Galbraith; 7129,
Clark; 7246, Bangham.
MANGERS: 2910, Grebanier; 3637, Cooke.
MANICURES: 3638, Moore.
MANNERS: 2744, Anthony; 3198, Holmes;
3182, Magee; 3416, Wheeler; 5211,
Anthony; 6595, Rosenfield.

MANY: 4540, Coblentz.
MAPLE TREES: 1612, Richter; 3504, Coatsworth.
MAPS: 3643, Engle; 3644, Bailey; 3645, Woods; 5267, Laing.
MARBELHEAD, MASSACHUSETTS: 4352, Hollander.
MARCH: 221, Abbe; 1339, Seager; 3604, Levine; 3649, Thomson; 3833, Sward.
MARCH WIND: 3653, Graham.
MARCHES: 3499, Tse-Tung.
MARGINS: 3655, Booth.
MARIN, JOHN: 5212, Nichols.
MARKETS: 3049, Nicolas.
MAROONED: 3665, Hillyer.
MARQUAND, JOHN PHILLIPS, 1893-1960: 3964, Gordon.
MARQUIS, DON, 1878-1937: 2607, Watt.
MARRIAGE: 9, Swift; 159, Usk; 564, Moraes; 816, Hull; 1488, Chadwick; 2049, Merrill; 2227, Brady; 2681, Hammer; 2889, Graham; 2966, Ford; 3244, Everson; 3258, Hammer; 3666, Moss; 3667, Yamanguchi; 3967, Schiff; 4015, Jaffray; 4110, Galler; 4246, Chadwick; 4247, Wheeler; 4273, Morton; 5372, Brown; 6086, Richstone; 6744, McFarland; 7027, Chadwick; 7340, Seifer.
MARRIAGE - ADVICE: 51, Buchanan.
MARRIAGE - ANNIVERSARIES: 235, Graham; 3557, Jerome.
MARRIAGE - DOMESTIC PROBLEMS: 1305, Koshland; 1538, Barker; 2514, McGinley; 2570, Emmons; 3085, Bentley; 3692, Bradbury; 3847, Ellert; 4315, 4325, 4331, 4333, 4334, 4335, 4337, 4338, 4339, 4340, Bracken; 5033, Seifer; 5363, Richstone; 6798, Seifer.
MARRIAGE - HUSBANDS: 3337, Reingold; 5366, Newbold; 6567, Emans.
MARRIAGE - PARADOXES: 3669, Congdon.
MARRIAGE PROPOSALS: 2669, Thorpe.
MARRIAGE VOWS: 6556, Blackwelder.
MARRIAGE - WIVES: 804, Jaffray; 1459, Galbraith; 4344, 4346, 4347, Bracken; 5581, Armour; 7150, Fowler.
MARSHES: 3670, Jacobson.
MASKS: 1833, Dicker.
MARTINIS: 3676, Noll.
MARTYRS: 3677, Hughes; 6751, L'Heureux.
MARY OF BETHANY: 6558, Wilkinson.
MARY STUART, QUEEN OF SCOTLAND, 1542-1587: 4699, McGinley.
MARY TUDOR, QUEEN OF ENGLAND, 1516-1558: 3679, Coatsworth; 3677, Hughes.
MARY, VIRGIN: 199, Cotter; 3137, Gordon; 3371, Marz; 4004, Zaturenska; 4598, Claude of Jesus; 4600, Mary Immaculata; 4601, Taylor; 7258, Garlick.
MASKED MAN: 3683, Pierce.
MASKS: 1833, Dicker; 3681, Barker.
MASSES: 1130, McCarthy; 1966, Quinn; 3906, Bryan.
MASTER: 3688, Merwin.
MATADORAS: 3690, Crews.

MATERIALISM: 6713, Ziegler.
MATERIALISTS: 3695, Coblentz.
MATERNITY: 1547, Ward.
MATERNITY CLOTHES: 5563, Congdon.
MATERNITY WARDS: 3696, Richstone.
MATHEMATICS: 7309, Anderson.
MATINS: 929, Fandel.
MATISSE, HENRI, 1869-1954: 2540, Langland.
MATRONS: 3417, Evans; 3444, Lehon.
MATTHEW, ST.: 2057, Magaret.
MATURING: 414, Amihai.
MAUSOLEUMS: 3704, Tomlinson.
MAXWELL, CHARLIE: 1589, Nash.
MAY: 1597, Bell; 2635, Conway; 7122, Pierce.
MAYFLOWER, THE: 3706, Jaffray.
MAZES: 2911, Galler.
MEADOWS: 2427, Sarton; 3709, Powers; 3710, Burr; 3711, Kelley.
MEALS: 3712, Armour.
MEANING: 3478, Calkins; 4894, Marz.
MEASLES: 4192, Stewart; 4408, McFarland.
MEASUREMENTS: 3713, Stanford.
MEDICAL SCHOOLS: 3719, de Vito.
MEDICINE: 3693, Gleason; 4842, Jennison.
MEDICINE CABINETS: 5381, Schiff; 6415, Jaffray.
MEDICIS: 482, Stock.
MEDIEVAL MAN: 303, Lattimore.
MEDITATIONS: 3723, Wurdemann.
MEDITERRANEAN: 3725, Montale.
MEDIUMS: 3726, Morris.
MEETING OF FRIENDS: 3388, Kanfer.
MEETING PLACES: 5017, Wright.
MEETINGS: 3729, Bogan; 3737, Merchant; 6714, Das.
MELLOW: 3721, Herschberger.
MEMORIAL DAY: 3745, Chaffee; 5232, Bowser.
MEMORIALS: 2875, Rock; 2876, O'Gorman.
MEMORIES: 405, Heafield; 2134, Cunliffe; 2211, Coxe; 2339, Stuart; 3254, Grenville; 3599, Orlovitz; 3750, Grenville; 3752, Malody; 3753, Masters; 3834, Vazakas; 4437, Coblentz; 4707, Cresson; 4770, Rainer; 4883, Balch; 7083, Workman; 7300, Sider.
MEMORIZING: 5601, Sweet.
MEMORY: 1301, Love; 2496, Blackwell; 4222, Abbe; 6120, Eaton; 6363, Stafford.
MEN: 528, Pillin; 3757, Service; 4060, Giordan; 4132, Johnson; 4186, Emerson; 4799, Lister; 4886, Hammer; 5295, McFarland; 6130, 7134, Galbraith.
MEN AND HOUSEWORK: 351, Usk.
MEN DYING: 6352, Booth.
MEN - TEMPERAMENT: 5229, Merchant.
MENAGERIES: 3758, Rosenthal.
MENDELSSOHN, FELIX, 1809-1847: 4954, Strong.
MENDING: 3930, Jennison.
MENTAL ILLNESS: 1344, Feinstein.
MENUS: 3762, Jacobson.
MERCHANDISING MANAGERS: 1201, Martin.

MERCY: 3763, Merwin; 3765, Weaver;
   3970, Lindsay; 5595, Richardson.
MERLIN: 3767, Gunn.
MERMAIDS: 471, Watkins.
MERRIMACK COUNTY: 3769, Hall.
MERRONETH, WALES: 3766, Humphries.
MESA LAND: 3773, Kelley.
MESSAGES: 4010, Panigrahi.
MESSENGERS: 3776, Flexner.
MESSIAH: 1704, Harrisen; 5076, Karni.
METAMORPHOSES: 3779, Duncan.
METAPHYSICS: 2854, Tomlinson; 3782,
   Fitzgerald.
METH DRINKERS: 2360, Smith.
MEXICAN BOYS: 856, Burns.
MEXICANS: 3785, Nathan.
MEXICO: 3784, Landeweer; 3786,
   Tagliabue; 3787, Bartlett; 3788,
   Summers; 5488, Hull.
MIAMI, FLORIDA: 1394, Lang.
MICE: 1335, Stevens; 4423, Holmes;
   5760, Crews; 6509, Galbraith.
MICHELANGELO BUONARROTI: 3789, Lilly.
MIDAS: 3167, Moss.
MIDDLE AGE: 3116, McGinley; 3556,
   Savage; 6481, Barker.
MIDDLE-AGE: 379, Rich; 7189, Crews.
MIDDLE-OF-THE-ROADERS: 5074, Jones.
MIDGETS: 5697, Reid.
MIDNIGHT: 1996, Denney; 3797, Clark;
   3798, Fichman; 5385, Richardson.
MIDSUMMER: 3801, Bronk; 6437, Levine.
MIDSUMMER NIGHTS: 3804, Bevington.
MIGRANTS: 4599, Conway.
MIGRATION: 3809, Wagoner.
MILITARY FUNERALS: 3811, Thomas; 7244,
   Allard.
MILITARY LEADERS: 2058, Morris.
MILITARY POWER: 4281, Fitzell.
MILK: 4152, Raskin.
MILKING: 82, Everson.
MILTON, JOHN, 1608-1674: 366, Rosen.
MIND: 3814, Schwartz; 4656, Smith;
   4658, Claudel; 6478, Barker; 6734,
   O'Gorman.
MIND POISONING: 1846, Slemp.
MINDS: 1565, Schwartz; 3152, Nicholl;
   4238, Walton.
MINNESOTA: 2108, Hansen.
MINNOWS: 4480, 5962, Stafford.
MINSTRELS: 3818, Huff; 3819, Carter.
MIRACLES: 114, Coblentz; 1519, Walsh;
   3821, Goodman; 3822, Pasternak; 5232,
   Bowser; 6475, Harrington; 6716, Trent.
MIRRORS: 328, Janes; 1342, Doherty;
   3681, Barker; 4686, Vesely; 5344,
   Levertov; 5890, Engle; 5917,
   Nemerov; 6537, Hall; 6674, Donnely;
   6959, Booth.
MISERS: 3872, Kearns.
MISERY: 2836, Kinnell; 4807, Ashbery.
MISFITS: 3757, Service.
MISHAPS: 1194, Ford.
MISSILES: 5030, Starbuck; 5897,
   Armour.
MISSING: 2117, Dorheim; 3835,
   Coblentz.
MISSIONARIES: 2278, Starbuck; 5253,
   Collier.
MISSISSIPPI RIVER: 3837, Ward.

MISSOURI RIVER: 7030, Jacobs.
MISSTEPS: 3838, White.
MISTAKES: 576, Heath; 5683, Armour;
   7126, Galbraith.
MISTS: 557, Coblentz; 3839, Gregor;
   3842, Coblentz.
MISUNDERSTANDING: 3844, Burrowes.
MITTENS: 5359, Pardue.
MOBILES: 3849, Updike.
MOCKERY: 3851, Galler.
MOCKING BIRDS: 7370, Delattre.
MOCKINGBIRDS: 3262, Witt; 3852, Isler.
MODELS (ART): 4292, Watson.
MODERN MAN: 5882, Cooper.
MODEST GIRLS: 6085, Collins.
MOMENTS: 6882, Squires.
MONASTERIES: 716, McCarthy.
MONDAY: 672, Grenville.
MONDAY MORNING: 4340, Bracken.
MONDRIAN: 3870, Solomon.
MONET, CLAUDE, 1840-1926: 3872, Norse.
MONEY: 259, Nash; 1762, Schiff; 1850,
   Hagiwara; 1930, Schlitzer; 2033,
   Armour; 2273, Galbraith; 3872,
   Kearns; 3968, Nash; 4749, Wheeler;
   4787, Graham; 5070, Bogardus; 7316,
   Chadwick.
MONEY AND LIVING: 5628, Newmeyer.
MONKS: 3873, Mary Honora.
MONTGOMERY, ALABAMA: 467, Waterman;
   6594, Bentley.
MONUMENTS: 3934, Pitchford.
MOODS: 3878, Matthews; 3879, Blackwell;
   4556, Weiss; 4781, Raskin; 7157,
   Levine.
MOON: 123, Kinnell; 404, Friedrich;
   2251, Wheelock; 3224, Swenson; 3228,
   Nichols; 3593, Burr; 3880, Sato,
   3285, Ridler; 3595, Hall; 3881,
   Zilles; 3882, Hartley; 3885, Lipton;
   3906, Morris; 4085, Quinn; 4086,
   Savage; 6047, Kramer; 6729, Cregeen;
   6833, Mack; 6841, Jacobsen; 7114,
   Sato.
MOONLIGHT: 2647, Wilson; 2879, Warren;
   3886, Bock; 4614, Pomeroy; 4852,
   Elliott; 5552, Jacobson.
MOORE, MARIANNE, 1887-: 6829, Olson.
MOPS: 4321, Galbraith.
MORALS: 5023, Moss.
MORNING: 145, Roseliep; 1611, Simpson;
   1613, Beach; 1614, Karandikar; 1949,
   Hicks; 2349, Blackburn; 2913, Frimet;
   2914, di Giovanni; 3196, Mastin;
   3897, Tigner; 3903, Reid; 3908,
   Austin; 3910, Hall; 5005, Jones;
   5273, Facos; 5502, Strand; 5965,
   Norman; 6389, Galbraith; 6677, Aiken;
   6860, Perry; 7056, Salomon.
MORTALITY: 426, Ginsberg; 3914, Frost.
MOSES: 1687, Holmes; 3102, Roth; 3915,
   Gilboa; 3916, Kanfer.
MOSES, ANNA MARY ROBERTSON, 1860-:
   6309, Olson.
MOSQUITOES: 634, Lazarus.
MOSS: 6929, Viereck.
MOTELS: 6659, Douglass.
MOTHER GOOSE: 3858, Jennison; 5899,
   5900, Winsor.
MOTHER HUBBARD: 3922, Wolking.

MOTHER'S DAY: 3367, Johnston, 3919, Heller.

MOTHERHOOD: 6676, Fairchild.

MOTHERS: 1, Stockdale; 203, Van Doren; 290, Gohn; 460, Constantine; 530, Ellis; 2867, Moody; 2949, Soule; 2998, Kizer; 3002, McNeill; 3142, Stewart; 3185, Wood; 3366, Quinn; 3520, Galbraith; 3925, Marx; 3931, Miner; 4011, Wolf; 4251, McFarland; 4520, Richstone; 4672, Wuebker; 5161, Richstone; 5187, Pasley; 5230, Delattre; 5806, Hamilton; 6039, Galbraith; 6393, Henry; 6426, Jenney; 7368, de Vito.

MOTHERS - COATS: 1098, Wood.

MOTHERS - EXPERIENCES: 5827, De Jong.

MOTHERS - HOLIDAYS: 3928, Richstone.

MOTHERS - KNOWLEDGE: 4640, Nelson.

MOTHERS - PROBLEMS: 4146, Brasier.

MOTHERS - SONGS: 1773, Jennison.

MOTHERS - THOUGHTS: 4949, Douglass.

MOTHERS - TRIBUTES: 6669, Counselman.

MOTHERS - WISDOM: 4169, Bannon.

MOTHS: 2092, Donnelly; 3598, Snodgrass; 3918, Barker.

MOTION: 3273, Burford; 4212, Garrigue.

MOTION PICTURES: 3953, Rosenfield.

MOTORCYCLISTS: 6801, Gunn.

MOTORISTS: 5836, Armour.

MOTORS: 3932, Coblentz.

MOUNTAIN SCENERY: 845, Wangsgaard.

MOUNTAIN SHACKS: 5622, Graham.

MOUNTAIN STREAMS: 4648, Nemerov.

MOUNTAIN TOWNS: 5695, Tanaka.

MOUNTAIN-CLIMBING: 5967, Eberhart.

MOUNTAINS: 304, Graves; 794, Merwin; 833, Eff; 1109, Tanaka; 2551, Justice; 3909, Cooper; 3939, Ignatow; 3942, Landeweer; 3946, Lougee; 4382, Weismiller; 5085, Ginsberg; 5419, Bauer.

MOURNING: 147, Sarton; 1400, Dana; 3963, Sward; 5192, Frankenberg.

MOURNING DOVES: 4790, Posner.

MOVIES: 1713, Rosenfield; 2002, Pugh; 2614, Stone; 3876, Congdon; 5370, Malcolm; 7098, Newman.

MOVING: 2333, Nemerov; 3950, Stafford.

MOWING LAWNS: 4890, Galbraith.

MOZART, WOLFGANG AMADEUS, 1756-1791:   3957, Bandeira; 4126, Witt.

MUD-PIES: 3969, Galbraith.

MULBERRY TREES: 488, Stevens.

MUNCH, EDVARD: 3174, Hall.

MURDER: 2978, Vance; 3972, Wagoner; 3973, Nemerov; 3974, Allen.

MURDER MYSTERIES: 3971, Russell.

MURDERERS: 376, Wright; 6671, Kanfer.

MUSES: 1441, Watkins; 2750, Sinisgalli; 4087, Moira; 5779, Bishop.

MUSEUM PIECES: 3981, Carruth.

MUSEUMS: 717, Bohm; 2019, Whittemore; 3979, Tanikawa; 4569, Atherton; 5326, Freeman.

MUSIAL, STANLEY: 6752, Nash.

MUSIC: 1550, Gregory; 1766, Lilly; 2084, Cully; 2193, Burrows; 2329, Scovel; 2409, Weiss; 2506, Bower; 2736, Smith; 3465, McGinley; 4111, Davis; 5742, Coblentz; 5816, Posner; 7359, Freeman.

MUSIC BOXES: 765, Lee; 3982, Stevenson.

MUSIC, LISTENING TO: 4469, Lister.

MUSICIANS: 3689, Lilly; 3983, Lister; 5427, Nemerov.

MUSK OX: 3984, Lister.

MUSSEL HUNTERS: 3986, Plath.

MUSTANGS: 4135, Burrows.

MYSTERY: 813, Mary Immaculata; 922, Wheeler.

MYTHMAKERS: 4025, Coxe.

MYTHOLOGY: 5364, Kessler.

MYTHS: 1396, Plath.

NAKED: 4028, Graves.

NAMES: 134, Donnelly; 733, Singer; 2307, Lineaweaver; 3478, Calkins; 4031, Creeley; 4032, Katz; 4129, Wright; 5068, Elmer; 5150, Bonnefoy; 6051, Nash.

NANTUCKET, MASSACHUSETTS: 4034, Chadbourne.

NAPLES: 4035, Ciardi; 4036, Langland.

NAPS: 750, Chadwick; 6163, Eisenlohr; 6730, Crane.

NARCISSISM: 4037, Packard.

NARCISSUS: 3978, Kizer; 4038, Barker.

NATIVITY: 225, Maris Stella; 443, Sat R; 641, Patrick; 878, Thorley; 882, Hilberry; 1023, M. Chrysostom Koppes; 2284, Ignatia; 2317, Cunningham; 2506, Bower; 2910, Grebanier; 2922, O'Connell; 2956, Cooper; 4258, Friedrich; 4342, Nims; 4657, Mary Madeleva.

NATIVITY SCENES: 1465, Lattimore 3608, Besch; 7097, Pierce.

NATO: 5322, Sagittarius.

NATURE: 1152, Seg; 2206, Weinstein; 2337, Lister; 2600, Nemerov; 2817, Jerome; 3159, Collins; 4044, McBrown; 4364, Byron; 4857, Lang; 5419, Bauer; 5825, Riddle; 5846, Moss.

NATURE POETS: 1676, Nemerov.

NATURE WALKS: 4043, Nash.

NAZARETH: 4046, Patrick.

NECESSITIES: 3656, Galbraith.

NECKLACES: 5146, Raiziss.

NECROPHILIACS: 6473, Moore.

NEED: 1248, Kahn.

NEEDLEWORK: 3930, Jennison.

NEGROES: 300, Johnson; 644, Dufault; 2488, Fennell; 2726, Cuney; 2728, Walsh; 3186, 4054, Razaf; 4828, Willis; 6534, Kahn.

NEIGHBORS: 1384, Holmes; 1387, de Vito, 2417, Warsaw; 3063, Jennison; 3335, Evans; 4143, Schlitzer; 5708, Rosenfield; 6569, Raskin.

NEON LIGHTS: 4115, Magee.

NESTING BOXES: 1936, Graves.

NESTS: 4057, Lamb; 4058, McGrath; 6967, Rosenberg.

NEUTRALISTS: 4059, Armour.

NEUTRONS: 5782, Bishop.

NEW BEGINNINGS: 5637, Coolidge.

NEW BETHLEHEM, PENN.: 4068, Houghton.
NEW COMERS: 2450, Richman.
NEW HAMPSHIRE: 4077, Golffing.
NEW YEAR: 2060, Carter; 4094, Clark;
    4859, Menashe.
NEW YORK CITY: 1316, Feldman; 2712,
    Nash; 7093, Jaffray.
NEW YORK PUBLIC LIBRARY: 881,
    Deutsch.
NEW YORK STATE: 7347, McGonigal.
NEW YORK TIMES: 2112, Eff.
NEW YORKERS: 1053, Bishop.
NEWLYWEDS: 5371, Galbraith.
NEWMAN, BARNETT: 4444, Nemerov.
NEWSPAPER REPORTERS: 4914, Bernard.
NEWSPAPERS: 1051, Gemmell; 6523,
    Hall.
NEWTON, CRADOCK: 1271, Tomlinson.
NICAEA: 1035, Molton.
NIETZSCHE, FRIEDRICH, 1844-1900:
    2279, Weiss.
NIGHT: 286, Friedrich; 361, Bernard;
    1461, Cotter; 1706, Ogilvie; 2010,
    Simpson; 2648, Fleming; 2739, Elytis;
    3078, Frost; 3783, Smythe; 3805,
    Guenther; 4107, Irvine; 4114, Isler;
    4116, Neame; 4118, Frost; 4125,
    Di Giovanni; 4163, Friedrich; 4998,
    Singer; 5378, Beyer; 5586, Delattre;
    5805, Moffitt; 7115, Moynahan.
NIGHTBOATS: 4026, Deutsch.
NIGHTINGALES: 4127, Yosano; 6510,
    Groszmann.
NIGHTMARES: 5872, Manifold.
NIGHTSHADES: 570, Holmes.
NOAH: 298, Macpherson; 4159, Delattre;
    4160, Langland.
NOCTURNES: 4166, Pillin.
NOISES: 5886, Emmons.
NONPROFIT: 4170, Maguire.
NONSENSE VERSE: 2828, Robin.
NOON: 6103, Vance; 1672, Ostroff;
    4172, Greer; 5377, Woods.
NORMAN, HERBERT: 1392, Kizer.
NORTH: 2207, Horner; 6692, Eberhart.
NOSEGAYS: 4179, Long.
NOSTALGIA: 4180, Farrar; 4181,
    Miyoshi; 5936, Brennan.
NOTATIONS: 4198, Lieberman.
NOTHING: 228, Gunn; 4214, Gravens;
    7036, D'Andrade.
NOTRE DAME CATHEDRAL: 4221, Witt.
NOTRE DAME DE CHARTRES: 4220,
    Meredith.
NOUNS: 938, Lineaweaver.
NOVELISTS: 4223, Hall; 4224, Pomeroy.
NOVELS: 422, Gunn.
NOVEMBER: 1917, Van Doren; 3792,
    Ross; 4225, Faith; 4226, Bulkeley;
    4227, Averitt; 4229, Porter; 4231,
    Love.
NOW: 4232, Galbraith,
NUCLEAR WARFARE: 452, Kelley.
NUCLEAR WEAPONS: 6818, Lang; 6903,
    Sagittarius.
NUDES: 321, Stepanchev; 4028, Graves;
    5870, Williams.
NUDISTS: 594, Kumin.
NUNS: 1390, Stein; 2099, Dana; 4402,
    Stein; 6273, Shapiro.

NURSERIES: 2393, Broughton; 4249,
    Enright.
NURSERY RHYMES: 4252, Montague; 6429,
    Warren.
NURSES: 4248, White; 6910, Merchant.
NURSING HOMES: 6793, Turner.
NUT TREES: 2220, Shneur.
NUTRITION: 2420, Fabstein.
OAK TREES: 1419, Merrill.
OBEDIENCE: 1046, Bangham.
OBEISANCES: 7095, Nash.
OBESITY: 1876, Abbe; 5507, Kreiser;
    7095, Nash.
OBLATIONS: 4272, Bangham.
OBSESSIONS: 4024, O'Gorman.
OCEAN TRAVEL: 3660, Kroll.
OCEANS: 3661, Raiziss; 4030, 4108,
    Jenkins; 4278, Winston; 4813, Perry;
    6391, Supervielle; 7167, Long.
OCTOBER: 860, MacLow; 1184, Levant;
    3334, Chaffee; 4282, Dean; 4283,
    Long; 4285, Pomeroy; 4286, Grenville;
    4289, Jacobs; 4290, McKee; 5168,
    Langland; 5308, Petrie; 5471, Stewart;
    6908, McGinley.
ODDITIES: 7298, Lamb.
ODORS: 5870, Williams.
ODYSSEUS: 4306, Merwin.
OIL: 4367, Landeweer.
OKLAHOMA: 1835, Brittain.
OLD AGE: 819, Merrill; 3672,
    Schluneger; 4394, Harper; 4397,
    Eckman; 4985, Davidson; 5038, Merwin;
    5230, Delattre.
OLD LADIES: 2916, Antolini.
OLD MEN: 66, Middleton; 1483, Hughes;
    2599, Hughes; 3261, Eberhart; 3631,
    Grenville; 4111, Davis; 4385, Bishop;
    4391, Merrill; 4395, Macpherson;
    4396, Keith; 4399, MacGillivray;
    4400, Long; 5819, Brinnin; 6467,
    Rothenberg.
OLD ONES: 6773, Merwin.
OLD SOLDIERS: 4407, Nemerov.
OLD WOMEN: 4415, Barnes; 5288, Morrah.
OMNISCIENCE: 1328, Wolf.
ONE: 4540, Coblentz.
ONENESS: 3850, Nemerov.
ONIONS: 5362, Blackburn.
OPEN MINDS: 5091, Cumin.
OPERAS: 2371, Levy.
OPHELIA: 1325, Mann.
OPINIONS: 4571, Galbraith.
OPOSSUMS: 4951, Eliot.
OPPORUNITY: 1582, Lucy; 6237, Braley.
OPPOSITE SEX: 6131, Galbraith.
ORACLES: 2292, Milne; 4501, Plath.
ORANGE PICKERS: 4574, Ignatow.
ORANGES: 3467, Sorrentino; 4575,
    Krolow.
ORATORS: 4576, Waddington; 4671,
    Lilly.
ORCHARDS: 4, Barker; 2915, Friend;
    3310, Lineaweaver; 4578, Hubler;
    4579, Stone; 5920, Corke.
ORCHESTRAS: 1170, Ginsberg.
ORDER: 4580, Hay.
ORDINATION: 4088, Doherty.
ORDINATION RITES: 3402, Roseliep.
ORPHEUS: 4584, Scott; 4585, Slavitt;
    4587, Untermeyer; 6430, Fitzgerald.

ORTHODONTISTS: 3317, Armour.
ORTHODOXY: 4588, Paddock.
OUT-OF-DOORS: 3777, Sears.
OUTDOOR COOKING: 458, Thorson.
OUTDOORS: 4616, Galler.
OUTER BANKS: 4617, Drewry.
OUTSIDERS: 4622, Graves.
OVERSHOES: 4627, Smith.
OVERSUPPLIED: 4629, Zimmerman.
OVERWEIGHT: 6322, White.
OWLS: 2569, Steegmuller; 2628,
   Eberhart; 3816, Welch; 5459, Benet;
   5460, Russo; 6345, Ciardi.
OXFORD UNIVERSITY: 4633, Dickey.
OYSTER FARMS: 4636, Landeweer.
OYSTERS: 242, Heringman.
PACTS: 805, Sagittarius.
PAELIGNI: 181, Humphries.
PAGAN LEARNING: 296, Hollander.
PAIN: 4643, Grossman; 4644, Van Hise;
   5636, Appleton; 6122, Vance.
PAINTERS: 4646, Ashbery.
PAINTINGS: 2964, Bynner; 4759, Armour.
PALM SUNDAY: 879, Waugaman; 2641,
   Pierce; 4405, Engle.
PALMISTRY: 6485, Jaffray.
PALMS: 4651, Whittemore.
PANTHERS: 4653, Eff.
PANTOMINE: 5018, Stone.
PAPER CHAINS: 7019, Henley.
PARABLES: 4324, Kelley.
PARACHUTES: 6565, Wagoner.
PARADES: 711, Moore; 3042, Simpson;
   4660, Hammer; 4661, Neely.
PARADISE: 4662, Anwar; 4664, Menashe;
   4666, Thornton.
PARALYTICS: 6476, Pierce.
PARASOLS: 3390, Swann.
PARENTS: 762, Richstone; 1438, Pierce;
   1854, Richstone; 2222, Jacobs;
   2224, Talman; 2320, Richstone; 4047,
   Stewart; 4669, Neely; 4721, Otis;
   4925, Brasier; 5537, Galbraith;
   5938, Stefanile; 6198, Smith; 6571,
   Barkins.
PARIS, FRANCE: 3755, Ciardi; 4670,
   Drouet.
PARKING: 5063, Jacobson.
PARKING SPACES: 5774, Bishop.
PARKS: 49, Clark; 211, Urdang; 6629,
   Maino.
PARODIES: 189, Stern; 650, Moore;
   699, Shores; 2309, Jones; 2779,
   Nash; 2789, Black; 2796, Chadwick;
   3085, Bentley; 3680, Lamb; 3738,
   Morrah; 3741, Hagelstange; 4067,4254,
   Sagittarius; 4691, Counselman; 5059,
   Wood; 5288, Morrah; 6023, Goodwell;
   6062, Wylie; 6429, Warren; 6447,
   Atherton; 6713, Ziegler; 6942,
   Jones; 7239, Meyers.
PARTIES: 6595, Rosenfield.
PARTING: 3320, Kahn; 4677, Hay;
   4678, Walujati.
PARTS OF SPEECH: 4757, Koch.
PASSAGES: 2883, Walton.
PASSION: 5067, Laing; 5821, O'Gorman.
PASSION WEEK: 5292, M. Jeremy.
PASSIONS: 2134, Cunliffe.
PASSOVER: 2146, Fiedler; 4692, Wolf;
   4693, Hameiri.

PAST: 3530, Sexton; 4392, Burke;
   4694, Goodman.
PAST, THE: 389, Galbraith; 3210,
   Wheeler.
PASTORAL POETS: 1572, Stow.
PASTORS: 4703, Schreiber.
PATCHWORK WIVES: 5171, Colvin.
PATHS: 2778, Tomlinson.
PATIENCE: 6638, Patmore.
PATIENCE OF PARENTS: 6656, Smith.
PATRON SAINTS: 3442, Giordan.
PAUL, ST.: 2890, Gunn; 4711, Hazo;
   5405, Janes; 5406, Richardson; 5625,
   McGinley.
PAULINUS OF NOLA: 4712, Cotter.
PAUPERS: 4714, di Giovanni.
PAVANS: 4716, DeJong; 4718, Bernard.
PAVLOVNA, ANNA: 4713, Marz.
PAYDAYS: 7316, Chadwick.
PEACE: 262, Foster; 767, Trent; 777,
   Merwin; 1210, Ponsot; 1302, Bunner;
   1512, Merrill; 1813, Brooks; 1826,
   Eckhardt; 2013, Carter; 3013,
   Davidson; 3461, Turner; 4060,
   Giordan; 4720, Loyal; 4722, Trent;
   4723, White; 4981, Patrick; 5592,
   McGinley; 5650, Grimm; 7290, James.
PEACE CONFERENCES: 480, Noyes.
PEACE-MAKERS: 3717, Amihai.
PEACH ORCHARDS: 3951, Nathan.
PEACOCKS: 4728, Witt.
PEAKS: 4324, Kelley.
PEALE, NORMAN VINCENT, 1898-: 202,
   Bentley.
PEARLS: 4263, Barker; 4729, Grace;
   5501, Lilly.
PEARLY GATES: 3135, Minck.
PEASANT GIRLS: 1250, Kondo.
PEASANTS: 4730, Wolf.
PEDANTRY: 4904, Honig.
PEDDLERS: 4735, Ginsberg.
PEDESTRIANS: 5044, Schneider.
PEEPERS: 4736, Cane.
PEER GYNT: 4737, Kinnell.
PEGUY, CHARLES, 1873-1914: 935,
   Trouster.
PELICANS: 612, Otis.
PENELOPE: 4739, Bagg.
PENITENCE: 3038, Angoff; 4027, D;
   4740, McCarthy.
PENITENTS: 5006, Roseliep.
PENMANSHIP: 7248, Pritchard.
PENNY ARCADES: 4742, Atherton.
PENSIONS: 6587, White.
PENTECOST: 4088, Doherty.
PEONIES: 4743, Quinn.
PEOPLE: 1913, Jennison; 3952,
   O'Gorman; 4744, Donnelly; 4745, Otis;
   6652, Franklin.
PERAZA, GUILLEN: 4827, Merwin.
PERCEPTION: 4747, Van Hise.
PERFECTION: 1195, Grenville.
PERFECTIONISTS: 1525, Honig.
PERFUMES: 4326, Bracken; 4752, Speer.
PERMANENT WAVES: 6292, Seifer.
PERSEPHONE: 4760, Hopkins; 6739,
   Plath.
PERSONALITY: 4763, Touster.
PERSONNEL: 4766, Brooks.
PESSIMISM: 1799, Yellem.

PESSIMISTS: 4771, Barker.
PESTLES: 4772, Tiempo.
PETER, SAINT: 329, Dudley.
PETER, ST.:   4775, O'Connell; 5328,
    Magaret.
PETRARCH: 330, Roseliep.
PETS: 4773, Lund; 4774, Wheeler.
PHARISEES: 4780, Janes.
PHARYNXES: 3635, Stevens.
PHILADELPHIANS: 4941, J.
PHILANDER: 4782, Jerome.
PHILANTHROPISTS: 3231, Burrows.
PHILATELISTS: 4783, Ebright.
PHILIP DE LA CASAS: 5407, Logan.
PHILLIPS, WALTER, CAPTAIN, U.S.M.C.:
    2058, Morris.
PHILOSOPHERS: 4785, Jones.
PHILOSOPHY: 3306, Quinn; 4432, Wright.
PHOBIAS: 2002, Pugh.
PHOENIXES: 4790, Posner; 4791,
    Whitman; 4792, Aiken; 4793, Owen.
PHONOGRAPH RECORDS: 3191, Leviant.
PHONOGRAPHS: 3355, Sharp.
PHOTOGRAPHS: 2310, Burr; 4104,
    Ignatow; 4794, Shapiro.
PHOTOGRAPHY: 451, Witt.
PHYSICIANS: 1528, 1529, Markle; 1851,
    Kenny; 7248, Pritchard.
PHYSICIANS' WAITING ROOMS: 6421,
    Armour.
PHYSICISTS: 383, Huntiers; 1968,
    Platt; 7022, Schenck.
PIANISTS: 3010, Swenson; 4461, Pillin;
    4795, Gibbs.
PIANO: 4796, Burns.
PIANO LESSONS: 714, Isler.
PIANO RECITALS: 5162, Baker.
PIANOS: 4436, Aucourt.
PICASSO, PABLO: 4798, Lohf; 5655,
    Laing.
PICNICS: 238, Pratt; 2315, Dufault;
    4801, M. Maura; 4802, Bock; 6679,
    Corke.
PICTURES: 6654, Rich.
PIGEONS: 130, Scott; 6839, Coe.
PIGGY BANKS: 888, Galbraith.
PIGS: 4812, Saunders.
PIGTAILS: 4887, McKee.
PINE TREES: 6026, Belitt.
PINK: 2741, Grossman.
PIONEERS: 4819, Whitman.
PIPERS: 4822, Dufault.
PIQUED DAMES: 4823, Lang.
PLACE NAMES: 7093, Jaffray.
PLACES: 2760, Todrin; 6338, Cunliffe.
PLAGUES: 2210, Alterman.
PLANETS: 5197, D.
PLANS: 6346, Otis.
PLANTS: 4831, Shiffert.
PLASTICS: 3694, Holloway.
PLATITUDES: 1361, Simon.
PLAY: 2298, Cotter.
PLAYGROUNDS: 5158, Hopkins.
PLAYING POSSUM: 6150, Neely.
PLAYS: 5452, Alleman.
PLAZA DE TORES, IOWA: 4837,
    Stoutenberg.
PLEDGES: 4847, Pritam.
PLENTY: 3218, Barker.
PLOWMEN: 2521, Jacobson; 3956, Lucy.

PLUMBING: 657, Updike.
PLUMBLINES: 5045, Ratliff.
PLYWOOD: 234, Shaw.
POE, EDGAR ALLAN, 1809-1849:   4850,
    Fadiman.
POEMS: 1914, Whittemore; 4505,
    Leverton; 4888, Stefanile; 6435,
    Whittemore; 7339, Duncan.
POETRY: 309, O'Gorman; 997, Hitchcock;
    1502, Caeiro; 1552, Richman; 2201,
    Claudel; 2318, Johnson; 2871, Moore;
    2885, Casey; 2887, Moore; 3172,
    Schwartz; 3890, Wright; 4189,
    Gerkle; 4839, Graves; 4858, Melo
    Neto; 4903, Farjeon; 4905, Holmes;
    4906, Kitasono; 4907, Engonopoulos;
    4909, Kaplan; 5143, Duncan; 5504,
    Zeldis; 5769, Tagliabue; 5771,
    Joost; 6320, Stock; 6379, Eastman;
    6904, Kenny.
POETS: 107; O'Gorman; 269, Dunn;
    415, Pessoa; 1348, Pasternak; 1391,
    Joshi; 1443, Kaneko; 1476, Claudel;
    1572, Stow; 1655, Fandel; 1892,
    Goddard; 4462, Abse; 4465, Lister;
    4546, Hillyer; 4560, Root; 4829,
    Kizer; 4839, Graves; 4897, Touster;
    4898, Stefanile; 4899, Justice;
    4900, De Kay; 4901, Hanford; 4910,
    Burford; 4942, Humphries; 4970,
    Ciardi; 5002, Wylie; 5272,
    Fitzgerald; 5524, Delattre; 5675,
    Morse; 6540, Lowenfels; 6660, Tse-
    Tung; 6899, Smith; 7044,
    Ferlinghetti.
POINTS OF VIEW: 3313, Bolton; 5455,
    Schenck.
POKER: 3920, Weiss.
POLE VAULTERS: 4912, Murano.
POLICEMEN: 4913, Anthony; 6413,
    White.
POLITICIANS: 4916, Glaze; 6349, Hall.
POLITICS: 4915, Lazarus; 4917,
    Nemerov.
POMEGRANATES: 6227, Nash.
POMPEII: 4919, Grossman.
PONDS: 2354, Kunitz; 4921, Steiner;
    6144, Mayhall; 7203, Ballielt.
PONY CARTS: 2304, Graham.
POODLES: 4923, Solomon.
POOLS: 5331, Barker.
POPCORN: 5887, Galbraith.
POPLAR TREES: 4926, Swenson; 7116,
    Chi.
POPPIES: 4927, Shneur.
PORCHES: 3910, Hall.
PORTRAITS: 2150, Urdang; 2267,
    Squires; 4280, Hedden; 4935, Johnson;
    4936, Walton; 4943, Young.
PORTS: 4931, Howes.
POSSESSION: 1235, Engle; 6834,
    Galbraith.
POSSESSIONS: 4558, Fretz.
POSTERS: 6004, Spear.
POSTMASTERS: 7044, Ferlinghetti.
POSTMEN: 4956, Carlile.
POSTMORTEMS: 4957, De Jong.
POSTWAR: 1119, Fall.
POTIONS: 4504, Moss.
POTTING PLANTS: 4964, Thomas.

POUND, EZRA, 1885-: 1820, Guthrie; 2065, Ciardi.
POVERTY: 3246, Hoskins; 4350, Bell.
POWER: 3478, Calkins; 5258, Burrowes; 5599, La Bombard.
PRAIRIES: 5785, Barker.
PRAISE: 3572, Halacy; 4971, Sitwell.
PRAYER: 931, Delattre; 1164, Janes; 1212, Mullins; 1726, Powers; 1781, Nationek; 2825, Sandeen; 2884, Coblentz; 3716, Clark; 4259, Wolf; 4731, Gray; 4973, Coleridge; 4974, Hamizah; 4986, Hager; 5190, Burrowes; 7283, Cully.
PRAYERS: 41, Katz; 137, Ely; 327, Kreymborg; 566, Merchant; 636, Kreiser; 893, Hughes; 1083, Patrick; 1182, Adams; 1347, 1421, Cully; 2557, O'Connor; 2898, Freeman; 2928, Clark; 3374, Sharp; 4705, Sandeen; 4724, Gray; 4972, Brenneman; 4975, Heafield; 4976, Benet; 4977, Griffith; 4978, Osborne; 4982, Nash; 4985, Davidson; 4995, Finks; 5791, Kay; 6264, Terry; 7265, Karni.
PRAYING MANTIS: 924, Holmes.
PRECARIOUS: 4987, Walton.
PREGNANCIES: 2447, Ponsot; 4990, Butler.
PREGNANCY: 2808, Turnbull; 4989, Koch.
PREGNANT WOMEN: 7264, Torres.
PREMONITIONS: 4994, Levine.
PREPAREDNESS: 1131, Pierce.
PRESENT: 4241, Gaines.
PRESIDENCY: 4254, Sagittarius.
PRESLEY, ELVIS: 1415, Pathan.
PRESSMEN: 3211, Frumbin.
PRIDE: 4062, Galbraith; 5004, Jennings; 6614, Pierce; 6681, Howes.
PRIESTS: 1159, O'Gorman.
PRIMERS: 1972, Rubin.
PRIMROSES: 6765, Hardy.
PRINCES: 339, Galler4875, O'Gorman.
PRINCESSES: 5673, Fuller.
PRINTING: 6713, Kaser.
PRINTING PRESSES: 5633, Winslow.
PRISONER OF WAR: 5014, Vance.
PRISONERS: 5015, Kabir.
PRIVACY: 2756, Nash; 6231, Hammer.
PROCRASTINATION: 5765, Chadwick.
PROFESSIONS: 6375, Jaffray.
PROFESSOR, DEATH OF: 6109, Roseliep.
PROFESSORS: 359, Stafford; 2490, Hanford; 5027, Ryskind; 5028, Mary Jeremy; 6109, Roseliep; 6880, Laing.
PROFIT AND LOSS: 952, Garrigue.
PROGRESS: 1128, Nash; 1292, Galler; 3641, Masters; 4151, Roche; 5032, Eisenlohr.
PROMISED LAND: 1806, Rich.
PROMISES: 5039, Warren.
PRONOUNS: 1683, Feinstein; 3133, Solovay.
PROPHETS: 57, Wilbur; 3087, Flatto; 5045, Ratliff; 5047, Richardson; 5508, Lilly; 5510, Galbraith.
PROSERPINE: 2711, Carruth; 5048, Freeman.
PROSPERITY: 7353, Bewas.
PROSTITUTES: 516, 1587, Hughes;

1980, Shapiro; 2271, Wright; 2595, Stepanchev; 3144, O'Doherty; 3658, 3658, Sagittarius; 4649, Singer; 6106, Plath.
PROTESTS: 5050, 5051, Burket.
PROVERBS: 6436.
PROVISION: 5055, Winchester.
PRUNING: 5056, Todd.
PSALMS: 3264, M. Paulinus; 4545, Shapiro.
PSYCHIATRISTS: 6949, Bauer.
PSYCHOANALYSIS: 1521, Warfel.
PSYCHOANALYSTS: 3215, Saroyan; 5061, Jones.
PSYCHOLOGY: 6182, Chadwick.
PTOLEMAIC SYSTEM: 1739, Hillyer.
PUBLIC GARDENS: 2917, Betjeman.
PUDDLES: 6972, Eisenlohr.
PUERTO RICANS: 6998, Steiner.
PULLMAN CARDS: 970, Krieger.
PUNCTUATION: 1138, Solovay.
PUPPETS: 3559, Wilbur.
PURITANS: 5069, Henley; 5132, Masters.
PURITY: 3067, Hall.
PURPLE: 2897, Pomeroy; 3596, Plunkett.
PURSUITS: 5072, Plath.
PUSSY CATS: 2569, Steegmuller.
PYGMALION: 5080, Friend.
PYROMANIACS: 5081, Porter.
PYTHONS: 5010, Ciardi.
QUAIL: 772, Engle; 1457, Smythe.
QUAKERESSES: 4943, Young.
QUAKERS: 1960, Groom.
QUARRIES: 1402, Warren.
QUARRELS: 1969, Grenville.
QUEENS: 5088, Bennett; 7117, Fuller.
QUESTIONERS: 5096, Lipton.
QUESTIONS: 5097, Scott.
QUESTS: 3294, Fandel.
QUIET: 5233, Engle.
QUIZZES: 6701, Wheeler.
RABBIS: 5928, Shapiro.
RABBITS: 1113, Merrill; 1242, Duryee; 3887, Jacobson; 7118, Solomon.
RACE: 6660, Pierce.
RACHEL: 1648, Johnson; 5106, Clark.
RACHMANINOFF, SERGEI, 1873-1945: 4483, O'Hara.
RACISM: 4593, Bender; 4982, Nash.
RADAR: 4276, MacLeod.
RADAR TOWERS: 592, Coxe.
RADICALS: 5109, Caton.
RADIOS: 5110, O'Hara; 5111, Whittemore.
RAFTS: 5112, Lloyd.
RAILROAD TRACKS: 6340, De Jong.
RAILROADS: 7101, Galler.
RAIN: 87, Page; 405, Heafield; 1090, Nemerov; 1559, Middleton; 1970, Kumin; 2603, Warren; 2839, McInery; 4709, Pomeroy; 4804, Howard; 4959, Emans; 5115, Armour; 5116, Blevins; 5117, Ciardi; 5118, Creeley; 5119, Levine; 5120, Moss; 5121, Nabokov; 5122, Nishiwaki; 5125, Humphries; 5126, Reid; 5128, Scollard; 5129, Landeweer; 5976, White; 6779, Merchant; 7054, Perdue; 7336, Richter.
RAIN CROWS: 5124, Berry.
RAINBOWS: 851, Blackburn; 5130, Landers; 5131, Fleming.

RAINFALL: 5132, Masters.
RAINY SEASONS: 5133, Blackwell.
RAMA: 6902, Schneider.
RANCH: 4638, Levine.
RAPHAEL (ARCHANGEL): 5135, Maris
    Stella.
RAPTURE: 5861, Lamb.
RASPBERRIES: 5138, Riggs.
RAT RACES: 5140, Blagden.
RATS: 437, Honig; 1822, Starbuck.
RAVENSBRUECK: 6058, Heisenfuttel.
READING: 362; 722, Counselman; 1771,
    Shapiro; 1971, Hilberry; 2743,
    Power; 4485, Cuomo; 5064, Updike;
    6217, Selby; 6417, Hurianek; 6618,
    Van Doren; 7261, Dudley.
READING INTERESTS: 4844, Watkins.
REALITY: 334, Steinman; 2151, Chang;
    6496, Davidson.
REASON: 3715, Bartlett; 5932, Rolland;
    6845, Eberhart.
REBELS: 5154, Adib; 5156, Stepanchev.
REBIRTH: 1136, Summers; 5157,
    Thornton.
REBUILDING: 5564, Johnson.
RECESSIONS: 3502, Chadwick.
RECIPES: 6620, Armour.
RECITALS: 987, Richstone; 5163,
    Merrill.
RECOGNITION: 5165, Wagoner.
RECORDS: 6990, Kessler.
REDBIRDS: 2578, Ellert.
REDEEMER: 5579, Thomas.
REDUCING: 2682, Chadwick.
REDWOODS: 2888, Witt.
REEDS: 5178, Tomlinson.
REEFS: 1229, Pierce.
REFLECTIONS: 5182, Workman; 2724,
    Horiguchi; 4917, Nemerov.
REFLECTIONS IN WATER: 6975, Swenson.
REFORMERS: 7370, Delattre.
REFRAINS: 2424, Huss.
REFRIGERATORS: 6406, Neely; 7132,
    Read.
REFUGE: 1046, Bangham.
REFUGEES: 4074, Boyle.
REGRET: 332, Stone.
REHABILITATION CENTERS: 5198, Kumin.
REJOICE: 4867, Schwartz.
RELATIVES: 1675, Wagoner; 2302,
    McGinley; 5200, Huhn.
RELATIVITY: 1602, Aller.
RELAXATION: 5202, Lister.
RELEASE: 5204, Keith.
RELIEF: 4388, Campbell.
RELIGION: 701, Nemerov; 3940,
    Knowlton; 5206, Hall; 5498, Grossman;
    5500, Bentley; 5746, Ostrander;
    6748, Mullins.
RELUCTANCE: 5492, Graves.
REMARKS: 4687, Mundell.
REMEMBERING: 1526, D.;; 2811, Nash;
    7123, Kemp.
REMEMBRANCE: 5213, Mounts.
REMORSE: 4157, Sarabhai.
RENDEZVOUS: 5220, Facos; 5221,
    Jacobson.
RENEWAL OF RELATIONSHIPS: 6740,
    Wheelock.
RENOIR, PIERRE AUGUSTE, 1841-1919:
    4668, Morris; 5224, Mills.

REPARTEE: 7234, Warsaw.
REPENTANCE: 5190, Burrowes; 5219,
    Weaver; 5227, Colby.
REPLACEMENT DEPOTS: 396, Wright.
REPORT CARDS: 22, Jenkins.
REPORTERS: 4446, Summers.
REQUIEMS: 5234, Hurshman; 5236,
    L'Heureux; 5237, Kessler.
RESENTMENT: 6294, Lilly.
RESERVOIRS: 5241, Adler.
RESIGNATION: 4520, Richstone.
RESISTANCE: 3662, Rich.
RESOLUTIONS: 6399, Jaffray; 6996,
    Dean.
RESPONSIBILITIES: 5245, Hoskins.
RESTAURANTS: 4519, Moss; 6225, W.
RESURRECTION: 1379, Jones; 1380,
    Kenseth; 2153, Molton; 2939,
    Sullivan; 3895, Cotter; 5049, Mullins;
    5250, O'Gorman; 5490, Moffitt; 6588,
    Stuart; 7324, Richardson.
RETIREMENT: 5251, Merchant; 5252,
    Vesely; 6825, Patterson.
RETORTS: 5254, Hall.
RETREATS: 5256, Caedmon.
RETRIBUTION: 5257, Coblentz.
RETROSPECT: 2884, Coblentz.
RETURNING: 5259, Howard.
REUTHER, WALTER: 1927, Eff; 2467,
    Ryskind.
REVEILLE: 3852, Isler.
REVELATION: 1329, Schmidt; 3820,
    Calkins; 5274, D.
REVELATIONS: 3497, Dufault.
REVENGE: 5278, Congdon.
REVISITS: 5553, McCarthy.
REVOLUTIONARIES: 6599, Rosenthal.
RHINOCEROSES: 5285, Maruyama.
RHODODENDRONS: 2821, His Majesty the
    Emperor of Japan.
RHYMING: 752, Nash.
RIBBONS: 4431, O'Hara.
RICE PUDDING: 5289, Zaw.
RICH YOUNG RULER: 4558, Fretz.
RICHES: 5293, Eberhart.
RIDDLES: 5295, McFarland; 5767, Wun.
RIDES: 1121, Huff.
RIGHTS: 2109, Freeman.
RIMBAUD, ARTHUR, 1854-1891: 1044,
    Plath.
RIMER, PENNSYLVANIA: 5299, Merwin.
RITES: 3650, Ford.
RITOURNELLE, PARIS: 5309, Ponsot.
RIVEN: 6535, Wells.
RIVER PORTS: 4176, Warsaw.
RIVERS: 25, Kinnell; 2405, Hope;
    2425, Stuart; 4825, Abbe; 5310,
    Crews; 5313, Lee; 5314, Perrings;
    5668, Hugo; 5712, Denney.
RIVERS, LARRY: 4490, O'Hara.
RIZZUTO, PHIL: 1479, Nash.
ROAD SIGNS: 6979, Hicks.
ROADS: 455, Graves; 495, Peterson;
    1007, Keith; 1709, Coxe; 1808,
    Grenville; 4090, Hagiwara; 4168,
    Rizzardi; 4435, Gilboa; 4632, Seager;
    5318, Taylor; 5321, Speer; 5858,
    Whitman.
ROBINS: 5325, Merrill.
ROBINSON, EDWIN ARLINGTON: 6543, Obear.

ROBINSON CRUSOE: 1300, Boylan.
ROCK AND ROLL: 5330, McGinley.
ROCKETS: 4594, Stafford; 6582,
   Singer.
ROCKS: 3560, Crews; 5327, Langland;
   5329, Padgaonkar.
RODIN, AUGUSTE, 1840-1917: 5326,
   Freeman.
RODS: 5351, Barker.
ROETHKE, THEODORE: 6724, McClure.
ROMAN CANDLES: 5334, Ames.
ROMAN CATHOLIC CHURCH: 1749,
   Sylvester.
ROMAN FORUM: 5335, Jennings.
ROME: 2139, Gerlach; 3976,
   Ackerson; 4406, Singer; 4533, Lynch;
   5384, Ciardi; 6938, Bogardus.
ROOFERS: 5340, Hemschemeyer.
ROOKS: 5342, Feringhetti.
ROOMS: 3188, Merchant; 5343, Berg;
   5346, Smith.
ROOSEVELT, ELEANOR: 1872, Caswell.
ROOSEVELT, THEODORE: 6223, Hall.
ROOSTER'S DAWN: 379, Stafford.
ROOSTERS: 6760, Merchant.
ROOTS: 2239, Bynner; 5937, Langland
ROSE GROWERS: 709, Graves.
ROSE TREES: 4541, Char.
ROSENFIELD, ISAAC: 2045, Blum; 2077,
   Ray.
ROSES: 632, Eisenlohr; 2547, Triem;
   2989, Rilke; 4304, Pessoa; 4871,
   Williams; 5350, O'Gorman; 5351,
   Barker; 5352, Zitner; 5353, 6914,
   Galbraith.
ROSH HASHANAH: 377, Rich; 1891,
   Shapiro.
ROUTES: 5361, Singleton.
ROWING: 5367, Pomeroy; 6146, Lock.
ROYALTY: 3302, Rubin.
RUGS: 1599, Galbraith.
RUINS: 3542, Eberhart.
RULES: 5374, Logue.
RUNNING: 973, Frost; 4803, Nemerov.
RURAL LIFE: 6893, Ostroff.
RUSES: 5597, Herschberger.
RUTH: 5380, Weiss.
SACRIFICE: 119, Hilberry.
SACROILIACS: 5845, Rosenteur.
SADAKO: 6422, Yoneda.
SADNESS: 613, Grenville.
SAILBOATS: 5392, Hicky; 5393, Francis.
SAILING: 942, Booth; 5394, Pasternack.
SAILORS: 869, Todd.
SAINT JOSEPH: 5403, Claudel.
SAINTLINESS: 2039, Brotherson.
SAINTS: 673, Duryee; 3383, Howes;
   5395, Feldman; 5410, Baro.
SALESMEN: 5412, Frumkin.
SALMON: 3170, Huff; 5414, Grenville.
SALOME: 5415, Merrill.
SAMELA: 5418, Greene.
SAN FRANCISCO, CALIFORNIA: 5445,
   Updike.
SAN THOME: 6863, Singer.
SAND: 971, Ratliff; 2523, Bock.
SAND DUNES: 6932, Weaver.
SANDBARS: 985, Rukeyser.
SANDBOXES: 966, Johnson.
SANDPIPERS: 5421, Nemerov.

SANITY: 6392, Henry.
SANS SOUCI: 5422, Mueller.
SANTA CLAUS: 1491, Turner; 2429,
   Sullivan; 3771, Nash; 4568, Ryskind;
   5423, Sagittarius; 6706, Moore; 7334,
   McGinley.
SAPPHIRES: 5425, Goodman.
SAPPHO: 1743, 5426, Wright.
SARAH: 5428, Schwartz.
SATELLITES: 4233, 4239, Ginsberg.
SATIRE: 1560, Overmyer; 3445, Bradford.
SATYRS: 1094, Guthrie; 5433, Williams.
SAUNTERERS: 599, Plutzik.
SAUVIES ISLAND: 5424, Stafford.
SAVANTS: 3235, Jammes.
SAVINGS: 3484, Warsaw.
SAYINGS: 5436, Stafford.
SCANDAL: 760, Galbraith.
SCARECROWS: 5440, Armour; 5441,
   Grenville; 5442, Jacobson.
SCARLET TANAGERS: 6247, Carrier.
SCARS: 1341, Kunitz; 2082, Stuart;
   5439, Hillyer.
SCHOLARS: 5447, Kenny.
SCHOOL: 786, Schiff; 1359, Mergard;
   1511, Maruyama; 3456, Wright; 5284,
   Hartich; 5448, Ginsberg; 5451,
   Isler; 5453, Mitchel; 5656, Starbuck;
   6036, Miner; 6497, Stockdale; 6644,
   Shyer; 7132, Read.
SCHOOL BUSES: 5449, Freneau.
SCHOOL LIBRARIES: 1962, Craven; 5998,
   Spear.
SCHOOL PLAYS: 3629, Douglass.
SCIENCE: 559, Rawling; 1603, Speiser;
   1604, White; 1991, Delattre; 2398,
   Frost; 3859, Boggs; 6713, Ziegler.
SCIENCE FICTION: 5454, Wheeler.
SCIENTISTS: 1603, Speiser; 6516,
   Stuart; 6517, Crown; 6528, Darcy;
   7284, Freeman.
SCOFFERS: 650, Moore.
SCORPIONS: 3548, Schevill.
SCOTSMEN: 5457, Johnson.
SCOURGES: 1775, Mary Jeremy.
SCREENS (DOORS, WINDOWS, ETC.): 634,
   Lazarus.
SCRIBES: 3414, Shapiro.
SCROLLS: 5462, Winslow.
SCROOGE: 5463, Nash.
SCULPTORS: 27, Chadbourne.
SCULPTURE: 3789, Lilly.
SEA: 479, Myers; 522, McFarland; 591,
   Scott; 593, De Longchamps; 600,
   Broughton; 930, Beum; 1096, Hare;
   1304, Rainer; 1453, O'Gorman; 1760,
   Burgander; 1868, Duncan; 2408,
   Finkel; 3217, Erba; 3496, Sampley;
   3513, Morse; 4470, Ciardi; 4876,
   Abse; 4933, Rizzardi; 5464, Burford;
   5465, Byron; 5472, Burford; 5477,
   Eaton; 5541, Sylvester; 6210,
   Bokudo; 6347, Duncan.
SEA-FOG: 2907, Morse.
SEA-MARKS: 5473, Frost.
SEA AND MAN: 5466, Landeweer.
SEA GULLS: 5469, Tagliabue; 5470,
   Gibbs.
SEA HORSES: 7262, Miller.
SEA MONSTERS: 5474, Merwin.

SEA OF GALILEE: 3204, Pierce.
SEA SHELLS: 1104, Smith; 5570,
    Merchant; 5571, Perry.
SEAHORSES: 4016, Legg.
SEALS: 1223, Booth.
SEAMARKS: 1792, Perse.
SEARCHERS: 5480, Berkowits.
SEAS: 5268, Hart; 5467, Lattimore;
    5471, Stewart; 5478, Merwin.
SEASALTER: 5481, Sparshott.
SEASCAPES: 5482, Deutsch; 5483,
    Frezza.
SEASONS: 110, Mezey; 890, Colt;
    1630, Lee; 3206, Pomeroy; 4563,
    Wheldon; 5543, Hall; 6650, Hardy;
    6668, Watkins.
SEAWEEDS: 3742, Howard.
SEBASTIAN, SAINT: 5408, Merwin.
SECOND ADVENT: 6361, Pierce.
SECOND COMING OF CHRIST: 1364, Smith;
    1711, Rowland; 4317, St. John of the
    Cross; 5490, Moffitt.
SECRETS: 4486, Galbraith; 5465,
    Byron; 5496, Bendre; 5497, Senge;
    5827, De Jong; 6747, Kernan.
SECTARIANS: 5499, Burket.
SEDLEY, SIR CHARLES, 1639?-1701: 121,
    Howard.
SEEDS: 4702, Ross; 5413, Cooper.
SEEING-EYE DOGS: 5503, Carlisle.
SEGREGATION: 1899, White; 2172,
    Smith; 4593, Bender; 6402, Cooper;
    6594, Bentley; 7106, Pierce; 7120,
    Winters.
SEINERS: 5509, Booth.
SELF: 1787, Creekmore; 2419, Carrier;
    2724, Horiguchi; 3043, Robertson;
    5832, Whitman; 6546, Curnow; 6846,
    Richardson.
SELF-IMPORTANCE: 5181, Stafford.
SELF-KNOWLEDGE: 5862, Schwartz.
SELF IMPORTANCE: 606, Otis.
SELF KNOWLEDGE: 4607, Coblentz.
SELF PITY: 6633, Molton.
SELF RESPECT: 1524, Burton.
SELLING: 1940, Galbraith.
SELVES: 7327, Weeks.
SENTRIES: 3415, MacAfee.
SEPTEMBER: 5526, Carpenter; 5540,
    Bishop; 5818, Wise.
SEQUENCES: 5529, Kahn.
SERENADES: 5530, Bentley.
SERENITY: 5532, Bartlett.
SERMONS: 5534, Ciardi; 5535, Elmer.
SERPENTS: 7307, Whittemore.
SERVICE STATIONS: 1953, Rosenfield.
SETTING-UP EXERCISES: 5544, Talman.
SEWING: 2043, McGonigal.
SEX: 6353, Thornton; 7245, Steiner.
SHAD: 7075, Burgess.
SHADOWS: 1249, Booth; 1543, Laing;
    5554, Coblentz; 5555, Stuart; 5556,
    Krolow; 7047, Richardson.
SHAGS: 5557, Booth.
SHAKESPEARE, WILLIAM, 1564-1616:
    2281, Dufault; 2335, Schwartz;
    3131, Kline; 4485, Cuomo;
    6686, Nash.
SHAMPOOS: 3470, Strachan; 5560,
    Bishop.

SHAVING: 6568, Rank.
SHEBA, QUEEN OF: 5087, Mueller.
SHELLEY, PERCY BYSSHE, 1795-1821:
    4797, Witt.
SHELLS: 5572, Nemerov.
SHELTER: 406, Shook.
SHELTERS: 5573, Derwood.
SHEPHERDS: 5575, Stafford; 5576, Hicks;
    5577, 5871, Crites; 6411, O'Gorman.
SHEPHERDESSES: 6843, Smith.
SHIELDS: 5578, Weiss.
SHIP LAUNCHING: 3268, Petrie.
SHIPMATES: 6496, Davidson.
SHIPS: 4725, Koehler; 6056, Shalom;
    6359, Wheeler.
SHIPS' BARS: 475, McCord.
SHIPWRECKS: 5583, Masefield; 5584,
    Merwin.
SHIRTS: 5585, Morris.
SHOALS: 5586, Delattre.
SHOES: 127, Hammer; 4654, Workman.
SHOES - TYING: 7131, McFarland.
SHOPPERS: 498, Neely.
SHOPPING: 5588, Collins.
SHOPPING CENTERS: 6185, Blackwell.
SHORE LINES: 5589, Weaver.
SHORES: 164, Pierce.
SHOWER BATHS: 1112, Kernan.
SHOWERS: 1885, Dickey.
SHRINES: 4131, Morris.
SHROUD OF TURIN: 5596, Cotter.
SIBYLS: 5598, Golffing.
SICK: 1517, Rosenteur; 5603, Engle.
SICKNESS: 4122, Levine.
SIDEWALKS: 5606, Appel.
SIERRAS: 5607, Jacobson.
SIGNS: 5605, Helfer.
SILENCE: 249, Edelman; 1000, Schwartz;
    1166, Supervielle; 1206, Graham;
    1345, Wheelock; 1475, Miles; 1960,
    Groom; 2255, Edelman; 2930, Kraft;
    5388, White; 5617, Pomeroy; 5618,
    Goodman; 5630, Kessler; 6398,
    Tagliabue; 7384, Stepanchev.
SIMON PETER: 587, Bangham.
SIMPLE LIFE: 6710, Lape.
SIMPLE WAYS: 5850, Gilboa.
SIMPLICITY: 4444, Nemerov; 5627,
    De Ford.
SIN: 4732, 5642, Mullins; 6667, Clark;
    7139, Patchen.
SINCERITY: 5631, Merton.
SINGING: 1646, Hardy; 2289, Engle;
    2763, Ardayne; 3879, Blackwell;
    4351, Wheeler.
SINGLE MEN: 5640, Holmes.
SIREN SOUNDS: 5643, Wolf.
SIRENS: 2111, Carlisle.
SISTERS: 5647, Kessler; 5649, Adler;
    6738, Muir; 6739, Plath.
SISYPHUS: 6222, Miles.
SITES: 1004, Church.
SIZES: 5657, Richstone.
SKATERS: 5658, Stepanchev.
SKATING: 5659, Graves; 6554, Daiches.
SKELETONS: 686, Duncan.
SKEPTICS: 5446, Petrie.
SKI RUNS: 5660, Barker.
SKID ROW: 5661, Gilbert.
SKIES: 2070, Clark; 5665, Merrill;
    5667, Rago.

SKIING: 6696, Updike.
SKILLS: 3213, Gass.
SKIN: 5662, Moss.
SKIPPING: 3457, Armour; 6495, Graham.
SKY: 2198, Coblentz; 5464, Burford;
    5666, Nathan.
SKY-WRITING: 3095, Dufault.
SKYLARKS: 1505, Hagiwara; 2486,
    Welch.
SLAYING: 470, Ciardi.
SLEEP: 212, Wain; 282, Oppenheimer;
    544, Solovay; 1653, Francis; 2297,
    Donnelly; 2813, Roethke; 3657,
    Lattimore; 3714, Williams; 3817,
    Redman; 4451, Meredith; 4452,
    Howes; 4880, Disher; 5195, Love,
    5568, Carmi; 5634, Creeley; 5670,
    Ardayne; 5671, Solum; 5674, Simpson;
    5676, Tagliabue; 5686, Galbraith;
    6390, Jennings; 7180, Davison.
SLEEPWALKERS: 5676, Crawford.
SLOOPS: 6253, De Kay.
SLOTHS: 5684, Eff.
SLUGS: 5687, Roethke.
SLUMBER: 6148, Neely.
SLUMS: 5186, MacDiarmid, 6647, Hall.
SMALL THINGS: 5689, Roethke.
SMALL TOWNS: 5700, Rubin.
SMELLS: 5705, Merchant.
SMILES: 202, Bentley; 2623, Barker;
    7374, Burket.
SMITH, HOKE: 3106, Smith.
SMOKERS: 5707, .
SMOKING: 4142, Galbraith.
SNACKS: 3796, Isler.
SNAILS: 87, Page; 2249, Wallace;
    5710, Earle; 7146, Gardner.
SNAKE CHARMERS: 1522, Pierce.
SNAKE PARK: 2919, Plomer.
SNAKES: 726, Crown; 3117, Moore; 4834,
    Walt; 6600, Levertov; 5711, Witt;
    7255, Hay.
SNORING: 4117, Armknecht.
SNOW: 188, Galler; 287, Saunders;
    573, Seager; 1001, Lewin; 1200,
    Havard; 1668, Berry; 1845, Loeser;
    1973, Riggs; 1974, Walton; 1975,
    Sloat; 2526, Hollander; 2805,
    Jammes; 2971, Robson; 3076, Wooten
    3340, Gleason; 4767, Mergard; 4952,
    Neely; 5255, Goodman; 5717, McKeehan;
    5718, Petrie; 5719, Pierce; 5721,
    St. Martin; 5722, Pasternak; 5723,
    Merrill; 5724, Longfellow; 5726,
    Hazen; 5727, Woods; 5728, Stuart;
    5730, Galler; 5730, Stepanchev;
    5736, Justice; 5802, Wagoner; 6055,
    Gibbs; 6105, Trent; 7078, Hoskins;
    7184, Merrill; 7202, Trent; 7228,
    Watson.
SNOW CRYSTALS: 5720, Heafield.
SNOW FLOWERS: 5725, Freeman.
SNOW SCENES: 5731, Mayo.
SNOWFALLS: 3651, Richter.
SNOWFLAKES: 5735, Donnelly.
SNOWMEN: 5731, Plath; 5736, Berrigan.
SNOWSUITS: 5733, Fairchild.
SOCIAL CHANGE: 2555, Nickerson.
SOCIAL SCIENTISTS: 5745, Jones.
SOAP: 7091, Wegert.
SODOM: 3536, Thompson.
SOEURS DE CHARITE: 5747, Brady.
SOIREES: 5754, Weiss.
SOLDIERS: 1723, Graves; 2232, Poster;
    5337, Lattimore; 5756, Ridland;
    5757, Eberhart; 5758, Oga; 5759,
    Zimmerman.
SOLDIERS' WIDOWS: 7039, Brecht.
SOLITARY TYPES: 5558, Lister.
SOLITUDE: 2432, Hillyer.
SONGS: 2665, McFarland; 3259, Chapin;
    3483, Moss; 3885, Lipton; 3911,
    Moffitt; 4399, MacGillivray; 5077,
    Char; 5793, McFarland; 5838, Whitman;
    5849, Gregor; 6098, Ekulkar; 6741,
    Woods.
SONIC BOOMS: 5852, Updike.
SONNETS: 311, 312, 313, 314, 315,
    Orlovitz; 3018, Stock; 3082,
    Ronsard; 5873, Vega; 6171, Coughlin.
SONS: 368, Schlitzer; 1488, Pierce;
    1627, Rittell; 1884, Petrie; 2087,
    Dell; 2088, Coxe; 2091, Richardson;
    2452, Stewart; 2485, Stone; 2843,
    Congdon; 3129, Heath; 3687, Dejong;
    4018, Kaplan; 4250, McCarthy; 4376,
    Wood; 4494, Sandeen; 5000, Wright;
    5025, Coxe; 5398, Wolf; 6329,
    Douglas; 6559, Silkin; 6572, Petite.
SONS GROWING UP: 6061, Ciardi.
SONS, NEWBORN: 5874, Rex.
SORROW: 1298, Nicholl; 2382, Mary
    Immaculata; 4267, Humphries; 5800,
    Murray; 5880, Koshland.
SOULS: 147, Sarton; 1298, Nicholl;
    2179, Shapiro; 4658, Claudel; 5223,
    Roethke; 5396, Richardson; 5792,
    Kreymborg; 6766, Freedman.
SOUNDS: 1408, Landeweer; 1691, Fleming;
    2388, Ammons; 2484, Bishop; 2941,
    Miles; 3296, Lattimore; 4119, Clower;
    5750, Emans; 5891, Cuomo; 6112, Lee.
SOUTH: 4982, Nash.
SOUTH AMERICA: 4268, Ryskind.
SOUTH, THE: 4177, Merrill.
SOUTHERN CROSS: 477, Thornton.
SOUTHWELL, ROBERT, CA 1561-1595: 1397,
    Logan.
SOUTHWEST: 2579, Armknecht.
SPACE: 3511, Nathan; 3855, Updike;
    4327, Cardozo; 4549, Penny; 5899,
    Winsor; 6469, Hitziz.
SPACE AGE: 5877, Zylstra; 5897,
    Armour.
SPACE BALLOONS: 5898, Burford.
SPACE HELMETS: 6035, Jacobson.
SPACE PROGRAM: 921, Trent.
SPACE TRAVEL: 5902, Lamb.
SPAIN: 3903, Reid; 5199, Sagitarrius;
    5903, Anzai; 6631, Feldman.
SPARROWS: 1622, Kinnell; 5907,
    Newton; 5908, Carruth; 5909, Bock.
SPEAKERS: 86, Otis; 489, Schlitzer;
    3845, Tadlock; 4144, Grenville; 5915,
    Spring.
SPEAKERS AT GRADUATIONS: 4362,
    Eisenlohr.
SPEAKING: 3039, Hoffman; 5148,
    Wheeler.
SPECTACLES: 2312, Updike.

SPEECH: 165, Sward; 1816, Tadlock;
3039, Hoffman; 4120, Hutchinson.
SPEECHES: 5920, Corke.
SPEED: 5921, Rukeyser.
SPIDERS: 3156, Nixon; 4458, Galbraith;
5923, Eberhart; 5924, Witt; 5925,
Schwartz; 6200, Deutsch; 6519,
Hackett; 7089, Wright.
SPINACH: 5685, Armour.
SPINNING: 5927, Valery.
SPINSTERS: 4424, Galbraith.
SPIRIT: 198, Shimoni; 3914, Frost.
SPIRITUAL JOURNEYS: 5931, Grace.
SPIRITUALITY: 5932, Rolland.
SPITE: 3475, Singer; 5934, Koshland.
SPOONS: 447, Smith.
SPORTS CARS: 5942, Wheeler.
SPRING: 18, Hillyer; 180, Lamb; 201,
Shook; 331, Stafford; 597, Cone;
866, Nash; 915, Solum; 1056, Starbuck;
1227, Isler; 1977, Stockdale; 1981,
Templin; 2123, Watkins; 2673, Payne;
2717, Hunter; 2892, MacCollom; 3119,
Cotter; 3260, Ross; 3731, Freeman;
3866, Hearst; 4182, Rottmann; 4370,
Schevill; 4818, Mansfield; 4967,
Grenville; 5022, Redman; 5244,
Marshall; 5638, Emerson; 5646,
Blackburn; 5822, Cotter; 5945, Boyle;
5948, Lowenfels; 5950, Rainer; 5955,
Sarton; 5956, Greet; 5961, Singleton;
5963, Robbins; 5966, Simon; 5968,
Coxe; 5969, Galbraith; 5971, Kelley;
5972, Carruth; 6113, Zimskind; 6191,
Anthony; 6256, Kahn; 6395, Ellis;
6441, Reid; 6705, Scrutton; 6815,
Stuart; 7014, Lee; 7364, Howard.
SPRING, COMING OF: 5778, Jacobs.
SPRING DANCES: 1334, Cole.
SPRING DAYS: 5960, Moffitt; 6525,
Wright.
SPRING EQUINOX: 2952, Hammer; 4877,
Corke.
SPRING FEVER: 5957, Usk.
SPRING FLOWERS: 1610, Roethke.
SPRING FREEZES: 5958, Merchant.
SPRING MORNINGS: 3904, Ginsberg;
5965, Norman.
SPRING SIGNS: 5613, Hite.
SPRING SONGS: 5788, Burroway; 5789,
Coatsworth; 5795, 5796, Scrutton;
5973, Ginsberg; 5974.
SPRING SOUNDS: 5974, Auxier.
SPRING TIDES: 5975, Cousens.
SPRING WEATHER: 7002, Whittemore.
SPRINGS: 5946, De Ford; 5947, Guri.
SPRINTERS: 5977, Dickey.
SPUTNIK: 5979, Pierce; 5980,
Whittemore.
SQUASHES: 6239, Whittemore.
SQUATTERS: 3642, Bishop.
SQUIRES: 4820, Levant.
SQUIRRELS: 1185, Smith; 5983, Swenson.
ST. CHRISTOPHER: 5399, Bogan.
ST. FRANCIS OF ASSISSI: 5401, Salomon.
ST. FELIX FEAST: 4712, Cotter.
STAINS: 1599, Galbraith.
STAIRS: 4604, Anthony.
STANCES: 6025, Clower.
STANDING: 6341, Harrington.

STARLINGS: 6031, Hall.
STARS: 197, Plutzik; 894, Frost; 1089,
Hassmer; 1473, Cotter; 2059, Henley;
2487, Reid; 5840, Dunbar; 5943,
Carter; 6027, Clark; 6028, Stafford;
6029, Lineaweaver; 6032, Berrigan;
6033, Merrill; 6034, Lister; 6589,
Blake.
STATES: 6372, Walton.
STATIONS OF THE CROSS: 6299, Roseliep.
STATISTICS: 1907, Parrish; 3619,
Kline; 6708, Lape; 6991, Chadwick.
STATUES: 1399, Ashbery; 3383, Howes;
5706, Seferis.
STATUS: 558, Watt.
STATUS QUO: 6041, Merrill.
STATUTES: 6042, Nemerov.
STEADFASTNESS: 5349, Lilly.
STEALING: 3743, Barker.
STEAM SHOVELS: 5594, Waring.
STEIN, GERTRUDE, 1874-1946: 4945,
Neville.
STENOGRAPHERS: 4203, Armour.
STEPHEN, ST.: 1890, Johnson.
STEPLADDERS: 1841, Galbraith.
STEPS: 4555, Heafield.
STEVENS, WALLACE: 2869, Smith; 4902,
Morse.
STEVENS, WALLACE, 1879-1955: 4433,
D'Andrade; 4683, Kroll; 4970, Ciardi.
STILES: 6052, Pudney.
STILL SPIRITS: 6054, Eberhart.
STILL-BORN: 2050, Ponsot.
STILLNESS: 5376, Nemerov.
STONE-BREAKERS: 6057, Nirala.
STONES: 204, Ignatow; 1081, Ammons;
1766, Lilly; 2793, Gilboa; 7048,
Reynolds.
STONEWORKS: 1477, Ciardi.
STORKS: 6064, Eff.
STORM WARNINGS: 6074, Lineaweaver.
STORM WINDOWS: 6075, Nemerov.
STORMS: 1119, Fandel; 2504, Rukeyser;
2990, White; 3149, Carruth; 3898,
Merrill; 4154, Bock; 4688, Pasternak;
6066, Rothberg; 6068, Whittemore;
6069, Huntress; 6070, Hughes; 6076,
Stoutenburg.
STORYTELLING: 282, Grenville; 5679,
Chadwick.
STRANGERS: 2040, Morse; 2795, Graham;
6088, Jennings.
STRATFORD-ON-AVON: 6718, Zukofsky.
STRAWBERRIES: 3748, Justice.
STREAMS: 512, Nemerov; 1028, Lennen;
1414, Watkins; 1790, U Tam'si; 3944,
Russell; 6095, Auden.
STREETCARS: 971, Harrington.
STRENGTH: 5505, Clark; 6099, Freeman;
7026, Galbraith.
STRENGTHENING: 5396, Richardson.
STROKES: 6104, Stafford.
STROLLS: 3913, Moffitt.
STRUGGLE: 33, Ponsot.
STUDENTS: 6514, Solovay; 589, Willis.
STUDY HABITS: 6109, Armour.
STYLE: 2245, Eberhart.
STYLES: 1080, Rosenfield; 6109,
Eisenlohr.
SUBMARINES: 384, Bracker.

SUBURBIA: 1541, Jennison; 1560,
    Overmyer; 6115, Hammer.
SUBURBS: 2575, Russell; 4789, Polikoff;
    5841, Mack; 6111, Updike.
SUBWAYS: 6116, Zacks.
SUCCEEDING: 4816, Johnson.
SUCCESS: 1337, Galbraith; 3295,
    Simpson; 6117, Hearst; 6118, Pack;
    7154, Bramley.
SUCKLING, SIR JOHN, 1609-1642: 755,
    Nash.
SUFFERING: 2767, Hagiwara.
SUICIDE: 6203, Sterling; 1679, Hart.
SUGGESTIONS: 5456, Richstone.
SUMMER: 105, Kennedy; 178, Hay; 369,
    Liddell; 486, Raynor; 1132, Coles;
    1371, Grover; 1858, Andrews; 3802,
    Lindbergh; 3945, Schwartz; 4257,
    Lathan; 4698, Morrison; 4866,
    Schwartz; 5632, Hammer; 5667, Rago;
    5698, Thomas; 6125, Shook; 6132,
    Kroll; 6133, Levine; 6134, O'Gorman;
    6137, Barnes; 6138, Lineaweaver;
    6139, Schwartz; 6142, Isler; 6145,
    Gardner; 6148, Neely; 6149, Merwin;
    6153, Hecht; 6154, Keith; 6711,
    Lape.
SUMMER RESORTS: 1085, Denney; 6130,
    Galbraith.
SUMMER SCHOOLS: 848, Whittemore.
SUMMER WINDS: 6152, Arnold.
SUMMIT CONFERENCES: 1789, Sagittarius;
    4268, Ryskind.
SUMMITS: 6157, Ryskind.
SUN: 773, Sorrentino; 744, Mueller;
    2527, Claudel; 4969, Wolf; 5037,
    Riddle; 5240, Cassin; 5525,
    Carnicelli; 5761, Morris; 5780,
    Bruce; 6158, Nishiwaki; 6366,
    Weaver; 6806, Merrill; 6822, Waslsh;
    6953, Kreymborg.
SUNBATHERS: 6159, O'Gorman; 6160,
    Sexton.
SUNDAY: 1468, Hay; 6114, Posner; 6162,
    Necker; 6164, Eberhart; 6165,
    Swenson; 6167, Rorke; 6354,
    Schoeberlein; 6687, Armour.
SUNDIALS: 6169, Graham.
SUNKEN SHIPS: 3250, Parone.
SUNLIGHT: 6172, Mueller; 7031,
    Armknecht.
SUNRISE: 3896, Pausch; 6173, Cunliffe;
    6174, Ackerson.
SUNSET: 6170, Merrill.
SUNSETS: 6175, Kaplan.
SUPERNATURAL: 6178, Guha.
SUPPER: 1616, Howes.
SUPPERTIME: 6180, Grenville.
SUPREME BEING: 193, Coblentz.
SURGERY: 6187, Armstrong.
SURGES: 1779, Barker.
SURPRISES: 6788, Pogue.
SURVIVAL: 5095, Tobin.
SURVIVORS: 6196, Merwin.
SUSPENSE: 6200, Middleton.
SUWANEE RIVER: 6201, Glaze.
SWALLOWS: 1978, Landeweer; 6072, Bly;
    6394, Garrigue.
SWAMPS: 474, Moore.
SWANS: 1394, Lang; 6093, Levertov.

SWANSONGS: 6204, Barker.
SWEATERS: 6205, Duke.
SWIFT, JONATHAN: 4503, Vance; 6211,
    Schwartz.
SWIM SUITS: 144, Jaffray.
SWIMMERS: 2103, Morris; 6212, Pierreau-
    Saussine; 6213, Moss.
SWITZERLAND: 2389, Singer.
SWORDS: 6214, Dicker.
SYCAMORE TREES: 6216, Grenville.
SYMBOLISM: 6217, Selby.
SYMPATHY: 4824, Scovel; 6218,
    Berryman; 7247, Akins.
SYNAGOGUES: 6632, Whitman.
SYNCRETISM: 6220, Koski.
SYNTHETIC FABRICS: 7271, Jennison.
SYNTHETICS: 6221, De Vito.
SYRIA: 4140, Sagittarius.
TABLE GRACE: 4328, Rittell.
TABLECLOTHS: 674, Marz.
TACT: 5041, Jaffray; 6521, Galbraith,
TAILORS: 3397, Perrings; 6233,
    Blackwell.
TAIWAN: 6235, MacInnis.
TALENTS: 5276, Zawadsky.
TALK: 2801, Richardson.
TALKING BOOKS: 6243, Barker.
TALKING TO ONE'S SELF: 5775, Wilbur.
TANAGERS: 6247, Carrier.
TAPESTRIES: 3385, Vazakas; 6254,
    Williams; 6255, Abrahams.
TARDINESS: 4456, Gabler.
TASKS: 6260, Morris.
TASTES: 23, Lineaweaver.
TAX EXEMPTIONS: 1880, Neely.
TAXES: 7291, Spring.
TAXIS: 3046, Nash.
TAYLOR, HAROLD: 6263, Redivivus.
TEA: 685, Lister; 2147, Gilbert.
TEACHERS: 209, Ashbery; 244,
    Whittemore; 923, Robbins; 4092,
    Congdon; 5375, Montgomery; 5713,
    Evans; 6234, Solovay; 6265,
    Bevington; 6443, Rigotti; 6591,
    Henley; 6799, Cox; 7351, Brooks.
TEACHERS AND TEACHING: 5431, Roethke.
TEACHING: 310, 544, Solovay; 589,
    Willis; 1065, Solovay; 1708, M.
    Dolores; 1719, Mooney; 3023, Zlotnik;
    3266, Solovay; 3364, Tovatt; 4128,
    Solovay; 4680, Camp; 5034, Royster;
    5528, Peters; 5773, Cuomo; 6267,
    Flaumenhaft; 6268, 6269, Owen; 6584,
    Scholsser; 6799, Cox.
TEACHING HISTORY: 2596, Gleason.
TEARS: 2125, Booth; 2550, Coblentz;
    5602, Iqbal; 6272, Armour.
TECHNOLOGY: 4836, Coblentz; 6274,
    Starbuck.
TEDDY BEARS: 2347, Young.
TEEN-AGERS: 5605, Helfer.
TEENAGERS: 24, 914, Armour; 6275,
    Galbraith.
TEETH: 6811, Todd.
TELEMACHOS: 6286, Scott.
TELEPHONE BOOTHS: 5323, Moody.
TELEPHONE CALLS: 1608, Whittemore.
TELEPHONE MESSAGES: 6279, Funk.
TELEPHONES: 1537, Grenville; 4334,
    Bracken; 6278, Freeman.

TELESCOPES: 6280, Edelman.
TELEVISION: 3988, Young; 4050, Henry; 4419, Flaumenhaft; 5916, McGinley; 6281, Schiff; 6894, Leichty; 7348, Willson.
TELLER, EDWARD: 4754, F, H.
TELLING: 2799, Moss.
TEMPER TANTRUMS: 6252, Richstone.
TEMPERAMENTS: 1904, de Vito.
TEMPERS: 1247, Jaffray; 2470, Parrish; 3575, Galbraith.
TEMPLES: 6290, Montgomery.
TEMPTATIONS: 3429, Armknecht.
TENANTS: 4302, Wilbur.
TENNIS: 6295, White.
TENNIS COURTS: 7015, Kemp.
TENNYSON, ALFRED LORD: 135, Whittemore.
TENORIO, JUAN: 1539, Campbell.
TENSIONS: 4842, Jennison; 6236, Talman; 6296, Wheeler.
TERESA DE CEPEDA: 6301, Hazo.
TERMINOLOGY OF DRINKING: 5600, Nash.
TERRACES: 6303, Akins.
TERRORS: 4628, Coblentz.
TERYLENE: 2886, Updike.
TEST PILOTS: 4499, Legler.
TESTS: 4271, Lazarus.
TEXTILE WORKERS: 2838, Che.
THAMES RIVER: 3807, Roche.
THANKSGIVING: 3551, McGinley; 5820, Thompson; 6224, Merrill; 6314, Howe; 6315, Nicolas; 6316, Hicky.
THAWS: 3079, Rainer; 6328, Schofield.
THEATER: 7190, Everson.
THEATERS: 2104, Garrigue; 2106, Olson; 3628, Galbraith; 3698, Mayhall.
THEATRES: 4022, Morris.
THEBES: 275, Kunitz.
THEOLOGY: 6334, McGinley; 7082, Vannenbergh.
THERAPY: 6336, Morton.
THERMOSTATS: 7072, Isler.
THICKETS: 6414, Ciardi.
THIEVES: 6360, Kunitz; 6361, Pierce.
THIN MEN: 5842, Murray.
THINGS: 916, Smith; 6291, Greenslet; 6364, Richardson; 7349, Ridgway.
THINKING: 2755, Lister; 5389, Jacobson.
THIRDS: 245, Garrigue.
THIRST: 1257, Clark; 5946, De Ford.
THOMAS, DYLAN: 81, Johnson; 1678, Sitwell; 2874, Barker.
THOMAS, DYLAN, 1914-1953: 1601, Thomas; 6423, Ciardi.
THOR: 341, You.
THOREAU, HENRY DAVID, 1817-1862: 1931, Beston.
THORN TREES: 5830, Barnes.
THOUGHTS: 1548, Singleton; 2545, Caeiro; 3207, Giulaini; 4851, Amihai; 5520, Birnbaum; 6409, Noyes; 6410, Jacobs; 7092, Sarton.
THREATS: 6538, Zitner.
THRESHOLDS: 1346, Hassmer.
THRIFT: 4019, Chadwick.
THRUSHES: 6454, Kroll; 6455, Eberhart; 6456, Pasternak.

THUNDER: 7217, Merrill.
TIDES: 961, Chapin; 3576, White; 6461, Swenson; 6462, Pierce.
TIGERS: 6465, Eff.
TIME: 60, Parrish; 158, Thomas; 218, McCrane; 237, Clark; 520, Pierce; 1033, Cassity; 1252, Van Doren; 1320, Delattre; 2062, Clark; 2402, Gibson; 2924, Sarton; 3477, Reid; 3861, Kirrup; 3863, Cully; 4094, Clark; 4281, Fitzell; 4426, Batchelder; 4655, Berrigan; 4684, Astier; 5319, Sexton; 6194, North; 6287, Plath; 6333, Morse; 6439, Whittemore; 6451, Cochrane; 6466, Pierce; 6468, Zaturenska; 6469, Hitziz; 6470, Swenson; 6472, Auden; 6478, Barker; 6603, Miles; 6682, Howes.
TIME PAYMENTS: 3035, Wheeler.
TIMING: 5770, Williams.
TIPPLERS: 6487, Richter.
TIRED: 2131, Conklin.
TIRESIAS: 6488, Kay.
TOADS: 780, Ciardi.
TOASTS: 6608, Siden.
TOBACCO: 6610, Merwin.
TODAS: 6601, Singer.
TODDLERS: 4185, Smith; 6611, Harrington.
TOGETHERNESS: 2399, Marshall; 4189, Gerkle.
TOIL: 2212, Shlonsky.
TOLERANCE: 7126, Galbraith.
TOMBS: 381, Smith.
TOMOKU UNIVERSITY: 5519, Kirkup.
TOMORROWS: 4849, Wesley; 6617, Wood.
TONES: 441, Berigan.
TONGUES: 6997, Usk.
TOOLS: 1933, Wheeler.
TOOTH-ACHE: 937, Murry.
TOOTHACHES: 4523, Lister.
TOOTHBRUSHES: 4017, McGinley.
TORNADOES: 4113, Jacobs.
TORTOISES: 6624, Hagiwara.
TOUGHS: 3405, Gunn.
TOURISTS: 13, Ashbery; 6151, Barker; 6628, Moss; 6630, Starbuck; 6631, 6656, Shapiro.
TOWERS: 6373, Mayo.
TOWNS: 796, Ebright; 1256, Strachen; 2122, McCulloch; 2616, Miner; 2829, Dejong; 4299, Watkins; 5333, Dreyer; 5701, Havard; 7055, Lennen.
TOXICOLOGISTS: 6635, Van Valen.
TOYS: 3055, Jennison; 4449, Molloy; 6636, Sandeen; 6637, Levine; 6777, Deutsch.
TOYS FOR CHILDREN: 5043, Schlitzer.
TRACKS: 7090, Kinnell.
TRADERS: 6639, Armour.
TRAFFIC: 100, Eckman; 7218, Jacobs.
TRAFFIC DEATHS: 182, Rennert.
TRAFFIC TICKETS: 7074, Otis.
TRAIN BUTCHERS: 6641, Ferril.
TRAINS: 101, Kondo; 305, Kempher; 2176, Smith; 2764, Fiedler; 2837, Fuller; 3339, Weiss; 3799, Riordan; 4204, Lattimore; 4682, Howe; 5506, Levertov, 7069, Everson.
TRANQUILIZERS: 6645, Fleming.

TRANSATLANTIC TRANSPORTS: 6646, Nash.
TRANSIENCE: 6649, Irvine.
TRANSLATIONS: 2411, Weales.
TRANSPARENCIES: 3829, Brown.
TRAPS: 6653, Galler.
TRAVEL: 1067, Rawlins; 2495, McFarland; 3173, Rukeyser; 5098, Bishop.
TRAVELERS: 64, Gibson; 5614, Johnson; 6486, Longfellow; 6658, Chakravarty.
TRAVELING: 6655, De Jong.
TRAVELING SALESMEN: 4165, Warren.
TRAVELOGUES: 6662, Sagittarius.
TREASURE: 7094, Hine.
TREE HOUSES: 6666, Ford.
TREES: 200, Kahn; 256, Ponsot; 293, Coxe; 675, Scott; 1239, Blackburn; 2240, Josephs; 2263, Jacobs; 2280, Lance; 2283, Doyle; 2416, Blackwell; 2722, Hall; 2734, Peel; 3310, Lineaweaver; 4075, Plutzik; 4418, Shapiro; 4713, Marz; 4761, Solomon; 5341, Colvin; 5356, Levine; 5738, Hanson; 6043, Gleason; 6598, Valery; 6665, Maris Stella; 6947, Kunitz; 6970, Schevill; 7084, Crown.
TRESPASSES: 538, O'Gorman.
TRICKS: 4049, Galbraith.
TRIPS: 3472, Van Doren.
TRIREMES: 2412, Decavalles.
TRIUMPH: 1135, Morse.
TROUBLE: 2483, Stewart.
TROY: 6689, Coffin.
TRUCK STOPS: 6690, Landeweer.
TRUCKS: 3400, Eisenlohr; 6691, Grossman.
TRUMAN, HARRY S., 1884-: 609, Fadiman.
TRUST: 4753, Zukofsky; 5349, Lilly; 6693, Coblentz.
TRUTH: 211, Urdang; 2090, Richardson; 2323, Patrick; 2466, Kumin; 3933, Russell; 4066, Chadbourne; 4217, Lazarus; 6464, White; 6683, Howes.
TRYING: 4816, Johnson.
TRYSTS: 6694, Carleton.
TUNISIA: 5339, Sagittarius.
TURIN: 381, Smith.
TURKEYS: 2322, Congdon; 2679, Nash; 5784, Stevens.
TURPENTINE: 6702, Lister.
TURTLES: 6703, Williams.
TWENTY-FIRST CENTURY: 6609, Lister.
TWILIGHT: 6643, Moffitt; 6716, Trent; 6885, Smith.
TWINS: 1276, Gleason; 1880, Neely.
TWO-YEAR OLDS: 6750, Landewear.
TYCOONS: 1693, Buchanan.
TYPE: 4848, Chin-trai.
TYPEWRITERS: 6753, Smith.
UCELLO, PAOLO, 1397-1475: 515, Belitt.
UGLINESS: 5647, Kessler.
UGLY DUCKLINGS: 6755, Kanfer.
ULYSSES: 3243, Coxe.
UMBRELLAS: 6758, Hall.
UNCERTAINTY: 4621, Reid.
UNCLES: 6763, Burrows.
UNCONSCIOUS: 7263, Hughes.
UNDERSTANDING: 1247, Janes; 3509, Neely; 5751, Carter; 5768, Ciardi; 6305, Eberhart.

UNESCO: 2156, Sagittarius.
UNION OF SOVIET SOCIALIST REPUBLICS: 2576, Pasternak.
UNIONS: 4691, Counselman.
UNITED NATIONS: 5035, Ryskind; 6816, Caswell.
UNITED STATES - OFFICIALS AND EMPLOYEES: 37, Whittemore.
UNIVERSE: 2030, Gibson; 5385, Richardson; 7299, Clark.
UNKNOWN, THE: 4542, Clark.
UNMARRIED WOMEN: 7051, Moore.
UNPROTECTED: 6794, Hearst.
UNYIELDING: 539, Morgan.
URIROTSTOCK: 4509, Goodman.
USSR: 4009, Eff.
VACATIONS: 1712, Davidson; 4953, Jacobs; 6147, Alkus; 6821, Kemp; 6822, Walsh; 6823, Johnson.
VACUUMING: 54, Armour.
VAGABONDS: 6651, Char.
VALENTINES: 291, Muldoon; 519, Sagittarius; 734, Milbrath; 928, Emmons; 990, Stockdale; 3220, Howard; 3620, Pratt; 5409, Ericson; 6444, Van Duyn; 6826; 6830, Cully; 6831, Humphries; 6832, Merrill.
VALLEYS: 26, Baro; 2367, Ashberry.
VALUES: 6835, Merchant.
VAN GOGH, VINCENT: 6874, Iris.
VANITY: 6837, Victor.
VEBLEN, THORSTEIN: 4733, Clark.
VENEGEANCE: 3307, Plath.
VENICE: 3872, Norse; 6960, Morse.
VENUS: 347, Bentley; 483, Goodman; 623, Carruth; 624, Rukeyser; 625, Urdang.
VERMEER, JOHANNES: 358, Tomlinson.
VERMONT: 6978, Earle.
VERMONT, LORD RICHARD: 3813, Sitwell.
VERNAL EQUINOX: 6847, Moore.
VERTEBRAE: 5926, Lamport.
VETERANS: 2233, Ginsberg.
VETERANS' DAY: 3746, Rosenthal.
VIEWPOINTS: 6867, Balch; 6868, Douglass.
VIEWS: 1054, Matthews; 3161, Morse; 6862, Miles.
VILLAGES: 4041, 6870, Tanaka.
VILLAS: 378, Wright; 2017, Sitwell.
VINDICTIVENESS: 1247, Jaffray.
VINES: 1598, Hoskins.
VIOLENCE: 6875, Bloom; 6876, Jerome.
VIOLINS: 132, Haber.
VIRGIN MARY: 6877, Claudel.
VIRGINS: 206, Bode; 6425, Lattimore.
VIRTUES: 602, Herschberger.
VIRUSES: 6881, Groszmann.
VISION: 5682, Furlong; 6627, Schevill; 6883, Lord; 6887, Bock.
VISIONS: 2707, Coblentz; 3868, Fandel; 6884, Schniebaum; 6886, Dickey; 6888, Rosen.
VISITING: 2548, Rosenfield.
VISITORS: 4958, Galbraith; 6895, Cousins; 6897, Lilly.
VISITS: 73, Roberts; 6621, Raskin; 6889, Litsey; 6890, Ponsot; 6893, Ostroff.
VITAMINS: 2938, Power; 3146, Schlitzer.

VITELLI, VITELLOZZO: 1398, Feldman.
VOCAL CORDS: 1553, Armour.
VOICES: 3534, Merwin; 4671, Lilly;
   6745, Morse; 6900, Kahn; 6901, Olson;
   6904, Kenny; 6907, Zaturenska.
VOLCANIC ISLANDS: 1407, Merwin.
VOLITION: 6909, Richstone.
VOWS: 6605, Duncan.
VOYAGES: 6912, Tremayne.
VULNERABLE: 1429, Clark.
VULPIUS, MELCHIOR, 1560(?)-1615: 3740,
   Moore.
VULTURES: 3086, Delattre; 3240, Dickey.
WADERS: 6916, Neely.
WAGES: 6917, Wheeler.
WAIST LINES: 6918, Carruth.
WAITERS: 4386, Hemphill.
WAITING: 933, Collins; 1330, Rajan;
   2113, Mok; 4190, Schlitzer; 6323,
   Thompson; 6384, Tremayne; 6919,
   Stepanchev; 6922, Hoffman.
WAKING: 74, Fandel; 171, Rank; 392,
   Laing; 682, Rukeyser; 2753, Toland;
   2764, Fiedler; 3912, Vance; 5653,
   Beum; 6924, Coxe.
WALES: 4175, Morris.
WALKING: 97, Facos; 1278, Brand;
   1623, Frost; 2207, Horner; 2686,
   M. Paulinus; 2856, Lynch; 6386,
   Frazee-Bower; 6555, Hoskins; 6728,
   Scott; 6929, Viereck; 6930, Morris;
   6931, Merrill; 6932, Weaver; 7155,
   Goldberg.
WALKS: 433, Bynner; 4108, Jenkins;
   6927, Whittemore; 7168, Lineaweaver.
WALL STREET: 7303, Swenson.
WALLS: 2396, Goodman; 4518, Montale;
   5357, Goodman; 6934, Enrico; 6935,
   Jones; 6937, St. Martin.
WALTZING: 6943, Bentley.
WANDERING: 6992, Kanfer.
WANDERERS: 3409, Logan; 6944, Wesley.
WANG WEI, 699-759: 4207, Berryman.
WAR: 197, Plutzik; 1454, Calkins;
   2038, Norman; 2058, Morris; 2439,
   Trent; 3214, Humphries; 6288,
   Plath; 6520, Kinnick; 6557, Ciardi
   6873, Sullivan; 7039, Brecht; 7290,
   James.
WAR DEAD: 4527, Engle; 6948,
   Coblentz.
WAR DREAMS: 4412, Whitman.
WAR ORPHANS: 3148, Eckhardt; 6950,
   Sitwell.
WARBLERS: 850, Kinnell.
WARNINGS: 3535, Clark; 6955, Meyer
   6956, Stoutenburg; 6958, Wagoner.
WARRIORS: 5869, Kinsey.
WARS: 3686, Sagittarius; 5458,
   Raskin.
WASHING DISHES: 6809, Ellis.
WASHING MACHINES: 572, Updike.
WASHINGTON, D. C.: 6963, Hazel.
WASHINGTON, GEORGE: 950, Merchant;
   4490, O'Hara; 6962, Ciardi.
WASPS: 6966, Belitt.
WATCHES: 713, Zimmerman; 4962, Nash.
WATER: 2245, Eberhart; 2794, La
   Bombard; 3194, Baro; 3222, Dickey;
   4242, Amihai; 4879, Woods.

WATER-LILLIES: 6577, Hughes.
WATER COLORS: 6973, Mooney.
WATER LILLIES: 6974, Zilles.
WATER POWER: 5317, Boyle.
WATER PURIFICATION: 4091, Fast.
WATER SURFACE: 6976, Kitahara.
WATER WITCHING: 4377, Freeman.
WATERS: 5282, Watkins.
WAVES: 164, Pierce; 2921, Gustafson;
   4535, Barker; 6335, Hollander.
WEAK KNEES: 58, Lieberman.
WEALTH: 2149, Pitts; 3430, Galbraith;
   4746, Kessler.
WEANING OF INFANTS: 6550, Wells.
WEAPONS: 999, Kunitz.
WEATHER: 264, Delattre; 661, Merchant;
   926, Burrows; 1169, Summers; 1297,
   4704, Grenville; 5511, Whittemore;
   5580, Roethke; 6698, Canaday; 6933,
   Grenville; 7000, Holmes; 7001,
   Grenville; 7002, Whittemore; 7004,
   Usk.
WEATHER FORECASTS: 2118, Nemerov;
   2119, Grenier.
WEBERN, ANTON: 2872, Mueller.
WEDDING ANNIVERSARIES: 230, Isler;
   2336, Walton.
WEDDINGS: 52, Kanfer; 743, Blanchard;
   1284, Barker; 1738, Weinstein; 4955,
   Strong; 5053, Morris; 6872, Betjeman;
   7008, Bomse; 7009, Ponsot.
WEEDS: 1269, Kroll; 4702, Ross; 7011,
   Drake.
WEEKENDS: 7012, Balliett; 7013,
   Blackwell; 7107, Dallas.
WEEPING: 3486, Gilboa; 4368, Kitahara.
WEIGHING: 2828, Robin.
WEIGHT CONTROL: 4158, Pugh.
WELCOME: 2798, Dunbar; 5207, Jaffray.
WELFARE: 3774, Ryskind.
WELFARE STATE: 1848, Sagittarius.
WELL-HOUSES: 7018, Warren.
WELLS: 1257, 5106, Clark; 7016,
   Johnson.
WELLS CATHEDRAL: 7029, Ackerson.
WELSH FARMERS: 4524, Stone.
WEST: 7028, Witt.
WEST, THE: 439, Peck; 7152, Boylan.
WESTERN POWERS: 4153, Sagittarius.
WESTERN TOWNS: 7033, Shapiro.
WESTMINSTER ABBEY: 3096, Hodes.
WHALERS: 7034, Merwin.
WHALES: 3494, Kanfer.
WHARVES: 6735, Goodman.
WHEEL: 7059, Nemerov.
WHIRLING: 5179, Updike.
WHIRLWINDS: 1770, Gilboa.
WHISPERS: 7099, Bandypadhyay..
WHISPS: 7063, L..
WHISTLES: 7102, Jenney.
WHISTLING: 7100, Congdon; 7102,
   Jenney.
WHITE: 662, Morris; 6071, Duncan.
WHITETHROATS: 7121, Hoffman.
WHITMAN, WALT: 4303, Garcia Lorca.
WHO'S WHO IN AMERICA: 6661, Armour.
WIDOWS: 3765, Weaver; 7140, Giordon;
   7141, Lineaweaver; 7142, Kizer; 7144.
WILDERNESS: 7011, Drake; 7153, Pierce.
WILDFLOWERS: 791, Zilles.

WILL: 1285, Carter; 1464, Shapiro.
WILLIAMS, ESTHER: 4738, Watt.
WILLIAMS, PAUL WIGHTMAN: 4301,
  Golffing.
WILLIAMS, TENNESSEE: 2975, Ryskind.
WILLIAMS, WILLIAM CARLOS: 4515,
  Langton; 6536, Eberhart.
WILLOWS: 6902, Schneider; 7282, Drake.
WILSON, WOODROW, 1856-1924: 5918,
  Fadiman.
WIND: 112, Gilboa; 660, Gordon; 2323,
  Patrick; 2675, Woods; 2995, Scott;
  3110, Ammons; 3434, Gibbs; 4188,
  Richards; 4537, Van Doren; 5623,
  Robson; 5645, 6642, Howes; 6723,
  Klopp; 7159, Hughes; 7163, Woodall;
  7164, Barker; 7166, Mok.
WIND INSTRUMENTS: 6128, Perry.
WINDOW SHOPPERS: 7171, Wheeler.
WINDOW-GAZING: 2553, Graves.
WINDOWPANES: 7173, Char.
WINDOWS: 19, Jaffray; 1420, Tremayne;
  2208, Swenson; 3853, Gregor; 4544,
  Pitchford; 6857, Hillyer.
WINDY DAYS: 4279, Bohm.
WINDYARDS: 7175, Reaney.
WINE: 258, Maura; 2597, Spingarn.
WINGS: 7179, Pierce.
WINNERS: 6579, Turner.
WINTER: 154, Graham; 163, Eisenlohr;
  201, Shook; 980, Nathan; 1297,
  Grenville; 1362, Ray; 1605, Merchant;
  1952, Montgomery; 2358, Collins;
  2493, Grenville; 2563, Coxe; 2568,
  Hopkins; 2733, Woolley; 3019, Merwin;
  3064, Swann; 3165, Collins; 3473,
  Weiss; 3507, Ward; 3682, Watkins;
  3793, Walton; 4270, Merrill; 4696,
  Nathan; 4868, Stuart; 5175, Hess;
  5359, Pardue; 5493, Plath; 6479,
  Merrill; 6856, Lee; 6952, Ward;
  7072, Isler; 7119, Frost; 7181,
  Langland; 7182, Kelley; 7183,
  Nicholson; 7186, Merrill; 7188,
  Franklin; 7195, Takamura; 7196,
  Merrill; 7197, Smith; 7199, Henry;
  7202, Trent; 7208, Facos; 7209,
  Nathan; 7210, Wright; 7213,
  Whittemore; 7216, Bock; 7220,
  McBrown; 7221, Patrick; 7223,
  Grenville; 7224, Seager; 7225,
  Rosenberg; 7227, Solomon.
WINTER, END OF: 5802, Wagoner; 7222,
  Brasier.
WINTER MORNINGS: 7204, Amen; 7205,
  Emans.
WINTER NIGHTS: 7190, Merwin; 7206,
  Long; 7207, Raha.
WINTER SCENES: 7212, Carroll.
WINTER WALKS: 7219, Chisholm.
WISDOM: 59, Summers; 2087, Dell;
  2324, Fosdick; 3772, Nichols; 4511,
  Wirt; 4729, Grace; 5390, Coblentz;
  5860, Kay; 7220, McCandless; 7230,
  Flynn; 7231, Pierce.
WISE MEN: 7097, Pierce.
WISHES: 4870, Weiss; 4911, Larraud;
  7232, Kayko; 7233, Rich; 7312,
  Hammer.
WIT: 7235, Bishop; 7251, Grenville.

WITCHCRAFT: 2567, Pedrick; 3646,
  Smith.
WITCHES: 7236, Fuller; 7237, Nemerov.
WITNESSES: 6782, Starbuck.
WITS: 4606, Thomas.
WIVES: 223, Schiff; 1176, Chadwick;
  1216, Brown; 1221, De Vito; 1509,
  Gleason; 1538, Barker; 1869, Sexton;
  1993, McGinley; 2480, Rudd; 2534,
  Armour; 2570, Emmons; 2589,
  Galbraith; 2659, Lincoln; 3227,
  Legler; 3680, Lamb; 3727, Richstone;
  3836, Rosenfield; 3967, Schiff; 4019,
  Chadwick; 4190, Schlitzer; 4334, 4346,
  4347, Bracken; 4639, Galbraith; 5170,
  Emmons; 5478, Merwin; 5545, Rexroth;
  5581, Armour; 5634, Creeley; 5679,
  Chadwick; 5693, Usk; 6828, Summers;
  7147, Taylor; 7148, Hart; 7150,
  Fowler.
WIVES AS AUTOMOBILE DRIVERS: 3319,
  Jaffray.
WOES: 2664, Collins.
WOMAN: 3312, Laing; 4680, Vesely.
WOMANHOOD: 357, Walton.
WOMEN: 607, Galbraith; 2125, Booth;
  2862, Paz; 3180, Lamport; 3303, Reid;
  3316, Zacks; 3391, Kinnell; 3393,
  Weiss; 3516, Nemerov; 3831, Roseliep;
  4534, Gokak; 4624, Armour; 4853,
  Gilman; 5287, Akins; 5566, Wilbur;
  5620, Kennedy; 5625, McGinley; 5702,
  Merwin; 6293, Smith; 6989, Wheeler;
  7045, Nixon; 7134, Galbraith; 7253,
  Clower; 7254, Williams; 7255, Hay;
  7256, Graves; 7259, Gilbert; 7260,
  Milne; 7266, Feldman; 7267,
  Hitchcock; 7270, Waddington; 7288,
  Twiggs.
WOMEN AND CLOTHES: 1997, Swenson.
WOMEN AS NATURALISTS: 7136, Neely.
WOMEN DRIVERS: 4445, Usk.
WOMEN GOSSIPS: 4603, Creason.
WOMEN GUESTS: 1313, Armour.
WOMEN TALKING: 463, Neely.
WOMEN TENNIS PLAYERS: 7269, Hatch.
WOMEN'S CLOTHES: 6767, Rosenfield.
WOMEN'S CONVENTIONS: 4777, Hammer.
WOMEN'S DRESSES: 1176, Chadwick;
  6796, Hammer; 7268, Redgrove.
WOMEN's FIGURES: 35, Richstone.
WONDER: 4063, Ewing; 5494, Nicholl;
  5766, Trent.
WOOD ENGRAVING: 3174.
WOODCOCKS: 7275, Tanaka.
WOODLANDS: 2686, M Paulinus.
WOODPECKERS: 7277, Laughlin.
WOODS: 3163, Sexton.
WORD, THE: 7294, Campbell.
WORD OF GOD: 2385, Carlisle.
WORDLESSNESS: 7286, Gordon.
WORDS: 165, Sward; 596, Apin; 2052,
  Humphries; 2507, Curnow; 2670,
  Mary Timothy; 3632, Koehler; 3933,
  Russell; 4460, Merchant; 4522,
  Douglass; 4697, Lennen; 5002, Wylie;
  5184, Edwards; 5839, Eaton; 6266,
  Carlisle; 6704, Levy; 6802, Elliott;
  7278, Pierce; 7286, Gordon; 7287,
  Morse; 7297, Abse; 7310, Macpherson.

WORDSWORTH, DOROTHY: 6371, Little.
WORK: 459, Armstrong; 2341, Nakano;
    4776, Gibbs; 5003, Richstone.
WORK BENCHES: 7257, Armour.
WORKING: 1791, Thornton.
WORKMEN: 7304, Morris.
WORLD: 1621, Freeman; 2337, Lister;
    2482, Eberhart; 2591, Haines; 2997,
    Jacobson; 3854, Alkus; 4263, Barker;
    5294, Friend; 7056, Salomon; 7305,
    Appleton; 7306, Fox; 7311, Hall;
    2561, Barker; 7314, Engle.
WORRY: 3533, Galbraith; 6076, Long;
    7138, Richstone.
WORSHIP: 1560, Overmyer; 2168, Victor;
    2974, Miller; 3288, Barker; 3721,
    Hough; 7221, Patrick; 7315, Tigner.
WORTH: 6834, Galbraith.
WOUNDS: 640, Fussell.
WRATH: 454, Talman.
WREATHS: 7318, Plath.
WRENS: 5332, Walton.
WRIST WATCHES: 1982, Grenville.
WRITERS: 65, Harris; 436, Lowenfels;
    5853, Amihai; 7322, MacDonald.
WRITING: 3093, Pierce; 4238, Walton;
    5159, Thompson; 6270, Wagoner; 7354,
    Sweet.
WRONG: 4260, Pierce.
X RAYS: 3510, Veenendaal; 5108,
    Jacobsen.
YANKEE STADIUM: 6252, Updike.
YAWNS: 1831, Tagliabue.
YEARNING: 7380, Rokeah.
YEARS: 2426, Booth; 5024, Catheron.
YELLOW PAGES: 78, Wagoner.
YELLS: 7335, Lister.
YEWBERRIES: 7342, Wolf.
YIDDISH: 4477, Victor.
YOGI: 561, Lee.
YOM KIPPUR: 7344, Harrison; 7345,
    Rainer.
YOU: 2254, Warren; 6311, Engle
YOUTH: 494, Lindbergh; 541, Carruth;
    1139, Ronsard; 1692, Davidson; 2351,
    Lazarus; 3062, Hall; 3530, Sexton;
    3995, Gibson; 4489, Krausz; 4605,
    Ashberry; 5166, Galbraith; 6526,
    Solovay; 6861, Smith; 7359, Freeman;
    7371, Cunliffe; 7375, Lee; 7376,
    Roseliep; 7377, De Jong.
YOUTH AND AGE: 364, Rich; 5208,
    Galbraith.
YOUTH AND DYING: 3795, Gordon.
YUCATAN: 6675, Weiss.
ZEAL: 7378, Lilly.
ZILPAH: 1174, Haber.
ZIPPERS: 7383, Anthony.
ZOOS: 103, Flaumenhaft; 7385, Ostroff.
ZULUS: 5626, Updike.
ZWINGLI, ULRICH, 1484-1531: 2683,
    McGinley

About the Compiler

JEFFERSON D. CASKEY is Professor of Library Science at Western Kentucky University. He is the co-author of *Samuel Taylor Coleridge: A Selective Bibliography of Criticism, 1935-1977* (Greenwood Press, 1978) and the author of articles published in *Library Services Journal, The Reference Librarian,* and *Language Arts.*